T0320465

Spaceborne Synthetic Aperture Radar Remote Sensing

This book provides basic and advanced concepts of synthetic aperture radar (SAR), PolSAR, InSAR, PolInSAR, and all necessary information about various applications and analysis of data of multiple sensors. It includes information on SAR remote sensing, data processing, and separate applications of SAR technology, compiled in one place. It will help readers to use active microwave imaging sensor-based information in geospatial technology and applications.

This book:

- Covers basic and advanced concepts of synthetic aperture radar (SAR) remote sensing.
- Introduces spaceborne SAR sensors, Calibration, Speckle Reduction, and Polarimetric SAR interferometry (PolInSAR).
- Discusses applications of SAR remote sensing in earth observation.
- Explores utilization of SAR data for solid earth, ecosystem, and cryosphere, including imaging of extra-terrestrial bodies.
- Includes PolSAR and PolInSAR for aboveground forest biomass retrieval, as well as InSAR and PolSAR for snow parameters retrieval.

This book is aimed at researchers and graduate students in remote sensing, photogrammetry, geoscience, image processing, agriculture, environment, forestry, and image processing.

Spaceborne Synthetic Aperture Radar Remote Sensing

Techniques and Applications

Edited by
Shashi Kumar, Paul Siqueira, Himanshu Govil and
Shefali Agrawal

CRC Press
Taylor & Francis Group
Boca Raton London New York

CRC Press is an imprint of the
Taylor & Francis Group, an **informa** business

First edition published 2023
by CRC Press
6000 Broken Sound Parkway NW, Suite 300, Boca Raton, FL 33487-2742

and by CRC Press
4 Park Square, Milton Park, Abingdon, Oxon, OX14 4RN

CRC Press is an imprint of Taylor & Francis Group, LLC

ISBN: 9781032069050 (hbk)
ISBN: 9781032069098 (pbk)
ISBN: 9781003204466 (ebk)

DOI: 10.1201/9781003204466

Typeset in Times
by Newgen Publishing UK

Contents

Preface

Synthetic aperture radar (SAR) remote sensing has been widely used in applications of solid earth, ecosystem, and cryosphere. Recognizing the importance of SAR remote sensing, many space agencies have launched state-of-the-art sensors into space and planned for many unique feature sensors in the future. The NASA-ISRO synthetic aperture radar (NISAR) mission is a unique spaceborne SAR mission with dual-frequency capability that will be launched in the future. Similarly, the P-band BIOMASS mission of the European Space Agency (ESA) will be the first mission in space dedicated to the biomass of the tropical forest. It is essential to recognize the requirements of advanced SAR remote sensing techniques, advancements in data processing, and innovation in modeling approaches for the characterization of manmade and natural features. The synthetic aperture radar (SAR) remote sensing technique has shown its significance for retrieving information on manmade and natural features and has been widely used for land use and land cover mapping. Recently, many advances have been made in SAR remote sensing techniques to improve accuracy of the biophysical and geophysical characterization of manmade and natural features from a local level to a global scale. The active microwave imaging SAR system has the potential not only to characterize object parameters but also to measure the height of the terrain and vegetation cover, velocity of glacier and sea ice, movement of tectonic plates, lava flow direction of a volcanic eruption, and subsidence in the earth's surface with very high accuracy. Spaceborne and airborne polarimetric SAR data have been used for different applications, including soil moisture estimation, forest aboveground biomass estimation, snow parameter retrieval, dielectric characterization, and oil spill detection ship identification, among others. Polarimetric SAR tomography (PolTomSAR) and polarimetric SAR interferometry (PolInSAR) are being developed as emerging techniques to derive forest parameters for canopy height and aboveground biomass retrieval. The PolInSAR inversion-based approaches use complex coherence optimization to retrieve forest height, and the PolTomSAR technique is implemented for forest height estimation using a large number of polarimetric acquisitions to create vertical resolution. The ability of quad-pole and hybrid-pole SAR data has been not only evaluated for the Earth's surface but also used for the surface and sub-characterization of planetary bodies. Several valuable studies have been conducted with the help of SAR remote sensing to characterize the surface and subsurface of planetary bodies.

To date, several spaceborne SAR missions have been launched, and datasets are available for land use and land cover mapping and monitoring. Several spaceborne SAR missions have been planned by different space agencies to be launched in the future. Understanding the different applications and implementation of modeling approaches on the SAR data for information retrieval can be difficult for both researchers and learners. This book provides basic and advanced concepts of spaceborne SAR, PolSAR, InSAR, PolInSAR, and all necessary information about various applications and data analysis of multiple sensors. The chapters of this book have been written with the aim of compiling in one place all information on SAR remote sensing, including basic and advanced concepts, data processing, and separate applications of SAR technology. This book will be very useful for those who want to use active microwave imaging sensor-based information in geospatial technology and applications.

Editor Biographies

 **Shashi Kumar**, PhD, received an MSc in Physics from Patna University, Patna, India, in 2006; an MSc in Geoinformatics under the joint education program of the Indian Institute of Remote Sensing (IIRS), Dehradun, India, and the International Institute for Geo-Information Science and Earth Observation (ITC), Enschede, the Netherlands, in 2009; and a PhD from the Indian Institute of Technology (IIT), Roorkee, India, in 2019. Since 2009, he has been working as a scientist with the Indian Institute of Remote Sensing (IIRS), Indian Space Research Organisation (ISRO), Dehradun, India. Dr. Shashi Kumar is a dedicated researcher contributing to capacity building through education and research in the field of advanced synthetic aperture radar (SAR) remote sensing, including polarimetric SAR (PolSAR), polarimetric SAR interferometry (PolInSAR), and polarimetric tomographic SAR (PolTomSAR), its data processing techniques, and applications. Over the past 14 years, Dr. Shashi Kumar has shown intellectual prowess in cutting-edge research works on PolSAR remote sensing and has over 200 publications. He has shown excellent collaborative skills through collaborative research work with scientists and professors from various universities and institutions. He has edited two journal issues on the special topics of 'Advances in Spaceborne SAR Remote Sensing for Characterization of Natural and Manmade Features – I &II' for the COSPAR journal *Advances in Space Research (ASR)*. Currently, Dr. Kumar is a guest editor for a special issue of *Advances in Space Research (ASR)* on 'Synergistic Use of Remote Sensing Data and In-Situ Investigations to Reveal the Hidden Secrets of the Moon', as well as a special issue of AGU Wiley's *Earth and Space Science* on 'Synthetic Aperture Radar Remote Sensing for Characterization of Land Use and Land Cover'.

Dr. Shashi Kumar worked as a member of the SAR Task Group to develop SAR protocols under the partnership of the Government of India (GoI) and the United States Agency for International Development (USAID) Forest-PLUS in collaboration with the University of Massachusetts, Amherst. He has also performed his duties as a committee member for the Commonwealth Scholarship 2016 at the Department of Higher Education, Ministry of Human Research Development. He is a science team member for the NASA-ISRO Synthetic Aperture Radar (NISAR) mission for the Science Products, Calibration, and Tools Development team as well as for the Chandrayaan-2 mission's Working Group 3 for Lunar Poles and Microwave Remote Sensing. As a science team member of the NISAR mission, Dr. Shashi Kumar has contributed to PolSAR calibration and processing of fully and hybrid polarimetric Airborne L- & S-band SAR data acquired for India's calibration sites and the United States and as a science team member of Chandrayaan-2 mission, Dr. Shashi Kumar did the polarimetric analysis and dielectric characterization of L-band DFSAR data for the craters of permanently shadowed regions (PSRs). One of his significant contributions has been the development of a methodological framework for polarimetric calibration (PolCal) of airborne and spaceborne fully polarimetric and hybrid/compact-pol SAR data to minimize distortions for scattering-based characterization of manmade and natural objects. In recognition of outstanding contributions toward 'polarimetric calibration of SAR data and development of PolSAR' and 'PolInSAR modelling approaches for scattering-based characterization of manmade and natural objects', the Indian Society of Remote Sensing (ISRS) conferred the Indian National Geospatial Award 2021 on Dr. Kumar.

Paul Siqueira, PhD, was a senior engineer with the Radar Science and Engineering Section, Jet Propulsion Laboratory, Pasadena, CA, USA. He was a visiting scientist with the Joint Research Center, European Commission, Ispra, Italy. He is currently a professor with the Department of Electrical and Computer Engineering, University of Massachusetts–Amherst, Amherst, MA, USA. He is also the co-director of the university's Microwave Remote Sensing Laboratory (MIRSL), where he is involved in the design, development, and use of microwave remote sensing instruments for earth science applications, such as deployable three-frequency weather radar (Ku-, Ka-, and W-band) and two-frequency polarimetric radiometers (KPR and KaPR) for characterizing rain and snowfall. He has also developed a two-frequency (S- and Ka-band) airborne interferometric SAR that can measure the surface topography and the volume scattering characteristics of natural targets (e.g. vegetation and snow). He teaches courses in microwave engineering, microwave metrology, and microwave systems engineering.

Dr. Siqueira is Principal Investigator for NASA's Terrestrial Ecology and Earth Science Technology programs, the Science Definition Team Ecosystems Lead for NASA's next-generation SAR (NISAR) that will launch in 2022, and Science Advisor for JAXA's ALOS-2 instrument. He was a recipient of the Harvard Forest Bullard Fellowship and the chairman of the Alaska Satellite Facilities' User Working Group. He also participates in the National Academy of Sciences' Committee on Radio Frequencies (CORF).

Himanshu Govil, PhD, received an MSc in Geology from Aligarh Muslim University, India, in 2006; a PG Diploma in Geoinformatics under the joint education program of the Indian Institute of Remote Sensing (IIRS), Dehradun, India, and the International Institute for Geo-Information Science and Earth Observation (ITC), Enschede, the Netherlands, in 2008; and a PhD from Aligarh Muslim University (AMU), Aligarh, India, in 2015. Since 2015, he has been working as an assistant professor in the Department Applied Geology, National Institute of Technology (NIT), Raipur, Chhatisgarh, India. Dr. Govil is handles research announcement (RA) projects related to the NASA-ISRO synthetic aperture radar (NISAR) and NASA-ISRO hyperspectral mission (AVIRIS-NG) missions. His research interests include hyperspectral remote sensing, thermal remote sensing, and SAR remote sensing with special emphasis on mineral mapping, subsidence, and subsurface monitoring.

Shefali Agrawal is a physicist at the Indian Institute of Remote Sensing with academic qualifications obtained both in India and in abroad (ITC, Netherlands). Her academic interests include both fundamental and applied aspects of remote sensing, GIS, and allied spatial technology, with an emphasis on satellite photogrammetry, Lidar remote sensing, hyperspectral remote sensing, UAV remote sensing, underwater image processing, and advanced image processing related to land use/land cover characterization and vegetation physics dynamics. She has had many accomplishments in her professional career and has contributed to various national and international projects, such as mapping and monitoring of land use/land cover vegetation types across south-central Asia for the first time, using SPOT vegetation satellite data for spectral modeling under the European Commission program. She is currently group head of the Geospatial Technology and Outreach Programme Group, which consists of all technology departments at IIRS, and is engaged in 3-D surface characterization and simulation through the integration of satellite stereo imageries, terrestrial laser scanning (TLS), and UAV-based data at IIRS for natural resources and archaeological applications. She has over 25 years of experience and has produced around 100 papers in national and international journals.

Contributors

Aghababaei, Hossein
Faculty of Geo-Information Science and
  Earth Observation
University of Twente
Enschede, Netherlands

Bhattacharya, Avik
Microwave Remote Sensing Lab
Indian Institute of Technology Bombay
Powai, Mumbai, Maharashtra, India

Bhaumik, Pralay
Department of Applied Geology
National Institute of Technology (NIT) Raipur
Chhattisgarh, India

Chang, Ling
Faculty of Geo-Information Science and
  Earth Observation
University of Twente
Enschede, Netherlands

Chatterjee, Rajat Subhra
Geosciences Department
Indian Institute of Remote Sensing
  (IIRS), ISRO
Dehradun, Uttarakhand, India

Chaudhary, Vaishali
Clayton H. Riddell Faculty of Environment,
  Earth, and Resources
University of Manitoba
Winnipeg, Manitoba, Canada

Dey, Subhadip
Microwave Remote Sensing Lab
Indian Institute of Technology Bombay
Powai, Mumbai, Maharashtra, India

Dwivedi, Ramji
GIS Cell
Motilal Nehru National Institute of
  Technology Allahabad
Prayagraj, India

Garg, Rajat
School of Computer Science
University of Petroleum and Energy Studies
Dehradun, Uttarakhand, India

Govil, Himanshu
Department of Applied Geology
National Institute of Technology (NIT) Raipur
Raipur, Chhattisgarh, India

Jayasri, P. V.
National Remote Sensing Centre
  (NRSC), ISRO
Hyderabad, Telangana, India

Kandasamy, Vignesh
Thazhal Geospatial Analytics Private Limited
Tirunelveli, Tamil Nadu, India

Kulshrestha, Anurag
Faculty of Geo-Information Science and
  Earth Observation
University of Twente
Enschede, Netherlands

Kumar, Anil
School of Computer Science
University of Petroleum and Energy Studies
Dehradun, Uttarakhand, India

Kumar, Shashi
Photogrammetry and Remote Sensing
  Department
Indian Institute of Remote Sensing
  (IIRS), ISRO
Dehradun, Uttarakhand, India

Kumar, Vinay
Photogrammetry and Remote Sensing
  Department
Indian Institute of Remote Sensing
  (IIRS), ISRO
Dehradun, Uttarakhand, India

Kumari, E. V. S. Sita
National Remote Sensing Centre
  (NRSC), ISRO
Hyderabad, Telangana, India

Tomar Sangita Singh
Department of Geography
Norwegian University of Science and
  Technology (NTNU)
Trondheim, Norway

Lopez-Sanchez, Juan M.
Institute for Computer Research (IUII)
University of Alicante
Alicante, Spain

Maithani, Sandeep
Urban and Regional Studies Department
Indian Institute of Remote Sensing
   (IIRS), ISRO
Dehradun, Uttarakhand, India

Mascolo, Lucio
Institute for Computer Research (IUII)
University of Alicante
Alicante, Spain

Meghanadh, Devara
GIS Cell
Motilal Nehru National Institute of Technology
   Allahabad
Prayagraj, India

Mishra, Varun N.
Amity Institute of Geo-Informatics and
   Remote Sensing (AIGIRS)
Noida, Uttar Pradesh, India

Mukhopadhyay, Ritwika
Department of Forest Resource Management
Swedish University of Agricultural Sciences
Umeå, Sweden

Niharika, K.
National Remote Sensing Centre
   (NRSC), ISRO
Hyderabad, Telangana, India

Persello, C.
Faculty of Geo-Information Science and
   Earth Observation
University of Twente
Enschede, Netherlands

Prasad, Ashutosh Venkatesh
National Centre for Polar and Ocean Research
   (NCPOR)
Vasco da Gama, Goa, India

Rajendran, Sankaran
Environmental Science Center
Qatar University
Doha, Qatar

Ryali, H. S. V. Usha Sundari
National Remote Sensing Centre
   (NRSC), ISRO
Hyderabad, Telangana, India

Shafai, Shahid Shuja
Faculty of Geo-Information Science and
   Earth Observation
University of Twente
Enschede, Netherlands

Sharma, Aanchal
Photogrammetry and Remote Sensing
   Department
Indian Institute of Remote Sensing
   (IIRS), ISRO
Dehradun, Uttarakhand, India

Singh, Awinash
Faculty of Geo-Information Science and
   Earth Observation
University of Twente
Enschede, Netherlands

Singh, Shashwati
Remote Sensing Applications Centre,
   Uttar Pradesh (RSAC-UP)
Lucknow, Uttar Pradesh, India

Stein, Alfred
Faculty of Geo-Information Science and
   Earth Observation
University of Twente
Enschede, Netherlands

Thakur, Praveen K.
Water Resources Department
Indian Institute of Remote Sensing
   (IIRS), ISRO
Dehradun, Uttarakhand, India

Tomar, Kiledar Singh
Department of Geography
University of Calgary
Calgary, Alberta, Canada

Tripathi, Akshar
Department of Civil Engineering
Indian Institute of Technology Ropar
Rupnagar, Punjab, India

Tserendulam, Nyamaa
Centre for Space Science and
    Technology Education in Asia Pacific
    (CSSTEAP)
Dehradun, Uttarakhand, India

Venkatachalaperumal, Shenbaga Rajan
Faculty of Geo-Information Science and
    Earth Observation
University of Twente
Enschede, Netherlands

1 Synthetic Aperture Radar Remote Sensing

Shashi Kumar and Aanchal Sharma

CONTENTS

1.1   INTRODUCTION

Synthetic aperture radar (SAR) remote sensing is an active imaging remote sensing technique that is conducted in the microwave region of the electromagnetic spectrum to generate high-resolution, two-dimensional images based on the scattering properties of the targeted objects. The first spaceborne SAR was SEASAT, which was launched in 1978, followed by the Soviet SAR Kosmos 1870 in 1987, the European remote sensing satellites ERS-1 in 1991 and ERS-2 in 1995, the Japanese environmental satellite JERS-1 in 1992, the Canadian RADARSAT-1 in 1995, and ESA's C-band ENVISAT ASAR in 2002.

In 2012 and 2009, the Indian Space Research Organisation (ISRO) launched all-weather capability radar imaging satellites C-band RISAT-1 and X-band RISAT-2, respectively, to take images of the earth. The joint SAR mission of the National Aeronautics and Space Administration (NASA) and the ISRO will be the first spaceborne earth observation mission launched in 2024 to acquire dual-frequency SAR data with L- and S-bands. The SAR sensors transmit the electromagnetic waves towards the earth's surface; scattering from the targeted objects produces backscattered energy that received by the sensors, and the images are generated based on the backscattered energy, which depends upon the sensor and the parameters of the targeted objects. SAR sensor parameters include wavelength, angle of incidence, and resolution; the object parameters of shape, size, orientation, roughness, and dielectric properties mainly control the backscatter amount. Generally, a 1 mm to 100 cm wavelength range of the electromagnetic spectrum is used in SAR remote sensing. Since the SAR sensor is operated in the microwave region of the electromagnetic spectrum, it becomes easy for the microwaves transmitted by the SAR sensor to penetrate the cloud cover of the troposphere to provide a clear image of the earth's surface after interaction with targets. Figure 1.1 shows VH and VV polarizations of Sentinel-1A SAR data for an area near Varanasi, India. The natural and false color composite (FCC) products of the Sentinel-2B multi-spectral imager (MSI) of 24 February 2021 show a clear view of the landform. The MSI product has full cloud cover as of 15 January 2021 and does not show any landscape visibility as a result. Figure 1.1 shows the data acquisition capability of a SAR sensor to retrieve earth surface information even through the cloud cover.

DOI: 10.1201/9781003204466-1

1

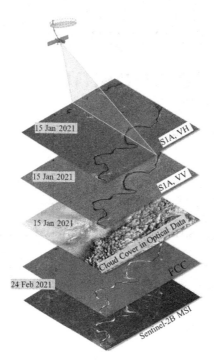

FIGURE 1.1   SAR data acquisition to retrieve earth surface information in the cloud cover.

TABLE 1.1
Microwave Bands Used in SAR Remote Sensing

Microwave Band	Wavelength	Frequency
K_a-band	0.75 – 1.13 cm	40.0 – 26.5 GHz
K-band	1.13 – 1.67 cm	26.5 – 18.0 GHz
K_u-band	1.67 – 2.40 cm	18.0 – 12.5 GHz
X-band	2.40 – 3.75 cm	12.5 – 08.0 GHz
C-band	3.75 – 7.50 cm	08.0 – 04.0 GHz
S-band	7.50 – 15.0 cm	04.0 – 02.0 GHz
L-band	15.0 – 30.0 cm	02.0 – 01.0 GHz
P-band	30.0 – 100 cm	01.0 – 0.30 GHz

Table 1.1 shows the microwave band of the electromagnetic spectrum that is used in SAR remote sensing [1], [2]. As can easily be seen in Table 1.1, the frequency of the microwave band is decreasing with an increase in wavelength.

More than one sensor is used to collect data for any given location in order to obtain SAR data in multiple frequencies. Typically, a spaceborne SAR system provides a dataset in a specific frequency range of microwave bands during its entire working life, so multiple SAR sensors are used to obtain multifrequency data for a particular region. Each microwave band has some advantages and limitations compared to other microwave bands. For example, the long-wavelength range of the microwave band shows high penetration efficiencies in the canopy and soil, but it delivers high attenuation and scintillation due to the ionospheric propagation of electromagnetic waves due to low energy. While the short wavelength range of the microwave band offers less penetration into the vegetation canopy and soil, is has less attenuation and scintillation due to the ionosphere.

1.1.1 Coherent Radar

Radar systems used in imaging are coherent and defined on the phase stability/consistency between transmitted pulses. Coherence is the ability of the radar system to do accurate phase measurement of the received signals and to maintain an integer multiple of wavelength between the two successive pulses [3]. Coherent radar stores the record of the phase information of the transmitted pulses, and the coherency in the radar systems is accomplished by the stable local oscillator (StaLO). If R represents the range distance from the sensor to the target and λ is the wavelength of the microwave band, then the phase delay in the returning pulse after scattering from the point target is given by Equation 1.1 [4].

$$\Delta\varnothing = -2\pi \times \frac{2R}{\lambda} = \frac{-4\pi R}{\lambda},$$ (1.1)

where $\Delta\varnothing$ is the delay in phase of the returned signal relative to the StaLO phase. In the NASA ISRO synthetic aperture radar (NISAR) mission, the control and timing board (CTB) will preserve a continual count of clock cycles produced by the instrument's 10 MHz StaLO [5].

1.2 SYNTHETIC APERTURE RADAR (SAR) GEOMETRY

Figure 1.2 shows the geometry of a synthetic aperture radar in which R represents the distance from the sensor to the target, θ is the angle of incidence, α is the look angle, γ is the depression angle, and β is the grazing angle. The radar system/sensor is shown above a particular altitude from the nadir point. There are two directions, namely azimuth or flight direction and range direction, which are responsible for the two spatial resolutions within the single SAR resolution cell. The angle of incidence is the angle between the point at which the electromagnetic wave transmitted by the SAR

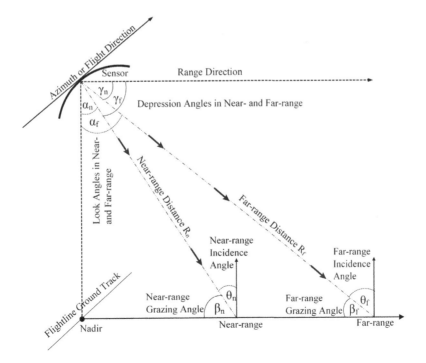

FIGURE 1.2 The geometry of the radar system for data collection.

sensor hits the target or earth surface and the normal drawn perpendicular to the point of incidence on the surface.

The radar sensor transmits microwave energy towards the earth's surface. When the microwave energy (electromagnetic waves) is transmitted towards the earth's surface, a portion of the targeted area is illuminated; the portion of the illuminated area that appears near to the nadir is called the near range and the portion that is on the far side is known as the far range. The illuminated area is an elliptical footprint across the track that defines the swath of the image, and this depends on the width (W) of the antenna and the wavelength (λ) of the transmitted electromagnetic wave of the microwave band.

The angles shown in Figure 1.2 vary from near to far range. As per the geometry, the figure clearly shows that if the terrain is flat, the surface is smooth, and the earth's curvature does not play an important role, then the angle of incidence will be exactly equal to the look angle. Generally, in the case of airborne sensors, for which platform altitude is much less, the earth's curvature does not show a very high influence that may cause a difference in look angle and incidence angle. But in the case of spaceborne sensors, where the platform height is around several hundred kilometers, the two angles could not be considered equal due to the earth's curvature [6], [7]. Figure 1.3 shows the spaceborne imaging geometry of a SAR system with an altitude H above the earth's surface. From the geometry, it is clear that the incidence angle is not equal to the look angle due to the curvature of the earth's surface. In Figure 1.3, α (∠ORS), θ (∠NSR), R, R_E, R_G, and H are SAR look angle, angle of incidence, distance from sensor to target, radius of the earth, sub-platform track on the earth's surface (ground range), and altitude of the platform of the spaceborne SAR system from the earth's surface, respectively. The angle ξ (∠CSR) is the angle between the line joining a point on the surface to the center of the earth and the incident electromagnetic wave to the surface point. The angle χ (∠OCS) is the angle subtended by the arc OS to the center (point C) of the earth.

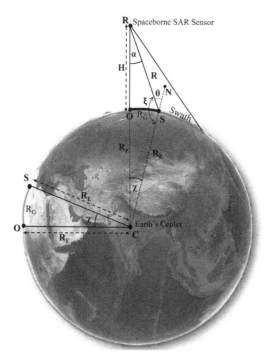

FIGURE 1.3   Spaceborne SAR geometry over the spherical Earth curvature.

Source: Image credit: Image courtesy Google Earth.

From Figure 1.3, it is clear that the angle of incidence will be equal to the difference of π and ξ. It could also be written as in Equation 1.2.

$$\theta = \pi - \xi. \tag{1.2}$$

From the law of sines for the relationship between sides and angles [8], as shown in Figure 1.3, the relation between the angles and the sides can be written as follows.

$$\frac{R_E}{\sin \alpha} = \frac{(R_E + H)}{\sin \xi} = \frac{(R_E + H)}{\sin(\pi - \theta)} = \frac{(R_E + H)}{\sin \theta}. \tag{1.3}$$

$$\sin \theta = \frac{(R_E + H) \times \sin \alpha}{R_E}. \tag{1.4}$$

The angle of incidence of the spaceborne SAR sensor can be measured by including the value of the radius of the earth, the platform altitude of the SAR sensor from the earth's surface, and the SAR look angle.

1.3 NORMALIZED RADAR BACKSCATTER CROSS-SECTION

Studies have shown that for scientific investigations, absolute calibration accuracy of 1 dB or better is essential for radiometric calibration to measure the radar cross-section from the scattering areas or pixel sizes [9]. Radiometric calibration of SAR data is generally performed by assuming the flat terrain includes the angle of incidence information in addition to the system parameters. Radiometric calibration is the procedure to obtain the normalized measure of the radar return from a distributed target, and the amount of the return signal from the scatter in the direction of the radar is the backscattering; the radar cross-section of the backscattered signal will be the backscattering cross-section (also known as the backscattering coefficient) and is usually represented by sigma naught [10].

The normalized radar backscatter cross-section of the targeted object in the SAR imagery can be calculated by using the SAR system parameters during image acquisition and the local incidence angle. The normalized backscattering cross-section for the alternating polarization slant-range complex products of ENVISAT ASAR is shown in Equation 1.5 [11].

$$\sigma_{i,j}^0 = \frac{DN_{i,j}}{K} \left(\frac{1}{G(\alpha_{i,j})^2} \right) \left(\frac{R_{i,j}}{R_{ref}} \right)^4 \sin(\theta_{i,j}) \tag{1.5}$$

for i = 1,2,............L and j = 1,2,...................M

where,

$DN_{i,j} = I^2 + Q^2$ = pixel intensity of power image at the ith image line and jth column;

K = absolute calibration constant;

$\sigma_{i,j}^0$ = sigma naught at image line and column "i,j";

$G(\alpha_{i,j}) = 4\pi \dfrac{S}{\lambda^2}$· = two-way antenna gain at the distributed target look angle corresponding to pixel "i,j" [11];

λ = wavelength of the microwave;

$$\pi = 3.14 \text{ or } \left(\frac{22}{7}\right);$$

S = surface area of the radar antenna;

η = illumination efficiency;

$\alpha_{i,j}$ = look angle corresponding to pixel "i,j";

$R_{i,j}$ = slant range distance to the pixel of ith line and jth column;

R_{ref} = reference slant range distance (800 km for all beams and modes); and

$\theta_{i,j}$ = incidence angle at the pixel of the ith row (line) and jth column.

1.4 LOCAL ANGLE OF INCIDENCE

To measure the actual radar cross-section for a resolution cell for undulating terrain, retrieval of local incidence angle for the corresponding locations in the SAR imagery is required. Calculation of local incidence angle requires information on radar incidence angle, the slope of the terrain, aspect angle, and viewing azimuth of the sensor [12]–[14]. Figure 1.4 shows a diagram of SAR image acquisition over undulating terrain. The angle of incidence of the incident electromagnetic waves is represented by θ_1 and the local angle of incidence is represented by θ. It is clear from Figure 1.4 that the radar angle of incidence that is calculated from Equation 1.4 is different than the local incidence angle.

Equation 1.6 is used to calculate the local incidence angle of each resolution cell of the SAR data for undulating terrain [12].

$$\theta_i = \cos^{-1}\left(\cos\theta_1 \cos\mu - \sin\mu\sin\theta_1 \cos(\alpha - \delta)\right), \tag{1.6}$$

where θ_1 is the radar incidence angle, θ_i is the local incidence angle for the ith pixel, μ is the local slope, δ is the terrain's aspect angle, and α is the SAR viewing angle.

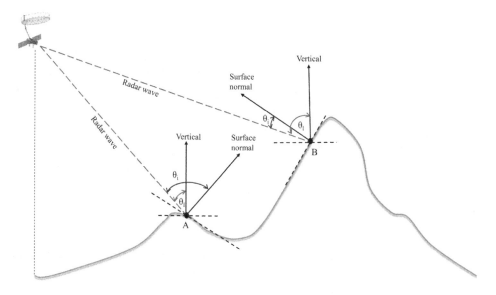

FIGURE 1.4 SAR image acquisition over an undulating terrain for analyzing the difference between radar angle of incidence and local incidence angle.

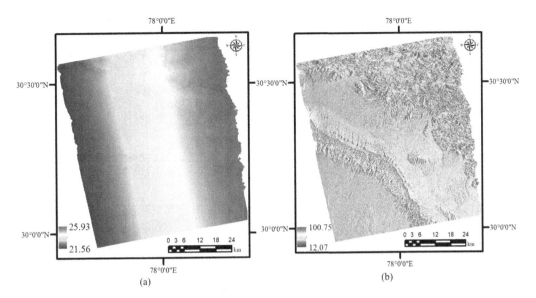

FIGURE 1.5 Incidence angle images of ALOS-2 PALSAR-2 data (a) radar incidence angle image from ellipsoid and (b) local incidence angle image.

Figure 1.5 shows the images of radar incidence angle and local incidence angle images of stripmap mode ALOS-2 PALSAR-2 data acquired over the Doon Valley forest ranges in Uttarakhand, India.

It is visible in the radar incidence angle map from the ellipsoid that it does not have sensitivity towards the undulating terrain because the angle of incidence is smoothly varying between 21.56° and 25.93°. The radar angle of incidence as shown in Figure 1.5a is generated using the radius of the earth, the platform altitude of the SAR sensor from the Earth's surface, and the SAR look angle, which varies from near to far range. Figure 1.5b is the local incidence angle map, generated with the help of SAR imaging geometry and terrain parameters; it shows sensitivity towards the topographic variation and undulation in the terrain.

1.5   SAR POLARIZATIONS

The electromagnetic wave consists of an electric field vector and magnetic field vector; these remain perpendicular to each other and mutually perpendicular to the direction of propagation of the electromagnetic wave. In imaging active microwave remote sensing, only one component, the electric field, is used to collect the information. Polarization refers to the vibration of the electric field perpendicular to the direction propagation. In an unpolarized electromagnetic wave, the electric field vibrates in all of the possible directions perpendicular to the propagation axis. Polarization restricts vibration of the electric field in either the horizontal or vertical direction. The electric field of a horizontally polarized electromagnetic wave oscillates in a plane parallel to the surface and the electric field oscillates vertically to the surface when polarized vertically [15]. A maximum of four polarimetric combinations can be received at a time, depending on the horizontal and vertical transmit and receive modes of a SAR system. The maximum four polarimetric combinations of the SAR data are horizontal transmit and horizontal receive (HH), horizontal transmit and vertical receive (HV), vertical transmit and horizontal receive (VH), and vertical transmit and vertical receive (VV). If a SAR system can acquire only one polarimetric combination out of the four possible polarimetric combinations, the data will be single polarized SAR data. If any two polarimetric combinations are acquired by the SAR system, then the data will be dual polarimetric and the system will be the dual-polarized

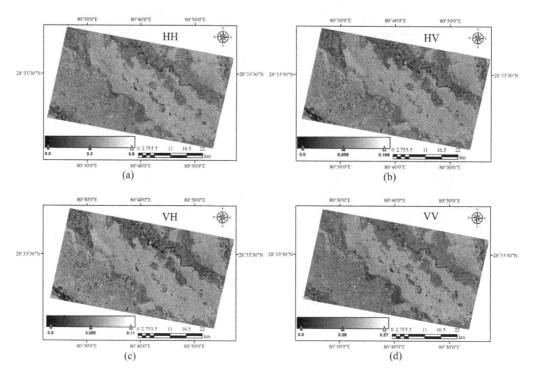

FIGURE 1.6　Quad-pol ((a) HH-polarization, (b) HV-polarization, (c) VH-polarization, and (d) VV-polarization) fully polarimetric C-band SAR data of RADARSAT-2 for Dudhwa National Park, Uttar Pradesh, India.

SAR system. Most spaceborne SAR systems operate in linear polarization to provide a linearly polar combination of horizontal and vertical polarization, but while maintaining a 90° phase shift between the horizontal and vertical components of the electric field during transmission, it is also possible to generate circularly polarized electromagnetic waves [16].

Figure 1.6 shows the quad-pol fully polarimetric data of RADARSAT-2 acquired on 20 November 2015 over Dudhwa National Park, Uttar Pradesh, India. It is visible in Figures 1.6 (a), (b), (c), and (d) that the different objects in the imaged area show different scattering behavior, and accordingly, the variation in different polarimetric combinations for each object/feature/class could be observed.

1.6　SAR IMAGING MODE

SAR sensors are operated in stripmap, spotlight, and ScanSAR modes to acquire the data. The highest spatial resolution is obtained with spotlight mode and the largest coverage is provided by ScanSAR mode. The high spatial resolution in the azimuth direction in the spotlight mode SAR is obtained by pointing the antenna towards the targeted object for the entire duration of data acquisition, as shown in Figure 1.7. The SAR antenna remains steered towards the targeted area in the spotlight mode as the airborne/spaceborne SAR system passes by the targeted location. The targeted area is illuminated for an extended time to get a higher effective synthetic aperture length.

Figure 1.8 (a) shows the staring spotlight mode data of TerraSAR-X, which was acquired on 25 December 2014 over the Manali region of Himachal Pradesh, India. The staring spotlight image of Manali has a 0.168 m range resolution and 0.45 m azimuth resolution. The final pixel size is 0.64 m after slant to ground range conversion and multilooking. The number of range and azimuth looks were 1 and 4 respectively in multilooking operation. Multilooking enhances the radiometric

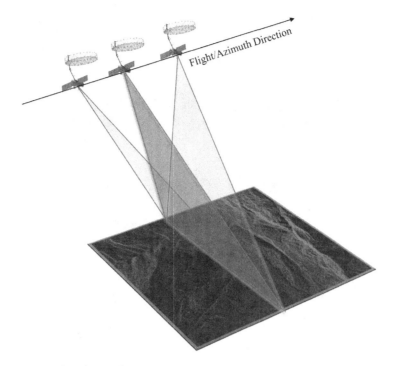

FIGURE 1.7   Spotlight imaging mode.

property of the SAR data to improve the image interpretability. The canopy of the individual trees could be easily seen and the canopy coverage and other parameters could be easily extracted from the staring spotlight TerraSAR-X data. The VV polarization backscatter data is represented by a color scheme, as shown in Figure 1.8 (a), in which low backscatter is shown in blue, moderate scatter is shown in green, and the very high backscatter is shown in red. Figure 1.8 (b) shows the staring-spotlight SAR data of TerraSAR-X over Delhi Airport Terminal 3, which was acquired on 28 November 2021. In the high-resolution SAR data terminal buildings, the runway, taxiway, aircraft stands, Aerocity, and other features are visible.

The stripmap mode data acquisition is generally performed by keeping a fixed off-nadir angle (look angle) when the electromagnetic waves illuminate the ground swath by pointing the antenna beam to a fixed azimuth angle. Figure 1.9 (a) shows the imaging geometry of stripmap mode SAR. Figure 1.9 (b) shows the stripmap image of the L-band spaceborne SAR data of the phased array L-band synthetic aperture radar-2 (PALSAR-2) of Advanced Land Observing Satellite-2 (ALOS-2). The L-band SAR data of ALOS-2 PALSAR-2 was acquired over Dehradun, Uttarakhand, India, on 9 August 2015 in stripmap mode with a 23.876° angle of incidence. Figure 1.9 shows the Pauli RGB representation of the quad-pol data in which surface, double-bounce, and volume scattering elements are represented by blue, red, and green respectively. It can be seen in Figure 1.9 that the dry river channels and smooth surface show the dominance of surface scattering elements, highlighted in blue. Vegetation-covered land shows the dominance of volumetric scattering elements and is represented in green. All objects (mainly urban structures) that contribute to double-bounce scattering are represented in red.

ScanSAR imaging mode is also known as "burst mode" or "wide swath mode" and is used for acquiring SAR data for a large swath coverage by periodically switching the antenna look angle of the SAR system in multiple swaths. A large swath coverage in ScanSAR imaging mode is obtained at the expense of azimuth resolution. ScanSAR imaging mode of a SAR system is shown in Figure 1.10 (a). Figure 1.10 (b) shows ScanSAR mode image acquisition of Sentinel-1A for the

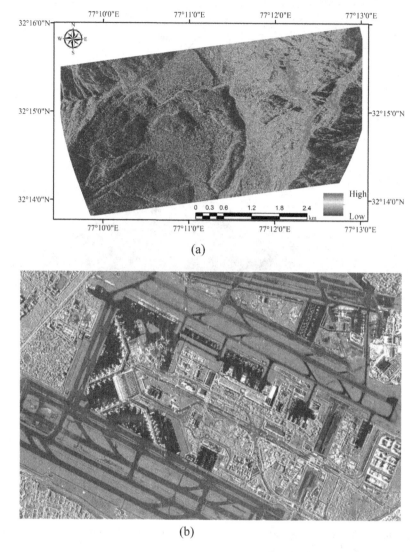

(a)

(b)

FIGURE 1.8 Staring-spotlight mode data of TerraSAR-X over (a) Manali region of Himachal Pradesh, India, and (b) Delhi Airport Terminal 3.

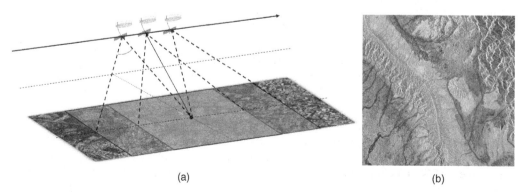

(a)   (b)

FIGURE 1.9 (a) Stripmap mode imaging and (b) stripmap mode quad-pol Pauli RGB of ALOS-2 PALSAR-2 data.

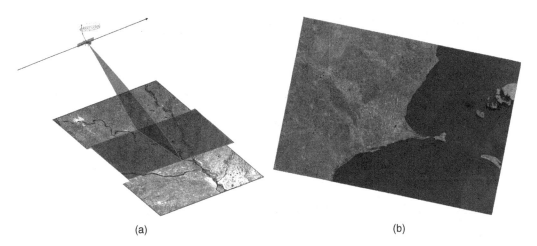

(a)   (b)

FIGURE 1.10   (a) ScanSAR mode imaging and (b) interferometric wide swath (IW) mode (ScanSAR mode data of Sentinel-1A).

Ram Setu (also known as Rama's Bridge) area, located between Rameswaram Island, off the southeastern coast of Tamil Nadu, India, and Mannar Island, off the north-western coast of Sri Lanka. The figure shows a full-resolution RGB decomposition for a radiometric terrain corrected granule of GRD SAR data from the Sentinel-1 mission, processed using GAMMA software. (This product was generated by ASF DAAC HyP3 2022 using the hyp3_gamma plugin version 5.1.4 running GAMMA release 20210701.) The interferometric wide swath (IW) mode of the Sentinel-1 SAR system is a new ScanSAR mode that is also known as terrain observation with progressive scan (TOPS) SAR. This false-color image facilitates visual interpretation by decomposing the signals into surface scattering with some volume scattering (red band), high volume scattering (green band), and low surface and volume scattering (blue band).

REFERENCES

[1]   K. Y. You, "Introductory chapter: RF/Microwave applications," in *Emerging Microwave Technologies in Industrial, Agricultural, Medical and Food Processing*, K. Y. You, Ed. Rijeka: IntechOpen, 2018, pp. 3–10.

[2]   K. Herndon, F. Meyer, A. Flores, E. Cherrington, L. Kucera, and Earth Science Data Systems, "What is synthetic aperture radar?," 2020. https://earthdata.nasa.gov/learn/backgrounders/what-is-sar (accessed Jan. 03, 2022).

[3]   B. R. Mahafza, *Introduction to Radar Analysis, Second Edition*, 2nd ed. New York: Chapman and Hall/CRC, 2017.

[4]   R. J. Sullivan, *Radar Foundations for Imaging and Advanced Concepts*, Indian Rep. New Delhi: Prentice-Hall of India & SciTech Publishing House, 2004.

[5]   C.-L. Chuang et al., "NISAR L-band digital electronics subsystem: A multichannel system with distributed processors for digital beam forming and mode dependent filtering," *2016 IEEE Radar Conference (RadarConf)*, 2016, pp. 1–5. https://doi.org/10.1109/RADAR.2016.7485225.

[6]   J. van Zyl and Y. Kim, *Synthetic Aperture Radar Polarimetry*. Hoboken, NJ: John Wiley & Sons, 2011.

[7]   C. Oliver and S. Quegan, *Understanding Synthetic Aperture Radar Images*. Herndon, VA: SciTech Publishing House, 2004.

[8]   I. M. Gelfand and M. Saul, *Trigonometry*. Boston, MA: Birkhäuser, 2001.

[9]   J. J. van Zyl, B. D. Chapman, P. Dubois, and J. Shi, "The effect of topography on SAR calibration," *IEEE Trans. Geosci. Remote Sens.*, vol. 31, no. 5, pp. 1036–1043, 1993. https://doi.org/10.1109/36.263774.

[10] European Space Agency, "Sentinel-1 SAR user guide," *Report*, 2022. https://sentinels.copernicus.eu/web/sentinel/technical-guides/sentinel-1-sar (accessed Feb. 22, 2022).

[11] B. Rosich and P. Meadows, "Absolute calibration of ASAR Level 1 products generated with PF-ASAR," 2004. https://earth.esa.int/web/guest/-/absolute-calibration-of-asar-level-1-products-generated-with-pf-asar-4503.

[12] D. Paluba, "A correction of the local incidence angle of SAR data: A land cover specific approach for time series analysis," Charles University, 2021.

[13] D. Paluba, J. Laštovička, A. Mouratidis, and P. Štych, "Land cover-specific local incidence angle correction: A method for time-series analysis of forest ecosystems," *Remote Sens.*, vol. 13, no. 9, pp. 1743:1–24, 2021. https://doi.org/10.3390/rs13091743.

[14] M. Hinse, Q. H. J. Gwyn, and F. Bonn, "Radiometric correction of C-band imagery for topographic effects in regions of moderate relief," *IEEE Trans. Geosci. Remote Sens.*, vol. 26, no. 2, pp. 122–132, 1988. https://doi.org/10.1109/36.3012.

[15] Alaska Satellite Facility, "Introduction to SAR," 2022. https://hyp3-docs.asf.alaska.edu/guides/introduction_to_sar/ (accessed Feb. 01, 2022).

[16] NASA's Jet Propulsion Laboratory, "Polarimetry," *NASA ISRO SAR (NISAR) Mission*, 2021. https://nisar.jpl.nasa.gov/mission/get-to-know-sar/polarimetry/ (accessed Feb. 01, 2022).

2 Speckle Reduction in SAR Images

Hossein Aghababaei and Alfred Stein

CONTENTS

2.1 INTRODUCTION

Synthetic aperture radar (SAR) imagery has many advantages over standard optical satellites, most notably that it can cover the entire Earth on all days and in all weather conditions, something that thousands of currently operating optical satellites cannot do. The most important factor in SAR imaging is the coherent active sensing system, where the sensor provides its own energy source for illumination. Microwave signals emitted by the sensor and reflected by the ground return to the sensor differently depending upon the material, texture, and moisture of targets, providing useful information on the characteristics and location of the observed targets. With radar imagery, however, the characteristic parameters of a target must be estimated from unreliable data because they are not directly accessible [1]. They are called unreliable because SAR images are subject to large variations and fluctuations due to speckle that is inherent in coherent images. Speckle can be clearly

DOI: 10.1201/9781003204466-2

13

FIGURE 2.1   ICEYE amplitude image over London, United Kingdom.

seen in Figure 2.1, where the amplitude image of the ICEYE satellite exhibits a salt-and-pepper effect, i.e., random and grainy aspects, that limits the possibilities of visual interpretation and analysis of the scene. Therefore, derived parameters such as texture or radiometric properties, as well as interferometric and polarimetric information, exhibit a strong signal-dependent variance. This affects not only the visual appearance of the images but also the performance of image analysis and information extraction techniques, which is detrimental for SAR image applications. Therefore, before performing information extraction techniques, speckle reduction is an important and often necessary step to reduce some of the strong variation in SAR images.

Speckle reduction or despeckling of SAR images is a preprocessing step that aims to reduce noise variance with minimal degradation of image quality. The simplest method to reduce speckle is to spatially average the pixels in a small window around the target pixel. This method is similar to the conventional mean filter, but it is not very successful because speckle has a multiplicative property [2]. Nevertheless, this simple strategy is well applicable to interferometric and tomographic data and leads to a uniform reduction of speckle [3]. This spatial averaging is a simple and basic form of despeckling, which comes with resolution losses and the possible mixing of different signals, affecting image quality and features such as edges, artificial structures, and fine textures. Robust despeckling, however, requires more sophisticated adaptive algorithms based upon the multiplicative speckle noise model. To apply it, despeckling must be carefully planned to avoid loss of resolution, loss of useful information and local mean backscatter, and degradation of fine features [4]. Over the last four decades, and since the advent of SAR technology, the design of efficient speckle suppression filters has been a long-standing research problem, with the first attempts at a statistical optimal linear approximation of multiplicative noise dating back to the 1980s [5]. The need to develop robust and efficient denoising strategies has significantly accelerated research activities, and successful methods have been developed, including local and adaptive strategies based on image models in spatial [5–7] and transformed domains [8, 9].

A special class of despeckling algorithms are the *nonlocal* (NL) techniques, which have been shown to be very effective in preserving detail while removing noise [1]. NL techniques are based upon the analysis of patches information, i.e., information within a small rectangular image region, typically a small square window. Unlike a local method such as the well-known intensity-driven adaptive neighborhood (IDAN) filter [10] that considers connected pixels, far-spaced pixels whose patch information is similar to the patch of that target pixel can be combined, justifying the widely used *nonlocal* name. In the last decade, several NL algorithms [11–16] for despeckling have appeared in the literature. The main difference between the algorithms lies in the definition of the similarity criterion and the function used to merge similar pixels or patches. A detailed review of these strategies is presented in the next sections.

Recently, deep learning (DL) has achieved great success in speckle reduction of SAR images. Its data-driven nature provides improved flexibility and the ability to capture a variety of features from SAR images. Besides the design and definition of the network architecture, two main aspects of this new strategy are 1) definition of the cost function and 2) training of the network. In the literature, the mean square error (MSE) [17] between the reference data and the output of the network is usually used as the cost function, while in some cases the MSE is combined with a regularization of the total variation [18, 19]. In addition, some studies [20, 21] have included statistical properties of SAR images in the definition of the cost function. Three different strategies have been explored for training the network. The first is based upon supervised training with reference data. In this strategy, the network matches the noisy images (as input) to the reference image (as output of the network). Since a noise-free reference image is not available for real SAR data from air or space, the challenge in using this strategy is to produce a simulated dataset. The second strategy is based upon the use of co-registered pairs of multi-temporal SAR images, while the third strategy is based upon a single SAR image without relying on reference or multi-temporal data. The details of these strategies are described in the next sections.

In this chapter, the underlying ideas and principles of SAR despeckling are explained in a general framework ranging from a single intensity SAR image to more sophisticated SAR modalities such as polarimetric and interferometric datasets. The statistical speckle model and basic and state-of-the-art filtering operations in local and nonlocal frames as well as advanced promising deep learning strategies are described. In addition, the chapter includes an overview of the established and widely used metrics for evaluating the quality of speckle filtering, both with- and without-reference metrics. Before delving into the core of the despeckling, the various modalities of SAR imaging are presented.

2.2 SAR IMAGING MODALITIES

SAR imaging proceeds as follows. An imaging radar with a mounted antenna on a platform transmits a microwave signal towards the Earth's surface in a side-looking direction. The reflected signal is backscattered from the surface and, in the case of a monostatic radar, is received by the same antenna. A complex SAR image is then created from the amplitude and phase of the received backscattered signal during the focusing process [22]. SAR images, however, can represent much more than just a two-dimensional (2D) reflectivity map. They contain a wealth of information that is useful for a variety of applications, from environmental studies to 3D or 4D (space and time) mapping. These applications can be performed using various SAR imaging modalities, which are briefly discussed below, while these modalities all share the common requirement of despeckling

2.2.1 AMPLITUDE/INTENSITY MODALITY

The simplest configuration of the SAR imaging modality represents the backscattered signal with a complex image along the coordinate system of the azimuth-slant range. The magnitude of the backscattered signal, indicating the radar cross-section (RCS), is usually given by an amplitude image (or an intensity image equal to the square of the magnitude). An example of an amplitude image is shown in Figure 2.1.

2.2.2 Polarimetric Modality

Polarimetric SAR (PolSAR) systems transmit and receive the radar waves with different polarization channels, allowing deeper insight into the backscattering mechanisms within the SAR image pixel. Two orthogonal polarization states are usually required, and PolSAR systems typically use a pair of horizontal and vertical polarizations [23]. When the transmitting and receiving antennas exchange their roles and the waves are transmitted and collected at the same position, PolSAR records three complex values for each resolution cell, taking into account the reciprocity theorem. If the waves are collected at a different position than the one transmitted, however, even four complex values are recorded.

2.2.3 Multi-Frequency Modality

In SAR systems, the recorded backscatter waves are a function of the frequency or the wavelength. Therefore, multiple images can be recorded at different frequencies [24, 25], increasing the dimensionality of the data and, consequently, the possibility of gaining deeper knowledge about the observed scene. This is called the multi-frequency modality.

2.2.4 Interferometric Modality

In SAR interferometry (InSAR) modality, two or more SAR images of the same scene from slightly different positions are combined to generally obtain elevation information or ground displacement maps [26].

2.2.5 Polarimetric-Interferometric Modality

In this modality, polarimetric and interferometric data are combined to provide information on the vertical structure of the targets and the nature of the scattering patterns [27]. The simple and important modality of polarimetric SAR interferometry (PolInSAR) uses two PolSAR data obtained under interferometric conditions and consists of six complex backscattering records (assuming that both polarimetric images obtain under the reciprocity theorem).

All these modalities require despeckling in their preprocessing stage. Accordingly, speckle filtering techniques fall into two categories: 1) single-image or single-channel techniques, and 2) multi-channel techniques. In the first category, the goal is to remove speckle from a single amplitude or intensity SAR image, while in the second case, multiple available images of the same scene are filtered together and the second-order covariance matrix of these batch data is estimated. This is usually the case when dealing with PolSAR, InSAR, multi-frequency, and PolInSAR modalities. This chapter thus presents the organization of content based on single and multi-channel filtering frameworks.

2.3 SINGLE-CHANNEL SAR IMAGES RESTORATION

2.3.1 Speckle Model

The signal returned by a rough surface[1] for a pixel consists of the incoherent sum of several backscattered waves reflected from many elementary scatterers, as shown with the well-known illustrations in Figure 2.2. The number and distribution of scatterers within each pixel, as well as their nature and structure, are random. Accordingly, the summation of the echoes can be either high or low depending on the constructive or destructive interference of the backscattered waves. This interference creates a granular noise in SAR images called speckle [28]. Typically, in SAR images, as can be seen in the ICEYE image in Figure 2.1, there is a random alternation of bright and dark

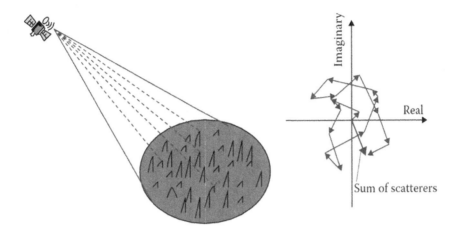

FIGURE 2.2   Illustration of speckle formation [23].

spots related to the constructive and destructive interference within pixels that gives rise to the speckle. Closer inspection reveals that speckle noise in homogeneous regions, such as river, is usually fully uncorrelated and random. In such cases, it can be assumed that the number of scatterers in each resolution cell is sufficiently large and none of them provides a much stronger reflected signal than the others (distributed scatterers). In this situation, the real and imaginary parts of the resulting complex signal are independent, and speckle is said to be *fully developed* [28].

For pixels where the returned signal is largely determined by the response of one (point scatterer) or a few elements, such as a corner reflector in built-up areas, however, the random effect is negligible, and the received signal power is related to the reflection coefficient of the individual scatterer. Therefore, the optimal design of a despeckling filter requires the separate treatment of a homogeneous area (with distributed scatterers) and pixels with point-like scatterers.

A well-adapted and experimented model in the literature for speckle is the multiplicative fading random process given as:

$$y(p) = x(p)\, s(p), \tag{2.1}$$

where $y(p)$ is the pth pixel in amplitude or intensity of an observed noisy SAR image, the quantity $x(p)$ presents unspeckle or noise-free reflectivity, and $s(p)$ represents the speckle fading term. Recall that in Equation (2.1) the additive white Gaussian noise is ignored, since in SAR images the additive noise is generally negligible compared to the signal-dependent speckle term. Thus, despeckling can be said to restore x from the observed noisy measurement y for each resolution cell (p) in the image. A despeckling filter is ideal and efficient if it is able to restore a noise-free reflectivity image without compromising the information content, to maintain the edges and sharpness of the feature boundaries, and to preserve the details [23].

As mentioned earlier, the real and imaginary parts of the observed noisy complex image under the fully developed speckle condition are independently and identically distributed with zero-mean Gaussian variables and a variance of $\sigma/2$. Consequently, the noisy complex image can be described by a complex Gaussian distribution. From this, the probability distribution function (pdf) of the amplitude image can be derived (Figure 2.3 (a) (b)) as the following Rayleigh distribution model [23]:

$$f_A\left(a\right) = \frac{2L^L}{\sigma^{2L}\left(L-1\right)!} a^{2L-1} exp\left(-\frac{La^2}{\sigma^2}\right), \tag{2.2}$$

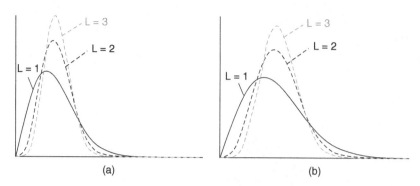

FIGURE 2.3 Pdfs of amplitude (a) and speckle (b) with different number looks L.

where $f_A(.)$ is the Rayleigh pdf of amplitude image, L is the number look, a indicates the pixel's values in an amplitude image, i.e., $a = y$, and $(.)!$ is the factorial operator. Moreover, the noise term of amplitude image can be described by the square root gamma distribution as:

$$f_s(s) = \frac{2L^L}{\Gamma(L)} s^{2L-1} exp\left(-Ls^2\right), \tag{2.3}$$

where Γ is the so-called gamma function and s is the speckle fading variable. The above models are valid only under the assumption that the mapped scene is characterized by distributed scatterers. Knowledge of the distribution model is the basis for the development of various despeckling filters, e.g., the nonland filter presented by Ferraioli et al. [14].

2.3.2 Despeckling Filters

In Equation (2.1), the measured noisy amplitude (or intensity) $y(p)$ can be viewed as a random variable whose mean is equal to the noiseless reflectivity $x(p)$ (i.e., $E[y(p)] = x(p)$, where $E[.]$ is the expectation operator), but which has a large variance. The principle of despeckling filters is therefore based on reducing this large variance of y to obtain a better estimate of its mean or noiseless reflectivity [23]. The expectation $E[y(p)]$ can be computed from L independent realizations of an amplitude (or intensity). Since the different realizations are not available for each amplitude, however, the expectation is unknown. Therefore, the expectation $E[y(p)] = x(p)$ is *commonly* approximated by spatially averaging similar pixels in the image as:

$$\hat{x} = \frac{1}{L} \sum_{l=1}^{L} y\left(p_l\right), \tag{2.4}$$

where $y(p_l)$ indicates the lth similar pixel to the target pixel. The selection and detection of valid similar pixels is an intensive research topic, where the objective is to find the most similar samples that have the same statistical distribution as the target pixel. In the following subsections, two general frameworks for finding similar samples and the spatial averaging procedure are discussed.

2.3.2.1 Local Framework

Local filters are based upon the idea of neighborhood operation, where a set of pixels surrounding a target pixel is used during the filtering process. A neighborhood of any target pixel (p) is a group of pixels defined by their position relative to that pixel. As shown in Figure 2.4 (a), the neighborhood can usually be defined using a rectangular window (3×3, 5×5, 7×7, ...) that is centered on the target pixel p. Thus, filtering can be viewed as a neighborhood operation where the value of any

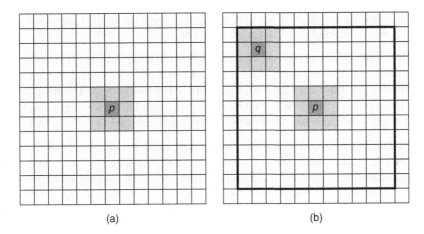

(a)   (b)

FIGURE 2.4   Representation of (a) local and (b) nonlocal frameworks.

target pixel in the output image is determined by applying a standard algorithm to the values of the pixels in the neighborhood or in the defined sliding rectangular window. As mentioned earlier, the mean or so-called boxcar filter is a simple averaging technique in which the target pixel is replaced by the mean of the pixels in a sliding window. This filter reduces the standard deviation of the noise by the square root of the total number of pixels in the window, but can result in loss of resolution and some over-smoothing effects, especially for larger sliding windows. This simple and basic noise filtering and even similar filters such as the median filter, however, cannot efficiently deal with multiplicative speckle noise. Therefore, more sophisticated techniques are required.

In the context of local despeckling, more successful filters have been reported through the development of Bayesian techniques. These filters aim at obtaining an estimate of the noise-free reflectivity $\hat{x}$ based upon a priori information about the signal model or its distribution. Depending upon the definition of the error function to be minimized, i.e., $\varepsilon = x - \hat{x}$, different estimators can be defined. The details of the various minimization strategies can be found in the reference by Argenti et al. in [4]. Here we provide an overview of some basic Bayesian filters that are still efficient in SAR despeckling.

Lee filters [5]: This filter is based upon the concept of using local mean and local variance estimated using a local window to deal with multiplicative speckle noise, additive noise, or a combination of both types. It assumes that the restored noise-free reflectivity $\hat{x}$ can be obtained by a linear combination of local mean $\bar{x}$ and the noisy measurement y, as $\hat{x} = a\bar{x} + by$ where the parameters a and b are estimated to minimize the mean squared error. The solution of this minimization is given by $a = 1 - b$, and consequently the estimate of the noise-free reflectivity is given by:

$$\hat{x} = \overline{x} + b\left(y - \overline{x}\right), \tag{2.5}$$

where $\bar{x} = \bar{y}$. The parameter $b = \text{variance}(x) / \text{variance}(y)$ can be viewed as a weighing between $\bar{x}$ and the original pixel value y. Indeed, the Lee filter has the adaptive specification. In homogeneous regions of a SAR image, the reflectivity is mostly constant and the variance of x is close to zero, and consequently $b = 0$. Thus, estimation of the filter boils down to the average of pixel values in a local neighborhood, i.e., $\hat{x} = \bar{x}$. For textured regions with moderate heterogeneity, the filter's solution is a linear combination between the local mean and the original pixel value. For extremely heterogeneous regions, however, $\text{variance}(x) \approx \text{variance}(y)$, so that the estimate of reflectivity is equal to its measurement, i.e., $\hat{x} = y$. An example of such a region is the neighborhood of a point or persistent scatterer, so such pixels should be left unfiltered and unprocessed, since these scatterers are intrinsically noise-free. Different solutions for parameter b are presented. In particular, this parameter differs in reference [29] with the term of $(1 + \sigma_s^2)^{-1}$ from Lee's original derivation, where σ_s^2 denotes the variance of noise. In the original work, it is assumed that $(1 + \sigma_s^2) \approx 1$, which could hold for multi-look data, while for single-look images may not be valid.

Kuan filters [6]: Kuan filters implement the expression of the local statistic in Equation (2.5), while another algorithm is used to compute the local variance of the noisy image, i.e., the variance of y. The development of this filter emerged out of a common problem with the Lee filter, i.e., the noise in edge areas is not properly smoothed. With the Kuan filter, speckle noise at the edges is less prominent, and the Kuan filter decreases the smoothing ability as compared to the Lee filter.

Refined Lee [30]: The refined Lee filter is designed to solve the common Lee filter's problem related to noisy edge regions in the filtered image. For this purpose, eight 7×7 windows are used to detect edge alignments. If no edge is detected, the estimation of $\hat{x}$ is performed using the whole 7×7 window; otherwise, the local mean and variance are calculated using only the pixels in the detected edge-oriented window, and then the expression of local statistics (Equation 2.5) is implemented. Although the filter works well on edge areas, artifacts can occur in structured regions, resulting in an overly segmented filtered image. Also, the kernel or window size in this filter is fixed at 7×7. An example of filtering operation using RadarSAT images in HH polarization over Flevoland (Netherlands) is shown in Figure 2.5. The data were acquired in April 2009 with a spatial resolution of 4.7 × 4.8 (azimuth, range), and the image has been released by Canadian Space Agency. As can be seen, the blurring or over-smoothing effect in heterogeneous build-up regions is evident with the result of the boxcar filter (Figure 2.5 b), highlighting that plain averaging is not the optimal strategy for despeckling in structured regions. This problem can largely be addressed with the Lee filter (Figure 2.5 c) and especially with the refined Lee filter (Figure 2.5 d). As an alternative, anisotropic diffusion [31], efficiently preserves structures such as lines or other details well in filtered images. Reducing image noise while preserving image edges and important parts of image content is generally a difficult task, while some studies reported the significance of exploring the anisotropic strategy for edge preservation [14, 32].

Other despeckling techniques: The linearized model in Equation (2.5) is the basis for the development of several despeckling filters in the literature, such as the Frost filter [33], the enhanced Frost filter [34], and the local adaptive filter [35]. The maximum a posteriori probability (MAP) filter [36, 37] is another classic but important filter for SAR despeckling. The filter is based upon the assumption that both radar reflectivity and the speckle noise follow a gamma distribution. The solution of the MAP filter lies between y and $\bar{x}$, which is the case for the linearized model. The sigma filter is another despeckling technique proposed by Lee [38]. This filter defines two sigma ranges for multiplicative noise $(y - 2\sigma_s y, y + 2\sigma_s y)$, and if the value of the target pixel is within the upper and lower sigma bounds, the estimation of $\hat{x}$ is performed using the average of the pixels in the local window. Otherwise, the target pixel is left unfiltered. The filter is efficient in enhancing contrast features, while it needs to be applied repeatedly with decreasing values of σ_s to prevent or alleviate the problem of the appearance of dark spots in the filtered image [4].

The above techniques belong to a class of filters that operate in the spatial domain. There are other types of filters that implement despeckling in the transformed domain. In some studies, multiplicative speckle noise has been converted into additive noise by the logarithm transformation. Reference [39] is the first work that employs this transformation to reduce the speckle effect using Lee's additive filter [5]. The advantage of such a transformation is the possibility of using various advanced techniques developed in the digital image processing community to reduce additive noise in optical images. After such a transformation, however, the dynamic range of the original image is compressed, and the local mean and variance in the transformed domain may not have the same specification as the values computed in the spatial domain. The wavelet transform is another way of filtering in the transform domain. Its main advantage is that a wavelet sub-band can be assigned to a speckle contribution that can be computed and filtered out [4]. For some interesting techniques based upon the wavelet transform, the reader is referred to [7, 40–45]. Finally, regularization of total

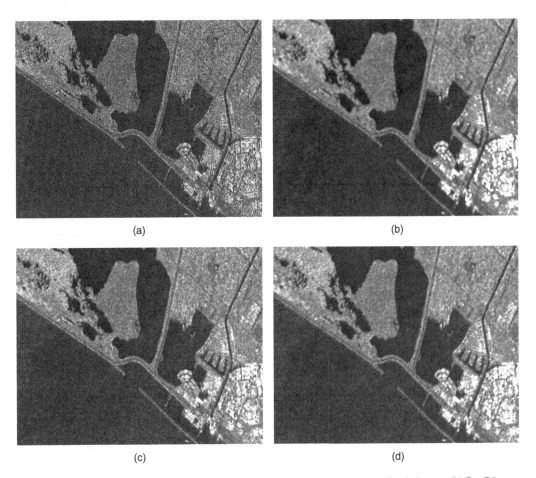

(a)

(b)

(c)

(d)

FIGURE 2.5 Example of some local filters: (a) original single-look noisy amplitude image, (b) 7 × 7 boxcar filter, (c) 7 × 7 Lee filter, (d) 7 × 7 refined Lee.

variation is a popular denoising method as well. This type of denoising aims to minimize a suitable cost function, which is a combination of a term for data fidelity and a priori that enforces smoothing while preserving edges. For more details, see [46–48].

2.3.2.2 Nonlocal Framework

The first breakthrough in SAR despeckling was achieved by introducing the nonlocal filtering framework, where a similar sample from the local neighborhood of a target pixel is extended to the whole image or to a search window. In this framework, the estimate of noise-free reflectivity can be recovered by the following equation:

$$\hat{x}(p) = \frac{\sum_{l=1}^{L} w(q_l) y(q_l)}{\sum_{l=1}^{L} w(q_l)}, \qquad (2.6)$$

where w is the weight indicating the importance of each sample used during averaging. Note that many local methods, such as the conventional boxcar, either set the importance of all samples equal, i.e., $w(l) = 1$, or compute the importance of samples based on the spatial distance to the target pixel, similar to the standard Gaussian filter where the weights are sampled in the sliding window from the 2D Gaussian function. In the nonlocal framework, however, the idea is to compute weights based on not only their spatial distance from the target pixel but also their similarity to this pixel. Thus, even far distant pixels can be included in filtering, based upon similarity measured by the difference between their observed value and the value of the target pixel.

A NL framework is thus efficient as it avoids enforcing the sample selection to belong to a restricted class of neighborhood signals. In this framework, for a target pixel p to be filtered, a search window is defined, represented by a black rectangular box in Figure 2.4 (b), where the target pixel is usually located in the center of the search window. The goal is then to find similar pixels in the search window that have statistical similarities with the target pixel p. The pixel-based similarity, i.e., comparing only the values of pixels p and q, is usually rather coarse and results in the observed values being amplified by strong noise. To solve this problem and make the similarity robust to the noise, similarity of a sample in the search window, such as pixel q in Figure 2.4 (b), with the target pixel q in a nonlocal frame, is computed by defining two patches of the same shape and dimension centered on pixels p and q, respectively. For instance, the patches in Figure 2.4 (b) are defined with rectangular 3×3 windows. Accordingly, the similarity of two pixels p and q is determined by comparing the information in their patches, which is equivalent to comparing two 9×1 vectors. The estimated similarities of all pixels in the search window are then converted into weights, and aggregation of the pixels is performed according to Equation (2.6).

In order to implement this simple structure of the nonlocal framework, three important points must be considered, which are discussed below.

2.3.2.2.1 Selection of Patch and Search Window

The first point relates to the identification of the patches and the search window. The patch can typically be defined from a set of 3×3 to 11×11 pixels, while the search window is defined with a rectangular box of 21×21 to 39×39 pixels [1]. It is apparently possible to use larger or smaller sizes depending on the resolution of the image and the area of interest. A larger search window provides the opportunity to find more similar samples, resulting in robust restoration of noise-free reflectivity, but at the cost of higher computational overhead. A small patch size may still result in some coarse similarity, while a larger patch size increases the computational cost and may introduce different information, as the patch may contain pixels with different properties than the target pixel. Therefore, the optimal patch size should be chosen to find a trade-off between these aspects.

2.3.2.2.2 Definition of Similarity Measure

Similarity can be defined by comparing the information of two noisy patches P and Q centered on pixels p and q. Assuming that each patch in a single-channel amplitude (or intensity) image contains M pixels, the information of the patches P and Q can be represented as follows:

$$
\begin{aligned}
\mathbf{y}_P &= \begin{bmatrix} y(p_1) & y(p_2) & y(p_3) & \cdots & y(p_M) \end{bmatrix}^T \\
\mathbf{y}_Q &= \begin{bmatrix} y(q_1) & y(q_2) & y(q_3) & \cdots & y(q_M) \end{bmatrix}^T,
\end{aligned}
\tag{2.7}
$$

where ^{T} denotes the transpose operation and $\mathbf{y}_p, \mathbf{y}_q \in \mathbb{R}^{M \times 1}$. A pair of noisy patches P and Q is called similar if $\mathbf{y}_p$ and $\mathbf{y}_Q$ follow the same distributional model. The Euclidean distance serves as a simple criterion that calculates the similarity between two noisy patches. It is efficient only for additive Gaussian noise, a common model for optical data. Since the noise properties of SAR are fundamentally different, the comparison of SAR noisy patches is also likely to be different. Several similarity measures were presented in [49] and a brief description of the most important similarity criteria is given here.

Generalized likelihood ratio test: The similarity between patches is formulated as a hypothesis test:

$$\begin{aligned} \mathbf{H}_0 &: \mathbf{x}_P = \mathbf{x}_Q = \mathbf{x}\; nullhypothesis \\ \mathbf{H}_1 &: \mathbf{x}_P \neq \mathbf{x}_Q\; alternativehypothesis, \end{aligned} \tag{2.8}$$

where $\mathbf{x}_p$ is deterministic or noise-free component of observer noisy patch, i.e., $\mathbf{y}_P = \mathbf{x}_P \odot \mathbf{s}_P$, where s_P is speckle term of noisy patch, and $\odot$ denoted the element wise product. In Equation (2.8), the null hypothesis $\mathbf{H}_0$ indicates the similarity of patches, while the alternative hypothesis $\mathbf{H}_1$ assumes $\mathbf{H}_0$ does not hold, i.e., the two patches are different. The generalized likelihood ratio test then equals [49]:

$$\delta_{PQ} = \frac{\max\limits_{x}\big(f(\mathbf{y}_P|\mathbf{x})f\big(\mathbf{y}_Q|\mathbf{x}\big)\big)}{\max\limits_{x_P}\big(\big(f(\mathbf{y}_P|\mathbf{x}_P)\big)\big)\max\limits_{x_Q}\big(\big(f(\mathbf{y}_P|\mathbf{x}_Q)\big)\big)}, \tag{2.9}$$

where $f(.)$ is the distribution of patches under where $\mathbf{H}_0$ and $\mathbf{H}_1$ are appropriate. An example of the application of this criterion to single-channel amplitude images can be found in the works of Deledalle et al. [12, 13].

Statistical distribution model: The distance between the distributions of patches is computed using the Kolmogorov–Smirnov (KS) distance [50]. In this case, the empirical distribution models from two noisy patches are compared using the following KS equation.

$$\delta_{PQ} = \max\big(\big\|F_{dp} - F_{dQ}\big\|\big), \tag{2.10}$$

where F_{dP} and F_{dQ} are the vectors obtained by sampling the empirical cumulative distribution functions (ECDFs) of the independent and identically distributed observations in the vectors $\mathbf{y}_p$ and $\mathbf{y}_Q$, respectively.

A geometric similarity measure: Reference [51] defines a geometric similarity measure that satisfies the particularities of SAR data based upon the ratio of the patch information. This measure provides some interesting invariance properties and is based on the squared distance between observations after applying a homomorphic transformation to the patch data, i.e.,

$$\delta_{PQ} = \big\|\log(\mathbf{d}_P) - \log(\mathbf{d}_Q)\big\|_2^2, \tag{2.11}$$

where $\|A\|_2$ indicates the L^2 norm of A.

These similarity measures are commonly used in nonlocal denoising of SAR images, while a variety of similarity measures exists, such as joint-likelihood criteria [49] and mutual-information kernels [52], that can be used in a nonlocal framework. The covariance matrix was defined from the patch information in [53], while the generalized likelihood ratio test was used following the distribution of the covariance matrix as the similarity index. In [11, 14], the statistical distribution strategy was extended and the patch ratio was compared with a known model. The details of this model are described in the next subsection.

2.3.2.2.3 Similarity to Weight Conversion

In Equation (2.6), the importance of all pixels in the search window should be computed to recover the noise-free estimate of reflectivity for the target pixel p. The weight or importance of the pixels can be determined by the degree of similarity of each pixel to the target pixel. There are several techniques for converting the estimated similarities into weighting values. A simple technique is the exponential kernel [54]:

$$w(q) = \exp\left(\frac{-\delta_{PQ}}{h}\right). \tag{2.12}$$

With this conversion, large values of δ indicating large differences between patches receive small weighing values, and consequently dissimilar pixels have a small contribution only to the aggregation or restoration process. In (11), the parameter $h > 0$ is a filtering bandwidth parameter. The problem with this technique is that a specific value of the filtering parameter may have the same effect when the size of the patches and the number of looks are changed. To deal with this issue, reference [55] estimated the kernel parameter as $h = F^{-1}(0.99)$, where F^{-1} is the inverse cumulative distribution function of δ under the hypothesis that the two patches are similar. Additionally, in reference [13], an extension of the exponential kernel is given by $w(q) = \psi[F(\delta_{PQ})]$, where F is the cumulative distribution function of δ and the mapping function ψ corresponds to the exponential kernel. Another strategy for converting similarity to weights is proposed in [14]. They used the pdf of δ to convert similarity into weights, i.e., $w(q) = \mathrm{pdf}(\delta_{PQ})$. Interested readers can refer to [56], where several definitions of a weight function have been provided.

Based upon the NL framework, several nonlocal methods have been presented in the literature, and this simple denoising structure yielded surprisingly good denoising performance and reduced the annoying phenomenon of smearing edges [1]. The first work to use a nonlocal framework was the introduction of the nonlocal mean (NL-means) [54], which considered a relatively large patch and estimated similarity using the Euclidean distance between any local patch in the search window and the patch centered at the target pixel. NL-means formed the starting point of the development of several efficient noise reduction filters. Here the details of two important nonlocal algorithms are presented.

NLSAR technique [1]: This is a unified patch-based technique for despeckling single and multi-channel SAR data. It is model based and its similarity criterion is based on a fully developed speckle assumption. For the NLSAR technique, the information of each patch is represented in the form of a data intensity vector; cf. Equation (2.7). Among the different possibilities for comparing the patch information, the NLSAR technique uses the generalized likelihood ratio-based measure (see Equation (2.9)), which shows significant performance and satisfies several invariance properties. This similarity criterion has been shown to be an efficient method with SAR data. The efficiency of NLSAR depends upon the assumption of a fully developed speckle model. In particular, in extremely heterogeneous areas, the distribution of the data may not match the given model under the assumption of a fully developed speckle model. In such a case, the loss of likelihood of the estimation may not be negligible

Noland technique [14]: The Noland technique is specified in the context of model-based filtering and uses the amplitude image for filtering. Let us represent the noisy amplitude image $y(p)$ as a product of the deterministic $x(p)$ and the noise terms $s(p)$ based upon the given model in Equation (2.1). For two noisy patches with information given by the vectors $\mathbf{y_P}$ and $\mathbf{y_Q}$ in Equation (2.7), the ratio patch is generated as follows:

$$d_{PQ} = \frac{y_P}{y_Q} = \left[\frac{y(p_1)}{y(q_1)} \quad \frac{y(p_2)}{y(q_2)} \quad \frac{y(p_3)}{y(q_3)} \quad \cdots \quad \frac{y(p_N)}{y(q_N)}\right]^T. \tag{2.13}$$

Suppose that we can assume the noise term in (1) to follow a square root gamma distribution given in Equation (2.3). For two similar pixels p and q whose deterministic or noise-free components are equal, i.e., $x(p) = x(q)$, the ratio between their amplitudes corresponds to the ratio between their speckle components, i.e., $\mathbf{d}_{PQ} = \mathbf{y}_P/\mathbf{y}_Q = \mathbf{s}_P/\mathbf{s}_Q$. In such a case, the ratio between two fully developed speckle noises can be modeled according to the following probability distribution function [7]:

$$f_d(d) = \frac{2\Gamma(2L)d^{2L-1}}{\Gamma(L)^2 \left(d^2 + 1\right)^{2L}}. \tag{2.14}$$

The Noland technique is based upon the idea of determining the ratio patch between the patch P containing the pixel p to be restored and the patch Q containing a similar candidate pixel q. If the deterministic parts of the two patches are equal, the corresponding ratio patch is expected to follow the statistical distribution given in Equation (2.14). But if the deterministic parts of the patches are different, the distribution of the ratio patch deviates from the model in Equation (2.14). Therefore, similarity of the two patches is measured using the Kolmogorov–Smirnov test:

$$\delta_{PQ} = max = \left(\left\|F_{dpQ} - F_{dmodel}\right\|\right), \tag{2.15}$$

where F_{dmodel} is the cumulative distribution function of $f_d(.)$ given in equation (2.14), and F_{dPQ} is the vector obtained by sampling the empirical cumulative distribution function of the independent and identically distributed observations in the vectors $\mathbf{d}_{PQ}$ in (2.13). Once the similarity is computed, it is converted into weight values using the pdf of δ.

In some cases, the patch-based technique may not be able to optimally restore the images with sharp edges. A specific aspect of the Noland technique is the use of the anisotropic strategy to solve this problem. This strategy involves computing the KS distances in four main directions (horizontal, vertical, and the two main diagonals) such that the distances in (2.15) are computed four times using patches centered in p and q and extended into the four directions considered. Once the distances in four directions have been computed, they are merged by taking their average. This strategy has been shown to be useful for edge sharpening.

An example of nonlocal filtering by the NLSAR and Noland techniques using the RadarSAT image in the Flevoland image is shown in Figures 2.6 (a) and (b), respectively. A qualitative comparison of the filtered images by nonlocal techniques with those obtained by conventional local filtering confirms the superiority and importance of the nonlocal techniques.

In addition to the nonlocal despeckling techniques mentioned earlier, several interesting techniques have been presented in the literature. These include the block-matching 3D filter (BM3D)

(a)   (b)

FIGURE 2.6 Example of some nonlocal filters: (a) NLSAR, (b) Noland.

[57], which takes advantage of both the nonlocal frame and the wavelet representation; the model-free nonlocal despeckling [11] with a generic similarity measure suitable for both homogeneous and heterogeneous regions; the Bayesian nonlocal framework [58], which incorporates the sigma filter into the nonlocal framework; and the SAR-BM3D filter [15], which follows the structure of the BM3D algorithm but modifies its main processing steps to account for the specificities of SAR images, probabilistic patch-based (PPB) filter [12], nonlocal filter based on geometrical comparison of pixel values [51], FANS filter [20], and nonlocal mean variants [59]. In addition, reference [13] provides an overview of the main patch-based methods for speckle reduction in SAR images.

2.3.2.3   Deep Learning Strategies for SAR Image Despeckling

The second breakthrough in SAR despeckling was made by deep learning-based strategies. Indeed, after the use of AlexNet convolutional neural network (CNN) [60] in digital image classification, a variety of methods have been developed for various image processing applications. CNNs are particularly successful in processing image data because they enforce some priorities that are perfectly suitable for digital images. Besides CNNs, generative adversarial networks (GAN) [61] have been developed. The research findings of most studies in the literature are that such deep learning methods are capable of building sophisticated models and achieving amazing performance [62]. These promising results have drawn the attention of researchers to the use of deep learning methods for SAR image denoising. Unlike the earlier model-based techniques (local and nonlocal), DL are defined as data-driven because deep neural networks learn a mapping between an input and the corresponding output based on some training data, which usually must be sufficiently large and contain pairs of input-reference examples. Thus, training a neural network involves finding optimal parameter values that minimize the given cost or loss function.

In the context of despeckling with deep neural networks, the training strategy is a crucial and challenging step. Despeckling with DL methods requires noisy SAR images as input data and noise-free images as reference data. In reality, however, it is not possible to capture clean SAR images without speckle contribution. Based upon the adapted training strategy, the despeckling techniques can be divided into supervised and self-supervised methods.

2.3.2.3.1   Supervised Learning Techniques

This is a conventional set of techniques to training networks, where the goal is to create a large number of training sets with pairs of noisy (y) and noise-free (x) images. To generate pairs of noise-free reference images and corresponding noisy images, two strategies can be used: 1) *synthesis strategies* and 2) *temporal multi-looking strategies*.

Synthetic strategies usually rely on the use of optical images to simulate noisy SAR images. Here, the optical image is considered as a noise-free reflectivity image (either amplitude or intensity), while the noisy image can be created using the model of Equation (2.1) and the statistical characterization of the speckle (e.g., Equation (2.3)). The advantage of this strategy is that the simulation of the training data pairs is quite simple, while the disadvantage is that this technique neglects speckle correlations and additionally the synthetic noisy image may not reflect the actual characteristics of the real SAR data. For example, the speckle model given in (2.3) is not suitable for simulating noisy data in heterogeneous built-up regions and in areas with geometric distortions (layover areas). Moreover, the optical image cannot fully represent the radiometric, spatial, and geometric properties of SAR data as for instance strong point scatterers are not present in the optical data. When a network trained with synthetic training data is used to denoise a real SAR image, the mentioned discrepancy between the simulated and real SAR features can lead to problems with artifacts, hallucinations of patterns, or over-smoothing and *cartoon-like* despeckled image might be produced [14] [62] (see the results of Figure 2.8).

To address the problems associated with synthetic data, the second method relies on reducing speckle fluctuations by temporal averaging of images from a long time-series. The main challenge

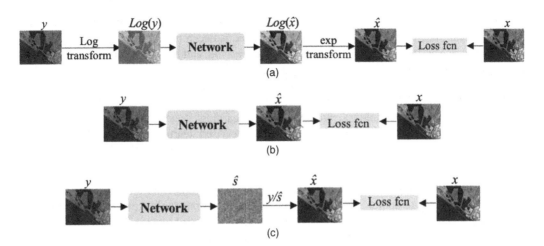

FIGURE 2.7 The structures of supervised networks: (a) network in the transformed domain, (b) network in original domain, (c) network with residual architecture.

with this strategy is access to a sufficiently large inventory of registered multi-temporal images of the same scene. In addition, there may be changes in the ground land cover of the scene, resulting in poor performance in the affected regions. Despite these challenges for both techniques, good and stunning despeckling results are reported in the literature [63].

Network architecture: When considering supervised learning, three different structures can be designed. As shown in Figure 2.7, these structures are:

1) *Network in the transformed domain*, where the goal is to train the network to work with additive noise rather than multiplicative noise. For this purpose, logarithm and exponential transformations are usually applied to the input images before the deep neural network and to the output of the network, respectively. An interesting framework for data transformation is based on the MuLog [64] method, where the goal is to fit the transformed data to the Fisher-Tippett distribution of log-transformed SAR speckle. Several networks have been designed in the transformed domain, and important examples of this technique can be found in references [65–67].
2) *Network in the original spatial domain*, where the goal is to train the network with original noisy and noise-free SAR images without performing any transformation. Thus, when training the network, the goal is to minimize a defined cost function based on the mapping of the noisy image (y) to noise-free data (x). For examples of the design of networks with this type of structure, see references [21, 68, 69].
3) *Network with residual architectures*, where the goal is to train the network to learn the mapping between the speckled image and the estimated pure speckle noise. Pure speckle noise is subtracted from the noisy image to obtain the estimate of despeckled or noise-free image. There are a large number of despeckling filter in the literature that use this design, and examples of interesting networks can be found at [70–72].

Loss function: The goal of the training process is to adjust the network parameters to minimize the defined loss function. For deep neural network based on the supervised training strategy, for which pairs of input and reference images are available, a cost function based on the L2 distance (or L1 distance) is commonly used in the literature [63]. Moreover, the literature also considers the loss function of the total variation when additional terms are included in the L2 distance. For example, in reference [21], a multicentric loss function was used to ensure better agreement with the actual statistics of real SAR data. In addition to the L2 distance between the reflectivity of the estimated and reference images, their gradient, to ensure edge preserving, and the KS distance between pdf of noise, to ensure the statistics of the real SAR data, are also used.

2.3.2.3.2 Self-Supervised Learning Techniques

Self-supervised learning techniques point to another learning strategy to avoid the limitations mentioned in supervised techniques. For the self-supervised learning techniques, learning is performed only with noisy images, without the need for noise-free reference images. Two frameworks can be considered.

Self-supervised – Noise2Noise: The Noise2Noise technique is based on the assumption that the speckle between multi-temporal SAR images is decorrelated in time. In this case, co-registered SAR images of the same scene taken at two different time points are used to train the network. Usually, the image of the first date is the input of the network and the image of the second date is considered as the output. So, the goal is to estimate an image that is close or similar to the second image. The idea is based on the fact that the co-registered multi-temporal SAR images have the same deterministic component and the network wants to get this similar term in two noisy images. Reference [73] has taken this idea and used two noisy images to train the network, still taking into account the L2 distance, but the important point is that independent realizations of the noise is required. Nowadays, the Noise2Noise despeckling-based technique is becoming more and more common; some studies in this subject are [74–76].

Self-supervised – Noise2Void: The Noise2Void technique is comparable to the Noise2Noise strategy, but only a single image is used to train the network, i.e., the input and output of the network is a single noisy image. For this technique, the speckle noise is assumed to be spatially uncorrelated and statistical information priors are available over the image. This technique originated in [77, 78], where the idea is to recover the noise-free reflectivity for each target pixel based on its neighborhood information. In this case, the goal of the network is to estimate the target pixel from its receptive field by minimizing a loss function, e.g., minimizing the L2 distance between the noisy pixel value and the predicted value. Another example of the development of a despeckling filter using this technique can be found in [79].

Application example of deep learning: Figure 2.8 shows an application example of despeckling with a deep neural network using the RadarSAT image over Flevoland. Despeckling was performed with a trained network based upon the supervised technique in the original spatial domain using the technique in [21]. A total of 57526 optical images, each 64 ×64 pixels in size, were used to simulate a noisy amplitude image and train the network. A detailed comparison of the results confirms that the denoised image by this technique is comparable to the one obtained by the nonlocal Noland technique in Figure 2.6 (b).

2.3.3 Despeckling Evaluation Metrics

After purification of speckle, the performance of filtering is evaluated and noise reduction is carried out. As mentioned in [23], an ideal speckle filter is expected to adaptively smooth speckle noise, maintaining sharpness of edges and details. From the point of view of conventional image processing, despeckling can be evaluated similarly to any standard filtering in terms of blurring homogeneous regions and preserving details in heterogeneous regions. However, SAR image reflectivity and radiometric information are essential for many applications, so radiometric preservation should also be considered. The possible methods for despeckling assessment can usually be defined qualitatively and quantitatively, and a brief overview of existing assessments of despeckling performance is given below.

FIGURE 2.8   Example of deep learning based despeckling.

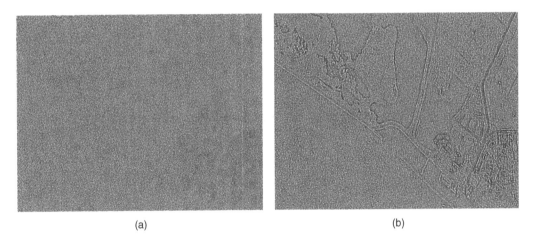

(a)   (b)

FIGURE 2.9   Example of ratio images using (a) Noland and (b) boxcar despeckling filters.

2.3.3.1   Qualitative Assessments

This method relies mainly on the visual inspection of the despeckled image. Through visual inspection, it is possible to verify the degree of smoothing in the filtered image and the ability to preserve edges and details. In addition to visual inspection of the filtered image, it is also possible to generate a ratio image, typically by dividing the original noisy image into the filtered image, and qualitatively evaluate this ratio image. As a rule of thumb, the ratio image represents the estimated speckle image (see the relationship in Equation (2.1)). Thus, by visually inspecting the ratio image, the filtering performance can be assessed in terms of signal leakage and noise correlation. In homogeneous regions, the ratio image is expected to follow the distribution model given in Equation (2.3). In general, the ratio image should contain only speckle without structures. Figure 2.9 shows an example of the ratio image obtained by two filtering techniques, Noland and boxcar. As can be seen in the ratio image by Noland, fewer structures remain in the homogeneous regions and the speckles have a random pattern, which underlines the better performance of Noland over the conventional boxcar method where the ratio image is affected by the remaining structures.

2.3.3.2 Quantitative Assessments

Visual assessment alone may not be sufficient to quantify the performance of various despeckling filters. To address this problem, several numerical evaluation metrics have been developed in the literature, which can be classified into reference and non-reference metrics and are explained below.

Reference metrics: As expected, these metrics assume the availability of a noise-free or reference image. Therefore, the estimated $\hat{x}$ and the noise-free x images can be compared using different indices, the most common being:

- *Mean squared error (MSE)*, which measures the average similarity between x and $\hat{x}$, where MSE is zero for an ideal despeckled image. This measure is formulated as:

$$MSE = E\left\{\left(x - \hat{x}\right)^2\right\}. \tag{2.16}$$

- *Signal to noise ratio (SNR)*, which measures the signal quality and noise reduction capability. The higher the SNR, the better the filtering performance. It is defined as

$$SNR = 10\log_{10}\left(\frac{\sigma_x}{E\left\{\left(x - \hat{x}\right)^2\right\}}\right), \tag{2.17}$$

where σ_x indicated the standard deviation of x.
- *Structural similarity index measurement (SSIM)*, which measures the similarity between x and $\hat{x}$. It is defined as

$$SSIM = \frac{\left(2E(x)E\left(\hat{x}\right) - c_1\right)\left(2\sigma_{x\hat{x}} + c_2\right)}{\left(E(x)^2 + E\left(\hat{x}\right)^2 + c_1\right)\left(\sigma_x^2 + \sigma_{\hat{x}}^2 + c_2\right)}, \tag{2.18}$$

where $c_1 = (0.01z)^2$ and $c_2 = (0.03z)^2$ are two variables used to stabilize the division with weak denominator, and z is the dynamic range of the pixel values. For an ideal filter SSIM=1.

In addition to the above indices, there are other metrics such as peak SNR, energy SNR [4], mean SSIM [80], edge correlation index [81], and Pratt's figure of merit [32] that can be used as reference metrics.

No-reference metrics: The referenceless metrics are more common in the evaluation of SAR despeckling filters, since the noise-free reference image is usually not available. There is no generic index that evaluates different aspects of denoising filters, and typically each index can evaluate a particular aspect of denoising methods. In the following, some of these common indices are presented.

- *Equivalent number of look (ENL)*, which measures the degree of smoothness in homogeneous areas. The index is based on the ratio between the squared power of the mean and the variance of the filtered image, as [5]:

$$ENL = \frac{E(\hat{x})^2}{\sigma_{\hat{x}}}.$$

(2.19)

A higher *ENL* indicates a better performance of noise suppression.

- *B index*, which is indicative of bias in noise reduction. Typically, the empirical mean and variance of the ratio image are expected to be close to the respective theoretical statistical mean and variance of the speckle noise process. Based upon this assumption, reference [82] introduced bias index evaluation of denoised images using Equation (2.20).

$$B = E\left(\frac{y - \hat{x}}{y}\right).$$

(2.20)

- *KL distance*, which assesses the statistical distribution of the denoised image. In homogeneous regions, the ratio image or estimated speckle is expected to follow the distribution model given in Equation (2.3). In order to achieve this, the *KL* distance between the empirical pdf of the ratio image $f_{\hat{s}}(.)$ and the known model $f_s(.)$ is used to evaluate the denoising filter. It is defined as

$$KL = \sum_k f_{\hat{s}}(k)\left[\log_2 \frac{f_{\hat{s}}(k)}{f_s(k)}\right].$$

(2.21)

- *M index*, which assesses the ability to remove speckle along with the ability to preserve detail. The metric is given as a combination of following indices [83]:

$$M = rENL, \mu + \delta h,$$

(2.22)

where for K homogeneous patches, $r_{ENL,\mu}$ is defined as

$$rENL, \mu = \frac{1}{2}\sum_k \left(rENL(k) + r\mu(k)\right),$$

$$rENL(k) = \frac{\left|ENL_{noisy}(k) - ENL_{ratio}(k)\right|}{ENL_{noisy}(k)}.$$

(2.23)

$$r\mu(k) = \left|1 - \mu_{\hat{s}}(k)\right|,$$

where ENL_{noisy} and ENL_{ratio} are the ENL computed in noisy and ratio images. The term $\delta h = 100 |h_o - h_g|/h_o$ is the distance between the homogeneity h_o of ratio image compared with the homogeneity h_g of the random permuted the ratio image.

Other metrics such as the coefficient of variation [84], the target to clutter ratio [19], the ratio edge-based index, and α-β indices [85] are also broadly employed in the literature for assessing the denoising capability.

2.4 MULTI-CHANNEL SAR IMAGES RESTORATION

2.4.1 SPECKLE MODEL

Multi-channel data are either polarimetric or interferometric images, or polarimetric-interferometric data, where *N* co-registered SLC images are typically available. Unlike the single-channel case, the characteristics of multi-channel data are not limited to amplitude, but also include phase information. The data information at each resolution cell p can be represented by an N-dimensional complex scattering vector as:

$$y(p) = \begin{bmatrix} y_1(p) & y_2(p) & y_3(p) & \cdots & y_N(p) \end{bmatrix}^T \in \mathbb{C}^{N \times 1}, \tag{2.24}$$

where $y_n(p)$ represents the complex value of pixel p in the nth image. For fully polarimetric data sets, the informative data vector is given as $\mathbf{y}(p) = [y^{hh}(p)\ y^{hv}(p)\ y^{vv}(p)]^T \in \mathbb{C}^{N \times 1}$, where the complex scattering coefficient y^{kl}, indexed as $k, l = \{h, v\}$, represents the electromagnetic signal emitted through the polarization channel l and received on the channel k. Note that in the case where the roles of the transmitting and receiving antennas are interchanged, such as in the reciprocity theorem, the polarization channels hv and vh are equal, i.e., $y^{hv} = y^{vh}$ [23]. However, in the general case, the informative data vector for polarimetric, interferometric or polarimetric-interferometric images can be represented by Equation (2.24). This N-dimensional complex vector follows a circular complex Gaussian distribution under fully develop speckle model assumption [86]:

$$f_\mathbf{y}(\mathbf{y}|\Sigma) = \frac{1}{\pi^N |\Sigma|} exp(\mathbf{y}^\dagger \Sigma^{-1} \mathbf{y}), \tag{2.25}$$

where $\Sigma \in \mathbb{C}^{N \times N}$ is the noise-free complex covariance matrix and the operator † denotes the Hermitian transpose. In Equation (2.25), the dependences of the scattering data vector and of Σ on the pixel coordinate p is not explicitly indicated for the sake of notation simplicity. The well-known multiplicative model in Equation (2.1), in case of multi-channel data, can be written as:

$$\begin{aligned} \mathbf{y}(p) &= \mathbf{x}(p) \odot \mathbf{s}(p) \\ &= \begin{bmatrix} y_1(p) & y_2(p) & y_3(p) & \cdots & y_N(p) \end{bmatrix}^T \odot \begin{bmatrix} y_1(p) & y_2(p) & y_3(p) & \cdots & y_N(p) \end{bmatrix}, \end{aligned} \tag{2.26}$$

where the vectors $\mathbf{x}$ and $\mathbf{s}$ denote the deterministic and noise components of the observed data vector $\mathbf{y}$, respectively. Therefore, the relationship in Equation (2.26) with second-order information can be represented as follows:

$$\mathbf{C} = \Sigma^{\frac{1}{2}} \mathbf{S} \Sigma^{\frac{1}{2}}, \tag{2.27}$$

where $\mathbf{C}$ is the noisy covariance matrix of data vector, commonly known as the *pre-estimated sample covariance matrix* (SCM). It is typically computed using a bounded spatial averaging of the neighboring pixels. Moreover, the speckle and deterministic signal covariance matrices are defined with $\mathbf{S} = E[\mathbf{ss}^\dagger]$ and $\Sigma = E[\mathbf{xx}^\dagger]$, respectively. Due to the unavailability of the signal realizations, the true covariance matrix Σ is unknown. It is straightforward, however, to approximate it by the sample covariance matrix (SCM) $\hat{\mathbf{R}}$ thorough the maximum likelihood estimation of L spatially *similar* scattering vectors.

$$\hat{\mathbf{R}}(p) = \frac{\sum_{l=1}^{L} w(q_1)\mathbf{y}(q_1)\mathbf{y}(q_1)^\dagger}{\sum_{l=1}^{L} w(q_1)}. \tag{2.28}$$

If $L \geq N$, then $\hat{\mathbf{R}}$ is a full-rank matrix that can be described by the complex Wishart distribution given by:

$$f_{\widehat{\mathbf{R}}}\left(\widehat{\mathbf{R}}|\Sigma\right) = \frac{L^{NL}\left|\widehat{\mathbf{R}}\right|^{L-N}}{\Gamma_N(L)|\Sigma|^L} exp\left(-L\,tr\left[\Sigma^{-1}\widehat{\mathbf{R}}\right]\right),$$

(2.29)

where $tr(.)$ is the trace operator, and $\Gamma_N(L) = \pi^{N(N-2)/2}\prod_{n=1}\Gamma(L-n+1)$, and $\Gamma(.)$ is the standard Euler gamma function. It should be noted that the given model in Equations (2.28)~(2.29) is the basis of several developed despeckling filters in the literatures.

The goal in despeckling of multi-channel data sets is to estimate the sample covariance matrix $\widehat{\mathbf{R}}$ using Equation (2.28). This estimation problem can be solved in local, nonlocal, or deep learning frameworks. An ideal multi-channel despeckling filter aims to estimate $\widehat{\mathbf{R}}$ such that 1) the scattering characteristics, edge sharpness, and point targets are preserved while the noise effects are smoothed, and 2) the polarimetric or interferometric properties are preserved and cross-talk is avoided. To this end, it is important to filter each term of the covariance matrix similarly and independently in the spatial domain.

2.4.2 DESPECKLING FILTERS

In this subsection, despeckling of multi-channel images by providing an overview of denoising methods within local, nonlocal, and deep learning frameworks is given.

2.4.2.1 Local Framework

Refined Lee [30]: The principle of this filtering is the same as the concept of the refined Lee filtering for single-channel image. Similarly, eight 7×7 windows are used to detect edge orientations. If no edge is detected, the estimation of $\widehat{R}$ is performed using the entire 7×7 window, while otherwise only the pixels in the detected edge-oriented window are used for the estimation process in Equation (2.28). In the refined Lee technique, edge alignment detection requires the use of amplitude or intensity images. Therefore, in the case of multi-channel images, the span image is generated by averaging the intensities of the different channels, and the edge is detected based upon this image. The span image generally has a lower noise rate than the individual channels and contains scattering response of features that may look different in each channel. Once the correct window is selected based upon the edge alignment, the sample covariance matrix can be calculated using the linearized model as follows:

$$\widehat{\mathbf{R}}(p) = \bar{\mathbf{R}}(p) + b(\mathbf{C}(p) - \bar{\mathbf{R}}(p)),$$

(2.30)

where each element of $\bar{\mathbf{R}}$ is the local mean covariance matrix whose elements are computed using the average of the pixels in the detected edge-aligned window. As mentioned earlier, $\mathbf{C}$ is a pre-estimated sample covariance matrix that can be computed using pixels with bounded samples, e.g., using the boxcar approach with 3×3 window size. Finally, we note that the parameter b can be estimated in the same way as in the single-channel case and with the span image.

IDAN [10]: The intensity-driven adaptive neighborhood (IDAN) technique is based upon a region-growth technique for generating an adaptive neighborhood in covariance matrix estimation. It uses only intensity information to select pixels for the adaptive neighborhood. The early core of each adaptive neighborhood is a starting pixel, which is derived from a median value in the 3×3 centered neighborhood. The main drawback of this method is its high computational complexity, while the most interesting outcome of this approach is that the number of homogeneous pixels to be averaged is increased, leading to an increase in filtering performance.

Other despeckling filters: In addition to the above-mentioned multi-channel filters, there are several methods developed in the literature. For example, the speckle reduction anisotropic diffusion (SRAD) [32] method uses a diffusion coefficient that is edge sensitive. If the gradient of the image is relatively large, diffusion is stopped, and when the gradient of the image is relatively small, diffusion occurs. Speckle filtering based upon a scattering model [87] relies upon the identifying pixels that share the same scattering mechanisms. This filter consists of three steps: 1) applying a target scattering decomposition technique to identify the scattering mechanisms of pixels, 2) unsupervised Wishart classification [88], and 3) filtering pixels that are in the same class and the same scattering category with the linearized model and usually with a local window of 9×9 pixels. For other standard approaches of despeckling, the readers may refer to [89–91]. Similar to the IDAN approach above, higher filter performance can be achieved if the number of similar pixels in the aggregation process is increased in Equation (2.28). In the standard filters, the search for similar pixels is performed using the diagonal elements or the span of the covariance matrix, while the off-diagonal elements are neglected. The way to consider all the information of the covariance matrix in the search for similar pixels has resulted into the introduction of the concept of distance, which mainly led to the development of nonlocal filtering, explained in the next subsection. An example of local-based filtering operation, when refined Lee and IDAN methods are implemented using fully polarimetric RadarSAT images over Flevoland (Netherlands), is shown in Figure 2.10 (b and c).

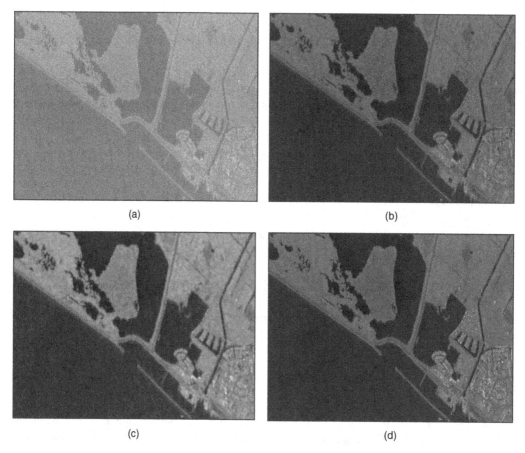

(a)   (b)

(c)   (d)

FIGURE 2.10 Example of some multi-channel filters using a fully polarimetric image: (a) noisy Pauli image, (b) refined Lee, (c) IDAN, and (d) NLSAR.

2.4.2.2 Nonlocal (NL) Framework

The NL framework can be also used to design a filter for denoising multi-channel images. The main difference between nonlocal filtering of single-channel and multi-channel images is in the definition of the similarity measure. As mentioned earlier, in the case of single-channel data, the information of each patch, e.g., patch P, can be represented in a vector containing the amplitude or intensity of all pixels of the patch. In the case of multi-channel data, the information of each patch containing M pixels can be represented by M *pre-estimated sample covariance matrices*, i.e., $C(p_1)$, $C(p_2)$, ... $C(p_M)$. Thus, the definition of the similarity measure between two patches P and Q in this case would be more complex than the case of single-channel data. Reference [49] evaluated some metrics commonly used in the denoising literature, while a brief overview of three strategies for estimating similarity is given here.

- **Similarity based on generalized likelihood ratio test:** The similarity between two patches can be formulated as a hypothesis test given as:

$$\begin{aligned} \mathbf{H}_0 : \; &\Sigma_P = \Sigma_Q \; \textit{nulhypothesis} \\ \mathbf{H}_1 : \; &\Sigma_P \neq \Sigma_Q \; \textit{alternativehypothesis}. \end{aligned} \tag{2.31}$$

It can be shown that the generalized likelihood ratio test from multi-channel data leads to a criterion represented in the following log formula [92].

$$\delta_{PQ} = 2L \sum_{m=1}^{M} \log \left(\frac{\frac{1}{2} |C(p_m) + C(q_m)|}{\sqrt{|C(p_m) \cdot C(q_m)|}} \right), \tag{2.32}$$

where L is the number of pixels used to compute the pre-estimated sample covariance matrices. This criterion computes the similarity of two noisy patches and is often used in nonlocal filtering of polarimetric and interferometric datasets. For example, this criterion is the fundamental component of the developed nonlocal filters in [12] [93].

- **Similarity based upon Kullback–Leibler divergence:** The divergence is based upon the quantification of the information shared by the distributions parameterized by two patches. Assuming a specific model of multi-channel SAR distributions, it can be shown that divergence (or similarity) can be determined using the following criterion [94].

$$\delta_{PQ} = L \sum_{m=1}^{M} tr \left(C(p_n)^{-1} C(p_n) + C(q_n)^{-1} C(p_n) \right). \tag{2.33}$$

- **Geometric similarity:** Geometric similarity estimates the similarity of two noisy patches P and Q using the following criterion [51].

$$\delta_{PQ} = L \sum_{m=1}^{M} \left\| C(p_n)^{-\frac{1}{2}} C(q_n) C(p_n)^{-\frac{1}{2}} \right\|_{FR}^{2}, \tag{2.34}$$

where $\|.\|_{FR}$ represents the Frobenius norm.

In addition to the above measures, which are often used for multi-channel datasets, the similarity criterion based upon the Frobenius distance can also be applied. Moreover, empirical distributions of target vectors in two patches can be compared with the KL distance as used in [95] to estimate the sample covariance matrix with interferometric time-series data. The peculiar aspect of this measure is its model-free property that could be valid for any area in the images; hence, this measure only uses the diagonal elements of the pre-estimated sample covariance matrix. An extension of this similarity measure is given in [3, 11], which includes ratio patch information. These statistical tests are however limited to the use of the amplitude or intensity information of the data covariance matrices, since the tests can be applied mainly to real data vectors. A test based upon the use of complex data covariance matrices to estimate the similarity of two patches is presented in [96]. Moreover, an interesting similarity criterion-based tomographic reconstruction can be found in [97].

Once the similarity is computed with multi-channel data, it is converted into weight values and used in Equation (2.28) to estimate the sample covariance matrix. The typical conversion techniques outlined in subsection 2.3.2.2 can be used here as well to calculate weight values from similarity values. Based upon this framework, several nonlocal filtering approaches have been reported in the literature. An example of an efficient nonlocal approach is the NLSAR technique, which is widely used in various applications of multi-channel data, including polarimetric, interferometric, and tomographic reconstructions [11, 13, 98–101]. The similarity measure in NLSAR with multi-channel images is computed using the generalized likelihood criterion, and an expansion of the exponential kernel is used to convert the similarity into a weight. Figure 2.10 (d) shows an example of the implementation of NLSAR for denoising a fully polarimetric image of RadarSAT. An important point in NLSAR technique is the bias reduction process. Namely, the weighted averaging in Equation (2.28) can lead to over-smoothed images and spread the bright structures that have several orders of magnitude higher intensity than their surrounding background, such as point scatterers. To recover such bright targets, the convex combination between the NL estimate and the noisy covariance matrices is performed using the following equation

$$\hat{\Sigma}(p) = \hat{\mathbf{R}}(p) + b\left(\mathbf{C}(p) - \hat{\mathbf{R}}(p)\right). \tag{2.35}$$

This equation is very similar to the formula given in (29). The final estimate of NLSAR $\hat{\Sigma}(p)$ is a linear combination of the pre-estimated SCM $\mathbf{C}$ and the nonlocal sample covariance matrix $\hat{\mathbf{R}}$, where the parameter b is estimated based on the variance of the intensity images in a homogeneous region.

2.4.2.3   Deep Learning Framework

In analogy to denoising of single-channel images, deep learning has revolutionized the denoising of multi-channel images. The explained possible strategies of deep learning denoising filters, including supervised and self-supervised techniques, can be perfectly applied to multi-channel images. The difference is the expansion of the number of input parameters, from only one amplitude or intensity image in the single-channel case to N complex images in multi-channel data. Two major challenges arise when using multi-channel data compared to single-channel images.

2.4.2.3.1   Training Network

The first challenge in denoising multi-channel images with supervised deep learning concerns training of the network. As mentioned earlier, good and solid training requires a large number of noisy images and reference images. In the single-channel case, the simulation is started by multiplying random noise with the optical image to produce a noisy amplitude image, while the optical image is considered as a noise-free reference image. For multi-channel cases, the simulation process is not as simple as for the single-channel amplitude image. For example, the correlation of noise between channels is to be considered. Moreover, in the case of polarimetric images, the simulated datasets should cover various backscattering mechanisms and not only the canonical ones, such as pure odd-bounce or double-bounce scattering mechanisms. Moreover, for interferometric datasets where the images of different baselines are obtained in time sequence, the temporal decorrelation with short- and long-term effects must also be considered. The simulation of such a large number of multi-channel images is therefore a more cumbersome task. For all these reasons, the temporal multi-looking approach is used mainly for training supervised networks. This temporal multi-looking strategy would be applicable for polarimetric images, where multiple time-series polarimetric images are averaged to produce a noise-free polarimetric super-image. For interferometric data, where the temporal decorrelation of the channels must be considered, this temporal multi-looking strategy cannot be used as a technique to generate noise-free multi-channel time-series data. Therefore, in such a case, the self-supervised strategies should be considered.

2.4.2.3.2 *Complex Values*

Currently, most deep learning building blocks and architectures are based on real-valued operations. Dealing with polarimetric or interferometric multi-channel SAR images forces the equation of complex-valued channels with real-valued data in order to avoid complex-valued operations. Thus, the use of deep learning techniques for denoising complex multi-channel SAR images generally requires finding an optimal form of SAR data as input to the networks. For this purpose, two simple methods have mostly been considered: 1) treating the complex-valued SAR images as real-valued data by directly partitioning them into real and imaginary channels, and 2) treating the complex-valued SAR images as real-valued amplitude and phase channels. These two simple strategies avoid complex-valued operations, while in the latter case the representation form and information of the original complex-valued data are better preserved. In addition to these two methods, there is an interesting technique presented in [64], where the complex-valued multi-channel images are decomposed into real-valued channels with an approximately stabilized variance. This technique decomposes complex images into independent real-valued channels to which deep learning can be easily applied. Such conversion strategies, however, may not be able to exploit all the features of the complex data covariance matrix in the deep learning processes. Therefore, a number of recent studies have focused on replicating the success of the real-valued network by developing a network architecture that retains the building blocks of the existing model while being able to handle complex-valued data [102, 103]. For examples of dealing with complex multi-channel SAR images in deep learning, see [104] [66]. Techniques developed in the context of deep learning specifically for multi-channel denoising are not yet sufficiently mature and extensive work is still needed to achieve an improved model for denoising polarimetric and interferometric images. Some studies on this topic are [105, 106].

2.4.3 DESPECKLING EVALUATION METRICS

Evaluating the performance of multi-channel denoising filters is also more complicated than evaluating single-channel despeckling filters. The ideal multi-channel denoising filter should not only adaptively smooth the speckle noise and preserve the sharpness of edges and details, but also preserve the statistical relationship and correlation between the different channels. For example, in the case of polarimetric images, an ideal filter should preserve the scattering characteristics and avoid cross-talk between channels. In analogy to the single-channel assessment, multi-channel denoising evaluation can be performed *qualitatively* and *quantitively*.

Qualitative methods are usually based upon visual inspection of the intensity and phase (either polarimetric or interferometric) of the various elements of the complex covariance matrix. For polarimetric images, a typical strategy is to generate the Pauli color-coded image and evaluate it visually to check the degree of smoothing in the filtered image, the ability to preserve edges and details, and the ability to preserve scattering mechanisms. It is almost needless to point out that the Pauli image is capable of representing the scattering mechanisms of the observed scene, since the channels of the Pauli images are associated with the surface, dihedral, and volumetric scattering mechanisms. For example, a visual comparison of the IDAN and NLSAR filters in Figure 2.10 (c) and (d) confirms that NLSAR outperforms IDAN in terms of scattering mechanism

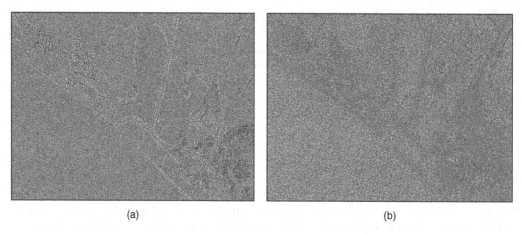

(a)   (b)

FIGURE 2.11   Example of ratio images using polarimetric image: (a) refined Lee and (b) NLSAR.

preservation, as building regions with dihedral scattering mechanism are better highlighted with red in the NLSAR-filtered image.

In addition to visually inspecting the filtered images, it is also possible to calculate the ratio covariance matrix, which gives the estimated speckle matrix for each resolution cell using the following equation.

$$\widehat{\mathbf{S}}(p) = \widehat{\mathbf{R}}(p)^{-\frac{1}{2}} \mathbf{C}(p) \widehat{\mathbf{R}}(p)^{-\frac{1}{2}}. \tag{2.36}$$

A Pauli image can also be generated from the estimated speckle matrix in Equation (2.36) – let's call this the ratio Pauli image. This ratio image should typically represent random patterns without any structures remaining. As an application example, the ratio Pauli images are computed with the refined Lee and NLSAR filters and shown in Figure 2.11. The higher percentage of structures left in the ratio image with the refined Lee filter indicates poor performance of this filter as compared to the NLSAR filter.

For quantitative evaluation, both reference and referenceless metrics of single-channel images explained in subsection 2.3.3 can be used here to evaluate the span image of the denoised multi-channel covariance matrix. All these metrics are applicable if diagonal element of the covariance matrix is the subject of evaluation. Any optimal evaluation requires the assessment of all aspects and information of the covariance matrix of the data. In this sense, for polarimetric images, target scattering decomposition techniques over pre-estimated and sample covariance matrices is performed, and then the ability of the denoising filter in preserving polarization parameters is quantitatively and qualitatively evaluated. Similarly, for interferometric data sets, the interferometric phase is analyzed. An important point in this case is that the noise term in the interferometric phase image is not multiplicative, but additive. This is important when computing the estimate of speckle noise in InSAR phase images. Moreover, in [11], a generic statistical quality index was introduced to evaluate the similarity of the ratio covariance with the properties derived from the pure speckle model. This generic approach can be used to evaluate the noise reduction capability in polarimetric, interferometric and polarimetric-interferometric images.

2.5   OPEN ISSUES AND FUTURE TRENDS

Despeckling of synthetic aperture radar images with different modalities is an important research topic in remote sensing. Apart from several standard local despeckling techniques, such as the refined

Lee and the sigma filters, most new development of filters is in the nonlocal or patch-based framework. The reported patch-based techniques have shown an excellent performance in speckle reduction of single- and multi-channel SAR images as compared to conventional local-based techniques. We see that the current horizons of despeckling are moving towards this nonlocal framework. The heart of the patch-based approach is the definition of the similarity criterion, while several measures have been developed so far that are not only useful for despeckling, but can also be used for classification, change detection, and target identification. Some open issues still remain to be resolved, although the patch-based framework has already come a long way since its inception. The invalidity of model-based similarity measures in non-homogenous regions on the one hand, and reliance of model-free similarity criteria on diagonal or real-valued elements of images on the other hand, forces a nonlocal approach to introduce more accurate and generic similarity models that are suitable for different SAR scenarios. In addition, automatic schemes for despeckling without user intervention in parameter setting should also be considered.

Apart from nonlocal despeckling, the new horizons for despeckling will in the near future be towards deep learning-based techniques. Considering the tremendous advances in the field of deep learning-based image processing, new developments to SAR despeckling are undoubtedly expected. With the increasing diffusion of multiprocessor systems, computational problems with deep learning approaches are also likely to be limited and resolved. Given the limitation of supervised training with synthetic data and the availability of a large number of remote sensing images with current and new generations of satellites, network training with multi-temporal data is likely to be a robust strategy alongside self-supervised approaches. Moreover, the development of networks with architecture and building block suitable for processing complex SAR data is an essential task that will remain the focus of research in the years to come.

NOTE

1 Roughness is typically defined on the scale of the radar wavelength.

REFERENCES

[1] C.-A. Deledalle, L. Denis, G. Poggi, F. Tupin, and L. Verdoliva, "Exploiting patch similarity for SAR image processing: The nonlocal paradigm," *IEEE Signal Processing Magazine*, vol. 31, no. 4, pp. 69–78, 2014.

[2] J.-S. Lee, "Speckle analysis and smoothing of synthetic aperture radar images," *Computer Graphics and Image Processing*, vol. 17, no. 1, pp. 24–32, 1981.

[3] H. Aghababaei, "On the assessment of non-local multi-looking in detection of persistent scatterers using SAR tomography," *Remote Sensing*, vol. 12, no. 19, p. 3195, 2020.

[4] F. Argenti, A. Lapini, T. Bianchi, and L. Alparone, "A tutorial on speckle reduction in synthetic aperture radar images," *IEEE Geoscience and Remote Sensing Magazine*, vol. 1, no. 3, pp. 6–35, 2013.

[5] J.-S. Lee, "Digital image enhancement and noise filtering by use of local statistics," *IEEE Transactions on Pattern Analysis and Machine Intelligence*, vol. 2, no. 2, pp. 165–168, 1980.

[6] D. T. Kuan, A. A. Sawchuk, T. C. Strand, and P. Chavel, "Adaptive noise smoothing filter for images with signal-dependent noise," *IEEE Transactions on Pattern Analysis and Machine Intelligence*, vol. 7, no. 2, pp. 165–177, 1985.

[7] R. Touzi, A. Lopes, and P. Bousquet, "A statistical and geometrical edge detector for SAR images," *IEEE Transactions on Geoscience and Remote Sensing*, vol. 26, no. 6, pp. 764–773, 1988.

[8] F. Argenti and L. Alparone, "Speckle removal from SAR images in the undecimated wavelet domain," *IEEE Transactions on Geoscience and Remote Sensing*, vol. 40, no. 11, pp. 2363–2374, 2002.

[9] G. Franceschetti, V. Pascazio, and G. Schirinzi, "Iterative homomorphic technique for speckle reduction in synthetic-aperture radar imaging," *JOSA A*, vol. 12, no. 4, pp. 686–694, 1995.

[10] G. Vasile, E. Trouvé, J.-S. Lee, and V. Buzuloiu, "Intensity-driven adaptive-neighborhood technique for polarimetric and interferometric SAR parameters estimation," *IEEE Transactions on Geoscience and Remote Sensing*, vol. 44, no. 6, pp. 1609–1621, 2006.

[11] H. Aghababaei, R. Zamani, G. Ferraioli, V. Pascazio, and G. Schirinzi, "A model-free ratio based nonlocal framework for denoising of SAR and TomoSAR data," in *EUSAR 2021; 13th European Conference on Synthetic Aperture Radar*, 2021: VDE, pp. 1–5.

[12] C.-A. Deledalle, L. Denis, and F. Tupin, "Iterative weighted maximum likelihood denoising with probabilistic patch-based weights," *IEEE Transactions on Image Processing*, vol. 18, no. 12, pp. 2661–2672, 2009.

[13] C.-A. Deledalle, L. Denis, F. Tupin, A. Reigber, and M. Jäger, "NL-SAR: A unified nonlocal framework for resolution-preserving (Pol)(In) SAR denoising," *IEEE Transactions on Geoscience and Remote Sensing*, vol. 53, no. 4, pp. 2021–2038, 2014.

[14] G. Ferraioli, V. Pascazio, and G. Schirinzi, "Ratio-based nonlocal anisotropic despeckling approach for sar images," *IEEE Transactions on Geoscience and Remote Sensing*, vol. 57, no. 10, pp. 7785–7798, 2019.

[15] S. Parrilli, M. Poderico, C. V. Angelino, and L. Verdoliva, "A nonlocal SAR image denoising algorithm based on LLMMSE wavelet shrinkage," *IEEE Transactions on Geoscience and Remote Sensing*, vol. 50, no. 2, pp. 606–616, 2011.

[16] W. Zhao, C.-A. Deledalle, L. Denis, H. Maître, J.-M. Nicolas, and F. Tupin, "Ratio-based multitemporal SAR images denoising: RABASAR," *IEEE Transactions on Geoscience and Remote Sensing*, vol. 57, no. 6, pp. 3552–3565, 2019.

[17] T. Zeng, Z. Ren, and E. Y. Lam, "Speckle suppression using the convolutional neural network with an exponential linear unit," in *Computational Optical Sensing and Imaging*, 2018: Optical Society of America, p. CW5B. 3.

[18] G. Chierchia, D. Cozzolino, G. Poggi, and L. Verdoliva, "SAR image despeckling through convolutional neural networks," in *2017 IEEE International Geoscience and Remote Sensing Symposium (IGARSS)*, 2017: IEEE, pp. 5438–5441.

[19] P. Wang, H. Zhang, and V. M. Patel, "SAR image despeckling using a convolutional neural network," *IEEE Signal Processing Letters*, vol. 24, no. 12, pp. 1763–1767, 2017.

[20] D. Cozzolino, S. Parrilli, G. Scarpa, G. Poggi, and L. Verdoliva, "Fast adaptive nonlocal SAR despeckling," *IEEE Geoscience and Remote Sensing Letters*, vol. 11, no. 2, pp. 524–528, 2013.

[21] S. Vitale, G. Ferraioli, and V. Pascazio, "Multi-objective CNN-based algorithm for SAR despeckling," *IEEE Transactions on Geoscience and Remote Sensing*, 2020.

[22] A. Moreira, P. Prats-Iraola, M. Younis, G. Krieger, I. Hajnsek, and K. P. Papathanassiou, "A tutorial on synthetic aperture radar," *IEEE Geoscience and Remote Sensing Magazine*, vol. 1, no. 1, pp. 6–43, 2013.

[23] J.-S. Lee and E. Pottier, *Polarimetric radar imaging: from basics to applications*. CRC Press, 2017.

[24] L. Ferro-Famil, E. Pottier, and J.-S. Lee, "Unsupervised classification of multifrequency and fully polarimetric SAR images based on the H/A/Alpha-Wishart classifier," *IEEE Transactions on Geoscience and Remote Sensing*, vol. 39, no. 11, pp. 2332–2342, 2001.

[25] K. Sarabandi, "/spl Delta/k-radar equivalent of interferometric SARs: a theoretical study for determination of vegetation height," *IEEE Transactions on Geoscience and Remote Sensing*, vol. 35, no. 5, pp. 1267–1276, 1997.

[26] R. Bamler and P. Hartl, "Synthetic aperture radar interferometry," *Inverse Problems*, vol. 14, no. 4, p. R1, 1998.

[27] S. R. Cloude and K. P. Papathanassiou, "Polarimetric SAR interferometry," *IEEE Transactions on Geoscience and Remote Sensing*, vol. 36, no. 5, pp. 1551–1565, 1998.

[28] J. W. Goodman, "Some fundamental properties of speckle," *JOSA*, vol. 66, no. 11, pp. 1145–1150, 1976.

[29] J.-S. Lee, L. Jurkevich, P. Dewaele, P. Wambacq, and A. Oosterlinck, "Speckle filtering of synthetic aperture radar images: A review," *Remote Sensing Reviews*, vol. 8, no. 4, pp. 313–340, 1994.

[30] J.-S. Lee, "Refined filtering of image noise using local statistics," *Computer Graphics and Image Processing*, vol. 15, no. 4, pp. 380–389, 1981.

[31] P. Perona and J. Malik, "Scale-space and edge detection using anisotropic diffusion," *IEEE Transactions on Pattern Analysis and Machine Intelligence*, vol. 12, no. 7, pp. 629–639, 1990.

[32] Y. Yu and S. T. Acton, "Speckle reducing anisotropic diffusion," *IEEE Transactions on Image Processing*, vol. 11, no. 11, pp. 1260–1270, 2002.

[33] V. S. Frost, J. A. Stiles, K. S. Shanmugan, and J. C. Holtzman, "A model for radar images and its application to adaptive digital filtering of multiplicative noise," *IEEE Transactions on Pattern Analysis and Machine Intelligence*, vol. 4, no. 2, pp. 157–166, 1982.

[34] A. Lopes, R. Touzi, and E. Nezry, "Adaptive speckle filters and scene heterogeneity," *IEEE Transactions on Geoscience and Remote Sensing*, vol. 28, no. 6, pp. 992–1000, 1990.

[35] K. S. Nathan and J. C. Curlander, "Speckle noise reduction of 1-look SAR imagery," in *IGARSS'87-International Geoscience and Remote Sensing Symposium*, vol. 2, pp. 1457–1462, 1987.

[36] A. Baraldi and F. Parmiggiani, "A refined Gamma MAP SAR speckle filter with improved geometrical adaptivity," *IEEE Transactions on Geoscience and Remote Sensing*, vol. 33, no. 5, pp. 1245–1257, 1995.

[37] A. Lopes, E. Nezry, R. Touzi, and H. Laur, "Structure detection and statistical adaptive speckle filtering in SAR images," *International Journal of Remote Sensing*, vol. 14, no. 9, pp. 1735–1758, 1993.

[38] J.-S. Lee, "A simple speckle smoothing algorithm for synthetic aperture radar images," *IEEE Transactions on Systems, Man, and Cybernetics*, no. 1, pp. 85–89, 1983.

[39] H. H. Arsenault and M. Levesque, "Combined homomorphic and local-statistics processing for restoration of images degraded by signal-dependent noise," *Applied Optics*, vol. 23, no. 6, pp. 845–850, 1984.

[40] M. I. H. Bhuiyan, M. O. Ahmad, and M. Swamy, "Spatially adaptive wavelet-based method using the Cauchy prior for denoising the SAR images," *IEEE Transactions on Circuits and Systems for Video Technology*, vol. 17, no. 4, pp. 500–507, 2007.

[41] T. Bianchi, F. Argenti, and L. Alparone, "Segmentation-based MAP despeckling of SAR images in the undecimated wavelet domain," *IEEE Transactions on Geoscience and Remote Sensing*, vol. 46, no. 9, pp. 2728–2742, 2008.

[42] H. Chen, Y. Zhang, H. Wang, and C. Ding, "Stationary-wavelet-based despeckling of SAR images using two-sided generalized gamma models," *IEEE Geoscience and Remote Sensing Letters*, vol. 9, no. 6, pp. 1061–1065, 2012.

[43] R. R. Damseh and M. O. Ahmad, "A low-complexity MMSE Bayesian estimator for suppression of speckle in SAR images," in *2016 IEEE International Symposium on Circuits and Systems (ISCAS)*, 2016: IEEE, pp. 1002–1005.

[44] H.-C. Li, W. Hong, Y.-R. Wu, and P.-Z. Fan, "Bayesian wavelet shrinkage with heterogeneity-adaptive threshold for SAR image despeckling based on generalized gamma distribution," *IEEE Transactions on Geoscience and Remote Sensing*, vol. 51, no. 4, pp. 2388–2402, 2012.

[45] P. Singh and R. Shree, "A new SAR image despeckling using directional smoothing filter and method noise thresholding," *Engineering Science and Technology, an International Journal*, vol. 21, no. 4, pp. 589–610, 2018.

[46] J. M. Bioucas-Dias and M. A. Figueiredo, "Multiplicative noise removal using variable splitting and constrained optimization," *IEEE Transactions on Image Processing*, vol. 19, no. 7, pp. 1720–1730, 2010.

[47] C. Li and Q. Fan, "Multiplicative noise removal via combining total variation and wavelet frame," *International Journal of Computer Mathematics*, vol. 95, no. 10, pp. 2036–2055, 2018.

[48] L. Rudin, P.-L. Lions, and S. Osher, "Multiplicative denoising and deblurring: theory and algorithms," in *Geometric Level Set Methods in Imaging, Vision, and Graphics*: Springer, 2003, pp. 103–119.

[49] C.-A. Deledalle, L. Denis, and F. Tupin, "How to compare noisy patches? Patch similarity beyond Gaussian noise," *International Journal of Computer Vision*, vol. 99, no. 1, pp. 86–102, 2012.

[50] F. J. Massey, Jr., "The Kolmogorov-Smirnov test for goodness of fit," *Journal of the American Statistical Association*, vol. 46, no. 253, pp. 68–78, 1951.

[51] O. D'Hondt, S. Guillaso, and O. Hellwich, "Iterative bilateral filtering of polarimetric SAR data," *IEEE Journal of Selected Topics in Applied Earth Observations and Remote Sensing*, vol. 6, no. 3, pp. 1628–1639, 2013.

[52] M. Seeger, "Covariance kernels from Bayesian generative models," *Advances in Neural Information Processing Systems*, vol. 2, pp. 905–912, 2002.

[53] X. Ma and P. Wu, "Multitemporal SAR image despeckling based on a scattering covariance matrix of image patch," *Sensors*, vol. 19, no. 14, p. 3057, 2019.

[54] A. Buades, B. Coll, and J.-M. Morel, "A review of image denoising algorithms, with a new one," *Multiscale Modeling & Simulation*, vol. 4, no. 2, pp. 490–530, 2005.

[55] C. Kervrann and J. Boulanger, "Local adaptivity to variable smoothness for exemplar-based image regularization and representation," *International Journal of Computer Vision*, vol. 79, no. 1, pp. 45–69, 2008.

[56] A. Foi and G. Boracchi, "Foveated nonlocal self-similarity," *International Journal of Computer Vision*, vol. 120, no. 1, pp. 78–110, 2016.

[57] K. Dabov, A. Foi, V. Katkovnik, and K. Egiazarian, "Image denoising by sparse 3-D transform-domain collaborative filtering," *IEEE Transactions on Image Processing*, vol. 16, no. 8, pp. 2080–2095, 2007.

[58] H. Zhong, Y. Li, and L. Jiao, "SAR image despeckling using Bayesian nonlocal means filter with sigma preselection," *IEEE Geoscience and Remote Sensing Letters*, vol. 8, no. 4, pp. 809–813, 2011.

[59] P. A. Penna and N. D. Mascarenhas, "(Non-)homomorphic approaches to denoise intensity SAR images with non-local means and stochastic distances," *Computers & Geosciences*, vol. 111, pp. 127–138, 2018.

[60] A. Krizhevsky, I. Sutskever, and G. E. Hinton, "ImageNet classification with deep convolutional neural networks," *Communications of the ACM*, vol. 60, no. 6, pp. 84–90, 2017.

[61] I. Goodfellow et al., "Generative adversarial nets," *Advances in Neural Information Processing Systems*, vol. 27, 2014.

[62] G. Fracastoro, E. Magli, G. Poggi, G. Scarpa, D. Valsesia, and L. Verdoliva, "Deep learning methods for synthetic aperture radar image despeckling: An overview of trends and perspectives," *IEEE Geoscience and Remote Sensing Magazine*, 2021.

[63] L. Denis, E. Dalsasso, and F. Tupin, "A review of deep-learning techniques for SAR image restoration," *arXiv preprint arXiv:2101.11852*, 2021.

[64] C.-A. Deledalle, L. Denis, S. Tabti, and F. Tupin, "MuLoG, or how to apply Gaussian denoisers to multi-channel SAR speckle reduction?," *IEEE Transactions on Image Processing*, vol. 26, no. 9, pp. 4389–4403, 2017.

[65] T. Pan, D. Peng, W. Yang, and H.-C. Li, "A filter for SAR image despeckling using pre-trained convolutional neural network model," *Remote Sensing*, vol. 11, no. 20, p. 2379, 2019.

[66] K. Zhang, W. Zuo, Y. Chen, D. Meng, and L. Zhang, "Beyond a gaussian denoiser: Residual learning of deep cnn for image denoising," *IEEE Transactions on Image Processing*, vol. 26, no. 7, pp. 3142–3155, 2017.

[67] K. Zhang, W. Zuo, and L. Zhang, "FFDNet: Toward a fast and flexible solution for CNN-based image denoising," *IEEE Transactions on Image Processing*, vol. 27, no. 9, pp. 4608–4622, 2018.

[68] K. Simonyan and A. Zisserman, "Very deep convolutional networks for large-scale image recognition," *arXiv preprint arXiv:1409.1556*, 2014.

[69] X. Tang, L. Zhang, and X. Ding, "SAR image despeckling with a multilayer perceptron neural network," *International Journal of Digital Earth*, vol. 12, no. 3, pp. 354–374, 2019.

[70] G. Huang, Z. Liu, L. Van Der Maaten, and K. Q. Weinberger, "Densely connected convolutional networks," in *Proceedings of the IEEE Conference on Computer Vision and Pattern Recognition*, 2017, pp. 4700–4708.

[71] O. Ronneberger, P. Fischer, and T. Brox, "U-net: Convolutional networks for biomedical image segmentation," in *International Conference on Medical Image Computing and Computer-Assisted Intervention*, 2015: Springer, pp. 234–241.

[72] Q. Zhang, Q. Yuan, J. Li, Z. Yang, and X. Ma, "Learning a dilated residual network for SAR image despeckling," *Remote Sensing*, vol. 10, no. 2, pp. 196, 2018.

[73] J. Lehtinen et al., "Noise2noise: Learning image restoration without clean data," *arXiv preprint arXiv:1803.04189*, 2018.

[74] E. Dalsasso, L. Denis, and F. Tupin, "SAR2SAR: A semi-supervised despeckling algorithm for SAR images," *IEEE Journal of Selected Topics in Applied Earth Observations and Remote Sensing*, vol. 14, pp. 4321–4329, 2021.

[75] S.-K. Kang, S.-Y. Yie, and J.-S. Lee, "Noise2Noise improved by trainable wavelet coefficients for PET denoising," *Electronics*, vol. 10, no. 13, pp. 1529, 2021.

[76] Y. Yuan, J. Guan, and J. Sun, "Blind SAR image despeckling using self-supervised dense dilated convolutional neural network," *arXiv preprint arXiv:1908.01608*, 2019.

[77] J. Batson and L. Royer, "Noise2self: Blind denoising by self-supervision," in *International Conference on Machine Learning*, 2019: PMLR, pp. 524–533.

[78] A. Krull, T.-O. Buchholz, and F. Jug, "Noise2void-learning denoising from single noisy images," in *Proceedings of the IEEE/CVF Conference on Computer Vision and Pattern Recognition*, 2019, pp. 2129–2137.

[79] S. Joo, S. Cha, and T. Moon, "DoPAMINE: Double-sided masked CNN for pixel adaptive multiplicative noise despeckling," in *Proceedings of the AAAI Conference on Artificial Intelligence*, 2019, vol. 33, no. 1, pp. 4031–4038.

[80] Z. Wang, A. C. Bovik, H. R. Sheikh, and E. P. Simoncelli, "Image quality assessment: from error visibility to structural similarity," *IEEE Transactions on Image Processing*, vol. 13, no. 4, pp. 600–612, 2004.

[81] F. Sattar, L. Floreby, G. Salomonsson, and B. Lovstrom, "Image enhancement based on a nonlinear multiscale method," *IEEE Transactions on Image Processing*, vol. 6, no. 6, pp. 888–895, 1997.

[82] S. Solbo and T. Eltoft, "A stationary wavelet-domain wiener filter for correlated speckle," *IEEE Transactions on Geoscience and Remote Sensing*, vol. 46, no. 4, pp. 1219–1230, 2008.

[83] L. Gomez, R. Ospina, and A. C. Frery, "Unassisted quantitative evaluation of despeckling filters," *Remote Sensing*, vol. 9, no. 4, p. 389, 2017.

[84] R. Touzi, "A review of speckle filtering in the context of estimation theory," *IEEE Transactions on Geoscience and Remote Sensing*, vol. 40, no. 11, pp. 2392–2404, 2002.

[85] L. Gomez, M. E. Buemi, J. C. Jacobo-Berlles, and M. E. Mejail, "A new image quality index for objectively evaluating despeckling filtering in SAR images," *IEEE Journal of Selected Topics in Applied Earth Observations and Remote Sensing*, vol. 9, no. 3, pp. 1297–1307, 2015.

[86] N. R. Goodman, "Statistical analysis based on a certain multivariate complex Gaussian distribution (an introduction)," *The Annals of Mathematical Statistics*, vol. 34, no. 1, pp. 152–177, 1963.

[87] J.-S. Lee, M. R. Grunes, D. L. Schuler, E. Pottier, and L. Ferro-Famil, "Scattering-model-based speckle filtering of polarimetric SAR data," *IEEE Transactions on Geoscience and Remote Sensing*, vol. 44, no. 1, pp. 176–187, 2005.

[88] J.-S. Lee, M. R. Grunes, E. Pottier, and L. Ferro-Famil, "Unsupervised terrain classification preserving polarimetric scattering characteristics," *IEEE Transactions on Geoscience and Remote Sensing*, vol. 42, no. 4, pp. 722–731, 2004.

[89] S. Goze and A. Lopes, "A MMSE speckle filter for full resolution SAR polarimetric data," *Journal of Electromagnetic Waves and Applications*, vol. 7, no. 5, pp. 717–737, 1993.

[90] A. Lopes and F. Séry, "Optimal speckle reduction for the product model in multilook polarimetric SAR imagery and the Wishart distribution," *IEEE Transactions on Geoscience and Remote Sensing*, vol. 35, no. 3, pp. 632–647, 1997.

[91] L. M. Novak, M. C. Burl, and W. Irving, "Optimal polarimetric processing for enhanced target detection," *IEEE Transactions on Aerospace and Electronic Systems*, vol. 29, no. 1, pp. 234–244, 1993.

[92] K. Conradsen, A. A. Nielsen, J. Schou, and H. Skriver, "A test statistic in the complex Wishart distribution and its application to change detection in polarimetric SAR data," *IEEE Transactions on Geoscience and Remote Sensing*, vol. 41, no. 1, pp. 4–19, 2003.

[93] G. Liu and H. Zhong, "Nonlocal means filter for polarimetric SAR data despeckling based on discriminative similarity measure," *IEEE Geoscience and Remote Sensing Letters*, vol. 11, no. 2, pp. 514–518, 2013.

[94] L. Torres, S. J. Sant'Anna, C. da Costa Freitas, and A. C. Frery, "Speckle reduction in polarimetric SAR imagery with stochastic distances and nonlocal means," *Pattern Recognition*, vol. 47, no. 1, pp. 141–157, 2014.

[95] A. Ferretti, A. Fumagalli, F. Novali, C. Prati, F. Rocca, and A. Rucci, "A new algorithm for processing interferometric data-stacks: SqueeSAR," *IEEE Transactions on Geoscience and Remote Sensing*, vol. 49, no. 9, pp. 3460–3470, 2011.

[96] M. Schmitt, J. L. Schönberger, and U. Stilla, "Adaptive covariance matrix estimation for multibaseline InSAR data stacks," *IEEE Transactions on Geoscience and Remote Sensing*, vol. 52, no. 11, pp. 6807–6817, 2014.

[97] C. Rambour et al., "Similarity criterion for SAR tomography over dense urban area," in *2017 IEEE International Geoscience and Remote Sensing Symposium (IGARSS)*, 2017: IEEE, pp. 1760–1763.

[98]   H. Aghababaee, A. Budillon, G. Ferraioli, V. Pascazio, and G. Schirinzi, "On the role of non-local filtering in forest vertical structure characterization using SAR tomography," in *2017 IEEE International Geoscience and Remote Sensing Symposium (IGARSS)*, 2017: IEEE, pp. 6032–6035.

[99]   H. Aghababaee, A. Budillon, G. Ferraioli, V. Pascazio, and G. Schirinzi, "Full 3D DEM generation in urban area by improving estimation from SAR tomography," in *IGARSS 2018 – 2018 IEEE International Geoscience and Remote Sensing Symposium*, 2018: IEEE, pp. 6087–6090.

[100]   H. Aghababaee, G. Ferraioli, G. Schirinzi, and M. R. Sahebi, "The role of nonlocal estimation in SAR tomographic imaging of volumetric media," *IEEE Geoscience and Remote Sensing Letters*, vol. 15, no. 5, pp. 729–733, 2018.

[101]   H. Aghababaee, B. Kanoun, S. Vitale, and G. Ferraioli, "The use of nl paradigm in sar applications," in *2019 IEEE 5th International Forum on Research and Technology for Society and Industry (RTSI)*, 2019: IEEE, pp. 120–123.

[102]   E. Cole, J. Cheng, J. Pauly, and S. Vasanawala, "Analysis of deep complex-valued convolutional neural networks for MRI reconstruction and phase-focused applications," *Magnetic Resonance in Medicine*, vol. 86, no. 2, pp. 1093–1109, 2021.

[103]   C. Trabelsi et al., "Deep complex networks," *arXiv preprint arXiv:1705.09792*, 2017.

[104]   B. N. Dash and N. Khare, "Deep complex neural network applications in remote sensing: an introductory review," in *Radar Sensor Technology XXV*, 2021, vol. 11742: International Society for Optics and Photonics, p. 1174208.

[105]   A. G. Mullissa, C. Persello, and J. Reiche, "Despeckling polarimetric SAR data using a multistream complex-valued fully convolutional network," *IEEE Geoscience and Remote Sensing Letters*, 2021.

[106]   X. Yang, T. Pan, W. Yang, and H.-C. Li, "PolSAR image despeckling using trained models on single channel SAR images," in *2019 6th Asia-Pacific Conference on Synthetic Aperture Radar (APSAR)*, 2019: IEEE, pp. 1–4.

3 Polarimetric Interferometric Decomposition

Shahid Shuja Shafai, Shashi Kumar, Hossein Aghababaei, and Anurag Kulshrestha

CONTENTS

DOI: 10.1201/9781003204466-3

45

3.1 INTRODUCTION

Earth observation has played a vital role in terms of monitoring and managing land use. It is useful to examine and analyze the changes in ground features and the spatial response of that change. Remote sensing has emerged significantly in the past 50 years and is one of the most important features of earth observation. It provides data that is needed to carry out such analysis utilizing satellite images, aerial photographs, LiDAR (light detection and ranging), RADAR (radio detection and ranging) data, etc.

Synthetic aperture radar (SAR) is a composite imaging architecture that captures the spatial attributes/characteristics of the earth's surface reflectivity by modeling polarimetric information of the backscattered wave [1]. The target is illuminated with a polarized electromagnetic pulse operated in the microwave band of the electromagnetic spectrum, and the reflected or scattered part is recorded by the sensor (hence the term backscatter). This backscattered response has information in terms of amplitude and phase that differs with different types of objects/targets [2]. Since the microwave region of the EM spectrum is used, it makes it possible to monitor at night time as well as in unfavorable weather conditions since microwaves can penetrate clouds and rain, and it does not have an effect of altitude on the spatial resolution [3]. Apart from this, it has a few other advantages over other imaging remote sensing techniques, such as sensitivity to shape, size, orientation, and dielectric properties of the object [4]. SAR polarimetry (PolSAR) and SAR interferometry (InSAR) are the two major techniques that have been developed using the SAR data, and they are widely used for applications such as disaster management, target characterization, biomass parameter retrieval and estimation, glacial studies, and so on and so forth.

The magnitude of backscattered waves related to the image scene has a spatial structure that normally correlates with underlying scattering intensities from which the scattering mechanism can be governed, but the underlying phase has no such correlation [5]. However, the underlying phase information can be yielded by performing scaler interferometry using another geometrically matched SAR image with a different spatial or temporal baseline [5], [6]. This technique is called InSAR. Using the InSAR approach, the target can be characterized on the basis of the coherence magnitude, which is the correlation between the observed phase differences within a resolution cell.

One of the extensive uses of PolSAR data is the classification of on-ground features and terrain [7]. An area observed from space or an airborne SAR system can be visualized or modeled for parameter inversion by processing the polarimetric information rendered in the scattering matrix [8]. The SAR image is generally rendered in σ^0 (sigma-naught), which is the backscatter per unit area [1]. However, to better interpret the content of SAR images, the interaction of radar signals with various land cover types (scatterers or targets in radar terminology) is expressed in terms of scattering mechanisms. Various targets backscatter the incident radar waves with different intensities and polarization and therefore show different scattering responses. There are three primary types of backscatter: surface/odd-bounce, volume, and double-bounce backscatter [2], [4].

In Figure 3.1, (a), (b), (c), (d), and (e) collectively represent surface scattering, (d), (e), and (f) collectively represent double-bounce scattering, and (g) represents volume scattering. The type of scattering observed mainly depends upon surface roughness, the orientation of the scatterer along the radar line of sight, and the frequency of the radar system [2]. The surface and double-bounce backscatter are characterized by co-polarization terms (H-H, V-V), and volume scattering is characterized by cross-polarization (H-V or V-H) terms. For each pixel of a SAR image, the PolSAR data comprises these polarization terms collectively in the form scattering matrix. From Figure 3.1, it is clear that the characterization of targets based on backscatter response is quite complex.

Therefore, the classification of ground features through the PolSAR approach is done using target decomposition theorems [9]. This method is broadly categorized as coherent and incoherent decomposition [10]. The former approach is done to characterize coherent or pure targets (targets that do not change the nature of polarization) and decomposes the scattering matrix directly. The main issue with the coherent decomposition approach is that the physical scattering models may not relate well

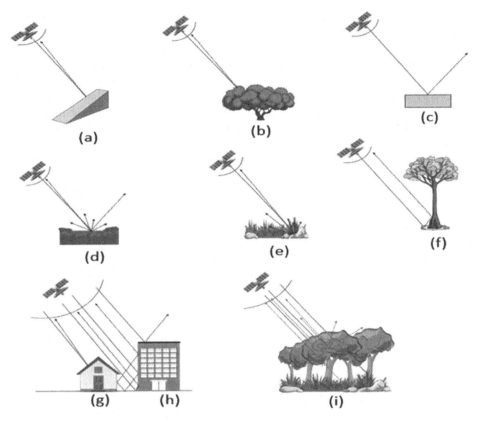

FIGURE 3.1 Different land cover types showing different scattering responses: (a) direct scattering from the surface, (b) direct scattering from the forest canopy, (c) forward scattering, (d) and (e) diffuse scattering, (f) diffused double-bounce scattering, (g) and (h) specular double-bounce scattering, and (i) volume scattering.

to the scattering response of distributed scatterers, i.e., different scatters within the same pixel having different backscattering responses [8]. These targets induce noise in the scattering process, which is termed speckle. To lower the effect of speckle, spatial averaging is performed; therefore, such an approach makes use of statistical information in the form of second-order statistics Hermitian covariance or coherency matrix to characterize the scattering mechanism and the associated target, also taking into account the scattering response from distributed scatterers [1], [2]. The geophysical characteristics are represented by a multi-band RGB image in which each band consists of decomposed scattering power. The red channels represent double-bounce, the blue represent surface, and the green represent volume scattering power.

3.2 LIMITATIONS IN TARGET IDENTIFICATION

Feature identification and characterization are important aspects of SAR application [14]. This can be done by using InSAR- and PolSAR-based methods. However, both approaches have certain limitations. Coherent change detection (CCD) is an approach in which the change in ground features is detected by analyzing the loss of coherence within two observable instances, i.e., the time interval within which the target was sensed [5]. However, the underlying scattering mechanism cannot be governed for the targets. Furthermore, the coherence is sensitive to various decorrelations and with relatively large temporal baselines, loss of coherence is undoubted. Low coherence estimates are not useful for InSAR applications, especially for target delineation [11]. In terms of polarimetric decompositions, clutter objects can be characterized by employing incoherent decomposition modeling as these relate well with the physical structure of the targets. Eigenvalue-based decomposition [12] and model-based decomposition [13], [14] are the two main target decomposition methods used in incoherent decomposition modeling. The former method uses the eigenvalues and eigenvectors of the coherency matrix along with the secondary parameters, namely entropy (denoting purity or dominance of scattering mechanism), alpha angle (denoting average scattering mechanism), and anisotropy (indicating dependency of non-dominant scattering mechanism) to get the account of the physical information of the target in terms of scattering mechanisms. The latter method directly decomposes the second-order scattering matrix into an ensemble canonical covariance/coherency matrix of the respective scattering mechanism [10]. Each canonical matrix corresponds to second-order descriptors of the simpler or canonical objects [8]. The urban targets can be characterized by their high double-bounce and/or direct surface backscatter, and the natural targets such as forest canopy can be characterized by their dominant volume backscatter response. However, various research and experiments show that incoherent decomposition models over-estimate volume scattering for the urban targets that i) have irregular geometry, ii) are established in compact spatial arrangement, iii) are along sloping terrains, and iv) are oriented along the radar line of sight [14]–[19]. These problems persist due to the imaging geometry of SAR systems. Due to side-looking acquisition geometry, the physical dimension, shape, spatial density, pattern, and orientation affect the backscatter response from the target. These variations increase the randomness of the scattering process, leading to predominant volume scattering response or an increase in received cross-pol intensities [15]. To compensate for the effect of orientation, the scattering matrix basis is rotated to lower the magnitude of cross-pol intensities. However, targets having an orientation shift of the order of $35°$ or more are eventually decomposed as volume scatterers [20]–[24]. Further, the problem of over-estimation of volume scattering is broadly observed in incoherent decomposition models (in both model-based and eigenvalue-based). For eigenvalue-based decomposition, such targets exhibit high entropy values, indicating random scattering. The high degree of randomness limits the precise characterization of the dominant scattering mechanism [10], [12]. For model-based decomposition, the problem cannot be solved directly because of the model framework and assumptions [15], [25]. The first assumption states that the correlation between co-pol and cross-pol terms is zero; this can be referred to as reflection symmetry and does not hold for distributed targets. The model also assumes all the scattering mechanisms do not correlate [13], [18], [26]; however, this assumption does not hold for distributed scattering cases. Furthermore, the internal design of the model itself serves as the shortcoming because for the current decomposition scheme, it is not possible to utilize complete information from the second-order statistics matrix (covariance/coherency matrix); the mathematical drawback can be seen with the number of equations used in decomposition modeling, which are fewer than the number of unknowns [25]. The alternative method, i.e., deorientation, also fails to subdue the predominant volume scattering induced from urban targets.

The problem can be summarized for both approaches. For InSAR-based methods, the problem is twofold: the inability to determine the underlying scattering mechanism or, in simple words, the reason for coherence loss and inability to characterize targets having low coherence estimates as an effect of various decorrelation. Similarly, for the PolSAR-based method, the problem is the scattering ambiguity of the underlying true scattering mechanism and predominant volume scattering induced from urban targets.

3.3 POLARIMETRIC INTERFEROMETRIC FUNDAMENTALS AND ADVANCEMENTS

In this section, various concepts that are necessary to understand the basics of polarimetric decomposition modeling have been studied. The polarimetric properties of microwaves, their

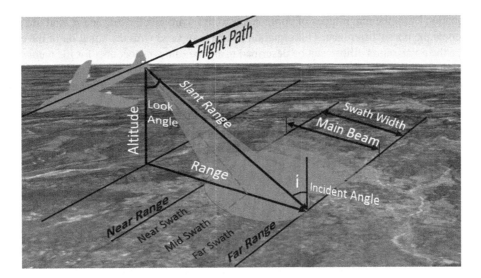

FIGURE 3.2   SAR imaging geometry.

response with targets, and the interpretation of the different scattering mechanisms have been discussed. Further, the SAR statistics-based scattering matrix and their decomposition modeling using different methods have also been explored.

3.3.1   RADAR IMAGING

Due to the complex geometry involved in SAR imaging (Figure 3.2), signal processing methods are required in range direction as well as in azimuth directions. This is because SAR regularly broadcasts phase-encoded pulses [3], [4]. These echoes, backscattered from the target, are recorded. Since the azimuth resolution is related to the antenna size, there is signal processing complicacy in the azimuth direction. The concept of "synthetic aperture" is employed to achieve high azimuth resolution. Using Doppler shifting anomalies, fine azimuth resolution cells are obtained. For every scatterer, the response of backscatter energy is captured as a distinct Doppler shift; consequently, this energy can be parted into fine azimuth resolution cells. Also, the Doppler shift makes it possible to achieve the azimuth resolution corresponding to antenna size, which could be several meters or kilometers wide [3].

3.3.2   POLARIZATION OF EM WAVES

The coordinate convention of an EM wave is a right-handed orthogonal set $(x,)$ described in three-dimensional space by three axes in which the z-axis represents the direction of propagation of wave and the x-axis and y-axis lie in a plane perpendicular to the z-axis [27]. One of the intrinsic properties of the electromagnetic wave is polarization [27]. It can also be interpreted as a trace of the orientation pattern and the form of the electrical field tip. The locus of the polarized wave describes the polarization of an electromagnetic wave [28]. Using the Maxwell equation, the polarized wave along the x and y axes for a temporal wave trajectory at a particular point $z = z_0$ can be deduced into an equation:

$$\left[\frac{E_x\left(z_0t\right)}{a_x}\right]^2 - 2\frac{E_x\left(z_0,t\right)E_y\left(z_0,t\right)}{a_xa_y}cos\phi + \left[\frac{E_y\left(z_0t\right)}{a_y}\right]^2 = \sin^2\left(\phi a_x\right) \qquad (3.1)$$

In Equation (3.1), the magnitudes of components x and y are given by a_x and a_y and the phases and ϕ denote the phase difference. This equation can be compared with the equation of the ellipse, and hence the polarization ellipse can be described using the same. ϕ accounts for the nature of the polarization ellipse. $\phi = 0°$ or $\pm180°$ represents linear polarization and $\phi = \pm45°$ represents circular polarization. The polarization ellipse (Figure 3.3) can be defined using three parameters, which are given below.

1. The amplitude, denoted by A, given as [29],

$$A = \sqrt{a_x^2 + a_y^2} \tag{3.2}$$

2. The angle made by the major axis with the X-axis of the ellipse, referred as the orientation angle, denoted by θ, is given as [29],

$$\tan 2\theta = 2 \frac{a_x a_y}{a_x^2 - a_y^2} \cos \phi \tag{3.3}$$

3. The ellipticity, denoted by $|\tau|$, is given as [29],

$$\left| \sin 2\tau \right| = 2 \frac{a_x a_y}{a_x^2 + a_y^2} \left| \sin \phi \right| \tag{3.4}$$

3.3.3 SCATTERING MATRIX

The scattering matrix gives the basic and primitive information of a target related to the scattering process. One of the ways to manifest polarimetric information is to model polarimetric signatures [28]. This can be done since the interaction of an object with an EM wave involves energy transition and absorption. Due to the energy transition, the absorbed energy is radiated or backscattered as a new wave. The backscattered wave is modulated to provide data on the interacted target's

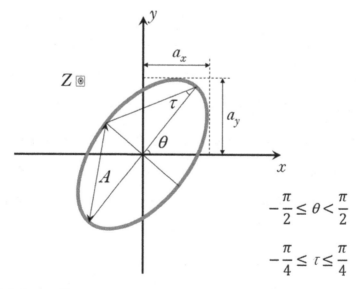

FIGURE 3.3   Polarization ellipse geometry [3], [32].

property. The backscatter response of a polarized wave incident on a target can have a contribution to both horizontal and vertical polarization irrespective of the polarization of the incident wave. The backscattered wave is modulated and information about the target in terms of dielectric properties, geometry, texture, etc., can be derived. To incorporate target properties that are smaller than the radar system's footprint, the radar cross-section (RCS) is introduced [30]:

$$\sigma = 4\pi r^2 \frac{\left|E_S\right|^2}{\left|E_I\right|^2} \tag{3.5}$$

E_I, E_S, and r are the incident and scattered EM wave associated with the target and the distance between target and radar respectively. For targets bigger than the footprint of RCS, also called distributed or extended targets [31], the scattering coefficient σ^0 is given as

$$\sigma^0 = \left\langle \frac{\sigma}{A_0} \right\rangle = 4\pi r^2 \frac{\left\langle \left|E_S\right|^2 \right\rangle}{\left|E_I\right|^2} \tag{3.6}$$

In Equation (3.6), σ^0 is the scattering coefficient. For a spherical surface with radius r, σ^0 is the ratio of the mean scattered power density to the mean incident power density. If the incident and the scattered wave are represented respectively by Jones vectors E_I and E_S, then, keeping the presumption of far-field valid, the backscattering mechanism can be expressed as a function of target properties in terms of scattering matrix as,

$$E_S = \frac{e^{-jkr}}{r} SE_I = \frac{e^{-jkr}}{r} \begin{bmatrix} S_{11} & S_{12} \\ S_{21} & S_{22} \end{bmatrix} E_I \tag{3.7}$$

The term e^{-jkr} relates to the propagation effect in amplitude and phase of EM wave. S is a 2×2 polarimetric scattering matrix or Sinclair scattering matrix [39]. It can also be represented in linear polarization basis, i.e., horizontal and vertical (H, V) as,

$$S = \begin{bmatrix} S_{HH} & S_{HV} \\ S_{VH} & S_{VV} \end{bmatrix} \tag{3.8}$$

VH polarization denotes the backscatter as vertical transmit (V) and horizontal receiving (H). In the same way, other elements of the scattering matrix can be defined. SPAN is the total scattering power and is given by,

$$SPAN = \left|S_{HH}\right|^2 + \left|S_{HV}\right|^2 + \left|S_{VH}\right|^2 + \left|S_{VV}\right|^2 \tag{3.9}$$

3.3.4 PolSAR

Polarimetric synthetic aperture radar, referred to as PolSAR, is an advancement of single-polarized SAR systems. The technique is used to acquire and synthesize the polarization state of the microwave spectrum. Therefore, complete information of on-ground targets or objects as scatterers can be identified by synthesizing the backscatter using different modes of polarization. Scattering matrices for point targets can be formed using full polarimetric information; therefore, the detection, categorization and segmentation of objects can be done using the PolSAR technique [29]. The coherent target can be characterized using the scattering matrix as a basic descriptor [8]. Kennaugh [27] introduced the idea of optimum polarization. This definition was used to create a new theory called Huynen, which coined the idea of radar phenomenology [32].

Spatio-temporal dynamics of the environment make the incoherent target (distributed targets) phenomenon more likely to appear than point targets. The polarimetric information as a function of stochastic scattering corresponding to such targets is given by second-order statistics covariance or coherency matrix. Pauli and lexicographic scattering vectors are used to derive these matrices.

3.3.5 SCATTERING VECTORS, COHERENCY MATRIX, AND COVARIANCE MATRIX

The scattering mechanism is projected into Pauli spin matrices so that they can be separated and interpreted. The majority of SAR systems are therefore mono-static under reciprocal constraints; the matrices are given as

$$P_1 = \frac{1}{\sqrt{2}}\begin{bmatrix} 1 & 0 \\ 0 & 1 \end{bmatrix}, \quad P_2 = \frac{1}{\sqrt{2}}\begin{bmatrix} 1 & 0 \\ 0 & -1 \end{bmatrix}, \quad P_3 = \frac{1}{\sqrt{2}}\begin{bmatrix} 0 & 1 \\ 1 & 0 \end{bmatrix} \tag{3.10}$$

Therefore, the scattering matrix is projected as

$$S = k_1 P_1 + k_2 P_2 + k_3 P_3 \tag{3.11}$$

and the Pauli scattering vector becomes

$$k_{p(H,V)} = \frac{1}{\sqrt{2}}\begin{bmatrix} S_{HH} + S_{VV} & S_{HH} - S_{VV} & 2S_{HV} \end{bmatrix}^T \tag{3.12}$$

The scattering vector of Pauli may indicate the structure of canonical scattering. The canonical surface or odd-bounce, even-bounce, or double-bounce and volume scattering mechanisms are represented as P_1, P_2, and P_3 by the spin matrices of Pauli. The scattering coefficients of the above-mentioned mechanisms are given by the vector $k_{p(H,V)}$. Using this vector, polarimetric coherency matrix T can be formed as:

$$T = \left\langle k_{P_{(H,V)}} k_{P_{(H,V)}}{}^H \right\rangle = \begin{bmatrix} T_{11} & T_{12} & T_{13} \\ T_{21} & T_{22} & T_{23} \\ T_{31} & T_{32} & T_{33} \end{bmatrix} =$$

$$\frac{1}{2}\begin{bmatrix} \left\langle |S_{HH} + S_{VV}|^2 \right\rangle & \left\langle (S_{HH} + S_{VV})(S_{HH} - S_{VV})^* \right\rangle & \left\langle 2(S_{HH} + S_{VV})S_{HV}{}^* \right\rangle \\ \left\langle (S_{HH} + S_{VV})^*(S_{HH} - S_{VV}) \right\rangle & \left\langle |S_{HH} - S_{VV}|^2 \right\rangle & \left\langle 2(S_{HH} - S_{VV})S_{HV}{}^* \right\rangle \\ \left\langle 2(S_{HH} + S_{VV})^* S_{HV} \right\rangle & \left\langle 2(S_{HH} - S_{VV})^* S_{HV} \right\rangle & \left\langle 4|S_{HV}|^2 \right\rangle \end{bmatrix} \tag{3.13}$$

Another way to vectorize the scattering matrix is by employing a lexicographic vector transform. Under the reciprocity condition and with linear polarization basis (HV), the vector is given as:

$$k_{L(H,V)} = \begin{bmatrix} S_{HH} & \sqrt{2}S_{HV} & 2S_{VV} \end{bmatrix}^T \tag{3.14}$$

The covariance matrix corresponding to second-order statistics can be defined as:

$$C = \left\langle k_{L_{(H,V)}} k_{L_{(H,V)}}^{H} \right\rangle = \begin{bmatrix} \left\langle |S_{HH}|^2 \right\rangle & \sqrt{2} \left\langle S_{HH} S_{HV}^* \right\rangle & \left\langle S_{HH} S_{HV}^* \right\rangle \\ \sqrt{2} \left\langle S_{HH}^* S_{HV} \right\rangle & 2 \left\langle |S_{HV}|^2 \right\rangle & \sqrt{2} \left\langle S_{HV} S_{VV}^* \right\rangle \\ \left\langle S_{HH}^* S_{HV} \right\rangle & \sqrt{2} \left\langle S_{HV}^* S_{VV} \right\rangle & \left\langle |S_{VV}|^2 \right\rangle \end{bmatrix} \quad (3.15)$$

The coherency and covariance matrix will be generated from the scattering matrix, and both matrices can be linearly transformed into one another as follows.

$$\langle T \rangle = N \langle C \rangle N^H \quad (3.16)$$

N is a unitary matrix, given as:

$$N = \frac{1}{\sqrt{2}} \begin{bmatrix} 1 & 0 & 1 \\ 1 & 0 & -1 \\ 0 & \sqrt{2} & 0 \end{bmatrix} \quad (3.17)$$

N^H is the transpose of the matrix, and $\langle \cdot \rangle$ denotes sample average.

3.3.6 Target Decomposition

To explore and interpret the polarimetric scattering mechanisms, J. R. Huynen incited polarimetric target decomposition over the theory of radar target phenomenology and coined Huynen decomposition or N-target decomposition [33]. The details of this breakdown are represented by a collection of Huynen parameters and the Kennaugh matrix dichotomy [34]. Polarimetric decomposition as a function of scattering phenomena is an effective technique to model land cover geophysical or bio-geophysical characteristics [10]. These comprise coherent and incoherent type decomposition. These point targets or coherent targets are decomposed using coherent decomposition, normally functioned on a scattering matrix. Cameron decomposition [28] and Krogager decomposition [30] are a few coherent decomposition methods [10].

The study or examination point targets or deterministic targets can be done by employing coherent decomposition; however, in contrast to ideal situations, we encounter distributed targets more often in a real-world scenario. Distributed targets can be effectively examined using incoherent decompositions [35]. Such types of decompositions require higher-order statistics to model scattering mechanisms as a function of the physical characteristics of the target. Incoherent decompositions can be broadly categorized as eigenvalue–eigenvector decomposition and model-based decomposition [36].

3.3.7 Model-Based Decomposition

This category of modeling features the disintegration of the polarimetric scattering matrix into a cumulative ensemble of the elementary canonical scattering matrix, each of which relates to a specific scattering mechanism. These scattering mechanisms can be a single-bounce, double-bounce, volume scattering, and helix scattering. The canonical scattering matrices can be modified according to the application of the decomposition used. The aim is to calculate the scatter power for each elementary scatter component and to decide the dominant scatter mechanism for the scatter with respect to space. Scattering mechanisms can be understood and interpreted well by employing model-based decomposition, as the physical structures of scatterers can be compared with canonical physical models directly, which gives this type of incoherent decomposition an advantage [10]. The first of its kind, the Freeman–Durden decomposition model is a generic incoherent model-based decomposition [13]. A further four-component scattering model [14] was proposed. These two models are the most commonly used models for polarimetric decompositions. Following on, various advances have been proposed, such as non-negative eigenvalue constraint [19], orientation angle compensation [37], generalizing scattering models [38], [15], [39], and modified model components on the basis of some parameters [40], [17], [41], [16], [42], [43], [44]. Few methods put the focus on the role of cross-polarization, induced from man-made targets and that introduced the component of dominant orientation angle [37], [45].

3.3.8 CLASSICAL THREE-COMPONENT DECOMPOSITION MODEL

Freeman–Durden decomposition [13] uses second-order polarimetric statistics-based covariance or coherency matrix to perform decomposition. The decomposition is segregated into three basic different scattering models, which are comprised of surface or odd-bounce scattering T_{odd}, even or double-bounce scattering T_{dbl}, and volume scattering T_{vol}. Therefore, the scattering mechanisms from targets constituted by "n" elemental scatter, which may be vegetation canopy, snow, and so on, show higher-order scattering-volume scattering. The scattering processes, such as the dihedral corner reflection produced by surface-wall compounds and/or surface-trunk features, are described by a double-bounce scattering. Nonetheless, odd-bounce scattering may reflect both single-bounce scattering from rough surfaces such as grassland and ocean and triple-bounce scattering from the woods (ground–trunk–ground structures) and corners of buildings (ground–wall–ground). This technique of decomposition considers the state of reflection symmetry valid, indicating that the cross-correlation among co-polarization and cross-polarization to be zero, i.e., $\left\langle S_{HH} S_{HV}^* \right\rangle = \left\langle S_{VV} S_{HV}^* \right\rangle = 0$. The scattering mechanisms are decomposed through the framework given below.

$$T = f_s \left\langle T_{odd} \right\rangle + f_d \left\langle T_{dbl} \right\rangle + + f_v \left\langle T_{vol} \right\rangle, \quad (3.18)$$

where, f_s, f_d, f_v are model coefficient for respective models and T is the total power.

3.3.9 FOUR-COMPONENT DECOMPOSITION MODEL

The four-component decomposition model was an advancement of the Freeman–Durden decomposition model, given by [14]. This model had a helix component to incorporate the backscattering from irregular or complicated structures. This additional component solves the problems that arise as a result of the previous model's assumption of reflection symmetry. The helix component in the model is associated with $\left\langle 2(S_{HH} - S_{VV}) S_{HV}^* \right\rangle$, i.e., $Im[T_{23}]$, which is the imaginary part of the coherency matrix. Using the same element, the model coefficient is determined. The mechanism of scattering is broken down through the framework below.

$$T = f_s \left\langle T_{odd} \right\rangle + f_d \left\langle T_{dbl} \right\rangle + + f_v \left\langle T_{vol} \right\rangle + f_c \left\langle T_{hel} \right\rangle, \quad (3.19)$$

where f_s, f_d, f_v, and f_c are model coefficients for respective models and T is the total power. Scattering mechanisms can be presumed and applicability can be investigated by calculating the power of individual components.

3.3.10 POLARIZATION ORIENTATION ANGLE (POA) COMPENSATION

To distinguish the state of polarization electromagnetic wave, the POA is one prime factor. It is influenced by terrain slopes in the direction of the road, oriented houses, and vegetation canopy. The scattering matrix's polarization base is rotated, causing POA change [46]. Due to this shift, the azimuth slope can be either maximized if the range slope is positive (towards the radar) or minimized if the range slope is negative (away from the radar) [20]. The following expression can be used to estimate POA.

$$\tan\theta = \frac{\tan\omega}{-\tan\gamma\cos\varphi + \sin\varphi}. \tag{3.20}$$

In Equation (3.20), θ is POA, $\tan\omega$ is the slope in the azimuth direction, $\tan\gamma$ is the slope in the ground range direction, and φ is the radar look angle.

The volume scattering power increases and double-bounce scattering power decreases because of the induced shift in polarization orientation angle, and the element of scattering matrix is affected, which leads to inaccurate information extraction from the coherency matrix or covariance matrix [20]. To resolve this, orientation compensation, also called deorientation, is done. The power of cross-polarization is reduced when the higher-order scattering matrix is rotated at a certain rotation angle, theoretically called the polarization orientation angle [46]. The POA angle is derived from the coherency matrix and forms the following expression.

$$\tan 4\theta = \frac{2Re\left(T_{23}\right)}{T_{22}-T_{33}}, \theta \in \left[-45^0, 45^0\right]. \tag{3.21}$$

After deorientation, the amount of contribution to total backscatter from volume scattering is reduced and an increase in the double-bounce scattering is observed, whereas a slight difference in the surface scattering is noticed [20]. Various algorithms were proposed to derive POA for applications such as oriented structures investigation, damage examination, ocean parameter estimations, etc. [21], [23], [24], [46]–[48]. Of all these algorithms, the most successful is the circular polarization algorithm, which estimates the POA using the correlation of the phase among co-polarization elements, i.e., the correlation between RR and LL circular polarizations.

$$4\theta = \arg\left(\left\langle S_{RR}S_{LL}^*\right\rangle\right) = \tan^{-1}\left(\frac{-4Re\left(\left\langle \left(S_{HH}-S_{VV}\right)S_{HV}^*\right\rangle\right)}{-\left\langle \left|S_{HH}-S_{VV}\right|^2\right\rangle + 4\left\langle \left|S_{HV}\right|^2\right\rangle}\right). \tag{3.22}$$

Further, the POA compensation method has been carried out in different studies [20], [22], [44], [46], [49], [50], to enhance the working of model-based decompositions.

3.4   POLARIMETRIC SAR INTERFEROMETRY (POLINSAR)

Polarimetric SAR interferometry [6] is a technique for combining two polarimetric images using interferometry that defines the polarimetric and interferometric correlation between the two images. PolInSAR combines pairs of polarimetric images using interferometry to acquire information [6]. In usage, either single-pass or repeat-pass data is required to derive the PolInSAR image. For the single-baseline method, after co-registration two Pauli scattering vectors k_1 and k_2 for an interferometric pair can be obtained. Assuming reciprocity, a $6\times6\,[T_6]$ matrix that is Hermitian positive semidefinite in nature can be derived as the outer product of k_1 and k_2 and is given as.

$$\left[T_6\right] = \left\langle \begin{bmatrix} k_1 & k_2 \end{bmatrix} \begin{bmatrix} k_1^H \\ k_2^H \end{bmatrix} \right\rangle = \begin{bmatrix} \left\langle T_{11}\right\rangle_{3\times3} & \left\langle \Omega_{12}\right\rangle_{3\times3} \\ \left\langle \Omega_{21}\right\rangle_{3\times3} & \left\langle T_{22}\right\rangle_{3\times3} \end{bmatrix}_{6\times6}. \tag{3.23}$$

T_{11} and T_{22} are the 3×3 generic Hermitian polarimetric coherence matrices for each acquisition of PolSAR. Ω_{12} is a 3×3 polarimetric interferometric phase correlation matrix. This matrix has information related to interferometric phase relations with respect to various polarimetric channels corresponding to different acquisitions.

3.4.1 POLARIMETRIC INTERFEROMETRIC DECOMPOSITION MODEL

PolSAR data renders a scattering response as quantification of amplitude and phase of the backscattered wave [5]. By performing vector interferometry on geometrically matched images, this underlying phase information can be turned into a function of polarization, i.e., interferograms of the polarized wave can be derived. This technique is called polarimetric SAR interferometry (PolInSAR) [6]. In simple words, PolInSAR data represents the correlation between backscatter responses from the same target over an extended spatial (for bi-static SAR system) or temporal (mono-static SAR system) baseline. The PolInSAR approach overcomes the limitation of PolSAR and InSAR and has a more effective application as compared to that of individual approaches. The coherence is observed to be high for the targets that have constant geophysical attributes in space and time, such as buildings. In contrast to this, the targets with dynamic spatio-temporal geophysical attributes exhibit low coherence [51]. A classic example of this case is sparse vegetation. It may change in terms of position (growth or shed), shape, and size (as they are under the effect of wind or seasonal change). Studies also show that natural scatterers are generally more prone to volume decorrelation. The sensitivity of PolInSAR coherence to volume decorrelation is circumscribed by the vertical arrangement of the scatterer. This approach can detect the phase centers of the scattering mechanism along with the indication of the cause of change in the coherence; therefore, it can be used to model scattering mechanisms as well [52]. The PolInSAR approach has a wide range of applications and has been extensively used for research associated with forestry and in the agriculture domain because of the relation of complex coherence with the type of scatterer [53]. PolInSAR data has been well applied for inversion modeling and biophysical parameters retrievals such as tree height and aboveground biomass [54], [55]. Related to the significance of PolInSAR data with the physical properties of the target, we can infer that PolInSAR coherence has the potential to counter the limitation of model-based decompositions. It is also advantageous to use PolInSAR coherence because i) it exhibits a strong relationship with the different types of scatterers, and ii) it is roll-invariant.

3.4.2 HYBRID DECOMPOSITION

The modified PolInSAR data-oriented model decomposes $[T_3]$ matrix ensemble of three major scattering mechanisms, namely, surface, double-bounce, and volume scattering. Freeman–Durden's three-component framework is altered such that urban features with over-estimated volume scattering are modeled empirically using PolInSAR coherence, entropy, and alpha angle. PolInSAR coherence, which is the main focus of the present study, has been used as a correlation between the scattering mechanisms, i.e., to separate the man-made targets that have a high measure of entropy and manifest false decomposition results.

In this subsection, PolInSAR decomposition modeling has been discussed in detail. The modeling procedure and computation of inputs to the model have also been described (Figure 3.4).

3.4.3 DATA PREPROCESSING

In radar imaging, the backscatter response is represented in terms of backscatter coefficient (σ^0) as the backscatter per unit area (average pixel value over a group of pixels) and is generally given as [56],

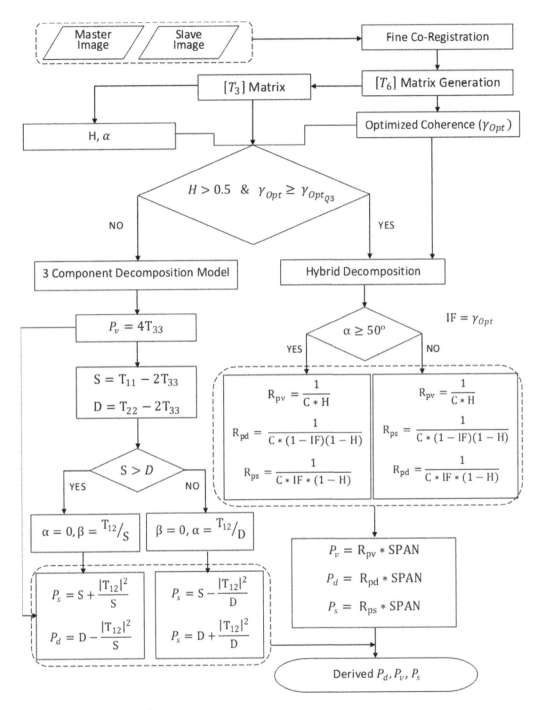

FIGURE 3.4 Model workflow.

$$\sigma^0 = 10 * \log_{10}\left(\frac{1}{n}\left(I_i^2 + Q_i^2\right)\right) + K \qquad (3.24)$$

In Equation (3.24), for each pixel, I and Q represent the complex information and K is the calibration factor. A relative calibration correction is required to make azimuth resolution independent of the target's range position [57]. In other words, radiometric calibration correction is required to represent true backscatter from the target. Single look complex (SLC) SAR data products are not radiometrically corrected, resulting in an improper representation of RCS (see Equation 3.6). The induced radiometric bias indicates that the true backscatter is not represented in the SAR image. Such data sets can be used for qualitative analysis but not for quantitative analysis, which is one of the utilities of polarimetric decomposition. Therefore, radiometric calibration becomes an essential step in SAR data processing. Radiometric calibration ensures that the radiometric bias is resolved and backscatter from the remotely sensed surface is truly related to the true value of backscattering in the image [58]. Further, PolInSAR data is derived from geometrically matched master and slave images, and the polarimetric interferometric phase correlation matrix is strongly polarization-dependent. For such datasets, it is important to perform radiometric calibration, especially for coherence optimization procedures [59], [60].

3.4.4   FINE CO-REGISTRATION

SAR interferometry has various applications such as digital elevation model (DEM) generation, coherence maps generation, deformation analysis, and so on. These applications rely on the phase information that is represented in the backscatter from the remotely sensed area extended over varying spatial or temporal baselines [59]. Co-registration refers to the geometrical alignment of two or more images such that the pixel in both images defines the same object. The sub-pixel co-registration is a mandate and critical procedure in InSAR data processing. For the generation of these secondary products, it is important that the pixel in the primary image and slave image overlap, which is the prerequisite for InSAR data manipulation. Initially, GCPs in master and slave points are generated and affine transformation parameters are derived using coarse co-registration. Then fine registration or sub-pixel co-registration is done by either the cross-correlation-based method or the coherence-based method, followed by oversampling of the co-registered secondary image.

3.4.5   POLINSAR COHERENCE ESTIMATION

PolInSAR coherence (γ) is the measure of backscatter correlation for a target observed in a different spatial or temporal baseline. In simple words, for a scatterer coherence can be defined as backscatter similarity of an InSAR pair [61]. PolInSAR coherence is derived by performing vector interferometry, where each vector corresponds to a different polarization channel. For a mono-static configuration, complex scattering coefficients μ_1 and μ_2 are defined for Pauli's scattering vectors k_1 and k_2 respectively. The feature vectors are projected on normalized projection vectors ω_1 and ω_2 to extend the scalar formulation into vector formulation [6]. This results in polarization-dependent interferograms. The scattering coefficients corresponding to the two different acquisitions are given as:

$$\mu_1 = \omega_1^H k_1 \quad \mu_2 = \omega_2^H k_2. \tag{3.25}$$

The interferograms formation can be given as:

$$\mu_1 \mu_1^H = \left(\omega_1^H k_1\right)\left(\omega_2^H k_2\right) = \omega_1^H \left[\Omega_{12}\right]\omega_2^H. \tag{3.26}$$

Using Equations (3.25) and (3.26), generalized complex γ is derived as [7]:

$$\gamma = \frac{\omega_1 \langle \Omega 12 \rangle \omega_2}{\sqrt{\langle \omega_1 \langle T11 \rangle \omega_1 \rangle \langle \omega_2 \langle T22 \rangle \omega_2 \rangle}}, 0 < \gamma < 1. \tag{3.27}$$

3.4.6 Coherence Optimization and Selection

Coherence optimization is done to yield the highest coherence estimates from a linear combination of polarization states. Optimization leads to best phase estimates resulting in better coherence estimates [62]. Normalized coherence is optimized in terms of ω_1 and ω_2 such that:

$$max_{\omega_1,\omega_2} \; \gamma: \left\| \omega_1 \right\| = \left\| \omega_2 \right\| = 1. \tag{3.28}$$

Optimum coherence (γ_{opt}) can be derived by optimizing Equation (3.27) based on the estimates [$T6$] matrix given in Equation (3.23). In simple words, optimization preserves the polarimetric information while maximizing polarization-dependent coherence. This can be done by using a complex Lagrangian function, which is given as [62]:

$$L = \omega_1^{*H} \left[\Omega_{12} \right] \omega_2 + \lambda_1 \left(\omega_1^{*H} \left[T_{11} \right] \omega_1 - 1 \right) + \lambda_2 \left(\omega_2^{*H} \left[T_{22} \right] \omega_2 - 1 \right). \tag{3.29}$$

λ_1 and λ_2 are Lagrange multipliers introduced to maximize the numerator in Equation (3.27) and keep the denominator constant. The optimization can be solved by partial differentiation of Equation (3.29) with respect to normalized projection vectors and equalizing to zero. By doing so, we get two 3×3 complex eigenvalue equations with non-negative real eigenvalues given as [62]:

$$v = \lambda_1 \lambda_2^H. \tag{3.30}$$

Further, the γ is affected by various decorrelations and is multiplicatively decomposed into decorrelation as given in the equation below [11].

$$\gamma = e^{j\varnothing_s} \gamma_{baseline} \gamma_{system} \gamma_{SNR} \gamma_{temporal} \gamma_{volume}. \tag{3.31}$$

In Equation (3.31), $e^{j\phi_s}$ is the interferometric phase term, $\gamma_{baseline}$, γ_{system}, and γ_{SNR} are processing-oriented decorrelation, and $\gamma_{temporal, volume}$ are target-based decorrelation. The target-based decorrelation has a good agreement with the geophysical characteristics of the target. As a general case, γ is comparatively low for non-uniform structures (vegetation, trees) and high for uniform structures (buildings). This difference in complex correlation is due to volume decorrelation [53]. The differential voluminous arrangement of natural scatterers, such as forest canopy, attenuates the interferometric phase within a fixed range called volume decorrelation [38]. For natural scatterers, volume decorrelation exhibits a strong agreement with temporal decorrelation, whereas urban scatterers are less affected by temporal decorrelation [52]. In the latter section, we will see how target-based decorrelation, i.e., temporal and volume, can be advantageous for modeling scattering mechanisms.

3.4.7 Entropy and Alpha Angle

Entropy and alpha angle are statistical parameters derived from eigenvalues of the coherency matrix [8]. These parameters are collectively used in H/A/α decomposition, also referred as eigenvalue decomposition. The coherency matrix can be expressed in terms of eigen states, which is given as [12]:

$$\langle T \rangle = U \Lambda U^H, \tag{3.32}$$

$$\langle T \rangle = \sum_{i-1}^{n} \lambda_i u_i u_i^H. \tag{3.33}$$

In Equation (3.33), $n = 3$ for a mono-static SAR system and $n = 4$ for a bi-static SAR system. In Equation (3.32), U is the eigenvector matrix and U^H is the conjugate transpose of the eigenvector matrix. Λ represents a diagonal matrix with non-negative real elements corresponding to eigenvalues. The polarimetric bases of input Pauli feature vector and eigenvector u are the same; hence, this decomposition is basis invariant [63]. The dominant scattering mechanism is determined from the highest eigenvector of $\langle T \rangle$ and is characterized using entropy (H), anisotropy (A), and alpha angle (α) [12]. The model assumes that the eigenvalues are in order $\lambda_1 > \lambda_2 > \lambda_3$, where λ_1 represents eigenvalue for a dominant scattering mechanism. These quantities are computed from eigenvalues and eigenvectors and are given as:

$$P_i = \frac{\lambda_i}{\sum_{n=1}^{3} \lambda_n}, 0 \le P \le 1, \tag{3.34}$$

$$H = -\sum_{i=1}^{n} P_i \log_3 P_i, 0 \le H \le 1, \tag{3.35}$$

$$A = \frac{\lambda_2 - \lambda_3}{\lambda_2 + \lambda_3}, 0 \le A \le 1 \tag{3.36}$$

$$\alpha = \sum_{i=1}^{3} P_i \cos^{-1} \left(\left| u_i(1) \right| \right), 0^0 \le \alpha \le 90^0. \tag{3.37}$$

In Equation (3.37), P_i represents the comparative influence of each eigen state to total scattering power, given in terms of probability. This representation, called entropy and denoted by H, is the quantification statistical disorder and related to the randomness of the scattering process [8], [12]. The randomness of the scattering process, the purity of the target (structural uniformity), and the corresponding dominant scattering mechanism are closely related to entropy [8]. For a pure scattering response, the entropy quantifies as 0 or 1. For all values within range [0, 1], the scattering event is random and indicates a partial or distributed target [12]. In this case, the dominant scattering mechanism cannot be uniquely determined and is indicated by the configuration of H and A values collectively, since A gives the relative importance of the other two eigenvalues [8], [12]. The resultant scattering mechanism is governed by the mean alpha angle. Having a close agreement with scattering physics, the alpha angle relates to the order of scattering and describes the internal degree of freedom for a scatterer. Therefore, the resultant scattering mechanism can be classified based on the alpha angle values, such as $\alpha = 0$ represents scattering from isotropic surfaces and $\alpha = 90$ denotes scattering from isotropic dihedral or helix. Isotropic surfaces generally undergo single-bounce scattering and dihedral surfaces show double-bounce scattering. The intermediate values of alpha angle represent anisotropic scattering [8], [12], [63]. Such scattering process has more entropy or random noise, and the average dominant scattering mechanism for such targets can be characterized in a 2-D H–α plane, which has different zones relating to a scattering response, with anisotropy denoting the relative importance of the other two scattering mechanisms [12].

3.4.8 Model Workflow and the Constraint Equation

In theory, a highly random scattering process observed over urban features causes over-estimation of volume scattering or, simply put, high entropy. To understand the model workflow better, we will label highly random urban scattering responses as pseudo-false scattering. For the hybrid decomposition scheme, we assume entropy is low urban targets. For pseudo-false scattering, the entropy values lie within range [0.5, 1] with correlated scattering mechanism [12]. Also, one of the reasons that most of the established models over-estimate volume scattering is the assumption of uncorrelated scattering mechanisms [18]. The over-estimated volume scattering for an urban target can also be accounted for as under-estimated double-bounce and/or surface scattering. In the modified work-flow, we use entropy and coherence to segregate man-made and natural targets and the scattering mechanisms, either surface or double-bounce, are characterized based on the alpha angle values. The dominant scattering mechanism is characterized by the measure of alpha angle (α). The pseudo-false scattering targets are selected on a pixel-to-pixel basis using the constraint equation, given as:

$$H > 0.5 \, \& \, \gamma_{Opt} \geq \gamma_{Opt_{Q3}}$$

(3.38)

where $\gamma_{Opt_{Q3}}$ is the value of optimum coherence corresponding to the third quantile. The condition $\gamma_{Opt} \geq \gamma_{Opt_{Q3}}$ signifies that the scatterers have high coherence magnitude and are less influenced by volume-time decorrelation, such as buildings or collectively urban targets. Coherence is sensitive to temporal decorrelation, and therefore, quantitative use of coherence has opted for the present study. For the PolInSAR RADARSAT2 data acquired over the study area, the value of $\gamma_{Opt_{Q3}}$ is 0.63, whereas the mean coherence value is 0.55. However, coherence alone is not a substantial parameter to segregate volumetric urban targets. As such scatterers are an ideal example of a mixed scattering phenomenon; entropy and coherence are collectively used to segregate urban targets from natural targets. The threshold value of entropy is taken as 0.5, as $H > 0.5$ represents multiple scattering phenomena [12]. Theoretically, Equation (3.38) delineates scattering processes that have high entropy measures and less phase decorrelation, i.e., pseudo-false scattering or distributed scattering of the urban targets. In a narrow sense, the constraint equation is the manifestation of synergic use of polarimetric interferometric information. For such scattering, the decomposition is given as:

$$P_v = SPAN * Rpv,$$

(3.39)

$$P_d = SPAN * Rps,$$

(3.40)

$$P_s = SPAN * Rpd.$$

(3.41)

In Equations (3.39), (3.40), and (3.41), P_s, P_d, and P_v represent surface, double-bounce, and volume scattering powers and R_* represents the corresponding reduction factor, respectively. SPAN represents the trace of the coherency matrix. Each reduction factor is a function of entropy and alpha angle, given as:

$$R_{pv} = \frac{1}{(C * H)}, \, R_{pv} \leq 0 \leq 1,$$

(3.42)

$$R_{pd} = \frac{1}{C * w_d (1 - H)}, \, R_{pd} \leq 0 \leq 1,$$

(3.43)

$$R_{ps} = \frac{1}{C * w_s (1 - H)}, \, R_{ps} \leq 0 \leq 1.$$

(3.44)

We have also used the model constant, denoted by C, to keep the reduction factors within range [0, 1]. The model constant was analyzed for boundary conditions given in eigenvalue decomposition. It was found that the most optimum value for C is 10. In Equations (3.42), (3.43), and (3.44), it can be observed that reduction factors corresponding to double-bounce and surface scattering are characterized by w_*, i.e., weight factor. Weight factor determines the dominant scattering power and is a function of coherence and alpha angle. The threshold $\alpha \geq 50°$ is used to segregate multiple scattering processes [12]. The calculation of the weight factor is as follows:

$$\alpha \ge 50° \begin{cases} w_d = (1 - \gamma_{Opt}), \\ w_d = \gamma_{Opt} \end{cases} \tag{3.45}$$

$$\alpha < 50° \begin{cases} w_s = (1 - \gamma_{Opt}). \\ w_d = \gamma_{Opt} \end{cases} \tag{3.46}$$

The reduction factors are introduced to keep the model workflow adaptive and dynamic for all of the scattering mechanisms. The novel method approach manifests synergic use of eigenvalue and model-based decomposition elements in the decomposition scheme, which is therefore termed a hybrid decomposition model. The decomposition of the proposed model is given below.

$$\begin{bmatrix} SPAN & 0 & 0 \\ 0 & SPAN & 0 \\ 0 & 0 & SPAN \end{bmatrix} = \frac{1}{R_s} \begin{bmatrix} P_s & 0 & 0 \\ 0 & 0 & 0 \\ 0 & 0 & 0 \end{bmatrix} + \frac{1}{R_d} \begin{bmatrix} 0 & 0 & 0 \\ 0 & P_d & 0 \\ 0 & 0 & 0 \end{bmatrix} + \frac{1}{R_v} \begin{bmatrix} 0 & 0 & 0 \\ 0 & 0 & 0 \\ 0 & 0 & P_v \end{bmatrix}. \tag{3.47}$$

Using Equations (3.42), (3.43), (3.44), and (3.47), the decomposed scattering powers can be deduced as:

$$P_v = \frac{SPAN}{(C * H)}, \tag{3.48}$$

$$P_d = \frac{SPAN}{w_d * C(1 - H)}, \tag{3.49}$$

$$P_s = \frac{SPAN}{w_s * C(1 - H)}. \tag{3.50}$$

The model retains the equalities corresponding to pure target condition. In other words, the cumulative power within each resolution cell will be less than or equal to SPAN. The weight factor equals the target that retains absolute coherence, i.e., when $\gamma = 1$. This represents the scattering event having maximum entropy and coherence, for which, P_d and P_s have an equal scattering response.

At $\gamma = 1$,

$$P_v = \frac{SPAN}{(C * H)}, \tag{3.51}$$

$$P_s = P_d = \frac{SPAN}{C(1 - H)}. \tag{3.52}$$

The estimated scattering power images are fed to RGB channels. The P_d image is fed to the red channel, P_s to blue, and P_v to green. The remotely sensed features are identified in the decomposed image according to the color values of the pixel. For urban features, such as town areas, the representing pixels should exhibit high-intensity values in the red channel. Similarly, higher intensity is shown in the green channel for vegetation features.

3.5   EXPERIMENT WITH SPACEBORNE DATA

This study was done on level 1.1 SLC RADARSAT-2 repeat-pass PolInSAR data acquired over the Dehradun region, India. The data for each acquisition consists of four single look complex images in linear HH, HV, VH, and VV polarization. The data has been acquired over the Dehradun region in Uttarakhand, India. The state capital, Dehradun, is located in the Doon valley. The geographic extent of the study area lies between latitudes $29°58'$ N and $31°2'$ N and longitudes $77°34'$ E and $78°18'$ E. It lies between the Shivalik mountain range and the middle Himalayan mountain range.

3.5.1   COHERENCE SELECTION

Coherence maps in the linear basis (γ_{HH}, γ_{HV}, γ_{VV}) were derived using Equation (3.27). A sensitivity analysis concerning window size was done (Figure 3.5). For the present study, coherence estimates showed sudden changes when computed using different window sizes. The experiment with window size concludes the size-coherence disproportionality, i.e., the smaller the window size, the greater the coherence magnitude and vice versa.

The temporal baseline for the present PolInSAR data is 24 days, and therefore, coherence estimates are affected by temporal decorrelation. For such data, an increase in window size can result in very poor estimates of coherence, which is evident from Figure 3.5 and Figure 3.6. An increase in window size reduces the mean of the estimated coherence by a considerable extent, indicating loss of coherence. For window size 7, the value of mean coherence is less than 0.3, which is not useful for the coherence-based analysis.

For the selected window size of 3, the estimated coherence follows a normal distribution. The histogram plots for other window sizes were also observed for all linear coherence (Figure 3.7). For each linear coherence at a window size more than 5, the majority of the coherence values are below

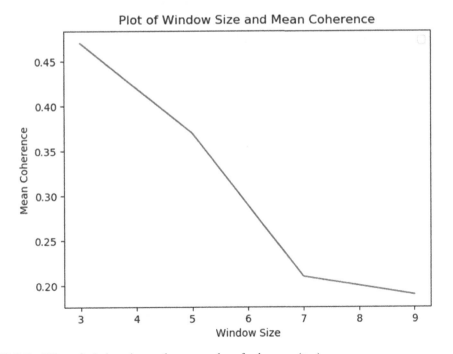

FIGURE 3.5   Effect of window size on the mean value of coherence (γ_{HH}).

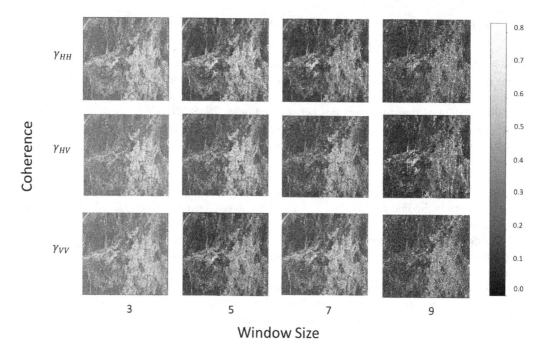

FIGURE 3.6   Effect of window size on the mean value of coherence (γ_{HH}).

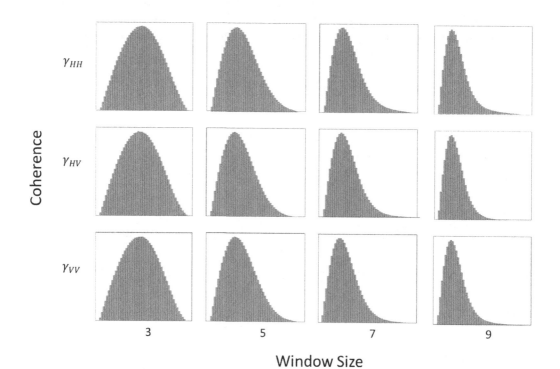

FIGURE 3.7   Histograms of linear coherence images with varying window size.

0.3. This depicts the sensitivity of coherence to window size irrespective of the polarization basis of the projection vector from which it is derived.

3.5.2 COHERENCE OPTIMIZATION

Linear coherences are maximized to lower the effect of decorrelation sources, which refers to optimization. Coherence optimization [62] has been done, and three optimum coherences were derived using the window size of 3. Optimum coherence 1 is the brightest, depicting high coherence values (Figure 3.8) as compared to the other two derived coherences, with optimum 3 being the darkest.

The optimized coherences are statistically evaluated through density plots. Optimum coherence 1 replicates a normal distribution within a range of 0.2 to 0.8 and has the highest mean of 0.56. Such characteristics depict that it is more sensitive to all types of scatterers in the study area [18]. Optimum coherence 2 and optimum coherence 3 also replicate a normal distribution but have comparatively a narrow range (see Figure 3.9). Based on the statistical evaluation, optimum coherence 1 has opted for PolInSAR decomposition modeling.

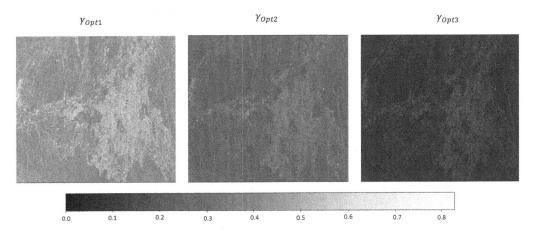

FIGURE 3.8 Optimum coherence maps of the Dehradun region.

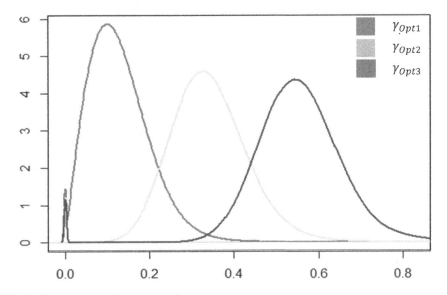

FIGURE 3.9 Density plots of optimum coherences.

3.5.3 Scattering Ambiguity in Generic Decomposition Models

This section reflects the problem of conventional decomposition models in resolving the scattering ambiguity of man-made and natural targets. RADARSAT-2 radiometrically calibrated co-registered PolInSAR data has been used for decomposition modeling. The generic three-component Freeman–Durden (FRE3) [13] decomposition model and four-component Yamaguchi (Y40) [14] model have been used initially to model man-made and natural targets (Figure 3.10). These models are efficient in characterizing forest areas or open surfaces (roads, dry rivers, fallow lands) and urban targets that are aligned along the radar line of sight. However, most of the established models over-estimate the

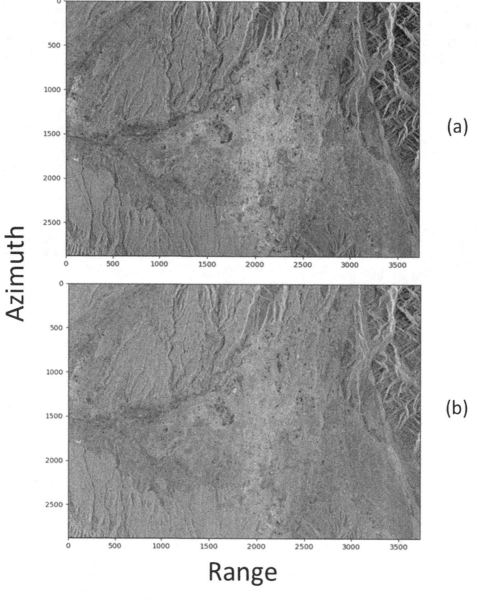

FIGURE 3.10 Decomposed images of the Dehradun region: (a) RGB composite FRE3 model and (b) Y40 model.

FRE3   Y40   Optical Image

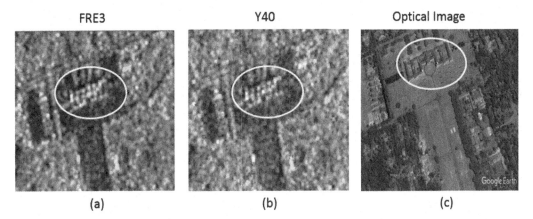

(a)   (b)   (c)

FIGURE 3.11 Forest Research Institute (FRI) locality shown in (a) FRE3 decomposed image, (b) Y40 decomposed image, (c) and optical image. The main building highlighted by the yellow illustration should show double-bounce scattering but has volume scattering as backscatter response.

FRE3   Y40   Optical Image

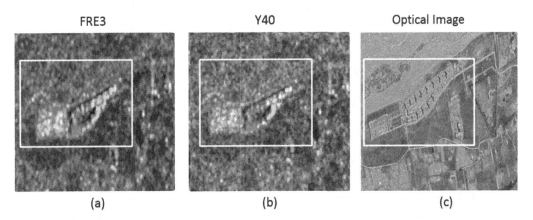

(a)   (b)   (c)

FIGURE 3.12 Uttaranchal University building is shown in (a) FRE3 decomposed image, (b) Y40 decomposed image, and (c) optical image. The buildings shown in the figure have irregular shapes and are deoriented along the radar line of sight. This target is an ideal example of pseudo-false scattering.

volume scattering element for the urban targets that have low to moderate orientation to the radar line of sight. This reflects the limitations mentioned in section 3.1.

Further, the problem of scattering ambiguity persists for a major portion of Dehradun city even after deorientation (Figures 3.11, 3.12, and 3.13). Some famous and historic urban features have been analyzed for scattering response after decomposition modeling (see Figures 3.11, 3.12, and 3.13).

The targets described in Figures 3.11, 3.12, and 3.13 are limited double-bounce scattering. Since the generic model fails to characterize these targets efficiently, we will synthesize interferometric information with model-based decomposition, i.e., a hybrid decomposition model. The targets illustrated by Figures 3.11, 3.12, and 3.13 will be evaluated for decomposition results of the hybrid and available decomposition models.

3.6 CONSTRAINT EQUATION

The value of entropy (H > 0.5) relates to higher-order scattering processes that are zoned as multiple scattering events [12], and therefore, it has also been taken as the threshold for segregating

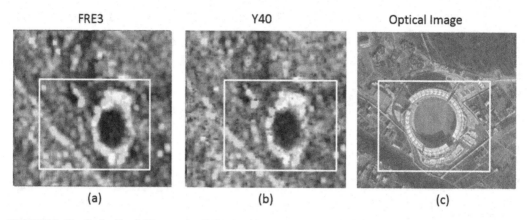

FIGURE 3.13   Rajiv Gandhi International Cricket Stadium is shown in (a) FRE3 decomposed image, (b) Y40 decomposed image, and (c) optical image.

FIGURE 3.14   Conditioned optimum coherence image.

pseudo-false scattering. Using coherence alone for characterizing urban targets is not meaningful. There is a possibility that a pixel representing natural land cover (forest canopy or vegetation) can have coherence values that resemble man-made targets or vice versa. This can be explained by coherence conditioning. Coherence conditioning was done such that the values that were greater than the mean values of coherence (0.56) were set to 1 and vice versa to 0 (see Figure 3.14).

The human-made targets are exclusively visible and have a bright tone; however, the same representation is observed over forest or vegetation land cover with a noisy appearance. This bright tone visible in vegetation or forest-dominant areas represents natural scatterers that are comparatively

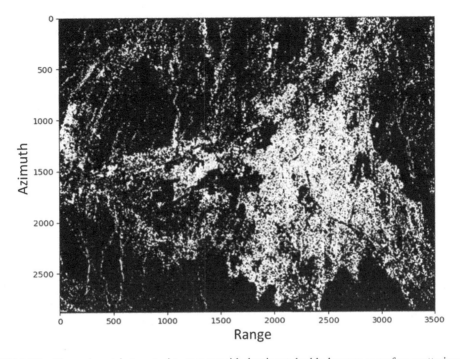

FIGURE 3.15 Non-volumetric targets, i.e., targets with dominant double-bounce or surface scattering.

less affected by decorrelation. For an anisotropic scatterer, such as a tree, the scattering response from the ground or trunk can dominate for low vertical profiles, and such targets can have a relatively better phase correlation. Therefore, a short vertical profile of such a scatterer can exhibit high coherence magnitude as compared to the long vertical profile [38]. This variation in coherence magnitude is due to the volume decorrelation. Since coherence is computed statistically by spatial averaging, coherence estimates for such targets can resemble the coherence estimates of the urban targets. Both urban and non-urban features correspond to the temporal decorrelation, and this agreement of time phase correlation is the foundation of the proposed decomposition scheme. However, scientific observations point out that temporal and volume decorrelation are convolved, which complicates the individual terminal characterization from each decorrelation [52]. Therefore, in the proposed model, entropy has been used to address this problem. Low entropy dipole scattering is observed from isolated dipole scatterers with significant channel imbalance, and scattering response from the ground (ground–trunk scattering) can dominate; however, the entropy for such a scattering process is lower than 0.5. On the other hand, the scattering response from oblate spheroidal targets (such as a leaf and collectively dense forest) have entropy measures more than 0.5 [12], but due to their dynamic nature, they exhibit low coherence estimates. Therefore, collectively using entropy and coherence to segregate the man-made targets is meaningful and advantageous as compared to the individual use of coherence. Since the coherence is dynamic and varies from area to area, therefore, a statistical parameter is opted for finding the threshold coherence value, as given in Equation (3.38). The targets corresponding to pseudo-false scattering are delineated by the constraint equation, as shown in Figure 3.15.

Comparing Figure 3.14 and Figure 3.15, it is evident that most of the vegetation cover has been omitted, leaving only dominant urban or man-made targets. Also, a dry river area is included in the category. For such targets, the underlying dominant scattering mechanism will be characterized by the hybrid decomposition approach.

3.7 RESULTS OF HYBRID DECOMPOSITION MODEL

The hybrid decomposition model is an extended version of the FRE3 decomposition model in which the decomposition of pseudo-false scattering areas (Figure 3.16) is done by the hybrid decomposition approach. The RADARSAT2 co-registered, multi-looked image is decomposed by the novel method. A window size of 3 has opted for the decomposition. The grayscale decomposed scattering power images (Figure 3.17) derived for the study area demonstrate the ability of the hybrid model in target characterization. The man-made targets have shown a bright tone in the P_d image, whereas natural targets have shown a dark tone depicting low double-bounce backscatter. The man-made targets orthogonal to radar line of sight have shown a relatively bright tone indicating major double-bounce scattering. The area consisting of forest cover showing a bright tone is a P_v image indicating high volume backscatter, and a comparatively dark tone is observed for urban land cover.

3.7.1 COMPARATIVE ANALYSIS

For qualitative analysis, the decomposition results have been matched with the optical image of Dehradun city, mainly consisting of urban targets and the Forest Research Institute locality, Uttaranchal University, and Rajiv Gandhi International Cricket Stadium, collectively shown in Figure 3.19. These targets have shown a red color in the proposed model decomposed image that evidences double-bounce scattering.

The urban targets compared for decomposition results show strong double-bounce scattering in the hybrid model image composite. The volumetric scattering from urban targets (red illustration in Figure 3.18) oriented about the radar line of sight has been reduced without limiting volume scattering for natural land cover. Furthermore, the buildings orthogonal to the radar line of sight show a relatively brighter tone for double-bounce scattering power, indicating enhanced P_d. The vegetation surrounded by buildings (yellow illustration in Figure 3.18) can be distinguished. The specific targets shown in

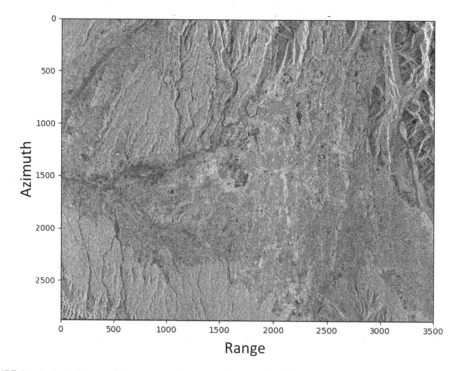

FIGURE 3.16 Hybrid model decomposed image color-coded to RGB.

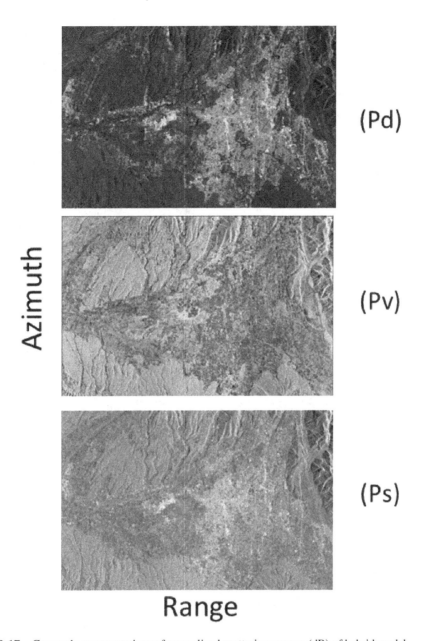

FIGURE 3.17   Greyscale representations of normalized scattering powers (dB) of hybrid model.

Figure 3.19 have been decomposed as dominant double-bounce scatterers irrespective of their shape, geometry, and orientation about radar line of sight. The proposed model gives a better overview of targets in terms of visual representation. In the next subsection, experiments of established models and proposed models are compared and evaluated for various land covers.

3.7.2   Comparison with Existing Decomposition Models

For the Forest Research Institute (FRI) building and cricket stadium, a visual comparison of decomposition results obtained from the proposed decomposition model with generic FRE3 and Y40

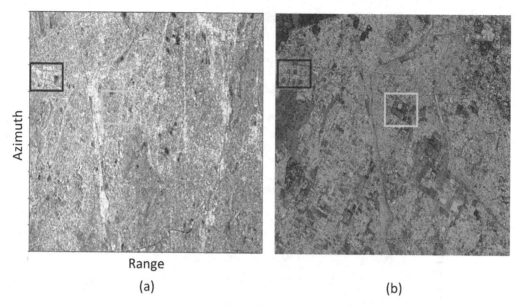

FIGURE 3.18 Comparison of hybrid model decomposed image with optical image for target characterization.

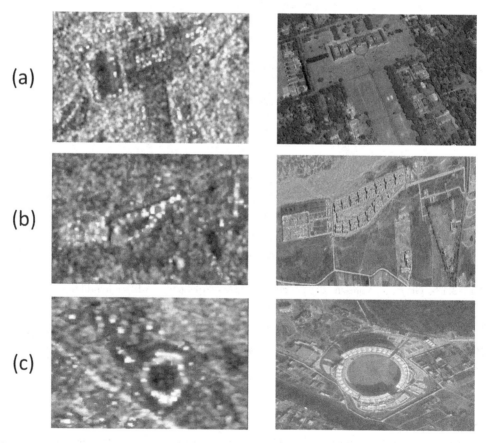

FIGURE 3.19 Comparison of the hybrid model image composite with the optical image: (a) FRI locality, (b) Uttaranchal University, and (c) Rajiv Gandhi International Stadium.

(a)   (b)   (c)

(d)   (e)   (f)

FIGURE 3.20 Image subsets representing (a) FRI locality decomposed by FRE3, (b) Y40, (c) BF4, (d) i6SD, and (e) hybrid decomposition model. Image (c) represents the optical image of the target.

decomposition models; a Bhattacharya and Frery four-component (BF4) decomposition model [16]; and a Singh six-component (i6SD) decomposition model [64] have been performed.

The visual comparison of the decomposition results highlights the robustness of the hybrid model in limiting the volume scattering for the application of target characterization. As the visual observation follows, the hybrid model has significantly reduced P_v observed for the FRI building. The FR3 and Y40 model over-estimate volume scattering for the same. The results also show that BF4 and i6SD models have shown reduced P_v observed over the FRI building. Further, the yellow illustration in Figure 3.20 represents buildings that are surrounded by forest canopies, and these have been decomposed as natural land cover by other decomposition models by showing a dominant volume scattering response. Only the proposed model has rightly identified these targets as buildings by showing dominant double-bounce scattering.

The sphere-shaped cricket stadium (Figure 3.21) lies in far-range and shows a dominant volume scattering response in FR3 and Y40 model decomposed images. Outperforming the compared models, the hybrid model has identified the cricket stadium as a dominant double-bounce target within minimum ambiguity. The BF4 and i6SD models have shown better decomposition results in contrast to FRE3 and Y40 models; however, the hybrid model renders a better visual representation of decomposition results compared to all generic and existing decomposition models. The experiments and outcomes of said models will be compared with relevant quantitative analysis for scattering powers observed over homogeneous urban and forest areas.

The density plot will provide the distribution of normalized power values for each interval. In simple words, it will give the range of each scattering power observed over the region of interest. The x-axis of the density plot represents normalized power values in dB, and the y-axis represents the density estimate or the concentration of the corresponding value. The high density represents the high frequency of the corresponding value. A density plot is derived for each scattering power observed over the urban patch (red illustration in Figure 3.22). For the proposed model, P_d lies within 2 dB to 6 dB interval with a maximum density of 1.6 observed at 5 dB magnitude, i.e., the majority of the observed P_d values are of the order of 5 dB. Out of the other models, the BF4 model

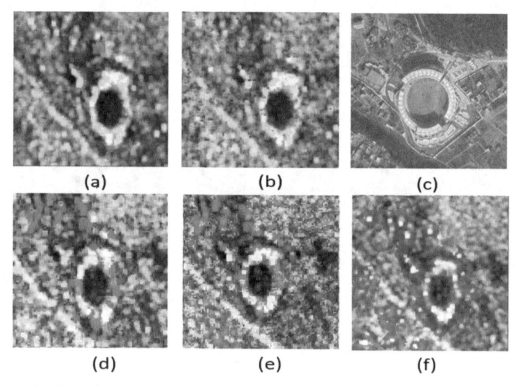

FIGURE 3.21 Image subsets representing Rajiv Gandhi International Stadium decomposed by (a) FRE3, (b) Y40, (c) BF4, (d) i6SD, and (e) hybrid decomposition model; (c) represents the optical image of the target.

has shown enhanced P_d values, followed by i6SD, Y40, and FRE3 models. Only the proposed model and BF4 model have unimodal distribution and non-negative values of P_d, as seen in the scattering distribution profile (see Figure 3.23). The hybrid model intrinsically resolves the negative power problem. Further, FRE3, Y40, and i6SD models have a bimodal distribution with a peak observed in the negative interval, denoting inconsistent results with negative powers. P_s observes the same response with significant enhancement given by the proposed model.

For P_v, which is the primary concern, the proposed model has shown a comparable response as that of the FRE3 model with a slight deviation. The i6SD model shows the lowest P_v, followed by the BF4 model and Y40 model. The proposed model has not significantly reduced P_v for urban targets. The proposed model is developed to keep the model results consistent with the observations. As seen in the case of POA compensation, the reduction is observed in volume scattering observed over the forest cover.

The concept of scattering ambiguity shifts the subject from urban to forest scatterers, with volume scattering being under-estimated. The direct increase or decrease of any scattering power can lead to inconsistent decomposition results and can be critical for applications where P_v is the parameter of interest, such as biophysical parameter estimation. Therefore, the hybrid model does not reduce or limit P_v, but it enhances the dominant scattering mechanism for the target of concern. In this vein, the model keeps the decomposition results constant. Furthermore, to quantify the relative change in the scattering powers decomposed by each model, mean power estimates for the illustrated patch were derived in the form of a pie chart for each scattering power. For each decomposed scattering power, the pie chart represents the ratio of individual scattering power to the cumulative maximum from all models. This ratio is represented as a percentage that shows the relative change.

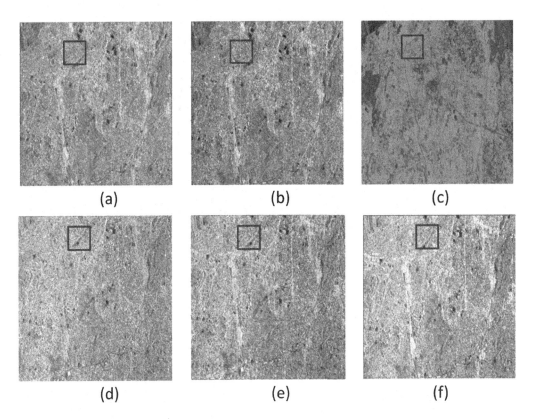

FIGURE 3.22 The subset represents the Dehradun city area with urban targets oriented about the radar line of sight. The subsets are decomposed using (a) FRE3, (b) Y40, (c) BF4, (d) i6SD, and (e) hybrid model, respectively.

The mean power estimates show the relative change in each scattering power decomposed by various models. The results (Figure 3.24) show that the hybrid model yields maximum double-scattering power for the urban region with a total contribution of 29.6% to the cumulative maximum. On comparing the hybrid model with a generic FRE3 and Y40 model, the results evidence a relative increase of 18.1% and 13%, respectively, for double-bounce scattering power. In contrast to the newly established BF4 and i6SD model, the relative increase for P_d is 6.5% and 10.3%, respectively. A similar response has been observed for surface scattering with an overall contribution of 28.7% to the cumulative maximum. For P_v, the proposed has an overall contribution of 21.9%, whereas FRE3 and Y40 models have an overall contribution of 23.5% and 22.1%, respectively. Based on the quantitative analysis, it is evident that the proposed model has brought a remarkable increase in P_d and P_s power estimated for the homogeneous urban area. The model has efficiently reduced the volume scattering and outperformed other decomposition models in urban target characterization.

The direct reduction of volume scattering powers can lead to inconsistent decomposition results. Since the proposed model has enhanced P_d significantly, the decomposition results are analyzed for natural land cover, to examine inconsistency in the results, if any. Initially, a subset representing vegetation and forest cover has been compared visually with the FRE3 model. Further, the results will be compared for volume and surface scattering powers observed over a dense forest patch. A bar chart representation is derived for the aforementioned scattering powers. The pie chart representation quantifies the relative change in the scattering response.

The red ROI in the Figure 3.25 represents the vegetated agriculture field with a sparse built-up area. Most of the buildings present in the locality are shown as natural land cover by the FRE3

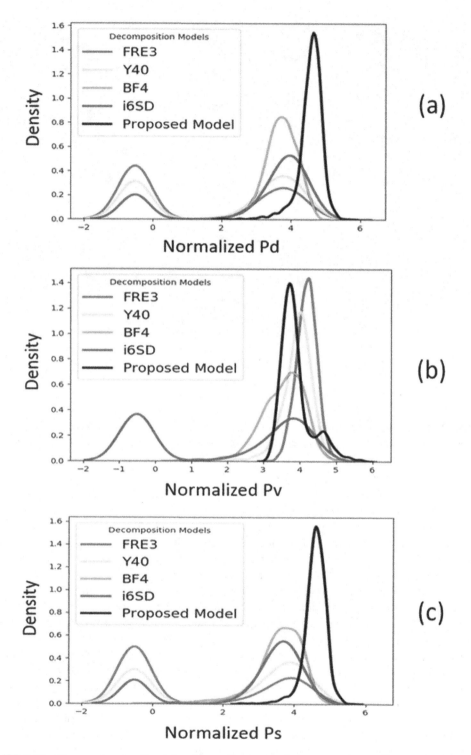

FIGURE 3.23 Comparative density plots of normalized scattering powers observed over a homogeneous urban patch: (a) double-bounce, (b) volume, and (c) surface scattering powers.

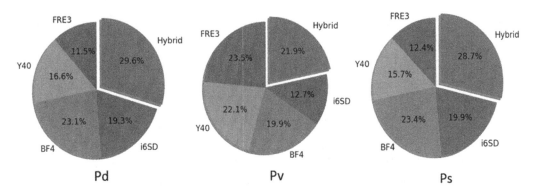

FIGURE 3.24 Mean power estimates of decomposed scattering power observed over a homogeneous urban patch.

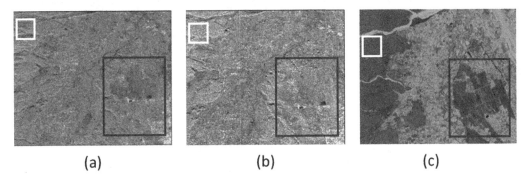

FIGURE 3.25 (a) FRE3 model and (b) hybrid model decomposed image subsets representing vegetative land cover and dense forest. (c) represents the optical image of the subset.

model. The proposed model has delineated these buildings within vegetated areas. Apart from differentiating urban targets within agriculture fields, the proposed model has enhanced volume scattering for the same (red illustration in Figure 3.25). Also, the scattering response from the forest patch is similar for FRE3 and the proposed model. The visual comparison shows that the model has produced consistent decomposition results for natural land cover. A bar chart representation of P_v and P_s discerned over the dense forest area (yellow rectangle illustrated in Figure 3.25) is given in Figure 3.26 to compare the decomposition results of each model. The vertical axis of the bar chart represents the cumulative decomposed scattering observed over the area.

Surface scattering has been included in the analysis because the dataset has been acquired at an imaging frequency of 5.4 GHz (C-band), which has low penetration power. For targets such as dense forest, P_s can dominate the scattering response. Mean power estimates were derived for surface and volume scattering to compare the change in decomposed scattering powers given by various models. The hybrid model has enhanced P_v discerned over the dense forest patch. Figure 3.27 shows that the highest P_v and P_s are given by hybrid model power. The relative increase in surface scattering power decomposed by the hybrid model is of a similar trend as observed from the BF4 and Y40 models.

In contrast to the FRE model, the mean power estimates signify a 1.6% and 7.4% hike for hybrid model decomposed P_v and P_s, respectively. The hybrid model P_s is comparable to the Y40 and BF4 models.

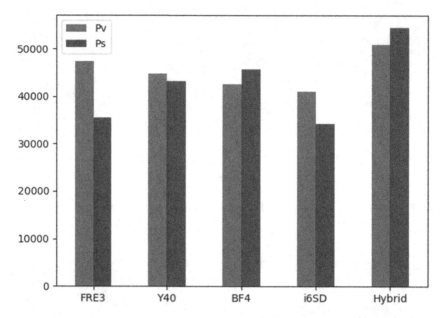

FIGURE 3.26   Total volume and surface scattering powers observed over dense forest patch.

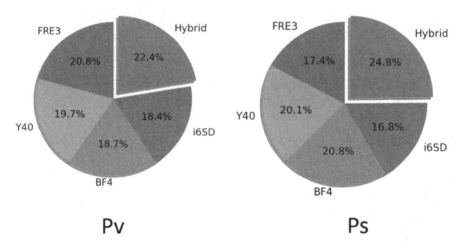

FIGURE 3.27   Mean power estimates of volume and surface scattering powers observed over a homogeneous dense forest patch.

3.7.3 SCATTERING ENTROPY EVALUATION

The problem of predominant volume scattering was also explored in terms of eigenvalue-based decomposition parameters. The scattering process observed from forest canopy or vegetation has moderate to high entropy values similar to that of the urban targets exhibiting volume scattering. The change in entropy has been analyzed for theoretical validation of the proposed model. After incoherent decomposition modeling, assuming that each pixel represents a coherent scatterer, the subsequent entropy has been analyzed. The diagonal elements of the coherency matrix are replaced with hybrid model decomposed scattering powers such that $T11$ is replaced with P_s, $T22$ is replaced with P_d, and $T33$ is replaced with P_v. This notion resembles the coherent decomposition scenario.

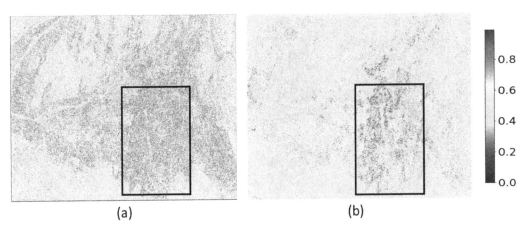

FIGURE 3.28 Modified entropy maps: (a) original entropy, (b) FRE3 model-based entropy, and (c) hybrid model-based entropy.

This will result in a new 3 × 3 coherency matrix, and entropy estimates of this matrix are termed modified entropy. Modified entropy has been derived by replacing diagonal elements of the coherency matrix with FRE3 model decomposed powers and proposed model decomposed powers. Both entropy images are compared with the original entropy image.

From Figure 3.28, it is evident that the proposed model has reduced the entropy estimates to a lower range for urban targets, as seen in the black illustration. The generic entropy derived from the FRE3 model shows high entropy estimates for the urban targets. For natural targets such as forest canopy, the modified entropy is of the order of 0.5 and above, which resembles the original entropy image. In another way, the results of this section can be paralleled as the validation of the hybrid model, as the range of entropy values for urban targets constructed using hybrid model composites replicates the values of the dihedral scattering process.

3.7.4 Limitation of POA Compensation

The rotated T^θ matrix was decomposed into the surface, volume, and double-bounce scattering powers by using the FRE3 and Y40 models. The reduction in decomposed volume scattering power from urban targets is apparent; however, the results are not satisfactory for the study area.

The problem of predominant volume scattering from urban targets persists, as is evident from Figure 3.29 (also see Figure 3.22). Further, POA shift values for the study area were analyzed to identify the range for compact urban targets. It was found that the volumetric urban targets have a POA shift magnitude of the order of ±30° and greater (Figure 3.30).

For urban scatterers with high POA shift magnitudes, of the order of ±30° and greater, POA compensation renders ineffective and cannot subdue the over-estimated volume scattering [18].

The visual evaluation indicates that POA compensation reduces the volume scattering power over natural land cover such as forest and agriculture (Figures 3.31 and 3.32). This can be observed since the image brightness values for the corresponding targets show a considerable reduction. For a quantitative evaluation, the volume power profile of a homogeneous forest patch is analyzed for pre- and post-POA compensation; see ROI in Figure 3.32.

Density plots of normalized volume scattering power (P_v) were derived for the subset before (red ROI Figure 3.32) and after (yellow ROI in Figure 3.32) POA compensation. The density plot estimates show (Figure 3.33) a significant decrease in estimated volume scattering power after POA compensation. The P_v values without deorientation have higher density estimates, between −5 and −10 dB for actual, whereas the P_v values with deorientation have lower density estimates and peak

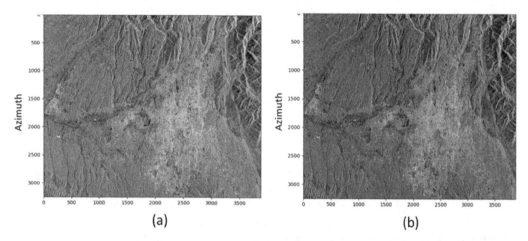

FIGURE 3.29   Images of the study area: (a) FRE3 and (b) Y40.

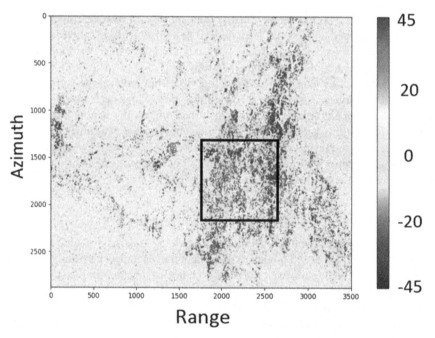

FIGURE 3.30   Estimated POA shift image of the study area. The ROI in the figure represents the urban patch shown in Figure 3.19.

values. POA compensation has caused a remarkable reduction in volume scattering powers for natural targets as well. POA compensation for such targets will lead to under-estimation of volume scattering, which can be critical for the utility of biophysical parameter retrieval.

3.8   DISCUSSIONS

3.8.1   Factors Affecting PolInSAR Coherence

One of the advantages of using PolInSAR coherence is its dependency on polarization channels. The magnitude of coherence estimated in different polarization combinations is different for the

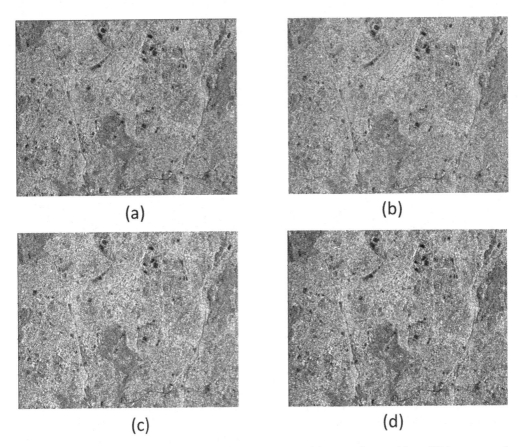

FIGURE 3.31 (a), (b) are FRE3 and Y40 model decomposed image subsets without POA compensation respectively and (c), (d) are FRE3 and Y40 model decomposed image subsets with POA compensation, respectively. The subset represents the Dehradun city area with urban targets.

same target. This shows the polarization-dependent property of PolInSAR coherence and its sensitivity to various scattering mechanisms [6]. The coherence derived in the HH and VV polarization basis is influenced mainly by double-bounce scatterings such as trunk–ground and canopy–ground interactions. On the other hand, coherence derived in HV polarization basis is influenced mainly by volume scattering interactions [38]. For a forest canopy, HV coherence will have relatively higher estimates as compared to that of HH or VV and vice versa for scatterers such as a building. The coherence is a multiplicative product of various decorrelation and sensitive to variations in phase estimates [65]. These decorrelations vary depending upon the sensor system used (spaceborne or airborne), type of acquisition (mono-static or bi-static), frequency of the sensor, error induced in phase estimates due to data processing, temporal baseline, weather conditions, and topography and land cover of the remotely sensed surface [11]. The effect of the decorrelation can be reduced to some extent; however, the error model that estimates the effect of each parameter needs further development.

3.8.2 PolInSAR Coherence and Decomposition Modeling

PolInSAR coherence can be a potential prospect for the polarimetric decomposition modeling. Its sensitivity to polarization and physical structure of the scatterers in terms of temporal and vertical decorrelation is of great importance for decomposition modeling. Coherence has been used

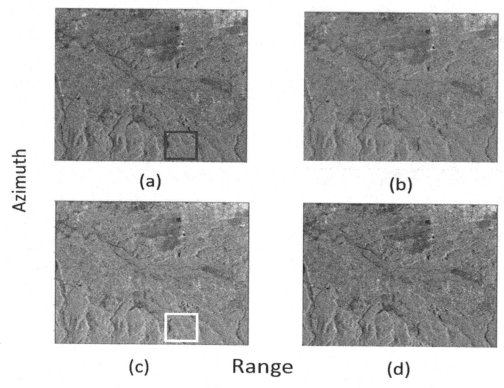

FIGURE 3.32 (a), (b) are FRE3 and Y40 model decomposed image subsets without POA compensation respectively and (c), (d) are FRE3 and Y40 model decomposed image subsets with POA compensation, respectively. The subset majorly represents vegetation and forest patch.

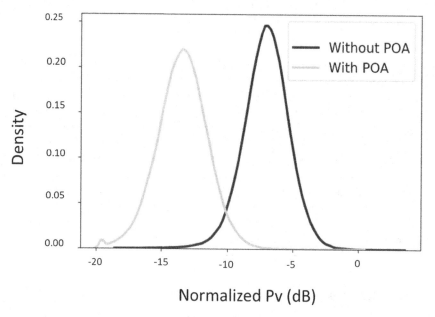

FIGURE 3.33 Density plot estimated of normalized Pv before and after POA compensation.

to design and modify the volume scattering mechanism model [18]; the same has been done in the present study as well. The statistical properties of the PolInSAR cross-correlation matrix are similar to that of the PolSAR higher-order statistics scattering matrix [5]; hence, it is possible to fuse polarimetric decomposition with phase correlation information. PolInSAR coherence allows to model phase centers that can be used to differentiate scattering mechanisms inside a ground resolution cell. The sensitivity of PolInSAR coherence to voluminous properties of land cover and temporal correlation between scattering mechanisms are modeled to develop the PolInSAR decomposition model.

3.8.3 STATISTICAL SIGNIFICANCE OF PolInSAR COHERENCE

The statistical properties of coherence make it possible to differentiate human-made and natural targets, even at low estimates. Optimum coherence and entropy are used in the proposed model to delineate pseudo-false scattering targets based on the constraint Equation (3.38). The value corresponding to the third quantile was used as a threshold value for coherence. For the study area, the γ_{Opt1} image can be modeled as N(0.56,0.1058), i.e., a normal distribution with mean as 0.56 and standard deviation as 0.1058. For this distribution, the value corresponding to the third quantile is 0.63. The distribution (the area under the curve) above this value is 0.26. The same analysis was done for γ_{Opt2} and γ_{Opt3}, where, γ_{Opt2} is modeled as N(0.33,0.0088) and γ_{Opt3} as N(0.12,0.0707). The distribution above the third quantile is the same for each optimized coherence; however, the estimates are different. Therefore, the use of statistical properties makes it possible to use any coherence irrespective of magnitude to delineate pseudo-false scattering targets. The use of low coherence estimates can deflect model results.

3.9 CONCLUSION AND RECOMMENDATIONS

PolSAR decomposition is the state-of-the-art method that can characterize targets based on their scattering process manifesting an easy physical interpretation. The scope of the present study has been limited to the scattering characterization of man-made and natural features or differentiation of urban and non-urban targets. The shortcomings of any method used in decomposition modeling cannot be generalized as it highly depends on the utility of decomposition specific to the application. However, during the present research, shortcomings of a few methods have been observed. The novelty and objective of this study were to develop a PolSAR backscatter and PolInSAR coherence-based decomposition model to limit the over-estimation of volume scattering elements and from urban structures/targets. Initially, conventional models were used to analyze the extent of scattering ambiguity for the study area. It was found that generic PolSAR decomposition models showed over-estimation of volume scattering observed over urban areas.

Deorientation is employed as an alternate method to limit P_v estimated over the man-made features. The results conclude that POA compensation is not very effective in reducing the predominant volume scattering from urban targets (Figures 3.22 and 3.32). Also, the decomposed volume scattering power over natural targets such as cropland or forest canopy is reduced due to deorientation (Figure 3.33). The available decomposition models and auxiliary methods were not very effective in limiting the volume scattering power observed over the urban features. The limitation of POA compensation was discussed in the section for deorientation or POA compensation. It is not recommended to use the POA compensation method for applications such as biomass or tree height estimation as it reduces the volume scattering contribution. As noted in the aforementioned section, POA compensation changes the estimates of PolInSAR coherence, and it is not recommended to use POA compensation in data-based PolInSAR studies. Furthermore, for low-frequency operating SAR sensors, surface scattering can be a predominant scattering, which can also be under-estimated. However, POA compensation is a valuable method to enhance double-bounce scattering and can be used in studies where urban targets are of the main focus.

PolInSAR coherence has been the main focus of the present study. Its sensitivity to various decorrelations makes it a potential technique to differentiate various land covers. It is noteworthy that coherence can differentiate man-made targets because these are less affected by decorrelations, but the use of coherence alone is not recommended for such target delineation. Furthermore, it was observed that unconstrained coherence (without established boundary conditions) should not be used for decomposition modeling equations. Furthermore, the use of coherence alone is not substantial since the decorrelation (volume and temporal) aspects that make it possible to use PolInSAR coherence in decomposition modeling are not separable. Following this, the qualitative use of coherence and its implementation in decomposition modeling was explored, which led to the development of the hybrid decomposition model.

The hybrid decomposition model developed in the present study was efficiently able to characterize the land cover as man-made or natural and significantly reduced volumetric urban scattering. The hybrid model intrinsically solves the limitation of InSAR- and PolSAR-based approaches in target characterization. For InSAR-based characterization, the use of entropy and coherence collectively can segregate man-made and natural targets, and the underlying scattering mechanism is characterized by the proposed model (one such example is the scattering characterization of dry rivers and buildings). Furthermore, the proposed model can characterize targets even on low coherence estimates; in this vein, the proposed model framework can address the limitation of InSAR for target characterization, which has been reflected on in section 3.2. For PolSAR-based approaches, the model can determine the actual scattering mechanism and reduce the predominant volume scattering for targets that have a complex shape, compact spatial arrangements, and/or sloping terrains and are oriented about the radar line of sight. The proposed model has proven its robustness in addressing the problem faced by InSAR and PolSAR methods for target characterization. Also, the model has intrinsically separated the volume and temporal decorrelation by collective use of entropy and coherence. The research concludes that the statistical properties of coherence work better for decomposition results as compared to default normalized values. The proposed model has the potential to use low coherence estimates in decomposition modeling. This can be done by using machine learning for designing weights and will be worked upon shortly.

REFERENCES

[1] C. López Martínez, *Multidimensional Speckle Noise, Modelling and Filtering Related to SAR Data.* 2004.

[2] Cloude, S. *Polarisation: Applications in Remote Sensing.* Oxford University Press, 2009, vol. 63.

[3] Wang, B.-C. *Digital Signal Processing Techniques and Applications in Radar Image Processing.* Hoboken, NJ: John Wiley & Sons, Inc., 2008.

[4] Lee, J.-S., and Pottier, E. Electromagnetic vector scattering operators. In *Polarimetric Radar Imaging*, Lee, J.-S., and Pottier, E., Eds. CRC Press, 2017, pp. 53–100.

[5] West, R. D., and Riley, R. M. Polarimetric interferometric SAR change detection discrimination. *IEEE Trans. Geosci. Remote Sens.* 2019, *57*, 3091–3104, doi:10.1109/TGRS.2018.2879787.

[6] Cloude, S. R., and Konstantinos, P. Papathanassiou polarimetric SAR interferometry. In *Dictionary Geotechnical Engineering/Wörterbuch GeoTechnik.* Berlin: Springer, 2014, vol. 36, pp. 1021–1021.

[7] Xiang, D., Tang, T., Hu, C., Fan, Q., and Su, Y. Built-up area extraction from PolSAR imagery with model-based decomposition and polarimetric coherence. *Remote Sens.* 2016, *8*, doi:10.3390/rs8080685.

[8] Earthnet, *Polarimetric Decompositions.* 2011.

[9] Ainsworth, T. L., Schuler, D. L., and Lee, J.-S. Polarimetric SAR characterization of man-made structures in urban areas using normalized circular-pol correlation coefficients. *Remote Sens. Environ.* 2008, *112*, 2876–2885, doi:10.1016/j.rse.2008.02.005.

[10] Cloude, S. R., and Pottier, E. A review of target decomposition theorems in radar polarimetry. *IEEE Trans. Geosci. Remote Sens.* 1996, *34*, 498–518, doi:10.1109/36.485127.

[11] Gens, R., and Van Genderen, J. L. SAR interferometry—Issues, techniques, applications. *Int. J. Remote Sens.* 1996, *17*, 1803–1835, doi:10.1080/01431169608948741.

[12] Cloude, S. R. An entropy based classification scheme for polarimetric SAR data. In Proceedings of the 1995 International Geoscience and Remote Sensing Symposium, IGARSS '95. Quantitative Remote Sensing for Science and Applications. IEEE, 1997, vol. 3, pp. 2000–2002.

[13] Freeman, A., and Durden, S. L. A three-component scattering model for polarimetric SAR data. *IEEE Trans. Geosci. Remote Sens.* 1998, *36*, 963–973, doi:10.1109/36.673687.

[14] Yamaguchi, Y., Moriyama, T., Ishido, M., and Yamada, H. Four-component scattering model for polarimetric SAR image decomposition. *IEEE Trans. Geosci. Remote Sens.* 2005, *43*, 1699–1706, doi:10.1109/TGRS.2005.852084.

[15] Arii, M., Van Zyl, J. J., and Kim, Y. Adaptive model-based decomposition of polarimetric SAR covariance matrices. *IEEE Trans. Geosci. Remote Sens.* 2011, *49*, 1104–1113, doi:10.1109/TGRS.2010.2076285.

[16] Bhattacharya, A., Muhuri, A., De, S., Manickam, S., and Frery, A. C. Modifying the Yamaguchi four-component decomposition scattering powers using a stochastic distance. *IEEE J. Sel. Top. Appl. Earth Obs. Remote Sens.* 2015, *8*, 3497–3506, doi:10.1109/JSTARS.2015.2420683.

[17] Duan, D., and Wang, Y. An improved algorithm to delineate urban targets with model-based decomposition of PolSAR data. *Remote Sens.* 2017, *9*, 1037, doi:10.3390/rs9101037.

[18] Chen, S., Wang, X., Li, Y., and Sato, M. Adaptive model-based polarimetric decomposition using PolInSAR coherence. *IEEE Trans. Geosci. Remote Sens.* 2014, *52*, 1705–1718, doi:10.1109/TGRS.2013.2253780.

[19] Van Zyl, J. J., Arii, M., and Kim, Y. Model-based decomposition of polarimetric SAR covariance matrices constrained for nonnegative eigenvalues. *IEEE Trans. Geosci. Remote Sens.* 2011, *49*, 3452–3459, doi:10.1109/TGRS.2011.2128325.

[20] Lee, J.-S., and Ainsworth, T. L. The effect of orientation angle compensation on coherency matrix and Polarimetric target decompositions. *IEEE Trans. Geosci. Remote Sens.* 2011, *49*, 53–64, doi:10.1109/TGRS.2010.2048333.

[21] Kimura, H. Radar polarization orientation shifts in built-up areas. *IEEE Geosci. Remote Sens. Lett.* 2008, *5*, 217–221, doi:10.1109/LGRS.2008.915737.

[22] An, W., and Xie, C., Yuan, X., Cui, Y., and Yang, J. Four-component decomposition of polarimetric SAR images with deorientation. *IEEE Geosci. Remote Sens. Lett.* 2011, *8*, 1090–1094, doi:10.1109/LGRS.2011.2157078.

[23] Iribe, K., and Sato, M. Analysis of polarization orientation angle shifts by artificial structures. *IEEE Trans. Geosci. Remote Sens.* 2007, *45*, 3417–3425, doi:10.1109/TGRS.2007.905973.

[24] Lee, J.-S., Schuler, D. L., and Ainsworth, T. L. Polarimetric SAR data compensation for terrain azimuth slope variation. *IEEE Trans. Geosci. Remote Sens.* 2000, *38*, 2153–2163, doi:10.1109/36.868874.

[25] Chen, S.-W., Wang, X.-S., Xiao, S.-P., and Sato, M. *Target Scattering Mechanism in Polarimetric Synthetic Aperture Radar.* Singapore: Springer, 2018.

[26] Yamaguchi, Y., Sato, A., Sato, R., Yamada, H., and Boerner, W. M. Four-component scattering power decomposition with rotation of coherency matrix. In *Proceedings of the 2010 IEEE International Geoscience and Remote Sensing Symposium.* IEEE, 2010, pp. 1327–1330.

[27] Kennaugh, E. M. Polarization properties of radar reflections. The Ohio State University, 1952.

[28] Cameron, W. L., and Leung, L. K. Feature motivated polarization scattering matrix decomposition. In *Proceedings of the IEEE International Conference on Radar.* IEEE, 1990, pp. 549–557.

[29] Radar Polarimetry. [Online]. Available: https://www.nrcan.gc.ca/maps-tools-publications/satellite-imagery-air-photos/remote-sensing-tutorials/microwave-remote-sensing/radar-polarimetry/9275 (accessed on Nov. 25, 2019).

[30] Krogager, E. New decomposition of the radar target scattering matrix. *Electron. Lett.* 1990, *26*, 1525, doi:10.1049/el:19900979

[31] Skolnik, M.I. *Introduction to Radar Systems*, 2nd ed. Tata: McGraw-Hill, 1962.

[32] Huynen, J. R. Phenomenological theory of radar targets. Delft University of Technology, 1970.

[33] Huynen, J. R. Towards a theory of perception for radar targets. In *Inverse Methods in Electromagnetic Imaging*, Boerner, W.-M., Brand, H., Cram, L. A., Gjessing, D. T., Jordan, A. K., Keydel, W., Schwierz, G., and Vogel, M., Eds. Dordrecht: Springer Netherlands, 1985, pp. 797–822.

[34] Cloude, S., *Polarization: Applications in Remote Sensing*. Oxford University Press, 2009.

[35] Chen, S-W., Wang, X-S., Xiao, S-P., and Sato, M. *Target Scattering Mechanism in Polarimetric Synthetic Aperture Radar*. Springer, 2018.

[36] Wolfgang-Martin, B. et al. Polarimetric Decompositions. [Online]. Available: https://earth.esa.int/documents/653194/656796/Polarimetric_Decompositions.pdf (accessed on Aug 20, 2019).

[37] Xiang, D., Tang, T., Ban, Y., Su, Y., and Kuang, G. Unsupervised polarimetric SAR urban area classification based on model-based decomposition with cross scattering. *ISPRS J. Photogramm. Remote Sens.* 2016, *116*, 86–100, doi:10.1016/j.isprsjprs.2016.03.009

[38] Neumann, M., Ferro-Famil, L., and Reigber, A. Estimation of forest structure, ground, and canopy layer characteristics from multibaseline polarimetric interferometric SAR data. *IEEE Trans. Geosci. Remote Sens.* 2010, *48*, 1086–1104, doi:10.1109/TGRS.2009.2031101

[39] Lee, J., Ainsworth, T. L., and Wang, Y. Generalized polarimetric model-based decompositions using incoherent scattering models. *IEEE Trans. Geosci. Remote Sens.* 2014, *52*, 2474–2491, doi:10.1109/TGRS.2013.2262051

[40] Shuang, Z., Shuang, W., and Bo, C. *Modified Hybrid Freeman / Eigenvalue Decomposition for Polarimetric SAR Data*. 1985, 2015.

[41] Bhattacharya, A., Singh, G., Manickam, S., and Yamaguchi, Y. An adaptive general four-component scattering power decomposition with unitary transformation of coherency matrix (AG4U). *IEEE Geosci. Remote Sens. Lett.* 2015, *12*, 2110–2114, doi:10.1109/LGRS.2015.2451369

[42] An, W., Cui, Y., and Yang, J. Three-component model-based decomposition for polarimetric SAR data. *IEEE Trans. Geosci. Remote Sens.* 2010, *48*, 2732–2739, doi:10.1109/TGRS.2010.2041242

[43] Zou, B., Zhang, Y., Cao, N., and Minh, N. P. A four-component decomposition model for PolSAR data using asymmetric scattering component. *IEEE J. Sel. Top. Appl. Earth Obs. Remote Sens.* 2015, *8*, 1051–1061, doi:10.1109/JSTARS.2014.2380151

[44] Yamaguchi, Y., Sato, A., Boerner, W.-M., Sato, R., and Yamada, H. Four-component scattering power decomposition with rotation of coherency matrix. *IEEE Trans. Geosci. Remote Sens.* 2011, *49*, 2251–2258, doi:10.1109/TGRS.2010.2099124

[45] Lee, J., and Ainsworth, T. L. The effect of orientation angle compensation on polarimetric. *IEEE Trans. Geosci. Remote Sens.* 2011, *49*, 849–852, doi:10.1109/TGRS.2010.2048333.

[46] Lee, J-S., Schuler, D. L., Ainsworth, T. L., Krogager, E., Kasilingam, D., and Boerner, W.-M. On the estimation of radar polarization orientation shifts induced by terrain slopes. *IEEE Trans. Geosci. Remote Sens.* 2002, *40*, 30–41, doi:10.1109/36.981347

[47] Schuler, D. L., Lee, J. S., Kasilingam, D., and Pottier, E. Measurement of ocean surface slopes and wave spectra using polarimetric SAR image data. *Remote Sens. Environ.* 2004, *91*, 198–211, doi:10.1016/j.rse.2004.03.008.

[48] Schuler, D. L., Lee, J.-S., and Ainsworth, T. L. Compensation of terrain azimuthal slope effects in geophysical parameter studies using polarimetric SAR data. *Remote Sens. Environ.* 1999, *69*, 139–155, doi:10.1016/S0034-4257(99)00017-6

[49] Souissi, B., and Ouarzeddine, M. Analysis of orientation angle shifts on the polarimetric data using Radarsat2 images. *IEEE J. Sel. Top. Appl. Earth Obs. Remote Sens.* 2016, *9*, 1331–1342, doi:10.1109/JSTARS.2016.2516766

[50] Chen, S., Ohki, M., Shimada, M., and Sato, M. Deorientation effect investigation for model-based decomposition over oriented built-up areas. *IEEE Geosci. Remote Sens. Lett.* 2013, *10*, 273–277, doi:10.1109/LGRS.2012.2203577

[51] Schneider, R. Z., Papathanassiou, K., Hajnsek, I., and Moreira, A. Polarimetric interferometry over urban areas: information extraction using coherent scatterers. In Proceedings of the Proceedings. *IEEE International Geoscience and Remote Sensing Symposium, 2005*. IGARSS '05., 2005, vol. 2, pp. 1089–1092.

[52] Chen, S.-W., Wang, X.-S., Xiao, S.-P., and Sato, M. *Target Scattering Mechanism in Polarimetric Synthetic Aperture Radar*. Singapore: Springer Singapore, 2018.

[53] Lavalle, M., and Hensley, S. Extraction of structural and dynamic properties of forests from polarimetric-interferometric SAR data affected by temporal decorrelation. *IEEE Trans. Geosci. Remote Sens.* 2015, *53*, 4752–4767, doi:10.1109/TGRS.2015.2409066

[54] Joshi, S. K., Kumar, S., and Agrawal, S. Performance of PolSAR backscatter and PolInSAR coherence for scattering characterization of forest vegetation using TerraSAR-X data. *L. Surf. Cryosph. Remote Sens. III* 2016, *9877*, 987707, doi:10.1117/12.2223898

[55] Ballester-Berman, J. D., Lopez-Sanchez, J. M., and Fortuny-Guasch, J. Retrieval of biophysical parameters of agricultural crops using polarimetric SAR interferometry. *IEEE Trans. Geosci. Remote Sens.* 2005, *43*, 683–694, doi:10.1109/TGRS.2005.843958.

[56] Zuhlke, M., Fomferra, N., Brockmann, C., Peters, M., Veci, L., Malik, J., and Regner, P. SNAP (sentinel application platform) and the ESA Sentinel 3 toolbox. In *Proceedings of the Sentinel-3 for Science Workshop*, 2015, vol. 734, p. 21.

[57] Bürgmann, R., Rosen, P. A., and Fielding, E. J. Synthetic aperture radar interferometry to measure earth's surface topography and its deformation. *Annu. Rev. Earth Planet. Sci.* 2000, *28*, 169–209, doi:10.1146/annurev.earth.28.1.169

[58] Frulla, L. A., Milovich, J. A., Karszenbaum, H., and Gagliardini, D. A. Radiometric corrections and calibration of SAR images. In *Proceedings of the IGARSS '98. Sensing and Managing the Environment* 1998 *IEEE International Geoscience and Remote Sensing. Symposium Proceedings.* IEEE, 1998; vol. 2, pp. 1147–1149.

[59] Veci, L., Prats-Iraola, P., Scheiber, R., Collard, F., Fomferra, N., and Engdahl, M. *The Sentinel-1 Toolbox*, 2014.

[60] Ferretti, A., Monti-Guarnieri, A., & Claudio Prati, F.R. *InSAR Principles: Guidelines for SAR Interferometry Processing and Interpretation*, 2007.

[61] Cloude, S. R., and Papathanassiou, K. P. Polarimetric optimisation in radar interferometry. *Electron. Lett.* 1997, *33*, 1176–1178, doi:10.1049/el:19970790

[62] Cloude, S. R., and Papathanassiou, K. P. Coherence optimisation in polarimetric SAR interferometry. In *Proceedings of the IGARSS'97. 1997 IEEE International Geoscience and Remote Sensing Symposium Proceedings. Remote Sensing – A Scientific Vision for Sustainable Development.* IEEE, 1997, vol. 4, pp. 1932–1934.

[63] Ferro-Famil, L., Pottier, E., and Lee, J. Sen unsupervised classification of multifrequency and fully polarimetric SAR images based on the H/A/Alpha-Wishart classifier. *IEEE Trans. Geosci. Remote Sens.* 2001, *39*, 2332–2342, doi:10.1109/36.964969

[64] Singh, G., and Yamaguchi, Y. Model-based six-component scattering matrix power decomposition. *IEEE Trans. Geosci. Remote Sens.* 2018, *56*, 5687–5704, doi:10.1109/TGRS.2018.2824322

[65] Neumann, M., Ferro-Famil, L., and Reigber, A. Multibaseline polarimetric SAR interferometry coherence optimization. *IEEE Geosci. Remote Sens. Lett.* 2008, *5*, 93–97, doi:10.1109/LGRS.2007.908885

4 Implementation of Machine Learning Classification Models on Multifrequency Band SAR Dataset

Anil Kumar, Rajat Garg, and Shashi Kumar

CONTENTS

4.1 INTRODUCTION

The application of SAR data for the LULC classification has a long history and undoubtably many advantages. Due to various features of the SAR data, it is used for many applications, including crop and vegetation monitoring, management of natural resources, natural disaster management, study of geological and urban applications, and weather and hydrological forecasting. The LULC is also used by various global agencies for the planning, management, and development of new and existing urban places. It is difficult to analyze the remote sensing data due to low resolution, orientation problems, and speckle noise in the data, though the technology has been enhanced, and many high-resolution consistent SAR data is available from different space agencies. The most important advantage of SAR data over optical data is its independence of atmospheric interference. The LULC SAR data mapping are cost effective, multi-temporal, spatially extensive, and time-saving [1]. The purpose of SAR data classification is to convert data into meaningful information. Various state-of-the-art classification models, both parametric and non-parametric, have been proposed and used for LULC purposes using SAR data [2]. The machine learning models used for classification always require a sufficiently large volume of labeled datasets to train the model. It has introduced an alternative model for the SVM that is able to classify with good accuracy even a small-sized training dataset [3]. Over the last decades, various state-of-the-art classifier models, like RF, SVM, KNN, and MLP, have received the exceptional attention of the research community

DOI: 10.1201/9781003204466-4

and have been used to implement classification on various types of SAR data, including ALOS-2/ PALSAR-2, RADARSAT-2, TerraSAR-X, and UAVSAR. has been found that Decision Tree (DT) J48 was the most suitable classifier to discriminate natural vegetation cover and urban areas. Aside from this RF, MLP, and SVM have been implemented on the Brazilian tropical savanna biome and proved to be the best classifiers [4]. The Maximum Likelihood Classifier (MLC), classification tree analysis, object-based classification, fuzzy ARTMAP (a neural network-based classifier), KNN, and SVM have been implemented on ALOS-PALSAR L-band and RADARSAT-2 C-band data for tropical moist-region land cover classification. In this work, the overall accuracy achieved using the L-band dataset was 72.2% and the same for the C-band was only 54.4% [5]. It is observed that the feature mapping of the L-band dataset is better than the C-band. Wang et al. present permafrost landscape mapping that uses TerraSAR-X data and information of interferometric coherence. It implemented a Classification and Regression Tree (CART) and Object-oriented Image Analysis (OBIA) and achieved an overall accuracy of 98% to classify rock and water, and an accuracy of 79% to discriminate vegetation types [6]. A novel algorithm for LULC, based on four component polarimetric decomposition supported by object-oriented image analysis and a decision tree algorithm proposed on RADARSAT-2 dataset, achieved an overall accuracy of 86.64% [7]. Urban and peri-urban land cover classification is done in Zhu et al. using ALOS-PALSAR data to map 17 land cover categories in Greater Boston, MA, USA. It implemented the Random Forest classifier and achieved a highest accuracy of 93.82% by combining the Landsat and PALSAR datasets [8]. The West African land cover map was assessed to find the impact on regional climate and ecosystem services. It used a combination of Moderate Resolution Imaging Spectroradiometer (MODIS), TanDEM-X, and TerraSAR-X datasets, which were implemented on Random Forest classifiers and achieved an accuracy of 80% for 9 classes and 73% for 14 classes [9]. This study projected the LULC in the region of Brazil, Roraima, using Sentinel-1 SAR data, and implemented Random Forest and Multi-Layer Perceptron (MLP) classifiers to classify rainforest, water, savannas, and sandbank/outcrop classes [10]. Many of the studies have applied various state-of-the-art machine learning models for landslide prediction and susceptibility as a part of earth surface studies [11]– [13]. It used the temporal RADARSAT-2 dataset captured over Greater Toronto and implemented a semi-supervised stochastic expectation-maximization (SEM) algorithm for LULC of the detailed urban area to get better classification accuracy [14]. The multiple space nearest neighbor (msNN) is an extension of KNN and was implemented on the LANDSAT-5 and ALOS-PALSAR datasets of Minas Gerais in Brazil to classify six different land cover classes. It achieved an accuracy of 70% for msNN in comparison with 58% for SVM and 55% using KNN [15]. It is restricted with not only conventional machine learning algorithms but also advance deep learning models like DeepLabv3+ , and many more have also been implemented for semantic segmentation of SAR data for LULC purposes and have analyzed the earth surface with good accuracy [16]. One of the major study areas is ship detection, and SAR datasets are widely used for this purpose [17].

4.2 STUDY AREA

The study focuses on the much-discussed San Francisco Bay Area located in California (US), which has been selected due to the obtainability of multiple classes and features within the targeted study area. The multifrequency SAR band to segment the target class is discussed. The target area is shown in Figure 4.1. SAR data from ALOS PALSAR2, GF3, RADARSAT-2, and TerraSAR-X2 are used to demonstrate the work. All the data with parameters are discussed in Table 4.1.

4.3 METHODOLOGY

It is important to classify the various land covers based on type and characteristics that help to analyze the land usage. Much research has been done by the researcher to optimally utilize the

TABLE 4.1
Details of Multifrequency SAR Datasets Used

SAR system parameter	ALOS-2/PALSAR-2	TerraSAR-X	RADARSAT-2	GF-3
Platform	Spaceborne	Spaceborne	Spaceborne	Spaceborne
Satellite	Advanced Land Observing Satellite-2 (ALOS-2)	TerraSAR-X	Radar Imaging Satellite (RISAT-2)	GaoFen-3
Sensor	Phased array type L-band Synthetic Aperture Radar (PALSAR-2)	SAR	C-band, SAR	SAR
Date of acquisition	14 April 2016	11 March 2015	24 January 2014	5 August 2017
Pass	Ascending	Descending	Ascending	
Altitude	628 km	514 km	798 km	
Data type	Single Look Complex (SLC)	Complex	Single Look Complex (SLC)	Single Look Complex (SLC)
Polarization	Fully polarimetric quad-pol (HH+HV+VH+VV)	Fully polarimetric quad-pol (HH+HV+VH+VV)	Fully polarimetric quad-pol; (HH+VV+HV+VH)	Quad-pol (HH+HV+VH+VV)
Mode of acquisition	Strip-map mode	Strip-map mode	Strip-map mode	Quad-Polarization Strip Map 1 (QPS1)
Frequency	1.236 GHz	9.65 GHz	5.40 GHz	5.4 GHz
Look direction	Right	Right	Right	Left or Right

land cover. This section discussed the models, focused on the areas and tried to implement various classifiers to efficiently segment the regions with good accuracy. The model uses the different algorithms supported by the pre-processing task, as shown in Figure 4.1.

The work flow starts with input data of multifrequency band SAR data.

4.4   PRE-PROCESSING

Radiometric calibration and multi-looking are the important phases of pre-processing SAR data. All of the available SAR dataset used in this work was already calibrated, so only multi-looking needed to be performed. Since SAR is a side-looking sensor, slant-range distortion occurs, which causes near-range objects to appear compressed relative to far-range objects. This results in a variation of captured image scale from near to far range. Multi-looking is the process by which square pixels are generated. The number of looks is determined by the image statistics. The ALOS-2/PALSAR-2 SAR data is multi-looked to generate square pixels of 5.78 m in size. In the case of GF-3 C-Band SAR data, the purpose of multi-looking is to suppress speckle noise [18]. No pre-processing is performed on the TerraSAR-X data. Pre- processing of RADARSAT-2 data requires geometric correction. In addition, to reduce the noise and preserve the detailed information, an enhanced frost filter with a window size of 7 × 7 is used [19].

4.5   POLSAR DECOMPOSITION

Barnes decomposition [20] on multifrequency band SAR data is used; this generates three single target vectors, k_{01}, k_{02}, and k_{03}, which are derived in Equations (4.1), (4.2), and (4.3).

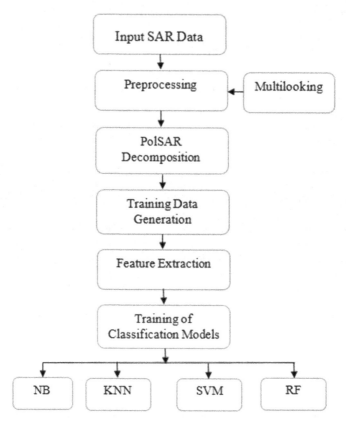

FIGURE 4.1 Workflow of the methodology implemented for semantic segmentation using various state-of-the-art machine learning models.

The three normalized target vectors can be obtained as [21]:

$$k_{01} = \frac{\langle [T] \rangle q_1}{\sqrt{q_1^{T^*} \langle [T] \rangle q_1}} = \frac{1}{\sqrt{\langle 2A_0 \rangle}} \begin{bmatrix} \langle 2A_0 \rangle \\ \langle C \rangle + j\langle D \rangle \\ \langle H \rangle - j\langle G \rangle \end{bmatrix}, \tag{4.1}$$

$$k_{02} = \frac{\langle [T] \rangle q_2}{\sqrt{q_2^{T^*} \langle [T] \rangle q_2}} = \frac{1}{\sqrt{2(\langle B_0 \rangle - \langle F \rangle)}} \begin{bmatrix} \langle C \rangle - \langle G \rangle + j\langle H \rangle - j\langle D \rangle \\ \langle B_0 \rangle + \langle B \rangle - \langle F \rangle + j\langle E \rangle \\ \langle E \rangle + j\langle B_0 \rangle - j\langle B \rangle - j\langle F \rangle \end{bmatrix}, \tag{4.2}$$

$$k_{03} = \frac{\langle [T] \rangle q_3}{\sqrt{q_3^{T^*} \langle [T] \rangle q_3}} = \frac{1}{\sqrt{2(\langle B_0 \rangle + \langle F \rangle)}} \begin{bmatrix} \langle H \rangle + \langle D \rangle + j\langle C \rangle + j\langle G \rangle \\ \langle E \rangle + j\langle B_0 \rangle + j\langle B \rangle + j\langle F \rangle \\ \langle B_0 \rangle - \langle B \rangle + \langle F \rangle + j\langle E \rangle \end{bmatrix}, \tag{4.3}$$

where A_0, B, B_0, C, D, E, F, G, and H are the same parameters as used in Hyunen's Muller Matrix.

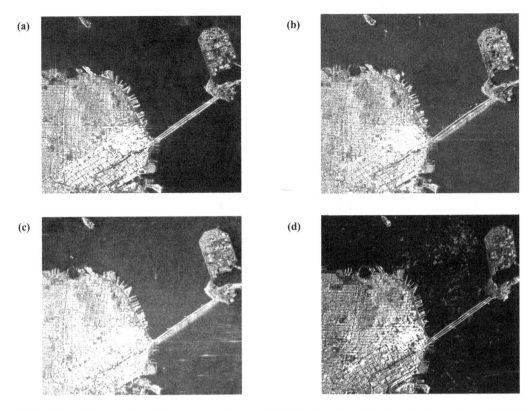

FIGURE 4.2 Representing the decomposed results of the San Francisco Bay Area for the captured PolSAR dataset: (a) ALOS-2/PALSAR-2, (b) GF-3, (c) RADARSAT-2, and (d) TerraSAR-X.

Figure 4.2 presents the output of Barnes decomposition for the input SAR datasets ALOS-2/PALSAR-2, GF-3, RADARSAT-2, and TerraSAR-X for the location of the San Francisco Bay Area in California, USA.

4.6 TRAINING DATA GENERATION

The labeled dataset is always required to train the classification models. The decomposed results are divided into patches per the adoptability of the models and labeled with respect to the ground truth. A number of testing and training datasets are created. A sample of decomposed results and its corresponding data patch is shown in Figure 4.3. Both patches belong to San Francisco. The four different class labels – urban, ground, water, and forest – are shown in their corresponding color coding in Figure 4.3. Of the complete dataset, made up of different data sources including ALOS-2/PALSAR-2, GF-3, RADARSAT-2, and TerraSAR-X, 80% of the data is used for training and the remaining 20% for testing and validation purposes.

4.7 METHODS FOR MACHINE LEARNING CLASSIFIERS

Various state-of-the-art machine learning models that help to predict the class label of the input dataset have been discussed and implemented. The selected models are k-Nearest Neighbor (KNN), Naïve Bayes (NB), Random Forest (RF), and Support Vector Machine (SVM). All of the models are validated on the common target area of San Francisco. The multifrequency band SAR data of

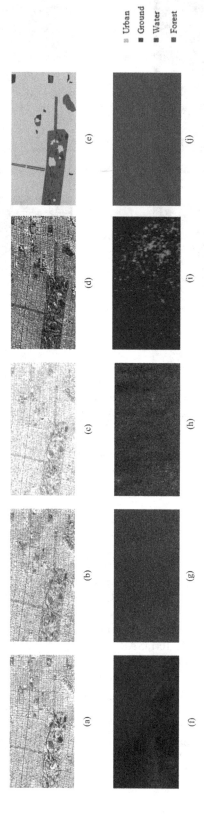

FIGURE 4.3   Representing decomposed image and corresponding processed and labeled images of one part of San Francisco in the USA: (a), (f) ALOS-2/PALSAR-2, (b), (g) GF-3, (c), (h) RADARSAT -2, (d), (i) TerraSAR-X, (e), (j) its corresponding label.

this region has been captured and then implemented with the listed models. Many of the studies implemented spaceborne optical multispectral data and multifrequency SAR data to implement in LULC [22]. The results must also be validated. For this purpose, ground truth validation is always required with predicted values, as shown in Figure 4.4.

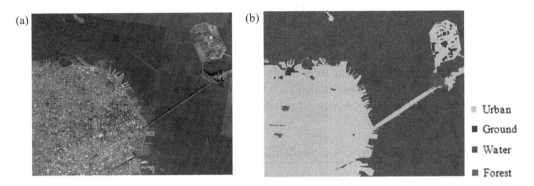

FIGURE 4.4 Representing (a) the Google map image of San Francisco, USA, considered as ground truth, and (b) the corresponding labeled image depicting four class labels of urban, ground, water, and forest.

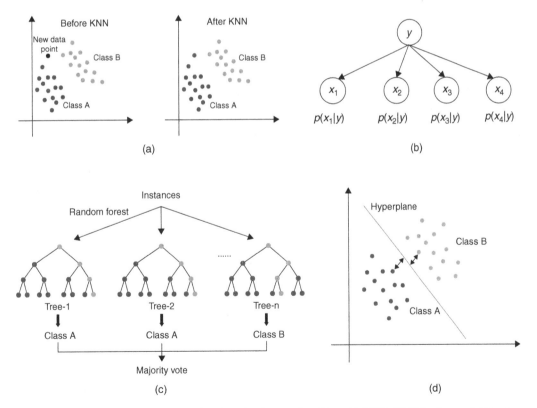

FIGURE 4.5 Schematic architecture of land use land cover classifiers: (a) KNN, (b) Naïve Bayes, (c) Random Forest, and (d) SVM.

4.7.1 k-Nearest Neighbor (KNN) Classification Model

The KNN model is assumed as a non-parametric algorithm. It works on the principle of neighborhood by assuming that elements of a similar class lie near to each other; the schematic architecture of the model is represented in Figure 4.5(a). Various distance measures and techniques are used to calculate the distance between the data points, e.g., Euclidian, Manhattan, Minkowski. For the set of sample data, observations are available and predictions are made based on nearest distance. The majority vote is considered as the target class. To implement the KNN model, the following selections are required: (i) the optimal distance metrics to assess the similarity in feature space; (ii) a technique of weighting the predictor variables into distance measures; (iii) techniques for weighting each neighbor during predictions; and (iv) a number k of the nearest neighbor's possibly odd selection [23]. The KNN model is also known as a lazy learner because it takes more time to train compared to other machine learning models because it has to calculate distance from every point in its neighborhood [24].

Algorithm 4.1 k-Nearest Neighbor Classification

Input:	X: Barnes decomposed multifrequency SAR image used labeled training data, Y: class labels of X, v: testing and validation dataset

Output: P: Prediction of v
1.   **for** $i = 1$ **to** m **do**, where m is the number of samples
2.   Compute distance $d(X_i, v)$
3.   **end for**
4.   Compute set I containing indices for the k smallest distances $d(X_i, v)$
5.   **return** majority label for $\{Y_i$ where $i \in I\}$

The steps of the KNN classification model are discussed in Algorithm 4.1. The prediction results of the KNN model are shown in Figure 4.6. It is implemented on multifrequency bands of SAR data captured by the sensors of ALOS-2/PALSAR-2, GF-3, RADARSAT-2, and TerraSAR-X. It is observed that on TerraSAR-X data, the KNN pixel accuracy is 91.37% and the F1-score achieved is 0.93, which is the highest result when compared to the ALOS-2/PALSAR-2, GF-3, and RADARSAT-2 datasets. With ALOS-2/PALSAR-2, the KNN model predicts with the lowest accuracy, of about 78.77%, as listed in Table 4.2. Overall, the data format of the selected bands enabled the identification of most of the class labels, except for the region containing the oriented building as shown in Figure 4.6(a)–4.6(c). Only the TerraSAR-X results are able to identify the oriented building with the correct class label, as shown in Figure 4.6(d).

4.7.2 Naïve Bayes Classification

The Naïve Bayes (NB) classification model is based on the Bayesian theory that deals with conditional probability and event prediction supported by strong (naïve) independent assumptions (Figure 4.5 (b)). The NB model assumes that the absence or presence of a given feature of a class

TABLE 4.2
Details of Performance of KNN Classifier on Multifrequency Band SAR Dataset

	ALOS-2/PALSAR-2	GF-3	RADARSAT-2	TerraSAR-X
Accuracy	78.77	86.2	79.39	91.37
F1-score	0.86	0.89	0.85	0.93

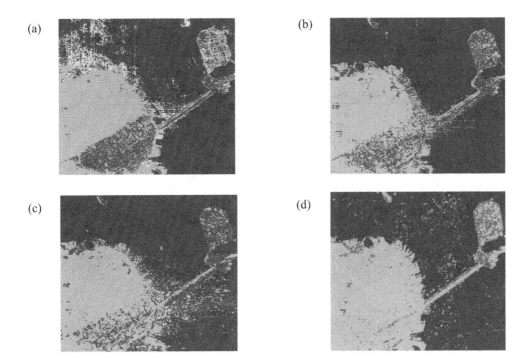

FIGURE 4.6 Representing the KNN classification model results of the San Francisco Bay Area for the captured PolSAR dataset of multifrequency band illustrated here: (a) ALOS-2/PALSAR-2, (b) GF-3, (c) RADARSAT-2, and (d) TerraSAR-X.

is independent of the absence or presence of any other feature [4]. This model is postulated by Equation (4.4) [25].

$$P(H \mid E) = \frac{P(E \mid H) * P(H)}{P(E)}. \tag{4.4}$$

where H = Hypothesis and E = Evidence.

$P(H \mid E)$ is the posterior probability of the hypothesis given that the evidence is true.

$P(E \mid H)$ is the likelihood of the evidence given that the hypothesis is true.

$P(H)$ is the prior probability of the hypothesis.

$P(E)$ is the prior probability that the evidence is true.

Algorithm 4.2 Naïve Bayes Classification

Input:	T: Barnes decomposed multifrequency SAR image used labeled training data, $F = (f_1, f_2, f_3, \ldots f_n)$ represents the predictor variables in testing dataset, v = testing data
Output:	P: Prediction of v (greatest likelihood)
1.	**Read** T, the number of training dataset;
2.	Compute mean and standard deviation of the predictor variables in each class;
3.	**Repeat**
4.	Compute the probability of f_i using the gauss density function for each class;
5.	**Until** the probability of all predictor variables $(f_1, f_2, f_3, \ldots f_n)$ of v has been calculated;
6.	**Compute** likelihood_each_class;
7.	**return** greatest_likelihood;

TABLE 4.3
Details of Performance of Naïve Bayes Classifier on Multifrequency Band SAR Dataset

	ALOS-2/PALSAR-2	GF-3	RADARSAT-2	TerraSAR-X
Accuracy	94.23	82.57	48.57	81.34
F1-score	0.94	0.85	0.41	0.87

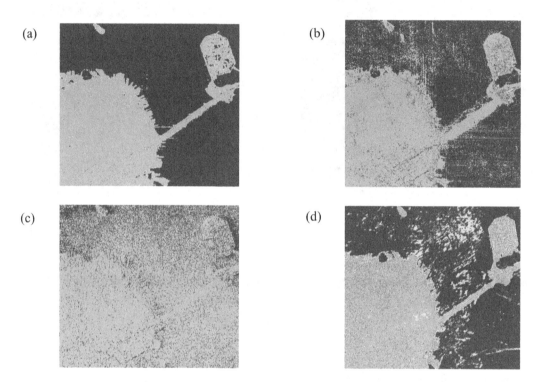

FIGURE 4.7 Representing the Naïve Bayes classification model results of the San Francisco Bay Area for the captured PolSAR dataset of multifrequency band illustrated here: (a) ALOS-2/PALSAR-2, (b) GF-3, (c) RADARSAT-2, and (d) TerraSAR-X.

The steps of the Naïve Bayes classification model are discussed in Algorithm 4.2. The prediction results of the NB model are shown in Figure 4.7. It is observed that the pixel accuracy and F1-score of the NB model on ALOS-2/PALSAR-2 are about 94.23% and 0.94, respectively, which is better than the GF-3 (Figure 4.8(b)), RADARSAT-2 (Figure 4.8(c)), and ALOS-2/PALSAR-2 (Figure 4.8(a)) datasets. The NB model does not perform well for the RADARSAT-2 dataset, which achieved pixel accuracy and F1-score for the same data band of 48.57% and 0.41, respectively, as shown in Table 4.3.

4.7.3 RANDOM FOREST CLASSIFICATION

Random Forest (RF) is a state-of-the-art machine learning model developed by Breiman [26]. The RF model is devised by merging a sizable number of random decision trees (DTs). Each DTs gives only one final class vote for each instance, and the final prediction is calculated based on consensus, i.e., the majority vote of all the DTs, as demonstrated in Figure 4.5(c) [27], [28]. Many current studies have advocated that the RF classifier performs better compared to other classifiers for land use land cover (LULC) classifications [29], [30]. The model used two major parameters called "n_estimators" and "max_depth" and used the default values of these as the part of sklearn library in Python.

Algorithm 4.3 Random Forest Classification

Input:	D: Barnes decomposed multifrequency SAR image used a labeled training data, $F = (f_1, f_2, f_3, ..., f_n)$ represents the predictor variables in testing dataset, N: Build N number of tree
Output:	N_i: Build tree and majority class will be final class

1.   To generate c classifiers;
2.   **for** $i = 1$ to n **do**
3.   Randomly sample the training data D with replacement to produce D_i
4.   Create a root node, N_i containing D_i
5.   Call Build_Tree(N_i)
6.   **end**
7.   **Build_Tree(N):**
8.   **if** N contains instances of only one class **then**
9.   return
10.   **else**
11.   Random selection of feature F_i, the possible splitting features in N
12.   Selection of feature F_i based on highest information gain
13.   Create n child nodes of N, $N_1, ..., N_n$, where F has n possible features
14.   **for** $i = 1$ to n **do**
15.   Set the contents of N_i to D_i, where D_i is all instances in N that match F_i
16.   Call Build_Tree(N_i)
17.   **end for**
18.   **end if**

The steps of the Random Forest classification model are discussed in Algorithm 4.3. The prediction results of the RF model are shown in Figure 4.8 for the different frequency band SAR datasets. It is observed that the pixel accuracy and F1-score of the RF model on the TerraSAR-X dataset are about 91.65% and 0.93, respectively, which is better than the GF-3, RADARSAT-2, and ALOS-2/PALSAR-2 datasets. The least supported SAR dataset with the RF model is ALOS-2/PALSAR-2, which achieved a pixel accuracy and F1-score of 78.28% and 0.85, respectively, as shown in Table 4.4. It can be observed from the predicted results of RF shown in Figure 4.8(a) that the RF model failed to correctly label the oriented buildings for the ALOS-2/PALSAR-2 dataset. The RF model performs extraordinarily in labeling the oriented buildings using the TerraSAR-X dataset, as shown in Figure 4.8(d).

TABLE 4.4
Details of Performance of Random Forest Classifier on Multifrequency Band SAR Dataset

	ALOS-2/PALSAR-2	GF-3	RADARSAT-2	TerraSAR-X
Accuracy	78.28	86.29	85.18	91.65
F1-score	0.85	0.90	0.89	0.93

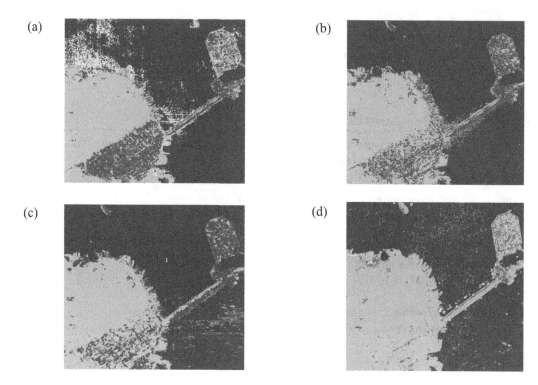

FIGURE 4.8 Representing the random forest classification model results of the San Francisco Bay Area for the captured PolSAR dataset of multifrequency band illustrated here: (a) ALOS-2/PALSAR-2, (b) GF-3, (c) RADARSAT-2, and (d) TerraSAR-X.

4.7.4 SUPPORT VECTOR MACHINE CLASSIFICATION

The Support Vector Machine (SVM) classification model is conceptualized on a decision hyperplane that describes the decision boundaries. A decision plane defined by SVM separates a set of data points having different class memberships. SVM is a non-parametric machine learning model [31]. It was initially designed to solve binary classification problems [32]. The fundamental idea behind this model is to maximize the margin of hyperplane (either side of a hyperplane that separates two data classes), as shown in Figure 4.5(d). It will help to reduce the upper bound of the predicted generalization error. The SVM model supports both classification and regression tasks and is capable of handling continuous and categorical values. This model is supported by number of support vectors that are the bordering samples. The multiclass problems are solved by pairwise classification. The SVM model carries the linear and non-linear kernel functions as per the suitability of the problems. The purpose of kernels is to transform the dataset; for instance, a non-separable 2D dataset can be transformed in separable 3D. In a few cases, SVM produces tremendous results for LULC [33]–[35].

Algorithm 4.4 Support Vector Machine Classification

Input:	T: Barnes decomposed multifrequency SAR image used a labeled training data;
	$F = (f_1, f_2, f_3, ...f_n)$ represents the predictor variables in testing dataset;
	T_{in}: Number of input vectors; T_{sv}: Number of support vectors;
	T_f: Number of features in support vector; SV[T_{sv}]: Array of support vector;
	IN[T_{in}]: Input vector array; b*: Bias
Output:	D: Decision function output

1.   To generate c classifiers;
2.   **for** $i = 1$ **to** T_{in} **by** 1 **do**
3. $\mathcal{D} = 0$
4.   **for** $j = 1$ **to** T_{sv} **by** 1 **do**
5. $dist = 0$
6.   **for** $k = 1$ **to** T_f **by** 1 **do**
7. $dist + = (SV[j].F[k] - IN[i].F[k])^2$
8.   **end for**
9. $\kappa = \exp(-Y \ x \ dist)$
10. $F + = SV[j]. \ \alpha^* \ x \ \kappa$
11.   **end for**
12. $F = F + b^*$
13.   **end for**

The steps of the SVM classification model are discussed in Algorithm 4.4. The prediction results of the SVM model are shown in Figure 4.9 for different frequency band SAR datasets. It is observed that the pixel accuracy and F1-score of RSVM model on TerraSAR-X are about 94.74% and 0.95, respectively, which is better than the GF-3 (Figure 4.9(b)), RADARSAT-2 (Figure 4.9(c)), and ALOS-2/PALSAR-2 (Figure 4.9(a)) datasets. The least supported SAR dataset with the SVM model is ALOS-2/PALSAR-2, which achieved pixel accuracy and F1-score of 80.87% and 0.87, respectively, as shown in Table 4.5. It can be observed from the predicted

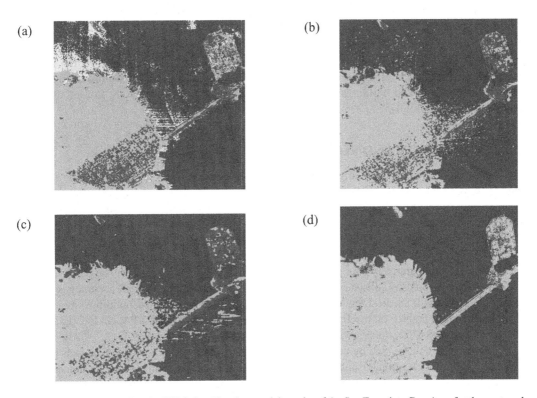

FIGURE 4.9   Representing the SVM classification model results of the San Francisco Bay Area for the captured PolSAR dataset of multifrequency band illustrated here: (a) ALOS-2/PALSAR-2, (b) GF-3, (c) RADARSAT-2, and (d) TerraSAR-X.

TABLE 4.5
Details of Performance of SVM Classifier on Multifrequency Band SAR Dataset

	ALOS-2/PALSAR-2	GF-3	RADARSAT-2	TerraSAR-X
Accuracy	80.87	86.41	85.45	94.74
F1-score	0.87	0.89	0.89	0.95

TABLE 4.6
Details of Performance Measures of Implemented ML Models on Multifrequency Band SAR Dataset

ML Models	SAR Data	ALOS-2/PALSAR-2	GF-3	RADARSAT-2	TerraSAR-X
RF	Accuracy	78.28	86.29	85.18	91.65
	F1-score	0.85	0.90	0.89	0.93
KNN	Accuracy	78.77	86.20	79.39	91.37
	F1-score	0.86	0.89	0.85	0.93
SVM	Accuracy	80.87	86.41	85.45	94.74
	F1-score	0.87	0.89	0.89	0.95
NB	Accuracy	94.23	82.57	48.57	81.34
	F1-score	0.94	0.85	0.41	0.87

results of SVM shown in Figure 4.9(a) that the RF model failed to correctly label the oriented buildings for the ALOS-2/PALSAR-2 dataset. The SVM model performs extraordinarily to predict the label of oriented buildings and the water label using the TerraSAR-X dataset, as can be observed in Figure 4.9(d).

4.8 CONCLUSION AND RECOMMENDATIONS

The outcomes of this study are aligned with previous research. The SVM classification model is found to have the best pixel accuracy and F1-score of 94.74% and 0.95, respectively, when compared to other models for the purpose of land cover and land use classification, as shown in Table 4.6. The performance of the models is graphically represented in Figure 4.10. It is also observed that the Naïve Bayes classification model gives tremendously better results compared to SVM, RF, and KNN for the ALOS-2/PALSAR-2 dataset, which are 94.23% accuracy and a 0.94 F1-score. However, it has comparatively poor performance for the RADARSAT-2 dataset. The performance of all implemented models is consistent for the GF-3 dataset. The average overall accuracy is 85.36% and the F1-score is 0.88. In a few results, it is observed that the oriented buildings are correctly classified by SVM and RF on the TerraSAR-X dataset, NB on the ALOS-2/PALSAR-2 dataset, and KNN on the TerraSAR-X dataset with small disturbances.

This work can be extended by adopting many other frequency bands of SAR datasets and also extending in terms of a greater number of classes. Another major challenge is the unavailability of common open-source training datasets with ground truth; annotation of this large number of datasets is very time consuming and takes greater effort. So, this work can continue in the same direction and also adopt many other advanced deep learning models to enhance classification accuracy.

(a)

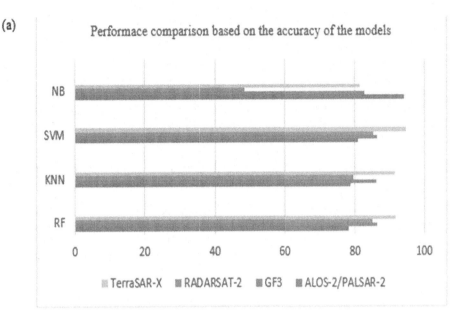

(b)

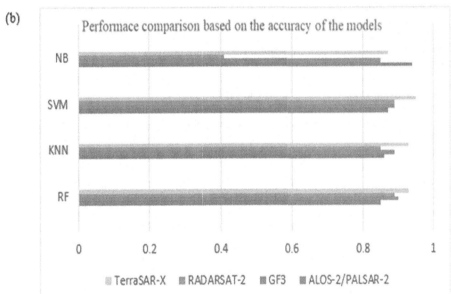

FIGURE 4.10 Representing the performance measures based on (a) accuracy and (b) F1-score of the NB, SVM, KNN, and RM models on TerraSAR-X, RADARSAT-2, DF-3, and ALOS-2/PALSAR-2 datasets.

REFERENCES

[1] J. Hoffmann, "The future of satellite remote sensing in hydrogeology," *Hydrogeol. J.*, vol. 13, no. 1, pp. 247–250, 2005, doi: 10.1007/s10040-004-0409-2.
[2] G. Mountrakis, J. Im, and C. Ogole, "Support vector machines in remote sensing: A review," *ISPRS J. Photogramm. Remote Sens.*, vol. 66, no. 3, pp. 247–259, 2011, doi: 10.1016/j.isprsjprs.2010.11.001.
[3] M. Chi, R. Feng, and L. Bruzzone, "Classification of hyperspectral remote-sensing data with primal SVM for small-sized training dataset problem," *Adv. Sp. Res.*, vol. 41, no. 11, pp. 1793–1799, 2008, doi: 10.1016/j.asr.2008.02.012.

[4] F. F. Camargo, E. E. Sano, C. M. Almeida, J. C. Mura, and T. Almeida, "A comparative assessment of machine-learning techniques for land use and land cover classification of the Brazilian tropical savanna using ALOS-2/PALSAR-2 polarimetric images," *Remote Sensing*, vol. 11, no. 13. 2019, doi: 10.3390/rs11131600.

[5] G. Li, D. Lu, E. Moran, L. Dutra, and M. Batistella, "A comparative analysis of ALOS PALSAR L-band and RADARSAT-2 C-band data for land-cover classification in a tropical moist region," *ISPRS J. Photogramm. Remote Sens.*, vol. 70, pp. 26–38, 2012, doi: 10.1016/j.isprsjprs.2012.03.010.

[6] L. Wang, P. Marzahn, M. Bernier, and R. Ludwig, "Mapping permafrost landscape features using object-based image classification of multi-temporal SAR images," *ISPRS J. Photogramm. Remote Sens.*, vol. 141, pp. 10–29, 2018, doi: 10.1016/j.isprsjprs.2018.03.026.

[7] Z. Qi, A. G.-O. Yeh, X. Li, and Z. Lin, "A novel algorithm for land use and land cover classification using RADARSAT-2 polarimetric SAR data," *Remote Sens. Environ.*, vol. 118, pp. 21–39, 2012, doi: 10.1016/j.rse.2011.11.001.

[8] Z. Zhu, C. E. Woodcock, J. Rogan, and J. Kellndorfer, "Assessment of spectral, polarimetric, temporal, and spatial dimensions for urban and peri-urban land cover classification using Landsat and SAR data," *Remote Sens. Environ.*, vol. 117, pp. 72–82, 2012, doi: 10.1016/j.rse.2011.07.020.

[9] U. Gessner et al., "Multi-sensor mapping of West African land cover using MODIS, ASAR and TanDEM-X/TerraSAR-X data," *Remote Sens. Environ.*, vol. 164, pp. 282–297, 2015, doi: 10.1016/j.rse.2015.03.029.

[10] V. H. R. Prudente et al., "SAR data for land use land cover classification in a tropical region with frequent cloud cover," in *IGARSS 2020 – 2020 IEEE International Geoscience and Remote Sensing Symposium*, 2020, pp. 4100–4103, doi: 10.1109/IGARSS39084.2020.9323404.

[11] P. Kainthura and N. Sharma, "Machine learning driven landslide susceptibility prediction for the Uttarkashi region of Uttarakhand in India," *Georisk Assess. Manag. Risk Eng. Syst. Geohazards*, vol. 0, no. 0, pp. 1–14, 2021, doi: 10.1080/17499518.2021.1957484.

[12] P. Kainthura and N. Sharma, "Machine learning techniques to predict slope failures in Uttarkashi, Uttarakhand (India)," *J. Sci. Ind. Res. (JSIR)*, vol. 80, no. 01, pp. 67–74, 2021. [Online]. Available: http://nopr.niscair.res.in/handle/123456789/55853.

[13] P. Kainthura and N. Sharma, "Probabilistic approach to predict landslide susceptibility based on dynamic parameters for Uttarkashi, Uttarakhand (India)," *J. Sci. Ind. Res.*, vol. 80, no. 08, pp. 716–725, 2021. [Online]. Available: http://nopr.niscair.res.in/handle/123456789/57980.

[14] X. Niu and Y. Ban, "An adaptive contextual SEM algorithm for urban land cover mapping using multitemporal high-resolution polarimetric SAR data," *IEEE J. Sel. Top. Appl. Earth Obs. Remote Sens.*, vol. 5, no. 4, pp. 1129–1139, 2012, doi: 10.1109/JSTARS.2012.2201448.

[15] F. de T. Martins-Bedê, M. S. Reis, E. Pantaleão, L. Dutra, and S. Sandri, "An application of multiple space nearest neighbor classifier in land cover classification," in *2014 IEEE Geoscience and Remote Sensing Symposium*, 2014, pp. 1713–1716, doi: 10.1109/IGARSS.2014.6946781.

[16] R. Garg, A. Kumar, N. Bansal, M. Prateek, and S. Kumar, "Semantic segmentation of PolSAR image data using advanced deep learning model," *Sci. Rep.*, vol. 11, no. 1, p. 15365, 2021, doi: 10.1038/s41598-021-94422-y.

[17] A. Grover, S. Kumar, and A. Kumar, "Ship detection using Sentinel-1 SAR data," *ISPRS Ann. Photogramm. Remote Sens. Spat. Inf. Sci.*, vol. IV–5, pp. 317–324, 2018, doi: 10.5194/isprs-annals-IV-5-317-2018.

[18] Z. Pan, L. Liu, X. Qiu, and B. Lei, "Fast vessel detection in Gaofen-3 SAR images with ultrafine strip-map mode," *Sensors*, vol. 17, no. 7. 2017, doi: 10.3390/s17071578.

[19] H. Guo et al., "Study of RADARSAT-2 synthetic aperture radar data for observing sensitive factors of global environmental change," *J. Appl. Remote Sens.*, vol. 8, no. 1, pp. 1–19, Feb. 2014, doi: 10.1117/1.JRS.8.084593.

[20] R. M. Barnes, *Roll Invariant Decompositions for the Polarisation Covariance Matrix*. Lexington, MA, USA: MIT Press, 1988.

[21] Y. Maghsoudi, "Analysis of Radarsat-2 full polarimetric data for forest mapping," PhD thesis, Dept. of Geomatics, Univ. of Calgary, Calgary, Alberta, Canada, 2012.

[22] R. Garg, A. Kumar, M. Prateek, K. Pandey, and S. Kumar, "Land cover classification of spaceborne multifrequency SAR and optical multispectral data using machine learning," *Adv. Sp. Res.*, vol. 69, no. 4, pp. 1726–1742, 2021, doi: 10.1016/j.asr.2021.06.028.

[23] G. Chirici et al., "A meta-analysis and review of the literature on the k-Nearest Neighbors technique for forestry applications that use remotely sensed data," *Remote Sens. Environ.*, vol. 176, pp. 282–294, 2016, doi: 10.1016/j.rse.2016.02.001.

[24] G. K. Guo G., Wang H., Bell D., Bi Y., "No title," in *KNN Model-Based Approach in Classification*, vol. 2888, 2003, doi: 10.1007/978-3-540-39964-3_62.

[25] N. Friedman, D. Geiger, and M. Goldszmidt, "Bayesian network classifiers," *Mach. Learn.*, vol. 29, no. 2, pp. 131–163, 1997, doi: 10.1023/A:1007465528199.

[26] L. Breiman, "Random forests," *Mach. Learn.*, vol. 45, no. 1, pp. 5–32, 2001, doi: 10.1023/A:1010933404324.

[27] J. H. Hastie, T. J. Tibshirani, and R. J. Friedman, *The Elements of Statistical Learning: Data Mining, Inference, And Prediction*. NY, USA: Springer, 2009.

[28] M. Belgiu and L. Drăguţ, "Random forest in remote sensing: A review of applications and future directions," *ISPRS J. Photogramm. Remote Sens.*, vol. 114, pp. 24–31, 2016, doi: 10.1016/j.isprsjprs.2016.01.011.

[29] J. Reynolds, K. Wesson, A. L. J. Desbiez, J. M. Ochoa-Quintero, and P. Leimgruber, "Using remote sensing and random forest to assess the conservation status of critical cerrado habitats in Mato Grosso do Sul, Brazil," *Land*, vol. 5, no. 2. 2016, doi: 10.3390/land5020012.

[30] S. Talukdar et al., "Land-use land-cover classification by machine learning classifiers for satellite observations – a review," *Remote Sensing*, vol. 12, no. 7. 2020, doi: 10.3390/rs12071135.

[31] B. E. Boser, I. M. Guyon, and V. N. Vapnik, "A training algorithm for optimal margin classifiers," in *Proceedings of the 5th Annual ACM Workshop on Computational Learning Theory*, 1992, pp. 144–152.

[32] A. E. Maxwell, T. A. Warner, and F. Fang, "Implementation of machine-learning classification in remote sensing: an applied review," *Int. J. Remote Sens.*, vol. 39, no. 9, pp. 2784–2817, May 2018, doi: 10.1080/01431161.2018.1433343.

[33] A. M. Abdi, "Land cover and land use classification performance of machine learning algorithms in a boreal landscape using Sentinel-2 data," *GIScience Remote Sens.*, vol. 57, no. 1, pp. 1–20, Jan. 2020, doi: 10.1080/15481603.2019.1650447.

[34] C. Huang, L. S. Davis, and J. R. G. Townshend, "An assessment of support vector machines for land cover classification," *Int. J. Remote Sens.*, vol. 23, no. 4, pp. 725–749, Jan. 2002, doi: 10.1080/01431160110040323.

[35] A. Mathur and G. M. Foody, "Land cover classification by support vector machine: towards efficient training," in *IGARSS 2004. 2004 IEEE International Geoscience and Remote Sensing Symposium*, 2004, vol. 2, pp. 742–744, doi: 10.1109/IGARSS.2004.1368508.

5 Implementation of Neural Network-Based Classification Models on Multifrequency Band SAR Dataset

Anil Kumar, Rajat Garg, and Shashi Kumar

CONTENTS

5.1 INTRODUCTION

In the last few decades, the neural network models have evolved to advanced deep learning models and successfully achieved better classification accuracy for many applications [1]. Feature extraction is one of the most powerful capabilities of deep learning models. For example, the various CNN models are capable of learning high- and low-level features from raw data supported by pooling and hidden layers, and then applying these extracted features to computer vision tasks like pattern recognition, object identification, and semantic segmentation [2], [3]. The adaptation of various neural network models in the field of remote sensing is widely accepted and is increasing exponentially, especially in the field of climate change and urbanization supported by LULC classification [4]. The deep belief network model was proposed to learn complex data patterns and deploy deep learning architectures. The probabilistic multilayered NN used restricted Boltzmann machines and achieved an overall accuracy of 81.74% for LULC on RADARSAT-2 PolSAR data of the Greater Toronto area [5], [6]. One of the prompt applications of SAR using deep learning models has been automatic target detection, used for defense and other purposes. In one application, a single layer of CNN is applied to learn the features automatically using the SAR image dataset. After the steps of convolution and pooling, an input SAR image dataset is transformed into a series of feature maps. These feature maps are used to train the model using the SoftMax activation function and achieved a target classification accuracy of 90.1% for three class targets and

DOI: 10.1201/9781003204466-5

84.7% for ten class targets [7]. Another state-of-the-art algorithm, deep convolutional networks (ConvNets), has achieved state-of-the-art results for computer vision and speech recognition. The same model has been implemented for SAR-ATR (SAR automatic target recognition) and then extended to moving and stationary TAR (MSTAR) and has achieved an accuracy of 99% on ten class target classifications [8]. It has been applied to a CNN model for ship–iceberg differentiation. This discrimination is implemented on a CNN model using TerraSAR-X strip-map images. An advanced deep NN is used to identify ships using Sentinel-1 and RADARSAT-2 ScanSAR imagery of the South African exclusive economic zone. One of the major issues of the deep learning models is unavailability of labeled training samples. Creating a labeled dataset is a cumbersome and time-consuming task. It is resolved somehow with the support of various data augmentation techniques, in which the data is translated, rotated, and interpolated [9]. The deep belief network (DBN) for SAR-ATR supported by RBM was introduced, which helped to extract hierarchical features and then fed these to a trainable classifier [10]. Deep learning models are very effective for extracting the features. It implemented deep convolutional auto-encoder (DCAE) to extract features and performed classification. The DCAE comprises in the first layer a handcrafted convolution layer that contains the gray level co-occurrence matrix (GLCM) and Gabor filters. The second layer of the model contains a handcrafted scale transformation that helps to reduce the influence of noise. This model is implemented on TerraSAR-X dataset to extract efficient features and perform better classification. The presence of speckle noises can reduce the accuracy of a classifier. It used a graph-cut-based regularization after implementing the deep supervised and contractive NN (DSCNN) model on SAR datasets that yielded superior classification results. The DBN classification model is used for land use and land cover (LULC) mapping on PolSAR data of urban areas and found an improvement in accuracy [5]. It implemented the adaptive boosting of the RBM model to PolSAR image data for object-oriented ensemble classification based on homogeneous regions [11]. A complex value CNN (CVCNN) model is proposed to process the complex values in PolSAR data that employs complex weight and operations on different layers and is used for better classification on PolSAR data. The various state-of-the-art machine learning models like SVM, random forest, and KNN are implemented on L-band ALOS-2 PALSAR-2, C-band RISAT-1, and X-band TerraSAR-X spaceborne multifrequency SAR datasets and achieved a LULC classification accuracy of 0.7948 for the water region using the performance measure of intersection over union (IoU). This showed improvement over the classification accuracy of Sentinel-2 data for same region and has an IoU of 0.7366 [12]. With the help of DeepLabv3+, an advanced deep learning model that internally uses an atrous convolution, it implemented the LULC classification and tried to resolve the problem of misclassification of urban area into forest cover. This work was applied on UAVSAR data of Houston, Texas, USA, and achieved an overall pixel accuracy of 85.65% and a precision of 0.9228, which is a superior result compared to the others [13].

5.2 NEURAL NETWORK MODELS

Various state-of-the-art neural network models have been developed to perform the classifications. Due to the strong feature extraction, the NN models have high demand in computer vision and speech recognition. This section of the chapter will discuss the strong neural network model that is used to classify the SAR dataset.

5.3 MULTI-LAYER PERCEPTRON (MLP) CLASSIFICATION MODEL

5.3.1 STUDY AREA

The study focuses on the much-discussed San Francisco Bay Area located in California (US), which has been selected due to the obtainability of multiple classes and features within the targeted study area. The multifrequency SAR band to segment the target class is discussed. The target area is

TABLE 5.1
Details of Multifrequency SAR Datasets Used

SAR system parameters	ALOS-2/PALSAR-2	TerraSAR-X	RADARSAT-2	GF-3
Platform	Spaceborne	Spaceborne	Spaceborne	Spaceborne
Satellite	Advanced land observing satellite-2 (ALOS-2)	TerraSAR-X	Radar imaging satellite (RISAT-2)	GaoFen-3
Sensor	Phased array type L-band synthetic aperture radar (PALSAR-2)	SAR	C-band, SAR	SAR
Date of acquisition	14 April 2016	11 March 2015	24 January 2014	5 August 2017
Pass	Ascending	Descending	Ascending	
Altitude	628 km	514 km	798 km	
Data type	Single look complex (SLC)	Complex	Single look complex (SLC)	Single look complex (SLC)
Polarization	Fully polarimetric quad-pol (HH+HV+VH+VV)	Fully polarimetric quad-pol (HH+HV+VH+VV)	Fully polarimetric quad-pol; (HH+VV+HV+VH)	Quad-pol (HH+HV+ VH+VV)
Mode of acquisition	Strip-map mode	Strip-map mode	Strip-map mode	Quad-polarization strip-map 1 (QPS1)
Frequency	1.236 GHz	9.65 GHz	5.40 GHz	5.4 GHz
Look direction	Right	Right	Right	Left or right

shown in Figure 5.1. SAR data from ALOS PALSAR2, GF3, RADARSAT-2, and TerraSAR-X2 are used to demonstrate the work. All the data with parameters are discussed in Table 5.1.

5.3.2 METHODOLOGY

It is important to classify the various land covers based on type and characteristics that help to analyze the land usage. Much research has been done by the researcher to optimally utilize the land cover. This section discussed the models, focused on the areas and tried to implement various classifiers to efficiently segment the regions with good accuracy. The model uses the different algorithms supported by the pre-processing task, as shown in Figure 5.1. The work flow started with input data of multifrequency band SAR data.

5.3.3 PRE-PROCESSING

Radiometric calibration and multi-looking are the important phases of pre-processing SAR data. All of the available SAR dataset used in this work was already calibrated, so only multi-looking needed to be performed. Since SAR is a side-looking sensor, slant-range distortion occurs, which causes near-range objects to appear compressed relative to far-range objects. This results in a variation of captured image scale from near to far range. Multi-looking is the process by which square pixels are generated. The number of looks is determined by the image statistics. The ALOS-2/PALSAR-2 SAR data is multi-looked to generate square pixels of 5.78 m in size. In the case of GF 3 C-Band SAR data, the purpose of multi-looking is to suppress speckle noise [14]. No pre-processing is performed on the TerraSAR-X data. Pre- processing of RADARSAT-2 data requires geometric correction. In addition, to reduce the noise and preserve the detailed information, an enhanced frost filter with a window size of 7×7 is used [15].

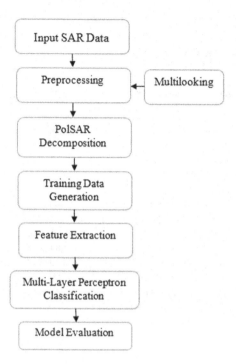

FIGURE 5.1 Workflow of the methodology implemented for semantic segmentation using various state-of-the-art machine learning models.

5.3.4 PoLSAR Decomposition

Barnes decomposition [16] n multifrequency band SAR data is used; this generates three single target vectors, k_{01}, k_{02}, and k_{03}, which are derived in Equations (5.1), (5.2), and (5.3). The three normalized target vectors can be obtained as [17]:

$$k_{01} = \frac{\langle[T]\rangle q_1}{\sqrt{q_1^{T*}\langle[T]\rangle q_1}} = \frac{1}{\sqrt{\langle 2A_0\rangle}}\begin{bmatrix}\langle 2A_0\rangle \\ \langle C\rangle + j\langle D\rangle \\ \langle H\rangle - j\langle G\rangle\end{bmatrix}, \tag{5.1}$$

$$k_{02} = \frac{\langle[T]\rangle q_2}{\sqrt{q_2^{T*}\langle[T]\rangle q_2}} = \frac{1}{\sqrt{2(\langle B_0\rangle - \langle F\rangle)}}\begin{bmatrix}\langle C\rangle - \langle G\rangle + j\langle H\rangle - j\langle D\rangle \\ \langle B_0\rangle + \langle B\rangle - \langle F\rangle + j\langle E\rangle \\ \langle E\rangle + j\langle B_0\rangle - j\langle B\rangle - j\langle F\rangle\end{bmatrix}, \tag{5.2}$$

$$k_{03} = \frac{\langle[T]\rangle q_3}{\sqrt{q_3^{T*}\langle[T]\rangle q_3}} = \frac{1}{\sqrt{2(\langle B_0\rangle + \langle F\rangle)}}\begin{bmatrix}\langle H\rangle + \langle D\rangle + j\langle C\rangle + j\langle G\rangle \\ \langle E\rangle + j\langle B_0\rangle + j\langle B\rangle + j\langle F\rangle \\ \langle B_0\rangle - \langle B\rangle + \langle F\rangle + j\langle E\rangle\end{bmatrix}, \tag{5.3}$$

where A_0, B, B_0, C, D, E, F, G, and H are the same parameters as used in Hyunen's Muller Matrix.

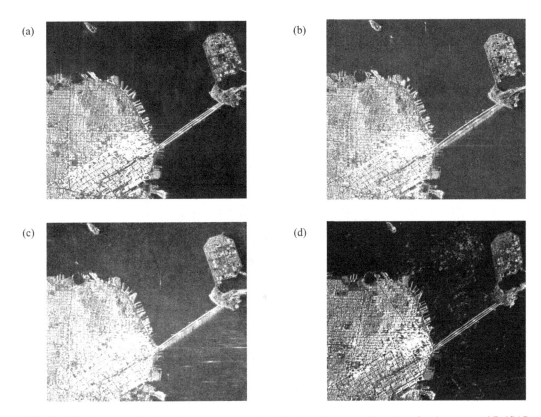

FIGURE 5.2 Representing the decomposed results of the San Francisco Bay Area for the captured PolSAR dataset: (a) ALOS-2/PALSAR-2, (b) GF-3, (c) RADARSAT-2, and (d) TerraSAR-X.

Figure 5.2 presents the output of Barnes decomposition for the input SAR datasets ALOS-2/ PALSAR-2, GF-3, RADARSAT-2, and TerraSAR-X for the location of the San Francisco Bay Area in California, USA.

5.3.5 TRAINING DATA GENERATION

The labeled dataset is always required to train the classification models. The decomposed results are divided into patches per the adoptability of the models and labeled with respect to the ground truth. A number of testing and training datasets are created. A sample of decomposed results and its corresponding data patch is shown in Figure 5.3. Both patches belong to San Francisco. The four different class labels – urban, ground, water, and forest – are shown in their corresponding color coding in Figure 5.4. Of the complete dataset, made up of different data sources including ALOS-2/ PALSAR-2, GF-3, RADARSAT-2, and TerraSAR-X, 80% of the data is used for training and the remaining 20% for testing and validation purposes.

5.3.6 ARCHITECTURE OF MULTI-LAYER PERCEPTRON (MLP) CLASSIFICATION MODEL

The multi-layer perceptron (MLP) is the general NN model most widely used for classification, recognition, approximation, and prediction. The generic MLP model is shown in Figure 5.5. It consists of three different layers – the input layer, the hidden layer, and the output layer. The input layer receives the input data, which is processed by hidden layers, and then classification and prediction

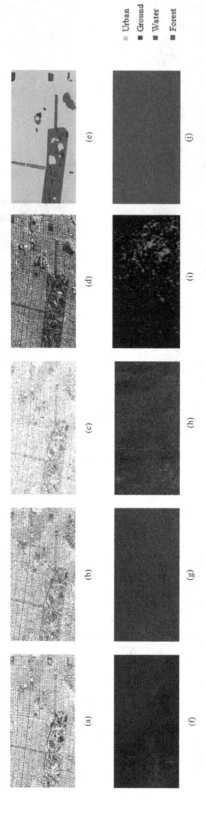

FIGURE 5.3 Representing decomposed image and corresponding processed and labeled images of one part of San Francisco in the USA: (a), (f) ALOS-2/PALSAR-2, (b), (g) GF-3, (c), (h) RADARSAT -2, and (d), (i) TerraSAR-X, (e), (j) its corresponding label.

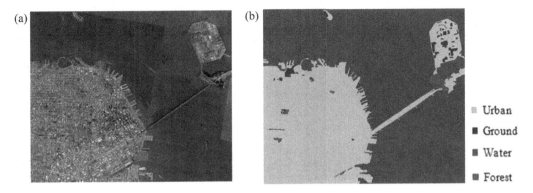

FIGURE 5.4   Representing (a) the Google map image of San Francisco, USA, considered as ground truth, and (b) the corresponding labeled image depicting four class labels of urban, ground, water, and forest.

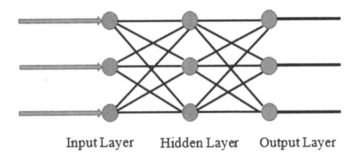

Input Layer   Hidden Layer   Output Layer

FIGURE 5.5   The multi-layer perceptron (MLP) model.

TABLE 5.2
Details of Performance of MLP Classifier on Multifrequency Band SAR Dataset

	ALOS-2/PALSAR-2	GF-3	RADARSAT -2	TerraSAR-X
Accuracy	63.77	70.2	71.89	78.57
F1-score	0.70	0.77	0.79	0.85

is done by the output layer. In other words, the output layer is the computational engine of the MLP model [18].

The MLP model is used for SAR image despeckling using a time-series data of SAR images. In this work, the model has multiple hidden layers designed for feed-forward network training, and back propagation gradient descent is used to reduce the error between the target output and neural network output. The model was tested on the TerraSAR-X dataset and provided satisfactory results on noise reduction [19]. One part of the work was used to establish a database of SAR image features to train an MLP model, which will classify the water, ice, and unknown class labels. The MLP is enhanced to allow uncertainty regarding each pixel's location, which helps to reduce misclassification [20]. The combination of the MLP model and the Weibull multiplicative model (WMM) is implemented on 60 ENVISAT and ERS2 image dataset of dark spots indicating the oil spills, which achieved an average classification accuracy of 94.65% [21]. The MLP model is now applied on the multifrequency-based SAR dataset; its classification results are shown in Figure 5.6, and its performance measures are listed in Table 5.2. It can be observed that the MLP classifier

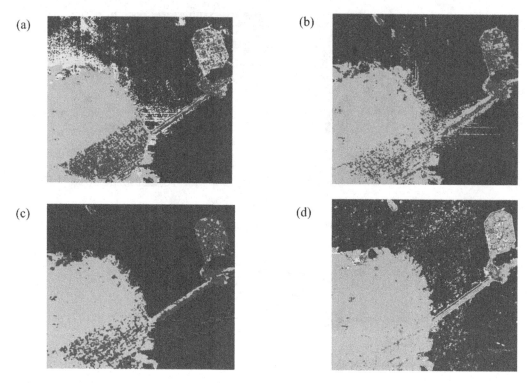

FIGURE 5.6 Representing the MLP classification model results of San Francisco for the captured PolSAR dataset of multifrequency band illustrated here: (a) ALOS-2/PALSAR-2, (b) GF-3, (c) RADARSAT-2, and (d) TerraSAR-X.

works better than others on the TerraSAR-X dataset and achieved an accuracy of 78.57% and an F-score of 0.851. The details of the performance measures for different bands of SAR datasets are depicted in Table 5.2.

5.4 COMPACT CNN CLASSIFICATION MODEL USING SLIDING-WINDOW OPERATIONS

The compact CNN classification model illustrated in Figure 5.7 was implemented on the C-band SAR dataset of the San Francisco Bay Area, USA. An N × N window of the electromagnetic channel of each pixel is fed as an input to a compact and adaptive 2D CNN. The CNN helps to determine the label of the center pixels. The number of utilized EM channels defines the size of the CNN input layers. One important hyper-parameter of this model is the size of the sliding windows. Changes in size varies the accuracy. The model is best performed for the window sizes of 21 × 21 and 23 × 23, giving accuracies of 0.9807, 0.9939 and 0.9911, 0.9908 for 3,4-channels, respectively. The L-band AISAR of the San Francisco Bay Area data covers mainly the five information classes of water, urban, forest, bare soil, and natural vegetation. It has an image size of 900 × 1024 with a pixel resolution of 10 × 10 m [22]–[24]. Figure 5.7 illustrates that at the initial phase of the model, the pre-processing task is performed on the PolSAR image dataset input for despeckling, using Lee speckle filtering, and also performed its linear scaling. After that, adaptive 2D CNN was used, proceeded by the SoftMax activation function that helps to improve classification, and the final mask was generated.

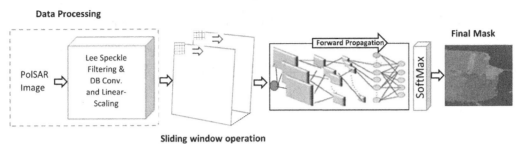

FIGURE 5.7   PolSAR data-based compact CNNs using sliding-window operation [25].

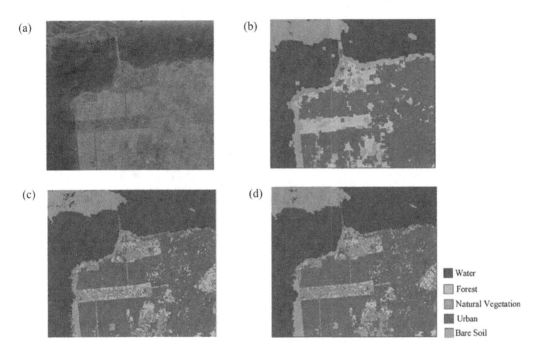

FIGURE 5.8   Representing the final segmentation results of the compact CNN for San Francisco of AIRSAR L-band PolSAR data: (a) input image, (b) and (c) representing the segmentation mask obtained after using 4-channel input with 21 × 21 and 7 × 7 pixel windows respectively, and (d) the segmentation results by 3-channel input with 7 × 7 pixel window [25].

The final segmentation results are shown in Figure 5.8, which used 3,4-channels of 21 × 21 pixel windows and 7 × 7 pixel windows, respectively. The model achieved an overall classification accuracy of 99.39% for 4-channel input and window size of 21 [25].

The compact CNN model is also implemented on the RADARSAT-2 C-band dataset of San Francisco and for the five different classes of high-density urban, low-density urban, water, vegetation, and developed, as mentioned in Figure 5.9. The overall classification accuracy achieved for the RADARSAT-2 C-band PolSAR dataset is 95.32%, as listed in Table 5.3.

TABLE 5.3
Details of Performance of Compact CNN Classifier on L-Band SAR Dataset

	Dimensions	#class	Train size/class	Total ground truth size	Maximum iteration	Overall accuracy
AIRSAR L-band	900 x 1024	5	292	123,459	40	99.39%
RADARSAT-2 C-band	1426 x 1876	5	500	252,500	400	95.32%

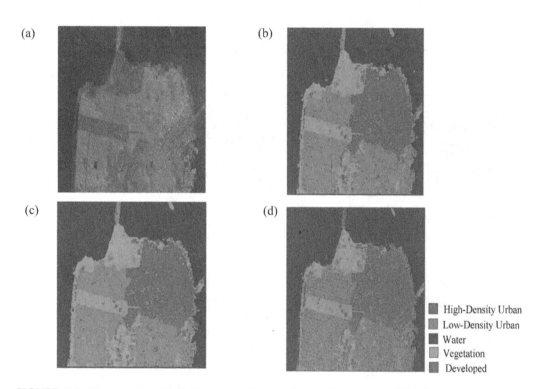

FIGURE 5.9 Representing the final segmentation results of the compact CNN for San Francisco of RADARSAT-2 C-band PolSAR data: (a) input image, (b) and (c) representing the segmentation mask obtained after using 3- and 4-channel input with 17 × 17 and 19 × 19 pixel windows respectively, and (d) the segmentation results by 3-channel input with 7 × 7 pixel window [25].

5.5   THE DEEPLABV3+ CLASSIFICATION MODEL

One of the advanced deep learning models, DeepLabv3+, works better than the traditional machine learning models even with a small training dataset with high classification accuracy. The L-band data from airborne sensor UAVSAR used in this work is taken from the open platform of NASA-JPL of Houston, Texas, USA [26]. The details of the input UAVSAR dataset are listed in Table 5.4. It is fully quad-pol SAR data and implemented G4U decomposition, as shown in Figure 5.10 [27]. Figure 5.10(b) shows the false composite image, in which green highlights the signature of the volume scattering, red of double-bounce, and blue of odd-bounce scattering.

The most common semantic segmentation in the deep learning model are fully convolutional networks (FCN). This model has only pooling and convolution layers that allow arbitrarily sized inputs and are also used for LULC classification purposes [29]. DeepLabv3+ is the extension of the

TABLE 5.4
Details of UAVSAR Data and Instrument [28]

SAR system parameters	Details
Platform	Airborne
Flight	Uninhabited aerial vehicle synthetic aperture radar (UAVSAR)
Date of acquisition	2 Sep 2017
Acquisition mode	PolSAR
Frequency	1.26 GHz
Wavelength	23.79 cm
Bandwidth	80 MHz
Pulse duration	5-50 μs
Transmit power	3.1 kW
Look angle range	25° – 65°
Data type	Multi-look complex (MLC)
Polarization	Fully polarimetric quad-pol (HH+HV+VH+VV)
Swath width	16 km
Range resolution (meters)	4.99 m (MLC product)
Azimuth resolution (meters)	7.2 m (MLC product)

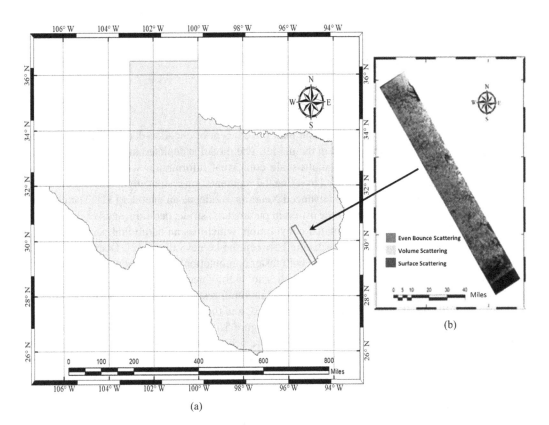

(a)

(b)

FIGURE 5.10 Represents the location of the study area compiled using ArcGIS v10.6 (https://desktop.arcgis.com/en/arcmap/): (a) the boundary of Texas state (obtained from https://gis-txdot.opendata.arcgis.com/) and (b) the G4U decomposition-based false color composite image of UAVSAR data for part of Houston, Texas (USA) generated using an open-source remote sensing tool, PolSARPro v6.0 (open access at https://step.esa.int/main/download/polsarpro-v6-0-biomass-edition-toolbox-download/).

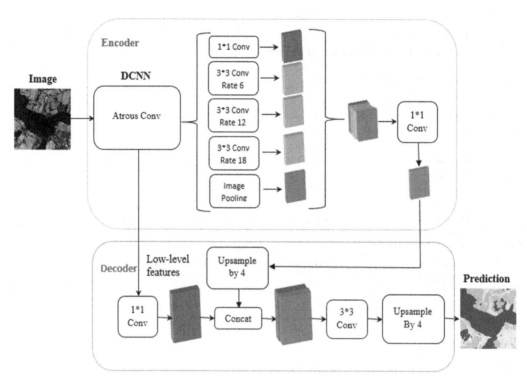

FIGURE 5.11   Encoder–decoder-based structure of DeepLabv3+ [30].

DeepLabv3 model of the DeepLab series and uses the concept of encoder–decoder and atrous spatial pyramid pooling (ASPP) integrated in the model. The model is depicted in Figure 5.11.

The encoder is used to encode the multi-scale contextual information with support of atrous convolutions. The decoder module is used to refine the segmentation results aligned to object boundaries. The DeepLabv3+ model uses an advanced Xception model as an encoder [31]. The convolution is performed with the support of three different parameters: stride, padding, and kernel size. The atrous convolution is also known as dilated convolution, which has an additional parameter called the dilation rate; this is responsible for spacing between the kernel values [32]. DeepLabv3+ more effectively recovers sharp object boundaries with faster computation. The segmentation result of the DeepLabv3+ is shown in Figure 5.12. Three patches are highlighted in Figure 5.12 as patch A, patch B, and patch C. It is observed that SVM, KNN, and random forest classifiers have wrongly classified some portion of the water class of patch A and patch B, and the forest class in patch C. However, it is correctly classified by DeepLabv3+, as shown in Figure 5.12(f). It also misclassified the oriented urban building as vegetation class, as shown in Figure 5.12(b). The DeepLabv3+ model is able to correctly classify even the oriented urban targets under the urban class with minimal classification [13]. Figure 5.12 represents the classification results of UAVSAR data of the city of Houston, USA; Figure 5.12(b) represents the G4U decomposed result of input UAVSAR data. The results of SVM, KNN, and random forest classification are compared with the DeepLabv3+ segmentation results; the model is found to have achieved an overall pixel accuracy of 85.65% and precision of 0.9228, which is better than all the mentioned classifiers.

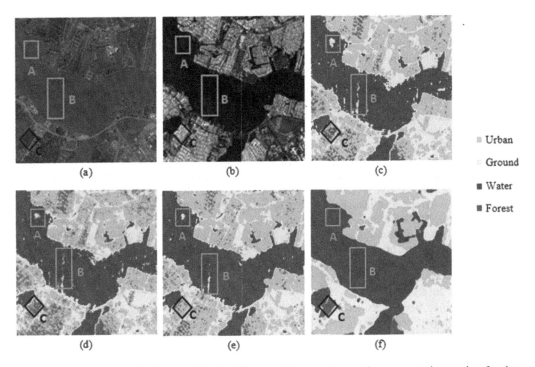

FIGURE 5.12 Representing the ground truth of Houston, Texas, and respective segmentation results of various classifiers: (a) Google Earth image as a ground truth, (b) false color composite image for G4U decomposition on UAVSAR data of a part of Houston, Texas (USA) and the respective image segmentation results for (c) RF classifier, (d) KNN classifier, (e) SVM classifier, and (f) DeepLabv3+.

5.6 CONCLUSION AND RECOMMENDATIONS

The outcomes of this study are aligned with previous research. The neural network models have been observed to be overwhelmingly good for LULC classification. In this chapter, three different NN models – MLP, compact CNN, and DeepLabv3+ – have been implemented on different SAR datasets. The MLP classifier is the basic NN model and has been applied on the TerraSAR-X, RADARSAT-2, GF-3, and ALOS-2/PALSAR-2 datasets; and the MLP is observed to work better for the TerraSAR-X dataset. The compact CNN model is implemented on the AIRSAR L-band and RADARSAT-2 C-band datasets. It achieved a classification accuracy of 99.39% for the AIRSAR L-band dataset for water, forest, natural vegetation, urban, and bare soil. The accuracy is 95.32% on the RADASAT-2 C-band dataset for five different classes: high-density urban, low-density urban, water, vegetation, and developed. Advanced deep learning models like DeepLabv3+ have been implemented and solved the problem of misclassification of oriented building as vegetation.

This study can be extended by taking on other and different frequency bands of the SAR dataset. The extension is also in terms of a greater number of classes. Another major challenge for the implementation of the neural network model is that it always requires a huge training dataset. The unavailability of common open-source training datasets with ground truth is another challenge; annotation of this large number of datasets is very time consuming and takes greater effort. So, this work can continue in the same direction and also adopt many other advanced deep learning models to enhance classification accuracy.

REFERENCES

[1] Y. LeCun, Y. Bengio, and G. Hinton, "Deep learning," *Nature*, vol. 521, no. 7553, pp. 436–444, 2015, doi: 10.1038/nature14539.

[2] Y. Guo, Y. Liu, T. Georgiou, and M. S. Lew, "A review of semantic segmentation using deep neural networks," *Int. J. Multimed. Inf. Retr.*, vol. 7, no. 2, pp. 87–93, 2018, doi: 10.1007/s13735-017-0141-z.

[3] Z. Zhao, P. Zheng, S. Xu, and X. Wu, "Object detection with deep learning: a review," *IEEE Trans. Neural Networks Learn. Syst.*, vol. 30, no. 11, pp. 3212–3232, 2019, doi: 10.1109/TNNLS.2018.2876865.

[4] X. X. Zhu et al., "Deep learning in remote sensing: a comprehensive review and list of resources," *IEEE Geosci. Remote Sens. Mag.*, vol. 5, no. 4, pp. 8–36, 2017, doi: 10.1109/MGRS.2017.2762307.

[5] Q. Lv, Y. Dou, X. Niu, J. Xu, J. Xu, and F. Xia, "Urban land use and land cover classification using remotely sensed SAR data through deep belief networks," *J. Sensors*, vol. 2015, p. 538063, 2015, doi: 10.1155/2015/538063.

[6] G. E. Hinton, S. Osindero, and Y.-W. Teh, "A fast learning algorithm for deep belief nets.," *Neural Comput.*, vol. 18, no. 7, pp. 1527–1554, Jul. 2006, doi: 10.1162/neco.2006.18.7.1527.

[7] S. Chen and H. Wang, "SAR target recognition based on deep learning," in *2014 International Conference on Data Science and Advanced Analytics (DSAA)*, 2014, pp. 541–547, doi: 10.1109/DSAA.2014.7058124.

[8] S. Chen, H. Wang, F. Xu, and Y. Jin, "Target classification using the deep convolutional networks for SAR images," *IEEE Trans. Geosci. Remote Sens.*, vol. 54, no. 8, pp. 4806–4817, 2016, doi: 10.1109/TGRS.2016.2551720.

[9] D. A. E. Morgan, "Deep convolutional neural networks for ATR from SAR imagery," in *Proc.SPIE*, 2015, vol. 9475, doi: 10.1117/12.2176558.

[10] Z. Cui, Z. Cao, J. Yang, and H. Ren, "Hierarchical recognition system for target recognition from sparse representations," *Math. Probl. Eng.*, vol. 2015, p. 527095, 2015, doi: 10.1155/2015/527095.

[11] F. Qin, J. Guo, and W. Sun, "Object-oriented ensemble classification for polarimetric SAR Imagery using restricted Boltzmann machines," *Remote Sens. Lett.*, vol. 8, no. 3, pp. 204–213, Mar. 2017, doi: 10.1080/2150704X.2016.1258128.

[12] R. Garg, A. Kumar, M. Prateek, K. Pandey, and S. Kumar, "Land cover classification of spaceborne multifrequency SAR and optical multispectral data using machine learning," *Adv. Sp. Res.*, vol. 69, no. 4, 2022, doi: 10.1016/j.asr.2021.06.028.

[13] R. Garg, A. Kumar, N. Bansal, M. Prateek, and S. Kumar, "Semantic segmentation of PolSAR image data using advanced deep learning model," *Sci. Rep.*, vol. 11, no. 1, p. 15365, 2021, doi: 10.1038/s41598-021-94422-y.

[14] Z. Pan, L. Liu, X. Qiu, and B. Lei, "Fast vessel detection in Gaofen-3 SAR images with ultrafine strip-map mode," *Sensors*, vol. 17, no. 7, 2017, doi: 10.3390/s17071578.

[15] H. Guo et al., "Study of RADARSAT-2 synthetic aperture radar data for observing sensitive factors of global environmental change," *J. Appl. Remote Sens.*, vol. 8, no. 1, pp. 1–19, Feb. 2014, doi: 10.1117/1.JRS.8.084593.

[16] R. M. Barnes, *Roll Invariant Decompositions for the Polarisation Covariance Matrix*. Lexington, MA, USA: MIT Press, 1988.

[17] Y. Maghsoudi, "Analysis of Radarsat-2 full polarimetric data for forest mapping," PhD thesis, Dept. of Geomatics, Univ. of Calgary, Calgary, Alberta, Canada, 2012.

[18] Z. Ali et al., "Forecasting drought using multilayer perceptron artificial neural network model," *Adv. Meteorol.*, vol. 2017, p. 5681308, 2017, doi: 10.1155/2017/5681308.

[19] X. Tang, L. Zhang, and X. Ding, "SAR image despeckling with a multilayer perceptron neural network," *Int. J. Digit. Earth*, vol. 12, no. 3, pp. 354–374, Mar. 2019, doi: 10.1080/17538947.2018.1447032.

[20] N. Asadi, K. A. Scott, A. S. Komarov, M. Buehner, and D. A. Clausi, "Evaluation of a neural network with uncertainty for detection of ice and water in SAR imagery," *IEEE Trans. Geosci. Remote Sens.*, vol. 59, no. 1, pp. 247–259, 2021, doi: 10.1109/TGRS.2020.2992454.

[21] A. Taravat and N. Oppelt, "Adaptive Weibull multiplicative model and multilayer perceptron neural networks for dark-spot detection from SAR imagery," *Sensors*, vol. 14, no. 12. 2014, doi: 10.3390/s141222798.

[22] T. Ince, M. Ahishali, and S. Kiranyaz, "Comparison of polarimetric SAR features for terrain classification using incremental training," in *2017 Progress in Electromagnetics Research Symposium – Spring (PIERS)*, 2017, pp. 3258–3262, doi: 10.1109/PIERS.2017.8262319.

[23] S. Uhlmann, S. Kiranyaz, M. Gabbouj, and T. Ince, "Polarimetric SAR images classification using collective network of binary classifiers," in *2011 Joint Urban Remote Sensing Event*, 2011, pp. 245–248, doi: 10.1109/JURSE.2011.5764765.

[24] S. Kiranyaz, T. Ince, S. Uhlmann, and M. Gabbouj, "Collective network of binary classifier framework for polarimetric SAR image classification: an evolutionary approach," *IEEE Trans. Syst. Man, Cybern. Part B*, vol. 42, no. 4, pp. 1169–1186, 2012, doi: 10.1109/TSMCB.2012.2187891.

[25] M. Ahishali, S. Kiranyaz, T. Ince, and M. Gabbouj, "Classification of polarimetric SAR images using compact convolutional neural networks," *GIScience Remote Sens.*, vol. 58, no. 1, pp. 28–47, Jan. 2021, doi: 10.1080/15481603.2020.1853948.

[26] "Uninhabited aerial vehicle synthetic aperture radar (UAVSAR)," 2021. [Online]. Available: https://uavsar.jpl.nasa.gov/cgi-bin/data.pl.

[27] A. Bhattacharya, G. Singh, S. Manickam, and Y. Yamaguchi, "An adaptive general four-component scattering power decomposition with unitary transformation of coherency matrix (AG4U)," *IEEE Geosci. Remote Sens. Lett.*, vol. 12, no. 10, pp. 2110–2114, 2015, doi: 10.1109/LGRS.2015.2451369.

[28] S. Hensley *et al.*, "The UAVSAR instrument: description and first results," in *2008 IEEE Radar Conference*, 2008, pp. 1–6, doi: 10.1109/RADAR.2008.4720722.

[29] E. Shelhamer, J. Long, and T. Darrell, "Fully convolutional networks for semantic segmentation," *IEEE Trans. Pattern Anal. Mach. Intell.*, vol. 39, no. 4, pp. 640–651, Apr. 2017, doi: 10.1109/TPAMI.2016.2572683.

[30] H. A. Liang-Chieh Chen, Yukun Zhu, George Papandreou, Florian Schroff, "Encoder–decoder with atrous separable convolution for semantic image segmentation," in *Computer Vision and Pattern Recognition*, 2018.

[31] F. Chollet, "Xception: deep learning with depthwise separable convolutions," in *2017 IEEE Conference on Computer Vision and Pattern Recognition (CVPR)*, 2017, pp. 1800–1807, doi: 10.1109/CVPR.2017.195.

[32] L.-C. Chen, G. Papandreou, F. Schroff, and H. Adam, "Rethinking atrous convolution for semantic image segmentation," in *Computer Vision and Pattern Recognition*, 2017.

6 Improved Data Fusion-Based Land Use/Land Cover Classification Using PolSAR and Optical Remotely Sensed Satellite Data
A Machine Learning Approach

Akshar Tripathi, Shashi Kumar, and Sandeep Maithani

CONTENTS

DOI: 10.1201/9781003204466-6

6.1   INTRODUCTION

The heterogeneity of urban land cover results in the mixing of other features like bare land, dry riverbeds, and fallow land with built-up areas during image classification [1]. Optical data relies mainly on the solar illumination of features on the earth's surface [2]. However, active RADAR data focuses on the surface roughness, which has its own energy that is sent to the target, and the backscatter from the target is recorded [3]. RADAR polarimetry is highly versatile and has a wide range of applications, such as oil spill monitoring and crop yield assessment, as well as many other fields with great potential in the land cover mapping [4]. The present study aims to integrate optical and SAR datasets for improving the accuracy of urban classification. Urbanization is taking place at a very fast rate in India, with the country's urbanization count standing at about 31.16% as of the 2011 census [5]. This is taking a heavy toll on available resources since competition for water and electricity is increasing; at the same time, more and more land is being converted for settlement purposes [6]. These developments make it imperative to study urban sprawl for a sustainable future and to ensure an adequate number of resources for future generations. Satellite remote sensing is a non-invasive tool that solves the purpose of mapping urban areas and monitoring their growth, along with LULC change, that occurs over time, simply and cost-effectively [7].

Optical remote sensing data that is frequently used for land cover (LC) mapping has its constraints; on the one hand, it does not have all-weather availability, and while on the other, spectral merging can be observed of urban build-up with fallow land, bare soil, and dry riverbeds [8]. This makes the delineation of urban targets and subsequent image classification a difficult task. Microwave or SAR (synthetic aperture RADAR) remote sensing has today developed as an advanced and highly sophisticated remote sensing tool; compared to any other remote sensing tool, it has unique features due to its varied range of applications and areas of research, which are not only versatile but also have a unique ability to make quantitative measurements [9]. Microwave remote sensing has added advantages of its own; it can penetrate through clouds, thus giving it an all-weather availability. It can even penetrate through soil, to some extent, and reveal information about topsoil, and the active microwave does not have to depend upon the sun for illumination, as is the case with optical data [10]. It also has various wavelength bands available, which have different interactions with different features on the ground and in turn reveal information that is not shown by optical remote sensing [11].

Among the various techniques in microwave remote sensing, PolSAR, or polarimetric synthetic aperture RADAR, remote sensing has been found highly useful for land use/land cover mapping, with unique abilities like various backscatter-based decomposition models and 3D visualization of features [12]. Polarization refers to the path traced by the tip of the electric field vector in an electromagnetic wave. Polarization can also be described by the orientation of the tip of the electric field vector in time and at a fixed location. Advantages of PolSAR over normal SAR remote sensing include that it not only reveals much information about the physical properties of the object but also helps in visualization and conceptualization of three-dimensional attributes changing with time

[13]. This makes PolSAR one of the most challenging aspects of SAR remote sensing. PolSAR has a distinct speciality of combining the enhanced spatial resolution available with SAR and properties of polarized electromagnetic energy [14]. The polarimetric backscatter signature from the target is a 3D saddle plot that is formed when the three components of polarimetry – ellipticity, orientation angle and amplitude of backscattered signal – are plotted [15]. As different features have different interactions with the polarized wave, each feature, be it man-made or natural, causes different scattering of the incident polarized wave [16]. This is studied in the backscatter and physical properties of targets are revealed, with feature delineation. Based on the relative backscatters and scattering mechanisms, several coherent and incoherent polarimetric decomposition models have been proposed [17]. This study aims to study and analyse a few of these decomposition models and use them for improved classification of man-made and natural features.

PolSAR data has an advantage over optical datasets due to its various polarimetric combinations; moreover, it has all-weather availability [18]. To overcome the shortcomings of both optical and PolSAR datasets, fusion of both datasets was attempted. Several fusion techniques were evaluated – wavelet transform, Gram–Schmidt fusion, and HSV fusion. Finally, the fused image was classified using both machine learning and object-based image classification (OBIC).

6.1.1 PROBLEMS IN MONITORING LAND USE/LAND COVER CHANGE

The increase in the human population has increased overutilization of resources while also giving momentum to rapid competition to grab as many resources as possible [19]. One such resource is land. The 2011 Indian census shows urbanization at 31.1% and still on the rise as more and more land is converted from forest to agriculture and agriculture to be built up to meet the demand of expanding cities and towns [20]. This is leading to loss of wildlife habitat, weaker monsoons, depletion of the groundwater table, and many more potential threats [21]. Given the current situation, it has become imperative to promptly and accurately map and monitor such changes in order to be well planned and prepared to meet any tragic situation [22]. Thus, land use/land cover mapping has been a crucial topic of study for remote sensing experts all over the world. With the advent of satellite-based remote sensing, the cost of mapping and monitoring not only has been reduced but also the time saving has increased [23]. Moreover, as a non-invasive tool, it is more robust and accurate and covers a larger area in less time as compared to tedious fieldwork [24]. The main problem with urban LULC mapping is the heterogeneity of urban areas, which makes it difficult to delineate urban features from bare soil, fallow land, and dry riverbeds [25], which have a similar tone. This problem has been encountered in the use of optical remote sensing data, which has led scientists to explore other domains of remote sensing, such as microwave and SAR remote sensing.

The properties of the target can be analysed by using polarimetric SAR, where the target is illuminated by the incident RADAR wave, which is scattered by the target in all directions [26]. It is the backscatter received by the antennae of the RADAR that is of actual importance. By studying the polarization of the incident and the backscattered wave, the target can be analysed and identified [27]. Conventional SAR transmits and receives on only one polarization channel [28], whereas quad-pol or fully polarimetric PolSAR transmit and receive in more than one polarization channel [29]. This results in four polarization channels – HH, VV, HV, VH – where relative phase and amplitude variations are observed [30]. PolSAR is a very powerful tool for information retrieval and feature identification for improved and accurate classification of man-made and natural features in imagery since each polarization is sensitive to varying surface features and characteristics [31].

6.1.2 SAR POLARIMETRY

Polarization, as shown in Figure 6.1 (www.intechopen.com/chapters/63701), refers to the path carved by the electric vector of an electromagnetic wave in space.

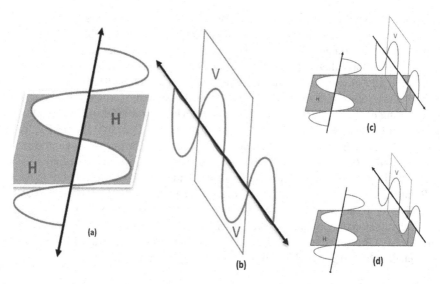

FIGURE 6.1 PolSAR linear polarization schemes: (a) HH polarization, (b) VV polarization, (c) VH polarization, and (d) HV polarization.

Polarization observed at a particular location can take the shape of an ellipse, line, or circle for fixed frequency waves. PolSAR identifies targets based on relative backscatter from targets [32]. Urban areas can be differentiated based on strong double scattering. Urban areas with large azimuth orientation angles (AOAs) give strong volumetric scattering showing similarity to vegetation [33]. If the wall of the building is parallel to the flight direction of the SAR sensor, the AOA is 0o. The range of AOA is $-\pi/4$ to $\pi/4$. For this study, AOA from 0 to $\pi/4$ was considered. Apart from AOA, the physical dimension, surface roughness, spatial density, and pattern were also seen to affect the scattering pattern in urban areas [34]. When the phase difference between two linearly polarized waves is changed, several polarization channels are seen [35]. When the phase difference is between 0 and π, a linearly polarized wave results, while a phase difference of $\pi/2$ and $3\pi/2$ circularly polarized waves are obtained [36]. For this study, linear polarized data of the X and C-band was used with HH, HV, VH, and VV polarization channels. When the electric field vector is parallel to the earth's surface, then it is termed horizontally polarized, while when it is at right angles to the earth surface, it is termed vertically polarized.

6.1.3 APPLICATION OF PolSAR IN LAND COVER (LC) CLASSIFICATION

There are several applications of LULC mapping using PolSAR data, like forest inventory mapping, urban sprawl mapping and monitoring, crop parameter and moisture retrieval, glacial and snow studies, wetland, and coastal management [37]. Many studies have shown that PolSAR data can provide valuable information on both mountainous and sub-mountainous areas that usually have cloud cover and thus optical and topographic data is not easily available [38]. Usage of PolSAR and its feature extraction and deformation mapping abilities have been used in several studies [39], [40]. In a few other studies, RADARSAT-2 C-band data was used to achieve up to 86% of classification accuracy using textural, interferometric, and polarimetric information [41], [42]. Single-frequency SAR data causes a lot of ambiguity in LC mapping; hence, for our study, X-band datasets of TerraSAR-X were taken. Multifrequency SAR datasets help to achieve better information retrieval because different frequency bands are sensitive to different land cover types [43]. The more of multitemporal datasets available, the easier the delineation of features, and one can easily differentiate between different LC classes [44].

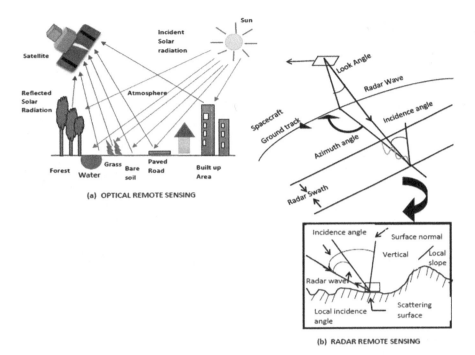

FIGURE 6.2   (a) Optical and (b) RADAR remote sensing.

6.1.4   ADVANTAGES OF POLSAR OVER OPTICAL DATASETS

Optical datasets show the mixing of urban and fallow land features with the same spectral signatures. Based on optical data features like spectral bands, if a standard false colour composite (FCC) is generated, it shows a cyan tone for both of these features, making their delineation and classification difficult as they both tend to merge [45]. The NDVI image generated from the optical dataset also cannot solve this difficulty since both of these areas are devoid of any vegetation [46]. Figure 6.2 (https://asf.alaska.edu/information/sar-information/what-is-sar/) shows the basic structure of optical and RADAR/PolSAR remote sensing.

PolSAR data, on the other hand, with its various modelling approaches and decomposition methods, minimize this ambiguity and give a detailed and more accurate LC classification [47]. The PolSAR dataset gives four linearly polarized channels in a quad-pol dataset; based on backscatter received, various polarimetric features like RADAR vegetation index (RVI), RADAR forest degradation index (RFDI), entropy, anisotropy, and alpha angle can be calculated, which give different information for various land use and land cover types [48]. Apart from this, the PolSAR data has various decomposition models to delineate features based on relative scattering mechanisms, where single or surface scattering holds good for water and fallow land and double-bounce scatter predominates in urban areas when the AOA is between 0 to $\pi/4$. For vegetated areas that have large AOAs, volumetric scattering predominates [38]. Whenever there is penetration of microwaves down to the ground in between vegetation, strong single bounce scattering patches are also observed.

6.2   MATERIALS AND METHODS

6.2.1   STUDY AREA AND DATASETS

6.2.1.1   Study Area

The study area selected is the city of Rudrapur, located in the Udham Singh Nagar district of Uttarakhand state in India [49]. Rudrapur covers an area of 27.65 km² and has good road, rail, and

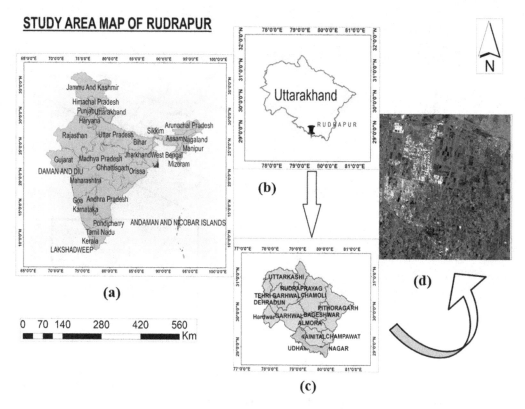

FIGURE 6.3 Study area map showing: (a) Map of India, (b) Uttarakhand boundary map with Rudrapur marked, and (d) TerraSAR-X RGB image of Rudrapur District, Uttarakhand, India.

TABLE 6.1
PolSAR Datasets Used

S.No.	Data	Date of acquisition	Mode of acquisition	Polarization	Resolution (range × azimuth) m	Incidence angle (degrees)
1.	TerraSAR-X and TanDEM-X Co-SSC	02/12/2015	Strip-map	Quad	1.67 × 6.6	45.45

air connectivity with all major cities in India. Rudrapur is located at 28.98° N and 79.40° E, latitude and longitude respectively, with an average of 253 m elevation above mean sea level. Rudrapur is a town with huge industrial setups, as shown in Figure 6.3.

6.2.1.2 Datasets

TerraSAR-X SAR and optical LISS-IV datasets from RESOURCESAT-2 were utilized for this study. The details of the datasets are shown in Table 6.1 and Table 6.2.

As mentioned in Table 6.1, the X-band dataset from TerraSAR-X was used for this study. The dataset was co-SSC (co-registered slant-range single look complex) from TerraSAR-X, which is one of two twin satellites (the other is TanDEM-X) from the German Space Agency-DLR [8].

LISS-IV (multispectral) optical data, of the same date as the PolSAR data, were acquired from the Indian remote sensing satellite RESOURCESAT-2 through the Indian Space Research Organization

TABLE 6.2
Optical Datasets Details

S.No.	Data	Date of acquisition	Mode of acquisition	Spatial resolution
1.	LISS-IV MS	2/12/2015	Descending	5.8 m

(ISRO), having a spatial resolution of 5.8 m [50]. This dataset was fused/integrated with the PolSAR data, and the results were then analysed for improved LULC classification. The details of optical datasets are shown in Table 6.2.

6.2.2 POLARIMETRIC DECOMPOSITION

There are two types of polarimetric decomposition methods – coherent and incoherent decomposition [51]. The coherent decomposition technique is based on a scattering matrix, and incoherent decomposition technique deals with coherency (T3) or covariance matrix (C3). Coherent decomposition can be used to study mainly permanent or coherent targets or point targets [52]. The following decomposition models were tested since they happen to be the few initially developed decompositions like the Freeman–Durden and are the most widely used, as suggested by studies [53].

6.2.2.1 Coherent Decompositions

Coherent decompositions are used mainly for coherent targets or point targets like built-up structures. These decompositions are based on a scattering matrix and consider the scattering mechanisms based on the interaction of RADAR waves with the target [14], [54].

6.2.2.1.1 *Pauli's Decomposition*

The most commonly used decomposition model in SAR polarimetry is Pauli's decomposition model. Pauli's decomposition of the scattering matrix is used for the representation of all scattering information on a SAR image. The scattering matrix is represented by [S] [18]:

$$[S] = \alpha \begin{bmatrix} 1 & 0 \\ 0 & 1 \end{bmatrix} + \beta \begin{bmatrix} 1 & 0 \\ 0 & -1 \end{bmatrix} + \gamma \begin{bmatrix} 0 & 1 \\ 1 & 0 \end{bmatrix}, \tag{6.1}$$

where $\alpha = (S_{hh} + S_{vv}) / \sqrt{2}$, $\beta = (S_{hh} - S_{vv})/ \sqrt{2}$, $\gamma = \sqrt{2}S_{hv}$ represent the different types of scattering, namely single bounce, double-bounce and 45 degrees rotated double-bounce scattering. The polarimetric information, of matrix [S], could be represented by combining the intensities $|S_{hh}|^2$, $|S_{vv}|^2$, and $2|S_{hv}|^2$. An RGB image can also be formed with intensity values $|\alpha|^2$ (red), $|\beta|^2$ (blue), and $|\gamma|^2$ (green), which correspond to physical scattering mechanisms. This study makes use of the following combination for generation of Pauli's RGB [55]:

$$Kp = \frac{1}{\sqrt{2}} \begin{bmatrix} S_{HH} + S_{VV} \\ S_{HH} - S_{VV} \\ 2S_{HV} \end{bmatrix}, \tag{6.2}$$

where, K_p is Pauli's vector, [HH + VV] corresponds to blue, [HH – VV] corresponds to red, and $2S_{HV}$ corresponds to green [56].

6.2.2.1.2 Sinclair's Decomposition

The polarization state of a plane monochromatic electric field is represented in its most compact form by the introduction of the Jones vector. For the monochromatic case, time dependence is neglected. With z = 0 [57],

$$\vec{E}(0) = \begin{pmatrix} E e^{i\sigma x} \\ E e^{i\sigma y} \end{pmatrix}. \tag{6.3}$$

$\vec{E}$ is called a Jones vector, which completely defines the phase and amplitude of complex orthogonal components of an electric field. If incident and scattered waves are characterized by their corresponding Jones vectors Ej and Es, the scattering process represented in terms of Jones vector is:

$$\mathrm{E_s} = \frac{e^{-jkr}}{r} \, \mathrm{E_j} = \frac{e^{-jkr}}{r} \begin{bmatrix} S11 & S12 \\ S21 & S22 \end{bmatrix}, \tag{6.4}$$

where matrix S is named as the scattering matrix and elements of it are referred to as complex scattering coefficients. Term $\dfrac{e^{-jkr}}{r}$ refers to propagation effects in amplitude and phase. The values of the complex scattering coefficients are coordinate system and polarization basis dependent [58].

6.2.2.2 Incoherent Decompositions

These decomposition models deal with coherency or covariance matrices and are used for distributed targets like vegetation [59]. These matrices can be used for partial polarized and scattering target decomposition. These decomposition techniques are of a further two types [60]:

1) **Eigenvalue decomposition.** This includes H-A-α parameter-based decomposition. These three parameters are based on eigenvalues, and usually, their higher values are considered since lower eigenvalues are observed to be affected by noise [61].
2) **Model-based decompositions.** In this decomposition method, the coherency or covariance matrix is taken to be representative of the scattering phenomenon of three mechanisms – single bounce, double-bounce, volumetric scattering [14]. Non-negligible power in off-diagonal terms is neglected by assuming reflection symmetry. This technique includes Freeman–Durden, Yamaguchi, and Van-Zyl decomposition.

The following incoherent decomposition models were tried for this study.

6.2.2.2.1 Freeman–Durden Decomposition

This decomposition models the covariance matrix in contribution from various targets. Canopy scatters from random dipoles, double-bounce scatters from surfaces with varying dielectric properties, and Bragg scatters for surfaces with moderate roughness. This method is used to derive decomposition using a covariance matrix, given as [52]:

$$\langle [C] \rangle = \begin{bmatrix} \langle |S_{HH}|^2 \rangle & \sqrt{2}\langle S_{HH.}S_{HV}^* \rangle & \langle S_{HH}S_{VV}^* \rangle \\ \sqrt{2}\langle S_{HV.}S_{HH}^* \rangle & \langle |S_{HV}|^2 \rangle & \sqrt{2}\langle S_{HV.}S_{VV}^* \rangle \\ \langle S_{VV.}S_{HH}^* \rangle & \sqrt{2}\langle S_{VV.}S_{HV}^* \rangle & \langle |S_{VV}|^2 \rangle \end{bmatrix} = [\vec{X}\vec{X}^{*T}]. \tag{6.5}$$

$\vec{X}$ is the complex scattering factor represented as [62]:

$$\bar{X} = [S_{HH} \cdot S_{HV} \cdot \sqrt{2}S_{HV}], \tag{6.6}$$

where the component "T" denotes the matrix transpose. Freeman–Durden decomposes the matrix into three scattering components [63]:

$$[C] = f_s \begin{bmatrix} |\beta^2| & 0 & \beta \\ 0 & 0 & 0 \\ \beta^* & 0 & 1 \end{bmatrix} + f_d \begin{bmatrix} |\alpha|^2 & 0 & \alpha \\ 0 & 0 & 0 \\ \alpha^* & 0 & 1 \end{bmatrix} + f_v \begin{bmatrix} 1 & 0 & 1/3 \\ 0 & 2/3 & 0 \\ 1/3 & 0 & 0 \end{bmatrix}. \tag{6.7}$$

The contribution in scattering can be estimated from the scattering powers P_s, P_d, and P_v, where they represent single, double, and volumetric scattering, respectively [19].

6.2.2.2.2 Yamaguchi Decomposition

An improvement to the Freeman–Durden model, this decomposition model was proposed in 2005 by adding a fourth helical component to the model [64]. This fourth component was to represent backscatter from heterogeneous targets. The covariance matrix [C] is given by [65]

$$[C] = f_s [C_{surface}] + f_d [C_{double}] + f_v [C_{volume}] + f_h [C_{helix}], \tag{6.8}$$

where f_s, f_d, f_v, and f_h are the expansion coefficients. This model gives a better and more generalized scattering mechanism. This is better for identifying plantations, forest patches, and agricultural fields, but urban areas tend to disappear since volumetric scattering predominates [66].

6.2.2.2.3 H-A-α Decomposition

This is an incoherent polarimetric decomposition model, based on the coherency matrix "T3" and its eigen decomposition. Let $\lambda 1, \lambda 2, \lambda 3$ be the eigenvalues of the matrix "T3," such that $\lambda 1 > \lambda 2 > \lambda 3 > 0$, and u1, u2, u3 are the corresponding eigenvectors; then, in this case [67],

$$Ui = \left[cos\alpha i, sin\alpha i \ cos\beta e^{j\sigma}, sin\alpha i \ cos\beta e^{j\gamma} \right]^T \tag{6.9}$$

From here, three secondary polarimetric parameters are obtained, which are entropy, anisotropy, and α angle.

6.2.2.2.4 Van-Zyl Decomposition

This model assumes that there is symmetrical backscatter and zero correlation between cross- and co-polarized channels. This decomposition model works well in the case of natural features such as soil, vegetation, and forests. With this, the covariance matrix "C3" can have an eigen decomposition where C3 is [68]

$$C3 = A1 \begin{bmatrix} \alpha^2 & 0 & \alpha \\ 0 & 0 & 0 \\ \alpha^* & 0 & 1 \end{bmatrix} + A2 \begin{bmatrix} \beta^2 & 0 & \beta \\ 0 & 0 & 0 \\ \beta^* & 0 & 1 \end{bmatrix} + A3 \begin{bmatrix} 0 & 0 & 0 \\ 0 & 1 & 0 \\ 0 & 0 & 0 \end{bmatrix}. \tag{6.10}$$

This model shows that the first two eigenvectors, A1 and A2, have similar mechanisms of scattering.

6.2.3 DATA FUSION TECHNIQUES USED

Many studies have been conducted to compare various image fusion techniques that describe image fusion as the process in which multiple imageries are combined into one output imagery. This leads to products with better and enhanced description of the scene, which is of more utility for human and machine perception for further image processing such as segmentation and classification [69]. Image fusion is defined as the combining of the relevant information from two or more images to extract more useful information from them. This study compares various image fusion techniques such as wavelet transform, principal component analysis, intensity hue saturation (IHS), and the high pass filtering method. The different image fusion techniques and their brief description and utilities, drawn from various studies, follow.

6.2.3.1 Principal Component Analysis (PCA)

This is a mathematical or rather statistical tool that transforms variables from correlated to uncorrelated variables, which are referred to as principal components, as found by [70]. The first principal component accounts for as much variance as possible in the data, while each successive component accounts for all the remaining variance, if any; this makes it a highly useful tool for image enhancement and classification [71]. One advantage of this system is that an arbitrary number of image bands can be used. Low-resolution multispectral images form the uncorrelated principal components.

6.2.3.2 Wavelet-Based Fusion

These are seen as extensions of image filtering techniques where the imagery is broken down or divided into several wavelets, and then these wavelets are selectively arranged together for fusion [72]. Wavelet-based fusion techniques give better performance than other fusion techniques as they tended to reduce colour distortions; moreover, standard methods together in combination with simple wavelets gave far superior results [73]. Its main advantage is that it provides desired output resolution over time and frequency domains. It is an improvement of Fourier transform that provides improved resolution only in the frequency domain [74]. In wavelet transform, the image is decomposed into informative and approximate coefficients at a specific level. Thereafter, fusion is applied, and these components are combined using inverse wavelet transform [75].

6.2.3.3 Intensity Hue Saturation Method

This technique has proven to be effective in converting an RBG image from RGB space to IHS space. The best advantage it has is that it offers variation in each component of the IHS easily and independently [76]. Due to this advantage, it is possible to swap one band from either of intensity, hue, or saturation with the RBG bands and fuse the imageries to retrieve more and productive information [77]. IHS fusion using fast Fourier transform uses a replaced intensity component along with the hue and saturation component and creates an RGB image by fusion performed by FFT. Intensity, hue, and saturation are the three colour components of an image that give it its visual interpretability. Hence, these need to be carefully combined. As one of the oldest fusion techniques, IHS fusion has the advantage that it carefully adds the details of high-resolution single-band imagery into the low-resolution multispectral image [78].

6.2.3.4 High Pass Filtering (HPF) Fusion

This technique is used to obtain a high-resolution multispectral image wherein the high frequency panchromatic (PAN) image passed through a high pass filter (HPF) is added to a low-frequency MSS image to obtain an image that is resultant of the two [79]. The main advantage of this type of image fusion is that a high-resolution multispectral image is obtained using this fusion in a much easier and quicker manner, using high frequency information from the high-resolution single-band image to the low-resolution multispectral image [80].

6.2.3.5 Average Method

This method uses an approximate value of all imageries that are to be fused and makes sure that all regions are always in focus [81]. Pixel values of all images are summed together and then divided by the number of input images [82]. The output imagery has a pixel value that is the average of all input pixel values. This process is speedy since it uses a fast-running process, but objects are of less clarity, and hence not much is used for image fusion [83]. Its advantage is its simplicity, since it combines the intensity values and intensities of input images and, based on an average value of these, gives a high-resolution multispectral image [84].

6.2.4 Selection of Classifiers

Once the features for classification are identified in imagery, based on visualization in optical and backscatter observed from different target features in PolSAR imagery, the next task is to select a suitable classifier that not only gives better delineation in classification for different features but also classifies the image with maximum accuracy. The classifiers can be broadly divided into two categories.

6.2.4.1 Parametric Classifiers

These classifiers consider that the classification dataset follows a Gaussian distribution function and is represented by statistical parameters like covariance matrix and mean vector [85]. Maximum likelihood is one of the most commonly used classifiers for statistical purposes used in RADAR image classification [86]. Maximum likelihood is supervised parametric image classification. The distribution of feature class values is usually modelled using a normal density function in a maximum likelihood classifier, but it depends upon the data type [67]. The non-parametric classifier gives better classification accuracies than the parametric classifier and the K-means nearest neighbourhood classifier was considerably better than the maximum likelihood classifier in every way [87].

6.2.4.2 Non-parametric Classifiers

These classifiers do not assume any probabilistic distribution function; nor do they consider any statistical parameter for class separability [88]. These are very useful for integrating non-intensity data to be used for the classification of SAR images. Among the most commonly used non-parametric classifiers are artificial neural networks, support vector machine, knowledge-based classifiers, decision trees, random forest classifiers, K-means nearest neighbourhood classifier, and object-based classifiers [40]. There are various advantages of non-parametric classifiers –

- They provide better classification accuracies.
- They can integrate various types of data from different sensors.
- They are good for handling multi-temporal data.

The few most commonly used non-parametric classifiers follow. [15]

6.2.4.3 K-means Nearest Neighbourhood Classifier (KNN)

The closest training samples from the feature space are used in the classification of the K-means nearest neighbourhood classifier. This non-parametric classifier stores all features and classifies them based on a similarity measure [73].

6.2.4.4   Support Vector Machine (SVM) Classification

This classifier is one of the most robust machine learning classifiers used for improved and accurate image classification. It fits a frontier line between two or more feature classes to ensure their separability from each other [89]. It uses kernels for this that are Gaussian-like radial basis function (RBF), non-Gaussian-like polynomial and linear, and hyperbolic kernels like the sigmoid kernel. Besides this, it also uses a misclassification penalty parameter function that controls the training momentum rate and prevents the feature classes from getting misclassified and in turn ensures the features are at a definite distance from the frontier line [90].

6.2.4.5   Artificial Neural Network (ANN) Classifier

This classifier works on a three-layer relationship: the input layer considers the information from the imagery, the intermediate layer is where the actual processing or classification takes place, and the output layer [91]. While the input layer is imagery dependent and depends upon the number of bands from the imagery taken as input, and the output layer depends on the number of classes, it is only the intermediate layer that can be controlled for better classification results [92]. This can be done by controlling the training momentum rate and misclassification penalty parameters so that feature class drainage is prevented apart from the classifier getting trapped in local minima [93].

6.2.4.6   Random Forest Classifier

This classifier divides the feature space into several sub-feature classes and thereafter fits decision trees in those sub-feature classes using averaging methods to improve the accuracy of a classification and best fitting of feature classes [94]. This classifier creates several random decision trees from a feature space and then averages the nodes from each tree to test and decide the final class of the object [95].

6.2.4.7   Object-Based Image Classification (OBIC)

This image classifier is found to have better and by far the highest accuracy among all image classification methods, especially more than pixel-based image classification techniques. This technique segments features into objects subject to a threshold value and makes its comparison with other such objects that are groups of pixels; the similar objects are grouped into one and form a class [96].

6.2.5   Methods

The methodology is shown in the flow chart in Figure 6.4. It deals with the pre-processing of PolSAR datasets. The datasets were first pre-processed for quad PolSAR data; orientation angle correction was performed, followed by coherence matrix generation since urban features are coherent features that change over a long time span. This was followed by speckle filtering of the datasets, which was done to remove any noise. The second part deals with polarimetric decomposition, wherein various decomposition models were tested to delineate ground targets based on relative backscatter mechanisms. Thereafter, RGBs were generated to show single bounce, double-bounce, and volumetric scatterings. After this, in the third part, double-bounce scatter band was fused with three bands of LISS-IV optical data, and the results were analysed. Thereafter, in the fourth part, various machine learning classification techniques like support vector machine (SVM), random forest classifier, K-means nearest neighbourhood (KNN), and artificial neural network (ANN) classifiers were used and their relative accuracies were assessed in the fifth part of the study, both with and without fusion/integration with optical data. In the fifth part itself of the methodology, the results were also compared for accuracy with object-based image classification. Ground truth validation was done to fine-tune the results obtained from classification. The methodology flow diagram is shown in Figure 6.4.

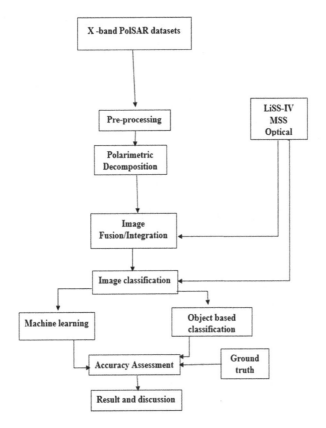

FIGURE 6.4   Methodology flow diagram.

6.3   RESULTS AND CONCLUSION

6.3.1   Polarimetric Decomposition

Different coherent and incoherent polarimetric decomposition techniques were applied, and the results are summarized in Table 6.3.

Figure 6.5 shows the different polarimetric decomposition results of TerraSAR-X quad-pol imagery, with different land use/land cover features.

From Table 6.3 and Figure 6.5, it can be inferred that Sinclair's decomposition is good for built-up delineation besides other LULC features; hence, the red band of Sinclair's decomposed RGB was used for fusion with LISS-IV optical imagery. The results of data fusion are shown in Figure 6.6.

From Figure 6.6 (c), it is seen that HSV-based fusion provides the highest feature class separability as compared to other fusion techniques. Hence, the HSV fusion results were utilized for further machine learning-based classifications.

6.3.2   Classification Results

6.3.2.1 KNN Classification

This study was undertaken by taking the value k = 1 and increasing it up to 100 in progression for 5000 training samples, using Euclidian distance to check the accuracy. The results showed more accuracy when k was an odd number. After increasing the value of k to more than 63, it was observed that the more the neighbourhood values, the more the accuracy of the KNN classifier. After

TABLE 6.3
Comparison of Coherent and Incoherent Polarimetric Decompositions

Decomposition model		Merits	Demerits
Coherent	Pauli's	Distinguished built-up target well	Couldn't distinguish between types of built-up
	Sinclair's	Distinguished built-up targets well	Couldn't distinguish natural targets well
Incoherent	Freeman–Durden	Distinguished built-up and non-built-up well	Couldn't distinguish natural targets well
	Yamaguchi	Distinguished natural targets well	Couldn't distinguish built-up from non-built-up
	H-A-α	Distinguished land cover features well	Couldn't distinguish between land use features
	Van-Zyl	Distinguished built-up from other features	Couldn't distinguish between natural targets

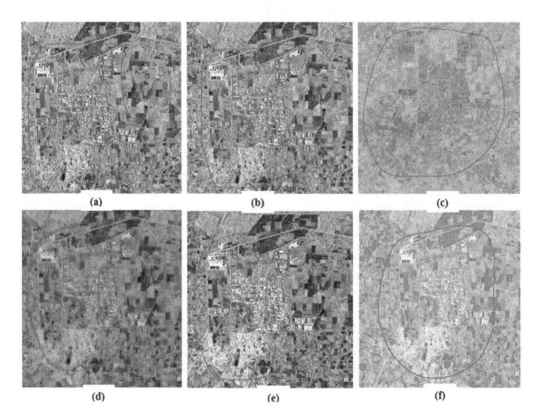

FIGURE 6.5 Polarimetric decomposition X-band, TerraSAR-X, RGBs showing study area: (a) Pauli's decomposition, (b)- Sinclair decomposition, (c) H-A-α decomposition, (d) Yamaguchi decomposition, (e) Van-Zyl decomposition, and (f) Freeman–Durden decomposition.

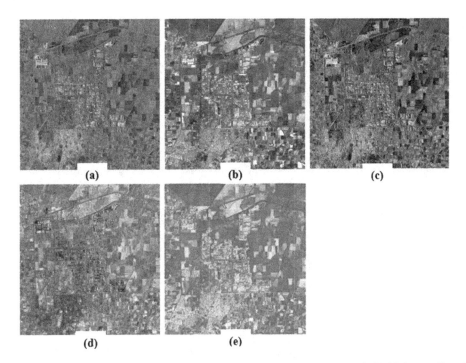

FIGURE 6.6 Sinclair's red band fused with LISS-IV MSS: (a) average method, (b) high pass filter (HPF) method, (c) hue saturation value (HSV) method, (d) PCA method, and (e) wavelet fusion.

varying the number of training samples and neighbours from 50 and 1 to 500 and 10 respectively, the optimum value was observed. Beyond 500 training samples, the misclassification was again found to increase. The classified image is shown in Figure 6.7 (a).

6.3.2.2 Random Forest (RF) Classification

In this study, it was seen that the performance of random forest increases in terms of classification accuracy by maximizing the individual tree strength and minimizing the correlation among the trees. This was done by proportionately increasing the number of trees with the number of training samples. Several trees close to 10% of training samples attained maximum accuracy, while an increase in the number of trees beyond this value led to misclassification of the imagery since the number of training samples is unevenly distributed in the trees. However, classification accuracy also depends upon the complexity of the dataset. The number of training samples was initially taken as 100, which was increased up to 5000, and the number of trees initially at 1 was increased up to 10. At values of 5000 and 10 for several training samples and trees respectively, the random forest classifier gave optimum classification. Beyond this value, misclassification was again found to increase, which was controlled to some extent by increasing the number of trees, but after a while, there was again a drastic increase in misclassification seen. The classified image is shown in Figure 6.7(b).

6.3.2.3 Artificial Neural Network (ANN) Classification

ANN, as a classifier, has proved to be a highly robust classification technique by giving high accuracy percentages overall in this study. However, this accuracy depends upon the values of ANN parameters like layer optimization, where the number of input layers was decided based on the input imagery, the learning rate "η," which has to be kept balanced as a lower value of η makes the network too slow to reach an optimum value while a higher value traps it in the local minima. The

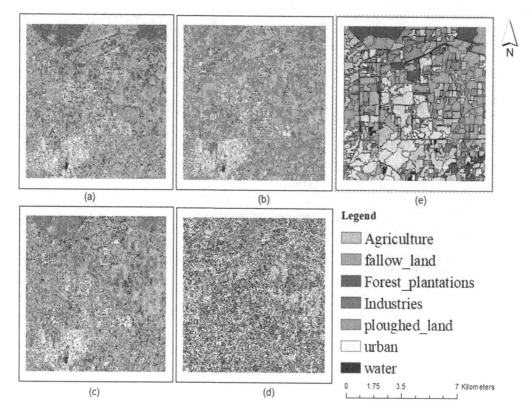

FIGURE 6.7 HSV-fused classified products using various machine learning techniques: (a) KNN, (b) RF, (c) ANN, (d) SVM, and (e) OBIC.

third parameter used was the training momentum function "α," which controls the learning rate from falling in the local minima. Its value needs to be optimized along with the number of iterations based on the type and size of the dataset or else a process drainage starts, which tends towards misclassification. The learning rate, "η," was varied in a range of 0–0.2 and, proportionately, the learning momentum rate, "α," was varied from 0 to 0.9. An optimum value giving high accuracy of classification was found at $\eta = 0.2$ and $\alpha = 0.9$, with several hidden layers at 1 and 800 iterations. Beyond these values, there was data drainage, and misclassification increased along with a decrease in feature separability. The classified image is shown in Figure 6.7(c).

6.2.4.4 Support Vector Machine (SVM) Classification

For SVM classification, it was found that the classification accuracy of an SVM classifier depends upon the distance of the class clusters from the frontier line or plane of separation. This is managed by controlling the spread of kernel function "γ" and misclassification penalty parameter "C." A low value of γ tends to lower the class separability, while a higher value increases misclassification. To achieve the best classification results, both γ and C have to be increased proportionately depending upon the dataset. In this study, the optimum values of both these parameters were found using Lib. SVM. The RBF (radial basis function) kernel yielded the most accurate results in this study among other SVM kernels. Here, the misclassification penalty parameter was varied from 100 to 150, and to control the spread of kernel, the classification probability threshold was varied from 0 to 1.5. It was found that almost all kernels of SVM gave the best and most accurate classification results at a misclassification penalty parameter value from 120 to 150 and probability threshold value of 0.5 to

1.5; beyond these values, the misclassification was seen to increase. The classified image is shown in Figure 6.7(d).

6.2.4.5   Object-Based Image Classification (OBIC)

In this study, the object-based image classification technique was found to be the most accurate and robust, and its classification accuracy depends upon the image segmentation. The more properly the image segments or objects are identified as a single entity, the better their classification. Here shape and compactness factors have a crucial role since they decide the size and shape of individual image segments. An optimum value of these two parameters along with the scale factor makes each segment identifiable as a separate object, which in turn increases the classification accuracy. Since object-based image classification depends a lot upon the shape, size, and distinctiveness of the individual segments, the scale factors for the division of the image into segments is very important. The value of scale factor was varied in this study from 50 to 150 and values of shape and compactness factor from 0 to 1. It was found that optimum values for the dataset used in this study were 150 for scale factor and 0.7 for shape and compactness factors, respectively. Beyond these values, the segments were too large and accommodated more than one feature class in them. The classified image is shown in Figure 6.7(e).

The classified maps using various machine learning techniques are shown in Figure 6.7.

The classification accuracies of various machine learning classification techniques for HSV-fused SAR and optical products as shown in Figure 6.7 are shown in Figure 6.8.

However, the classification accuracies of optical LISS-IV datasets using the same machine learning techniques are shown in Figure 6.9.

From Figures 1.8 and 1.9, it is seen that HSV-fused product gave a better classification accuracy as compared to an optical dataset that gave mixing of urban and fallow land features, hence resulting in lower classification accuracies.

6.4   CONCLUSIONS

The present study aims to assess the potential of PolSAR backscatter and optical reflectance for improved and accurate image classification. It can be inferred from the study that PolSAR data, with its several decompositions and modelling approaches, helps to minimize the ambiguity of merging of fallow land and urban features as happens in optical data. This problem of merging becomes

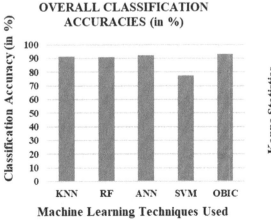
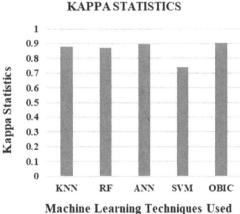

FIGURE 6.8   Classification accuracy % and kappa statistics for HSV SAR and optical-fused product.

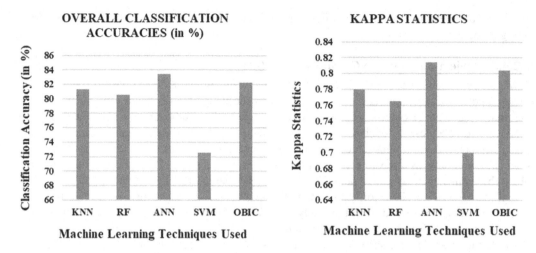

FIGURE 6.9 Classification accuracy % and kappa statistics for LISS-IV optical imagery.

more acute when the wheat crop is harvested in north India. Both quad and dual PolSAR data were able to minimize this ambiguity and gave improved and more accurate land cover classification as compared to its optical counterpart. The quad PolSAR data was tried with several coherent and incoherent decomposition models.

It was observed that the fused product gave high classification accuracy with both machine learning and object-based classification as compared to its optical counterpart. Moreover, there was the least misclassification with almost all classification algorithms. Out of the various machine learning algorithms, the ANN classification algorithm using the radial basis function kernel proved to be the most accurate, giving up to 92% classification accuracy, and was comparable to the object-based classification approach in terms of accuracy. After detailed research, it was found that with the used methodology, the ambiguity of merging of urban and fallow land features was minimized and a high level of classification accuracy was achieved. The major contributions made through this study are:

- PolSAR and optical data were successfully fused/integrated using HSV transform, showing maximum feature separability in the fused product compared to individual datasets.
- Improvement in the mapping of LULC change can be achieved by proper fusion/integration of high-resolution PolSAR and optical data along with using the optimum value of classification parameters; pixel-based machine learning classification techniques give high classification accuracy comparable to object-based classification.

REFERENCES

[1] S. Jalan, "Exploring the potential of object based image analysis for mapping urban land cover," *J. Indian Soc. Remote Sens.*, vol. 40, no. 3, pp. 507–518, 2012.

[2] M. Weiss, F. Jacob, and G. Duveiller, "Remote sensing for agricultural applications: A meta-review," *Remote Sens. Environ.*, vol. 236, p. 111402, 2020.

[3] Y. Wang, X. X. Zhu, and R. Bamler, "Retrieval of phase history parameters from distributed scatterers in urban areas using very high-resolution SAR data," *ISPRS J. Photogramm. Remote Sens.*, vol. 73, pp. 89–99, 2012.

[4] P. Marzahn and R. Ludwig, "On the derivation of soil surface roughness from multi parametric PolSAR data and its potential for hydrological modeling," *Hydrol. Earth Syst. Sci.*, vol. 13, no. 3, pp. 381–394, 2009.

[5] A. Siddiqui, S. Halder, P. Chauhan, and P. Kumar, "COVID-19 pandemic and city-level nitrogen dioxide (NO2) reduction for urban centres of India," *J. Indian Soc. Remote Sens.*, vol. 48, no. 7, pp. 999–1006, 2020.

[6] J. Niemczynowicz, "Urban hydrology and water management – present and future challenges," *Urban Water*, vol. 1, no. 1, pp. 1–14, 1999.

[7] J. Yin et al., "Monitoring urban expansion and land use/land cover changes of Shanghai metropolitan area during the transitional economy (1979–2009) in China," *Environ. Monit. Assess.*, vol. 177, no. 1, pp. 609–621, 2011.

[8] T. Esch, H. Taubenböck, A. Felbier, W. Heldens, M. Wiesner, and S. Dech, "Monitoring of global urbanization-time series analyses for mega cities based on optical and SAR data," in *2012 Second International Workshop on Earth Observation and Remote Sensing Applications*, 2012, pp. 21–25.

[9] M. Chini, R. Pelich, L. Pulvirenti, N. Pierdicca, R. Hostache, and P. Matgen, "Sentinel-1 InSAR coherence to detect floodwater in urban areas: Houston and hurricane Harvey as a test case," *Remote Sens.*, vol. 11, no. 2, pp. 1–20, 2019.

[10] R. N. Nof et al., "SAR interferometry for sinkhole early warning and susceptibility assessment along the Dead Sea, Israel," *Remote Sens.*, vol. 11, no. 1. 2019.

[11] D. Mandal et al., "Assessment of rice growth conditions in a semi-arid region of India using the generalized radar vegetation index derived from RADARSAT-2 polarimetric SAR data," *Remote Sens. Environ.*, vol. 237, p. 111561, 2020.

[12] Y. L. S. Tsai, A. Dietz, N. Oppelt, and C. Kuenzer, "Remote sensing of snow cover using spaceborne SAR: A review," *Remote Sens.*, vol. 11, no. 12, 2019.

[13] P. Patel, H. S. Srivastava, and R. R. Navalgund, "Use of synthetic aperture radar polarimetry to characterize wetland targets of Keoladeo National Park, Bharatpur, India," *Curr. Sci.*, vol. 97, no. 4, pp. 529–537, 2009.

[14] N. Agrawal, S. Kumar, and V. Tolpekin, "Polarimetric SAR interferometry-based decomposition modelling for reliable scattering retrieval," in *Proc.SPIE*, 2016, vol. 9877.

[15] J. Hu, P. Ghamisi, and X. X. Zhu, "Feature extraction and selection of Sentinel-1 dual-pol data for global-scale local climate zone classification," *ISPRS International Journal of Geo-Information*, vol. 7, no. 9. 2018.

[16] N. Dore, J. Patruno, E. Pottier, and M. Crespi, "New research in polarimetric SAR technique for archaeological purposes using ALOS PALSAR data," *Archaeol. Prospect.*, vol. 20, no. 2, pp. 79–87, 2013.

[17] L. Carin, R. Kapoor, and C. E. Baum, "Polarimetric SAR imaging of buried landmines," *IEEE Trans. Geosci. Remote Sens.*, vol. 36, no. 6, pp. 1985–1988, 1998.

[18] D. Varade, S. Manickam, O. Dikshit, G. Singh, and Snehmani, "Modelling of early winter snow density using fully polarimetric C-band SAR data in the Indian Himalayas," *Remote Sens. Environ.*, vol. 240, p. 111699, 2020.

[19] K. Li, B. Brisco, S. Yun, and R. Touzi, "Polarimetric decomposition with RADARSAT-2 for rice mapping and monitoring," *Can. J. Remote Sens.*, vol. 38, no. 2, pp. 169–179, Jan. 2012.

[20] P. Kumar et al., "Multi-level impacts of the COVID-19 lockdown on agricultural systems in India: The case of Uttar Pradesh," *Agric. Syst.*, vol. 187, p. 103027, 2021.

[21] W. M. Boerner and J. J. Morisaki, "Recent developments of radar remote sensing; air- and space-borne multimodal SAR remote sensing in forestry & agriculture, geology, geophysics (volcanology and tectonology): Advances in POL-SAR, IN-SAR, POLinSAR and POL-DIFF-IN-SAR sensing and imaging with applications to environmental and geodynamic stress-change monitoring," *2006 International Radar Symposium*, pp. 1–4, 2006.

[22] K. A. Prasad, M. Ottinger, C. Wei, and P. Leinenkugel, "Assessment of coastal aquaculture for India from Sentinel-1 SAR time series," *Remote Sens.*, vol. 11, no. 3. 2019.

[23] C. K. Singh, S. Shashtri, R. Avtar, S. Mukherjee, and S. K. Singh, "Monitoring change in land use and land cover in Rupnagar district of Punjab, India using Landsat and IRS LISS III satellite data," *Ecol. Quest.*, vol. 13, pp. 73–79, 2010.

[24] K. Rajitha, C. K. Mukherjee, and R. Vinu Chandran, "Applications of remote sensing and GIS for sustainable management of shrimp culture in India," *Aquac. Eng.*, vol. 36, no. 1, pp. 1–17, 2007.

[25] L. Karthikeyan, I. Chawla, and A. K. Mishra, "A review of remote sensing applications in agriculture for food security: Crop growth and yield, irrigation, and crop losses," *J. Hydrol.*, vol. 586, p. 124905, 2020.

[26] P. S. Roy, P. G. Diwakar, I. J. Singh, and S. K. Bhan, "Evaluation of microwave remote sensing data for forest stratification and canopy characterisation," *J. Indian Soc. Remote Sens.*, vol. 22, no. 1, pp. 31–44, 1994.

[27] P. Pampaloni and K. Sarabandi, "Microwave remote sensing of land," *Radio Sci. Bull.*, vol. 308, no. 308, pp. 30–48, 2004.

[28] T. W. Brakke, E. T. Kanemasu, and J. L. Steiner, "Microwave radar response to canopy moisture, leaf-area index, and dry weight of Wheat, corn, and sorghum*," *Remote Sens. Environ.*, vol. 11, no. 3., pp. 207–220, 1981.

[29] H. U. R. Mohammed, M. Dawood, and A. V. Alejos, "Experimental detection and characterization of Brillouin precursor through loamy soil at microwave frequencies," *IEEE Trans. Geosci. Remote Sens.*, vol. 50, no. 2, pp. 436–445, 2012.

[30] B. W. Barrett, E. Dwyer, and P. Whelan, "Soil moisture retrieval from active spaceborne microwave observations: An evaluation of current techniques," *MDPI Remote Sens.*, pp. 210–242, 2009.

[31] P. Hoekstra and A. Delaney, "Dielectric properties of soils at UHF and microwave frequencies," *J. Geophys. Res.*, vol. 79, no. 11, pp. 1699–1708, 1974.

[32] E. T. Engman, "Applications of microwave remote sensing of soil moisture for water resources and agriculture," *Remote Sens. Environ.*, vol. 226, pp. 213–226, 1991.

[33] M. C. Dobson and F. T. Ulaby, "Active microwave soil moisture research," *IEEE Trans. Geosci. Remote Sens.*, vol. GE-24, no. 1, pp. 23–36, 1986.

[34] J. P. Walker, P. R. Houser, and G. R. Willgoose, "Active microwave remote sensing for soil moisture measurement: a fi eld evaluation using ERS-2," *Hydrol. Process.*, vol. 1997, pp. 1975–1997, Feb. 2004.

[35] S. R. Oza, R. P. Singh, V. K. Dadhwal, and P. S. Desai, "Large area soil moisture estimation and mapping using space-borne multi-frequency passive microwave data," *J. Indian Soc. Remote Sens.*, vol. 34, no. 4, pp. 343–350, 2006.

[36] B. W. Barrett, E. Dwyer, and P. Whelan, "Soil moisture retrieval from active spaceborne microwave observations: An evaluation of current techniques," *Remote Sens.*, vol. 1, no. 3, pp. 210–242, Sep. 2009.

[37] S. S. Panda, G. Hoogenboom, and J. O. Paz, "Remote sensing and geospatial technological applications for site-specific management of fruit and nut crops: A review," *MDPI Remote Sens.*, pp. 1973–1997, 2010.

[38] D. Tapete, F. Cigna, and D. N. M. Donoghue, "'Looting marks' in space-borne SAR imagery: Measuring rates of archaeological looting in Apamea (Syria) with TerraSAR-X Staring Spotlight," *Remote Sens. Environ.*, vol. 178, pp. 42–58, 2016.

[39] D. Kumar, "Urban objects detection from C-band synthetic aperture radar (SAR) satellite images through simulating filter properties," *Sci. Rep.*, vol. 11, no. 1, p. 6241, 2021.

[40] J. M. Delgado Blasco, G. Verstraeten, and R. F. Hanssen, "Detecting modern desert to urban transitions from space in the surroundings of the Giza World Heritage site and Greater Cairo," *J. Cult. Herit.*, vol. 23, pp. 71–78, 2017.

[41] K. B. Katsaros, P. W. Vachon, W. T. Liu, and P. G. Black, "Microwave remote sensing of tropical cyclones from space," *J. Oceanogr.*, vol. 58, no. 1, pp. 137–151, 2002.

[42] N. Baghdadi, M. Zribi, and R. Ludwig, "Sensitivity of C-band polarimetric SAR data to the soil surface parameters over bare agriculture fields," in *2012 IEEE International Geoscience and Remote Sensing Symposium*, 2012, pp. 7039–7042.

[43] N. Baghdadi et al., "A potential use for the C-band polarimetric SAR parameters to characterize the soil surface over bare agriculture fields," *IEEE Trans. Geosci. Remote Sens.*, vol. 50, no. 10, pp. 3844–3858, 2012.

[44] I. Choudhury and M. Chakraborty, "Analysis of temporal SAR and optical data for rice mapping," *J. Indian Soc. Remote Sens.*, vol. 32, no. 4, pp. 373–385, 2004.

[45] R. Prakash, D. Singh, and N. P. Pathak, "A fusion approach to retrieve soil moisture with SAR and optical data," *IEEE J. Sel. Top. Appl. Earth Obs. Remote Sens.*, vol. 5, no. 1, pp. 196–206, 2012.

[46] Z. Qi, A. G.-O. Yeh, X. Li, S. Xian, and X. Zhang, "Monthly short-term detection of land development using RADARSAT-2 polarimetric SAR imagery," *Remote Sens. Environ.*, vol. 164, pp. 179–196, 2015.

[47] A. K. Agnihotri, A. Ohri, S. Gaur, Shivam, N. Das, and S. Mishra, "Flood inundation mapping and monitoring using SAR data and its impact on Ramganga River in Ganga basin," *Environ. Monit. Assess.*, vol. 191, no. 12, p. 760, 2019.

[48] S. Plank and S. Martinis, "Combined analysis of polarimetric SAR data and optical imagery for rapid landslide mapping in vegetated areas," in *EGU General Assembly Conference Abstracts*, 2020, p. 1301.

[49] A. Tripathi, S. Maithani, and S. Kumar, "Minimization of the ambiguity of merging of urban builtup and fallow land features by generating 'C2' covariance matrix using spaceborne bistatic dual pol SAR data," *IEEE XPLORE*, Mar. 2018.

[50] U. G. Sefercik, "Productivity of TerraSAR-X 3D data in urban areas: A case study in trento," *Eur. J. Remote Sens.*, vol. 46, no. 1, pp. 597–612, 2013.

[51] K. S. Tomar, S. Kumar, and V. A. Tolpekin, "Evaluation of hybrid polarimetric decomposition techniques for forest biomass estimation," *IEEE J. Sel. Top. Appl. Earth Obs. Remote Sens.*, vol. 12, no. 10, pp. 3712–3718, 2019.

[52] B. R. Parida and S. P. Mandal, "Polarimetric decomposition methods for LULC mapping using ALOS L-band PolSAR data in Western parts of Mizoram, Northeast India," *SN Appl. Sci.*, vol. 2, no. 6, p. 1049, 2020.

[53] V. Turkar, "Applying coherent and incoherent target decomposition techniques to polarimetric SAR data," pp. 23–29, 2011.

[54] G. G. Ponnurangam and Y. S. Rao, "The application of compact polarimetric decomposition algorithms to L-band PolSAR data in agricultural areas," *Int. J. Remote Sens.*, vol. 39, no. 22, pp. 8337–8360, Nov. 2018.

[55] H. Dong, "Gaofen-3 PolSAR image classification via XGBoost and polarimetric spatial information," *Sensors (Basel)*, vol. 18, no. 2, pp. 1–20, Feb. 2018.

[56] A. Mosavi, P. Ozturk, and K. Chau, "Flood prediction using machine learning models: Literature review," *Water*, vol. 10, no. 11, 2018.

[57] A. Tripathi, S. Kumar, and S. Maithani, "Spaceborne bistatic polarimetric SAR for scattering analysis and classification of man-made and natural features," in *2018 3rd International Conference on Microwave and Photonics, ICMAP 2018*, Jan. 2018.

[58] S. Mohanty, G. Singh, and Y. Yamaguchi, "Faraday rotation correction and total electron content estimation using ALOS-2/PALSAR-2 full polarimetric SAR data," in *2016 IEEE International Geoscience and Remote Sensing Symposium (IGARSS)*, 2016, pp. 4753–4756.

[59] A. Dehni and M. Lounis, "Remote sensing techniques for salt affected soil mapping: Application to the Oran region of Algeria," *Procedia Eng.*, vol. 33, pp. 188–198, 2012.

[60] J. Jung, D. Kim, S. Member, M. Lavalle, and S. Yun, "Coherent change detection using InSAR temporal decorrelation model: A case study for volcanic ash detection," *IEEE Trans. Geosci. Remote Sens.*, vol. 54, no. 10, pp. 5765–5775, 2016.

[61] U. Khati, G. Singh, and L. Ferro-famil, "Analysis of seasonal effects on forest parameter estimation of Indian deciduous forest using TerraSAR-X PolInSAR acquisitions," *Remote Sens. Environ.*, vol. 199, pp. 265–276, 2017.

[62] Z. Fu, B. L. Golden, S. Lele, S. Raghavan, and E. A. Wasil, "A genetic algorithm-based approach for building accurate decision trees," *INFORMS J. Comput.*, vol. 15, no. 1, pp. 3–22, Feb. 2003.

[63] A. K. Srivastava and S. Singh, "Citrus decline: Soil fertility and plant nutrition," *J. Plant Nutr.*, vol. 32, no. 2, pp. 197–245, Feb. 2009.

[64] X. Zhou, N.-B. Chang, and S. Li, "Applications of SAR Interferometry in Earth and Environmental Science Research," *Sensors*, vol. 9, no. 3, pp. 1876–1912, 2009.

[65] R. Dwivedi, A. B. Narayan, A. Tiwari, O. Dikshit, and A. K. Singh, "Multi-temporal SAR interferometry for landslide monitoring," *Int. Arch. Photogramm. Remote Sens. Spat. Inf. Sci. – ISPRS Arch.*, vol. 41, pp. 55–58, Jul. 2016.

[66] H. W. Chung, C. C. Liu, I. F. Cheng, Y. R. Lee, and M. C. Shieh, "Rapid response to a typhoon-induced flood with an SAR-derived map of inundated areas: Case study and validation," *Remote Sens.*, vol. 7, no. 9, pp. 11954–11973, 2015.

[67] B. Yekkehkhany, S. Homayouni, H. McNairn, and A. Safari, "Multi-temporal full polarimetry L-band SAR data classification for agriculture land cover mapping," in *2014 IEEE Geoscience and Remote Sensing Symposium*, 2014, pp. 2770–2773.

[68] J. M. Lopez-Sanchez and J. D. Ballester-Berman, "Potentials of polarimetric SAR interferometry for agriculture monitoring," *Radio Science*, vol. 44, no. 02. pp. 1–20, 2009.

[69] C. Kuenzer, A. Bluemel, S. Gebhardt, T. V. Quoc, and S. Dech, "Remote sensing of mangrove ecosystems: A review," *Remote Sens.*, vol. 3, no. 5, pp. 878–928, 2011.

[70] D. K. Sahu and M. P. Parsai, "Different image fusion techniques – a critical review," *Int. J. Mod. Eng. Res. Technol.*, vol. 2, pp. 4298–4301, 2012.

[71] S. K. Pal, T. J. Majumdar, and A. K. Bhattacharya, "ERS-2 SAR and IRS-1C LISS III data fusion: A PCA approach to improve remote sensing based geological interpretation," *ISPRS J. Photogramm. Remote Sens.*, vol. 61, pp. 281–297, 2007.

[72] B. A. K. Prusty, R. Chandra, and P. A. Azeez, "Temporal variation and distribution of selected alkali and alkaline earth metals in the sediment of A monsoonal wetland in India," *Fresenius Environ. Bull.*, vol. 18, no. 6, pp. 917–927, 2009.

[73] A. S. Yommy, R. Liu, S. O. Onuh, and A. C. Ikechukwu, "SAR image despeckling and compression using K-nearest neighbour based lee filter and wavelet," in *2015 8th International Congress on Image and Signal Processing (CISP)*, 2015, pp. 158–167.

[74] T. K. Jakka, Y. M. Reddy, and B. P. Rao, "GWDWT-FCM: Change detection in SAR images using adaptive discrete wavelet transform with fuzzy C-mean clustering," *J. Indian Soc. Remote Sens.*, vol. 47, no. 3, pp. 379–390, 2019.

[75] M. Acharyya, R. K. De, and M. K. Kundu, "Segmentation of remotely sensed images using wavelet features and their evaluation in soft computing framework," *IEEE Trans. Geosci. Remote Sens.*, vol. 41, no. 12, pp. 2900–2905, 2003.

[76] J. Engel, "A simple wavelet approach to nonparametric regression from recursive partitioning schemes," *J. Multivar. Anal.*, vol. 49, no. 2, pp. 242–254, 1994.

[77] A. B. McBratney, M. L. Mendonça Santos, and B. Minasny, "On digital soil mapping," *Geoderma*, vol. 117, no. 1, pp. 3–52, 2003.

[78] G. I. Metternicht and J. A. Zinck, "Remote sensing of soil salinity: potentials and constraints," *Remote Sens. Environ.*, vol. 85, pp. 1–20, 2003.

[79] R. J. Dekker, "Speckle filtering in satellite SAR change detection imagery," *Int. J. Remote Sens.*, vol. 19, no. 6, pp. 1133–1146, Jan. 1998.

[80] D. Devapal, S. S. Kumar, and C. Jojy, "A novel approach of despeckling SAR images using nonlocal means filtering," *J. Indian Soc. Remote Sens.*, vol. 45, no. 3, pp. 443–450, 2017.

[81] C. S. Hsieh, T. Y. Shih, J. C. Hu, H. Tung, M. H. Huang, and J. Angelier, "Using differential SAR interferometry to map land subsidence: A case study in the Pingtung Plain of SW Taiwan," *Nat. Hazards*, vol. 58, no. 3, pp. 1311–1332, 2011.

[82] A. Routray, U. C. Mohanty, K. K. Osuri, S. C. Kar, and D. Niyogi, "Impact of satellite radiance data on simulations of Bay of Bengal tropical cyclones using the WRF-3DVAR modeling system," *IEEE Trans. Geosci. Remote Sens.*, vol. 54, no. 4. Pp. 2285–2303, 2016.

[83] C. Surussavadee and W. Wu, "Evaluation of WRF planetary boundary layer schemes for high-resolution wind simulations in Northeastern Thailand," in *2015 IEEE International Geoscience and Remote Sensing Symposium (IGARSS)*, 2015, pp. 3949–3952.

[84] F. Chen, N. Masini, J. Liu, J. You, and R. Lasaponara, "Multi-frequency satellite radar imaging of cultural heritage: The case studies of the Yumen Frontier Pass and Niya ruins in the western regions of the Silk Road corridor," *Int. J. Digit. Earth*, vol. 9, no. 12, pp. 1224–1241, 2016.

[85] M. Hansen, R. Dubayah, and R. Defries, "Classification trees: An alternative to traditional land cover classifiers," *Int. J. Remote Sens.*, vol. 17, no. 5, pp. 1075–1081, Mar. 1996.

[86] E. Adam, O. Mutanga, J. Odindi, and E. M. Abdel-Rahman, "Land-use/cover classification in a heterogeneous coastal landscape using RapidEye imagery: evaluating the performance of random forest and support vector machines classifiers," *Int. J. Remote Sens.*, vol. 35, no. 10, pp. 3440–3458, May 2014.

[87] S. Singha and R. Ressel, "Arctic Sea ice characterization using RISAT-1 compact-pol SAR Imagery and feature evaluation: A case study over northeast Greenland," *IEEE J. Sel. Top. Appl. Earth Obs. Remote Sens.*, vol. 10, no. 8, pp. 3504–3514, 2017.

[88] V. Turkar and Y. S. Rao, "Applying coherent and incoherent target decomposition techniques to polarimetric SAR data," pp. 23–29, 2011.

[89] S. Abdikan, F. B. Sanli, M. Ustuner, and F. Calò, "Land cover mapping using sentinel-1 SAR data," *Int. Arch. Photogramm. Remote Sens. Spat. Inf. Sci. – ISPRS Arch.*, vol. 41, pp. 757–761, Jul. 2016.

[90] A. S. Yommy, R. Liu, and A. S. Wu, "SAR image despeckling using refined Lee filter," in *2015 7th International Conference on Intelligent Human-Machine Systems and Cybernetics*, 2015, vol. 2, pp. 260–265.

[91] M. Ramya and S. Kumar, "Feature extraction using multi-temporal fully polarimetric SAR data," in *Proc.SPIE*, 2016, vol. 9877.

[92] S. Saif, U. Kothyari, and A. Manoj, "ANN-based soil moisture retrieval over bare and vegetated areas using ERS-2 SAR data," *J. Hydrol. Eng.*, vol. 13, no. 6, pp. 461–475, Jun. 2008.

[93] H. Mcnairn, C. Champagne, J. Shang, D. Holmstrom, and G. Reichert, "ISPRS journal of photogrammetry and remote sensing integration of optical and synthetic aperture radar (SAR) imagery for delivering operational annual crop inventories," *ISPRS J. Photogramm. Remote Sens.*, vol. 64, no. 5, pp. 434–449, 2009.

[94] R. Grimm, T. Behrens, M. Märker, and H. Elsenbeer, "Soil organic carbon concentrations and stocks on Barro Colorado Island – digital soil mapping using random forests analysis," *Geoderma*, vol. 146, no. 1, pp. 102–113, 2008.

[95] W. S. Lee, V. Alchanatis, C. Yang, M. Hirafuji, D. Moshou, and C. Li, "Sensing technologies for precision specialty crop production," *Comput. Electron. Agric.*, vol. 74, no. 1, pp. 2–33, 2010.

[96] T. Blaschke, "ISPRS journal of photogrammetry and remote sensing object based image analysis for remote sensing," *ISPRS J. Photogramm. Remote Sens.*, vol. 65, no. 1, pp. 2–16, 2010.

7 Polarimetric SAR Descriptors for Rice Monitoring

Subhadip Dey, Lucio Mascolo, Avik Bhattacharya, and Juan M. Lopez-Sanchez

CONTENTS

7.1 INTRODUCTION

Agronomic management of rice and its yield is highly sensitive to accurate spatio-temporal information about plant growth. Moreover, the time of rice transplantation strongly determines the grain yield. Hence, it is essential to monitor rice phenological stages over a large area. In this regard, synthetic aperture radar (SAR) data play a vital role due to their high sensitivity to the dielectric and geometrical structure of the canopy. Alongside this, the variation in the transmit frequencies of SAR provides information about different crop canopy layers and underlying soil surface [6]. Notably, according to previous studies, one could adequately capture rice phenological stages with high-frequency SAR data [7], [33], [34], [41]. However, one should also note that the SAR backscatter signal is affected by the underlying soil surface condition during early vegetative stages of crops [36] and crop bio-physical parameters and types [12], [13], [14], [28], [29], [30], [26], [27] at advanced phenological stages.

In the early works, only backscattering coefficients available at single-polarization channels were mainly used to follow the development of rice fields. In the literature, the estimation of rice phenological characteristics using polarimetric descriptors can be mainly divided into two major categories: (1) utilizing target characterization parameters and (2) utilizing model-based scattering power components. Target characterization parameters contain information about the scattering mechanism from targets and the amount of randomness associated with it. In this regard, Cloude

DOI: 10.1201/9781003204466-7

et al. [5] pioneered the radar polarimetry study by proposing a target characterization parameter $\bar{\alpha}$. The scattering entropy parameter H is utilized along with $\bar{\alpha}$ for an unsupervised clustering scheme.

Discrimination of rice phenological stages using $H / \bar{\alpha}$ plane was shown by Lopez-Sanchez et al. [22], [21]. Their study showed the importance of the temporal correlation between HH and VV and their ratio concerning the rice morphological characteristics. At the beginning of the cultivation period, a dense data cluster was observed in medium entropy and low alpha region due to the fields' sparse vegetation. However, at the advanced phenological stages, the cluster density shifted towards the region of high entropy and high alpha in the $H / \bar{\alpha}$ plane.

Furthermore, Lopez-Sanchez et al. [23] utilized the dominant scattering-type information (α_1) instead of $\bar{\alpha}$. This study analyzes the temporal characteristics of α_1 and entropy with the development of rice phenological stages. It was observed from the study that the values of α_1 and entropy were low at the initial stage of rice, while they increased during the plant emergence stage. During the advanced vegetative stage, both parameters show the dominance of multiple scattering from the fields. In contrast, at the harvest stage, $\alpha_1 < 30°$ and the scattering entropy remained high due to the field roughness condition.

On the other hand, Praks et al. [37] proposed alternative scattering-type and randomness parameters equivalent to $\bar{\alpha}$ and H for clustering PolSAR data. These parameters were obtained from the elements of the coherency matrix. It was shown that the surface scattering fraction and the scattering diversity that are equivalent polarimetric descriptors could be utilized for classification, visualization, or interpretation. Further, Yin et al. [43] used the co-polarization ratio and their coherence to propose a new scattering-type parameter, α_B which captures various scattering mechanisms. The parameter could distinguish scattering from oriented and randomly distributed targets. In the same study, a new $\Delta\alpha_B / \alpha_B$ plane was proposed that showed better separation capability than the $H / \bar{\alpha}$ clustering plane. It was also stated that the stability of the proposed method was better with multi-temporal SAR data.

Ratha et al. [38] proposed a roll-invariant scattering-type parameter (α_{GD}), the scattering helicity parameter (τ_{GD}), and the scattering purity parameter (P_{GD}) using a geodesic distance (GD) between two Kennaugh matrices. A new P_{GD} / α_{GD} unsupervised classification scheme is proposed that is analogous to $H / \bar{\alpha}$. However, the P_{GD} / α_{GD} clustering plane showed better performance than earlier proposed schemes. Utilizing the concept of GD, two vegetation descriptors were developed: the generalized radar vegetation index (GRVI) [39, 31] for full-pol data, and the compact-pol radar vegetation index (CpRVI) [32, 25] for compact-pol data. Further, for dual-pol SAR data, the dominant scattering component is utilized along with the degree of polarization to formulate the dual-pol radar vegetation index (DpRVI) [30]. These vegetation descriptors have shown good sensitivity with the advances in the crop phenological stages.

Erten et al. [15] investigated the interferometric SAR (InSAR) and Pol-InSAR techniques for the inversion of crop height. It was observed that the root mean square error for Pol-InSAR was much lower than the differential InSAR technique. Romero-Puig [40] studied the effect of double-bounce decorrelation on the inversion of all RVoG model parameters. In their study, the vegetation height of rice is estimated with single-pass bistatic TanDEM-X data over a rice area in Spain.

Li et al. [20] utilized the Freeman–Durden, Cloude–Pottier, and Touzi decomposition parameters to map and monitor rice crops. The study showed that the decomposition parameters enhanced the ability to monitor rice due to changes in the scattering phase center with plant maturity. The Freeman–Durden decomposition produced the highest classification accuracy (83%) for rice identification, compared to the Touzi (82%) and the Cloude–Pottier (80%) decompositions.

Lopez-Sanchez et al. [24] investigated the differential variations of the scattering power components from the Freeman–Durden decomposition with rice growth stages. Unique signatures obtained from these scattering powers at each growth stage help to identify rice phenology. However, the Freeman–Durden decomposition power components are sensitive to the orientation of targets, and the volume scattering model uses an ensemble of uniformly distributed dipoles.

Recently, a paradigm shift in the theory of polarimetric scattering power decomposition has been observed with a model-free decomposition technique proposed by Dey et al. [8]. Their decomposition technique concurrently provides target characterization parameters (θ_{FP} and τ_{FP}) and four decomposed scattering power components. Moreover, this technique does not require any a priori information about the target and provides non-negative and roll-invariant scattering power components for polarimetric SAR data.

A suitable application of the target characterization parameter θ_{FP} along with scattering entropy H is shown over rice fields by Dey et al. [10]. In this study, the changes in the scattering mechanism are shown from the initial phenological stage to the advanced phenological stage of rice. Alongside this, an unsupervised clustering scheme with 12 zones was proposed to distinguish rice phenological stages. Following this, the model-free three decomposed power components [9] were utilized to classify different rice phenological stages over an Indian test site.

This chapter elaborates the use of the descriptors from the model-free decomposition technique proposed by Dey et al. [8] for temporal rice phenology monitoring over an Indian and a Spanish test site using RADARSAT-2 full polarimetric SAR data.

7.2 METHODOLOGY

In full polarimetric (FP) synthetic aperture radar (SAR) data, the 2×2 complex Sinclair matrix (**S**) contains the complete information about a target. Particularly for far-range radar polarimetry, **S** is expressed in the backscatter alignment (BSA) convention. For the linear horizontal (H) and linear vertical (V) polarization basis, **S** is expressed as,

$$\mathbf{S} = \begin{bmatrix} S_{HH} & S_{HV} \\ S_{VH} & S_{VV} \end{bmatrix} \Rightarrow \mathbf{k} = V([\mathbf{S}]) = \frac{1}{2}\text{Tr}(\mathbf{S}\Psi) \tag{7.1}$$

where, S_{HH} is the element for H-transmit and H-received, S_{VH} is the element for H-transmit and V-received, S_{HV} is the element for V-transmit and H-received, and S_{VV} is the element for V-transmit and V-received. $V(\cdot)$ is the vectorization operator on the scattering matrix, Ψ is the group of orthogonal basis matrix, and Tr is the sum of the diagonal elements of the matrix. In the monostatic backscattering case, the reciprocity theorem constrains the scattering matrix to be symmetric, i.e., $S_{HV} = S_{VH}$.

The concept of **S** is primarily limited to elementary and stationary targets. However, many observed targets in radar remote sensing require a multivariate statistical description due to the combination of coherent speckle noise and vector scattering components from different targets. For such targets, it is essential to generate the concept of an average or dominant scattering mechanism for the classification or inversion of the data. This averaging process leads to the concept of the distributed targets, which may not be entirely explainable with **S**.

The multi-looked Hermitian positive semi-definite coherency matrix **T** is obtained from the ensembled outer product of target vector $\mathbf{k}_p$. The expression of $\mathbf{k}_p$ is obtained from the involutory Pauli spin matrices, Ψ_p.

$$\Psi_P = \left\{ \sqrt{2}\begin{bmatrix} 1 & 0 \\ 0 & 1 \end{bmatrix}, \sqrt{2}\begin{bmatrix} 1 & 0 \\ 0 & -1 \end{bmatrix}, \sqrt{2}\begin{bmatrix} 0 & 1 \\ 1 & 0 \end{bmatrix} \right\} \tag{7.2}$$

Thus, the Pauli basis vector $\mathbf{k}_p$ for monostatic case becomes

$$\mathbf{k}_p = \frac{1}{\sqrt{2}}\begin{bmatrix} S_{HH} + S_{VV} & S_{HH} - S_{VV} & 2S_{HV} \end{bmatrix}^T,$$

and the expression of $\mathbf{T}$ is

$$\mathbf{T} = \langle \mathbf{k}_p \cdot \mathbf{k}_p^{*T} \rangle = \frac{1}{2} \begin{bmatrix} \langle |S_{HH} + S_{VV}|^2 \rangle & \langle (S_{HH} + S_{VV})(S_{HH} - S_{VV})^* \rangle & 2\langle (S_{HH} + S_{VV})S_{HV}^* \rangle \\ \langle (S_{HH} + S_{VV})(S_{HH} - S_{VV})^* \rangle & \langle |S_{HH} - S_{VV}|^2 \rangle & 2\langle (S_{HH} - S_{VV})S_{HV}^* \rangle \\ 2\langle (S_{HH} + S_{VV})S_{HV}^* \rangle & 2\langle (S_{HH} - S_{VV})S_{HV}^* \rangle & 4\langle |S_{HV}|^2 \rangle \end{bmatrix}$$

$$(7.3)$$

7.2.1 THE KENNAUGH MATRIX FRAMEWORK

The information content of a 3×3 complex coherency matrix $\mathbf{T}$ can also be represented in terms of power by the 4×4 real Kennaugh matrix ($\mathbf{K}$). In general, for the coherent case, the $\mathbf{K}$ matrix can be represented in terms of $\mathbf{S}$ as,

$$\mathbf{K} = \frac{1}{2}\mathbf{A}^*(\mathbf{S} \otimes \mathbf{S}^*)\mathbf{A}^H, \quad \mathbf{A} = \begin{bmatrix} 1 & 0 & 0 & 1 \\ 1 & 0 & 0 & -1 \\ 0 & 1 & 1 & 0 \\ 0 & j & -j & 0 \end{bmatrix}, \quad (7.4)$$

where $\otimes$ is the Kronecker product, and $j = \sqrt{-1}$. However, for the incoherent case, $\mathbf{K}$ can also be represented in terms of the elements of $\mathbf{T}$ as,

$$\mathbf{K} = \begin{bmatrix} \dfrac{T_{11} + T_{22} + T_{33}}{2} & \Re(T_{12}) & \Re(T_{13}) & \Im(T_{23}) \\ \Re(T_{12}) & \dfrac{T_{11} + T_{22} - T_{33}}{2} & \Re(T_{23}) & \Im(T_{13}) \\ \Re(T_{13}) & \Re(T_{23}) & \dfrac{T_{11} - T_{22} + T_{33}}{2} & -\Im(T_{12}) \\ \Im(T_{23}) & \Im(T_{13}) & -\Im(T_{12}) & \dfrac{-T_{11} + T_{22} + T_{33}}{2} \end{bmatrix} \quad (7.5)$$

$$= \begin{bmatrix} k_{11} & k_{12} & k_{13} & k_{14} \\ k_{12} & k_{22} & k_{23} & k_{24} \\ k_{13} & k_{23} & k_{33} & k_{34} \\ k_{14} & k_{24} & k_{34} & k_{44} \end{bmatrix} \quad (7.6)$$

Each element of $\mathbf{K}$ can be directly related to different physical characteristics of targets that can be interpreted from Huynen phenomenological theory [18]. According to this theory, the elements of $\mathbf{K}$ can be written in terms of nine parameters that are related to physical attributes of targets [19].

$$\mathbf{K} = \begin{bmatrix} A_0 + B_0 & C & H & F \\ C & A_0 + B & E & G \\ H & E & A_0 - B & D \\ F & G & D & -A_0 + B_0 \end{bmatrix} \quad (7.7)$$

where,

A_0 is the total scattered power from the regular part of a target,

B_0 is the total scattered power from the irregular part of a target,

$B_0 + B$ is the total symmetric or irregularity depolarized power,
$B_0 - B$ is the total asymmetric depolarized power,
C, D are the generator of target global and local shape, respectively,
E, F are the generator of target local twist and global twist or helicity, respectively,
G, H are the generator of target local and global coupling, respectively.

As $\mathbf{T}$ and $\mathbf{K}$ are interchangeable, the elements of $\mathbf{T}$ can be written in terms of $\mathbf{K}$ elements:

$$\mathbf{T} = \frac{1}{2}\begin{bmatrix} (k_{11} + k_{22} + k_{33} - k_{44}) & k_{12} - jk_{34} & k_{13} + jk_{24} \\ k_{12} + jk_{34} & (k_{11} + k_{22} - k_{33} + k_{44}) & k_{23} + jk_{14} \\ k_{13} - jk_{24} & k_{23} - jk_{14} & (k_{11} - k_{22} + k_{33} + k_{44}) \end{bmatrix} \tag{7.8}$$

7.2.2 Target Characterization Parameters

Utilizing the information of $\mathbf{K}$ as described in section 7.2.1, Dey et al. [9] proposed a target characterization parameter, θ_{FP}. This parameter, θ_{FP}, jointly utilizes the degree of polarization and the elements of $\mathbf{K}$. In this regard, the state of polarization of a partially polarized wave is captured by the utilization of the 3D Barakat degree of polarization [3], [4].

Barakat [4] proposed the $N-$ fold measure of his degree of polarization (also referred to as ND polarization measure) as

$$P_n(N) = \left(1 - \frac{N^n n! p_n(N)}{N^{(n)} p_1^n(N)}\right)^{1/2}; \quad n = 2,\dots,N, \tag{7.9}$$

where $N^{(n)} = N(N-1)\cdots(N-n+1)$ with $0 \le P_n \le 1$ and

$$p_1(N) = \sum \lambda_1(N) = \text{tr}(\Phi_N) \tag{7.10}$$

$$p_2(N) = \sum \lambda_1(N)\lambda_2(N) \tag{7.11}$$

$$\vdots \tag{7.12}$$

$$p_N(N) = \lambda_1(N)\lambda_2(N)\cdots\lambda_N(N) = \det(\Phi_N). \tag{7.13}$$

For $N = 3$, there are two corresponding polarization measures of Φ_3 as

$$P_3(3) = \left[1 - \frac{27 p_3(3)}{p_1^3(3)}\right]^{1/2} = \left[1 - \frac{27\det(\Phi_3)}{\text{tr}^3(\Phi_3)}\right]^{1/2}, \tag{7.14}$$

$$P_2(3) = \left[1 - \frac{3 p_2(3)}{p_1^2(3)}\right]^{1/2}. \tag{7.15}$$

where, Φ_N is the $N \times N$ coherency matrix and det and tr represent matrix determinant and trace respectively. Equation (7.14) is the so-called 3D Barakat degree of polarization (m_{FP}), whereas (7.15) represents the distance between the unpolarized state and any mixed state.

Therefore, m_{FP} from the 3×3 coherency matrix $\mathbf{T}$ for FP SAR data results:

$$m_{FP} = \sqrt{1 - \frac{27\det(\mathbf{T})}{\operatorname{tr}^3(\mathbf{T})}} \in [0,1], \tag{7.16}$$

Following this, two auxiliary parameters η_1 and η_2 are formulated as,

$$\eta_1 = \tan^{-1}\frac{k_{11} - k_{44}}{2m_{FP}k_{11}}, \quad \text{and} \quad \eta_2 = \tan^{-1}\frac{k_{11} + k_{44}}{2m_{FP}k_{11}}, \tag{7.17}$$

It may be noted that $(k_{11} - k_{44})/(2m_{FP}k_{11})$ denotes the fraction of power scattered from the regular part[1] of a target with respect to the total polarized power, and that $(k_{11} + k_{44})/(2m_{FP}k_{11})$ denotes the fraction of scattered power from the irregular part of a target with respect to the total polarized power. Thereafter, by using a simple relationship $(\tan\theta_{FP} = \tan(\eta_1 - \eta_2))$, the characterization parameter is obtained as,

$$\theta_{FP} = \tan^{-1}\frac{4m_{FP}k_{11}k_{44}}{k_{44}^2 - (1 + 4m_{FP}^2)k_{11}^2} \in [-45°, 45°], \tag{7.18}$$

In this regard, θ_{FP} is a roll-invariant quantity, i.e., the value of θ_{FP} does not vary with the orientation of target with respect to the radar line of sight. For any canonical target, $m_{FP} = 1$. Hence, for trihedral target (odd-bounce), $\theta_{FP} = 45°$, and for dihedral target (even-bounce) $\theta_{FP} = -45°$. For other standard volume targets [2, 16, 42] or diffused targets, $\theta_{FP} = 0°$.

Although θ_{FP} can characterize most of the canonical targets, it is still ambiguous between dihedral and helix targets. For both targets, $\theta_{FP} = -45°$. Helix scattering acts as the generator of circularity in the scattered wave when a deformation in the dihedral scatterer occurs. As a result, the dihedral reflection symmetry condition in the $\mathbf{T}$ of helix breaks. Therefore, helix can be represented as a combination of pure even-bounce scattering with an asymmetry part.

$$\mathbf{T}^{helix} = \frac{1}{2}\begin{bmatrix} 0 & 0 & 0 \\ 0 & 1 & \pm j \\ 0 & \mp j & 1 \end{bmatrix}.$$

Hence, a scattering asymmetry (helicity) characterization parameter, τ_{FP}, is introduced,

$$\tau_{FP} = \tan^{-1}\frac{|K_{14}|}{K_{11}} \in [0°, 45°] \tag{7.19}$$

where, $|\cdot|$ is the absolute value. For a complete symmetric target, $\tau_{FP} = 0°$, and for a complete asymmetric target, $\tau_{FP} = 45°$.

To explain the discrimination ability of τ_{FP}, we consider a mixture of dihedral and helix targets within a resolution cell. The mixture proportion is adjusted by $\lambda \in [0,1]$ and is expressed as

$$\mathbf{T}^{overall} = \lambda\mathbf{T}^{dihedral} + (1 - \lambda)\mathbf{T}^{helix}.$$

The variation of θ_{FP} and τ_{FP} for this mixture is shown in Figure 7.1. It can be observed that $\theta_{FP} = -45°$ for every values of λ. However, τ_{FP} varies with λ. This observation essentially confirms that θ_{FP} is ambiguous for discriminating helix and even-bounce scattering mechanisms, while τ_{FP} is able to distinguish them.

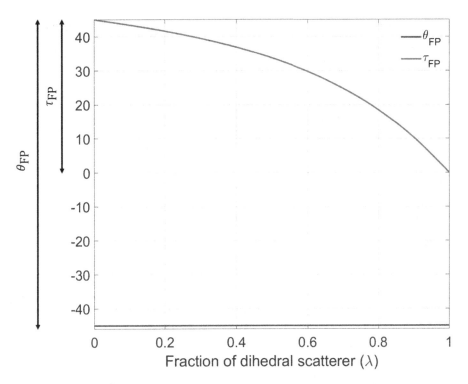

FIGURE 7.1 Variation of θ_{FP} and τ_{FP} for different proportion of dihedral in a dihedral-helix mixture.

7.2.3 SCATTERING POWER DECOMPOSITION

The information of θ_{FP} and τ_{FP} is utilized to derive the four scattering power components [8]. The helix power component P_c (7.20) is obtained by modulating the total polarized power (i.e., $2m_{FP}K_{11}$) by the scattering asymmetry parameter, τ_{FP}. The diffused scattering power component P_v (7.21) is obtained as the depolarized fraction (i.e., $1-m_{FP}$) of the total power. The residual power component P_r (7.22) is accordingly calculated, which is equal to the sum of the helix and the diffused power components subtracted from the total scattered power ($2K_{11}$). This residual power component represents the fraction of the polarized scattering power components. This polarized fractional power is then redistributed among odd (P_s (23)) and even (P_d (7.24)) power components using the geometrical factor ($1 \pm \sin 2\theta_{FP}$). This factor depends on the scattering-type parameter θ_{FP}.

$$P_c = 2m_{FP}K_{11}\sin(2\tau_{FP}), \tag{7.20}$$

$$P_v = 2(1-m_{FP})K_{11}, \tag{7.21}$$

$$P_r = 2K_{11} - (P_c + P_v)$$

$$= 2m_{FP}K_{11}(1-\sin(2\tau_{FP})), \tag{7.22}$$

$$P_s = \frac{P_r}{2}(1+\sin(2\theta_{FP})), \tag{7.23}$$

$$P_d = \frac{P_r}{2}(1-\sin(2\theta_{FP})). \tag{7.24}$$

Let us now characterize m_{FP}, θ_{FP}, and τ_{FP} along with the four scattering power components for a few particular scattering scenarios:

For a pure diffused scattering-type, i.e., when $m_{FP} = 0$, then $P_v = 2K_{11} = \text{Span}$, and $P_s = P_d = P_c = 0$.

For polarized scattering types, i.e., when $m_{FP} = 1$, two cases arise:

1. If $\theta_{FP} = 45°$, and $\tau_{FP} = 0°$, then $P_s = 2K_{11} = \text{Span}$, and $P_d = P_v = P_c = 0$.
2. If $\theta_{FP} = -45°$, and:
   a. $\tau_{FP} = 0°$, then $P_d = 2K_{11} = \text{Span}$, and $P_s = P_v = P_c = 0$.
   b. $\tau_{FP} = 45°$, then $P_c = 2K_{11} = \text{Span}$, and $P_d = P_v = P_s = 0$. In this case, the scattering is purely asymmetric.

For $\theta_{FP} = 0°$, i.e., when either $m_{FP} = 0$, or $K_{44} = 0$, then,

1. If $m_{FP} = 0$, and if $\tau_{FP} = 0°$, then $P_s = P_d = P_c = 0$, and $P_v = 2K_{11} = \text{Span}$.
2. If $K_{44} = 0$, and if $\tau_{FP} = 0°$, then $P_c = 0$ with $P_s = P_d$, and P_v varies with $m_{FP} \in [0,1]$.

It should be noted that the characterization parameters θ_{FP} and τ_{FP}, and the scattering power components P_d, P_s, P_v, and P_c, are non-negative and roll-invariant.

7.3   STUDY AREA AND SATELLITE DATA

This study considers rice crops over two different test sites from India and Spain. In the following sections, we provide descriptions of the test sites, respectively.

7.3.1   INDIAN TEST SITE

The study area is located near the city of Vijayawada in the state of Andhra Pradesh, India (16°24′6.2″N,8°41′2.4″E) as shown in Figure 7.2 [11]. The climatic zone varies from sub-humid to humid within the study area, with primarily clayey soil texture in this region. The spatial coverage of this test site is $\approx 25\text{km} \times 25\text{km}$. Rice is a major crop grown in this area. Depending on the variety and cultivation practices, the sowing period of rice varies from mid-June to mid-July. However, in general, cultivation starts after the pre-monsoon rain, and rice is harvested during mid-December. The average field size is $\approx 60\text{m} \times 60\text{m}$. In each field, two sampling locations were chosen for in-situ measurements. Information about the crop growth stage, management practices, and bio-physical parameters was noted during a field campaign conducted from June to December 2019.

7.3.1.1   Satellite Dataset and Pre-Processing

Fine quad wide (FQW) mode RADARSAT-2 images were acquired from July to November 2019 over the test site, as shown in Table 7.1. These images were multi-looked by a factor of 2×3 pixels in the range and azimuth directions, respectively, to generate $\approx 15\text{m} \times 15\text{m}$ square pixel images. During rice cultivation, typically, many adjacent fields are cultivated together. Therefore, the region appears homogeneously cropped, even though each parcel's size is small. Hence, a 3×3 boxcar filter [19] was applied to reduce speckle. Dual co-polarimetric (DP) SAR data (HH-VV) were extracted from the FP data and are subsequently co-registered with a root mean square error (RMSE) $\leq 0.25\text{m}$.

7.3.2   SPANISH TEST SITE

The test site consists of an area of $30\text{km} \times 30\text{km}$ in the mouth of the Guadalquivir River, Seville, in the southwest of Spain, where rice is cultivated annually from approximately May to October

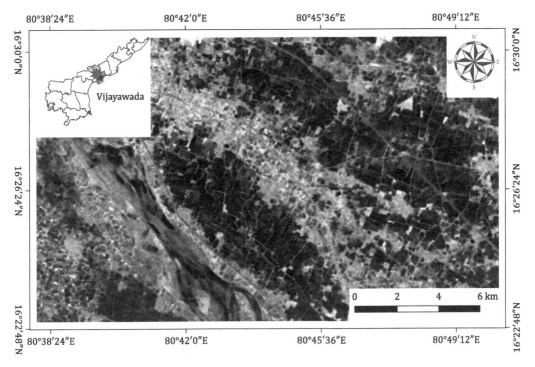

FIGURE 7.2 Pauli RGB image acquired on 24 July 2019 over the JECAM test site over Vijayawada, India.

TABLE 7.1
RADARSAT-2 Data Acquired for the Indian Test Site

Acquisition date	Beam mode	Incidence angle range (°)	Orbit	Azimuth (m) × range (m)
6 June 2019		33.73–36.65		
24 July 2019		33.73–36.65		
17 August 2019		33.73–36.65		
10 September 2019	FQ15W	33.73–36.65	Ascending	4.73 × 5.11
4 October 2019		33.73–36.64		
21 November 2019		33.73–36.64		

(Figure 7.3). The geographic location of this area is 37°2′29.45″N,6°2′57.24″W. This area has a Mediterranean climatic zone, with varying soil types of cambisol, cromic luvisol, and rendsic leptosol [17]. The areal coverage of this test site is ≈ 16×8km². The average size of each field is ≈ 300×300m². Information about the crop types was recorded during field campaigns carried out from May to October 2014.

7.3.2.1 Satellite Dataset and Pre-Processing

Over Seville, Spain, fine quad wide (FQW) mode RADARSAT-2 images were acquired at two different incidence angles from May to September 2014, as shown in Table 7.2. For FQ8W, the incidence angle range is 26.3° to 29.3°, while for FQ19W, the incidence angle range is 37.7° to 40.4°. These images were multi-looked by a factor of 9×9 pixels in the range and azimuth directions, respectively, to generate ≈ 5m × 5m square pixel images. These images are further co-registered with

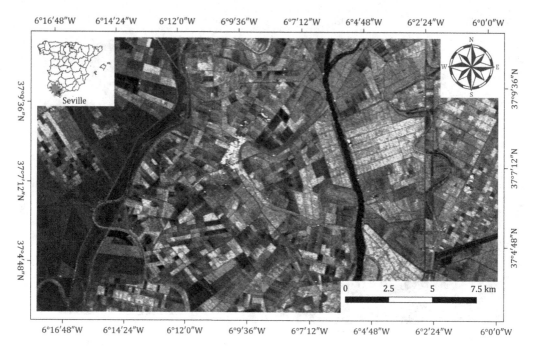

FIGURE 7.3 Pauli RGB image acquired on 9 July 2014 over Seville, Spain

TABLE 7.2
RADARSAT-2 Data Acquired for the Spanish Test Site

Acquisition date	Beam mode	Incidence angle range (°)	Orbit	Azimuth (m) × range (m)
22 May 2014	FQ8W	26.30–29.30	Ascending	5 × 5
15 Jun 2014				
9 Jul 2014				
2 Aug 2014				
26 Aug 2014				
19 Sep 2014				
5 Jun 2014	FQ19W	37.70–40.40	Ascending	5 × 5
29 Jun 2014				
23 Jul 2014				
16 Aug 2014				
9 Sep 2014				

root mean square error (RMSE) ≤ 0.12m. As discussed earlier, the adjacent fields are also cultivated with rice, making the area appear homogeneous.

7.3.3 In-Situ Measurement Procedures and Rice Morphology

In this study, over an Indian test site, two sampling locations at each field were selected for soil moisture measurements. The arrangement of these locations was set at two parallel transects along the row direction. In this regard, the separation between transects was set to ≈ 40m. For soil moisture measurement, Theta-probes were used. Over the area, the soil remains saturated throughout the rice-growing season due to either rainfall or irrigation. Similar to soil moisture, vegetation parameter

TABLE 7.3
Description of Rice Morphology at Different Growth Stages Over Indian Test Site

Date	Growth stage	Description
6 June 2019	Bare field (BF)	Complete soil layer is exposed with no standing crop
24 July 2019	Early tillering (ET)	1 to 3 tillers detectable
17 August 2019	Advanced tillering (AT)	Maximum number of tillers detectable
10 September 2019	Booting (B)	Flag leaf sheath swollen
4 October 2019	Flowering (F)	Anthers visible on most spikelets
21 November 2019	Maturity (M)	Grain becomes hard and plants appear yellowish

TABLE 7.4
Statistics (mean ± standard deviation) of Bio-Physical and Soil Parameters at Different Phenology Stages of Rice Over Indian Test Site

Date	PH (cm)	PAI (m^2 m^{-2})	SM (%)	Growth stage
6 June 2019	NA	NA	31.92 ± 6.10	Bare field
24 July 2019	22.30 ± 3.21	0.60 ± 0.10	Saturated	Early tillering
17 August 2019	49.26 ± 7.12	1.86 ± 0.36	Saturated	Advanced tillering
10 September 2019	96.16 ± 8.76	6.03 ± 0.80	Saturated	Booting
4 October 2019	98.93 ± 4.76	6.16 ± 0.13	44.60 ± 0.72	Flowering
21 November 2019	99.32 ± 1.82	5.86 ± 0.62	41.16 ± 8.04	Maturity

Note: Here, PH: plant height, PAI: plant area index, SM: soil moisture and NA: no measurements available.

measurements were conducted at two points in each field. At each point, the plant area index (PAI), plant height, and phenology were measured using non-destructive methods. Hemispherical digital photography was used to determine PAI. For this measurement, ten photos at each sample point along two transects with a separation of 2 m were collected by a wide-angle lens mounted on a digital camera. All photos were post-processed using the CanEYE software (www6.paca.inra.fr/can-eye), which calculates an estimate of the PAI. Table 7.3 shows the distinct morphological stages of rice, while Table 7.4 shows the statistics of rice bio-physical and soil parameters.

Over the Spanish test site, six fields were monitored during the 2014 ground campaign. In this case, rice phenology described by the BBCH (form *Biologische Bundesanstalt, Bundessortenamt und CHemische Industrie*) scale, measured throughout the season. This scale subdivides rice phenology into principal stages, from germination to senescence, as shown in Table 7.5. Each of these stages is subdivided into secondary stages, resulting in codes ranging from 0 to 99. For this study, we analyze one of the monitored fields, named "Colinas". The BBCH stages of these fields at the RADARSAT-2 acquisition dates are listed in Table 7.6 and Table 7.7, for the beam FQ8W and FQ19W, respectively.

7.3.3.1 Morphological Characteristics of Rice Across Its Phenological Stages

The morphological developments of rice across its various phenological stages are shown in Figure 7.4. Rice growth stages consist of mainly three phases: vegetative, reproductive, and maturity. Over the test sites, rice cultivation majorly depends on rainfall events. The growing period of rice primarily relies on the variety of rice. However, in general, the period varies from 100 days to 140 days. Short-duration cultivation lasts for 100–120 days, medium-duration for 120–140 days,

TABLE 7.5
BBCH Scale for Rice

Principal stage	BBCH
Germination	00–09
Leaf development	10–19
Tillering	21–29
Stem elongation	30–39
Booting	41–49
Inflorescence emergence	51–59
Flowering	61–69
Fruit development	71–77
Ripening	83–89
Senescence	92–99

TABLE 7.6
BBCH Stages for Field Colinas at the RADARSAT-2 Dates (Beam FQ8W)

Acquisition date	BBCH stage
22 May 2014	3
15 Jun 2014	18
9 Jul 2014	25
2 Aug 2014	32
26 Aug 2014	45
19 Sep 2014	69

TABLE 7.7
BBCH Stages for Field Colinas at the RADARSAT-2 Dates (Beam FQ19W)

Acquisition date	BBCH stage
5 Jun 2014	11
29 Jun 2014	22
23 Jul 2014	29
16 Aug 2014	37
9 Sep 2014	58

and long-duration for almost 160 days [1]. The vegetative stage of rice starts with the germination of the seed and completes with fully developed plants. In this period, the number of tillers increases, and stems elongate. The germination phase consists of seed and radicle development. During booting, the thickening of stem and flag leaf development is observed. Also, due to the vertical structure of plants, rice is known as an erectophile plant. Subsequently, during panicle emergence and heading stages, significant leaf inclination is visible. The fruit development stage starts with the appearance of grain. Later, these grains become milky, and the anther development starts. Subsequently, the dough stage followed by the ripening condition of rice leads to the final harvest.

FIGURE 7.4 Crop morphological characteristics across phenological stages.

During the advanced ripening, rice appears to be dry due to the drop in the crop-water content. The fully grown structure of rice becomes random as grains become heavy, while the number of leaves decreases [35].

7.4 RESULTS AND DISCUSSION

In this section, the behavior of the target characterization parameters and decomposed scattered powers, derived from the RADARSAT-2 data collected over the Indian and Spanish test sites, is analyzed as a function of rice phenology.

7.4.1 TEMPORAL ANALYSIS OVER TWO TEST SITES AND DIFFERENT INCIDENCE ANGLE

The temporal analysis of θ_{FP}, τ_{FP}, P_d, P_s, P_v, and P_c is shown for the rice fields in Vijayawada and Seville. In this regard, since the Seville dataset consists of two different beams collected at two different incidence angles (see Table 7.2), a multi-angle analysis is carried out.

Regarding the Vijayawada dataset, the center incidence angle is $\approx 35°$. The temporal variations of θ_{FP} and τ_{FP} are shown in Figure 7.5, and the temporal variations of P_d, P_s, P_v, and P_c are shown in Figure 7.6. One can observe that the median of θ_{FP} during 6 June is around 20°, indicating odd-bounce scattering from the field. During this period, most fields possess bare conditions, and hence high odd-bounce scattering power components are observed in Figure 7.6. In addition, the existence of a minor P_v component (≈ -12dB) is due to the soil surface roughness.

On 24 July, the overall roughness in the field increased due to the appearance of early tillers in the rice crop. Hence, during this time $\theta_{FP} \approx 10°$. Also, the value of P_s and P_d are similar, which indicates that the scattering from regular and irregular parts of a target is almost equal. Further decrease in the values of $\theta_{FP} \approx -5°$ is observed on 17 August, when rice achieved the advanced tillering stage. During this period, the scattering from the tillers and underlying water in the fields changed the scattering mechanism to even-bounce. As a result, dominant even-bounce scattering is observed. The multiple interactions of EM waves within rice tillers also increased due to the increased number of tillers. Hence, a slight increase in the P_v component is observed on 17 August as compared to 24 July.

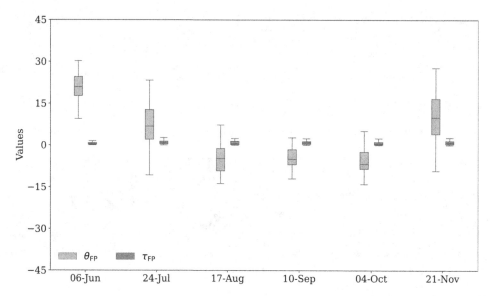

FIGURE 7.5 Temporal variations of θ_{FP} and τ_{FP} over Vizayawada, India, at center incidence angle $\approx 35°$.

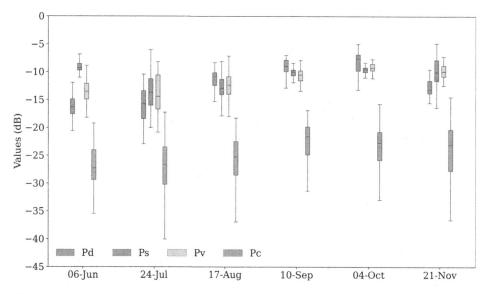

FIGURE 7.6 Temporal variations of model-free scattering power components over Vizayawada, India, at center incidence angle $\approx 35°$.

Beyond 17 August, the decrease in θ_{FP} is marginal because the overall crop height and distribution of crop canopy increase during the booting and flowering stage. Hence, an increase in the P_v component is observed on 10 September and 4 October. On 21 November, the rice fields reached the maturity stage, and the grains became firm and heavy. At this point, the crop becomes dry, whereas the moisture content in grains remains $\approx 20\%$. Due to the weight of the grains, the lodging of rice is usually visible in the fields, due to which the morphological condition becomes further complicated than the dough stage. Consequently, P_s and P_v components increased during this period. In contrast,

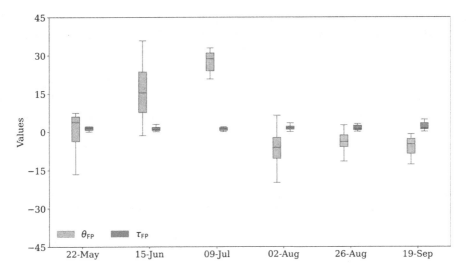

FIGURE 7.7 Temporal variations of θ_{FP} and τ_{FP} over the field Colinas, Seville, Spain, at center incidence angle ~28° (FQ8W).

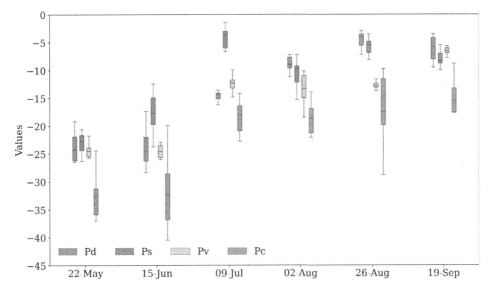

FIGURE 7.8 Temporal variations of model-free scattering power components over the field Colinas, Seville, Spain, at center incidence angle ~28° (FQ8W).

the changes in τ_{FP} are marginal throughout the phenological cycle of rice but hold a unique pattern. Also, the P_c component is much lower than other scattering power components.

Regarding the Seville dataset, Figure 7.7 and Figure 7.8 show the temporal evolution of θ_{FP} and τ_{FP} (P_d, P_s, P_v, and P_c) for the field Colinas at: ~28° incidence angle.

Also in this case, τ_{FP} is stable around 0 for the whole growing cycle. Regarding the other parameters, on 22 May the field is completely flooded, being at stage BBCH 3 (see Table 7.6). Hence, since the total backscattered power from the water layer is very low, the median value of θ_{FP} is ~5°, while P_d, P_s, and P_v (P_c) are around −24dB (−33dB). On 15 June, when the field is at BBCH 18, while

P_d, P_v, and P_c are almost unchanged, while θ_{FP} is : 15°, which leads to an increase in P_s of about 7dB. Although some plantselements (i.e., leaves) are present in the field, a non-negligible odd-bounce scattering is observed, driven by the wind-induced roughness on the underlying water layer. Then, on 9 July, although the field is in the middle of tillering (BBCH 25), odd-bounce dominates the radar response, with θ_{FP} (P_s) being around 30° (−5dB). Nonetheless, P_d, P_v, and P_c increased substantially of about 10dB, 12dB, and 20dB, respectively. This denotes that, at this stage, the double-bounce between the water and the tillers, the volume scattering from the tillers, and, finally, asymmetric scattering also contribute to the total received power.

This situation changes on 2 August, when the field is at stage BBCH 32 (early stem elongation). Here, $\theta_{FP} \approx -7°$ which, along with $\tau_{FP} \approx 0°$, indicates that double-bounce dominates. Accordingly, P_d (≈ -9dB) is slightly larger than P_s. Regarding P_v and P_c, they are more or less unchanged with respect to the previous acquisition. On 26 August, the field is at BBCH 45. Regarding θ_{FP}, it is $\sim -3°$, while both P_d and P_s increase about 5dB, with P_d being still larger than P_s. Such an increase is not observed for P_v, which is still at ~ -12dB. This is because plants are mainly vertical at this stage. Hence, the oriented volume scattering due to the vertical stems dominates over the diffuse scattering. Finally, on 19 September, when plants approach the maturation phase (BBCH 69), θ_{FP} is still around −3°, while, driven by the development in the upper part of the canopy, P_v increases ~ 7dB, being similar to P_d and P_s (which are more or less unchanged). Regarding P_c, its median value is stable at ~ -15dB at the last two acquisitions.

We now turn to analyze, for the same rice field, the behavior of these parameters extracted from the images collected at an incidence angle $\sim 39°$. The evolution of θ_{FP} and τ_{FP} is shown in Figure 7.9, while P_s, P_d, P_v, and P_c are shown in Figure 7.10. On 5 June, the field is at stage BBCH 11 (beginning of leaf development; see Table 7.7), for which the contribution from the underlaying water dominates, with $\theta_{FP} \approx 16°$ and $P_s \approx -17$dB. Regarding P_d and P_v (P_c), their median value is around −23dB (−30dB). Then, on 29 June, plants are at the early tillering stage (BBCH 22). Here, a large variation is observed in θ_{FP}, with its median value being around −14°. This is due to the double-bounce between the water and the first tillers, for which P_d, which is ~ -19dB, is slightly larger than P_s. Note that this is not observed in the image collected on 9 July at $\sim 28°$ incidence angle, when plants are at BBCH 25. Hence, as expected, such a large incidence angle variation allows observing a different scattering mechanism at approximately the same phenological stage. Regarding P_v and P_c, they are more or less unchanged. The dominant double-bounce is even more noticeable on 23 July, when the field has the maximum tillers (BBCH 29). In this case, θ_{FP} is much narrower, around −14°, with P_d (≈ -9dB) being above P_s (≈ -12dB). P_v increases significantly of ~ 9dB, as a consequence of the large amount of tillers, while P_c increases up to −17dB. Then, at BBCH 37 on 16 August, oriented scattering from the elongated vertical stems is in place, for which θ_{FP} approaches $\sim -4°$, while P_d and P_s increase about 3.5dB and 5dB, respectively. Accordingly, P_v and P_c remain approximately stable at −14dB and −17dB, respectively. Finally, on 9 September, plants are in the middle of the maturation phase (BBCH 58), for which θ_{FP} is around −4°; P_d and P_s are almost equal (≈ -7dB); $P_v \approx -10$dB ($P_c \approx -14$dB).

7.4.2 RICE PHENOLOGY CLASSIFICATION

This section shows the classification of rice phenological stages using model-free scattering power components, P_d, P_s, P_v, and P_c. The phenology classification using random forest (RF) classifier is shown in Figure 7.11. In this study, the number of trees from RF is limited to 600 as the out-of-box (OOB) error rate is minimum in this configuration. The quantitative measures in terms of user's accuracy (UA) and producer's accuracy (PA) are shown in Table 7.8. Alongside this, the global measures from Table 7.8 are aggregated in Table 7.9.

It can be seen from Table 7.8 that PA is 100% during bare field condition. This high PA essentially indicates that all the pixels of BF are correctly classified as BF. During BF, the surface roughness

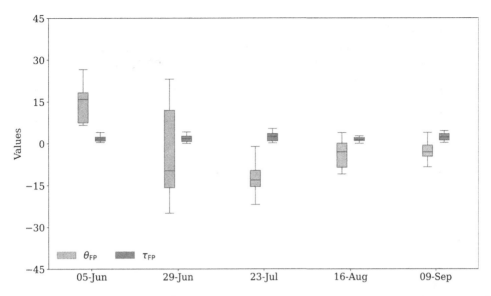

FIGURE 7.9 Temporal variations of θ_{FP} and τ_{FP} over Colinas, Seville, Spain, at center incidence angle ~ 39°
(FQ19W).

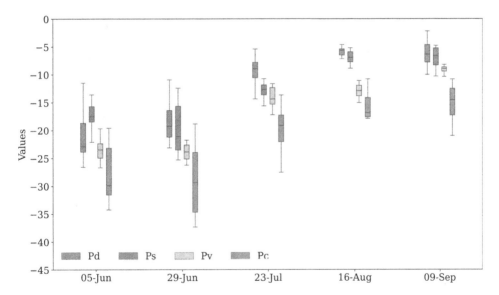

FIGURE 7.10 Temporal variations of model-free scattering power components over Colinas, Seville, Spain,
at center incidence angle ~ 39° (FQ19W).

remains low, and hence high P_s power and low P_c power make the scattering pattern unique from the
rest of the phenological stages. On the other hand, UA during BF is 93.01%. The high value of UA
is due to the misclassification of other phenological stages as BF for rice crops.

During the early tillering (ET) stage, PA drops to 88.14. One of the important causes of this drop
is the similarity of scattering characteristics with the advanced tillering (AT) stage. A similarity
among P_d, P_s, and P_v values can also be seen in Figure 7.6. Moreover, the increased variance during
the ET stage might also be responsible for such confusion with the AT stage. Due to this reason,
many AT pixels are classified as ET pixels, which increases the UA at the ET stage.

TABLE 7.8
Producer's and User's Accuracy of Phenology Stages of Rice for MF4CF Decomposed Power Components Using A RF Classifier

Accuracies	Phenology stage					
	BF	ET	AT	B	F	M
PA (%)	100.00	88.14	86.72	84.91	97.97	100.00
UA (%)	93.01	96.26	84.92	92.38	91.37	100.00

Note: BF: bare field, ET: early tillering, AT: advanced tillering, B: Booting, F: flowering, M: maturity, PA: producer's accuracy, UA: user's accuracy

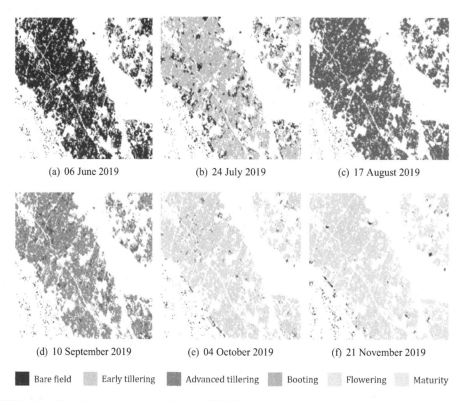

(a) 06 June 2019   (b) 24 July 2019   (c) 17 August 2019

(d) 10 September 2019   (e) 04 October 2019   (f) 21 November 2019

■ Bare field   Early tillering   ■ Advanced tillering   Booting   Flowering   Maturity

FIGURE 7.11 Variations in clusters using the MF4CF scattering power components for the rice-growing season.

Further, a decrease in PA and UA is observed at AT stage. At this stage, the PA and UA drop to 86.72% and 84.92%, respectively. As discussed earlier, AT stage has high confusion with ET. Also, a marginal similarity of AT with the booting (B) stage is observed in rice branching structure and scattering mechanism due to the stem and underlying water interaction. However, during the booting stage, the high amount of diffused scattering power P_v raises a significant difference in the signature pattern due to which both PA and UA increased to 89.91% and 92.38%, respectively.

During the flowering stage (F), the visible anthers on most spikelets change the values of $P_d, P_s,$ and P_v powers. Moreover, a change in P_c power makes the pattern different from the ET, AT, or B stages. Hence, significant increase of PA to ≈ 13% and UA to ≈ 8% is observed as compared to the

TABLE 7.9
Global Measures for MF4CF Decomposition Techniques

Overall accuracy (%)	κ	p-value
93.42	0.93	1.14×10^{-8}

B stage. During the maturity and harvest stage (M), both PA and UA are 100%. This phenomenon indicates that all pixels with stage M are correctly classified as M, which might be due to the change in scattering mechanisms due to the initiation of harvest. Also, during this time, crop lodging is observed due to the matured heavy grains. These lodged rice crops also increase the P_s power while the remaining rice structure produces a significant P_v power component.

Apart from PA and UA, the overall classification accuracy is shown in Table 7.9. One can observe that the achieved overall classification accuracy is 93.42% with high Kappa (κ) coefficient of 0.93 and low P-value of 1.14×10^{-8}. These global measures essentially confirm the promising results of rice phenology classification. The analysis-ready products of rice phenological stages at each date over the area are shown in Figure 7.11.

7.5 CONCLUSIONS

This chapter introduces model-free target characterization parameters and scattering power decomposition techniques for full polarimetric (FP) synthetic aperture radar (SAR) data. In this context, the model-free target characterization parameters are derived using the Kennaugh matrix elements and the nD Barakat degree of polarization. Further, the scattering-type parameters (θ_{FP} and τ_{FP}) are utilized as geometrical factors to derive the model-free decomposed power components (MF4CF). In this regard, full polarimetric C-band RADARSAT-2 data is used over Indian and Spanish test sites to monitor the rice phenological development. These target characterization parameters, θ_{FP} and τ_{FP} are observed to be highly sensitive to the phenological stages of rice due to the change in the scattering mechanisms based on morphological changes. Further, the potential of scattering power components for rice growth characterization is also assessed.

The results and the temporal variation of scattering power components also confirm their sensitivity to crop morphological changes. Hence, the scattering power components is used to classify different rice phenological stages. Moreover, it is essential to note that the scattering purity of the scattered electromagnetic (EM) wave changes with the advancement of rice phenology. This change in scattering purity also gets captured in the scattering power components. The overall classification accuracy for rice phenology classification is promising. The achieved overall classification accuracy is 93.42%. In addition, a high Kappa coefficient indicates the high inter-rater reliability. Alongside this, high values of producer's accuracy (PA) and user's accuracy (UA) infers the equivalent classification performance at each rice phenological stage.

One should note that the decomposition technique is model-free. Therefore, the scattering power components are unique and unambiguous. Alongside this, the target characterization parameters are roll-invariant. All the scattering power components of MF4CF are non-negative and stable (i.e., the scattering power components do not change abruptly with a small perturbation of the coherency matrix). One can also expand this method to other sites and other crop types. Future studies may also include radar images acquired at X- and L-band, such as the TerraSAR-X and ALOS-2 satellites. At high frequencies, X-band could discriminate the initial growth stages from advanced growth stages. However, at lower frequencies, less sensitivity is expected to the initial emergence of the plants, and, as such, L-band might be helpful to discriminate more advanced phenology stages of crops. These multi-frequency analyses would lead to a better understanding of crop phenology to the farming user community.

ACKNOWLEDGMENTS

RADARSAT-2 Data and Products © MacDonald, Dettwiler and Associates Ltd. (2014) – All Rights Reserved. RADARSAT-2 is an official trademark of the Canadian Space Agency. The data over the Spanish test site were provided under the SOAR Education International Initiative (SOAR-EI-5158).

The field data of the Spanish test site were kindly provided by the Federacion de Arroceros de Sevilla.

The authors would like to thank the Canadian Space Agency and MAXAR Technologies Ltd. (formerly MDA) for providing RADARSAT-2 images over Vijayawada, India, through the Joint Experiment for Crop Assessment and Monitoring (JECAM) SAR Inter-comparison Experiment network. The authors are also thankful to the Andhra Pradesh Space Application Centre (APSAC), ITE & C Department, Government of Andhra Pradesh for their support during field campaigns.

NOTE

1 A general radar target is called regular when the S_{11} and S_{22} elements of the scattering matrix $\mathbf{S}$ are equal in magnitude and phase. In this respect, a sphere is a purely symmetric and regular target, while a corner reflector is non-symmetric and irregular.

REFERENCES

[1] B Adhikari, MK Bag, MK Bhowmick, and C Kundu. Status paper on rice in West Bengal. *Rice Knowledge Management Portal*, 2011.

[2] Wentao An, Yi Cui, and Jian Yang. Three-component model-based decomposition for polarimetric SAR data. *IEEE Transactions on Geoscience and Remote Sensing*, 48(6):2732–2739, 2010.

[3] Richard Barakat. Degree of polarization and the principal idempotents of the coherency matrix. *Opt. Commun.*, 23(2):147–150, 1977.

[4] Richard Barakat. n-fold polarization measures and associated thermodynamic entropy of N partially coherent pencils of radiation. *Opt. Acta*, 30(8):1171–1182, 1983.

[5] Shane R Cloude and Eric Pottier. An entropy based classification scheme for land applications of polarimetric SAR. *IEEE Transactions on Geoscience and Remote Sensing*, 35(1):68–78, 1997.

[6] Malcolm WJ Davidson, Thuy Le Toan, Francesco Mattia, Giuseppe Satalino, Terhikki Manninen, and Maurice Borgeaud. On the characterization of agricultural soil roughness for radar remote sensing studies. *IEEE Transactions on Geoscience and Remote Sensing*, 38(2):630–640, 2000.

[7] Caleb G De Bernardis, Fernando Vicente-Guijalba, Tomas Martinez-Marin, and Juan M Lopez-Sanchez. Estimation of key dates and stages in rice crops using dual-polarization SAR time series and a particle filtering approach. *IEEE Journal of Selected Topics in Applied Earth Observations and Remote Sensing*, 8(3):1008–1018, 2015.

[8] Subhadip Dey, Avik Bhattacharya, Alejandro C Frery, Carlos López-Martnez, and Yalamanchili S Rao. A model-free four component scattering power decomposition for polarimetric SAR data. *IEEE Journal of Selected Topics in Applied Earth Observations and Remote Sensing*, 14:3887–3902, 2021.

[9] Subhadip Dey, Avik Bhattacharya, Debanshu Ratha, Dipankar Mandal, and Alejandro C Frery. Target characterization and scattering power decomposition for full and compact polarimetric sar data. *IEEE Transactions on Geoscience and Remote Sensing*, 59(5):3981–3998, 2020.

[10] Subhadip Dey, Avik Bhattacharya, Debanshu Ratha, Dipankar Mandal, Heather McNairn, Juan M Lopez-Sanchez, and YS Rao. Novel clustering schemes for full and compact polarimetric SAR data: An application for rice phenology characterization. *ISPRS Journal of Photogrammetry and Remote Sensing*, 169:135–151, 2020.

[11] Subhadip Dey, Narayanarao Bhogapurapu, Avik Bhattacharya, Dipankar Mandal, Juan M Lopez-Sanchez, Heather McNairn, and Alejandro C Frery. Rice phenology mapping using novel target characterization parameters from polarimetric sar data. *International Journal of Remote Sensing*, 42(14):5519–5543, 2021.

[12] Subhadip Dey, Ushasi Chaudhuri, Narayana Rao Bhogapurapu, Juan M Lopez-Sanchez, Biplab Banerjee, Avik Bhattacharya, Dipankar Mandal, and YS Rao. Synergistic use of tandem-x and

landsat-8 data for crop-type classification and monitoring. *IEEE Journal of Selected Topics in Applied Earth Observations and Remote Sensing*, 13:8744–8760, 2021.

[13] Subhadip Dey, Ushasi Chaudhuri, Dipankar Mandal, Avik Bhattacharya, Biplab Banerjee, and Heather McNairn. Biophynet: A regression network for joint estimation of plant area index and wet biomass from sar data. *IEEE Geoscience and Remote Sensing Letters*, 18(10): 1701–1705, 2020.

[14] Subhadip Dey, Dipankar Mandal, Laura Dingle Robertson, Biplab Banerjee, Vineet Kumar, Heather McNairn, Avik Bhattacharya, and YS Rao. In-season crop classification using elements of the Kennaugh matrix derived from polarimetric radarsat-2 SAR data. *International Journal of Applied Earth Observation and Geoinformation*, 88:102059, 2020.

[15] Esra Erten, Juan M Lopez-Sanchez, Onur Yuzugullu, and Irena Hajnsek. Retrieval of agricultural crop height from space: A comparison of SAR techniques. *Remote Sensing of Environment*, 187:130–144, 2016.

[16] Anthony Freeman and Stephen L Durden. A three-component scattering model for polarimetric SAR data. *IEEE Transactions on Geoscience and Remote Sensing*, 36(3):963–973, 1998.

[17] Juan F Gallardo. *The soils of Spain*. Springer, 2015.

[18] J R Huynen. *Phenomenological theory of radar targets*. PhD dissertation, Technical Univ., Delf, The Netherlands, 1970.

[19] Jong-Sen Lee and Eric Pottier. *Polarimetric radar imaging: from basics to applications*. CRC Press, 2017.

[20] Kun Li, Brian Brisco, Shao Yun, and Ridha Touzi. Polarimetric decomposition with RADARSAT-2 for rice mapping and monitoring. *Canadian Journal of Remote Sensing*, 38(2):169–179, 2012.

[21] JM Lopez-Sanchez, SR Cloude, and JD Ballester-Berman. Rice phenology monitoring by means of SAR polarimetry at X-band. *IEEE Transactions on Geoscience and Remote Sensing*, 50(7):2695–2709, 2012.

[22] Juan M Lopez-Sanchez, J David Ballester-Berman, and Irena Hajnsek. First results of rice monitoring practices in spain by means of time series of TerraSAR-X dual-pol images. *IEEE Journal of Selected Topics in Applied Earth Observations and Remote Sensing*, 4(2):412–422, 2011.

[23] Juan M Lopez-Sanchez, Shane R Cloude, and J David Ballester-Berman. Rice phenology monitoring by means of SAR polarimetry at X-band. *IEEE Transactions on Geoscience and Remote Sensing*, 50(7):2695–2709, 2012.

[24] Juan M Lopez-Sanchez, Fernando Vicente-Guijalba, J David Ballester-Berman, and Shane R Cloude. Polarimetric response of rice fields at C-band: Analysis and phenology retrieval. *IEEE Transactions on Geoscience and Remote Sensing*, 52(5):2977–2993, 2014.

[25] Dipankar Mandal, Avik Bhattacharya, and Yalamanchili Subrahmanyeswara Rao. Biophysical parameter retrieval using compact-pol SAR data. In *Radar Remote Sensing for Crop Biophysical Parameter Estimation*, pp. 155–176. Springer Singapore, 2021.

[26] Dipankar Mandal, Avik Bhattacharya, and Yalamanchili Subrahmanyeswara Rao. Biophysical parameter retrieval using full- and dual-pol SAR data. In *Radar Remote Sensing for Crop Biophysical Parameter Estimation*, pp. 107–153. Springer Singapore, 2021.

[27] Dipankar Mandal, Avik Bhattacharya, and Yalamanchili Subrahmanyeswara Rao. Radar vegetation indices for crop growth monitoring. In *Radar Remote Sensing for Crop Biophysical Parameter Estimation*, pp. 177–228. Springer Singapore, 2021.

[28] Dipankar Mandal, Mehdi Hosseini, Heather McNairn, Vineet Kumar, Avik Bhattacharya, YS Rao, Scott Mitchell, Laura Dingle Robertson, Andrew Davidson, and Katarzyna Dabrowska-Zielinska. An investigation of inversion methodologies to retrieve the leaf area index of corn from c-band SAR data. *International Journal of Applied Earth Observation and Geoinformation*, 82:101893, 2019.

[29] Dipankar Mandal, Vineet Kumar, Heather McNairn, Avik Bhattacharya, and YS Rao. Joint estimation of plant area index (PAI) and wet biomass in wheat and soybean from c-band polarimetric SAR data. *International Journal of Applied Earth Observation and Geoinformation*, 79:24–34, 2019.

[30] Dipankar Mandal, Vineet Kumar, Debanshu Ratha, Subhadip Dey, Avik Bhattacharya, Juan M Lopez-Sanchez, Heather McNairn, and Yalamanchili S Rao. Dual polarimetric radar vegetation index for crop growth monitoring using sentinel-1 SAR data. *Remote Sensing of Environment*, 247:111954, 2020.

[31] Dipankar Mandal, Vineet Kumar, Debanshu Ratha, Juan M Lopez-Sanchez, Avik Bhattacharya, Heather McNairn, YS Rao, and KV Ramana. Assessment of rice growth conditions in a semi-arid region of India using the generalized radar vegetation index derived from radarsat-2 polarimetric SAR data. *Remote Sensing of Environment*, 237:111561, 2020.

[32] Dipankar Mandal, Debanshu Ratha, Avik Bhattacharya, Vineet Kumar, Heather McNairn, Yalamanchili S Rao, and Alejandro C Frery. A radar vegetation index for crop monitoring using compact polarimetric SAR data. *IEEE Transactions on Geoscience and Remote Sensing*, 58(9):6321–6335, 2020.

[33] Heather McNairn, Xianfeng Jiao, Anna Pacheco, Abhijit Sinha, Weikai Tan, and Yifeng Li. Estimating canola phenology using synthetic aperture radar. *Remote Sensing of Environment*, 219:196–205, 2018.

[34] Heather McNairn and Jiali Shang. A review of multitemporal synthetic aperture radar (SAR) for crop monitoring. In *Multitemporal Remote Sensing*, pp. 317–340. Springer, 2016.

[35] KEWC Moldenhauer and Nathan Slaton. Rice growth and development. *Rice Production Handbook*, 192:7–14, 2001.

[36] Simonetta Paloscia. A summary of experimental results to assess the contribution of SAR for mapping vegetation biomass and soil moisture. *Canadian Journal of Remote Sensing*, 28(2):246–261, 2002.

[37] Jaan Praks, Elise Colin Koeniguer, and Martti T Hallikainen. Alternatives to target entropy and alpha angle in SAR polarimetry. *IEEE Transactions on Geoscience and Remote Sensing*, 47(7):2262–2274, 2009.

[38] D. Ratha, E. Pottier, A. Bhattacharya, and A. C. Frery. A PolSAR scattering power factorization framework and novel roll-invariant parameter-based unsupervised classification scheme using a geodesic distance. *IEEE Transactions on Geoscience and Remote Sensing*, 58(5):3509–3525, 2019.

[39] Debanshu Ratha, Dipankar Mandal, Vineet Kumar, Heather Mcnairn, Avik Bhattacharya, and Alejandro C. Frery. A generalized volume scattering model-based vegetation index from polarimetric SAR data. *IEEE Geoscience and Remote Sensing Letters*, 16(11):1791–1795, 2019.

[40] Noelia Romero-Puig, Juan M Lopez-Sanchez, and J David Ballester-Berman. Estimation of rvog scene parameters by means of polinsar with tandem-x data: Effect of the double-bounce contribution. *IEEE Transactions on Geoscience and Remote Sensing*, 58(10):7283–7304, 2020.

[41] Grant Wiseman, Heather McNairn, Saeid Homayouni, and Jiali Shang. RADARSAT-2 polarimetric SAR response to crop biomass for agricultural production monitoring. *IEEE Journal of Selected Topics in Applied Earth Observations and Remote Sensing*, 7(11):4461–4471, 2014.

[42] Yoshio Yamaguchi, Toshifumi Moriyama, Motoi Ishido, and Hiroyoshi Yamada. Four-component scattering model for polarimetric SAR image decomposition. *IEEE Transactions on Geoscience and Remote Sensing*, 43(8):1699–1706, 2005.

[43] Junjun Yin, Wooil M Moon, and Jian Yang. Novel model-based method for identification of scattering mechanisms in polarimetric SAR data. *IEEE Transactions on Geoscience and Remote Sensing*, 54(1):520–532, 2015.

8 Synergistic Fusion of Spaceborne Polarimetric SAR and Hyperspectral Data for Land Cover Classification

Vinay Kumar, Shenbaga Rajan Venkatachalaperumal, and C. Persello

CONTENTS

DOI: 10.1201/9781003204466-8

8.1 INTRODUCTION

8.1.1 BACKGROUND

LULC classification is an important application of satellite images. Retrieval of authentic information about earth surface features is required to provide effective solutions for solving land and environmental problems (Townshend et al. 1991). Many satellite datasets are now available due to the launch of multiple types of remote sensing satellites. The sensors on board each satellite have their own advantages and disadvantages when it comes to extracting information about the earth surface features. Many natural and man-made materials are difficult to distinguish with moderate resolution optical sensors (Borghys et al. 2007). Due to the limitations of such sensors, information retrieved from them affects land cover classification and its accuracy. In the case of hyperspectral sensors, hyperspectral refers to excessive spectral information, which consists of a large number of contiguous spectral bands. The narrow spectral resolution enables differentiation of spectrally similar features and is useful in material-level feature identification. Polarimetric SAR synthetic aperture RADAR (radio detection and ranging) works in four polarization channels and measures backscattered signals of targeted objects of different characteristics. One of the significant advantages of SAR is its long wavelength, as it is not affected by atmospheric interference. This property of SAR has increased its usage for earth observation (Chandola 2014). Man-made features such as urban areas can be extracted clearly from SAR images based on surface roughness as well as geometric and scattering properties of the objects. But identification of different vegetation types is difficult using SAR imagery as trees produce a bright backscatter, as do buildings (Borghys et al. 2007). It means extracting information from a single sensor does not provide an efficient solution. It is necessary to make use of information from different sources for better interpretation and classification; each of the sensors provides different, useful, and complementary information. The process of combining or integrating information from different sensors is termed image fusion (Knödel, Lange, and Voigt 2007). The data fusion preserves the primacy of information and utilizes the interdependent information about the multiple sensors (Li et al. 2013). Fusion of the data depends on different levels of processing and results in three different levels of fusion methods: pixel, feature, and decision (Pohl and Van Genderen 1998). Image fusion from different sensors has been found more productive, as the content from multiple sources is combined, which improves classification

(Dong et al. 2009). The satellite data used for image fusion vary, with spatial as well as spectral characteristics, which provide detailed information about the features observed (Pohl, Munro, and van Genderen 1997).

Many aspects have to be looked at for multi-sensor data fusion. These are objective/application of the user, selection of sensors based on complementary characteristics such as spatial, spectral, and temporal resolutions, necessary pre-processing of the data, and, most importantly, the best fusion technique to be applied (Pohl and Van Genderen 1998). Apart from these aspects, there are several other challenges faced by researchers in multi-sensor fusion, including the integration of a greater number of spectral bands, which increases processing complexity; high-resolution images that require higher geometric correction accuracy; geometric and radiometric correction requirements; and shadow features that may appear due to sensors' different observation angles (Pohl and van Genderen 2014). Apart from these challenges, the selection of bands is an important consideration to be taken into account for the fusion process. Band selection comes into the picture when some fusion processes take only three input bands for processing, for example, the intensity hue saturation (IHS) fusion technique. As reviewed by Pohl and van Genderen (1998), band selection could be accomplished with optimum index factor, and feature extraction to select the uncorrelated components could be done using principle component analysis (Pohl and Van Genderen 1998).

There are three different levels of fusion techniques. Pixel level refers to the lowest processing level of image fusion by merging the measured physical parameters. Fusion at feature level requires the extraction of objects recognized in the various data sources. Decision-level fusion represents a method that uses value-added data where the input images are processed individually for information extraction. There are several objectives and achievements that can be attained using multi-sensor image fusion techniques. The main goals of applying fusion techniques could be to sharpen the image by improving the spatial and spectral resolution of the fused image; to enhance the extraction of certain features and information; to initiate change detection that depends on the temporal aspects of the different sensors; to improve classification by combining multiple sources of data for processing; or to replace defective data, as the images acquired by satellites are influenced by numerous effects such as noise, cloud cover, and blurred features (Pohl and Van Genderen 1998).

The lowest processing level of fusion is pixel-level fusion, in which the measured physical parameters from two or more images are merged. As reviewed by Pohl and van Genderen (2015), there are several pixel-level fusion algorithms, categorized in general as either colour-related or statistical-related fusion techniques. Colour-related techniques include IHS fusion, red, green, blue transformation fusion, and YIQ fusion, where Y represents the luma information that is the brightness of an image and I and Q represent the chrominance of the image. Statistical and the numerical methods include principal component analysis (PCA), wavelet transform, high-pass filter (HPF), regression variable substitution, Brovey transform, and component substitution. PCA works on the principle of principal component transformation. The optical imagery is first resampled and transformed into principal components, and the first component is replaced with the panchromatic (PAN) image to fuse with the optical imagery using inverse PCA to get a fused product with high spectral and spatial content (Metwalli et al. 2010). Brovey transform is based on arithmetic operations. Wavelet fusion and high-pass filter fusion are based on the extracting high-frequency information content using filters, and component substitution is similar to the PCA method. PC fusion works based on forward transformation of optical data and then follows component substitution, where the new data space is replaced with the high-resolution band. Finally, the fused result is obtained by the inverse transform back to the original space. Regression variable-based pixel-level fusion was performed by using Kriging (Meng, Borders, and Madden 2010). Here the correlation is between the response variable (an image that needs to be fused) and the predictor variable (image with finer spatial resolution).

An improved intensity hue saturation (IHS) transform–based, pixel-level fusion was used to fuse IKONOS multispectral and SAR HH band images (Ghanbari and Sahebi 2014). Both spectrally and spatially, the fused image was comparatively good with other fusion techniques such as Brovey and HIS. The performances of different techniques such as PCA, Brovey, Ehler's fusion, and wavelet transform were compared on fusing SAR and optical imagery (Amarsaikhan et al. 2010). The research determined that multi-sensor fusion could enhance feature extraction. The IHS transformation was used to integrate the high spectral resolution, provided by hyperspectral data and the surface texture information derived from radar data into a single image of an urban area (Chen, Hepner, and Forster 2003). A comparison of Radarsat 2 C-band and ALOS PALSAR L-band-fusion with Landsat TM mapper was made for land cover classification (Lu et al. 2011). Different pixel-level fusion techniques were used, such as wavelet fusion, HPF fusion, PCA and normalized multiplication. It was concluded that wavelet merge and HPF merge performed better compared with the other techniques.

Advanced and complex pixel-level fusion techniques like enhanced Gram–Schmidt spectral sharpening were performed by introducing a generalized intensity component for calculating a low-resolution PAN image for the fusion process by Aiazzi et al. (2006). The results proved that the preceding method outperformed regular Gram–Schmidt fusion in terms of spectral sharpness and high spatial quality. A comparative analysis of IHS, Brovey, and Ehler's fusion techniques was carried out on the image and multispectral SPOT images, and it was concluded that among the fusion techniques used, Ehler's fusion produced a better result (Abdikan et al. 2014).

Feature-level fusion involves the extraction of features from different data sources to form a single feature vector containing all the extracted features and then fusing them for further understanding. These extracted features correspond to the characteristics obtained from input images. In feature-level fusion, different features are targeted by each sensor, and the feature extraction process is carried out to obtain a combined feature vector from each sensor. The resulting feature vectors are then fused together and form a joint feature vector. The process of feature extraction or feature selection plays a significant role in this level of fusion. There are different feature-level fusion techniques, as discussed, including neural networks, Dempster Shafer's theory, expert systems, logical templates, Bayesian inference, and cluster analysis. Successful implementation of feature-level fusion is possible only with the proper extraction and selection of features from the datasets. There are two approaches defined for reducing the number of features: extracting the information contained in the original features through either linear or non-linear transformations to the original feature space (Bruzzone and Persello 2009). This method is usually called feature extraction, derived from a subset of the original set of features (bands) that allows separating the land cover classes. This process is commonly referred to as feature selection (Pohl and Van Genderen 1998).

A high correlation occurs when a large number of features (bands) are obtained, and this leads to the redundancy of information. This occurs when the sensor has a high spectral resolution (Bruzzone and Persello 2009) . Research on the kernel-based feature selection approach was conducted for the classification of hyperspectral data (Persello and Bruzzone 2016). This research focussed on selecting a subset of features from the hyperspectral image that helps in differentiating the defined classes and does not change across the source and target domains. This research involved study of two hyperspectral images to evaluate the domain stability in the kernel Hilbert space. Here the domain is referred to as the images captured in the different geographical area or at different time period. The experimental results showed an improvement in classification accuracy with high generalization capabilities. It was suggested that the reduction in features helps in improving the classification accuracy by handling the Hughes phenomenon and also reduces the computational burden (Swain and Davis 1981).

The extraction and selection of features from the datasets are the most important part of the feature-level fusion process for both spectral and SAR imageries, used for target discrimination and to reduce the effects of registration errors (Peli et al. 1999). The extracted features have also been classified into three categories: statistics-based, fractal-based, and correlation-based features. The statistics-based features use amplitude-based statistics to target or characterize a particular area.

Fractal-based features calculate fractal behaviour. The correlation-based features measure the level of correlation among the targets.

Another method of extracting features is through texture analysis. This is a way of extracting contextual information. Texture is one of the important parameters of SAR data. Texture-based feature extraction was researched, and the fusion of SAR and multispectral imageries was performed (Byun 2014). The grey level co-occurrence matrix approach was used by the author to extract texture information from the SAR amplitude image. Additional research on texture-based fusion of SAR and multispectral images was performed (Kiema 2002) . The author used the homogeneity measure obtained from the GLCM method for the fusion approach.

Very limited research has been performed in the past on feature-level fusion of multiple sensors. Artificial neural network–based feature-level fusion was conducted by Giampouras, Charou, and Kesidis (2013). Here the authors used principal component analysis (PCA) as a feature extraction method and formed a feature vector along with light detection and ranging (LiDAR) data, which was then fused and classified using the Bayesian regularization propagation algorithm. A conclusion was made that the classification could be done efficiently with the use of artificial neural networks (ANN). Using wavelet transform and neural networks, an efficient block-based feature-level image fusion technique was researched by Sheela Rani, Vijaya Kumar, and Sujatha (2012). Feature extraction and selection were performed based on spatial frequency, energy of gradient, edge information, contrast visibility, and variance. Research on feature-level fusion was conducted using a wavelet transform–based feature extraction method and support vector machine for the classification of the formed feature vector using the extracted features (Huang, Zhang, and Li 2008).

Decision-level fusion is the highest level of fusion among the three fusion levels. Decision-level fusion represents a method that uses value-added data where the input images are processed and classified individually for information extraction. The obtained information is then combined, applying decision rules to reinforce conventional interpretation and furnish a better understanding of the observed objects (Pohl and Van Genderen 1998). Decision-level fusion is a research area in the field of multi-sensor image fusion and very few research projects have previously been performed.

One aspect of the research investigates urban and industrial site identification with the fusion of SAR and hyperspectral imageries. Three types of decision-level fusion – namely the weighted majority vote, a method based on support vector machines, and a method based on a binary decision tree – were implemented on SAR and hyperspectral imageries for improved object recognition in the region of urban and industrial sites. It was concluded that fusion based on the decision tree provided a better result when compared with the other two fusion methods (Borghys et al. 2007). Change detection in urban scenes with the fusion of SAR and hyperspectral image was performed. The expert classifier method was used to implement decision-level fusion, concluding that adequate information of the changes in urban scenes was obtained (Borghys et al. 2007).

Support vector machine–based decision-level fusion is also a standard method adopted by researchers for fusing multi-sensor datasets. Dual support vector machine–based decision fusion of multi-sensor images was used (Waske, Menz, and Benediktsson 2007). Initially, the two sources were individually classified using SVM, and then the feature vector was formed from the obtained rule images from both classifications. The rule images contain the distance of a pixel to the decision boundary of the SVM, and the maximum value to the hyperplane determines the final class membership (Waske, Menz, and Benediktsson 2007). Again, a second SVM was used to classify the formed feature vector, and final class membership was decided. The research has concluded that the dual SVM-based decision fusion of multi-sensor data outperforms other techniques, such as majority voting, an absolute maximum voting scheme, and decision tree–based fusion.

One of the important applications of polarimetric synthetic aperture radar is terrain and land use classification. Polarimetric decomposition is the method used to extract the ground features based on the scattering properties of the same. The multi-component scattering model (MCSM) consists of five scattering components, namely the surface scattering component, double-bounce scattering component, helix scattering component, volume scattering component, and wire scattering component (Zhang et al. 2009). This model is the extended version of the four-component scattering model developed by Ma et al. (2014). The wire scattering component is the fifth component added to the MCSM model.

Each of the scattering components has significance in feature extraction. Double-bounce scattering, volume scattering, and surface scattering are used to describe the polarimetric backscatter of naturally occurring scatterers from a pair of orthogonal surfaces (in urban regions), from a cloud of randomly oriented dipoles and from moderately rough surface, respectively, and helix and wire scattering are used to describe the polarimetric backscatter of scatterers from man-made objects in urban areas (Zhang et al. 2009) . Decomposition is an important process in the case of classification of PolSAR images. MCSM, which is used to describe the polarimetric backscatter of both natural and man-made objects, proved useful in classification along with the texture parameter using SVM (Zhang et al. 2009).

In comparison with traditional and conventional classification methods, like maximum likelihood, the minimum distance to mean classifier, etc., SVM is more robust in handling complex data, such as high dimensionality high-resolution satellite images and hyperspectral images. It has been proven that SVM-based classification is more efficient, better in both the learning ability and the expressing ability in the classification of hyperspectral data (Dai, Huang, and Dong 2007). Another study on the ability of SVM to classify hyperspectral images was performed, and it was observed that SVM is more efficient than the other non-parametric classifiers, such as RBF neural network and KNN classifiers, and less sensitive to the Hughes phenomenon (Melgani and Bruzzone 2002). As SVM can handle more complex data, it is also widely used in the classification of SAR data. Research on target recognition using SVM on SAR was performed and a comparison was made for SVM-based target detection on SAR with other conventional classifiers (Zhao and Principe 2001). The results proved that the SVM outperformed all other classifiers in target detection. In addition, it has been concluded that the SVM is able to form a locally bounded decision function for each of the classes. Classification of SAR using SVM was performed on feature vectors such as polarimetric parameters after the decomposition technique and also on the texture properties of SAR (Fukuda and Hirosawa 2001).

The main objective of this research is to enhance LULC features and classification accuracy by integrating hyperspectral with C-band as well as L-band fully polarimetric SAR data individually using all the three different levels of fusion and their comparative analysis

8.2   STUDY AREA AND DATASETS USED

8.2.1   Study Area

The study area chosen for this research is in and around the city of Dhanbad, Jharkhand, India. The study area consists of built-up and industrial areas, areas of dense and sparse vegetation, cropland, barren land, water, and dry riverbeds; these are the potential classes on which the research work was carried out. Figure 8.1 shows the location map of the study area along with the FCC image of Hyperion data.

8.2.2   Datasets Used

The datasets used for this study were EO-1 Hyperion data, Radarsat-2 C-band, and ALOS PALSAR L-band fully polarimetric SAR data. The details of the data used (Table 8.1) are mentioned next.

8.2.2.1   EO-1 Hyperion Data

In November 2000, an earth observation (EO-1) satellite was launched under the NASA's new millennium program. One of the sensors in EO-1 was Hyperion, which was developed for providing

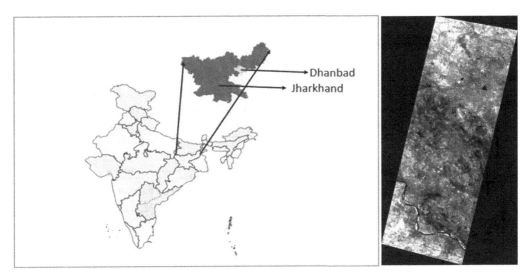

FIGURE 8.1   Location map of study area and FCC image of Hyperion data.

Source: **http://bhuvan.nrsc.gov.in/bhuvan_links.php.**

TABLE 8.1
Dataset Specifications

Specifications	Hyperion	Radarsat 2	ALOS PALSAR
Spatial resolution	30 metres	20 metres (after multilooking)	20 metres (after multilooking)
Spectral resolution	10 nm	–	–
Wavelength	220 bands (0.4–2.5 micrometre)	C-band	L-band
Polarimetric mode	–	HH, HV, VH, VV	HH, HV, VH, VV
Incidence angle	–	27.6 degree	25.6 degree

data of around 220 narrow spectral bands with a wavelength range of 357 nm–2576 nm. The narrow spectral resolution of the data was used for better characterization of the earth surface features. The swath width of this pushbroom sensor is 7.5 kilometres.

8.2.2.2   Radarsat-2 Data

The Radarsat-2 satellite is a jointly funded mission of the Canadian Space Agency (CSA) and MacDonald Dettwiler Associates Ltd. of Richmond, BC, and was launched in the year 2007. Radarsat-2 works in the fully polarimetric mode with a C-band imaging frequency at 5.405 GHZ and. The look direction of the Radarsat-2 antenna is left or right. Radarsat-2 offers data in all four polarization channels (HH, HV, VH, and VV).

8.2.2.3   ALOS PALSAR Data

The Japanese Aerospace and Exploration Agency (JAXA) launched the advanced land observing satellite (ALOS) on January 24, 2006. ALOS carried PALSAR and was launched into a sun-synchronous orbit. The revisit time of this satellite was 46 days. PALSAR's polarimetric mode offers the complete polarimetry of HH, HV, VV and VH polarizations.

8.3   RESEARCH METHODOLOGY

The aim of this research is to enhance LULC classification by fusing hyperspectral data with fully polarimetric C-band and L-band SAR data individually. The methodology adopted to achieve this goal is shown in Figure 8.2. Initially, Hyperion (L1R data) was pre-processed and converted to surface reflectance after atmospheric correction. Fully polarimetric Radarsat-2 C-band and ALOS PALSAR L-band SAR data were pre-processed and various polarimetric scattering parameters were extracted such as such as span (total intensity), surface, double-bounce, volume, helix, and wire

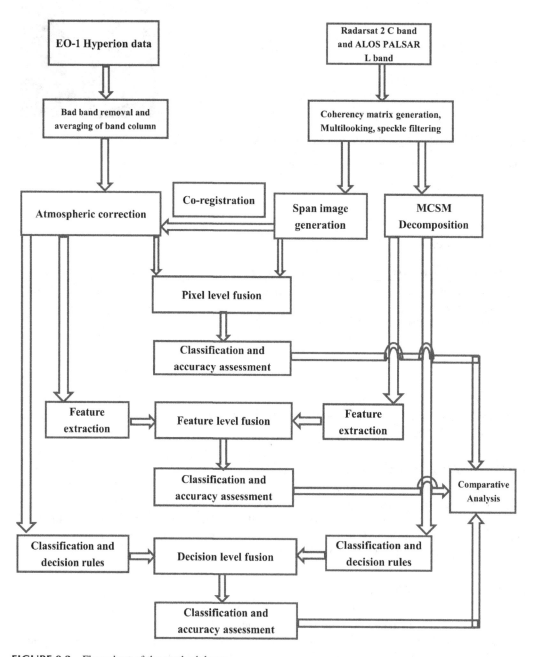

FIGURE 8.2   Flow chart of the methodology.

scattering. The extracted polarimetric parameters were co-registered with the Hyperion reflectance data. After that, different levels of image fusion techniques, i.e., pixel-, feature-, and decision-level fusion were performed. LULC classification of the fused products, as well as the individual datasets, was performed, followed by accuracy assessment. Comparative analysis was undertaken between the accuracy results to obtain the optimal level and the fusion pair (Hyperion + RS2 or Hyperion + ALOS PALSAR) to determine which gives the better overall accuracy.

8.3.1 PROCESSING OF THE DATASETS

Pre-processing is one of the essential steps of data fusion. The quality of the fused product and, further, the accuracy of the classification of the fused image depend on how well the pre-processing has been done. The Hyperion image obtained was at level 1, and the fully polarimetric data (Radarsat-2 and ALOS PALSAR) were at level 1 single look complex (SLC).

The images underwent the following pre-processing steps.

8.3.1.1 Pre-Processing of Hyperion Data

The pre-processing of Hyperion data includes sensor error and atmospheric correction. Some spectral bands of the Hyperion data appear completely dark or very noisy due to poor signal to noise ratio or to coinciding with atmospheric/water absorption bands. A total of 144 bands was left after the removal of no-information bands. Due to miscalibration, some of the bands of the Hyperion sensor had a dropped line error, which can be corrected using the method of averaging neighbouring pixels. Further, the sensor error–corrected hyperspectral data was converted to surface reflectance. The FLAASH (first line of sight atmospheric analysis of hypercubes) model, which is based on the MODTRAN radiative transfer model, was used for atmospheric correction (Hadjimitsis et al. 2010).

8.3.1.2 Processing of PolSAR Data

Fully polarimetric SAR data contains all four polarizations in the form of a 2 × 2 scattering matrix. The backscatter response from the four polarization channels is stored in a scattering matrix form, as shown below (Verma 2014).

$$[S] = \begin{bmatrix} S_{HH} & S_{HV} \\ S_{VH} & S_{VV} \end{bmatrix},$$ (8.1)

where,
S_{HH} = backscatter response of HH polarization,
S_{HV} = backscatter response of HV polarization,
S_{VH} = backscatter response of HV polarization, and
S_{VV} = backscatter response of HV polarization.

The scattering matrix only gives information for clear targets, but the materials on the earth's surface are complex in nature. As scattering matrix is insufficient to provide the desired information. The parameters derived from the generation of second-order statistics from the vectorized form of the scattering matrix S can help in understanding complex features on the earth's surface. The second-order matrix is known as a coherency matrix. The Pauli feature vector is the vectorized form of scattering matrix and can be given as:

$$K_p = \frac{1}{\sqrt{2}} \begin{matrix} S_{HH} + S_{VV} \\ S_{HH} - S_{VV} \\ 2S_{HV} \end{matrix}$$ (8.2)

The dot product of this Pauli vector with the transpose of itself generates the coherency matrix. The data was converted from a single look complex (SLC) to multilook complex image (MLC) to turn the slant range to ground range resolution. The coherency matrix is given in equation (8.3):

$$\langle[T]\rangle = \langle K_p K_P^\dagger \rangle = \begin{bmatrix} \left\langle \left|S_{HH}+S_{VV}\right|^2\right\rangle & \left\langle\left(S_{HH}+S_{VV}\right)S_{HH}-S_{VV}\right\rangle & 2\left\langle\left(S_{HH}+S_{VV}\right)S_{HV}\right\rangle \\ \left\langle\left(S_{HH}-S_{VV}\right)S_{HH}+S_{VV}\right\rangle & \left\langle\left|S_{HH}-S_{VV}\right|^2\right\rangle & 2\left\langle\left(S_{HH}-S_{VV}\right)S_{HV}\right\rangle \\ 2\left\langle S_{HV}\left(S_{HH}+S_{VV}\right)\right\rangle & 2\left\langle S_{HV}\left(S_{HH}-S_{VV}\right)\right\rangle & 4\left\langle\left|S_{HV}\right|^2\right\rangle \end{bmatrix}, \quad (8.3)$$

where,
† represents the conjugate and transpose, and
◇ represents the averaging over the whole data.

The sum of the diagonal elements of the matrix is the total intensity value, which is popularly known as span.

$$\textbf{Span} = \left\langle\left|S_{HH}+S_{VV}\right|^2\right\rangle + \left\langle\left|S_{HH}-S_{VV}\right|^2\right\rangle + 4\left\langle\left|S_{HV}\right|^2\right\rangle.$$

Multilooking was done by using equation (8.4).

$$\text{Slant range resolution to ground resolution} = C\tau/2\left(1/\sin\vartheta\right). \quad (8.4)$$

where,
$C\tau/2$ = pixel spacing in range direction, and
$\sin\vartheta$ = incidence angle.

Parameters	Radarsat-2	ALOS PALSAR
Ground range resolution	20 metres	20 metres
Incidence angle	27.6 degrees	25.6 degrees
Multilook factor	5.2	6.1

Various speckle filters were applied to reduce the speckles, and a Lee refined filter with a window size of 3 provided a good result.

8.3.1.3 Multiple-Component Scattering Model (MCSM) Decomposition

Multiple-component scattering model (MCSM) decomposition is an extension of the Yamaguchi four-component scattering model (Zhang et al. 2009). In this decomposition, wire scattering is added as fifth component, which is found to be very prominent for urban areas. The five scattering mechanisms of MCSM decomposition are double-bounce, volume, helix, surface, and wire scattering, which give the contribution of total backscatter value. These scatterings depend on the scattering behaviour of the scatterers based on their orientation, shape, surface roughness, geometrical structure, etc. MCSM decomposition is the linear combination of all five scattering mechanisms (Zhang et al. 2008).A detailed description of the MCSM based on the work of Verma (2014) is given next.

The coherency matrix of MCSM decomposition is written as,

$$[T] = f_s\left[T_s\right] + f_d\left[T_d\right] + f_v\left[T_v\right] + f_h\left[T_h\right] + f_w\left[T_w\right], \quad (8.5)$$

where, [T] = coherency matrix,

$[T_s]$, $[T_d]$, $[T_v]$, $[T_h]$, and $[T_w]$ are the coherency matrices of the surface, double-bounce, volume, helix, and wire scattering components, and f_s, f_d, f_v, f_h, and f_w are the coefficients of the five scattering components.

The individual matrix elements of surface, volume, helix, double-bounce and wire scattering components are explained next.

8.3.1.4 Surface Scattering

This scattering is more prominent in little rough surface regions, where the cross-polarization is negligible. Examples of surface scatterers are bare land, road features, and water bodies. The surface scattering coherency matrix is given as:

$$\langle [T_s] \rangle = \begin{bmatrix} 1 & \beta^* & 0 \\ \beta & |\beta|^2 & 0 \\ 0 & 0 & 0 \end{bmatrix}, Where \;\; \beta = \frac{R_H - R_V}{R_H + R_V} \;\; and \;\; |\beta| < 1, \tag{8.6}$$

Where, R_H and R_V are the Fresnel reflection coefficients.

8.3.1.5 Double-Bounce Scattering

Double-bounce scattering is prominent in urban areas where there are dihedral structures or ground tree trunks. The coherency matrix of this scattering is given as:

$$\langle |T_d| \rangle = \begin{bmatrix} |\alpha|^2 & \alpha & 0 \\ \alpha^* & 1 & 0 \\ 0 & 0 & 0 \end{bmatrix}, \;\; where \;\; \alpha = \frac{e^{2j\gamma} HR_{TH} R_{GH} + e^{2j\gamma} VR_{TV} R_{GV}}{e^{2j\gamma} HR_{TH} R_{GH} - e^{2j\gamma} VR_{TV} R_{GV}} \;\; and \;\; |\alpha| < 1, \tag{8.7}$$

where $R_{TH,}$ $R_{TV,}$ $R_{GV,}$ R_{GH} reflection coefficients of tree trunk and ground surface for horizontal and vertical polarization.

8.3.1.6 Volume Scattering

Volume scattering corresponds to the multiple scatterers, and its best example is forest canopy. The coherency matrix of volume scattering is given as:

$$[T_V] = \begin{bmatrix} 2 & 0 & 0 \\ 0 & 1 & 0 \\ 0 & 0 & 0 \end{bmatrix}. \tag{8.8}$$

8.3.1.7 Helix Scattering

Helix scattering is more prominent in urban areas with complex building structures (Zhang et al. 2008). Left- and right-handed circular polarization are generated by the helix target. The helix coherency matrix is given as:

$$[T_h] = \frac{1}{2} \begin{bmatrix} 0 & 0 & 0 \\ 0 & 1 & \pm j \\ 0 & \pm j & 1 \end{bmatrix}. \tag{8.9}$$

8.3.1.8 Wire Scattering

This scattering is contributed by thin canonical structures and building edges (Zhang et al. 2008).

$$[S_w] = \begin{bmatrix} \gamma & \rho \\ \rho & 1 \end{bmatrix}, \tag{8.10}$$

where $\gamma = \dfrac{S_{HH}}{S_{VV}}, \rho = \dfrac{S_{HH}}{S_{VV}}$.

The coherency matrix of the wire component is given as:

$$\langle [T_w] \rangle = \frac{1}{2} \begin{bmatrix} |\gamma+1|^2 & (\gamma+1)(\gamma-1)^* & 2(\gamma+1)\rho^* \\ (\gamma-1)(\gamma+1)^* & |\gamma-1|^2 & 2(\gamma-1)\rho^* \\ 2(\gamma+1)^*\rho & 2\rho(\gamma-1)^* & 4|\rho|^2 \end{bmatrix}. \tag{8.11}$$

The MCSM decomposition coherency matrix of the wire component is given as:

$$[T] = f_s \begin{bmatrix} 1 & \beta^* & 0 \\ \beta & |\beta|^2 & 0 \\ 0 & 0 & 0 \end{bmatrix} + f_d \begin{bmatrix} |\alpha|^2 & \alpha & 0 \\ \alpha^* & 1 & 0 \\ 0 & 0 & 0 \end{bmatrix} + \frac{f_v}{4} \begin{bmatrix} 2 & 0 & 0 \\ 0 & 1 & 0 \\ 0 & 0 & 1 \end{bmatrix} + \frac{f_h}{4} \begin{bmatrix} 0 & 0 & 0 \\ 0 & 1 & \mp j \\ 0 & \mp j & 1 \end{bmatrix}.$$

$$+ \frac{f_w}{2} \begin{bmatrix} |\gamma+1|^2 & (\gamma+1)(\gamma-1)^* & 2(\gamma+1)\rho^* \\ (\gamma-1)(\gamma+1)^* & |\gamma-1|^2 & 2(\gamma-1)\rho^* \\ 2(\gamma+1)^*\rho & 2\rho(\gamma-1)^* & 4|\rho|^2 \end{bmatrix} \tag{8.12}$$

The power of the five scattering components are as follows:

$$P_{s=} f_s \left(1+|\beta|^2\right) \tag{8.13}$$

$$P_{d=} f_d \left(1+|\alpha|^2\right) \tag{8.14}$$

$$P_v = f_v, \tag{8.15}$$

$$P_h = f_h, \tag{8.16}$$

$$P_w = f_w \left(1+|\gamma|^2 + 2|\rho|^2\right). \tag{8.17}$$

The expansion coefficients mentioned in the preceding equations can be obtained as follows.
From the T23 element we get

$$f_{h=2\,Im(T_{23})} \tag{8.18}$$

and

$$f_w = \frac{Re(T_{23})}{(\gamma-1)\rho^*}. \tag{8.19}$$

Therefore,

$$P_h = f_h \tag{8.20}$$

and

$$P_w = \frac{Re(T_{23})}{(\gamma-1)\rho^*}\left(1-|\gamma|^2+2|\rho|^2\right). \tag{8.21}$$

The volume scattering component is derived based on the co-polarized components, namely HH and VV.

$$10\log\left[\frac{\langle|S_{VV}|^2\rangle}{\langle|S_{HH}|^2\rangle}\right] = 10\log\left[\frac{T_{11}+T_{22}-2Re(T_{12})}{T_{11}+T_{22}+2Re(T_{12})}\right]. \tag{8.22}$$

$$For\, 10\,\log(\langle|S_{VV}|^2\rangle/\langle|S_{HH}|^2\rangle)<-2db, \langle|T_V|\rangle = \frac{1}{30}\begin{bmatrix}15&5&0\\5&7&0\\0&0&8\end{bmatrix}. \tag{8.23}$$

$$For\, -2db <10\,\log(\langle|S_{VV}|^2\rangle/\langle|S_{HH}|^2\rangle)<2db, \langle|T_V|\rangle = \frac{1}{4}\begin{bmatrix}12&0&0\\0&1&0\\0&0&1\end{bmatrix}. \tag{8.24}$$

$$For\, 10\,\log(\langle|S_{VV}|^2\rangle/\langle|S_{HH}|^2\rangle)>2db, \langle|T_V|\rangle = \frac{1}{30}\begin{bmatrix}15&-5&0\\-5&7&0\\0&0&8\end{bmatrix}. \tag{8.25}$$

Based on the coherency matrix of the volume scattering component, the power of volume scattering is obtained as:

$$P_v = 4T_{33} - 2P_h - 8f_w|\rho|^2 \; or\; P_v = \frac{15}{4}T_{33} - \frac{15}{8}P_h - \frac{15}{2}f_w|\rho|^2 \,. \tag{8.26}$$

The equations containing the coefficient for surface and double-bounce scattering is given as:

$$S = f_{s+}f_d|\alpha|^2 = T_{11} - \frac{P_v}{2} - \frac{f_w}{2}|\gamma+1|^2, \tag{8.27}$$

$$D = f_d|\beta|^2 + f_d = T_{22} - T_{33} - \frac{f_w}{2}\left(|\gamma-1|^2 - 4|\gamma+1|^2\right), \tag{8.28}$$

$$C = f_s\beta^* + f_d\alpha = T_{12} - \frac{f_w}{2}(\gamma+1)(\gamma-1)^*. \tag{8.29}$$

Based on the sign of Re $\langle S_{HH}S^*_{VV}\rangle$, surface and double-bounce scattering are estimated. In terms of coherency matrix elements, the Re $\langle S_{HH}S^*_{VV}\rangle$ term is estimated as:

$$C_0 = T_{11} + T_{22} + T_{33} + P_h. \tag{8.30}$$

If there is a dominance of surface scattering, then $\mathrm{Re}\langle S_{HH}S^*_{VV}\rangle > 0$, i.e., $C_0 > 0$. In this case, the double-bounce scattering is negligible. The surface and double-bounce scattering powers are given as:

$$P_s = f_s\left(1+|\beta|^2\right) = S + \frac{|C|^2}{D}, \tag{8.31}$$

$$P_d = f_d\left(1+|\alpha|^2\right) = D - \frac{|C|^2}{D}. \tag{8.32}$$

If $\mathrm{Re}\langle S_{HH}S^*_{VV}\rangle < 0$, then $\beta = 0$, and the double-bounce scattering is dominant. Then the power of the double-bounce and the surface scattering is obtained as:

$$P_s = f_s\left(1+|\beta|^2\right) = S - \frac{|c|^2}{D}, \tag{8.33}$$

$$P_d = f_d\left(1+|\alpha|^2\right) = D + \frac{|C|^2}{D}. \tag{8.34}$$

8.3.1.9 Geocoding of Extracted Polsar Parameters and Co- Registration with Hyperspectral Image

The PolSAR data are captured on the side-looking geometry, which leads to distortions like shadow, layover, and foreshortening. To correct these distortions and to geo-register the image, geocoding is required using the digital elevation model (DEM). The DEM used was the shuttle radar topographic mission (SRTM). PolSAR parameters extracted from both Radarsat-2 and ALOS PALSAR data were geocoded using the shuttle radar topographic mission (SRTM) digital elevation model (DEM). After that, the atmospherically corrected Hyperion data was precisely co-registered with the geocoded polarimetric parameters from Radarsat-2 and ALOS PALSAR.

8.3.2 Pixel-Level Fusion

In this level of fusion, Hyperion image was fused with the span image of Radarsat-2 and ALOS PALSAR images using three pixel-level fusion techniques, i.e., HPF fusion, wavelet fusion, and Gram–Schmidt fusion. The techniques chosen for fusion were able to preserve the spectral properties of the hyperspectral images in the fused output. The optimal fusion technique and also the best fusion pair were found based on the land cover classification and its accuracy. Various pixel-level fusion techniques used in this study are explained next.

8.3.2.1 High-Pass Filter Fusion

In this technique, a high-pass convolution filter is applied on high spatial resolution image, which results in the data containing high spatial frequency information. Then the same is added pixel wise to the low-resolution bands (Pohl and Van Genderen 1998).

The steps of the fusion algorithm are as follows:

- Read pixel sizes from the images and calculate R, where R is the ratio between low-resolution cell size and high-resolution cell size.
- Apply high-pass convolution filter to the to the high spatial resolution data and produce a high-pass filtered image. The kernel size is dependent on the value of R.
- Resample low-resolution data to the pixel size of the high-pass filtered data.

- Add HPF data to each band of low-resolution data. The HPF image is weighted relative to the global standard deviation of each low-resolution band.
- The fused image is stretched to match the mean and standard deviation of the low-resolution image.

Therefore, the parameters that need to be considered for HPF fusion are value R, kernel size, and the weight factor, which determines the crispness of the fused image.

8.3.2.2 Wavelet Fusion

In wavelet transform, the key element is the selection of the base waveform to be used. The base waveform is called the mother wavelet, which is used to represent the image. The input signal (image) is broken down into successively smaller multiples of this basis. A signal is decomposed into a multi-resolution representation with both low detail and high detail information content using discrete wavelet transform (Li, Kwok, and Wang 2002). When used for image fusion, the source images are first geometrically registered and then decomposed by DWT to the same resolution. Corresponding wavelet coefficients are combined, and the fused image is obtained by performing the inverse wavelet transform (Li, Kwok, and Wang 2002; Gonzalez and Woods 2001).

In inverse discrete wavelet transform (IDWT), the reduced images are then passed through low-pass and high-pass reconstruction filters to obtain the output image. This process is the inverse of DWT, where the sub-images are upsampled along the rows and convolved along the columns with the filters. The obtained outputs are combined and upsampled along columns and then are filtered row-wise to get the original image.

The algorithm for wavelet fusion (Li, Kwok, and Wang 2002) is given as follows.

- Decompose the high spatial resolution data using the wavelets through several iterations until the low-pass image is generated along with all of the corresponding high-pass images obtained during recursive decomposition.
- The generated low-pass image from the high spatial resolution image is replaced with the low spatial resolution image.
- Inverse decomposition takes place using the high-pass images derived from the decomposition and the high-resolution image was obtained.

8.3.2.3 Gram–Schmidt Fusion

Gram–Schmidt (GS) orthogonal transformation, which uses multivariate statistics, is the basis of this image fusion (Lu and Zhang 2014). The GS process consists of taking each vector and then subtracting the elements with the previously obtained vectors (Klonus and Ehlers 2007). The algorithm of GS fusion (S. Klonus and Ehlers 2009) is given as follows.

- A greyscale band is generated from the low spatial resolution spectral bands of hyperspectral data.
- GS transformation is applied on the simulated greyscale band and the spectral bands, using the simulated greyscale band as the first band.
- The high spatial resolution data band is swapped with the first GS band.
- The inverse of GS transformation is applied to form the fused product.

8.3.3 FEATURE-LEVEL FUSION

In feature-level fusion, the features were extracted from different sensors and then a feature vector was formed to perform SVM classification and accuracy assessment. The features from Hyperion were extracted using the kernel-based principal component analysis (KPCA) method and the features from fully polarimetric SAR data were extracted using MCSM decomposition. The main purpose of KPCA is to generalize the PCA method for the non-linear case as the higher dimensionality data is more sensitive to non-linearity. Also, KPCA considers the higher order information of the datasets and gives more principal components than normal PCA. In the case of SAR images, MCSM decomposition was used to extract information. Decomposition of polarimetric SAR is useful in extraction of features such as urban areas, vegetation, and smooth surface features such as barren land, water, road features, etc. MCSM it is useful in extracting prominent urban features based on their scattering property. Next, an explanation of feature extraction methods adopted for feature-level fusion is given.

8.3.3.1   Kernel-Based Principal Component Analysis Feature Extraction in Hyperion

Linear PCA is a linear dimensionality reduction and feature extraction technique that works on second-order statistics. In reality, the data is not linear; hence, the use of KPCA, which works on higher order statistics, comes into the picture (Fauvel, Chanussot, and Benediktsson 2006). Schölkopf, Smola, and Müller (1997) have shown that even if the mapped feature space F has arbitrarily large dimensionality, PCA can be performed for some choices of φ using the kernel functions. According to Schölkopf, Smola, and Müller (1997), a data x_k where $k = 1,...,l$ is mapped to high dimensionality feature space F as $\varphi(x_1) \ldots \varphi(x_l)$ and is centred at:

$$\sum_{k=1}^{l} \varphi(x_k) = 0. \tag{8.35}$$

Here l is the total number of representative samples.

After the mapping of data to higher dimensional space F, to find the PCA of the covariance matrix, necessary parameters referred to as eigenvalues λ and eigenvectors V need to be calculated. The covariance matrix is given as:

$$C = \frac{1}{l} \sum_{j=1}^{l} \varphi\left(x_j\right) \varphi\left(x_j^T\right). \tag{8.36}$$

Eigenvectors V ε F\ {0} and λ values ≥0, from which it is understood that,

$$\lambda V = CV. \tag{8.37}$$

Since the eigenvector lies between φ (x_1).......φ (x_k), the resulting equation is:

$$\lambda\left(\varphi(x_k).V\right) = C(\varphi(x_k).V), \text{ for all } k = 1....l, \tag{8.38}$$

$$V = \sum_{i=1}^{l} \alpha_i \varphi\left(x_i\right), \tag{8.39}$$

where α_i = coefficient.

By substituting V and C in the equation, we obtain:

$$l\lambda K \alpha = K^2 \alpha, \tag{8.40}$$

where K is the matrix of size l*l.

The solution for the above equation is obtained by solving the eigenvalue problem given below for the non-zero eigenvalues.

$$l\lambda\alpha = K\alpha. \tag{8.41}$$

By normalizing the solutions of α^k that belong to non-zero eigenvalues, and the corresponding vectors in F are also normalized, we get:

$$1 = \sum_{i,j=1}^{l} \alpha_i^k \alpha_j^k \left(\varphi(x_i) . \varphi(x_j) \right) = \left(\alpha^k . K \alpha^k \right) = \lambda_k \left(\alpha^k . \alpha^k \right). \tag{8.42}$$

To extract the principal components, projection of the image at a point onto the eigenvectors in F is computed as:

$$\left(V^k . \varphi(x) \right) = \sum_{i=1}^{l} \alpha_i^k \left(\varphi(x_i) . \varphi(x) \right), \tag{8.43}$$

where,
V^k = eigenvectors, and
α = column vectors.

Schölkopf, Smola, and Müller (1997) have found that the main advantage of using kernel-based PCA is that it improves the recognition capability of the non-linear PCA components when compared with the linear PCA components.

8.3.3.2 MCSM-Based Feature Extraction in Radarsat-2 and ALOS PALSAR

Extraction of features from the fully polarimetric datasets was performed using MCSM decomposition to obtain the surface, double-bounce, helix, volume, and wire scattering parameters.

8.3.4 Decision-Level Fusion

The third and highest level of fusion is decision-level fusion. Here the original source images, namely the Hyperion, extracted MCSM polarimetric parameters from Radarsat-2, and the ALOS PALSAR, were first classified and the obtained rule images were stacked together to form a feature vector. So, there were two feature vectors formed: one was for the Hyperion and Radarsat-2 pair and the other was for the Hyperion and ALOS PALSAR pair. These rule images are the priori output of the classification. These rule images consist of the membership values of the belongingness of a pixel to a particular class based on the distance from the fitted decision line. In general, the SVM multiclass classification works on two types of strategies. They are:

- One against all (OAA)
- One against one (OAO)

Since, in this research, SVM used was based on the one-against-all (OAA) strategy, eight rule images were obtained for the eight defined classes and a second SVM classification was applied to the feature vectors to decide the final class membership of each pixel based on the fitted decision line. The OAA strategy was used in this research as it is computationally better than the one-against-one (OAO) strategy. Finally, the accuracy assessment was performed for the information-fused outputs.

8.3.4.1 One-Against-All Multiclass SVM Classification

Initially, the SVM was developed as a binary classifier. Now it is being used to solve the multiclass problems. There are two generally used approaches, as already mentioned, namely OAA and OAO strategies, used to solve the preceding problem (B. Waske and van der Linden 2008). In the case of OAA strategy, there is a set of n binary classifiers trained to separate each class from the remaining classes (Waske, Menz, and Benediktsson 2007). Therefore, n rule images are obtained that consist of the maximum distance from the fitted decision line, and this decides the final class membership of a pixel (Aisen 2006).

8.4 CLASSIFICATION AND ACCURACY ASSESSMENT

8.4.1 CLASSIFICATION

All of the generated datasets after different-level fusion of hyperspectral with Radarsat-2 as well as ALOS PALSAR were classified using support vector machine (SVM). An NRSC level 2 classification scheme was adopted for classifying the study area. The SVM classification was chosen due to high dimensionality of the hyperspectral dataset, which caused curse of dimensionality. As data dimensionality increases after a certain point, classification accuracy decreased. This happens due to fewer training samples with respect to the number of bands of the hyperspectral data. In that case, data dimensionality reduction was performed for feature selection to the high dimensional dataset, but the SVM classifier is less sensitive to the Hughes phenomenon.

8.4.1.1 Support Vector Machines (SVM)

SVM is a non-parametric statistical learning classification technique that has no underlying assumption of the data (Mountrakis, Im, and Ogole 2011). Given a set of labelled data, the SVM algorithm finds a hyperplane that separates the dataset into the defined classes. The optimal separation hyperplane indicates the decision boundary that helps in minimizing the misclassifications. The SVM classifier is a linear binary classifier in its simplest form. In the linear case of SVM, the assumption is that the data are linearly separable in the input space (Mountrakis, Im, and Ogole 2011). An explanation of the support vector machines is described next, based on the work of Melgani and Bruzzone (2004). Let us consider a set of training samples I = 1, 2..., N in a feature space X_i and there are two classes that are linearly separable. Hence, it is possible to find an optimal hyperplane that separates the two classes. Therefore, the discriminant function is given as:

$$f(x) = W.x + b,$$ (8.44)

where,
W = vector that defines the hyperplane, and
b = bias that can separate two classes without errors.

To get the optimal hyperplane, parameters such as W and b have to be found. This is given as:

$$yi(W.Xi + b) > 0,$$ (8.45)

where $i = 1, 2...., N$.

The primary objective of SVM is to find the maximum distance between the training samples that are available closely and to the hyperplane that is separating. This distance is given as equal to 1/‖W‖ such that:

$$\min i\left(y_i\left(W.X_i + b\right)\right) \geq 1, \text{ where } i = 1, 2, ..., N.$$ (8.46)

Therefore, the geometrical margin between the two classes can be given as 2/‖W‖, and the optimal hyperplane is found by:

$$\begin{cases} \text{Minimize}: \dfrac{2}{\|w\|} \\ \text{Subject to}: y_i\left(w.X_i + b\right) \end{cases} \tag{8.47}$$

This optimization problem is translated into a dual problem using Lagrangian formulation AS:

$$\begin{cases} \text{maximize}: \displaystyle\sum_{i=1}^{N} \alpha_i - \frac{1}{2}\sum_{i=1}^{N}\sum_{j=1}^{N} \alpha_i \alpha_j y_i y_j \left(\mathbf{x_i} \cdot \mathbf{x_j}\right) \\ \text{Subject to}: \displaystyle\sum_{i=1}^{N} \alpha_i y_i = 0 \text{ and } \alpha_i \geq 0, \quad i = 1,2,\dots,N. \end{cases} \tag{8.48}$$

where α_i is the Lagrange multiplier.

Now the discriminant function becomes dependent on both the Lagrange multiplier and also the training samples:

$$f(X) = \sum_{I \in S} \alpha y_i \left(X_i.X\right) + b. \tag{8.49}$$

Corresponding to the non-zero Lagrange multipliers' S is then a subset of training samples. In determining the discriminant function, the Lagrange multipliers weight each of the training samples according to the importance of determining the discriminant function. Support vectors are the training samples associated to non-zero weights. These support vectors lie exactly at a distance 1/ ‖W‖ from the optimal hyperplane.

In real cases, linearly separable cases are not possible. In the case of non-separable data, the solution is that which expresses the combination of two criteria. The criteria are margin maximization, as in the previous case, and error minimization, to penalize the wrongly classified samples. Hence, the new function is given as:

$$\psi(W,\xi) = 1/2\left(\|W\|\right)^2 + C\sum_{i=1}^{N}\xi_i. \tag{8.50}$$

In equation (8.50), ξ_i, called the slack variable, is introduced to account for the non-separability of the data, and C is the regularization or the cost parameter that allows control for the penalty assigned for the misclassification of the samples. It should be noted that the larger the C value, the larger the penalty associated with the misclassification and vice versa.

To improve the preceding method of separating the two inseparable classes, it should be generalized to non-linear discriminant function using kernels. In general, a kernel corresponds to the inner dot product of two features in a feature space based on some mapping.

$$K\left(xi,xj\right) = \varphi(xi).\varphi(xj), \tag{8.51}$$

where φ is the mapping term.

According to Mercer's theorem, every semi-positive definite function is a kernel. To be a valid kernel in SVM, the kernel function needs to fulfil Mercer's theorem (Schölkopf and Smola 2002). Most standard kernel functions used in SVM are polynomial, sigmoid, and radial basis function kernels.

Linear kernel:

$$K\left(x,xi\right) = x.xi. \tag{8.52}$$

Polynomial kernel: This kernel computes the inner product of all monomials up to degree p:

$$K(x, xi) = (x.xi + 1)^P.$$ (8.53)

Radial basis function kernel:

$$K(x, xi) = \frac{exp(-\| x - xi \|)^2}{2\sigma^2}.$$ (8.54)

Sigmoid kernel:

$$K(x, xi) = tanh(x.xi + 1).$$ (8.55)

Use of the kernel can therefore avoid the computation effort and solve the dual problem, as it avoids computation of the inner products in the transformed space. Hence, the final discriminant function is expressed as:

$$f(X) = \sum_{i \in S} \alpha_{iy_i} k(X_i, X) + b.$$ (8.56)

8.4.2 ACCURACY ASSESSMENT

Accuracy assessment is one of the compulsory steps in validating the generated result. In this research, the cross-validation–based model, evaluation and accuracy assessment was adopted. In particular, the holdout method of cross-validation was performed with a training set, test set, and validation set. Following is the explanation of cross-validation in general, the holdout method of cross-validation, and the optimization of kernel parameters.

8.4.2.1 Cross-Validation

Cross-validation is also referred to as rotation estimation (Kohavi 1995). It is a model validation technique used to evaluate the results of how analysis based on statistics will generalize to an independent dataset. The basic idea of cross-validation is to train the classifier with the training set and test it with an entirely new test dataset. The different methods of cross-validation are holdout cross-validation, K-fold cross-validation, and leave one out cross-validation. The holdout method of cross-validation was used in this study and spatially uncorrelated samples were taken as training, validation, and test sets. Next is the description of the method.

8.4.2.2 Holdout Method with Parameter Tuning

This the simplest method of cross-validation. The holdout method was performed for this research to train the SVM classifier and to test it. This method is also referred to as the test sample estimation method, as the data is divided into two mutually exclusive subsets of the training set and a test set or a holdout set (Kohavi 1995). Additionally, a validation set was used to finetune the kernel parameters. The validation set is used to finetune the kernel parameters. In case of radial basis function, the parameter is gamma (ɣ) and the SVM cost parameter C. In a polynomial kernel, the parameters are degree, gamma, coefficient, and the SVM parameter C. In a sigmoid kernel it is gamma and coefficient along with the SVM parameter C. A grid search is one of the methods to define a set of candidate values for the parameter that is to be optimized. These parameters were tested and the optimum values of the parameters were obtained based on the higher accuracy on the validation set. An example of assigning values for each parameter in a grid search follows.

Cost C ϵ {1, 50, 100, 150, 200, 250, 300},
Degree p ϵ {1, 2, 3},

Coefficient C0 ϵ {1, 5, 10},
Gamma γ ϵ {0.05, 0.10, 0.15, 0.20,..., 1}.

The parameters have to be well optimized; if not, an overfitting or under-fitting problem of the model occurs.

8.4.3 Comparative Analysis

A comparative analysis was made between the fused products of hyperspectral and PolSAR data of C-band and L-band, using the three levels of fusion methods. The optimum level of fusion technique and also the best fusion pair was identified based on the classification and its accuracy.

8.5 RESULTS AND DISCUSSION

8.5.1 Results

8.5.1.1 Results of Pixel-Level Fusion

A comparative analysis was made from the results obtained from the three pixel-level fusion techniques using Hyperion and SPAN data extracted from PolSAR data (Radarsat-2 and ALOS PALSAR) and their classified outputs. The results of the classified outputs of the fused products are shown in Figure 8.3. The fusion of Hyperion + Radarsat-2 (span) and Hyperion + ALOS PALSAR (span) preserved the spectral characteristics of Hyperion with minimal spatial distortion. Wavelet fusion of Hyperion + Radarsat 2 and Hyperion + ALOS PALSAR preserved the spectral property of Hyperion to a certain extent, but there were spatial distortions in both the fused products. In Gram–Schmidt (GS) fusion, the spectral properties were not well preserved. Among all the fused results, high-pass filter (HPF) fusion performed well as it preserved the spectral properties of the hyperspectral data. After classifying the fused data, it was observed that the classification of HPF-fused data obtained from Hyperion and Radarsat-2 images (Figure 8.3d) was better in terms of overall accuracy and kappa value (Figure 8.4) when compared with the classified result of Hyperion and other fused products. The overall accuracy of classified results of the HPF-fused image of ALOS PALSAR and Hyperion data (Figure 8.3e) was better than the other fused classified results. The main reason could be due to its ability of to preserve the spectral properties of the hyperspectral data with minimal spatial distortions.

In the case of Gram–Schmidt fusion, the results were comparatively poor, which could be due to the multi-sensor fusion and overall accuracies of both Hyperion + Radarsat-2 and Hyperion + ALOS PALSAR reduced by 14 % (Figure 8.4). The classified images are shown in Figures 8.3f and g). It was found that the wavelet resolution merge for both pairs provided nearly the same results and did not affect much in the improvement of overall accuracy and kappa value (Figure 8.4) when compared with the original Hyperion classified image. Also, an important observation was that there was spatial distortion in the fused image. This could be one of the reasons for the reduced classification accuracy.

Accuracy of the classification depends on not only the overall accuracy and kappa values, but also the individual class accuracies. In different fused datasets, some of the classes have showed improved and better user and producer accuracy when compared with the others (Figures 8.5 and 8.6). Though the wavelet fusion of Hyperion and ALOS PALSAR provided slightly lesser accuracy when compared with Hyperion, due to the longer penetration capability of ALOS PALSAR, the class accuracy of dense forest was much better than the other products. In the case of barren land, due to the surface scattering and high penetration power of ALOS PALSAR, the fusion with Hyperion gave a better interpretation of barren land regions (Figure 8.3b and d). In addition, the producer accuracy

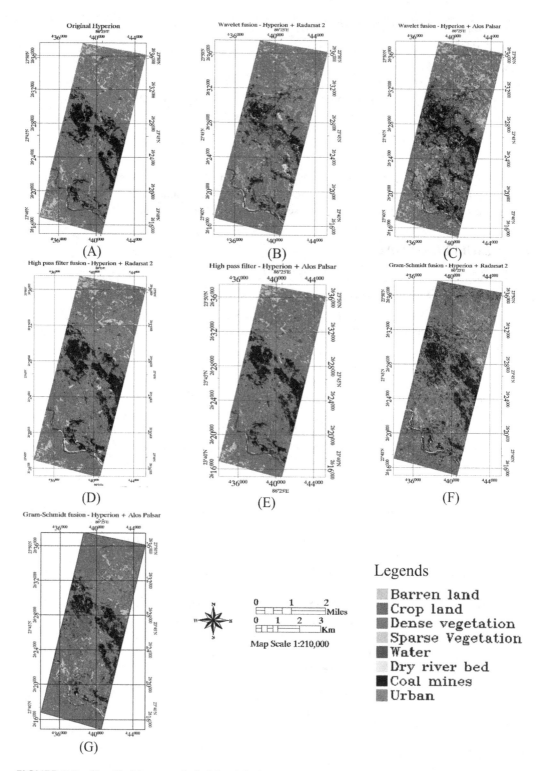

FIGURE 8.3 Classified images of pixel-level fusion: (A) Hyperion image, (B) wavelet fusion (Hyperion + Radarsat-2), (C) wavelet fusion (Hyperion + ALOS PALSAR), (D) HPF fusion (Hyperion + Radarsat-2), (E) HPF fusion (Hyperion + ALOS PALSAR), (F) Gram–Schmidt fusion (Hyperion + Radarsat-2), and (G) Gram–Schmidt fusion (Hyperion + ALOS PALSAR).

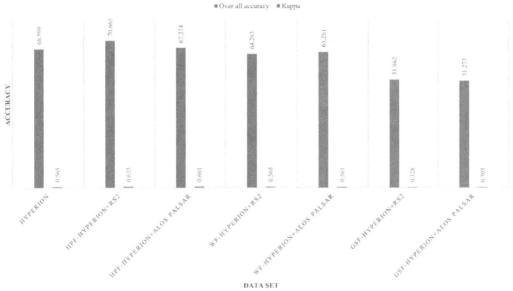

FIGURE 8.4 Comparison of overall accuracy and kappa of pixel-level fusion techniques.

of the same class in Hyperion and ALOS PALSAR fusion showed an improvement when compared with the other datasets (Figure 8.4). Due to the less penetration power of Radarsat-2, sparse vegetation, which includes shrubs and grasslands, showed a better producer accuracy in wavelet and HPF when compared with the other fused products, but not better than Hyperion. Another important observation was in the case of dry riverbeds. Due to the high penetration power of ALOS PALSAR, the dry riverbed showed an improvement in accuracy in wavelet and HPF fusion. Therefore, due to the high spectral property of hyperspectral, the urban areas and dry riverbed could be differentiated. The urban class showed a much better improvement in Radarsat-2 fusion with Hyperion using HPF. In case of the cropland class, the Radarsat-2 fusion with Hyperion using HPF and ALOS PALSAR fusion with Hyperion using HPF and wavelet showed improvement in producer accuracies (Figure 8.6). According to previous studies, Radarsat-2 is better for cropland identification when compared with ALOS PALSAR. But in this research, since the datasets acquired consisted of harvested cropland, both Radarsat-2 and ALOS PALSAR fusion showed accuracy improvement.

Overall, HPF fusion using Radarsat-2 and Hyperion gave improved overall accuracy and kappa value when compared with the original Hyperion. The accuracy of RS2 + Hyperion (HPF) was only slightly better, by around 3%, when compared with Radarsat-2 and ALOS PALSAR (HPF). But when analysed on the individual class accuracies, each of the fused products except Gram–Schmidt has some advantage in extracting information about each class. Though there were only a few percentage points of increase in the overall accuracy when compared with the original Hyperion, the individual class accuracies are important to obtain more information, which were inferred in the fused products. One more important point here is that the accuracies of the fused products were compared with the original low spectral resolution Hyperion image and not with the SAR, as the SAR datasets used were greyscale images and were not classified. Generally, from the literature, in case of pixel-level fusion the classification accuracy of the fused product was compared only with the high spectral resolution image and not with the high spatial resolution PAN or the greyscale image.

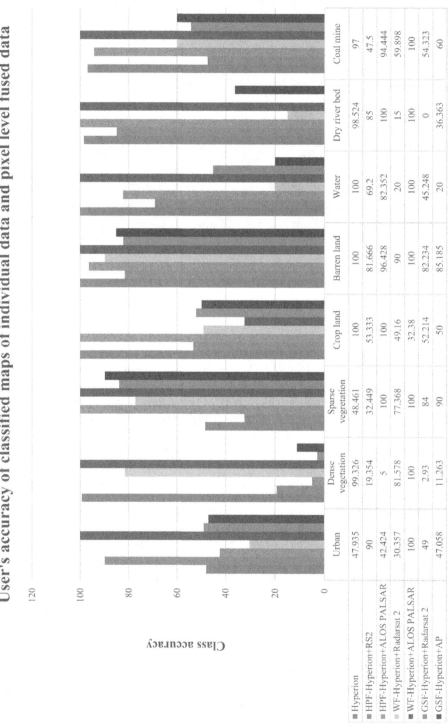

FIGURE 8.5 User accuracies of the defined classes from the classified outputs of the Hyperion- and pixel-level fused products.

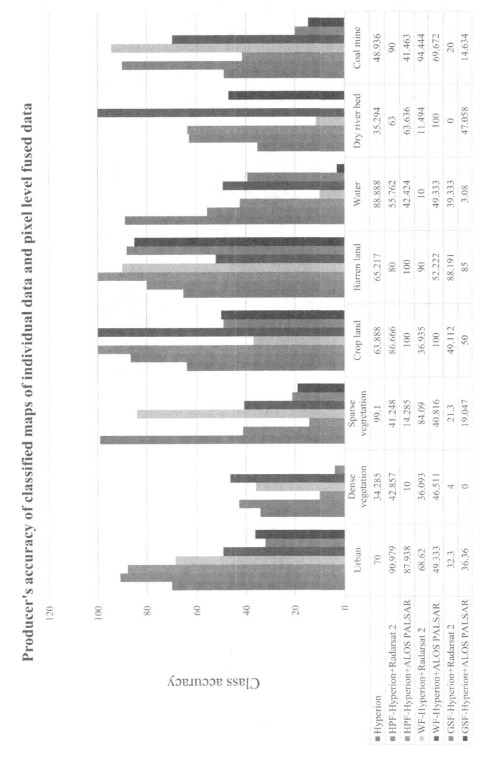

FIGURE 8.6 Producer accuracies of the defined classes from the classified outputs of the Hyperion- and pixel-level fused products.

8.5.1.2   Results of Feature-Level Fusion

The results obtained after feature-level fusion was performed by forming a feature vector of KPCA components extracted from Hyperion and the MCSM parameters extracted from the fully polarimetric SAR data. After extracting the feature vectors from hyperspectral and PolSAR data, the classification was performed using non-linear support vector machines. The kernel function used was the radial basis function for the classification of Hyperion and the feature vectors and polynomial kernel for the individual PolSAR datasets. The accuracy assessment was performed using the cross-validation–based holdout method. The spatially uncorrelated pixels were taken as the training set,

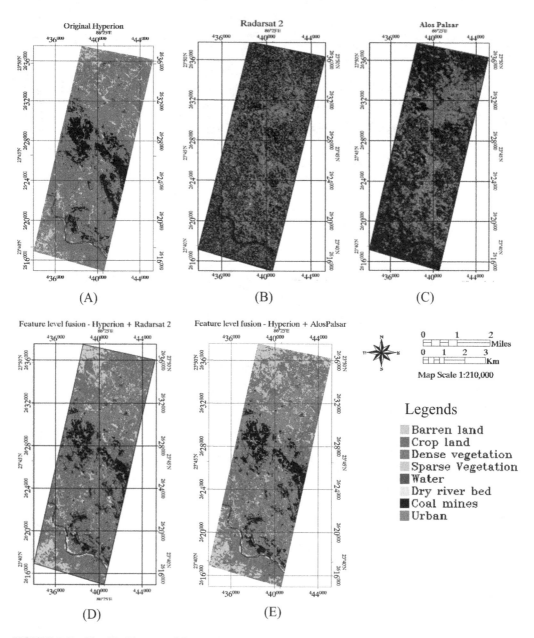

FIGURE 8.7   Classified images of feature-level fusion: (A) Hyperion, (B) Radarsat-2, (C) ALOS PALSAR, (D) Hyperion + Radarsat-2, and (E) Hyperion + ALOS PALSAR.

test set, and validation set for each of the feature vector and the fully polarimetric SAR datasets. The SVM model was finetuned based on the accuracy obtained using the validation set, and the kernel parameter gamma and the SVM parameter C were chosen. Figure 8.8 shows the accuracy obtained for the classification of the fused products. Figure 8.7 shows the classified images of the Hyperion, individual PolSAR data, and fused products at feature-level fusion. In these images, RS2 indicates Radarsat-2. The results of feature-level fusion were obtained through the information fusion of the extracted features: Hyperion through KPCA and SAR datasets through MCSM decomposition. Classification after the information fusion of Hyperion + RS2 and Hyperion + ALOS PALSAR has resulted in an increase in overall accuracy and kappa (Figure 8.8). The classified images are given in Figure 8.7a–e. There is an improvement of around 10% and 33% in the overall accuracy of Hyperion + ALOS PALSAR fusion when compared with the individual datasets, namely Hyperion and ALOS PALSAR. In the case of the other pair, there is around 7% and 36% improvement in the overall accuracy in comparison with Hyperion and Radarsat 2 (Figure 8.8).

In the case of class accuracies, urban class accuracy (both producer and user accuracy) was improved from the fusion of RS2 with Hyperion and ALOS PALSAR with Hyperion when compared with the individual datasets. The main reason could be the MCSM decomposition technique used for the extraction of features in SAR datasets. This decomposition technique is capable of extracting the urban region from the fully polarimetric data. The individual class accuracies of the dense vegetation and sparse vegetation also showed good improvement in the case of Hyperion + ALOS PALSAR and Hyperion + Radarsat-2, respectively (Figures 8.9 and 8.10). This could be due to the high penetration power of ALOS PALSAR to classify the dense vegetation correctly. Since Radarsat-2 has a low penetration power, sparse vegetation is better in the fusion of the latter. Due to surface scattering, which is prominent in moderately rough surface regions, there was an increase in producer and user accuracy of barren land in the information fusion of Hyperion with both RS2 and ALOS PALSAR. Also, the coal mining regions were classified, and the accuracy was improved,

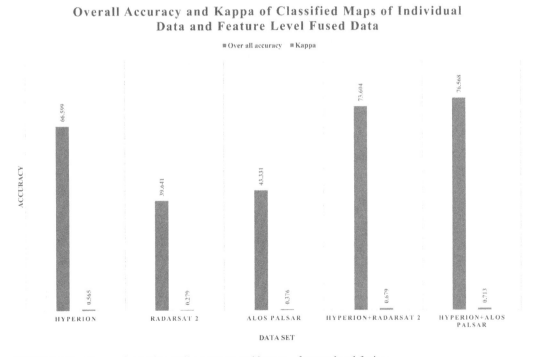

Overall Accuracy and Kappa of Classified Maps of Individual Data and Feature Level Fused Data

■ Over all accuracy ■ Kappa

66.599			73.604	76.568
	39.641	43.331		
0.565	0.279	0.376	0.679	0.713
HYPERION	RADARSAT 2	ALOS PALSAR	HYPERION+RADARSAT 2	HYPERION+ALOS PALSAR

DATA SET

FIGURE 8.8 Comparison of overall accuracy and kappa – feature-level fusion.

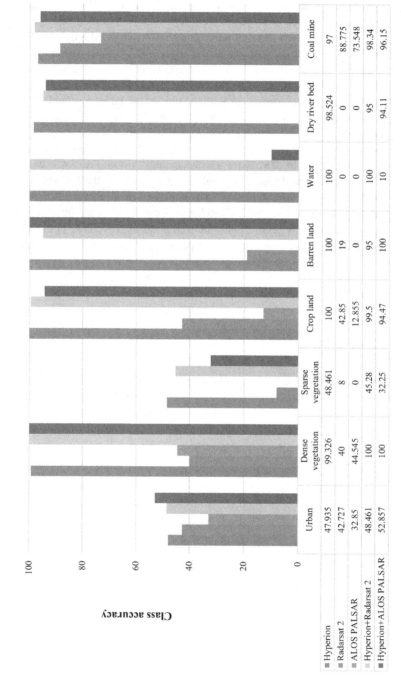

FIGURE 8.9 User accuracies of the defined classes from the classified outputs of the Hyperion, Radarsat 2, ALOS PALSAR, and feature-level fused products.

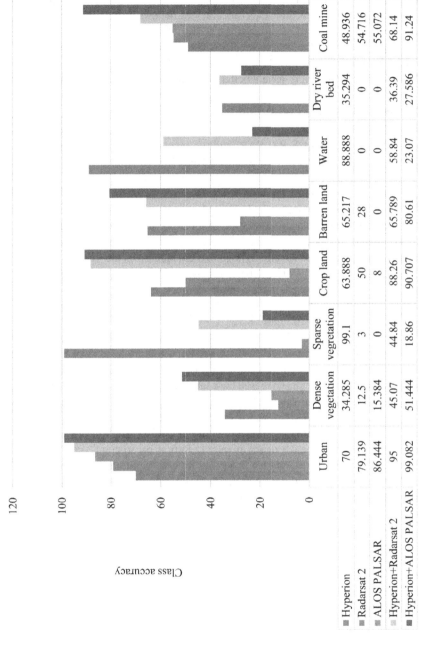

Producer's accuracy of classified maps of individual data and feature level fused data

	Urban	Dense vegetation	Sparse vegetation	Crop land	Barren land	Water	Dry river bed	Coal mine
Hyperion	70	34.285	99.1	63.888	65.217	88.888	35.294	48.936
Radarsat 2	79.139	12.5	3	50	28	0	0	54.716
ALOS PALSAR	86.444	15.384	0	8	0	0	0	55.072
Hyperion+Radarsat 2	95	45.07	44.84	88.26	65.789	58.84	36.39	68.14
Hyperion+ALOS PALSAR	99.082	51.444	18.86	90.707	80.61	23.07	27.586	91.24

FIGURE 8.10 Producer accuracies of the land use classes from the classified outputs of the Hyperion- and feature-level fused products.

which could also be due to the surface scattering parameter. The results of the accuracy assessment are given in the Figure 8.8. Main reasons for these results could be the feature extraction; in particular, the kernel-based non-linear transformation of the Hyperion data played a significant role in improving overall accuracy, and also some of the class accuracies of the classified feature vectors, namely the water and dry riverbed, which were not classified correctly in the individual ALOS PALSAR and RS2 images (Figures 8.9 and 8.10). In addition, the MCSM decomposition-based feature extraction in SAR improved the class accuracy of the urban class. The accuracies could have been further improved if the classification of the SAR datasets were performed better. Due to the surface scattering property of the coal mine class, dry riverbed class, barren land class, and water class created confusion and were misclassified (Figure 8.7b and c). Overall, the fusion of Hyperion and ALOS PALSAR comparatively gave a better result in terms of overall accuracy and kappa.

8.5.1.3   Results of Decision-Level Fusion

Decision-level fusion was performed on the rule images, which were the priori output of the SVM classification of Radarsat-2, ALOS PALSAR, and the Hyperion images. In total, eight rule images were obtained for each of the classes for all three datasets. The feature vectors obtained using the rule images were classified using the SVM a second time to obtain the final class membership of the pixels. The training, test, and validation samples were taken based on the membership values of each pixel belonging to a particular class. The value ranges from 0 to 1 and indicate the distance of the pixels to the fitted hyperplane of the SVM model. The lower the value, the closer the pixel is to the fitted hyperplane and vice versa. A decision was made such that a range was set from 0.80 to 1, and the pixels belonging to this specified range was considered as the training, test, and validation samples. Different kernels, such as radial basis function, polynomial and sigmoid, were tried, and the optimal kernel was chosen based on the overall accuracy. Figure 8.11 shows classified images of the original datasets and the information-fused datasets at decision-level fusion. A summary of the classification accuracy is shown in Figure 8.12.

In this level of fusion, different kernels, such as radial basis function, polynomial and sigmoid, were used to classify the Radarsat-2, ALOS PALSAR and feature vectors of Hyperion + RS2 and Hyperion + ALOS PALSAR. The initial output of this level of fusion was the rule images of RS2, ALOS PALSAR, and the Hyperion images. These are the priori outputs of the SVM classification, which consist of the membership values of each pixel belonging to a particular class. Later, the rule images of RS2 and ALOS PALSAR were stacked individually with the Hyperion. Then, SVM was applied based on the training samples obtained from the stacked rule images, and finally, the class memberships were decided for each of the pixels. Different parameters, such as gamma for RBF kernel; gamma, degree, and coefficient for polynomial kernel; and gamma and degree for sigmoid kernel were chosen based on a grid search method on the validation set.

From the obtained results, decision-level fusion significantly improved the classification accuracy of the fused product when compared with the original RS2 and ALOS PALSAR by a greater margin, but very less improvement was found in comparison with Hyperion. It was observed that the ALOS PALSAR and Hyperion fusion was better when compared with Radarsat 2 and Hyperion in terms of overall accuracy and kappa (Figure 8.12). The individual classification of the PolSAR images proved less useful in terms of the overall accuracy. This could be due to the similar backscatter range values for coal, barren land, dry riverbed, and water because of the smooth surface scattering. Highest overall accuracy and kappa were obtained when the polynomial kernel was used for the individual SAR images. In the SVM applied to the feature vectors, it was found that the RBF kernel improved the overall accuracy.

In the case of individual class accuracies, the urban, cropland, water, coal, and dense vegetation classes of the fused images improved in terms of producer accuracy in comparison with the individual images (Figures 8.13 and 8.14). The urban class improved due to the MCSM decomposition parameters extracted from PolSAR data. The accuracy of dense vegetation was high in the Hyperion

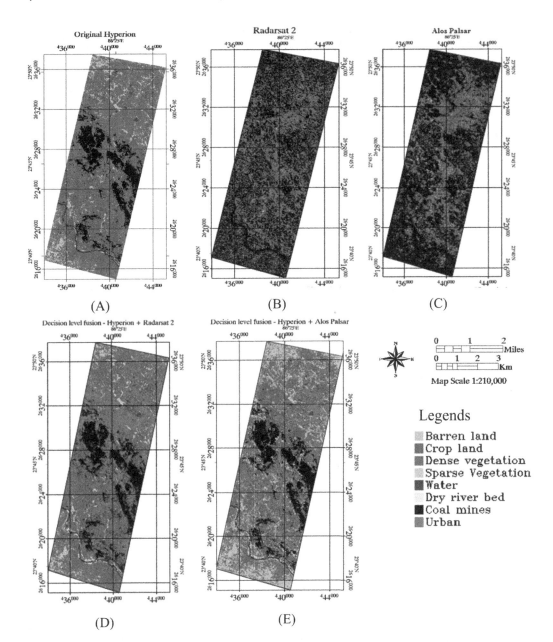

FIGURE 8.11 Classified images of decision-level fusion: (A) Hyperion, (B) Radarsat-2, (C) ALOS PALSAR, (D) Hyperion + Radarsat-2, and (E) Hyperion + ALOS PALSAR.

and ALOS PALSAR fusion results due to the higher penetration capability of ALOS PALSAR. The comparative analysis of the user and producer accuracies of the individual classes for decision-level fusion is shown in Figures 8.13 and 8.14. From the obtained results, there was not much improvement in the overall accuracy when compared with Hyperion. The reason could be due to the poor classification of the SAR datasets, which were of coarser spatial resolution, as well as the classes, namely the coal, barren land, dry riverbed, and water class, which had the same range of backscatter values due to the surface scattering property. This led to misclassification of the classes. Overall, the fusion of Hyperion and ALOS PALSAR proved to be better in comparison with Hyperion and

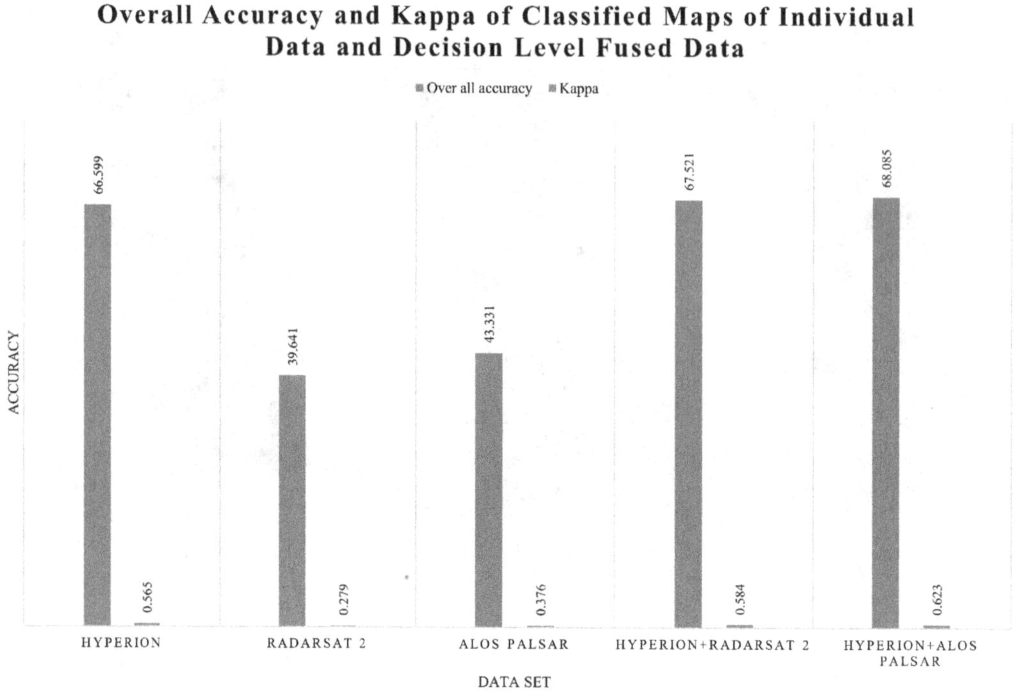

Overall Accuracy and Kappa of Classified Maps of Individual Data and Decision Level Fused Data

■ Over all accuracy   ■ Kappa

FIGURE 8.12 Comparison of overall accuracy and kappa – decision-level fusion.

Radarsat-2, which improved classification accuracy by around 1.5% when compared with Hyperion, the individual SAR dataset by around 28% in comparison with Radarsat-2, and 29% in comparison with ALOS PALSAR. Figures 8.13 and 8.14 show the user and producer class accuracies for the defined classes at decision-level fusion.

8.5.2 COMPARATIVE ANALYSIS OF ALL THE THREE LEVELS OF FUSION OF HYPERSPECTRAL AND PolSAR DATA

After analysing the classified results obtained from the three levels of fusion, the optimal fusion pair was chosen from each of the fusion levels for comparison. The optimal fusion pair was selected by observing the best classification accuracy. HPF fusion of Hyperion and Radarsat-2 was found to be the best optimal fusion pair among the pixel-level fusion outputs, whereas at feature-level and decision-level fusion, the Hyperion and ALOS PALSAR pair was observed as the best combination. Figure 8.15 shows the comparative analysis, overall accuracy, and kappa at all three fusion levels.

Based on the obtained results of all three levels of fusion, the optimal data pair that gave the highest overall accuracy and the kappa at each level of fusion was found to be:

Hyperion and Radarsat-2 for pixel-level fusion (Figure 8.3).
Hyperion and ALOS PALSAR for feature-level fusion (Figure 8.7).
Hyperion and ALOS PALSAR for decision-level fusion (Figure 8.11).

Comparative analysis was made in terms of overall accuracy and kappa (Figure 8.15) among the three, and the optimal fusion pair along with the level of fusion was obtained. Based on the analysis, the Hyperion and ALOS PALSAR pair have the highest overall accuracy at the feature level of fusion. The overall accuracy obtained was 76.568%, which was greater than the original Hyperion

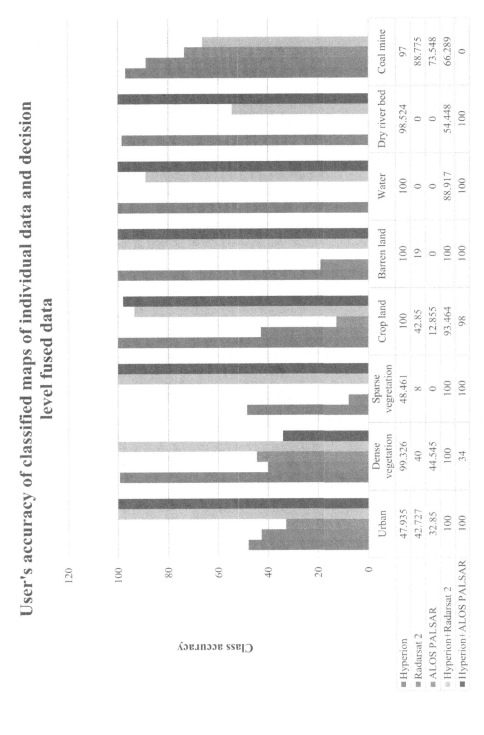

FIGURE 8.13 User accuracies of the defined classes from the classified outputs of the Hyperion, Radarsat-2, ALOS PALSAR, and decision-level fused products.

	Urban	Dense vegetation	Sparse vegetation	Crop land	Barren land	Water	Dry river bed	Coal mine
Hyperion	47.935	99.326	48.461	100	100	100	98.524	97
Radarsat 2	42.727	40	8	42.85	19	0	0	88.775
ALOS PALSAR	32.85	44.545	0	12.855	0	0	0	73.548
Hyperion+Radarsat 2	100	100	100	93.464	100	88.917	54.448	66.289
Hyperion+ALOS PALSAR	100	34	100	98	100	100	100	0

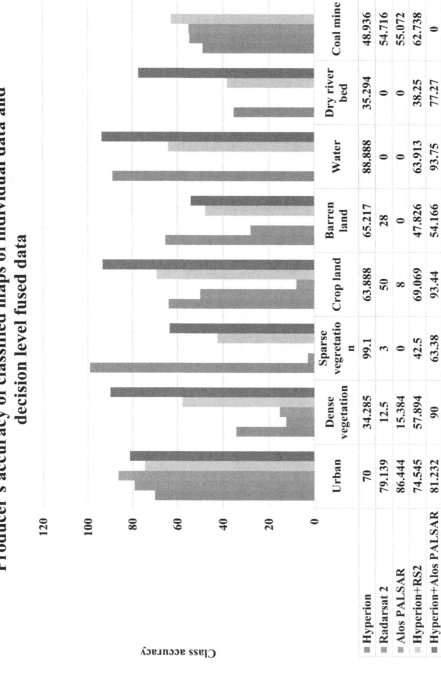

FIGURE 8.14 Producer accuracies of the defined classes from the classified outputs of the Hyperion, Radarsat-2, ALOS PALSAR, and decision-level fused products.

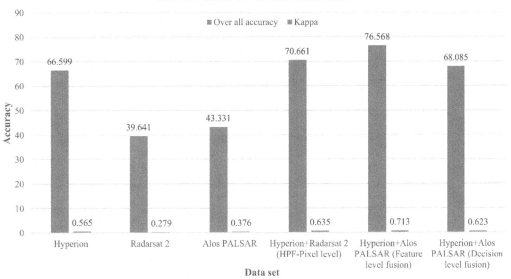

Overall Accuracy & Kappa of Classified Maps of Individual Data and all three levels of fused data

FIGURE 8.15 Comparison of overall accuracy and kappa of the classified maps of the Hyperion, Radarsat-2, ALOS PALSAR, and fused outputs at all three levels of fusion.

and Radarsat-2. At decision-level fusion, Hyperion and ALOS PALSAR fusion has the better overall accuracy, of around 68%. The producer accuracy of coal mines, cropland, and urban classes was improved at feature-level fusion of the Hyperion and ALOS PALSAR fusion pair (Figures 8.16 and 8.17). The main reasons for the obtained results on all three levels of fusion are:

- Effective feature extraction from both datasets could have resulted in high accuracy at feature-level fusion.
- The spectral preserving property of HPF is the main reason for improved accuracy at pixel-level fusion.
- At the decision level, there was not much improvement in accuracy when compared with the original Hyperion and the other fusion levels. This could be due to the improper classification of SAR datasets that resulted in an ineffective decision-making process.
- The coarser resolution of SAR datasets (20-metre resolution) was an important factor that had an effect on the obtained results.
- The penetration capability of each ALOS PALSAR and Radarsat-2.
- MCSM decomposition, which is prominent in extraction of urban features, was less effective in the classification process of the PolSAR datasets.

Figures 8.16 and 8.17 represent the individual class accuracies of LULC classes from the classified maps of the Hyperion, Radarsat-2, ALOS PALSAR, and fused outputs at all three levels of fusion.

8.6 CONCLUSION AND RECOMMENDATION

8.6.1 CONCLUSION

Multi-sensor fusion of satellite datasets normally enhances LULC classification, as fusion combines complementary information from different sensors for better interpretation of land cover features. In

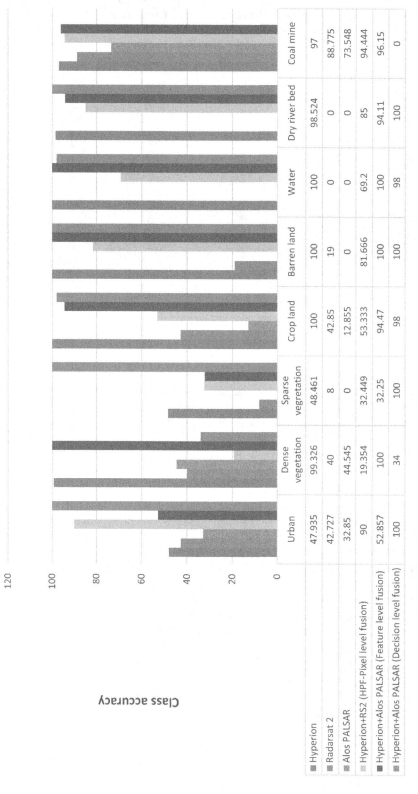

FIGURE 8.16 User accuracies of the land use classes from the classified maps of the Hyperion, Radarsat-2, ALOS PALSAR, and fused outputs at all three levels of fusion.

	Urban	Dense vegetation	Sparse vegetation	Crop land	Barren land	Water	Dry river bed	Coal mine
Hyperion	47.935	99.326	48.461	100	100	100	98.524	97
Radarsat 2	42.727	40	8	42.85	19	0	0	88.775
Alos PALSAR	32.85	44.545	0	12.855	0	0	0	73.548
Hyperion+RS2 (HPF–Pixel level fusion)	90	19.354	32.449	53.333	81.666	69.2	85	94.444
Hyperion+Alos PALSAR (Feature level fusion)	52.857	100	32.25	94.47	100	100	94.11	96.15
Hyperion+Alos PALSAR (Decision level fusion)	100	34	100	98	100	98	100	0

Producer's accuracy of classified maps of individual data and all three levels of fused data

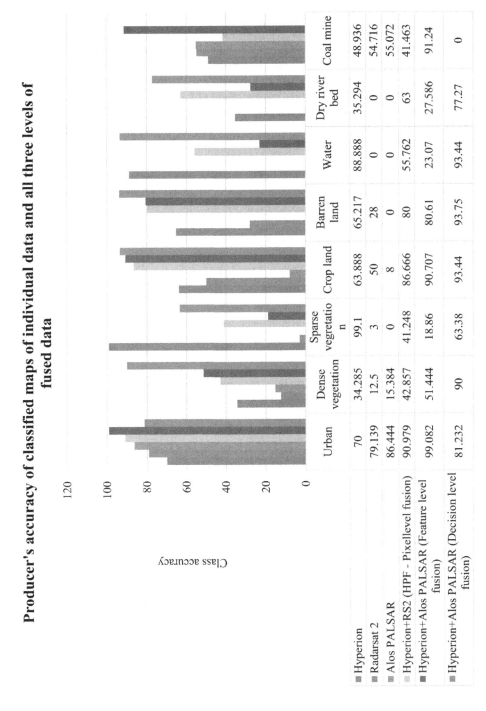

	Urban	Dense vegetation	Sparse vegretation	Crop land	Barren land	Water	Dry river bed	Coal mine
Hyperion	70	34.285	99.1	63.888	65.217	88.888	35.294	48.936
Radarsat 2	79.139	12.5	3	50	28	0	0	54.716
Alos PALSAR	86.444	15.384	0	8	0	55.762	0	55.072
Hyperion+RS2 (HPF - Pixellevel fusion)	90.979	42.857	41.248	86.666	80	55.762	63	41.463
Hyperion+Alos PALSAR (Feature level fusion)	99.082	51.444	18.86	90.707	80.61	23.07	27.586	91.24
Hyperion+Alos PALSAR (Decision level fusion)	81.232	90	63.38	93.44	93.75	93.44	77.27	0

FIGURE 8.17 Producer accuracies of the land use classes from the classified maps of the Hyperion, Radarsat-2, ALOS PALSAR, and fused outputs at all three levels of fusion.

this study, Hyperion data was fused separately with Radarsat-2 C-band and ALOS PALSAR L-band using three different levels of fusion, namely the pixel level, feature level, and decision level. The conclusions for the study are as follows:

- In the obtained results, significant improvement was observed in the individual class accuracies of LULC classes, such as urban, cropland, and vegetation, of the fused products in comparison with the individual sources. For example, the spectrally similar classes of dry riverbed and urban features were distinguished with the help of double-bounce, helix, and wire scattering as they are more dominant in urban regions. Hence, integrating hyperspectral data with polarimetric SAR data enabled enhancement of LULC classes.
- It was also observed that the classified image of Hyperion and ALOS PALSAR L-band fusion at feature-level fusion provided better classification accuracy than fusion of Hyperion and Radarsat-2 C-band and the individual sources.
- Due to extraction of polarimetric parameters, by using the MCSM decomposition technique significant improvement was observed in various classes, especially the urban class.
- Among the classified result of pixel-level fused products, the HPF-fused product of Hyperion and Radarsat-2 gave highest overall accuracy, as the spectral properties of the Hyperion data were preserved to a larger extent in the fused output.
- The kernel-based SVM classification played an important role in the improvement of the classification, and for the classification of feature vectors at the decision-level fusion, the polynomial kernel was found more effective. At pixel level and feature level, however, the radial basis function was found suitable for classification.

8.6.2 Recommendations

It is very important in any study to perform qualitative as well as qualitative analysis of the resultant product. Though significant improvement was observed in the accuracy of the fused output of hyperspectral and PolSAR data at the feature level in comparison with the other fused product and individually classified data, there are a few observations to consider in future work.

- Usage of very high-resolution spaceborne polarimetric data and hyperspectral data could improve the fusion performance.
- Feature selection technique like kernel-based Hilbert space independence criterion could be used to select the features based on the defined classes that are relevant for the classification process. This could further improve the performance of feature-level fusion.
- Texture parameters–based classification could be done if the polarimetric data is of high spatial resolution. This, in turn, would improve the classification of the individual SAR datasets as well as the performance of decision-level fusion.
- Decision-level fusion on the usage of the one-against-one strategy based SVM classification could improve decision-making and classification accuracy as it performs pairwise discrimination of each of the classes from the other, which causes a particular class differentiation. Though it is a time-consuming process, it could prove effective in classification and fusion.

REFERENCES

Abdikan, Saygin, Fusun Balik Sanli, Filiz Sunar, and Manfred Ehlers. 2014. "A Comparative Data-Fusion Analysis of Multi-Sensor Satellite Images." *International Journal of Digital Earth* 7 (8): 671–87. https://doi.org/10.1080/17538947.2012.748846.

Aiazzi, B., S. Baronti, M. Selva, and L. Alparone. 2006. "Enhanced Gram-Schmidt Spectral Sharpening Based on Multivariate Regression of MS and Pan Data." In *2006 IEEE International Symposium on*

Geoscience and Remote Sensing, 3806–9. Denver, CO, USA: IEEE. https://doi.org/10.1109/IGA RSS.2006.975.

Aisen, Ben. 2006. "A Comparison of Multiclass SVM Methods." 2006. http://courses.media.mit.edu/2006f all/mas622j/Projects/aisen-project/.

Amarsaikhan, D., H.H. Blotevogel, J.L. van Genderen, M. Ganzorig, R. Gantuya, and B. Nergui. 2010. "Fusing High-Resolution SAR and Optical Imagery for Improved Urban Land Cover Study and Classification." *International Journal of Image and Data Fusion* 1 (1): 83–97. https://doi.org/10.1080/19479830903562041.

Borghys, Dirk, Michal Shimoni, Gregory Degueldre, and Christiaan Perneel. 2007. "Improved Object Recognition by Fusion of Hyperspectral and SAR Data," 14.

Bruzzone, Lorenzo, and Claudio Persello. 2009. "Approaches Based on Support Vector Machine to Classification of Remote Sensing Data." In *Handbook of Pattern Recognition and Computer Vision*, edited by C. H. Chen, 4th ed., 329–52. World Scientific. https://doi.org/10.1142/9789814273398_0014.

Byun, Younggi. 2014. "A Texture-Based Fusion Scheme to Integrate High-Resolution Satellite SAR and Optical Images." *Remote Sensing Letters* 5 (2): 103–11. https://doi.org/10.1080/21507 04X.2014.880817.

Chandola, Shreya. 2014. "Polarimetric SAR Interferometry for Forest Aboveground Biomass Estimation," MS thesis, Faculty of Geo-information Science and Earth Observation, Univ. of Twente, Enschede, the Netherlands, 80.

Chen, C.-M., G. F. Hepner, and R. R. Forster. 2003. "Fusion of Hyperspectral and Radar Data Using the IHS Transformation to Enhance Urban Surface Features." *ISPRS Journal of Photogrammetry and Remote Sensing* 58 (1–2): 19–30. https://doi.org/10.1016/S0924-2716(03)00014-5.

Dai, Chen-guang, Xiao-bo Huang, and Guang-jun Dong. 2007. "Support Vector Machine for Classification of Hyperspectral Remote Sensing Imagery." In *Fourth International Conference on Fuzzy Systems and Knowledge Discovery (FSKD 2007)*, 77–80. Haikou, China: IEEE. https://doi.org/10.1109/FSKD.2007.550.

Dong, Jiang, Dafang Zhuang, Yaohuan Huang, and Jingying Fu. 2009. "Advances in Multi-Sensor Data Fusion: Algorithms and Applications." *Sensors* 9 (10): 7771–84. https://doi.org/10.3390/s91007771.

Fauvel, Mathieu, Jocelyn Chanussot, and Jon Benediktsson. 2006. "Kernel Principal Component Analysis for Feature Reduction in Hyperspectral Images Analysis." In *Proceedings of the 7th Nordic Signal Processing Symposium – NORSIG 2006*, 238–41. IEEE. https://doi.org/10.1109/NORSIG.2006.275232.

Fukuda, S., and H. Hirosawa. 2001. "Support Vector Machine Classification of Land Cover: Application to Polarimetric SAR Data." In *IGARSS 2001. Scanning the Present and Resolving the Future. Proceedings. IEEE 2001 International Geoscience and Remote Sensing Symposium (Cat. No.01CH37217)*, 1:187–89. Sydney, NSW, Australia: IEEE. https://doi.org/10.1109/IGARSS.2001.976097.

Ghanbari, Zeynab, and Mahmod R. Sahebi. 2014. "Improved IHS Algorithm for Fusing High Resolution Satellite Images of Urban Areas." *Journal of the Indian Society of Remote Sensing* 42 (4): 689–99. https://doi.org/10.1007/s12524-014-0364-x.

Giampouras, Paris, Eleni Charou, and Anastasios Kesidis. 2013. "Artificial Neural Network Approach for Land Cover Classification of Fused Hyperspectral and Lidar Data." In *Artificial Intelligence Applications and Innovations*, edited by Harris Papadopoulos, Andreas S. Andreou, Lazaros Iliadis, and Ilias Maglogiannis, 412:255–61. IFIP Advances in Information and Communication Technology. Berlin, Heidelberg: Springer Berlin Heidelberg. https://doi.org/10.1007/978-3-642-41142-7_26.

Gonzalez, Rafael C., and Richard E. Woods, eds. 2001. *Digital Image Processing*. Addison-Wesley.

Hadjimitsis, D. G., G. Papadavid, A. Agapiou, K. Themistocleous, M. G. Hadjimitsis, A. Retalis, S. Michaelides, N. Chrysoulakis, L. Toulios, and C. R. I. Clayton. 2010. "Atmospheric Correction for Satellite Remotely Sensed Data Intended for Agricultural Applications: Impact on Vegetation Indices." *Natural Hazards and Earth System Science* 10 (1): 89–95. https://doi.org/10.5194/nhess-10-89-2010.

Huang, X., L. Zhang, and P. Li. 2008. "A Multiscale Feature Fusion Approach for Classification of Very High Resolution Satellite Imagery Based on Wavelet Transform." *International Journal of Remote Sensing* 29 (20): 5923–41. https://doi.org/10.1080/01431160802139922.

Kiema, J. B. K. 2002. "Texture Analysis and Data Fusion in the Extraction of Topographic Objects From Satellite Imagery." *International Journal of Remote Sensing* 23 (4): 767–76. https://doi.org/10.1080/01431160010026005.

Klonus, S., and M. Ehlers. 2009. "Performance of Evaluation Methods in Image Fusion." In *Proceedings of 12th International Conference on Information Fusion*, 1409–16. Seattle, WA, 6–9 July.

Klonus, Sascha, and Manfred Ehlers. 2007. "Image Fusion Using the Ehlers Spectral Characteristics Preservation Algorithm." *GIScience & Remote Sensing* 44 (2): 93–116. https://doi.org/10.2747/1548-1603.44.2.93.

Knödel, Klaus, Gerhard Lange, and Hans-Jürgen Voigt. 2007. *Environmental Geology*. Berlin, Heidelberg: Springer Berlin Heidelberg. https://doi.org/10.1007/978-3-540-74671-3.

Kohavi, Ron. 1995. "A Study of Cross-Validation and Bootstrap for Accuracy Estimation and Model Selection," August, 1137–43.

Li, Shutao, James T. Kwok, and Yaonan Wang. 2002. "Using the Discrete Wavelet Frame Transform to Merge Landsat TM and SPOT Panchromatic Images." *Information Fusion* 3 (1): 17–23. https://doi.org/10.1016/S1566-2535(01)00037-9.

Li, Tong, Junping Zhang, Honglei Zhao, and Cuiping Shi. 2013. "Classification-Oriented Hyperspectral and PolSAR Images Synergic Processing." In *2013 IEEE International Geoscience and Remote Sensing Symposium – IGARSS*, 1035–38. Melbourne, Australia: IEEE. https://doi.org/10.1109/IGARSS.2013.6721340.

Lu, Dengsheng, Guiying Li, Emilio Moran, Luciano Dutra, and Mateus Batistella. 2011. "A Comparison of Multisensor Integration Methods for Land Cover Classification in the Brazilian Amazon." *GIScience & Remote Sensing* 48 (3): 345–70. https://doi.org/10.2747/1548-1603.48.3.345.

Lu, Xiaochen, and Zhang, Junping. 2014. "Panchromatic and Multispectral Images Fusion Based on Modified GS-SWT." In *2014 IEEE Geoscience and Remote Sensing Symposium*, 2530–33. IEEE. https://doi.org/10.1109/IGARSS.2014.6946988.

Ma, Shiwei, Li Jia, Xin Li, Ling Wang, Huiyu Zhou, and Xin Sun, eds. 2014. *Life System Modeling and Simulation*, vol. 461. Communications in Computer and Information Science. Berlin, Heidelberg: Springer Berlin Heidelberg. https://doi.org/10.1007/978-3-662-45283-7.

Melgani, F., and L. Bruzzone. 2002. "Support Vector Machines for Classification of Hyperspectral Remote-Sensing Images." In *IEEE International Geoscience and Remote Sensing Symposium*, 1:506–8. Toronto, Ont., Canada: IEEE. https://doi.org/10.1109/IGARSS.2002.1025088.

Melgani, F., and L. Bruzzone. 2004. "Classification of Hyperspectral Remote Sensing Images with Support Vector Machines." *IEEE Transactions on Geoscience and Remote Sensing* 42 (8): 1778–90. https://doi.org/10.1109/TGRS.2004.831865.

Meng, Qingmin, Bruce Borders, and Marguerite Madden. 2010. "High-Resolution Satellite Image Fusion Using Regression Kriging." *International Journal of Remote Sensing* 31 (7): 1857–76. https://doi.org/10.1080/01431160902927937.

Metwalli, Mohamed R., Ayman H. Nasr, Osama S. Farag Allah, S. El-Rabaie, and Fathi E. Abd El-Samie. 2010. "Satellite Image Fusion Based on Principal Component Analysis and High-Pass Filtering." *Journal of the Optical Society of America A* 27 (6): 1385. https://doi.org/10.1364/JOSAA.27.001385.

Mountrakis, Giorgos, Jungho Im, and Caesar Ogole. 2011. "Support Vector Machines in Remote Sensing: A Review." *ISPRS Journal of Photogrammetry and Remote Sensing* 66 (3): 247–59. https://doi.org/10.1016/j.isprsjprs.2010.11.001.

Peli, Tamar, Mon Young, Robert Knox, Kenneth K. Ellis, and Frederick Bennett. 1999. "Feature-Level Sensor Fusion." In *Proc. SPIE 3719, Sensor Fusion: Architectures, Algorithms, and Applications III*, edited by Belur V. Dasarathy, 332. Orlando, FL. https://doi.org/10.1117/12.341355.

Pohl, C., and J. L. Van Genderen. 1998. "Review Article Multisensor Image Fusion in Remote Sensing: Concepts, Methods and Applications." *International Journal of Remote Sensing*. Taylor & Francis. https://doi.org/10.1080/014311698215748.

Pohl, Christine, and John van Genderen. 2014. "Remote Sensing Image Fusion: An Update in the Context of Digital Earth." *International Journal of Digital Earth* 7 (2): 158–72. https://doi.org/10.1080/17538947.2013.869266.

Pohl, Christine, and John van Genderen. 2015. "Structuring Contemporary Remote Sensing Image Fusion." *International Journal of Image and Data Fusion* 6 (1): 3–21. https://doi.org/10.1080/19479832.2014.998727.

Pohl, Christine, Duncan Munro, and John L. van Genderen. 1997. "Enhanced Image Analysis Through Multilevel Data Fusion Techniques." In *Proc. SPIE 3068, Signal Processing, Sensor Fusion, and Target Recognition VI*, edited by Ivan Kadar, 32. Orlando, FL, USA. https://doi.org/10.1117/12.280821.

Schölkopf , Bernhard, and Alex Smola. 2002. "Support Vector Machines and Kernel Algorithms."

Schölkopf, Bernhard, Alexander Smola, and Klaus-Robert Müller. 1997. "Kernel Principal Component Analysis." In *Artificial Neural Networks — ICANN'97*, 583–88. https://doi.org/10.1007/BFb0020217.

Sheela Rani, C. M., V. Vijaya Kumar, and B. Sujatha. 2012. "An Efficient Block Based Feature Level Image Fusion Technique Using Wavelet Transform and Neural Network." *International Journal of Computer Applications* 52 (12): 13–19. https://doi.org/10.5120/8253-1780.

Swain, Philip H., and Shirley M. Davis. 1981. "Remote Sensing: The Quantitative Approach." *IEEE Transactions on Pattern Analysis and Machine Intelligence* PAMI-3 (6): 713–14. https://doi.org/10.1109/TPAMI.1981.4767177.

Townshend, John, Christopher Justice, Wei Li, Charlotte Gurney, and Jim McManus. 1991. "Global Land Cover Classification by Remote Sensing: Present Capabilities and Future Possibilities." *Remote Sensing of Environment* 35 (2–3): 243–55. https://doi.org/10.1016/0034-4257(91)90016-Y.

Verma, Ruchi. 2014. "Polarimetric Decomposition Based on General Characterization of Scattering From Urban Areas and Multiple Component Scattering Model," MS thesis, Faculty of Geo-information Science and Earth Observation, Univ. of Twente, Enschede, the Netherlands.

Waske, B., and S. van der Linden. 2008. "Classifying Multilevel Imagery From SAR and Optical Sensors by Decision Fusion." *IEEE Transactions on Geoscience and Remote Sensing* 46 (5): 1457–66. https://doi.org/10.1109/TGRS.2008.916089.

Waske, Bjorn, Gunter Menz, and Jon Atli Benediktsson. 2007. "Fusion of Support Vector Machines for Classifying SAR and Multispectral Imagery From Agricultural Areas." In *2007 IEEE International Geoscience and Remote Sensing Symposium*, 4842–45. IEEE. https://doi.org/10.1109/IGARSS.2007.4423945.

Zhang, Lamei, Bin Zou, Junping Zhang, and Ye Zhang. 2009. "An Extended Multiple-Component Scattering Model for PolSAR Images." *International Journal of Remote Sensing* 30 (21): 5515–25. https://doi.org/10.1080/01431160802653732.

Zhang, Lamei, Bin Zou, Hongjun Cai, and Ye Zhang. 2008. "Multiple-Component Scattering Model for Polarimetric SAR Image Decomposition." *IEEE Geoscience and Remote Sensing Letters* 5 (4): 603–7. https://doi.org/10.1109/LGRS.2008.2000795.

Zhao, Q., and J. C. Principe. 2001. "Support Vector Machines for SAR Automatic Target Recognition." *IEEE Transactions on Aerospace and Electronic Systems* 37 (2): 643–54. https://doi.org/10.1109/7.937475.

9 Marine Oil Slick Detection Using Synthetic Aperture Radar Remote Sensing Techniques

Vaishali Chaudhary and Shashi Kumar

CONTENTS

9.1   INTRODUCTION

Oil spills are the release of toxic hydrocarbons into oceans or any other water channel, contaminating the water. For decades now, oil spills have become a major problem, both economically and ecologically. Oil is absorbed into birds' feathers, making them heavy and vulnerable to temperature changes in their surroundings, which ultimately leads to death due to hypothermia. The oil creates a layer over the water surface that prevents the necessary amount of sunlight to get through, leading to a decrease in the level of oxygen dissolution. In addition, the area around the oil spill, or the part of the area that directly or indirectly depends upon the water body for food, also faces fatal effects. For example, Deepwater Horizon, an oil rig blowout on April 20, 2010, is considered the biggest oil spill in the Gulf of Mexico [1], threatening the lives of 11 workers and leaving 17 people severely injured. Oil and gas kept coming out of the well for 87, days and approximately 5 million barrels of oil were released into the water. Thousands of aquatic animals and birds have died due to these incidents. The difficult part has been accurately determining the adverse effects of these spills on smaller species. After the incident, the affected area came under numerous operational studies to investigate the degree of mortality within the region and also the effect of oil spills on the lives of humans who rely on these bodies of water.

These spills spread over the water surface and form a thin, shiny layer called sheen. The spread or the formation of this thin layer depends on the physical properties of the oil, such as viscosity, density, dielectric constant, specific gravity, adhesiveness, persistence, interfacial tension, the ratio of the emulsification, toxicity, and also the location of the spill. Another crucial aspect of an oil spill is the thickness factor. However, this area of research is in the development stage. There are only a few available methods for determining the thickness, and the instruments used for this purpose are very complex and require advanced tools [2]. The spilled oil appears different depending on the thickness. Generally, a 0.05–0.2µ thickness of oil generates a sheen effect, 0.3–3 µ thickness is responsible for rainbow sheen, and oil thickness above 3µ appears as brown/black. There are many reasons why oil spills happen. Fundamentally, oil spills in the oceans, rivers, or any other water channel occur due to accidents related to pipelines, tankers, rigs, storage equipment, etc. Sometimes natural disasters like a hurricane can also be responsible for the same. With every passing year, dependency on naval transportation for supplying goods and other utilities increased exponentially. And this traffic in the marine routes also gives rise to illegal discharges of oil.

9.2 TYPES OF OIL

Depending upon oil properties like volatility, viscosity, and toxicity, oil spills can be further categorized into five broad categories [3], [4]. Molecular-level knowledge about the oil type is crucial for planning countermeasure strategies. Some oil types are very volatile and hence are less toxic, and vice versa. The persistence of these oils in the environment also depends upon weathering processes. The climate of the region plays a crucial role in weathering the oil. However, some heavy oils persist in the marine ecosystem for quite a long time, even after being weathered. These heavy oils accumulate and make solid components that are misunderstood by marine animals as food; inhaling these substances damages their lungs. These accumulated substances also penetrate deep

TABLE 9.1
A Brief Description of Different Oil Types

Type	Properties	Example
Class 1	Highly volatile and concentrated, less persistent, strong odor, spreads quickly, prone to leave residue, high-quality crude oils	Jet fuel, gasoline
Class 2	Moderately concentrated and less toxic than Class 1, easy cleanup, does not leave residue, highly flammable, tends to exists in the environment longer than Class 1	Kerosene, light crude oil, heating oils, diesel
Class 3	Sticky oils, heavier than previous class categories, does not disperse into the water column, high probability of adhering to the water surface, cleanups are expensive, long-term effect on the ecosystem	Most crude oils, IFO 180
Class 4	Heavy crude oils, persists longer in the environment with very little or no weathering, much less evaporation, requires immediate cleanup countermeasures	Fuel oil (Bunker B/C or RFO – residual fuel oil), heavy crude oil
Class 5	Sinks in the water column and sit at the sea bed, contaminates the shoreline if spilled near it, negligible evaporation and dissolution, very harmful for aquatic animals in the long term	Slurry and residual oils

into birds' feathers, making them less insulating. A brief explanation of different types of oil has been provided in Table 9.1. The types are broadly divided into five classes, with their respective examples noted alongside.

9.3 WEATHERING PROCESSES

As discussed earlier, different oil types have different physical properties, and the weathering of the oil depends greatly on these properties. To sum it up scientifically, weathering describes the change in the physical and chemical properties of the oil when it comes in contact with the surrounding environment. When the oil enters the water, it is less viscous and less dense than water and tends to spread more easily. Due to these properties, fresh oil spills are considered more dangerous. Several studies [5], [6] have been carried out on the oil spill weathering procedure, and it can be summarized that the lifespan of an oil spill in water is affected greatly by changes in physical or chemical properties caused by weathering. As soon as the oil comes into contact with the water surface, it starts losing light molecular components (of low viscosity), leaving behind highly viscous residue. These residues sometimes become denser than the water and sink and may sit at the sea bed for months or even years. The process of weathering has several sub-processes, namely bio-degradation, adsorption (or sedimentation), dispersion, evaporation, photo-oxidation, dissolution, and emulsification [7] (see Figure 9.1).

As soon as the oil comes in contact with water, several phenomena start to occur. Hydrocarbons (oil) combine with oxygen in the presence of the sun in a process known as photo-oxidation. This operation can change the chemical properties of the oil. This aggregation results in the formation of resins that, after dissolving with water, create a water-in-oil emulsion [7]. At the same time, evaporation occurs when the lighter oil starts changing to vapor, meaning the remaining oil is more viscous and denser. This process may make the dispersion of the remaining oil very difficult. An oil type with a large percentage of light oil molecules and high volatility evaporates faster than heavy oil. Since heavy oils are made up of less volatile and heavy molecular weight components, their evaporation is generally less and slow, even after 8–10 hours. This is because evaporation shows sensitivity to the chemical and viscous properties of the oil. Moreover, the intermediate category of oil also shows similar properties to heavy oil and evaporates at a lesser rate. Typically, 75% of the light oil evaporates within the first few hours of exposure to the environment [7]. The sea

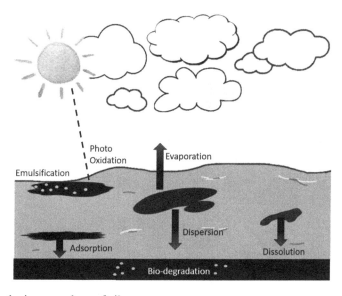

FIGURE 9.1 Weathering procedures of oil.

surface can be turbid at times, which leads to the emulsion phenomena. As already discussed in the photo-oxidation process, emulsification refers to the suspension of water molecules in the oil molecules, resulting in water-in-oil emulsion. Due to this combination, a change occurs in the oil properties, making the oil more viscous and even more persistent than the original form of the oil. However, lighter oil containing water-soluble molecules can easily dissolve into the water. This process is known as dissolution.

Some hydrocarbons, more precisely light aromatic compounds, e.g., toluene and benzene, have the highest degree of water solubility [8]. The dissolution process is highly dependent on the surface area of the oil and the degree of solubility. In cases when the oil is not soluble in water, oil molecules sometimes break into smaller droplets due to the effect of the rough waves. This breakdown procedure is called dispersion, and it can result in large droplets that may float back to the water surface and form another slick by combining with other similar drops. However, the lighter oil droplets may remain suspended in the water column. Moreover, the thin, lighter oil layer over the water surface is dispersed completely due to the effects of rough waves and turbulence. These suspended hydrocarbons are naturally consumed by micro bacteria and fungi to generate energy in a process is known as bio-degradation. These bacteria are commonly found in water bodies. To promote the bio-degradation process during a cleanup procedure, a dispersant is used to make the oil molecules dissolve into the water column effectually so that they can further be disintegrated by the bacteria. The bio-degradation of the oil droplets becomes very difficult if dispersion of the oil has not occurred. However, heavy suspended particles in the water associate with the oil molecules, forming suspended solids that sink and rest on the sea bed. Adsorption or sedimentation can be prevented before this occurs with the use of absorbents. The oil droplets must be absorbed by the adsorbents by spreading the oil over its surface.

9.4 MAJOR OIL SPILL INCIDENTS

Oil spills are generally accidental hazards. This is not always the case, however, as transportation ships also sometimes intentionally leak oils. Illegal ship activities are also responsible for oil spill incidents. Some areas in the sea are very prone to such accidents due to increased marine traffic. Figure 9.2 shows the location, year, and released oil quantity of some of the major oil spills in

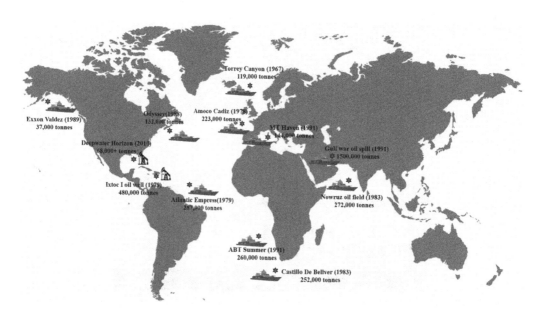

FIGURE 9.2   Major oil spills in the history.

history. While the Gulf of Mexico has witnessed many oil spill incidents over time, the Deepwater Horizon blowout is considered the worst oil spill in the history of the USA along with the Exxon Valdez oil spill.

Table 9.2 provides a summary of some of the largest oil spills in history. The release of these oils into the water not only contaminates the water but aquatic organisms and birds, depending on the water body, also face a severe threat and exposure to harsh ecosystem conditions that can ultimately result in their death. There have been numerous oil releasing incidents. The Deepwater Horizon blowout in the Gulf of Mexico in 2010 is considered one of the largest oil spills in American history, with approximately 780,000 m^3 US gallons of oil spilled into the water. During its operational control measures, approximately 7,000 m^3 of US gallons of dispersant were used, which adversely affected aquatic life. The oil spillage continued for a five-month long period, making it a spill with fatal socio-economic and environmental impacts. One of the most tedious tasks in

TABLE 9.2
Details of Some of the Major Oil Spills in the History

Oil Spill Incident	Date and Year	Location
Exxon Valdez [9]	March 24, 1989	Gulf of Alaska, Alaska, United States of America
Deepwater Horizon [1]	April 20, 2010	Gulf of Mexico, United States of America
Ixtoc I oil well [10]	June 3, 1979–March 23, 1980	Bay of Campeche, Gulf of Mexico
Atlantic Empress [11]	July 19, 1979	Caribbean Sea
Odyssey (1988) [12]	November 10, 1988	North Atlantic
Amoco Cadiz [13]	March 16, 1978	(1978)
Torrey Canyon [14]	March 18, 1967	United Kingdom
MT Haven [15]	April 11, 1991	Italy
Gulf War oil spill [16]	1991	Arabian Gulf
Nowruz oil field [17]	February 10, 1983	Persian Gulf, Iran
ABT Summer [18]	May 28, 1991	Off the coast of Angola
Castillo De Bellver [19]	August 6, 1983	South Africa

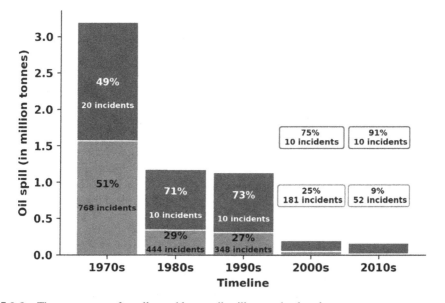

FIGURE 9.3   The percentage of smaller and larger oil spills over the decades.

planning countermeasure actions for these oil spill incidents is tracking the spread. If we look at the frequency of the oil that has been spilled over the last few decades, a gradual decline can be observed. According to ITOPF's Oil Tanker Spill Statics (2019) report, there have only been a few incidents of larger oil spills that are responsible for a high quantity of oil spilling into water bodies. During the 1970s, 49% of the oil was spilled only from 20 large incidents, compared with a 51% margin from 768 smaller incidents (see Figure 9.3).

The difference in the number of incidents is huge, while the amount of spilled oil does not vary so much in percentage. The same trend has been followed over the subsequent decades. It is quite obvious from the data that only a few big oil spills can cause fatal damage to the environment, as the amount of oil released into the water is much higher than in smaller oil spills. However, a good decrement in the occurrence of smaller oil-spill incidents can be observed in the 2000s and 2010s with larger incident showing almost constant frequency.

9.5   CLEANUP PROCEDURE AND ASSOCIATED COSTS

Oil spills are considered fatal due to their chemical, physical, and biological properties. An oil spill incident can easily muck up the surrounding area and the coastlines. Several different procedures and equipment have been designed to be used for routine oil spill cleanup. Depending upon the requirements of the situation, many countermeasure procedures are available for the cleanup operation. The most commonly used procedures are explained next.

The most commonly used method for oil spill cleanup is to use booms. These are used to collect the spreading oil. Booms are long, floating, interconnected barriers. The collected oil is then separated with the help of skimmers. The next method is the use of sorbents, which are absorbent substances specially designed to absorb only oil out of water. The physical properties of sorbents make them hydrophobic (water-repellent) and oleophilic (oil-attracting). The removal of oil is done by either absorption or adsorption. Sorbents remove the remaining oil traces from water (where skimmers cannot reach) and land areas. However, in-situ burning is most often used to clean the oil from the surface of the water. It is one of the most effective ways of removing the oil slick when the oil has been freshly spilled. This whole operation is performed in a very controlled manner. The main objective of burning oil on the site is to stop its adverse effects on the environment. However, burning also leaves residue behind, as well as some toxic gases in the atmosphere. Sometimes, a chemically loaded material (dispersant) is sprayed or used over the oil-affected regions. These chemicals separate the oil molecules from the water, turning the molecules into small droplets for microbes' consumption (bio-degradation), though the effectiveness of dispersant material may vary depending on the age of the oil spill. Moreover, sometimes all of the cleanup procedures are not sufficient. In those cases, help from manual methods is considered. Cleanup teams help in manually collecting oil from the water bodies. People with very little training, equipped with shovels, gloves, and equipment, can be deployed in coastal areas. This type of cleaning can be very time-consuming but also effective, as little or no training is required to clean the oil spilled on shorelines. All of the described options are very effective if used strategically. However, if the affected region is located remotely and has dense vegetation cover, then sometimes natural recovery becomes the most feasible option. The oil disperses into the water body over time; part of it bio-degrades with time, and ultimately the ecosystem recovers naturally. However, this whole process may take years depending upon the type of oil and the sea conditions.

9.5.1   MONETARY COSTS ASSOCIATED WITH OIL SPILLS

The overall procedure of oil cleanup is very costly for both oil industries and the public. The overall cleanup costs consist of many direct and hidden costs. These costs may be related to the oil company

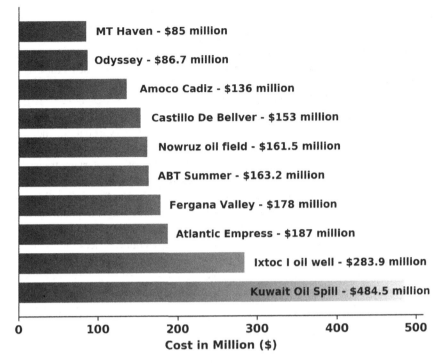

FIGURE 9.4   The cleanup costs of some of the biggest oil spills in history as of 2010.

and its infrastructure or to the manpower associated with it. These costs are briefly described next (figure 9.4).

Costs associated with the oil industry (private cost) include:

a) Overall damage caused to the oil rig/platform and the machinery.
b) Costs associated with the measures taken to stop further spillage of the oil.
c) Contemporary price of the amount of oil dispersed into the water.
d) The cleanup operations.
e) Penalty charges/fine.

Indirectly associated costs include:

a) Manpower casualty and fine payable towards the family.
b) Loss of business.
c) Loss of customers.
d) Damage to the area of operation (worksite).

These associated costs are highly dependable on several other factors, such as:

a) The type of the oil.
b) The location, time of year, and the sea condition.
c) The physical properties of the oil.
d) How effectively and timely the cleanup operation can be done etc.

9.6 OIL SPILL DETECTION PROCEDURE

The history of aerial photographs goes back to 1859 when the first aerial image was gained through a camera carried high with the help of a balloon. Aircraft these days are the most common airborne platform for remote sensing operations for both civilian and military purposes. Airborne platforms are highly efficient and sophisticated systems providing high spatial resolution. One such platform is Uninhabited Aerial Vehicle Synthetic Aperture Radar (UAVSAR). UAVSAR operating in microwave L-band has extensively captured oil spill sites in quad-polarimetric mode, that is, four polarizations: HH, HV, VH, and VV. The first H (horizontal) or V (vertical) in the combination represents the polarization of the transmitted wave, and the second term indicates polarization of the received wave. For example, HV polarization will be read as for H-polarized transmitted wave, V-polarized wave is received. In 1960, the first remote sensing satellite was launched for a meteorology mission. Since then, over a hundred satellites have been launched for several diverse missions.

Detection of a dark object (oil spill) can be done mainly in three ways: manual, semi-automatic, and automatic. In the manual procedure, human interpreters are trained to identify oil spills and discriminate between slicks and look-alikes. The second procedure is semi-automatic, which is a complex coupling of automatic and manual inspection done by humans. This procedure is the most widely used these days. The last procedure, i.e., fully automatic, is very complex due to the challenges it faces. These kinds of operations are still in a developing stage as the accuracy of these operations can still be dubious. For any system to be fully automatic, a high level of precision is required. Hence, this field is still under extensive research as long as oil spills are concerned.

One of the most reliable methods for tracking oil spillages is visual observation with the help of aircraft, ships, divers, or any digital imaging instrument, for example, airborne digital photography. Divers can only go up to a certain depth and operate within visible limits only. These limitations have been eliminated by remotely sensed data. With a sensor mounted on a spaceborne or airborne platform, the areas of interest can be monitored without directly coming in contact. In case of hazards like oil spillages, the system must be able to operate irrespective of the timeline and weather conditions. Using an active microwave sensor, the data can be acquired 24 hours a day, regardless of the weather conditions and illumination factor, as the area mapping can be done at night as well. Although a significant amount of oil can be dispersed deep into the water and lie at the sea bed, radar waves are not powerful enough to penetrate sufficiently deep through the water to detect it. Hence, very little in-situ data of the submerged oil is available, and to resolve this issue several experiments are being carried out worldwide. One of the most widely used remote sensing platforms for oil spill monitoring these days is synthetic aperture radar (SAR), a side-looking radar that gives information about the objects in a scene based on the backscattering that it receives from those objects. Surface roughness can also be estimated from this backscattering information of the water body. Principally, the backscattered data captured by the SAR sensor greatly relies on small surface waves, also known as gravity-capillary waves. The existence of oil spills on the water body dampens these capillary waves by diminishing the surface tension; due to this effect, the affected zone emerges smoother than the non-oil spill zone and thus the oil-covered zone will look darker in a SAR image compared to a non-oil zone. There are, however, other natural phenomena that might appear like an oil-spill dark patch in SAR imagery, like low wind zones, rain cells, natural oil seepage, internal waves, grease ice, and upwelling/downwelling stretches [20]. Every SAR imagery has some additional unwanted information attached to its pixel values. To be precise, the energy levels captured by a remote sensing platform differ from the actual energy levels. This mainly happens due to the sun's elevation and azimuth or the atmospheric conditions. This information can be related to the atmospheric interaction of the microwave or may be due to the radar's design mechanism. These values may create discrepancies that deviate from the whole study and result in completely non-practical results. The dataset must go through radiometric and atmospheric corrections before being further analyzed to determine the actual data values (figure 9.5).

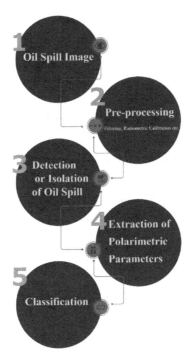

FIGURE 9.5 Basic strategy followed in detecting oil spills.

Radiometrically calibrated data follow normal distributions. Similarly, all the elements of the coherency matrix must follow a normal distribution of data. As the swath of the remotely sensed data can be quite large in area, especially in the case of spaceborne platforms, a smaller subset of the region of interest with oil spill patches can be taken out to speed up the process, although this is an optional step. Once the oil spills are isolated, different polarimetric parameters or mechanisms can be carried out for further assessment.

SAR sensors have a tendency to have noise elements (salt-and-pepper effect), generally known as speckle, that make the imagery very coarse in texture. When the signal traverses back to the sensor after hitting the target, a number of other coherent signals from other elements present in the scene also traverse back to the receiver. These signals interfere with each other both destructively and constructively (generating black-and-white pixels), giving a salt-and-pepper texture to the image; this kind of noise is random in nature. The presence of speckle reduces the detailed quality of the data and the property of the data and increases the chances of classifying the data incorrectly. In an unfiltered image, the visual interpretation of the scene is very difficult due to the interfering high and low frequencies. Also, the spills are not crisply visible. In other words, the contrast of the image is very low due to the presence of the noise. Applying a polarimetric filter to create a filtered image offers a better contrast.

The next step in oil spill detection involves backscattering analysis of the oil spills. Due to a higher degree of absorption and scattering in the water regions, the monitoring is very limited. If the sea surface is not rough enough, most of the transmitted radar waves will reflect back mostly away from the sensor. If the surface is smooth, then most of the incident energy will transmit away from the sensor. This type of scattering is known as specular reflection (see Figure 9.6(a)). With the increment in degree of roughness of the surface, the amount of the backscattering reaching the radar's receiver increases (see Figure 9.6(b) and (c)). Clearly, more backscattering energy is reaching the radar sensor in case of rough surfaces. Radar backscattering from the sea surface is

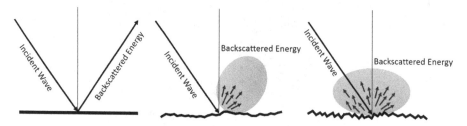

FIGURE 9.6 Various types of scattering from the surface with varying degree of roughness: (a) smooth surface, (b) slightly rough surface, and (c) very rough surface.

basically a complex interaction of the radar waves with the sea surface. Hence, the backscatter depends upon several factors, like the wavelength of the signal, dielectric and geometric properties of the target, etc.

Both oil and water will show surface scattering, but the oil-covered surface is relatively smoother (as the presence of oil suppresses the short gravity and capillary waves) compared to water. This leads to the formation of a darker signature of the oil spill. Apart from this, a vast number of diverse waves also exist in the ocean. Smaller waves mix with larger waves to form a periodic structure with one wave on top of another wave. These smaller waves are modified by larger waves. This whole mechanism makes the Bragg scattering model insufficient for the precise study of the backscattering behavior of marine bodies.

9.7 SAR REMOTE SENSING FOR OIL SPILL DETECTION

The image interpretation of oil spills with a microwave radar sensor can be different for varying circumstances. The spread of oil over the water body depends on the sea current and the wind up to a large extent. Wind speed also plays a vital role in ocean monitoring. Wind speeds have to be high enough to make the sea rough, which will help in getting a good strength of backscattered signal that is generally higher than the sensor's noise floor [21]. For instance, a fresh oil spill generates a very bright image compared to an old oil spill. To be precise, fresh and old oil spills may vary in visual interpretation depending upon several factors. For example, two images (with different capturing times) of UAVSAR L-band SAR data from an oil-on-water exercise called the Norwegian Radar Oil Spill Experiment (NORSE, June 2015) are utilized to show this.

In Figure 9.7, the change in the appearance, as well as signature, can be clearly seen between the two images. Figure 9.7(a) appears brighter as the spill was fresh. On the other hand, in Figure 9.7(b), the spill seems to have weathered with time. The effect of wind can also be observed on oil spills. Oil spills have some regions with lesser oil quantity than the other regions. These regions are weathered much more easily by the wind making the oil film very thin at those locations; hence, a fainter signature is captured. The color fringes from one end of the image to another end occur due to variation in incidence angle over the area of interest as a result of the low operational altitude ($\approx$13,800 meters) of UAVSAR.

Several famous SAR studies based on polarimetric features and properties have been carried out for more than a decade for successful detection and classification of oil spills from look-alikes and water [22], [23], [29]–[32].

Fundamentally, the radar signature for the oil slick is very similar to calm sea zones and the look-alike phenomena. Some of the studies are briefly identified in Table 9.3. Detecting the oil slick is considered a tedious task because of the dynamic nature of the sea. A number of parameters, such as wind, ocean current, temperature, the chemical composition of the spilled oil, quantity of oil spilled, and location, have a major role in accurately estimating the extent and effect of an oil spill incident.

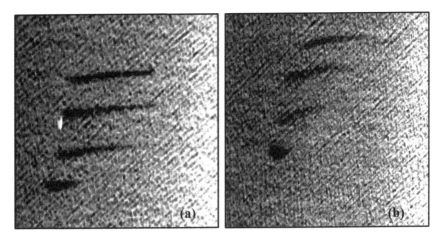

FIGURE 9.7 UAVSAR L-band imagery captured on June 10, 2015 in the North Sea during NORSE experiment at (a) 07:44:13 UTC and (b) 11:45:40 UTC.

TABLE 9.3
A Brief History of Some of the Previous Work Done on Oil Spills

Author	Methodology
Camilla Brekke, Anne H. S. Solberg [22]	Pattern recognition-based discrimination between the oil spill and look-alike
A. H. S. Solberg, C. Brekke, P. O. Husoy [23]	Algorithm for dark spot detection and classification
Stine Skrunes, Camilla Brekke, Torbjorn Eltoft [24]	Discrimination between oil slick types based on multi-polarization features characterization
R. Shirvany, M. Chabert, J-Y. Tourneret [25]	Degree of polarization based oil spill detection
B. Fiscella, A. Giancaspro, F. Nirchio, P. Pavese, P. Trivero [26]	Physical and geometrical features (area, perimeter, average NRCS, etc.)
Oscar Garcia-Pineda, Beate Zimmer, Matt Howard, William Pichel, Xiaofeng Li, Ian R. MacDonald [27]	Texture-classifying neural network algorithm (TCNNA) along with edge-detection filters
H. Espedal [28]	Development of supervised slick discrimination algorithm (direct/contextual analysis, drift/SAR EOM model)

9.7.1 POLARIZATION SIGNATURE ANALYSIS OF THE OIL SPILL PATCHES

Polarization signatures are the simplified 3D representation of the radar backscattering from the ground targets with different polarization basis. In electromagnetic theory, the scattering energy is a function of transmitted ψ (orientation angle) and χ (ellipticity) as well as the backscattered ψ and χ angles. For an electromagnetic wave, χ ranges from $-45°$ to $+45°$, and ψ lies between $0°$ and $180°$. The value of the scattering component (on the z-axis) along with ψ and χ angles (x- and y-axis) are represented as a 3D figure [33]. The shape of the polarization curve can explain the various properties of the target. In a remote sensing system, the calculation of backscattering behavior of the target under varying polarization state becomes very complex. Hence, polarization signatures are used with a much more simplified representation. The main objective of the polarization signature is to plot the variation in the radar backscattering intensity as a function of ψ and χ [34]. The polarization signatures are generated in two modes: co-polarization (transmitted and received signal are in same polarization, i.e., HH or VV) and cross-polarization (transmitted and received signal are orthogonal to each other, i.e., HV or VH).

Figure 9.8 represents the polarization signatures generated from two different UAVSAR L-band quad-pol datasets for the oil-covered and oil-free regions. Figures 9.8(a) and (b) represent the co- and cross-pol signatures for NORSE2015 (Norwegian Radar Oil Spill Experiment 2015), in the North Sea, Figures 9.8(c) and (d) show the co- and cross-pol signatures for the Gulf of Mexico region. In the oil spill detection problem, the polarization signature can provide information about the sea surface properties. The oil-covered surface is responsible for increments in unpolarized backscattering intensity. This change in polarization leads to increased pedestal height in polari-metric signatures compared to the oil-free water surface [35]. The change in pedestal height can be considered as an effective tool for discrimination between oil and water. A small change in pedestal height can be observed between the co-pol signature of Figure 9.8(a) and (b). The pedestal height of the oil-covered surface is slightly higher as compared to the oil-free surface. The same trend can be observed between the co-pol signature of Figure 9.8(c) and (d). Moreover, the change in pedestal height for Gulf of Mexico data is very significant. This change may be due to different underlying sea and wind conditions during the satellite capture.

(a)   North Sea: oil-covered
(b)   North Sea: oil-free
(c)   Gulf of Mexico: oil-covered
(d)   Gulf of Mexico: oil-free

9.7.2 DECOMPOSITION MODELS

Decomposition techniques can be seen as a vast field of techniques for manipulating different types of radar responses associated with the covariance/coherency matrix [36]. Polarimetric decompositions are the most widely used methods to study the scattering behavior of the targets. Broadly, the decomposition models are of two types: coherent and incoherent. The coherent decom-position model represents the scattering matrix as a grouping of scattering responses from several elements present in the cell. Typically, these models are used to study and analyze the behavior of pure targets (man-made structures). On the other hand, incoherent decomposition models are best suited to study distributed targets (forest/agricultural lands). Based on these fundamental principles, several decomposition models exist currently. Figure 9.9 represents a brief structure of the decom-position model hierarchy that is widely utilized in oil spill detection.

9.7.2.1 Coherent Decomposition Models

Pauli decomposition synthesizes the scattering matrix $[S]$ in Pauli basis. The resultant matrix is a combination of four individual 2×2 matrices, i.e., $[S]_a$, $[S]_b$, $[S]_c$, and $[S]_d$. However, in the case of a monostatic system (where transmitter and receiver are placed side by side), cross-component scattering matrices are considered equivalent, i.e., $S_{HV}=S_{VH}$. The resultant scattering matrix for Pauli decomposition can be represented as given in Equation 9.1.

$$S = \begin{bmatrix} S_{HH} & S_{HV} \\ S_{VH} & S_{VV} \end{bmatrix} = \alpha[S]_a + \beta[S]_b + \Upsilon[S]_c, \tag{9.1}$$

$$\text{Where} \qquad \alpha = \frac{S_{HH}+S_{VV}}{\sqrt{2}}, \tag{9.2}$$

$$\beta = \frac{S_{HH}-S_{VV}}{\sqrt{2}} \tag{9.3}$$

$$\gamma = \sqrt{2}S_{HV} \tag{9.4}$$

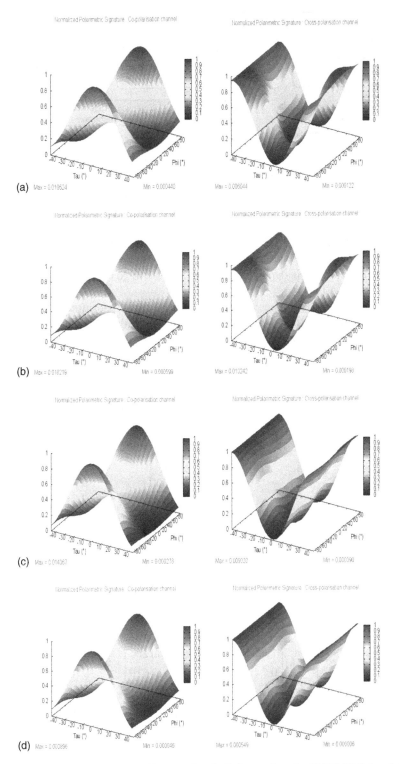

FIGURE 9.8 Polarization signatures for oil-covered and oil-free surface for UAVSAR L-band data of (a) – (b) North Sea captured on June 10, 2015 at 07:44:13 UTC and (c) – (d) Gulf of Mexico captured November 17, 2016 at 17:47:53 UTC.

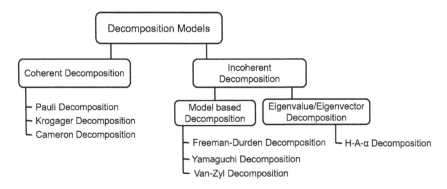

FIGURE 9.9 Classification of decomposition models.

In general, α is responsible for the odd or single-bounce scattering contribution to the scattering matrix, whereas, β and γ contribute to dihedral or double-bounce scattering and volume scattering respectively. For more details in depth, the reader is advised to go through online material on polarimetry provided by ESA [37].

Krogager decomposition is another very famous coherent decomposition model that is considered better than other coherent decomposition models in discriminating man-made structures from natural objects. In this decomposition, the scattering matrix is composed of surface (odd-bounce), diplane (volume), and helix scattering. Generally, Krogager decomposition is based on a circularly polarized scattering matrix, i.e., $S_{RL}(x,y)$. Here L is used for the left-hand circular element and R depicts the right-hand circular element [38]. The $S_{RL}(x,y)$ elements can be expressed as given in Equations 9.5, 9.6, and 9.7:

$$S_{RR}(x,y) = \frac{S_{HH}(x,y) - S_{VV}(x,y)}{2} + iS_{HV}(x,y), \tag{9.5}$$

$$S_{LL}(x,y) = \frac{S_{HH}(x,y) - S_{VV}(x,y)}{2} - iS_{HV}(x,y), \tag{9.6}$$

$$S_{RL}(x,y) = \frac{S_{HH}(x,y) - S_{VV}(x,y)}{2} + iS_{HV}(x,y). \tag{9.7}$$

The mathematical interpretation of Krogager decomposition in linear orthogonal basis (h,v) is presented as:

$$\begin{aligned}
\left[S_{(h,v)}\right] &= e^{j\varphi}\left\{e^{j\varphi_s}k_s\left[S\right]_s + k_d\left[S\right]_d + k_h\left[S\right]_h\right\} = \\
&e^{j\varphi}\left\{e^{j\varphi_s}k_s\begin{bmatrix}1 & 0 \\ 0 & 1\end{bmatrix} + k_d\begin{bmatrix}\cos 2\theta & \sin 2\theta \\ \sin 2\theta & -\cos 2\theta\end{bmatrix} + k_h e^{\mp j2\theta}\begin{bmatrix}1 & \pm j \\ \pm j & 1\end{bmatrix}\right\}.
\end{aligned} \tag{9.8}$$

In Equation 9.8, φ is the absolute phase, which is dependent on the distance between the satellite and target. Here, k_s, k_d, and k_h represents the power backscattered from sphere-like, diplane, and helix-like elements respectively.

9.7.2.2 Incoherent Decomposition Models

Coming to the incoherent decompositions, there are some very popular decomposition models in the SAR research domain. These are: Van Zyl decomposition, Freeman–Durden decomposition, and Yamaguchi decomposition. These models have been widely used in the literature, and many researchers have implemented them for the sole purpose of analyzing the backscattering behavior of oil spills [39]–[42]. Principally, when the radar wave interacts with an object, it majorly decomposes into three principle scattering behaviors. These scattering mechanisms are:

a) Surface scattering (backscattering governed by the first-order Bragg scatterers).
b) Double-bounce scattering (backscattering from dihedral structures).
c) Volume scattering (backscattering governed by randomly oriented dipoles).

With the increment of radar system utilization for various purposes, the need to extract physical information from the target is increasing day by day [36]. The basis of these techniques lies in the light scattering phenomena given by Chandrasekhar [43] and was later formalized by Huynen as target-based decomposition techniques [44]. With time, a number of decomposition theories were proposed. Some of the most commonly utilized decomposition techniques are briefly described next.

One of the foremost decomposition models is Freeman–Durden decomposition (Figure 9.10(a)). This model was implemented with three basic scattering mechanisms, i.e., canopy scattering (branches) from randomly oriented dipoles, double-bounce scattering (trunk–ground) mechanism from dihedral structures, and surface scattering (ground) from first-order Bragg scatterers. The model sums up the total backscattering contributed from each mechanism (see Equations 9.9 and 9.10) [45].

$$\langle [C] \rangle = f_s \left[C_{ground} \right] + f_d \left[C_{trunk-ground} \right] + f_v \left[C_{branches} \right], \tag{9.9}$$

$$\text{Where; } \left[C_{ground} \right] = \begin{bmatrix} |\beta|^2 & 0 & \beta \\ 0 & 0 & 0 \\ \beta^* & 0 & 1 \end{bmatrix}, \left[C_{trunk-ground} \right] = \begin{bmatrix} |\alpha|^2 & 0 & \alpha \\ 0 & 0 & 0 \\ \alpha^* & 0 & 1 \end{bmatrix}, \left[C_{branches} \right] = \begin{bmatrix} 1 & 0 & \frac{1}{3} \\ 0 & \frac{2}{3} & 0 \\ \frac{1}{3} & 0 & 1 \end{bmatrix}. \tag{9.10}$$

However, Freeman–Durden decomposition showed some values of covariance matrices as non-negligible for urban areas and topographic slopes. In the case of reflection symmetry, these values should be equal to zero. This limitation was recognized by Yamaguchi [46] and Yajima [47], and a

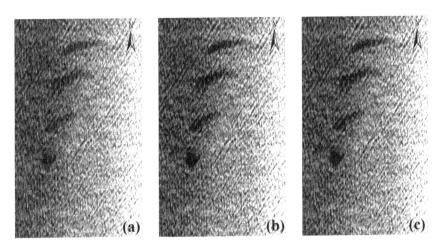

FIGURE 9.10 Representation of decomposition outputs for (a) Freeman–Durden, (b) Van Zyl, and (c) Yamaguchi decomposition for UAVSAR L-band (North Sea).

new decomposition model was proposed with an additional fourth component named as helix. This component represented the scattering of off-diagonal elements. According to the Yamaguchi model, when the reflection symmetry assumption holds true, 3-component Freeman–Durden decomposition can be applied effectively, but if there is a region that is not following the hypothesis, the Yamaguchi 4-component model with helix scattering power [48] becomes more appropriate. The modified covariance matrix with the fourth scattering element is given as:

$$\left\langle [C]^{HV} \right\rangle = f_s + \begin{bmatrix} |\beta|^2 & 0 & \beta \\ 0 & 0 & 0 \\ \beta^* & 0 & 1 \end{bmatrix} + f_d \begin{bmatrix} |\alpha|^2 & 0 & \alpha \\ 0 & 0 & 0 \\ \alpha^* & 0 & 1 \end{bmatrix} + \frac{f_v}{15} \begin{bmatrix} 8 & 0 & 2 \\ 0 & 4 & 0 \\ 2 & 0 & 3 \end{bmatrix} + \frac{f_c}{4} \begin{bmatrix} 1 & \pm j\sqrt{2} & -1 \\ \mp j\sqrt{2} & 2 & \pm j\sqrt{2} \\ -1 & \mp j\sqrt{2} & 1 \end{bmatrix},$$

(9.11)

where, f_s, f_d, f_v, and f_c in Equation 9.11 are the expansion coefficients for surface, double-bounce, volume, and helix scattering. Moreover, along with the development of these decomposition models, a major drawback in these techniques was reported by Van Zyl [49]. According to physics principles, the total power received by the radar system is directly proportional to the radar cross-section. Hence, the values of total power received should not be in negative terms. It was concluded by Van Zyl that every term of decomposition must produce a non-negative term for a properly modeled radar system [49]. The principle of Van Zyl decomposition [49] is founded on the hypothesis that the correlation between the co- and cross-polarized channel is zero and the reflection symmetry hypothesis is molded. The explained theory is correct in the case of natural elements like forestry and soil. With the help of these assumptions, the covariance matrix can be expressed as in Equation 9.12 [48].

$$C_3 = A_1 \begin{bmatrix} |\alpha|^2 & 0 & \alpha \\ 0 & 0 & 0 \\ \alpha^* & 0 & 1 \end{bmatrix} + A_2 \begin{bmatrix} |\beta|^2 & 0 & \beta \\ 0 & 0 & 0 \\ \beta^* & 0 & 1 \end{bmatrix} + A_3 \begin{bmatrix} 0 & 0 & 0 \\ 0 & 01 & 0 \\ 0 & 0 & 0 \end{bmatrix}.$$

(9.12)

9.7.2.3 Eigenvalue/Eigenvector Decomposition – $H - A - \alpha$ Decomposition

This technique was proposed by [50] based on the second-order statistics to extract the average target parameters from the data. The 3×3 elements of the coherency matrix, i.e., eigenvectors and their relative magnitudes (eigenvalues), were used to model the decomposition parameters. $H - A - \alpha$ decomposition is composed of three major elements, namely, entropy (H), anisotropy (A), and scattering angle (α). The entropy of a system is defined as the degree of randomness. Technically, for coherency matrix T, the value of H is computed through the logarithmic sum of its eigenvalues and written as in Equation 9.13:

$$H = -\sum_{i=1}^{i=3} P_i \log_3 \left(P_i \right).$$

(9.13)

Here, P_i is the probability to define the eigenvalues. Hence, P_i is given as in Equation 9.14:

$$P_i = \frac{\lambda_i}{\sum_{j=1}^{i=3} \lambda_j}.$$

(9.14)

For low values of H, the system is considered weakly depolarized and the scattering information about the dominant scatterer can be extracted. However, high values of H indicate strong depolarization of the system/signal, giving an indication of multiple scattering. In the case of oil spills, a clean water body generally possesses low H values. Moreover, the presence of oil slick on the water body increases the depolarization of signal and ultimately the value of H becomes high. The second parameter, anisotropy (A) calculates the statistical dominance of scattering between the probability of second and third eigenvalues. Hence, it is given by the formula in Equation 9.15.

$$A = \frac{\lambda_2 - \lambda_3}{\lambda_2 + \lambda_3}. \tag{9.15}$$

The values of A for an oil-covered area are typically higher than the oil-free areas. When both λ_2 and λ_3 are equal or 0, the value of A is also 0, indicating the presence of dominant scattering [51]. Similarly, $\alpha = 0°$ represents single-bounce (Bragg's) scattering, while $\alpha = 45°$ indicates the presence of dipole scattering and $\alpha = 90°$ gives information about dihedral or double-bounce scattering. Mathematically, α is represented as shown in Equation 9.16.

$$\alpha = \sum_{i=1}^{3} P_i \alpha_i. \tag{9.16}$$

9.8   SEPARABILITY ANALYSIS

After extracting the scattering behavior from both oil and water surfaces, the main task is to examine the degree of separation between the oil-covered and oil-free surfaces. For a successful oil spill detection, there must be a substantial difference between the backscattering values of water and oil. These goals are achieved with separability analysis [52] methods by taking random samples from both elements. The outputs from various decomposition models can be examined for this purpose [52][40]. The decomposition models with the highest degree of separation between the two samples are considered apt for further analysis. This quantitative methodology gives precise outcomes, as it is not easy to predict the extent of separation between two entities solely from visual representation (shown in Figure 9.11). Another way of determining separation between oil and water is

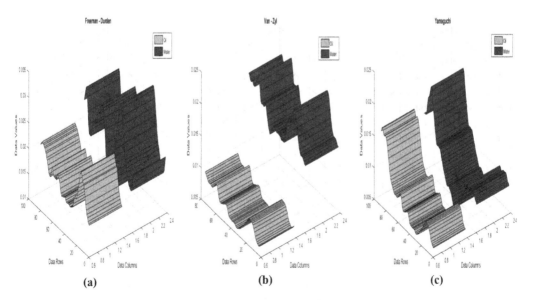

FIGURE 9.11   Plots showing the separability analysis outputs for (a) Freeman–Durden, (b) Van Zyl, and (c) Yamaguchi decomposition for UAVSAR L-band (North Sea).

texture-based analysis. The capillary and gravity waves are dampened by the oil layer, hence creating a smooth texture for the surfaces covered by oil. Similarly, the oil-free region naturally has a coarser texture than the oil-covered surfaces.

This difference in texture is captured by the SAR sensor, and a significant difference between the backscattering values can easily be noticed. Some texture-based techniques, e.g., gray-level co−occurrence matrix, have been widely used for distinguishing oil spills from the water body [53]–[55].

9.9 CLASSIFICATION TECHNIQUES

One of the major goals of an oil spill problem is to detect and classify the oil from the water body to get a clear identification. The classification procedure can be broadly divided into two major categories: unsupervised and supervised classification. Depending upon the complexity of the problem, either of the classifications can be selected. Most commonly, supervised classification is considered a better choice due to the training of the data as it gives the output based on the prior knowledge; hence, it is considered reliable. The selection of training sets is done manually by the interpreter based on the understanding of water–oil separation degree. A classification procedure in itself is a complete field of research. For any classification procedure to be useful, it is crucial that the elements are mapped correctly to the respective assigned classes. Incorrect mapping of a single class may lead to highly inaccurate results with a very high false accuracy percentage. This happens due to the sudden increment in one class's accuracy, and also, when oil and water have similar signatures, then it is very plausible for the classifier to consider one class as another. So, on the root level, the classifier falls into this trick and thinks that it is classifying the classes correctly, but on the contrary, the accuracy percentage falls abruptly, yielding highly incorrect outputs. It becomes necessary to accurately estimate the classification results and then finetune the classifier parameters accordingly. Two classifiers are used here to demonstrate the classification procedure: support vector machines and Wishart supervised classifiers. A number of supervised and unsupervised classifiers have been utilized over time for mapping oil spills, for example, random forest classifier, artificial neural network (ANN), convolutional neural network (CNN), maximum likelihood classification (ML), Wishart supervised/unsupervised classifier, K-means classifier, support vector machine, decision tree-based classifier, wavelet neural network, etc. [56]–[61].

9.9.1 SUPPORT VECTOR MACHINE

Support vector machines (or SVM) are a part of the supervised classification hierarchy generally used for classification, regression, and outlier detection. In technical terms, SVM works on finding a hyperplane within a feature space with n-dimension. With the help of this hyperplane, SVM distinguishes between the classes. The algorithm works as follows: 1. a hyperplane with maximized margin is defined, 2. a penalty term for the misclassified classes, 3. the data is mapped to higher dimensional space if needed, as it is easy to separate the data points along with linear decision surfaces. SVM classifier distinguishes between the classes principally based on the following approaches: maximal margin classifier and soft margin classifier. Another important aspect of SVM includes the use of kernels. A kernel is defined as the dot product between each input (x) and support vector (xi). The mathematical representation of linear kernel is given in Equation 9.17.

$$K\left(x, x_i\right) = sum\left(x * x_i\right). \tag{9.17}$$

The function measures distance or similarity between support vectors and the input data.

The linear separation of the dataset becomes difficult with the increasing size of the dataset, and this also hinders visualization of the dataset. Hence, using a linear kernel does not yield accurate results. To overcome this issue, SVM with polynomial and radial kernel is preferred for the sake of better precision in predictions. Here, SVM with radial kernel (see Equation 9.18) is applied to the dataset.

$$K\left(x, x_i\right) = exp\left(-\gamma * sum\left(x - x_i^2\right)\right). \tag{9.18}$$

In Equation 9.18, $0 \leq \gamma \leq 1$. For the application in this study, SVM with RBF (radial basis function) kernel is utilized. As the datasets used in this study have largely two classes, i.e., water and oil class, there will be two samples in the feature space. If the dataset contains more samples (or classes), SVM fails to draw precise classifications. Since the research problem discussed in this study consists of only two classes, SVM is preferred. Different RBF kernel values are used to classify the oil spills and the water. RBF is also known as gamma. This gamma parameter generally shows the extent of influence of a single training set. A low gamma value means that the influence will be up to far extents, while high gamma values define the close influence of the training set. Large values of gamma make the support vectors only include the support vector itself. In that case, even the regularization parameter C cannot prevent over-fitting. If the value of gamma is very small, then it makes the model too constrained to capture the shape or complexity of the data.

9.9.2 Wishart Supervised Classification

This classifier works on the Wishart distance measure in the dataset. The algorithm works by dividing the data into several clusters. The division of the cluster is done on the principle of differences in scattering contrast of the data images. The algorithm generates a relationship between the data and the potential classes depending upon the training data fed into the algorithm by the user. Mathematically, Wishart supervised classification is represented by Equation 9.19.

$$V_m = \frac{1}{N_m} \sum_{i=1}^{N_m} \langle T \rangle_i. \tag{9.19}$$

Here, T is the coherency matrix and V_m is the cluster; hence, the distance from T to V_m is considered the Wishart distance, which is given in Equation 9.20.

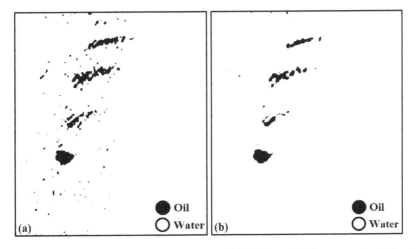

FIGURE 9.12 Classification outputs for UAVSAR data with SVM and Wishart supervised classification.

$$d\big(\langle T\rangle, V_m\big) = \ln\big|V_m + Tr\big(V_m^{-1}\langle T\rangle\big)\big|, \tag{9.20}$$

where ln() is a natural logarithmic function, $Tr(.)$ indicates the trace of matrix, and is the determinant of the matrix. For this study, several window sizes have been tested using Wishart supervised classification, e.g., $3\times3, 7\times7, 11\times11$, and 21×21. Out of all the window sizes, the classifier window size of 21×21 has provided the most suitable outcomes, with a minimum misclassification ratio. All classification outputs are given in Figure 9.12.

9.10 ACCURACY ASSESSMENT

9.10.1 AUC (Area Under the Curve) and ROC (Receiver Operating Characteristics)

AUC and ROC, collectively known as AUROC, are widely used for the statistical evaluation of classifier's outputs. Both AUC and ROC are interlinked, as AUC depicts the extent of separability, while ROC draws the probability curve. They both work collectively to state the precision of a classifier in identifying various classes precisely. The ROC curve is drawn against two axes, true positive rate (TPR) at the y-axis and false positive rate (FPR) at the x-axis. The formulas for both terminologies are shown in Equations 9.21 and 9.22.

TPR/sensitivity:

$$TPR = \frac{TP}{TP + FN}. \tag{9.21}$$

FPR/sensitivity:

$$FPR = \frac{FP}{TP + FN}. \tag{9.22}$$

The AUROC curve for all the tested parameters was calculated, but the curve for the parameters showing higher accuracy is included below. The AUROC of SVM classification with gamma parameter value k = 0.005 is showing a curve with AUC = 0.63, i.e., the accuracy is approximately 63%, showing that the classes are classified less accurately. Most of the resulting outputs had some percentage of misclassification. To reduce this percentage, a post-classification procedure, i.e., majority analysis, was carried out on all outputs. This procedure reduced the misclassified pixels to some extent, but still, the percentage of these pixels is high enough to yield a low-value AUROC curve. On the other hand, Wishart supervised classification with window size 21×21 shows an accuracy of approximately 83% without any post-classification analysis, showing the supremacy of Wishart supervised classification over SVM.

The AUROC curve has several points while testing the classifier's performance. But AUROC depicts a cut-off point representing the AUROC value at which the classifier performs better than other points to classify the classes accurately. This cut-off value gives the finest TPR against the FPR for a particular classification model.

When AUROC = 1, the classifier splits the features into respective classes without any datapoint overlay. Hence, after analyzing the outputs, it is clear that support vector machine classification is quite powerful but also possesses some limitations that rely on the dataset and the number of features it has. Also, there is a need for a post-classification process after SVM classification. On the other hand, Wishart supervised classification performs better with the same training dataset without any post-classification process.

9.11 CONCLUSIONS AND FUTURE WORK

Although the number of oil spill incidents has decreased over time, some of these incidents go unnoticed due to remote areas or less severity of the incident. Some of the major oil spills, like Deepwater Horizon, affected the ecosystem adversely. After a couple of years, the oil was cleaned from the shorelines, but a large amount of the dispersed oil sat on the sea bed, and according to several experiments, it is speculated that there is still an oil layer of good thickness lying over the seafloor. SAR satellites provide good resolution imagery with frequently repeated passes and have advantages over optical remote sensing. To extend the capabilities, an upcoming NISAR mission is planned to be launched in 2024, a joint endeavor of the National Aeronautics and Space Administration (NASA) and the Indian Space Research Organization (ISRO). The satellite will have a dual-frequency system, i.e., L- and S-bands. Under this mission, oil spills will also be observed as the repetition pass of the satellite is 12 days and covers a wide swath of 240 km. Many studies have been carried out about the detection of marine slicks. The main goal of an oil spill problem lies in separating the oil patches from similar phenomena and the drift/trajectory traversal of the slicks with given sea and wind conditions. This should be noted that knowing the extent of an oil drift correctly is very difficult as the oil patch keeps moving and the information within the pixel is not constant. Also, taking the pixel reference for the same is not practical.

REFERENCES

[1] R. Pallardy, "Deepwater Horizon oil spill – environmental disaster, Gulf of Mexico [2010]." Encyclopedia Britannica, 2010.

[2] M. Fingas, "The challenges of remotely measuring oil slick thickness," *Remote Sens.*, vol. 10, no. 2, 2018, doi: 10.3390/rs10020319.

[3] "Weathering processes affecting spills." Office of Response and Restoration. [Online]. Available: https://response.restoration.noaa.gov/oil-and-chemical-spills/oil-spills/weathering-proces ses-affecting-spills. [Accessed 14-Oct-2022].

[4] J. King, "Types of oil spills." Sciencing.com. [Online]. Available: https://sciencing.com/types-oil-spi lls-6593214.html. [Accessed 15-Oct-2022].

[5] P. Sebastião and C. G. Soares, "Modeling the fate of oil spills at sea," *Spill Sci. Technol. Bull.*, vol. 2, no. 2, pp. 121–131, 1995, doi: 10.1016/S1353-2561(96)00009-6.

[6] A. T. C. on M. of O. Spills, "State-of-the-art review of modeling transport and fate of oil spills," *Journal of Hydraulic Engineering*, vol. 122, no. 11, pp. 594–609, Nov. 1996, doi: 10.1061/ (ASCE)0733-9429(1996)122:11(594).

[7] M. F. Fingas, "A literature review of the physics and predictive modelling of oil spill evaporation," *J. Hazard. Mater.*, vol. 42, no. 2, pp. 157–175, 1995, doi: 10.1016/0304-3894(95)00013-K.

[8] M. Fingas, "Chapter 8 – introduction to spill modeling," in *Oil Spill Science and Technology*, M. Fingas, Ed. Boston: Gulf Professional Publishing, 2011, pp. 187–200.

[9] "Exxon Valdez oil spill | Response, animals, & facts." Encyclopedia Britannica. [Online]. Available: https://www.britannica.com/event/Exxon-Valdez-oil-spill. [Accessed: 25-Feb-2021].

[10] "Ixtoc I oil well." Oil in the Ocean. [Online]. Available: https://www.whoi.edu/oil/ixtoc-I. [Accessed 15-Oct-2022].

[11] "Atlantic Empress, West Indies, 1979." ITOPF. [Online]. Available: https://www.itopf.org/in-action/ case-studies/atlantic-empress-west-indies-1979/. [Accessed: 25-Feb-2021].

[12] "Odyssey, Off Canada, 1988." ITOPF. [Online]. Available: https://www.itopf.org/in-action/case-stud ies/case-study/odyssey-off-canada-1988. [Accessed 14-Oct-2022].

[13] "Amoco Cadiz, France, 1978." ITOPF. [Online]. Available: https://www.itopf.org/in-action/case-stud ies/case-study/amoco-cadiz-france-1978. [Accessed 14-Oct-2022].

[14] "Torrey Canyon, United Kingdom, 1967." ITOPF. [Online]. Available: https://www.itopf.org/in-act ion/case-studies/case-study/torrey-canyon-united-kingdom-1967. [Accessed 14-Oct-2022].

[15] "Haven, Italy, 1991." ITOPF. [Online]. Available: https://www.itopf.org/in-action/case-studies/case-study/haven-italy-1991. [Accessed 14-Oct-2022].

[16] J. Michel, "Chapter 37 – 1991 Gulf War Oil Spill," in *Oil Spill Science and Technology*, M. Fingas, Ed. Boston: Gulf Professional Publishing, 2011, pp. 1127–1132.

[17] "Nowruz Oil Field; Persian Gulf, Iran." NOAA Incident News. [Online]. Available: https://incidentn ews.noaa.gov/incident/6262. [Accessed 14-Oct-2022].

[18] "Abt Summer, off Angola, 1991." ITOPF. [Online]. Available: https://www.itopf.org/in-action/case-studies/case-study/abt-summer-off-angola-1991. [Accessed 14-Oct-2022].

[19] "Castillo de Bellver, South Africa, 1983." ITOPF. [Online]. Available: https://www.itopf.org/in-act ion/case-studies/case-study/castillo-de-bellver-south-africa-1983. [Accessed 14-Oct-2022].

[20] O. A. Ajadi, F. J. Meyer, M. Tello, and G. Ruello, "Oil spill detection in synthetic aperture radar images using Lipschitz-regularity and multiscale techniques," *IEEE J. Sel. Top. Appl. Earth Obs. Remote Sens.*, vol. 11, no. 7, pp. 2389–2405, 2018.

[21] M. Wilhelmsen, "Classification of marine oil spills and look-alikes in Sentinel-1 TOPSAR and Radarsat-2 ScanSAR images," master's thesis, Faculty of Science and Technology, Dept. of Physics and Technology, Arctic Univ. of Norway, 2018.

[22] C. Brekke and A. H. S. Solberg, "Oil spill detection by satellite remote sensing," *Remote Sens. Environ.*, vol. 95, no. 1, pp. 1–13, 2005.

[23] A. H. S. Solberg, C. Brekke, and P. O. Husoy, "Oil spill detection in Radarsat and Envisat SAR images," *IEEE Trans. Geosci. Remote Sens.*, vol. 45, no. 3, pp. 746–755, 2007.

[24] S. Skrunes, C. Brekke, and T. Eltoft, "Characterization of marine surface slicks by Radarsat-2 multipolarization features," *IEEE Trans. Geosci. Remote Sens.*, vol. 52, no. 9, pp. 5302–5319, 2014, doi: 10.1109/TGRS.2013.2287916.

[25] R. Shirvany, M. Chabert, and J.-Y. Tourneret, "Ship and oil-spill detection using the degree of polarization in linear and hybrid/compact dual-pol SAR," *IEEE J. Sel. Top. Appl. Earth Obs. Remote Sens. – IEEE J SEL TOP APPL EARTH Obs*, vol. 5, pp. 885–892, 2012, doi: 10.1109/ JSTARS.2012.2182760.

[26] B. Fiscella, A. Giancaspro, F. Nirchio, P. Pavese, and P. Trivero, "Oil spill detection using marine SAR images," *Int. J. Remote Sens.*, vol. 21, no. 18, pp. 3561–3566, 2000.

[27] O. Garcia-Pineda, B. Zimmer, M. Howard, W. Pichel, X. Li, and I. R. MacDonald, "Using SAR images to delineate ocean oil slicks with a texture-classifying neural network algorithm (TCNNA)," *Can. J. Remote Sens.*, vol. 35, no. 5, pp. 411–421, 2009.

[28] H. Espedal, "Detection of oil spill and natural film in the marine environment by spaceborne SAR," in *IEEE 1999 International Geoscience and Remote Sensing Symposium. IGARSS'99 (Cat. No.99CH36293)*, 1999, vol. 3, pp. 1478–1480.

[29] M. Migliaccio, A. Gambardella, and M. Tranfaglia, "SAR polarimetry to observe oil spills," *IEEE Trans. Geosci. Remote Sens.*, vol. 45, no. 2, pp. 506–511, 2007.

[30] F. Del Frate, A. Petrocchi, J. Lichtenegger, and G. Calabresi, "Neural networks for oil spill detection using ERS-SAR data," *IEEE Trans. Geosci. Remote Sens.*, vol. 38, no. 5, pp. 2282–2287, 2000, doi: 10.1109/36.868885.

[31] A. H. S. Solberg, G. Storvik, R. Solberg, and E. Volden, "Automatic detection of oil spills in ERS SAR images," *IEEE Trans. Geosci. Remote Sens.*, vol. 37, no. 4, pp. 1916–1924, 1999, doi: 10.1109/ 36.774704.

[32] P. Pavlakis, D. Tarchi, and A. J. Sieber, "On the monitoring of illicit vessel discharges using spaceborne sar remote sensing – a reconnaissance study in the Mediterranean sea," *Ann. Des Télécommunications*, vol. 56, no. 11, pp. 700–718, Nov. 2001, doi: 10.1007/BF02995563.

[33] "Polarization signatures." Natural Resources Canada. [Online]. Available: https://www.nrcan.gc.ca/ maps-tools-and-publications/satellite-imagery-and-air-photos/satellite-imagery-products/educatio nal-resources/tutorial-radar-polarimetry/polarization-signatures/9597. [Accessed 14-Oct-2022].

[34] "What is a radar polarization signature, and how is one used?" L3Harris. [Online]. Available: https:// www.l3harrisgeospatial.com/Support/Self-Help-Tools/Help-Articles/Help-Articles-Detail/ArtMID/ 10220/ArticleID/19641/1829. [Accessed 14-Oct-2022].

[35] M. Migliaccio, F. Nunziata, and A. Gambardella, "Polarimetric signature for oil spill observation," in *2008 IEEE/OES US/EU-Baltic International Symposium*, 2008, pp. 1–5, doi: 10.1109/ BALTIC.2008.4625555.

[36] S. R. Cloude and E. Pottier, "A review of target decomposition theorems in radar polarimetry," *IEEE Trans. Geosci. Remote Sens.*, vol. 34, no. 2, pp. 498–518, 1996, doi: 10.1109/36.485127.

[37] "Polarimetry tutorial | PolSARpro | ESA." [Online]. Available: https://earth.esa.int/web/polsarpro/polarimetry-tutorial. [Accessed: 29-Jan-2021].

[38] D. Gaglione, C. Clemente, L. Pallotta, I. Proudler, A. De Maio, and J. J. Soraghan, "Krogager decomposition and pseudo-Zernike moments for polarimetric distributed ATR," in *2014 Sensor Signal Processing for Defence (SSPD)*, 2014, pp. 1–5, doi: 10.1109/SSPD.2014.6943309.

[39] A. Kulshrestha, "Dark spot detection for characterization of oil spills using PolSAR remote sensing," MS thesis, Univ. of Twente, Eschende, the Netherlands, 2018.

[40] V. Chaudhary and S. Kumar, "Marine oil slicks detection using spaceborne and airborne SAR data," *Adv. Sp. Res.*, vol. 66, no. 4, pp. 854–872, Aug. 2020, doi: 10.1016/j.asr.2020.05.003.

[41] Y. Zou, S. Zhang, C. Liang, and W. An, "Research on detection oil spill information based on polarization decomposition," in *IGARSS 2018 – 2018 IEEE International Geoscience and Remote Sensing Symposium*, 2018, pp. 1206–1209.

[42] A. A. Matkan, M. Hajeb, and Z. Azarakhsh, "Target decomposition theory in oil spill detection from SAR data," *Int. J. Image Data Fusion*, vol. 7, no. 3, pp. 264–281, 2016, doi: 10.1080/19479832.2015.1068873.

[43] S. Chandrasekhar, *Radiative Transfer*. Dover, 1960.

[44] J. R. Huynen, "Phenomenological theory of radar targets," doctoral thesis, Faculty of Electrical Engineering, Technische Hoogeschool Delft, 1970.

[45] A. Freeman and S. L. Durden, "A three-component scattering model for polarimetric SAR data," *IEEE Trans. Geosci. Remote Sens.*, vol. 36, no. 3, pp. 963–973, May 1998, doi: 10.1109/36.673687.

[46] Y. Yamaguchi, T. Moriyama, M. Ishido, and H. Yamada, "Four-component scattering model for polarimetric SAR image decomposition," *IEEE Trans. Geosci. Remote Sens.*, vol. 43, no. 8, pp. 1699–1706, 2005.

[47] Y. Yajima, Y. Yamaguchi, R. Sato, H. Yamada, and W. Boerner, "POLSAR image analysis of wetlands using a modified four-component scattering power decomposition," *IEEE Trans. Geosci. Remote Sens.*, vol. 46, no. 6, pp. 1667–1673, 2008, doi: 10.1109/TGRS.2008.916326.

[48] Jong-Sen Lee, and Eric Pottier, *Polarimetric Radar Imaging: From Basics to Applications*. CRC Press, 2009.

[49] J. J. Van Zyl, M. Arii, and Y. Kim, "Model-based decomposition of polarimetric SAR covariance matrices constrained for nonnegative eigenvalues," in *IEEE Transactions on Geoscience and Remote Sensing*, 2011, vol. 49, no. 9, pp. 3452–3459, doi: 10.1109/TGRS.2011.2128325.

[50] S. R. Cloude and E. Pottier, "An entropy based classification scheme for land applications of polarimetric SAR," *IEEE Trans. Geosci. Remote Sens.*, vol. 35, no. 1, pp. 68–78, Jan. 1997, doi: 10.1109/36.551935.

[51] E. Pottier and S. R. Cloude, "Application of the H/A/alpha polarimetric decomposition theorem for land classification," in *Wideband Interferometric Sensing and Imaging Polarimetry*, 1997, vol. 3120, pp. 132–143, doi: 10.1117/12.278958.

[52] S. Kumar, H. P. Kattamuri, and S. Agarwal, "Dark spot detection for characterization of marine surface slicks using PolSAR remote sensing," in *Remote Sensing of the Oceans and Inland Waters: Techniques, Applications, and Challenges*, 2016, vol. 9878, p. 98780K, doi: 10.1117/12.2224415.

[53] M. Joseph, P. V Jayasri, S. Dutta, E. V. S. S. Kumari, and A. V. V Prasad, "Oil spill detection from RISAT-1 imagery using texture analysis," pp. 1–4, 2016.

[54] F. Zhang, W. Tian, and S. Wang, "Oil spill identification based on textural information of SAR image," in *IGARSS 2008 – 2008 IEEE International Geoscience and Remote Sensing Symposium*, 2008, pp. IV–1308, doi: 10.1109/IGARSS.2008.4779971.

[55] A. Misra and R. Balaji, "Simple approaches to oil spill detection using sentinel application platform (SNAP)-ocean application tools and texture analysis: A comparative study," *J. Indian Soc. Remote Sens.*, vol. 45, no. 6, pp. 1065–1075, Dec. 2017, doi: 10.1007/s12524-016-0658-2.

[56] Y. Zhang, Y. Li, Y. He, and T. Jiang, "Supervised oil spill classification based on fully polarimetric SAR features," in *2016 IEEE International Geoscience and Remote Sensing Symposium (IGARSS)*, 2016, pp. 1540–1543.

[57] D. Song, Y. Ding, X. Li, B. Zhang, and M. Xu, "Ocean oil spill classification with RADARSAT-2 SAR based on an Optimized wavelet neural network," *Remote Sens.*, vol. 9, no. 8, 2017, doi: 10.3390/rs9080799.

[58] A. Montali, G. Giacinto, M. Migliaccio, and A. Gambardella, "Supervised pattern classification techniques for oil spill classification in SAR images: preliminary results," *Eur. Sp. Agency, (Special Publ. ESA SP)*, 2006.

[59] H. Guo, D. Wu, and J. An, "Discrimination of oil slicks and lookalikes in polarimetric SAR images using CNN," *Sensors (Basel).*, vol. 17, no. 8, p. 1837, Aug. 2017, doi: 10.3390/s17081837.

[60] J. Fan, F. Zhang, D. Zhao, and J. Wang, "Oil spill monitoring based on SAR remote sensing imagery," *Aquat. Procedia*, vol. 3, pp. 112–118, 2015, doi: 10.1016/j.aqpro.2015.02.234.

[61] E. Ramsey III, A. Rangoonwala, Y. Suzuoki, and C. E. Jones, "Oil detection in a coastal marsh with polarimetric synthetic aperture radar (SAR)," *Remote Sens.*, vol. 3, no. 12, pp. 2630–2662, 2011, doi: 10.3390/rs3122630.

10 Spaceborne C-Band PolSAR Backscatter and PolInSAR Coherence-Based Modeling for Forest Aboveground Biomass Estimation

Ritwika Mukhopadhyay, Shashi Kumar, Hossein Aghababaei, and Anurag Kulshrestha

CONTENTS

10.1 A BRIEF HISTORY OF APPLICATIONS OF SYNTHETIC APERTURE RADAR (SAR) FOR BIOPHYSICAL PARAMETER RETRIEVAL

Forests play a vital role in the environment and for mankind as a source of tangible as well as intangible benefits [1]. Global forest cover has been recorded as decreasing from 31.6% to 30.6% during the 20-year interval years from 1995 to 2015 [1]. Forests also importantly contribute to the mitigation of atmospheric carbon. Atmospheric carbon is sequestered in tree trunks, branches, leaves, and roots. Therefore, the assessment of forest quality is a crucial step, performed based on the measurement of the biophysical parameters of the forests. The estimation of the biophysical parameters of forests are accomplished using remote sensing techniques. The three main types of remotely sensed data are optical, SAR, and LiDAR data. Among the three, SAR sensors have the advantage of penetrating through clouds, and data can also be acquired during both day and night, as well as in all-weather conditions. SAR sensors are immensely useful for height, volume, and biomass measurements of trees.

SAR is the application of a radar remote sensing technique that transmits radiation within the microwave range of the electromagnetic spectrum; the backscattered radiation from the target is received from the earth's surface [2]. SAR polarimetry (PolSAR) and polarimetric SAR interferometry (PolInSAR) are the advanced techniques of SAR remote sensing [2]. In the PolSAR technique, the backscatter from each SAR resolution cell of a fully polarimetric SAR data is measured for the characterization of the targets on the earth's surface [2], [3]. The backscattered signals depend on

DOI: 10.1201/9781003204466-10

235

the geometrical orientation of the target, as well as moisture content, permittivity, and ensemble average entropy of the targets [4], [5]. PolInSAR is a further extended technique of SAR that utilizes the benefits of both PolSAR and InSAR. The InSAR techniques deals with the characterization of the target in the vertical plane [6]. The PolInSAR coherency matrices describe the polarimetric as well as the interferometric properties of the images [2]. The coherence values retrieved from theses matrices denote the degree of correlation between two SAR datasets acquired at a certain interval of time [4].

SAR has an enormous application in different fields of study and has been implemented for the estimation of biophysical and structural parameters of trees [7]–[9]. Much work has been done for estimation of the biophysical parameters of forests utilizing datasets of different bands of micro-wave range, such as, X, C, L, and P [3], [9], [18], [10]–[17]. The backscatter and the coherence values retrieved from a fully polarimetric dataset using the PolSAR and PolInSAR techniques can be exploited and combined with the field data to estimate aboveground biomass (AGB) of forest. The relationship between the field data and the image data can be established by a machine learning (ML) algorithm or a parametric modelling approach. ML is an artificial intelligence method enab-ling supervised learning from the dataset and can be used for either regression or classification. The ML methods implemented with SAR studies are, namely, support vector machine (SVM), random forest (RF), rotation random forest (RoRF), classification and regression tree (CART), support vector regression (SVR), and random forest regression (RFR)[3], [19], [20]. RFR is a bootstrap aggregating algorithm in which each regression tree is trained, which forms the entire random forest model [19], [21], [22].

In this study, the PolSAR backscatter and PolInSAR coherence values were retrieved from the fully polarimetric SAR datasets. The relationship between the image parameters and field data was established using RFR algorithm. The novelty of this study was aimed at the coherent exploitation of the PolSAR backscatter and PolInSAR coherence values for the estimation of AGB. And, with the implementation of an RFR algorithm, the most important variable responsible for AGB estimation could be identified.

10.2 DOON VALLEY FORESTS AT A GLANCE

The study area selected for this study was Malhan Forest Range of the Doon Valley Forest Division, covering an area of 75.90 sq. km, as seen in Figure 10.1. The forest was homogenously dominated by Sal (*Shorea robusta*) trees as the keystone species [23]. The other species found in the forest range were Rohini (*Mallotus philippenensis*), Sagon (*Tectona grandis*), Sain (*Terminalia tomentosa*), Dhawri (*Lagerstromia parviflora*), and Peepal (*Ficus religiosa*). The forest range comprised four beats, namely, Sahansara, Kalyanpur, Kaluwala, and Malhan. The beats and compartments were demarcated by natural boundaries such as river channels and fire lines. The forest cover had a dense canopy, acting as a source of volume scattering. The surrounding agricultural lands with crops also contributed to volume scattering. Agricultural lands without crops along with nearby urban settlements contributed to surface scattering. Also, rocks and pebbles in the dried riverbed were a source of surface scattering. In addition, the orchard plantations with evident canopy gaps were a source for double-bounce scattering. Therefore, the selected forest area enabled us to study the different types of scattering mechanisms required for the study. The field photographs can be seen in Figure 10.2.

Field data was collected during the month of December. The sampling was carried out following the systematic sampling technique [25]. The entire study area was divided into 500 × 500 sq. m grids and the initial plot was chosen randomly, followed by successive plots laid at equal intervals of around 800 m in both directions. The sample plots were of 31.62 × 31.62 sq. m, covering an area of 0.1 ha. The field data consisted of the measurement of the girth at breast height (gbh) over bark (ob) and tree height for every individual tree in the sample plots. The field AGB was calculated using

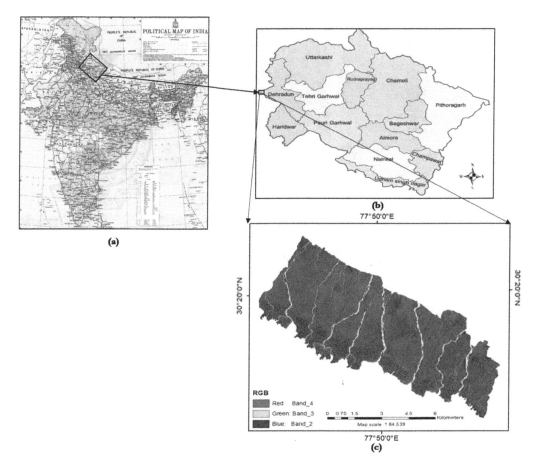

FIGURE 10.1 Study area [3]: (a) political map of India [24], (b) district map of Uttarakhand, and (c) Malhan Forest range.

species-specific allometric equations with diameter at breast height (dbh) as the independent variable. The dbh was estimated from the gbh following Equation 10.1.

$$dbh = gbh / \pi. \tag{10.1}$$

Further, the stem volume was calculated from the dbh (ob), followed by the AGB value estimation in Mg/ha units, using Equation 10.2.

$$AGB = stem\ volume\ x\ specific\ gravity. \tag{10.2}$$

The pair of fully polarimetric C-band datasets used for this study area were acquired by Radarsat-2 sensor. The acquisitions were 25 January 2019 and 18 February 2019, having a temporal interval of 24 days.

10.3 OVERVIEW OF THE FUNDAMENTALS AND METHODOLOGICAL DEVELOPMENT

The workflow followed for this study can be seen in Figure 10.3. The field data were collected using the systematic sampling technique discussed in section 10.2. The major reason for adapting

(a)   (b)

(c)   (d)

FIGURE 10.2   Field photographs [3].

this technique was because the vegetation was homogeneous, but also because this technique has advantages over other sampling techniques. The uniform interval between the plots could not be maintained for every plot due to the presence of dense undergrowth that made some regions completely inaccessible [3]. A total of 38 plots were sampled in the field, with approximately 9 plots per beat.

The PolSAR approach was adapted for retrieving the backscatter mechanisms for each SAR resolution cell of the first acquisition, i.e., master image. The master image was first calibrated and then speckle filtering was done. Finally, Yamaguchi four-component decomposition modelling was implemented in order to retrieve the scattering mechanisms, namely, surface, double-bounce, volume, and helix scattering. The Yamaguchi four-component decomposition model is modified based on the three-component decomposition model. In the four-component decomposition model, the reflection symmetry is not assumed and is denoted as $\left\langle S_{HH} S_{HV}^* \right\rangle \neq 0$ and $\left\langle S_{VV} S_{HV}^* \right\rangle \neq 0$ [26]. The resulting covariance matrices of the four-component decomposition model can be formulated as Equation 10.3.

$$C = f_s C_{surface} + f_d C_{double-bounce} + f_v C_{volume} + f_c C_{helix},$$ (10.3)

where, $f_s, f_d, f_v,$ and f_c are the expansion factors of the complex observables.

The PolSAR-based H-alpha decomposition modeling approach was implemented in order to retrieve the entropy, anisotropy, and the sigma-nought HV values [27].

The PolInSAR-based approach was implemented to retrieve the coherence values from the two SAR acquisitions. First, the master and the slave images – the first and the second acquisitions

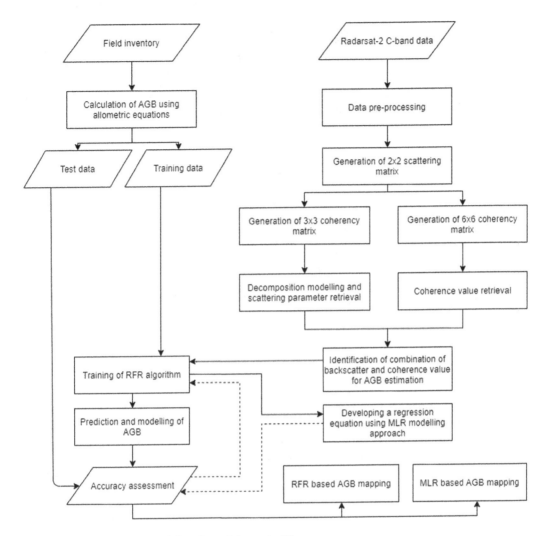

FIGURE 10.3 Methodological flowchart of the study [3].

respectively – were co-registered. Shifts of 2 rows and 43 columns were observed during co-registration of the two image acquisitions [3]. The $[T_6]$ coherency matrix was generated from the k_1 and k_2 Pauli vectors, as shown in Equation 10.4 [27].

$$k_1 = \begin{bmatrix} S^1_{HH} + S^1_{VV} \\ S^1_{HH} - S^1_{VV} \\ 2S^1_{HV} \end{bmatrix} \quad k_2 = \begin{bmatrix} S^2_{HH} + S^2_{VV} \\ S^2_{HH} - S^2_{VV} \\ 2S^2_{HV} \end{bmatrix},$$

$$[T_6] = < \begin{bmatrix} S^1_{HH} + S^1_{VV} \\ S^1_{HH} - S^1_{VV} \\ 2S^1_{HV} \\ S^2_{HH} + S^2_{VV} \\ S^2_{HH} - S^2_{VV} \\ 2S^2_{HV} \end{bmatrix} \begin{bmatrix} S^{1*}_{HH} + S^{1*}_{VV} & S^{1*}_{HH} - S^{1*}_{VV} & 2S^{1*}_{HV} & S^{2*}_{HH} + S^{2*}_{VV} & S^{2*}_{HH} - S^{2*}_{VV} & 2S^{2*}_{HV} \end{bmatrix},$$

$$\begin{bmatrix} T_6 \end{bmatrix} = \begin{bmatrix} \begin{bmatrix} T_{11} \end{bmatrix} & \begin{bmatrix} \Omega_{12} \end{bmatrix} \\ \begin{bmatrix} \Omega_{12} \end{bmatrix}^{*T} & \begin{bmatrix} T_{22} \end{bmatrix} \end{bmatrix}. \tag{10.4}$$

Superscripts 1 and 2 in Equation 10.4 indicate the two image acquisitions at the two extremes of the temporal baseline. The Hermitian coherency matrices of each acquisition are represented as $[T_{11}]$ and $[T_{22}]$, and, the non-Hermitian complex polarimetric–interferometric matrix is represented as $[\Omega_{12}]$ [2]. The complex coherences were obtained from Equations 10.5–10.8 [27].

$$\mu_1 = \omega_1^\dagger K_{p1}, \tag{10.5}$$

$$\mu_2 = \omega_2^\dagger K_{p2}, \tag{10.6}$$

$$\gamma = |\gamma| e^{i\phi} = \gamma_{(\omega_1 \omega_2)}, \tag{10.7}$$

$$\gamma_{(\omega_1 \omega_2)} = \frac{\langle \mu_1 \mu_2^\dagger \rangle}{\sqrt{\langle \mu_1 \mu_1^\dagger \rangle \langle \mu_2 \mu_2^\dagger \rangle}} = \frac{\omega_1^\dagger \Omega_{12} \omega_2}{\sqrt{\omega_1^\dagger T_{11} \omega_1 \omega_2^\dagger T_{22} \omega_2}}, \tag{10.8}$$

where,
ω_1 and ω_2 are the unitary projection vectors,
and
μ_1 and μ_2 are complex scalars due to the projection of the scattering vectors on ω_1 and ω_2.

The backscatter components – namely, volume, helix, surface, double-bounce, entropy, anisotropy, sigma-nought HV, sigma-nought VV, sigma-nought HH backscatter coefficients, backscatter mechanisms, and the HH, HV, VV, HH–VV, HH+VV, and HV+VH coherence values for the corresponding field plots – were used as training data for the RFR algorithm [3]. Two-thirds of the field data and the corresponding SAR variables were considered as a training dataset. The remaining one-third of the dataset was used for validation purposes. The variables were tested for sensitivity and in return their importance in the prediction of AGB.

The SAR variables with higher sensitivity derived from RFR models were used for establishing a statistical relationship between AGB and image variables through a multiple linear regression (MLR) modeling approach [3]. The multi-collinearity test was performed for the MLR model to identify the independent predictor variables for the prediction of AGB. Finally, the RFR and MLR models were validated against the validation dataset.

10.4   ILLUSTRATION OF THE OUTCOMES OF THE ANALYSIS

The tree-level field data for every individual plot contributed to the plot-level estimation of field AGB. The plot-level estimated AGB was ranged between 158.14 Mg/ha and 384.84 Mg/ha, as seen in Figure 10.4. Plot 17 was observed to behave as an outlier with a very high AGB value of 447.23 Mg/ha. The overall distribution of the field-estimated AGB was observed to follow a normal distribution with a wide range of AGB values for a homogeneous forest.

The PolSAR-based backscatter images were retrieved from the Yamaguchi four-component decomposition modeling and also the H/A/alpha decomposition modeling approach. From the four-component decomposition modeling, the surface, double-bounce, volume, and helix scattering parameters were retrieved, as seen in Figure 10.5. Figure 10.5(e) shows the RGB color composite image of the Yamaguchi four-component decomposition model where the vegetated areas contributed in volume scattering. The top surface of the canopy was observed to contribute to surface scattering. The rocks, pebbles, and sand in the dry riverbed was seen to contribute to both

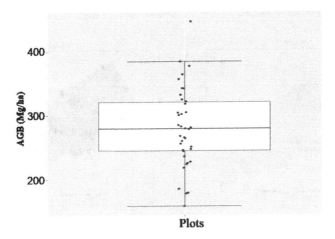

FIGURE 10.4   Boxplot representing the distribution of the field AGB and the outlier [3].

surface and double-bounce scattering. The H/A/alpha decomposition modeling the entropy, anisotropy, and sigma-nought HV parameters were retrieved.

These image parameters were extracted for the corresponding field plots and their distribution against the field AGB were studied. The coefficient of determination of the image parameters volume backscatter, sigma-nought HV backscatter co-efficient, anisotropy, and entropy with respect to field AGB were 0.479, 0.447, 0.006, and 0.218, respectively, as seen in Figure 10.6. The relation between these image parameters and field AGB were linear and positive except for the anisotropy values, which had a negative linear relationship with field AGB.

The complex coherences were retrieved from the PolInSAR-based approach for linear basis (HH, HV, VV), Pauli basis (HH+VV, HV+VH, HH−VV), and optimal basis (Opt-1, Opt-2, Opt-3). These coherence values were observed to range between 0 and 1. In Figure 10.7, which shows the color composite images of the linear, Pauli, and optimal bases, it was observed that the HV and HV+VH coherences were majorly contributed from the vegetated areas. HH+VV and HH−VV, representing surface and double-bounce scattering respectively, were observed to be contributed from the dry riverbeds and the canopy surfaces of the homogeneous forest. And, in the color composite image for the optimal coherences, the forest area was seen to be darker, representing high decorrelation from the vegetation.

In Figure 10.8, the highest correlation was observed for HV+VH polarization with respect to the field biomass, followed by HV polarization. Therefore, from this analysis, it was seen that the coherences from vegetated areas depend on the polarization basis and also behave differently for different scattering components.

The coherence values representing double-bounce and volume scattering were analyzed with respect to each other in order to study the dependency of coherence and the ground-to-volume scattering ratio, as seen in Figure 10.9. The distribution of HV and HV+VH were observed to be similar, having a low range in the y-axis representing high decorrelation of the vegetated areas. The range of HH, VV, HH+VV, and HH−VV were observed to be high, which represents stable scatterers such as rocks, pebbles, and sand. The distribution of the optimal coherences was observed to follow an equi-probable distribution with a gradual decrease in the range of the y-axis. Therefore, from this analysis, it could be said that for a forest region, the co-pol coherence values such as HH, VV, HH+VV, and HH−VV are more sensitive to ground scattering than the cross-pol coherences HV and HV+VH [3].

The RFR model hyperparameters were optimized with 250 regression trees and a training–testing ratio of 70:30. From the analysis of the variable importance for AGB prediction, as seen in

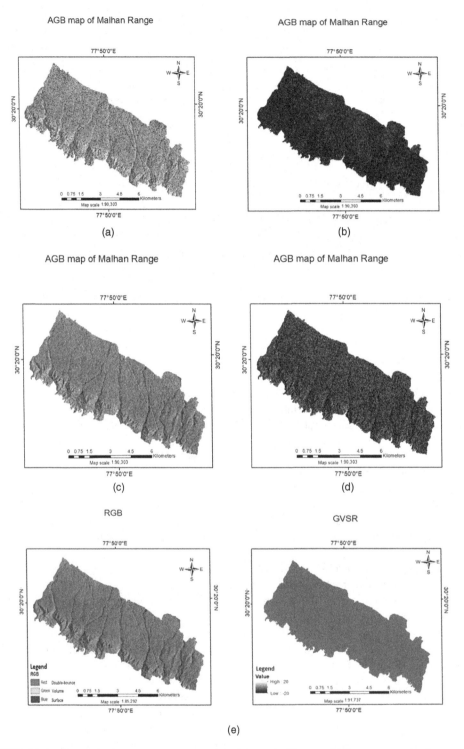

FIGURE 10.5 Shows the image parameters retrieved from the Yamaguchi four-component decomposition modelling [3]: (a) surface scattering, (b) double-bounce scattering, (c) volume scattering, (d) helix scattering, and (e) RGB image (red: double-bounce scattering, green: volume scattering, blue: surface scattering).

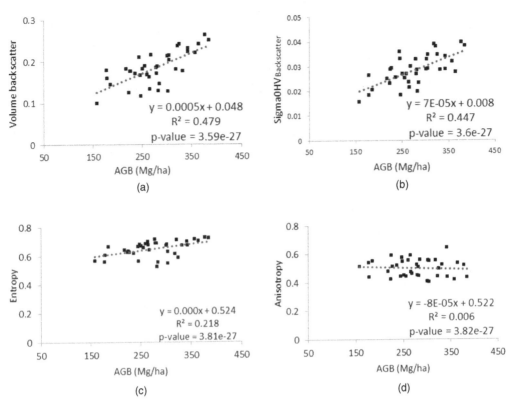

FIGURE 10.6 Shows the graphs indicating the relation between the field AGB and PolSAR image parameters [3]: (a) volume scattering, (b) sigma-nought HV scattering coefficient, (c) entropy, and (d) anisotropy.

Figure 10.10, it was observed that the volume backscatter component was successively followed by HV and HV+VH coherences, sigma-nought HV backscatter coefficient parameters. Therefore, it could be identified that the most sensitive and important parameters predicted AGB with high accuracy, yielding the lowest RMSE in return.

In the case of RFR model, the value of the coefficient of determination was 0.65, and the RMSE value yielded was 24.33 Mg/ha, as seen in Figure 10.11(a). In the case of the MLR model, the value of the coefficient of determination was 0.54, and the RMSE value yielded was 33.05 Mg/ha, as seen in Figure 10.12(a). Therefore, the RFR model was seen to be better than that of MLR for the prediction of AGB. The AGB prediction maps were generated from the two models for the entire study area, as seen in Figure 10.11(b) and 10.12(b). The map generated from the RFR model was seen to represent the proper distribution of the AGB values over the whole area, along with proper demarcation of low biomass areas and high biomass areas. The fire lines and the river channels were accurately identified with the RFR model, unlike the MLR model.

10.5 INFERENCES

In the earlier parts of this chapter, the fundamentals of SAR remote sensing techniques were described along with its applications in the estimation of AGB of forests, a sub-tropical forest in this case. The models illustrated in this chapter were applied for predicting and mapping AGB, exploiting the PolSAR and PolInSAR variables retrieved from an image pair of fully polarimetric Radarsat-2

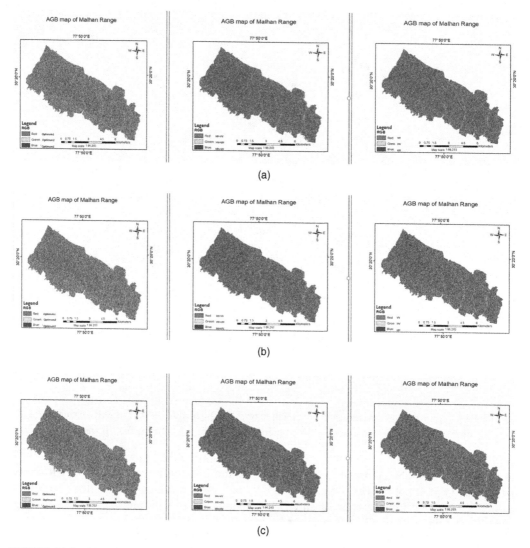

FIGURE 10.7 Shows the color composite images of the PolInSAR coherence values [3]: (a) linear basis, (b) Pauli basis, and, (c) optimal basis.

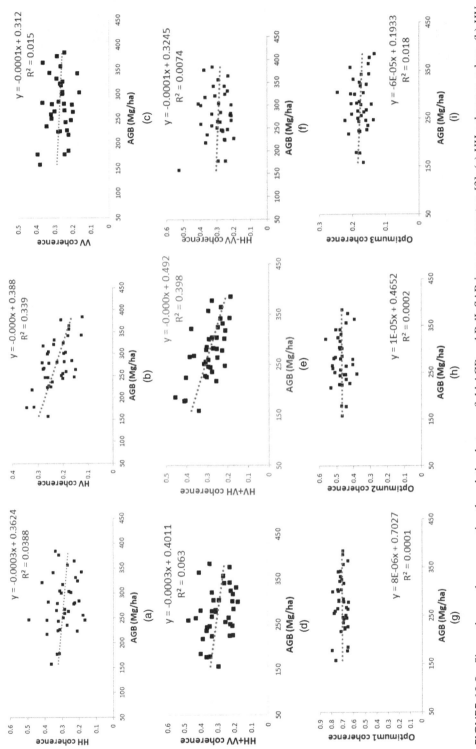

FIGURE 10.8 Shows the graphs representing the relation between field AGB and PolInSAR image parameters [3]: (a) HH coherence values, (b) HV coherence values, (c) VV coherence values, (d) HH+VV coherence values, (e) HV+VH coherence values, (f) HH−VV coherence values, (g) Opt-1, (h) Opt-2, and (i) Opt-3.

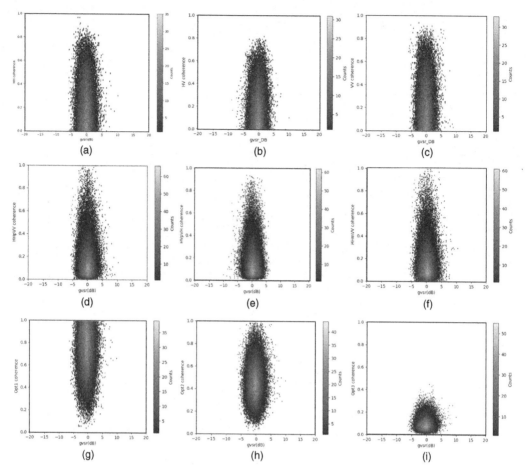

FIGURE 10.9 Shows the graphs representing the dependency of coherence values with respect to ground-to-volume scattering ratio [3]: (a) HH coherence values, (b) HV coherence values, (c) VV coherence values, (d) HH+VV coherence values, (e) HV+VH coherence values, (f) HH−VV coherence values, (g) Opt-1, (h) Opt-2, and (i) Opt-3.

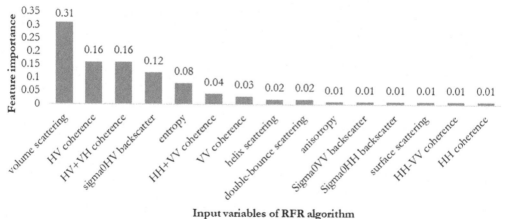

FIGURE 10.10 Shows the plot for variable sensitivity of the RFR model independent variables [3].

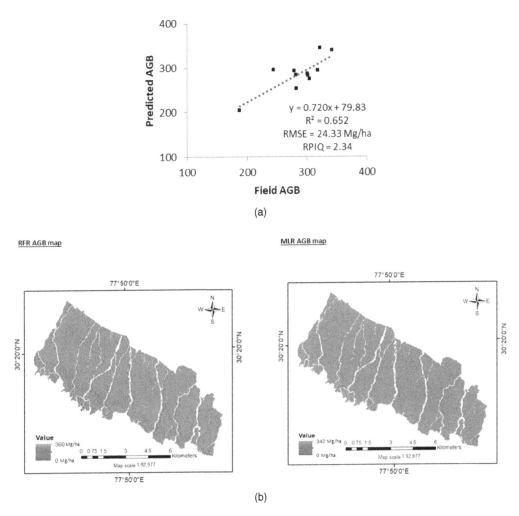

FIGURE 10.11 Shows the results of the RFR model [3]: (a) predicted AGB vs field AGB plot and (b) AGB prediction map.

C-band data; from these, RFR was observed to be more efficient in the prediction of AGB. The higher efficiency of RFR over MLR can be explained due to the flexibility of input variables. In the case of RFR, it can handle a large number of input variables, unlike MLR. From the two models, the most sensitive and important variables identified for the prediction of AGB were volume scattering, HV and HV+VH coherences, and sigma-nought HV backscatter coefficient components.

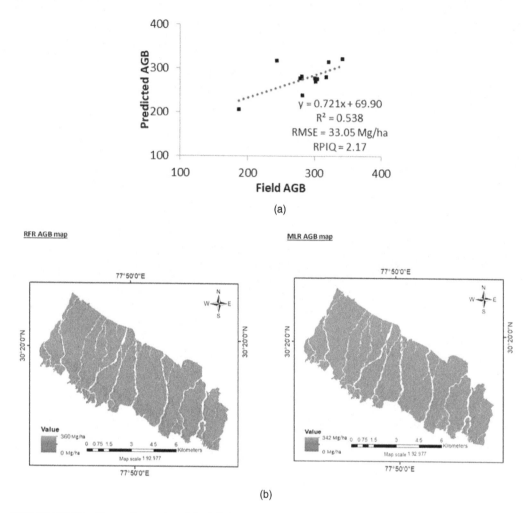

$$y = 0.721x + 69.90$$
$$R^2 = 0.538$$
$$RMSE = 33.05 \text{ Mg/ha}$$
$$RPIQ = 2.17$$

(a)

(b)

FIGURE 10.12 Shows the results of the MLR model [3]: (a) predicted AGB vs field AGB plot and (b) AGB prediction map.

REFERENCES

[1] FAO, *The State of World's Forests – 2018 – Forest Pathways to Sustainable Development*. 2018.

[2] S. Cloude, *Polarisation: Applications in Remote Sensing*. Oxford University Press, 2010.

[3] R. Mukhopadhyay, S. Kumar, H. Aghababaei, and A. Kulshrestha, "Estimation of aboveground biomass from PolSAR and PolInSAR using regression-based modelling techniques," *Geocarto Int.*, 2021, doi: 10.1080/10106049.2021.1878289.

[4] M. Neumann and L. Ferro-Famil, "Remote sensing of vegetation using multi-baseline polarimetric SAR interferometry (theoretical modeling and physical parameter retrieval)," *undefined*, 2009.

[5] G. Krieger, K. P. Papathanassiou, and S. R. Cloude, "Spaceborne polarimetric SAR interferometry: Performance analysis and mission concepts," *EURASIP J. Appl. Signal Processing*, vol. 2005, no. 20, pp. 3272–3292, Dec. 2005, doi: 10.1155/ASP.2005.3272.

[6] S. R. Cloude and K. P. Papathanassiou, "Polarimetric SAR interferometry," *IEEE Trans. Geosci. Remote Sens.*, vol. 36, no. 5 PART 1, pp. 1551–1565, 1998, doi: 10.1109/36.718859.

[7] E. L. Uneburg, "Aspects of Radar Polarimetry," *Turk. J. Elec. Engin.*, vol. 10, no. 2, pp. 219–243, 2002.

[8] D. Massonnet and J.-C. Souyris, *Imaging with Synthetic Aperture Radar*, 1st ed. New York, 2008.

[9] S. Chandola, "Polarimetric SAR Interferometry for Forest Aboveground Biomass Estimation," MS thesis, Faculty of Geo-information Science and Earth Observation, Univ. of Twente, Enschede, the Netherlands, 2014.

[10] M. D. Behera, P. Tripathi, B. Mishra, S. Kumar, V. S. Chitale, and S. K. Behera, "Above-ground biomass and carbon estimates of *Shorea robusta* and *Tectona grandis* forests using QuadPOL ALOS PALSAR data," *Adv. Sp. Res.*, vol. 57, no. 2, pp. 552–561, Jan. 2016, doi: 10.1016/j.asr.2015.11.010.

[11] F. Garestier, P. C. Dubois-Fernandez, D. Guyon, and T. Le Toan, "Forest biophysical parameter estimation using L- and P-band polarimetric SAR data," *IEEE Trans. Geosci. Remote Sens.*, vol. 47, no. 10, pp. 3379–3388, Oct. 2009, doi: 10.1109/TGRS.2009.2022947.

[12] J. Carreiras, J. Melo, and M. Vasconcelos, "Estimating the above-ground biomass in Miombo Savanna Woodlands (Mozambique, East Africa) Using L-band synthetic aperture radar data," *Remote Sens.*, vol. 5, no. 4, pp. 1524–1548, Mar. 2013, doi: 10.3390/rs5041524.

[13] P. Sai Bharadwaj, S. Kumar, S. P. S. Kushwaha, and W. Bijker, "Polarimetric scattering model for estimation of above ground biomass of multilayer vegetation using ALOS-PALSAR quad-pol data," *Phys. Chem. Earth*, vol. 83–84, pp. 187–195, Oct. 2015, doi: 10.1016/j.pce.2015.09.003.

[14] S. Kumar, R. D. Garg, H. Govil, and S. P. S. Kushwaha, "PolSAR-decomposition-based extended water cloud modeling for forest aboveground biomass estimation," *Remote Sens.*, vol. 11, no. 19, p. 2287, Sep. 2019, doi: 10.3390/rs11192287.

[15] S. Kumar, U. Pandey, S. P. Kushwaha, R. S. Chatterjee, and W. Bijker, "Aboveground biomass estimation of tropical forest from Envisat advanced synthetic aperture radar data using modeling approach," *J. Appl. Remote Sens.*, vol. 6, no. 1, p. 063588, Oct. 2012, doi: 10.1117/1.JRS.6.063588.

[16] N. Agrawal, S. Kumar, and V. A. Tolpekin, "Polinsar based scattering information retrieval for forest aboveground biomass estimation," in *International Archives of the Photogrammetry, Remote Sensing and Spatial Information Sciences – ISPRS Archives*, Jun. 2019, vol. 42, no. 2/W13, pp. 1913–1920, doi: 10.5194/isprs-archives-XLII-2-W13-1913-2019.

[17] M. Santoro, L. Eriksson, J. Askne, and C. Schmullius, "Assessment of stand-wise stem volume retrieval in boreal forest from JERS-1 L-band SAR backscatter," *Int. J. Remote Sens.*, vol. 27, no. 16, pp. 3425–3454, Aug. 2006, doi: 10.1080/01431160600646037.

[18] J. Singh, "PolInSAR and TLS data modeling for forest biophysical parameter characterization," MTech thesis, Andhra Univ., Visakhapatnam, India, 2015.

[19] R. Mangla, "Machine learning based regression model for forest aboveground biomass estimation using RISAT-1 PolSAR and TLS Lidar Data," MT MTech thesis, Andhra Univ., Visakhapatnam, India, 2015.

[20] M. Yazdani, S. Shataee Jouibary, J. Mohammadi, and Y. Maghsoudi, "Comparison of different machine learning and regression methods for estimation and mapping of forest stand attributes using ALOS/PALSAR data in complex Hyrcanian forests," *J. Appl. Remote Sens.*, vol. 14, no. 02, p. 1, May 2020, doi: 10.1117/1.jrs.14.024509.

[21] V. N. Vapnik, *The Nature of Statistical Learning Theory*. New York, Springer, 2000.

[22] M. Neumann, L. Ferro-Famil, and A. Reigber, "Estimation of forest structure, ground, and canopy layer characteristics from multibaseline polarimetric interferometric SAR data," *IEEE Trans. Geosci. Remote Sens.*, vol. 48, no. 3 PART 1, pp. 1086–1104, 2010, doi: 10.1109/TGRS.2009.2031101.

[23] H. G. Champion and S. K. Seth, *A Revised Survey of the Forest Types of India*. 1968.

[24] "Survey of India." https://surveyofindia.gov.in/ (accessed Apr. 24, 2021).

[25] B. Husch, J. A. Kershaw, and T. W. Beers, *Forest Mensuration*, 4th ed. New Jersey: John Wiley & Sons Inc., 2003.

[26] Y. Yamaguchi, Y. Yajima, and H. Yamada, "A four-component decomposition of POLSAR images based on the coherency matrix," *IEEE Geosci. Remote Sens. Lett.*, vol. 3, no. 3, pp. 292–296, Jul. 2006, doi: 10.1109/LGRS.2006.869986.

[27] J.-S. Lee and E. Pottier, *Polarimetric Radar Imaging: From Basics to Applications*, vol. 33, no. 2. Informa UK Limited, 2012.

11 Analysis of Polarimetric Techniques for Characterization of Glacial Feature

Shashwati Singh, Shashi Kumar, Praveen K. Thakur, and Varun N. Mshra

CONTENTS

11.1 INTRODUCTION

Glaciers are masses of ice formed by the recrystallization of snow precipitation; they contain a total of 69% of fresh water in the frozen form. Glaciers have been regarded as sensitive indicators

DOI: 10.1201/9781003204466-11

of climate change for a long time. Climate influences the mass balance of a glacier's surface. Recent trends in global warming have a direct impact on glaciers. Because Himalayan glaciers are positioned near the Tropic of Cancer, they get more heat, making them more vulnerable to climate change. The Himalayan glaciers feed Asia's major rivers, which are the only supply of fresh water for millions of people living on the Indian subcontinent; imbalances in glacier reservoirs can leads to a catastrophic situation at both regional and global levels. On a geographical basis, the Indian Himalaya is categorized into three parts, mainly known as the eastern, western, and central Himalayas, where Gangotri and Siachen Glaciers lie in the transitional zone between the Eastern–Western and Karakoram Range of the north-western part of the Himalayas respectively. Gangotri Glacier is an important source of water for people living in the Gangetic plain. Siachen is the largest non-polar glacier; thus, it has become important for researchers to keep an eye on them. Due to the difficult terrain and inaccessibility of some regions, satellite data is used to observe glaciers. However, rough high alpine places pose significant challenges, such as uneven distribution of solar light due to topography, cloud cover, and shadow on the spectral response of snow. Microwave-based synthetic aperture radar (SAR) imaging is an alternative and one of the most essential ways for collecting data in high mountainous areas. Microwaves can surpass rain and fog, cloud, and moist precipitation, allowing for all-weather monitoring regardless of time or solar light; nevertheless, extreme caution must be exercised when selecting the appropriate frequency range for a given application.

In this chapter, we have used fully polarimetric data of advanced land observation satellite-phased array-type L-band synthetic aperture radar (ALOS-PALSAR-2), which is acquired in HH, HV, VV, and VH polarization. To understand the nature of the target and identify the target during any season, PolSAR data acquired in different modes and SAR incidence angles >30° give better information for discriminating glacier facies [1]. When multiple targets are available in pixel, we need to study different polarized data, as polarimetric parameters differ depending upon different target parameters for e.g. sensor parameters, which include frequency, polarization, and incidence angle [2], and snow parameters, like snow density, volume, depth, internal layering, dielectric property, ice particle size and shape, and surface roughness (air–snow and ground–snow) [1]. Together, both parameters can change the scattering mechanism. The entire study discussed in this chapter was conducted without going into the field because of the prevailing Covid-19 pandemic situation in the country, so to validate the results, different polarimetric techniques are considered, and a detailed study of these parameters is considered to retrieve scattering mechanisms for different glacier facies.

In this study, analysis of different applied methods, such as backscattering coefficient, eigenvalue–eigenvector, Freeman–Durden three-component decomposition, and Stokes vector, is generated for glacier facies. The spaceborne SAR data were acquired during the accumulation period for Gangotri Glacier and the ablation period for Siachen Glacier. According to [3], the Indian Himalayan Region receives snowfall from mainly western disturbances and S-W monsoon, which also accumulates during winter till March and then melts April through August, with minimum snow cover by the end of August. In this chapter, the methods were applied to find out snow (wet or dry) and percolation zone in the accumulation zone and ice and debris in ablation. The terminology is explained in a such way to differentiate dry snow, where no melting takes place around the year, as such a type of glacier is absent in most part of the Himalayas because of the range's elevation and temperature. The percolation zone lies below the dry snow zone and above the wet snow zone, where melted water infiltrates down and refreezes, forming pipe-like channels, ice lenses, and layers. Such zones are found at a lower elevation, which also wets the upper part of the snow [4], [5]. The wet snow zone is where melting occurs during the melting season, with winter bringing about refreezing. The bare ice zone is located at a lower elevation, where melting takes place throughout the year; there is no accumulation of snow here. The debris-covered zone is found in the ablation zone, which is carved out of mountain due to friction produced from moving ice and snow. In SAR images, backscatter is dependent on snow and ice parameters [5]. The total backscattering from a dry snow–covered area is the sum of surface and volume scattering from air/snow, scattering inside the snow due to ice particles and scattering from ground/snow. Wet snow–covered areas are the sum of surface and volume scattering from air/snow interface [6] and multiple scattering from both surface and volume scattering [7]. Highly reflective surfaces, such as clean ice, produce surface scattering where radar waves cannot make it through ice due to its property of being dielectric. The presence of debris and moraines gives high backscattering due to its roughness, which causes volume-type scattering [8]; double-bounce scattering is caused by the presence of crevasses in the zones. Backscattering from snow is a function of SAR frequency and incidence angle; depending on the size of wavelength, dry snow can give a strong surface scattering response in cases of longer wavelength and a volume scattering response at shorter wavelengths [8]; at a small angle of incidence, a snow area can give a surface scattering response, and at large incidence angle a volume scattering response [9] .

The Gangotri Glacier is bifurcated into two zones, mainly accumulation and ablation zones. The exact ELA is not defined to differentiate the zones because it does not involve the aim of the study; an approximate area was taken from optical data to define accumulation and ablation zones. Part of Siachen Glacier is where some of ablation is been carried out while doing comparative analysis among three methods – backscattering coefficient and two decomposition methods. In the accumulation zone, the scattering σ^0 from wet/dry snow and percolation zone creates confusion when differentiating among them; similarly, in ablation zones, ice, debris, and crevasses were found to be ambiguous in both study areas. Stokes vector–based approach, CPR, resolves the striking discussion among them. CPR indicates the threshold value for ice greater than unity, and rest surfaces are below unity [10]. While comparing results, it was found that both decompositions produce quite similar result but are not satisfactory. On other side, the backscattering coefficient σ^0 for both zones of the studied area shows a very low sigma naught value, which signifies the presence of wet snow even in the ablation region, which also validated the results using optical data from the same period. The data was acquired during the accumulation period for Gangotri Glacier; the image shows snow pixels till the snout, and for Siachen Glacier it was acquired during the middle of the ablation period, which also shows snow pixels covering an area more than its actual position of accumulation zone. So, to produce concrete results, more parameters should to be taken together with field data.

11.2   STUDY AREA AND DATASETS

11.2.1   STUDY AREA

This section considers the relevant study area (see Figure 11.1).

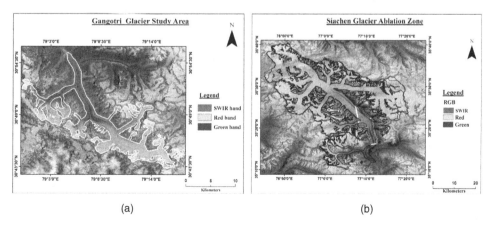

(a)   (b)

FIGURE 11.1   (a) Gangotri Glacier (left) and (b) Siachen Glacier (right).

11.2.1.1 Gangotri Glacier

In this present study, only part of the glacier has been studied to show the scattering mechanism in more precise way. Gangotri Glacier is located in the transitional zone between the Eastern–Western part of Himalaya, in the Garhwal district of Uttarakhand, which flows from the north-west and extends for 30 kilometers between latitudes 30°43'22" N and 30°55'.49" and longitudes 79°4'41" E and 79° 16'34"E. Gangotri Glacier has a surface elevation of 4000–7000 meters. The glacier's width ranges from 0.20 to 2.35 kilometers, covering an area of about 122 km² [11]. The Gangotri and its feeding glacier are estimated to cover a total area of 210.60 km² [12]. At the snout of the glacier at Gaumukh, it gives rise to the Bhagirathi River, which meets Alaknanda at Devprayag to form the river Ganga. The glacier has a total capacity of frozen ice and snow of 23.2±4.2 km², and in the upper zone, mainly the accumulation zone, the glacier is 540 meters thick; in the ablation zone, in lower reaches at the snout, the glacier is 50–60 meters thick [13]. Summer monsoons and winter snowfall are the main source of water for the Gangotri Glacier.

11.2.1.2 Siachen Glacier

Siachen Glacier has a geographical extension of 35°31'18.80" N and 76°57'3.77" E, situated in the Karakoram Range of the North-Western Himalayas. It is Asia's longest glacier, extending 72 kilometers. It is also the world's second longest valley glacier, after the Polar Regions, stretching northwest–southeast. The glacier's snout is at 3670 meters above sea level, while the accumulation zone's highest point is at 7200 meters [14]. The glacier has width of 1–8 km; inclusive of all feeding glaciers, Siachen Glaciers occupies a total 700 km² of an area that has feeding tributaries, mainly Teram-Sher and Lolofond. It is the source of the major river Indus. Extra tropical low- pressure systems known as western disturbances impact precipitation in the Karakoram Himalayas, whereas the Indian monsoon has a very minor impact in this area.

11.2.2 Datasets

This work utilizes the capacity of fully polarimetric advanced land observation satellite–phased array-type L-band synthetic aperture radar (ALOS-PALSAR-2). A detailed description of the quad-pol SAR data of ALOS-PALSAR-2 is given in Table 11.1.

11.4 METHODOLOGY

To study backscattering parameters of different glacial feature, SLC data of ALOS-PALSAR-2 was imported to process and analyze the data. SLC is an acronym for single look complex, which is level 1.1 processed data; this level of processed data gives better resolution in an azimuth direction. SLC products are good to work with for decomposition models because such a product retains the original complex value of image. Since it is measured by complex (I and Q) magnitude values, each image pixel contains both phase and amplitude details. The volume file of SLC data of ALOS-PALSAR-2 is imported to SNAP to perform the first step of radiometric calibration, where the output image was saved as a complex image. After radiometric correction, the SAR image was geometrically corrected using range doppler terrain correction using internal DEM of SRTM 1 sec.

11.4.1 Calculation of Backscattering Coefficient σ^0

The calibrated image is required to translate the DN values of these intensity images into their corresponding radar backscattering coefficient values for any meaningful and quantitative study of SAR images. The target attributes are studied using backscattered radar power, which is measured in decibels (dB) and expressed as $10\log_{10}$ (received power / incident power). Equation 11.1, where target-wise backscattering may be evaluated, creates σ^0 in the dB scale image during the calibration

TABLE 11.1
ALOS-PALSAR-2 Specification

Observation Mode	Full (Quad.) Polarimetry [6m]	
Obs. mode ID (code)	HBQ	
Date of acquisition	2015/06/05	2015/03/22
Area	Siachen Glacier	Gangotri Glacier
Band	L-band	L-band
Frequency	1.2 GHz	1.2 GHz
Incidence angle	37.61895°–40.28089°	32.31719°–35.28783°
Polarization	HH, HV, VV, VH	HH, HV, VV, VH
Look direction	Right	Right
Temporal resolution	14 days	14 days
Pass	Ascending	Ascending
Product type	SLC	SLC
Range resolution	5.13 m	5.13 m
Azimuth resolution	3.21 m	3.21 m
Level	1.1	1.1
Pixel spacing	5.13 m	5.13 m
Beam mode	Stripmap	Stripmap

procedure [1]. The log function is applied to the radar image to produce a normal distribution of values. Because bright values are moved towards the mean and dark values are extended over a broader color range, it converts pixel values into a logarithmic scale, resulting in higher contrasts [15].

$$\sigma^{\circ} = 20\ log_{10}\ (X) - k + 10\ log_{10}\ (sin\theta_{local}/\ sin\theta_{center}),$$ (11.1)

where X is the pixel value, k denotes the calibration constant in dB, θ_{local} denotes the local incidence angle, and θ_{center} denotes the nominal incidence angle at the scene center.

11.4.2 SCATTERING MATRIX

Polarimetry matrix generation and polarimetric speckle filtering are all part of the generation of SAR data before polarimetric decomposition [16]. Polarized electromagnetic waves of radar polarimetry are vector in nature; when a polarized wave strikes an object, it is reflected back. The 2×2 coherent backscattering matrix, also known as the Sinclair matrix, contains information regarding the orientation, reflectivity, and shape of the reflecting body [17].

$$S = \begin{bmatrix} S_{hh} & S_{hv} \\ S_{vh} & S_{hh} \end{bmatrix}.$$ (11.2)

When a horizontally polarized wave strikes a target, the backscattered wave might have horizontal and vertical polarization contributions. A vertically polarized incident wave also behaves in similar way. The backscattering attributes of the target may be entirely represented by a scattering matrix (S) because the horizontal and vertical components create a complete basis set to express the electromagnetic wave [18]. Complex backscattering coefficients are the elements of the scattering matrix S_{HH}, S_{VV}, and S_{HV}. In a co-polarized channel, the elements S_{HH} and S_{VV} produce power, while in a cross-polarized channel, the elements S_{HV} and S_{VH} produce power. For the backscattering situation, $S_{HV} = S_{VH}$ is assumed [8].

Before decomposing any of the Sinclair-based matrix image, the image needs to be transformed into 3 × 3 matrix form for any monostatic acquired image. In this chapter, an incoherent-based decomposition method is adopted; naturally, incoherent-based decomposition is dependent on coherency and covariance scattering matrix. The refined Lee filter with window size 5 × 5 is used before performing decomposition on the coherency matrix to reduce the speckle noise.

The scattering matrix is expressed as a complex sum of Pauli and lexicographic matrices in this decomposition.

11.4.3 Target Decomposition

Decomposition is used to distinguish between volume and surface scattering. The term "coherent" refers to a target that is pure, whereas "incoherent" refers to scattered scatterers. Only coherent or pure scatterers can be identified using the scattering matrix [S]. This matrix, on the other hand, cannot be used to characterize the scattered scatterers [6]. Thus, incoherent-based polarimetric decomposition can characterize incoherent scatterers. Depending on the type of snow pack, the scattering mechanism ranges from volume to surface scattering; polarimetric decompositions can be utilized to distinguish distinct zones of a glacier.

11.4.3.1 Eigenvalue–Eigenvector Decomposition

The 3 × 3 Hermitian averaged coherency (T_3) matrix of eigenvalue and eigenvector can be computed to yield a diagonal form of the coherency matrix that can be physically interpreted as statistical independence between a set of target vectors. To identify the scattering contributed by different scatterers within a SAR resolution cell, 3 × 3 Hermitian coherency matrices are used [19]. The 3 × 3 diagonal elements of the matrix comprise the eigenvalues of $\langle [T_3] \rangle$:

$$\left[\Sigma_3 \right] = \begin{bmatrix} \lambda_1 & 0 & 0 \\ 0 & \lambda_2 & 0 \\ 0 & 0 & \lambda_3 \end{bmatrix}, \tag{11.5}$$

where $\lambda_1 > \lambda_2 > \lambda_3 > 0$.

The three diagonal elements are represented as λ_1 = alpha angle (α), λ_2 = entropy (H), and λ_3 = anisotropy (A). On other hand, alpha also explains scattering mechanisms; its value spans between 0° and 90°.

If $\alpha = 0°$, then it represents surface scattering; if $\alpha = 45°$, then it represents volume scattering; and if $\alpha = 90°$, then it represents double-bounce scattering.

H quantifies the degree of randomness in the image and signifies unpredictable components in returned waves or energy. Entropy is also capable of differentiating the dominant scattering mechanism. Low entropy values imply that the target is weakly depolarizing, and the eigenvector corresponding to the greatest eigenvalue represents the dominating target scattering component. The target is depolarizing if entropy is high. The value of H spans from 0 to 1. Anisotropy shows relationship between the second eigenvalue and third eigenvalue. This parameter is very useful in distinguishing different scattering processes when entropy reaches a high value.

The eigenvector represents the kind of scattering pattern, whereas the eigenvalue indicates the scattering magnitude. The three elements derived from this decomposition, as shown in expression (11.5), give different scattering mechanisms representing different glacial surfaces, which is described later in this chapter.

11.4.3.2 Freeman–Durden Decomposition

This Freeman–Durden decomposition is the best exponent representation of model-based decomposition; the covariance matrix is modeled by the Freeman–Durden decomposition as the output of three scattering mechanisms. See [20] for calculation of the three scattering elements from Freeman–Durden decomposition.

The computed covariance matrix $[C_3]$ is expressed as follows using the Freeman decomposition.

$$[C3] = \left\langle [C_3] \right\rangle_v + [C_3]_d + [C_3]_s, \tag{11.6}$$

where subscript v corresponds to volume scattering, d to double-bounce scattering, and s to surface scattering.

- Volume scattering is modeled as a set of randomly oriented dipoles.
- Double-bounce scattering modeled by a dihedral reflector.
- Surface scattering modeled by first order Bragg surface scatterer.

11.4.4 STOKES PARAMETERS

Stokes parameters can be used to determine the polarization state of an electromagnetic wave. Rather than amplitudes and phases, the four Stokes parameters (intensity, polarization, rotation, circularity) are represented in terms of power. Stokes parameters are essential because, in addition to fully polarized waves or unpolarized wave, they can also characterize partially polarized waves [18]. The Stokes child parameter, circulation polarization ration (CPR), is derived using Stokes vector. The hybrid mode required for the Stokes parameter has an architecture of a 2×2 coherency matrix, but L-band quad-pol data are designed in a 3×3 coherency matrix that is later converted to a 2×2 coherency matrix to achieve Stokes parameters. The converted hybrid polarimetric architecture of PALSAR L-band is represented by equation (11.7) [18].

$$\begin{bmatrix} S_1 \\ S_2 \\ S_3 \\ S_4 \end{bmatrix} = \begin{bmatrix} |E_H|^2 + |E_V|^2 \\ |E_H|^2 - |E_V|^2 \\ 2\,Re\,|E_H\,E_{V*}| \\ -2\,Im\,|E_H\,E_{V*}| \end{bmatrix}, \tag{11.7}$$

where, S_1, S_2, S_3, and S_4 are four Stokes parameters, Re is a real and Im an imaginary channel of the product, and $\times$ expresses complex conjugate of polarization.

11.5 RESULTS AND DISCUSSION

11.5.1 BACKSCATTERING COEFFICIENT σ^o IMAGE INTERPRETATION

11.5.1.1 Siachen Glacier Ablation Zone

In the Figure 11.2, Siachen Glacier is bifurcated according to the definition of glacial geomorphology, mainly the ablation zone and the accumulation zone, but due to data availability, only part of the glacier is being studied. The average backscattering value ranges differently for like (HH, VV) and unlike (HV, VH) polarization; for example, in like polarization, the acquired σ^o scattering coefficient is −13.25 dB and −13.37 dB for VV and HH polarization, respectively, and −20.82 dB and −20.73 dB for HV and VH polarization, respectively. In the ablation zone in the middle of the ablation period, ice and debris are prominent with some melted snow. Even if there is L-band, no penetration of waves takes place because as snow wetness increases, the dielectric constant also increases, and as the SAR wave is sensitive to dielectric property, every scattering will take place at the surface of the snow [7]. As already stated, the backscattering coefficient is a function of the snow parameter; the presence of wet snow will give weak backscattering because of its dielectric property, and so much less energy is returned to SAR as most is absorbed (see Figure 11.2). In the Himalayan glacier, the ablation zone is mainly covered with debris. The surface roughness causes variation in backscattering from the ablation zone in the ablation period. The debris-covered area

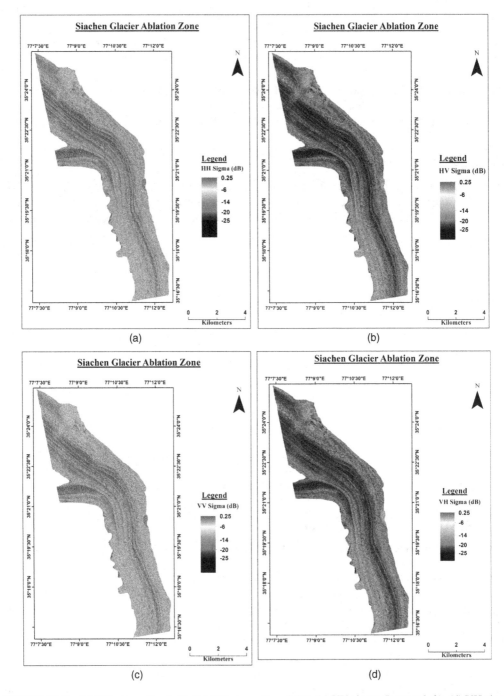

FIGURE 11.2 (a) HH sigma (top left), (b) HV sigma (top right), (c) VV sigma (bottom left), (d) VH sigma (bottom right). In every polarization, sigma naught shows very high and very low values, but to show better scattering, sigma naught is set to maximum and minimum value to fixed range.

has high backscattering signals, whereas bare ice has comparatively low backscattering [1]. In the ablation period, the bare ice zone shows the lowest value of > −14 dB approx., due to accumulation of snow during the winter period and wetness of snow during the summer as this does not allow signals to penetrate the snow pack. This higher backscattering of SAR signals can be caused due to contact of roughed and crevassed bare ice surfaces.

11.5.1.2   Gangotri Glacier

For Gangotri Glacier, only the main part of the glacier is being studied here; tributary glaciers are excluded for a focus on the accumulation and ablation zones of the main glacier. The average acquired σ^0 scattering coefficient for accumulation zone is −8.52 dB and −8.57 dB for VV and HH polarization, respectively, and −13.92 dB and −14.15 dB for VH and HV polarization, respectively. Gangotri Glacier is divided in its accumulation and ablation zones, as can be seen in Figure 11.3; by the end of the accumulation period, the accumulation zone comprises dry/ wet snow, with the percolation zone lying between them. The surface of dry snow has no significant effect on backscattered signals, because it has a small dielectric property, so it is penetrated in the background of the air–snow surface. According to L-band frequency and snow grain size, where Rayleigh scattering dominates, for wavelengths much larger than the size of particles low backscattering is given pertaining to the homogeneous surface. Increase in incidence angle leads to decrease in the total backscattering due to a fall in backscattering from snow–ground [7], and vice versa for a small incidence angle. In wet snow

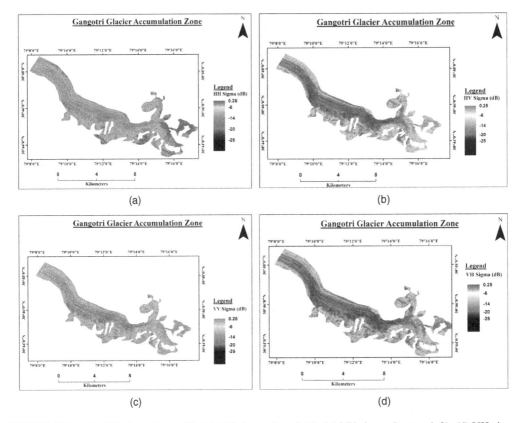

FIGURE 11.3   (a) HH sigma (top left), (b) HV sigma (top right), (c) VV sigma (bottom left), (d) VH sigma (bottom right). In every polarization, sigma naught shows very high and very low values, but to show better scattering, sigma naught is set to maximum and minimum value to fixed range.

regions, incident microwaves are absorbed by melt water inside the snow pack, and backscattering of the SAR signal from the wet snow region is lowest during summer [5]. It is higher in the winter because melt water refreezes, forming ice pipes and lenses that operate as strong scatterers, that is, produce high scattering as signals penetration and interact with them [1]. Frozen percolation zones produce high backscattering all year round but often give low backscattering due to exposure to high temperature. In Figure 11.3, at the head of glacier very high scattering is seen due to the percolation zone. In unlike polarization, where a lowest value > −14 dB approx. is seen at lower elevation due to wet snow, and in like polarization, a higher scattering coefficient is dominating, with lower value present mostly in the middle part of the glacier. Dry snow develops where the temperature never goes beyond melting point; even at very high altitudes, intense light over the Himalayan area prevents the development of dry snow, and thus such facies is absent in Gangotri Glacier [1].

Ablation zones of the Indian Himalayan glaciers have a similar composition, like debris, ice, and crevasses. In Figure 11.4, of the ablation zone, the average acquired value is around −7.17 dB and −7.29 dB for VV and HH polarization and −13.02 dB and −13.15 dB for VH and HV polarization. There will be a similar amount of backscattering from the ablation zone, as in the Siachen Glacier ablation zone. In the ablation zone, high scattering energy signifies debris or moraines and crevasses, while low scattering energy signifies for bare ice; however, there is more snow found in the ablation zone, which is spread till the snout, due to a data acquisition period at the end of the accumulation period. Figure 11.4 shows dominance of a lower scattering coefficient > −14 dB in unlike polarization and higher coefficient < −14 dB like polarization. As a result, high σ^0 backscattering is only received where there is the presence of such targets that are more susceptible for volume and double-bounce scattering, such as debris/moraines and crevasses, and comparatively low σ^0 backscattering is received from snow/bare ice. Since the acquired period of L-band data is at the end of the accumulation period, this area gives a lower backscattering coefficient than the snow due to the specular reflector and smooth ice surface of the bare ice zone in winter [22]. Snow that falls in this area melts rapidly owing to the higher temperatures, revealing the existing ice once more. The layer may give a very low scattering coefficient for wet snow in summer than in the bare ice zone, depending on the timing of snow precipitation, indicating snow in the area. Therefore, the σ^0 backscattering coefficient becomes significant in analysis of glaciers facies.

11.5.2 Results of H-A-α Decomposition

11.5.2.1 Gangotri Glacier

In Figure 11.5 of alpha and entropy, dominant scattering for the Gangotri Glacier accumulation zone is shown. The H-A-α decomposition can even show the perceived target's scattering angle and degree of randomness [23]. In the alpha image, the values are categorized as < 40° surface scattering, > 40°<50° volume scattering, and >50° double-bounce. And on the entropy image, values vary, with 0–5 considered low entropy, 5–9 medium entropy, and 9–10 high entropy [24], [25]. The entropy values closer to 1 are scattered from throughout the glacier, which is represented in black in the image. The pixel or area with high entropy values in the image appears to have a diffused kind of scattering, which denotes the combinations of two types of scattering mechanisms, mainly like double-bounce or both double-bounce and volume scattering in the area because here the alpha angle is above 40°. The alpha angle below and equal to 50° shown (Figure 11.5) in yellow and pink is equivalent to medium entropy, while values shown (Figure 11.5) in yellow present a medium degree of volume and surface scattering in the region. A high degree of polarization results in cases of low entropy values and gives back a specular surface reflection. Low surface scattering is present in very few pixels or areas in the glacier zone, which is shown in pink, where the alpha value has a pixel value below 40°, while a decrease in entropy value can be observed shown in pink. The average value for alpha angle and entropy in the accumulation zone are 43.46° and 0.83 respectively.

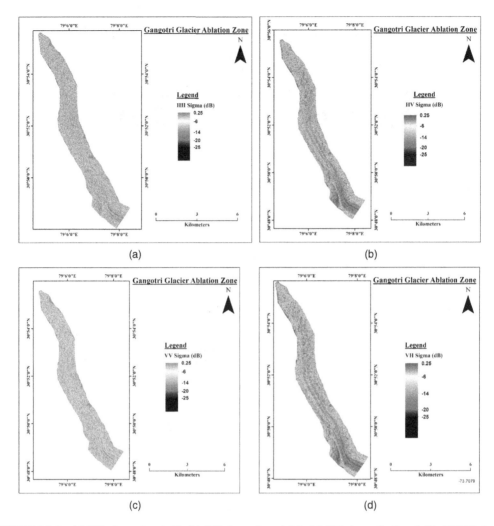

FIGURE 11.4   (a) HH sigma (top left), (b) HV sigma (top right), (c) VV sigma (bottom left), (d) VH sigma (bottom right). In every polarization, sigma naught shows very high and very low values, but to show better scattering, sigma naught is set to maximum and minimum value to fixed range.

In Figure 11.6 of alpha and entropy, dominant scattering for the Gangotri Glacier ablation zone is shown. In the glacier's ablation zone, the entropy value closer to 1 is a dominant scattering in the glacier, which is represented in black in the image, whereas in the alpha-derived image, values between 40° and 50° are a dominant scattering in the ablation zone and is shown in yellow. The alpha angle equal to and greater than 40° is equivalent to a higher entropy value in the image, which appears to have a diffuse kind of scattering; the consequences of diffuse scattering are explained in the earlier section regarding the accumulation zone. Medium entropy values are followed by a low alpha degree below 50°, representing both surface and volume scattering in pink and yellow. Alpha value below 40° is followed by surface scattering caused by specular reflection from target; the lower entropy results from high degree of polarization and surface reflection are observed in the image. The alpha below 40° is shown in pink, and low entropy is represented in pink. The low degree of surface reflection is found to be a lesser percentage. The average values for alpha and entropy in the ablation zone are 43.80° and 0.86 respectively.

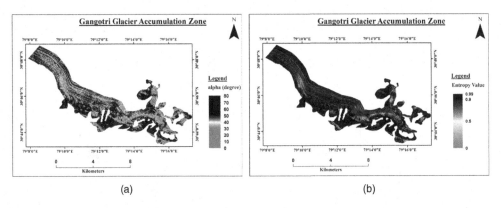

FIGURE 11.5   (a) Alpha angle image (top) and (b) entropy (bottom) of accumulation zone.

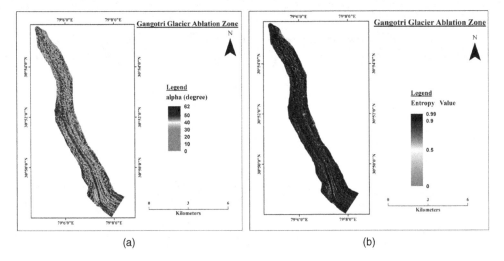

FIGURE 11.6   (a) Alpha angle image (top) and (b) entropy (bottom) of ablation zone.

11.5.2.2   Siachen Glacier

The alpha and entropy for the second research area are shown in Figure 11.7. On the ablation zone of Siachen Glacier, patterns identical to research area 1 were discovered. Alpha values equal to and above 40° are equivalent to entropy values closer to 1. A lower alpha angle below 50° and medium entropy values clearly signify surface scattering and volume scattering. Volume scattering and surface scattering were found to be dominant, with little contribution from the double-bounce scattering component. The average values for alpha and entropy in the ablation zone are 36.21° and 0.76 respectively.

11.5.3   Results of Freeman–Durden Decomposition

11.5.3.1   Gangotri Glacier

Figure 11.8 shows the Gangotri Glacier accumulation zone acquired during the end of the accumulation period (when dry snow is in the state of melting). The red color shows double-bounce, green volume, and blue surface scattering; the remaining secondary colors, like yellow, cyan, and magenta, are blends of red + green, green + blue, and blue + red, respectively, while white reflects scattering from all elements. Dominance of volume scattering in elevated areas is shown in green,

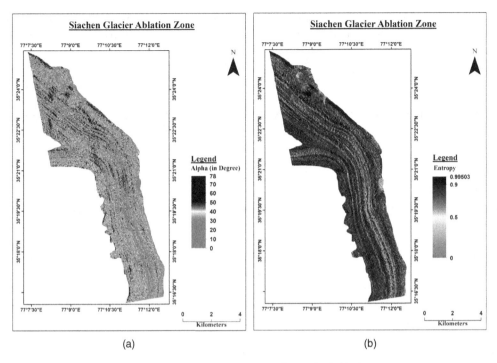

FIGURE 11.7   (a) Alpha angle image (top) and (b) entropy (bottom) of ablation zone.

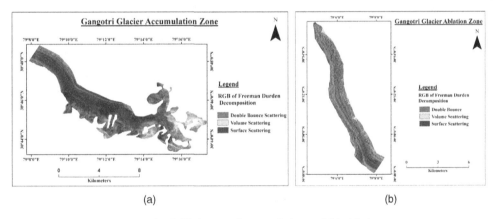

FIGURE 11.8   (a) Freeman–Durden RGB image of accumulation and (b) ablation zone.

and yellow and cyan represent low dominance of both type of scattering surface and double-bounce and surface and volume scattering, respectively. Below, where the surface is little settled not undulating much, the magenta color shows the dominance of double-bounce and surface scattering, while a comparatively low surface resenting in blue is seen. The factor drives backscattering signals, such as surface scattering from rough and dense surface like bare ice, low surface scattering from wet snow due to signals absorbed by liquid water, and volume scattering from dry snow and the percolation zone [26]. Snowpack with water content below 1% is considered dry snow [23]. The volume scattering from dry snow is mainly from the snow layer, which is governed by the size of the grain in comparison to the wavelength, and air–snow surface effect is ignored due to poor dielectric property in dry snow (the angle of refraction and wavelength displacement is a function of a dielectric constant, which is controlled by the density of snow) [6]. In the case of L-band, wavelength is much higher than the size of grain and the layer is considered as a smooth surface, giving the surface type of scattering. Increase in incidence angle leads to decrease in the total backscattering due to a fall in backscattering from snow–ground, and surface roughness for dry snow has almost no contribution to returned signals; thus, the area will have dominance of surface scattering [27], [6].

Snowpack with water content above 1% is considered wet snow [23]. All scattering takes places at the surface in the case of wet snow due to its absorption of SAR signals. Wetness of snow is inversely proportional to volume scattering and directly proportional to surface scattering. The wet snow at larger incidence angles (>30°) and older wet snow give the volume type of scattering [23]. During the accumulation period, there will be more surface scattering in comparison to the ablation period because the surface will have a smooth surface. Depending upon the season, the percolation zone can give surface and volume scattering. During the accumulation period, the percolation zone has very strong scattering due to frozen ice pipes/glands and ice lenses causing volume scattering [28], but once they are exposed to higher temperatures, their scattering changes due to melting [5]. The strong contribution of double-bounce can also be seen in the percolation zone in magenta [29], Crevasses in snow pack can also give a double-bounce contribution.

Figure 11.8 shows the ablation zone of Gangotri Glacier, where bare ice, ice with debris moraines, and crevasses are found. The green color in ablation shows the dominant color representing volume scattering. Magenta represents contribution of surface and double-bounce scattering, and much less scattering represents cyan and yellow. During the accumulation period, bare ice facies will have lower scattering than wet snow because bare ice surface will act as specular surface and smooth ice will cause lower scattering. And in summer, due to its melting condition, bare ice will have higher scattering in comparison to wet snow [22]. Surface roughness, which is a function of the local incidence angle and wavelength, can alter the radar backscattering coefficient. Debris on glacial ice in the ablation zone creates a rough surface, which returns a significant quantity of SAR signals to the receiving antenna, causing volume scattering [16]. High volume scattering in the ablation zone is because of the presence of crevasses, debris, and moraines in the zone, caused due to a multiple scattering process [8]. Double-bounce scattering can also be caused due to crevasses in the ablation zone. A point to notice: images acquired during early summer can have wet snow in ablation as well, which can also give surface type of scattering. The sigma naught images (Figures 11.3 and 11.4) show very low scattering values in both regions of glacier.

11.5.3.2 Siachen Glacier

(Figure 11.9 shows the ablation zone of Siachen Glacier, which shows similar results to the Gangotri ablation zone. We can see the dominance of green, which represents volume scattering in the zone. Similar to Gangotri, Siachen is also heavily covered with crevasses, debris, and moraines, which in return give multiple scattering from the surface. In the middle of the glacier, a linear pattern is formed that shows magenta (blend of red and blue); this color is formed from a combination of double-bounce and surface scattering. The presence of bare ice gives the surface scattering due to the specular nature of the surface and also the dielectric property of the surface during the summers, and the presence of heavy moraines gives double-bounce scattering. In addition, rock or moraines can also give surface scattering due to its smooth surface behavior.

11.5.4 Stokes Parameter-Based Approach

11.5.4.1 Circular Polarization Ratio (CPR)

Figure 11.10 depicts CPR for the two research areas, mainly the Gangotri Glacier accumulation and ablation zones. In his literature, [10] has mentioned that the Greenland ice sheet has a unique radar return property; no other terrestrial surfaces have this uniqueness. In his study, he mentions

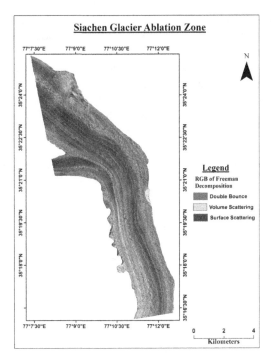

FIGURE 11.9 Freeman–Durden RGB image of accumulation zone.

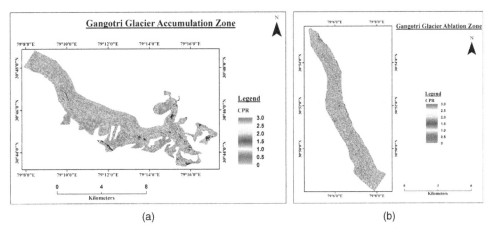

FIGURE 11.10 (a) Circular polarimetry ratio (CPR) image of accumulation (top) and, (b) ablation zone (bottom).

the extra-terrestrial study of Jupiter, which has a similar response to the Greenland ice sheet. But their strong radar responses generate from different products. On Jupiter, heterogeneity of products is because of years of meteoroid showers, while on the Greenland ice sheet, the heterogeneity of products is because of periodic melting and refreezing of snow. In his research, he has explained that at 5.6 and 24 cm wavelengths, the CPR was larger than unity at incidence angles of more than 30° and 45° respectively, and at larger wavelengths of 68 cm, CPR was less than 1 and dropped to 0.1; this is subject to changes in surface roughness, as the ratio increases with increase in surface roughness. He has also supported the hypothesis that volume scattering is mainly taken from subsurface and ice pipes, by which the return radar echoes are influenced to the greatest extent, and single scattering from firn deeply trapped under layers of snow or solidified ice bodies.

According to various studies, in the accumulation zone shown in Figure 11.10, wet snow, dry snow, and the percolation zone are found in most of the area. While comparing the result with H-A-α decomposition, high CPR value of more than 1 is found, as the ratio increases with surface roughness. Strong radar echoes from the under surface occur because of the presence of ice in the subsurface, which is due to seasonal melting and refreezing of snow or concentrated buried ice bodies causing volume type of scattering. The value greater than unity also represents surface scattering in the zone coming from the rough wet region. CPR values of 1 and below also dominate in the zone; the lower value can relate to the surface with double-bounce scattering, while compared to the decomposition result, and such a surface can have a comparatively less rough dihedral surface (see Figure 11.5).

Figure 11.10 shows the Gangotri Glacier ablation zone, which consists of bare ice, ice covered with debris, and crevasses, and is highly covered with moraines. According to [21], higher CPR values greater than 1 can be from ice or any surface giving double-bounce scattering; in this current chapter, the ablation zone comprises bare ice, crevasses, debris, and moraines; depending upon roughness, there is less scattering from bare ice than debris and moraines. The bare ice zone can be a highly reflective surface during winter and less reflective during summer, due to melting causing surface scattering, and with debris and moraines high backscattering is received due to its roughness, which deteriorates during winters due to snow, causing volume scattering. Dihedral scattering can be also from crevasses, as analyzed from decomposed images; in Figure 11.6, most of the pixels are above 1, and very few pixels fall below 1. So, highly rough surfaces like debris and ice as surface scattering show value above 1 [30].

11.6 CONCLUSION

The present study was carried out using ALOS-PALSAR-2 L-band data. The main conclusions of this work focus around findings of wet snow, dry snow, ice, and debris/moraines, using the potential of higher wavelength energy, although percolation zones, ice walls, and crevasses are also discussed in the chapter. To get desired results, various parameters were measured and analyzed; mainly, sigma naught value in dB scale, CPR, eigenvalue–eigenvector-based decomposition, and model-based decomposition were utilized to retrieve desired scattering from different glacial facies. This current work has been validated using different literature already present in the market, as field data collection was not possible due to the prevailing Covid-19 pandemic situation in the country. In this current chapter, a study of only part of the glacier is being carried out, and the exact ELA is not defined because it does not connect to the aim of the study; only an approximate area was bifurcated using optical data for identifying accumulation and ablation zone. We can distinguish regions of wet and dry snow, glacial ice, and debris by categorizing the glacier into distinct zones. Different backscattering coefficient σ^0 results for different targets in different polarization as the scattering coefficients are acquired in four different polarization modes, which shows the unique differences in like and unlike polarization. The average value of the Siachen and Gangotri ablation zones and the Gangotri accumulation zone for unlike polarization is higher than like polarization, and the mean value of the accumulation zone is higher than the mean value of the ablation zone. The sigma naught values for every snow facies are so complex that exact scattering cannot be considered for different snowpack from the sigma naught image, especially during the accumulation period, when ice and snow both have lower backscattering coefficient σ^0 and act as specular surfaces; therefore, there is need for the other parameter to cross-check the results. According to H-A-α decomposition, the elevated accumulation zone of Gangotri Glacier showed dominance of double-bounce scattering due to the presence of an internal structure of ice, while volume scattering was seen from dry snow or the percolation zone, with much surface scattering due to highly reflective surfaces like ice in the percolation zone or melted snow; on the gentle elevated surface below it, mixed scattering is found, like dominance of volume scattering, less surface, and double-bounce scattering (see Figure 11.5). And in the ablation zone of both study areas, a mixed type of scattering is analyzed throughout the surface, where high volume scattering is seen because of debris/moraines, double-bounce because of crevasses and moraines, and much less surface scattering due to the presence of ice in the zone (see Figure 11.6). Similarly, Freeman–Durden shows quite similar result to H-A-α decomposition, yet the results for the decomposition was not satisfactory; where pixel of H-A-α shows surface scattering and Freeman–Durden shows dominance of volume scattering for the same surface, the decomposition shows dominance of volume scattering in the region of Gangotri Glacier and contrasting results for Siachen Glacier. Such contrast results must be fulfilled using other techniques because they provide comparatively low target information in cases of ice and snow. An additional method like CPR is required to get the desired target information.

CPR is different from other decomposition models; this approach uses circular-based polarization in comparison to other decomposition methods, which are linearly polarized, and thus CPR is sensitive to object orientation. Researchers have derived thresholds for ice and other objects depending on their roughness. CPR clearly differentiated ice from snow, and the presence of ice under the percolation zone and in the ablation zone is clearly defined. CPR results show complementary results to H-A-α decomposition. In sigma naught image and in H-A-α decomposition, where some striking responses were observed between ice and wet snow, CPR uses its threshold value to discriminate between ice and other reflecting objects. The drawback of CPR is that it is unable to retrieve scattering mechanisms. H-A-α uses its invariant roll parameter for quantitative analysis, where the rest of the applied methods does not. The decompositions characterize the target based on dominant scattering element, but CPR characterizes subsurface target. The information retrieved from single methods is not sufficient to give any conclusion unless there are other parameters to validate the results, by which a concrete result can be made. Yet, SAR-based studies on glaciers contribute to bridging the gap between researchers and in-situ data collection. Further, such polarimetric studies on glaciers can be helpful to analyze upcoming projects by the NASA–ISRO mission and for beginners.

REFERENCES

[1] S. Kundu and M. Chakraborty, "Delineation of glacial zones of Gangotri and other glaciers of Central Himalaya using RISAT-1 C-band dual-pol SAR," *Int. J. Remote Sens.*, vol. 36, no. 6, pp. 1529–1550, 2015, doi: 10.1080/01431161.2015.1014972.

[2] F. Mazeh et al., "Numerical analysis of radar response to snow using multiple backscattering measurements for snow depth retrieval," *Prog. Electromagn. Res. B*, vol. 81, no. April, pp. 63–80, 2018, doi: 10.2528/PIERB18042803.

[3] P. K. Thakur et al., "Snow cover and glacier dynamics study using C- and L-band SAR datasets in parts of North West Himalaya," *Int. Arch. Photogramm. Remote Sens. Spat. Inf. Sci. – ISPRS Arch.*, vol. 42, no. 5, pp. 375–382, 2018, doi: 10.5194/isprs-archives-XLII-5-375-2018.

[4] P. Jansson, "Technical report TR-06-34: ice sheet hydrology – a review," *Phys. Geogr.*, Mar. 2007.

[5] W. Fu, X. Li, M. Wang, and L. Liang, "Delineation of radar glacier zones in the Antarctic peninsula using polarimetric SAR," *Water*, vol. 12, no. 9, p. 2620, 2020.

[6] G. Venkataraman and G. Singh, "Radar application in snow, ice, and glaciers," in *Encyclopedia of Snow, Ice and Glaciers*, V. P. Singh, P. Singh, and U. K. Haritashya, eds., Springer Netherlands, 2011, pp. 883–903.

[7] F. Mazeh et al., "Numerical analysis of radar response to snow using multiple backscattering measurements for snow depth retrieval," *Prog. Electromagn. Res. B*, vol. 81, no. June, pp. 63–80, 2018, doi: 10.2528/PIERB18042803.

[8] G. Singh, G. Venkataraman, Y. Yamaguchi, and S. E. Park, "Capability assessment of fully polarimetric alos-palsar data for discriminating wet snow from other scattering types in mountainous regions," *IEEE Trans. Geosci. Remote Sens.*, vol. 52, no. 2, pp. 1177–1196, 2014, doi: 10.1109/TGRS.2013.2248369.

[9] M. S. Mahmud, V. Nandan, S. E. L. Howell, T. Geldsetzer, and J. Yackel, "Seasonal evolution of L-band SAR backscatter over landfast Arctic sea ice," *Remote Sens. Environ.*, vol. 251, no. August, p. 112049, 2020, doi: 10.1016/j.rse.2020.112049.

[10] E. J. Rignot, S. J. Ostro, J. J. Van Zyl, and K. C. Jezek, "Unusual radar echoes from the Greenland ice sheet," *Science (80-).*, vol. 261, no. 5129, pp. 1710–1713, 1993, doi: 10.1126/science.261.5129.1710.

[11] S. Bhushan, T. H. Syed, A. V. Kulkarni, P. Gantayat, and V. Agarwal, "Quantifying changes in the gangotri glacier of central himalaya: Evidence for increasing mass loss and decreasing velocity," *IEEE J. Sel. Top. Appl. Earth Obs. Remote Sens.*, vol. 10, no. 12, pp. 5295–5306, 2017, doi: 10.1109/JSTARS.2017.2771215.

[12] A. Bhattacharya, T. Bolch, K. Mukherjee, T. Pieczonka, J. Kropáček, and M. F. Buchroithner, "Overall recession and mass budget of Gangotri Glacier, Garhwal Himalayas, from 1965 to 2015 using remote sensing data," *J. Glaciol.*, vol. 62, no. 236, pp. 1115–1133, 2016, doi: 10.1017/jog.2016.96.

[13] A. Agrawal, R. J. Thayyen, and A. P. Dimri, "Mass-balance modelling of Gangotri glacier," *Geol. Soc. Spec. Publ.*, vol. 462, no. 1, pp. 99–117, 2018, doi: 10.1144/SP462.1.

[14] A. Vijay Mahagaonkar, "Glacier surface velocity estimation & facies classification using InSAR and multi-temporal SAR techniques in Indian Himalaya," MS thesis, Faculty of Geo-information Science and Earth Observation, Univ. of Twente, Enschede, the Netherlands, Mar. 2019.

[15] A. Braun and L. Veci, "SENTINEL-1 Toolbox SAR Basics Tutorial," *Esa*, no. March 2015, pp. 1–20, 2020, [Online]. Available: http://sentinel1.s3.amazonaws.com/docs/S1TBX SAR Basics Tutorial.pdf.

[16] G. H. Yao, C. Q. Ke, X. Zhou, H. Lee, X. Shen, and Y. Cai, "Identification of alpine glaciers in the Central Himalayas using fully polarimetric L-band SAR data," *IEEE Trans. Geosci. Remote Sens.*, vol. 58, no. 1, pp. 691–703, 2020, doi: 10.1109/TGRS.2019.2939430.

[17] W. (Bill) Wei, "Advanced concepts," *Art Conserv.*, no. 1, pp. 109–143, 2021, doi: 10.1201/9781003162445-5.

[18] J-S. Lee and E. Pottier, *Polarimetric Radar Imaging: From Basics to Applications.* Boca Raton: CRC Press, 2009.

[19] S. Kumar, A. Babu, S. Agrawal, U. Asopa, S. Shukla and A. Maiti, "Polarimetric calibration of spaceborne and airborne multifrequency SAR data for scattering-based characterization of manmade and natural features," *Adv. Sp. Res.*, vol. 69, pp. 1684–1714, 2022.

[20] Y. Yamaguchi, *Polarimetric Synthetic Aperture Radar.* CRC Press, 2020.

[21] E. J. Rignot, S. J. Ostro, J. J. Van Zyl, and K. C. Jezek, "Unusual radar echoes from the Greenland ice sheet," *Science (80-).*, vol. 261, no. 5129, pp. 1710–1713, 1993, doi: 10.1126/science.261.5129.1710.

[22] L. Huang, Z. Li, B. Sen Tian, Q. Chen, J. L. Liu, and R. Zhang, "Classification and snow line detection for glacial areas using the polarimetric SAR image," *Remote Sens. Environ.*, vol. 115, no. 7, pp. 1721–1732, 2011, doi: 10.1016/j.rse.2011.03.004.

[23] Y. L. S. Tsai, A. Dietz, N. Oppelt, and C. Kuenzer, "Remote sensing of snow cover using spaceborne SAR: a review," *Remote Sens.*, vol. 11, no. 12, 2019, doi: 10.3390/rs11121456.

[24] C. Yonezawa, M. Watanabe, and G. Saito, "Polarimetric decomposition analysis of ALOS PALSAR observation data before and after a landslide event," *Remote Sens.*, vol. 4, no. 8, pp. 2314–2328, 2012, doi: 10.3390/rs4082314.

[25] K. Ji and Y. Wu, "Scattering mechanism extraction by a modified Cloude-Pottier decomposition for dual polarization SAR," pp. 7447–7470, 2015, doi: 10.3390/rs70607447.

[26] J. Arigony Neto, H. Saurer, R. Jaña, F. Rau, J. Simões, and H. Goßmann, "Monitoring snow parameters on the Antarctic Peninsula using satellite data – a new methodological approach," Jan. 2006.

[27] J. Koskinen, *Snow Monitoring Using Microwave Radars.* 2001.

[28] J. J. Sharma, I. Hajnsek, K. P. Papathanassiou, and A. Moreira, "Polarimetric decomposition over glacier ice using long-wavelength airborne PolSAR," *IEEE Trans. Geosci. Remote Sens.*, vol. 49, no. 1 PART 2, pp. 519–535, 2011, doi: 10.1109/TGRS.2010.2056692.

[29] G. Singh et al., "Retrieval of spatial and temporal variability in snowpack depth over glaciers in svalbard using GPR and spaceborne POLSAR measurements," *Water (Switzerland)*, vol. 12, no. 1, 2020, doi: 10.3390/w12010021.

[30] S. Mohan and A. K. Das, "Studies of polarimetric properties of lunar surface using Mini-SAR data," *Current Science*, vol. 101, no. 2, pp. 159–164, Jul. 2011.

12 Spaceborne SAR Application to Study Ice Flow Variation of Potsdam Glacier and Polar Record Glacier, East Antarctica

Kiledar Singh Tomar, Ashutosh Venkatesh Prasad, and Sangita Singh Tomar

CONTENTS

12.1 INTRODUCTION

The Antarctic ice sheet (AIS) has been losing its mass continuously in recent decades owing to increasing average temperatures, the warming ocean, and the retreating grounding line. Antarctica mainly loses its mass through the accelerated motion of its glaciers [1]. The Antarctic ice sheet contains an ice volume whose sea level equivalent (SLE) is 57.2 m [2]. The major portion of ice mass loss is happening in the West Antarctic ice sheet (WAIS) and Antarctic peninsula ice sheet (APIS), as shown by various studies focusing on glaciers like Pine Island Glacier, Thawites Glacier etc. [3–5]. In comparison to the WAIS and APIS, the East Antarctic ice sheet (EAIS) has experienced less mass loss in recent decades, but the impact can still be seen amid an increased flow rate of the glaciers and ice thinning [1, 6]. The EAIS is considered the largest reservoir of fresh water on earth and is capable of raising sea level by ~50 m [7].

Given the area covered by the EAIS is larger than the WAIS and APIS combined, it can contribute around 53.3 m to global mean sea level rise [8] if melted completely, and it is losing ice mass at the rate of -57 ± 52 Gt yr-1 [9]. Despite the large differences in areal coverage and potential for sea level rise, the EAIS is less studied in comparison to the WAIS and APIS. Most of the studies to date have concentrated on the western side of the Transantarctic Mountains, mainly due to ease of access and less harsh climatic conditions in comparison to the EAIS. This scenario is slowly changing owing to recent developments in the field of remote sensing technology. Microwave remote sensing is playing a major role by providing year-round data for conducting research in the remote polar environment.

In recent years, satellite observations have provided us with much needed support in increasing our understanding about the AIS. Different satellite-based techniques are now being utilized to observe and monitor different aspects of AIS, such as glacier ice flow [10–13], ice thickness change [14, 15], mass balance [4, 11, 16, 17, 18], grounding line fluctuation [19, 20], and changing gravitational attraction [21, 22].

Glacier velocity is one of the crucial parameters that needs regular monitoring to assess and understand glacier dynamics. Glacier velocity is sensitive to variations in temperature and precipitation, as any subtle changes in these two meteorological parameters may cause fluctuations in glacier flow velocity. Glacier velocity measurements give a direct indication of the changing climate, depending upon variations in temperature and precipitation. Here, Greenland and Antarctica are of prime concern as the ice sheets in these regions can contribute up to 7.2 m and 57.2 m of sea level rise respectively if melted completely. The glaciers present within these ice sheets are the source of surface meltwater runoff, through which they lose their ice mass into the ocean. The Antarctic peninsula has seen air temperatures rise 2.5 °C since 1950, and as a result is losing ice mass at a rapid rate. In such a scenario, monitoring of glacier velocity becomes utmost important. Increased mass loss from the ice sheets has been attributed to increase in air temperature, subsurface ocean temperature, basal melting, and surface meltwater runoff. The need to monitor the glaciers of the ice sheets regularly has increased, but it is quite difficult to carry out in situ observations in such remote and harsh weather and climatic conditions. In order to overcome this problem, we make use of earth observation technology, with which we can timely monitor the changes in the dynamics of the glacier through use of the satellite imagery.

Over the years, the optical datasets have been used to monitor glacier dynamics and other earth surface processes. However, one of the major drawbacks of optical datasets is that they are not capable of year-round monitoring of the Antarctic glaciers as half of the year Antarctica remains in complete darkness; it is impossible for optical satellites to capture the movement of the glaciers in those dark time periods. Obtaining cloud-free optical satellite imagery all year round is another drawback in Antarctica; this can be overcome by the use of active microwave remote sensing satellites, which operate year-round, providing all-weather as well as day and night observation. Synthetic aperture radar (SAR) satellites operate all year round, providing datasets even during the night. This nighttime monitoring capability of the SAR satellites has enabled researchers across the globe to efficiently monitor glacier surface changes. The microwave region of the electromagnetic spectrum has been widely utilized for studying glaciers and ice sheets as an alternative to optical data.

Considering the significance of spaceborne SAR in monitoring Antarctic surface and environment, this chapter will deliver information on SAR remote sensing applications in Antarctica and SAR data and methods utilized for glacier flow monitoring. The chapter focuses on DInSAR as well as the offset tracking based method to estimate glacier flow velocity. Two main areas are discussed: (a) application of spaceborne SAR techniques in glacier flow velocity estimation and (b) a case study on Potsdam Glacier and Polar Record Glacier, East Antarctica.

12.2 ROLE OF SPACEBORNE SAR IN ANTARCTICA

Spaceborne SAR has demonstrated its importance in glaciological advances over the last two decades in ice dynamics studies [23]. Spaceborne SAR has contributed to foremost progress in East Antarctica, demonstrating its application for ice flow variation estimations [24, 25], mass balance [25, 26], advance and retreat rates [27, 28], coastal mapping, digital elevation model (DEM) generation [29, 30], topography mapping [25, 26, 31], ice thickness estimation, grounding line estimation/

delineation [25, 32], study of glaciological properties of ice sheets [33], and ocean tides observation [34] etc.

The major applications of spaceborne SAR in Antarctic mapping and monitoring include (Figure 12.1) DEM generation, mapping of coastline, grounding line, surface ice flow, and surface melt flux. Over the years, a variety of approaches have been developed and implemented over the Antarctic region that have used remote sensing technology.

Rignot et al. used ERS-1 and ERS-2 data to demonstrate surface displacement patterns on the Filchner and Ronne ice shelves caused by ocean tides and compared this with tidal models, concluding that differential SAR interferometry can be used to validate the tidal models under the ice shelves [34].

Interferometric technique using SAR (InSAR) has proven to be very useful in accurately delineating grounding lines [35]. Differential InSAR reveals vertical motion at the grounding line, which helps identify its location and is typically due to the visco-elastic bending of ice in the region. The grounding line is a transition boundary where ice (such as marine terminating glaciers, ice sheets) meets with the ocean along the land periphery, such as in Antarctica. This boundary is essential to the study of ice sheets for different reasons, for instance, it is the boundary where ice flux going to the ocean is measured [36]. In addition, it is an essential input to numerical ice sheet models. Finally, it is important to locate the grounding line and its change because this is strongly linked to mass loss in Antarctica [36, 37]. A study focusing on nine East Antarctic glaciers – namely David, Ninnis, Totten, Mertz, Denman, Scott, Shirase, Lambert, and Stancomb-Wills – was carried out by [25] using the ERS-1/2 and RADARSAT-1 datasets. In this study, the InSAR technique was utilized to precisely delineate the grounding line and to estimate the glacier surface velocity. The ice flux for each glacier in this study has also been estimated by combining the surface velocity with the ice thickness at the flux gate of each glacier.

Making use of the RADARSAT ScanSAR images, Giles et al. measured sub-pixel displacements on the tongue of Mertz Glacier in East Antarctica with an accuracy of $\leq \pm 0.25$ pixels [38].

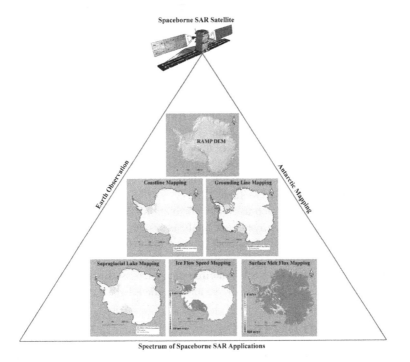

FIGURE 12.1   Spaceborne SAR applications in Antarctic mapping and monitoring.

Mouginot et al. mapped the ice velocity of Antarctica by combining different SAR sensor datasets, including Envisat ASAR, ERS-1 and ERS-2, ALOS-PALSAR, and RADARSAT-1 and RADARSAT-2 [39]. This was the first ever study carried out to estimate the ice flow of Antarctica using InSAR data from variety of SAR sensors. It presented a work flow or methodology that included processing, calibration, error-estimation, and mosaicking to generate a complete ice velocity map of Antarctica.

In a study carried out by [11] for Totten Glacier, they estimated its surface velocity using optical as well as InSAR data from eight different SAR satellites, including ERS-1, ERS-2, RADARSAT-1, RADARSAT-2, ALOS-PALSAR, TanDEM-X, TerraSAR-X, and COSMO-Skymed. They made use of different SAR datasets in order to cover a time period from 1989 to 2015, as different SAR satellites covered different time spans during the observation period of the study. They also in turn combined these velocity estimates with the ice thickness to determine the ice flux along the grounding line.

Baumhoer et al. utilized the Sentinel-1 imagery to extract the fronts of Antarctic glaciers and ice shelves using a deep learning approach [40]. They made use of the EW mode imagery of Sentinel as it covers a large spatial area with dual polarizations (HH + HV), which are helpful in ice type classification. The study incorporated different kinds of morphologies of Antarctic coastline like ice shelves, glacier tongue, and rocks.

Dirscherl et al. presented an automated approach to mapping of supraglacial lakes in Antarctica using the Sentinel-1 imagery, employing a deep learning technique [41]. This study was carried out using a total of 70 Sentinel-1 ground range detected (GRD) products in interferometric wide (IW) mode and single polarization as it provides better spatial resolution of 10 m in comparison to EW mode with dual polarization, which has 40 m spatial resolution.

In a study investigating the concurrent breakup of outlet glaciers in Porpoise Bay, East Antarctica [42], wide swath mode imagery of ENVISAT ASAR was used to detect changes in the terminus of six different outlet glaciers, revealing a calving event.

Han and Lee in [17] used COSMO-SkyMed and ICESat data to derive tide-corrected ice velocity maps and mass balance of four glaciers draining ice from the EAIS through the Transantarctic Mountains into the Ross Sea embayment: David Glacier, Mulock Glacier, Byrd Glacier, and Nimrod Glacier.

12.3 GLACIER VELOCITY ESTIMATION USING SPACEBORNE SAR

A variety of glacial processes, such as ice flow, surge, formation of glacial lakes and related hazards, and mass balance, can be determined through the study of glacier velocity [43, 44]. Several glaciers of East Antarctica have been studied in terms of their glacier flow velocity estimations. Spaceborne SAR-based techniques and approaches played a vital role in estimating the flow variations from glacier to ice shelf utilizing different bands of SAR sensors. An overview of the studies conducted on glaciers of East Antarctica is presented in Table 12.1.

Several SAR-based techniques, such as image correlation (IMCORR), speckle tracking, offset tracking, InSAR/DInSAR, and interactive image analysis system (IIAS), have been applied to study the glacier flow velocity in East Antarctica. Speckle tracking and InSAR have been widely utilized to monitor glacier velocity for most of the glaciers [13, 24, 25, 47, 49, 50, 51]. Glacier flow velocity has been estimated by exploiting SAR satellite data such as JERS, RADARSAT-1/2, ALOS-PALSAR, ERS-1/2, TerraSAR-X, Envisat ASAR, and Sentinel-1.

12.4 STUDY AREA AND DATASET

The present study focuses on two study sites: Potsdam Glacier and Polar Record Glacier (PRG) in East Antarctica. Potsdam Glacier is located north of Wohlthat Mountains and south of Schirmacher

TABLE 12.1

Overview of the Glacier Velocity Studies Conducted in East Antarctica Using SAR

Area/Region	Study Conducted	Methods	Spaceborne SAR Data
Shirase Glacier	[45]	Image correlation based	JERS-1, ALOS-PALSAR
	[46]	Image correlation based	JERS-1
	[47]	Speckle tracking	ERS
	[25]	Speckle tracking	ERS-1/2, RADARSAT
Polar Record Glacier	[48]	Offset tracking	Sentinel-1
	[49]	DInSAR	
Byrd Glacier	[50]	InSAR based	RADARSAT-1
	[51]	Speckle tracking	RADARSAT-1 & 2
	[52]	Speckle tracking	TerraSAR-X
Dalk Glacier	[13]	Offset tracking	Sentinel-1
Cook Glacier	[50]	InSAR based	RADARSAT-1
Fisher Glacier	[24]	Interferometric and speckle tracking approach	RADARSAT
	[50]	InSAR based	RADARSAT-1
Lambert Glacier	[24]	Interferometric and speckle tracking approach	RADARSAT
	[25]	InSAR and speckle tracking based	ERS-1/2, RADARSAT
	[50]	InSAR based	RADARSAT-1
Mellor	[24]	Interferometric and speckle tracking approach	RADARSAT
	[50]	InSAR based	RADARSAT-1
David Glacier	[25]	InSAR based	ERS-1/2
	[53]	Feature tracking and DInSAR	RADARSAT-1
Mulock	[50]	InSAR based	RADARSAT-1
Nimrod Glacier	[52]	Speckle tracking	TerraSAR-X
Ninnis	[25]	Speckle tracking	ERS-1/2
	[54]	Alaska SAR Facility (ASF) interactive image analysis system (IIAS) based	ERS-1&2, JERS-1
Mertz	[25]	Speckle tracking	ERS-1/2
	[55]	Image correlation (IMCORR) technique	RADARSAT-1 & Envisat ASAR
	[38]	IMCORR	RADARSAT-1
	[54]	ASF IIAS based	ERS-1&2, JERS-1
Totten	[25]	Speckle tracking	ERS-1/2
	[11]	Speckle tracking	ERS-1/2, RADARSAT-1/2, ALOS-PALSAR, TanDEM/TerraSAR-X (TDX/TSX), COSMO-Skymed (CSK)
	[56]	Speckle tracking	ALOS-PALSAR
Scott and Denman Glacier	[25]	Speckle tracking	ERS-1/2
Stancomb-Wills	[25]	InSAR and speckle tracking based	ERS-1/2, RADARSAT

Oasis. The glacier flow drains from the southeast into Nivlisen [57]. The presence of the Indian Antarctic Research Base Maitri lies northwest nearly ~40 km from the lower reaches and ~120 km towards the north from the upper reaches of the glacier. The estimated average ice thickness of Potsdam Glacier is reported to be ~1000 m [8]. The annual temperature at this glacier remains below −20 °C, and elevation range varies from 97 m to 2098 m. The geographical location of Potsdam Glacier is depicted in Figure 12.2.

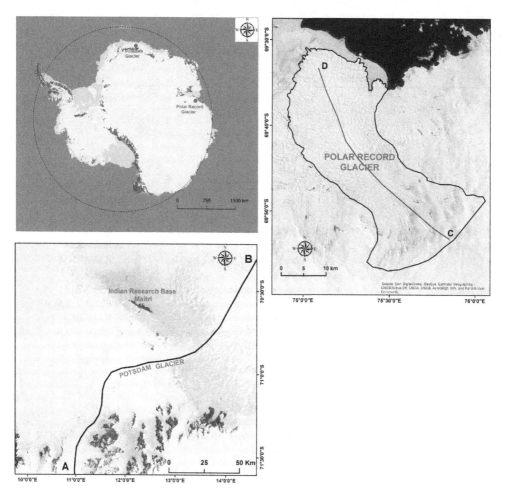

FIGURE 12.2 Location of the Potsdam Glacier (AB represents central flowline along the glacier) and Polar Record Glacier (CD represents central flowline along the glacier).

The other study site is PRG, which is one of the major outlet glaciers present in the Prydz Bay area near Larsemann Hills in East Antarctica [58]. The presence of PRG lies 69°45" S and 75°30" E on Princess Elizabeth land, surrounded by Meknattane Nunataks and Dodd Island [48]. Indian Research Base Bharati and Zhonshan station (China) are situated 50 km away to the east from PRG. It is reported that the glacier shows evidence of several calving events and losing mass during the period 1937 to 1990 [49, 59]. The geographical location of PRG is depicted in Figure 12.2.

The present study utilizes the European Space Agency's Sentinel-1 satellite images. The Sentinel-1 SAR single look complex (SLC) and GRD images of IW swath mode were used for DInSAR and the offset tacking approach, respectively. The data was acquired in C-band with horizontal transmit and horizontal receive (HH) polarization. The InSAR pair used for Potsdam Glacier has a temporal resolution of six days in ascending mode and the image pair used for PRG is present in descending mode. Specifications regarding Sentinel-1 data is mentioned in Table 12.2. Copernicus DEM were also used in the present study.

TABLE 12.2
Specification of Sentinel-1 SAR Data Utilized in the Study

| Parameters | Method Used for Processing | |
	DInSAR	Offset Tracking
Study glacier	Potsdam Glacier	PRG
Band	C	C
Product	SLC	GRD
Polarization	HH	HH
Acquisition date	20 Feb 2020, 26 Feb 2020	18 Feb 2020, 24 Feb 2020
Acquisition mode	IW	IW
Temporal resolution	6 days	6 days
Wavelength	5.6 cm	5.6 cm
Azimuth × range resolution	5 × 20 m	5 × 20 m

12.5 METHODOLOGY

To estimate glacier surface velocity, two remote sensing based techniques were used in this study. The DInSAR method was implemented on Sentinel-1 SLC data to estimate the glacier flow of Potsdam Glacier, while the offset tracking method was implemented on Sentinel GRD data to robustly determine the glacier flow of PRG. The detailed methodology is provided in the subsequent sections.

12.5.1 GLACIER VELOCITY ESTIMATION USING DINSAR

The method adopted in the present study to estimate glacier flow velocity using Sentinel-1 SAR data is represented in Figure 12.3. The steps involved to estimate glacier flow velocity starting from pre-processing of SAR data until final glacier flow estimates are briefly presented. The present study focuses on two repeat pass differential interferometry method over Potsdam Glacier in Schirmacher Oasis, East Antarctica. While choosing the InSAR pair, more emphasis has been given to temporal and perpendicular baselines. The chosen temporal baseline was six days, which is the shortest in our case to reduce temporal decorrelation. The perpendicular baseline was < 150 m in our case of displacement calculation. The master and slave image (InSAR pair) of Sentinel-1 SAR data was pre-processed first to generate the interferogram. Pre-processing starts with the configuration of both images through precise orbit information. Both images are co-registered using enhanced spectral diversity (ESD) to improve the accurate estimations. The gaps between adjacent bursts in the Sentinel imagery were eliminated using deburst through the co-registered product. Interferogram has been generated from the accurately co-registered interferometric pair, and coherence has been estimated as well. The estimated coherence represents the correlation of the pixel in the slave image corresponding to the pixel in the master image and ranges from 0 to 1, corresponding to least and highest degree of coherence, respectively. Furthermore, debursting was done in order to eliminate the gaps between adjacent bursts in the Sentinel-1 imagery. The phase difference present in the interferogram comprised of the topographic phase, the earth's curvature, atmospheric phase delay, and the displacement component. The phase due to the earth's curvature is subtracted, and the delay in atmospheric phase is assumed to be negligible or imperceptible [60]. The interferogram generated was comprised of topographic phase and displacement component. The topographic phase produced during interferogram generation was eliminated with an external DEM, resulting in a contribution

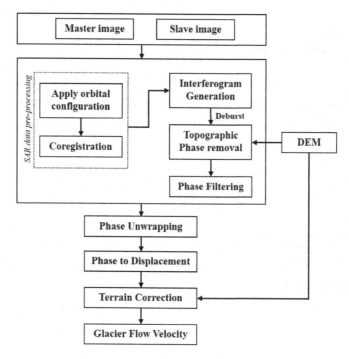

FIGURE 12.3   Flowchart of the DInSAR-based glacier velocity estimation.

from phase due to displacement (ice flow motion). The noise present in the displacement phase is filtered with the help of Goldstein phase filtering. The phase present in this differential interferogram was wrapped between $-\pi$ and π. This wrapped phase was unwrapped using SNAPHU-v1.4.2 [61] by applying a minimum cost flow (MCF) algorithm. This unwrapped phase was converted to displacement using equation 12.1:

$$\Delta d = \frac{\lambda}{4\pi}\Delta\phi, \tag{12.1}$$

where,
Δd: displacement,
$\Delta\phi$: differential phase, average of grain diameter,
λ: wavelength.

This displacement using the DInSAR approach is present in the line of sight (LOS) direction, which was further utilized to calculate the horizontal surface velocity using the slope of the glacier surface and incidence angle as in equation 12.2:

$$V_s = \frac{V_{LoS}}{\cos\alpha\cos\xi\sin\theta + \cos\theta\sin\alpha}, \tag{12.2}$$

where,
V_s: glacier surface velocity (horizontal),
V_{LoS}: LOS velocity calculated from displacement,
α: slope of glacier surface,
ξ: aspect angle between radar beam direction and glacier slope,
θ: look angle.

12.5.2   Glacier Velocity Estimation Using Offset Tracking

The offset tracking method is one of the most widely used methods, other than the DInSAR method, to estimate the flow rate of any glacier. The offset tracking method employs different approaches to monitor the flow rate of the glaciers. These approaches include intensity tracking, feature tracking, and speckle tracking. The intensity tracking approach is based on a pixel-to-pixel image correlation algorithm, which generates the offset fields from image patches of intensity images with a normalized cross-correlation algorithm [62] and estimates the relative displacement between image pairs. The feature tracking approach involves tracking of glacial features like crevasses, moraines etc. on co-registered image pairs in order to develop a 2D velocity field. Tracking of the features can be done in two ways, i.e. manual selection and automatic tracking. The requirement for this approach is that the glacial feature should remain undisturbed over the period of observation. The estimation of displacement can be inferred from the relative movement of the glacial features measured between the two images.

The offset tracking method measures the offsets in both azimuth and slant range direction, thus providing a 2D ground displacement field. One of the major advantages of the offset tracking method is that it can be applied where there is low coherence. It can be employed on SAR images with large acquisition time intervals.

In order to estimate the glacier flow rate between two observations, we utilized two Sentinel-1 GRD images, which were pre-processed before applying the offset tracking algorithm. The pre-processing procedure incorporates the apply orbit file function, which provides the SAR image file with the accurate orbital information. Then, thermal noise removal is performed, which is followed by the calibration. After the pre-processing of images, the image pair is co-registered using DEM-assisted co-registration with cross-correlation by utilizing high-resolution REMA DEM. This study used 128×128 window size with 40×40 pixel spacing as earlier used by [48] for the same glacier. The amount attributed to the cross-correlation surface shows the movement between the image pair (master and slave image) [63]. The estimated glacier movement is calculated in slant and azimuth directions over the glacier surface. The displacement D in slant and azimuth directions can be calculated as:

$$D = \sqrt{\left(R_{range}\Delta x_{range}\right)^2 + \left(R_{azi}\Delta x_{azi}\right)^2}, \tag{12.3}$$

where,

R_{range}: pixel spacing in range direction,

R_{azi}: pixel spacing in azimuth direction,

Δx_{range}: pixel shifts in range direction,

Δx_{azi}: pixel shifts in azimuth direction.

12.5.3   Field Measurements

Field measurements in Antarctica is always challenging due to its harsh environment, terrain, weather, crevasses, and minimal logistic support. This study was supported by the field work carried out during 38th and 39th Indian Scientific Expeditions to Antarctica. Helicopter support was required while traveling to reach the study sites. It takes around 45 minutes to reach Polar Record Glacier from either Indian Research Base Bharati or the ship *Vasiliy Golovnin*. Stakes were installed at PRG (Figure 12.4). A DGPS survey has been carried out at both glaciers to monitor the stakes in order to measure the ice flow movement.

FIGURE 12.4 Stakes installation and field measurements taken during the Indian Scientific Expedition to Antarctica.

12.6 RESULTS AND DISCUSSION

The study utilizes two different approaches for glacier velocity estimation: offset tracking and DInSAR. These two approaches were chosen to be able to efficiently measure the smaller displacements (Potsdam Glacier) and larger displacements (PRG) expected on these two glaciers. Offset tracking was employed on GRD product of Sentinel-1 SAR for PRG, while a DInSAR-based approach was used on the SLC product of Sentinel-1 SAR for Potsdam Glacier. Satellite image acquisition selection was performed during austral summer (February) of 2020. This section provides the surface velocity estimation results obtained from offset tracking and a DInSAR-based approach.

12.6.1 DInSAR-Based Glacier Velocity Estimation for Potsdam Glacier

In the present study, the DInSAR-based glacier velocity for Potsdam Glacier has been estimated. The present study is conducted during the last month of austral summer (February), and high seasonal glacier movement can be expected. The Potsdam Glacier region has a scarcity of satellite imagery for continuously monitoring its flow. Glacier surface velocity has been estimated for Potsdam Glacier from the SAR image pairs of ascending passes. The interferogram generated from the SAR image pair mentioned in Table 12.2 is presented in Figure 12.5. Figure 12.6 shows the velocity magnitude obtained using the DInSAR approach outlined in section 12.5.1, using the same data pair. This is the most favorable data selection for DInSAR, since it maximizes the coherence due to higher temporal resolution and reduces the fringe rate over the fast-flowing regions of the glacier, which in turn improves the phase unwrapping process results. In Figure 12.5, each color cycle of interferogram represents one fringe. This fringe (cycle of shading) represents half of wavelength displacement in the LOS direction. The generated interferogram represents good development of

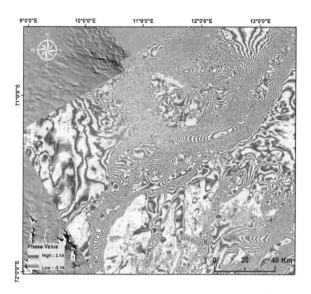

FIGURE 12.5 Interferogram generated using Sentinel-1 InSAR pair for Potsdam Glacier.

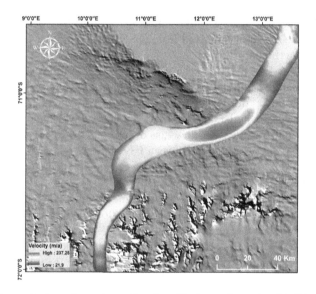

FIGURE 12.6 Ice flow velocity estimated over Potsdam Glacier surface using DInSAR.

fringes over the glacier, hence separating the interferogram from outside regions. For the selected Sentinel-1 SAR data pair with a six-day interval, it was observed that the coherence was preserved in most of the glacier area due to uniform motion. Coherence loss was observed mainly in the northwest portion of the glacier. The loss of coherence may be due to a large displacement of the glacier in this region. The area near the upper reaches (southeast) of the glacier is free from fringes, indicating stable areas.

The spatial distribution of glacier flow velocity derived from the Sentinel-1 InSAR pair of Potsdam Glacier is shown in Figure 12.6. The LOS motion was estimated using an ascending and descending InSAR pair of Sentinel-1 SAR data, which ultimately converted to horizontal velocity,

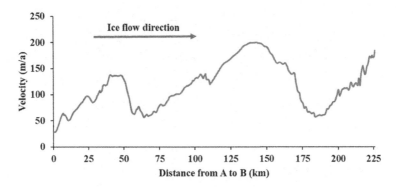

FIGURE 12.7   Glacier flow velocity along the flowline AB.

as outlined in section 12.5.1. The glacier exhibits direction of flow from A to B (Figure 12.2) with varying glacier velocity. The higher velocity exists in the middle region (towards the southeast of Maitri station) and lower reaches of the glacier near Nivlisen ice shelf (Figure 12.6). The interferogram is symmetrical about the central line of flow of the glacier. There are local maxima and minima in the phase pattern along the glacier axis, indicating the flow of the glacier is not constant.

The maximum velocity along the glacier surface-flow direction was observed as 237.2 m/a, with an average glacier flow velocity for the whole glacier surface of 115.9 m/a. The minimum glacier flow velocity over the glacier surface derived from the Sentinel-1 InSAR pair of Potsdam Glacier was observed as 21.9 m/a (Figure 12.6).

The study conducted by [57] to monitor basal melting at Nivlisen ice shelf covers a portion of the Potsdam Glacier, where ice flow speed was also calculated. They reported ice flow speed in the range of 100–200 m/a for the portion of Potsdam Glacier (close to Maitri station) that is close to the flow speed for the same portion in the present study. Another study using optical data for Potsdam Glacier, conducted by [64], reported ice flow speed during 2016 in the range of 18.6–285 m/a with an RMSE of 78 m/a. Surface velocity between F39 and F27 in [65] for Potsdam Glacier was reported in the range of 40–90 m/a. The maximum glacier velocity reported by [66] was 120 m/a in the lower portion of the glacier.

In Figure 12.7, the observed glacier velocity along the flowline AB ranges from 28.50 m/a to 200 m/a. The observed velocity is found to vary along the flowline with multiple local maxima and minima that can be majorly due to the turned geometry of the glacier. The maximum velocity along the glacier surface-flow direction was observed near the middle region of the glacier. The observed glacier velocity has large variability along the length of the glacier. There is significant rise in flow velocity in the passage between the nunataks and the middle of the glacier area along with the lower reaches (Figure 12.7).

12.6.2   OFFSET TRACKING BASED GLACIER VELOCITY ESTIMATION FOR PRG

The Sentinel-1 SAR data pair was processed using an offset tracking approach for PRG. The intensity offset tracking method was applied to the six-day image pair mentioned in Table 12.1. The velocity measured for six days is represented in m/a to be comparable with other reported values of the glaciers at an annual scale. Here, the velocity is assumed to be constant over the year. The chosen data pair selection was found to be the most favorable for offset tracking, since the ice motion contribution in a six-day time span is often below the noise floor of offset tracking measurements, especially in the slow movement region. This is also due to azimuth and range measurement biases that affect the Sentinel-1 pair. The spatial distribution of the resulting horizontal ice velocity magnitude

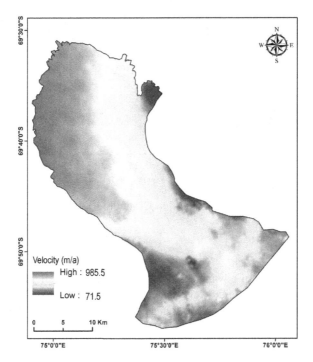

FIGURE 12.8   Ice flow velocity estimated over the PRG surface using offset tracking.

is shown in Figure 12.8. The spatial distribution shows the higher velocity as up to 985.5 m/a in the lower reaches of the glacier near the terminus, while the upper reaches show slower glacier movement. High velocities over ~900 m/a are observed in the western part of the glacier near the terminus. This is mainly due to lower coherence observed over this region, which shows significant changes might have occurred on the glacier surface. The estimated average glacier flow velocity of PRG was 692.08 m/a, which is near the maximum velocities reported earlier for PRG. This is because the ice flow velocity is expected to be high towards the end of austral summer in comparison to the rest of the year. Moreover, it has been observed that glacier flow velocity estimates varied in the range of 71.5 m/a to 985.5 m/a.

Glacier flow velocity has also been assessed along the flowline CD (Figure 12.9), showing flow velocity along flowline starting from C to D at an interval of 1 km (Figure 12.2). Average glacier velocity was observed to be 692.08 m/a, where the velocity range along the flowline was between 387 m/a to 913 m/a. This minimum velocity is significantly higher than the minimum velocity observed for the whole glacier. This relatively higher velocity along the glacier's central flowline is indicative of higher mass contribution from other regions of the glacier. In Figure 12.9, a dip in glacier velocity between 5 to 10 km is observed, starting from C. This reason for this dip in velocity is the presence of the grounding line. Apart from this dip, unlike the results obtained for Potsdam Glacier, the velocity increases constantly from C to D.

It is quite noticeable that when compared with the offset tracking results (Figure 12.8), the DInSAR-based estimates show an improvement in resolution, particularly in slow-moving regions where a much smoother pattern is observed (Figure 12.6).

The surface of PRG is heavily covered with crevasses, which makes field data collection difficult. Thus, the accuracy assessment of the estimated velocity was carried out using the data collected (Figure 12.4) outside the glacier near point C. The comparison with the collected data showed an error of 0.029 m/d.

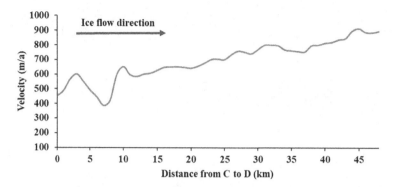

FIGURE 12.9 Glacier flow velocity along the flowline CD of PRG.

12.7 CONCLUSION

Spaceborne SAR exhibits several advantages over other electro-optical sensors, due to: (a) day–night, all-weather capability, and microwave systems represent the best approaches to collecting data for a given region at a given time; and (b) signals sent by radar systems are sensitive to the physical structure and moisture content of the surface being sensed and thus provide avenues to obtain results for earth observation applications that are not otherwise available. The present study uses a Sentinel-1 dataset to derive glacier surface flow of the two study glaciers, Potsdam Glacier and PRG. Two different techniques, i.e. DInSAR and offset tracking, were used to study the different magnitudes of displacements of these glaciers. Through these two techniques, the most recent ice flow velocity for the year 2020 has been estimated.

We have presented DInSAR-based processing of acquired Sentinel-1 SAR data for glacier velocity retrieval over the Potsdam Glacier. The DInSAR-based approach has demonstrated its potential to effectively monitor the ice flow variations at Potsdam Glacier. On a comparative note, the DInSAR-based approach has an advantage over this glacier to deliver high-resolution measurements as the glacier contained slow-moving regions. The spatial distribution of flow velocity over the glacier surface ranges from 21.9 m/a to 237.25 m/a. The observed mean glacier flow velocity for Potsdam Glacier is 93.44 m/a. Similarly, offset tracking based estimates were presented for PRG where displacements of large magnitude were expected. High velocities were observed during the end of the austral summer month of 2020. The spatial distribution of flow velocity over the glacier surface ranges from 71.5 m/a to 985.5 m/a. The estimated average glacier flow velocity of PRG was 692.08 m/a, which is near to maximum velocities reported earlier for PRG.

The less pronounced use of SAR in earth studies has led to developing algorithms for interpretation. There are recognized needs for further validation studies for existing image analysis as well as for interferogram applications. To ensure these developments, it is necessary to make SAR data vastly more accessible to stakeholders. Here, spaceborne SAR could play a major role towards continuing earth observing systems (EOS) in the future, and for some applications, it might be indispensable.

REFERENCES

[1] E. Rignot, J. Mouginot, B. Scheuchl, M. Van Den Broeke, M. J. Van Wessem, M. Morlighem, Four decades of Antarctic ice sheet mass balance from 1979–2017, *Proc. Natl. Acad. Sci. U. S. A.*, 116 (4) (2019) 1095–1103.

[2] M. Morlighem, E. Rignot, T. Binder, D. Blankenship, R. Drews, G. Eagles, O. Eisen, F. Ferraccioli, R. Forsberg, P. Fretwell, V. Goel, J. S. Greenbaum, H. Gudmundsson, J. Guo, V. Helm, C. Hofstede,

I. Howat, A. Humbert, W. Jokat, N. B. Karlsson, W. S. Lee, K. Matsuoka, R. Millan, J. Mouginot, J. Paden, F. Pattyn, J. Roberts, S. Rosier, A. Ruppel, H. Seroussi, E. C. Smith, B. Sun, M. R. va. den Broeke, T. D. va. Ommen, M. van Wessem, D. A. Young, Deep glacial troughs and stabilizing ridges unveiled beneath the margins of the Antarctic ice sheet, *Nat. Geosci.*, 13 (2) (2020) 132–137.

[3]　H. Han, J. Im, H. Cheol Kim, Variations in ice velocities of Pine Island Glacier ice shelf evaluated using multispectral image matching of Landsat time series data, *Remote Sens. Environ.*, 186 (2016) 358–371.

[4]　H. Konrad, A. E. Hogg, R. Mulvaney, R. Arthern, R. J. Tuckwell, B. Medley, A. Shepherd, Observations of surface mass balance on Pine Island Glacier, West Antarctica, and the effect of strain history in fast-flowing sections, *J. Glaciol.*, 65 (252) (2019) 595–604.

[5]　A. Shepherd, L. Gilbert, A. S. Muir, H. Konrad, M. McMillan, T. Slater, K. H. Briggs, A. V. Sundal, A. E. Hogg, M. E. Engdahl, Trends in Antarctic ice sheet elevation and mass, *Geophys. Res. Lett.*, 46 (14) (2019) 8174–8183.

[6]　B. Miles, J. Jordan, C. Stokes, S. Jamieson, G. H. Gudmundsson, A. Jenkins, Recent acceleration of Denman Glacier (1972–2017), East Antarctica, driven by grounding line retreat and changes in ice tongue configuration, *Cryosph. Discuss.*, (2020) 1–26.

[7]　L. A. Stearns, Dynamics and mass balance of four large East Antarctic outlet glaciers, *Ann. Glaciol.*, 52 (59) (2011) 116–126.

[8]　P. Fretwell, H. D. Pritchard, D. G. Vaughan, J. L. Bamber, N. E. Barrand, R. Bell, C. Bianchi, R. G. Bingham, D. D. Blankenship, G. Casassa, G. Catania, D. Callens, H. Conway, A. J. Cook, H. F. J. Corr, D. Damaske, V. Damm, F. Ferraccioli, R. Forsberg, Y. Fujita, Y. Gim, P. Gogineni, J. A. Griggs, R. C. A. Hindmarsh, P. Holmlund, J. W. Holt, R. W. Jacobel, A. Jenkins, W. Jokat, T. Jordan, E. C. King, J. Kohler, W. Krabill, M. Riger-Kusk, K. A. Langley, G. Leitchenkov, C. Leuschen, B. P. Luyendyk, K. Matsuoka, J. Mouginot, F. O. Nitsche, Y. Nogi, O. A. Nost, S. V. Popov, E. Rignot, D. M. Rippin, A. Rivera, J. Roberts, N. Ross, M. J. Siegert, A. M. Smith, D. Steinhage, M. Studinger, B. Sun, B. K. Tinto, B. C. Welch, D. Wilson, D. A. Young, C. Xiangbin, A. Zirizzotti, Bedmap2: Improved ice bed, surface and thickness datasets for Antarctica, *Cryosphere*, 7 (1) (2013) 375–393.

[9]　J. L. Chen, C. R. Wilson, D. Blankenship, B. D. Tapley, Accelerated Antarctic ice loss from satellite gravity measurements, *Nat. Geosci.*, 2 (12) (2009) 859–862.

[10]　L. A. Stearns, G. S. Hamilton, A new velocity map for Byrd Glacier, East Antarctica, from sequential ASTER satellite imagery, *Ann. Glaciol.*, 41 (2005) 71–76.

[11]　X. Li, E. Rignot, J. Mouginot, B. Scheuchl, Ice flow dynamics and mass loss of Totten Glacier, East Antarctica, from 1989 to 2015, *Geophys. Res. Lett.*, 43 (12) (2016) 6366–6373.

[12]　R. Gomez, J. Arigony-Neto, A. De Santis, S. Vijay, R. Jaña, A. Rivera, Ice dynamics of Union Glacier from SAR offset tracking, *Glob. Planet. Change*, 174 (2019) 1–15.

[13]　Y. Chen, C. Zhou, S. Ai, Q. Liang, L. Zheng, R. Liu, H. Lei, Dynamics of Dalk Glacier in East Antarctica derived from multisource satellite observations since 2000, *Remote Sens.*, 12 (11) (2020) 13–16.

[14]　M. McMillan, A. Shepherd, A. Sundal, K. Briggs, A. Muir, A. Ridout, A. Hogg, D. Wingham, Increased ice losses from Antarctica detected by CryoSat-2, *Geophys. Res. Lett.*, 41 (11) (2014) 3899–3905.

[15]　A. E. Hogg, L. Gilbert, A. Shepherd, A. S. Muir, M. McMillan, Extending the record of Antarctic ice shelf thickness change, from 1992 to 2017, *Adv. Sp. Res.*, 68 (2) (2021) 724–731.

[16]　F. Rémy, M. Frezzotti, Antarctica ice sheet mass balance, *Comptes Rendus – Geosci.*, 338 (14–15) (2006) 1084–1097.

[17]　H. Han, H. Lee, Tide-corrected flow velocity and mass balance of Campbell Glacier tongue, East Antarctica, derived from interferometric SAR, *Remote Sens. Environ.*, 160 (2015) 180–192.

[18]　A. S. Gardner, G. Moholdt, T. Scambos, M. Fahnstock, S. Ligtenberg, M. Van Den Broeke, J. Nilsson, Increased West Antarctic and unchanged East Antarctic ice discharge over the last 7 years, *Cryosphere*, 12 (2) (2018) 521–547.

[19]　T. Li, G. Dawson, S. Chuter, J. Bamber, Mapping the Antarctic grounding zone from ICESat-2 laser altimetry, *Cryosph. Discuss.*, (2020) 1–19.

[20] G. J. Dawson, J. L. Bamber, Measuring the location and width of the Antarctic grounding zone using CryoSat-2, *Cryosphere*, 14 (6) (2020) 2071–2086.

[21] S. B. Luthcke, T. J. Sabaka, B. D. Loomis, A. A. Arendt, J. J. McCarthy, J. Camp, Antarctica, Greenland and Gulf of Alaska land-ice evolution from an iterated GRACE global mascon solution, *J. Glaciol.*, 59 (216) (2013) 613–631.

[22] I. Velicogna, T. C. Sutterley, M. R. Van Den Broeke, Regional acceleration in ice mass loss from Greenland and Antarctica using GRACE time-variable gravity data, *Geophys. Res. Lett.*, 41 (22) (2014) 8130–8137.

[23] I. Joughin, B. E. Smith, W. Abdalati, Glaciological advances made with interferometric synthetic aperture radar, *J. Glaciol.*, 56 (200) (2011) 1026–1042.

[24] I. Joughin, Ice-sheet velocity mapping: A combined interferometric and speckle-tracking approach, *Ann. Glaciol.*, 34 (2002) 195–201.

[25] E. Rignot, Mass balance of East Antarctic glaciers and ice shelves from satellite data, *Ann. Glaciol.*, 34 (2002) 217–227.

[26] D. G. Vaughan, J. L. Bamber, M. Giovinetto, J. Russell, A. P. R. Cooper, Reassessment of net surface mass balance in Antarctica, *J. Clim.*, 12 (4) (1999) 933–946.

[27] M. B. Giovinetto, H. J. Zwally, Spatial distribution of net surface accumulation on the Antarctic ice sheet, *Ann. Glaciol.*, 31 (2000) 171–176.

[28] K. T. Kim, K. C. Jezek, H. G. Sohn, Ice shelf advance and retreat rates along the coast of Queen Maud Land, Antarctica, *J. Geophys. Res.*, 106 (C4) (2001) 7097–7106.

[29] K. C. Jezek, RADARSAT-1 Antarctic mapping project: Change-detection and surface velocity campaign, *Ann. Glaciol.*, 34 (2002) 263–268.

[30] H. Liu, K. C. Jezek, B. Li, Development of an Antarctic digital elevation model by integrating cartographic and remotely sensed data: A geographic information system based approach, *J. Geophys. Res. Solid Earth*, 104 (B10) (1999) 23199–23213.

[31] J. L. Bamber, R. A. Bindschadler, An improved elevation dataset for climate and ice-sheet modelling: Validation with satellite imagery, *Ann. Glaciol.*, 25 (1997) 439–444.

[32] Y. Mohajerani, S. Jeong, B. Scheuchl, I. Velicogna, E. Rignot, P. Milillo, Automatic delineation of glacier grounding lines in differential interferometric synthetic-aperture radar data using deep learning, *Sci. Rep.*, 11 (1) (2021) 1–10.

[33] K. C. Jezek, Glaciological properties of the Antarctic ice sheet from RADARSAT-1 synthetic aperture radar imagery, *Ann. Glaciol.*, 29 (1999) 286–290.

[34] E. Rignot, L. Padman, D. R. Macayeal, M. Schmeltz, Observation of ocean tides below the Filchner and Ronne ice shelves, Antarctica, using synthetic aperture radar interferometry: Comparison with tide model predictions, *J. Geophys. Res.*, 105 (C8) (2000) 19,615-19,630.

[35] E. Rignot, J. Mouginot, B. Scheuchl, Antarctic grounding line mapping from differential satellite radar interferometry, *Geophys. Res. Lett.*, 38 (10) (2011) 1–6.

[36] H. D. Pritchard, S. R. M. Ligtenberg, H. A. Fricker, D. G. Vaughan, M. R. Van Den Broeke, L. Padman, Antarctic ice-sheet loss driven by basal melting of ice shelves, *Nature*, 484 (7395) (2012) 502–505.

[37] K. M. Brunt, H. A. Fricker, L. Padman, T. A. Scambos, S. O'Neel, Mapping the grounding zone of the Ross ice shelf, Antarctica, using ICESat laser altimetry, *Ann. Glaciol.*, 51 (55) (2010) 71–79.

[38] A. B. Giles, R. A. Massom, R. C. Warner, A method for sub-pixel scale feature-tracking using Radarsat images applied to the Mertz Glacier Tongue, East Antarctica, *Remote Sens. Environ.*, 113 (8) (2009) 1691–1699.

[39] J. Mouginot, B. Scheuch, E. Rignot, Mapping of ice motion in antarctica using synthetic-aperture radar data, *Remote Sens.*, 4 (9) (2012) 2753–2767.

[40] C. A. Baumhoer, A. J. Dietz, C. Kneisel, C. Kuenzer, Automated extraction of Antarctic glacier and ice shelf fronts from Sentinel-1 imagery using deep learning, *Remote Sens.*, 11 (21) (2019) 1–22.

[41] M. Dirscherl, A. J. Dietz, C. Kneisel, C. Kuenzer, A novel method for automated supraglacial lake mapping in Antarctica using Sentinel-1 SAR imagery and deep learning, *Remote Sens.*, 13 (2) (2021) 197.

[42] B. W. J. Miles, C. R. Stokes, S. S. R. Jamieson, Simultaneous disintegration of outlet glaciers in Porpoise Bay (Wilkes Land), East Antarctica, driven by sea ice break-up, *Cryosphere*, 11 (1) (2017) 427–442.

[43] F. Paul, T. Bolch, A. Kääb, T. Nagler, C. Nuth, K. Scharrer, A. Shepherd, T. Strozzi, F. Ticconi, R. Bhambri, E. Berthier, S. Bevan, N. Gourmelen, T. Heid, S. Jeong, M. Kunz, T. R. Lauknes, A. Luckman, J. P. Merryman Boncori, G. Moholdt, A. Muir, J. Neelmeijer, M. Rankl, J. VanLooy, T. Van Niel, The glaciers climate change initiative: Methods for creating glacier area, elevation change and velocity products, *Remote Sens. Environ.*, 162 (2015) 408–426.

[44] P. Pandey, A. Ramanathan, G. Venkataraman, Remote sensing of mountain glaciers and related hazards, *Environmental Applications of Remote Sensing*, (2016) 131–162.

[45] K. Nakamura, K. Doi, K. Shibuya, Fluctuations in the flow velocity of the Antarctic Shirase Glacier over an 11-year period, *Polar Sci.*, 4 (3) (2010) 443–455.

[46] K. Nakamura, K. Doi, K. Shibuya, Estimation of seasonal changes in the flow of Shirase Glacier using JERS-1/SAR image correlation, *Polar Sci.*, 1 (2–4) (2007) 73–83.

[47] F. Pattyn, D. Derauw, Ice-dynamic conditions of Shirase Glacier, Antarctica, inferred from ERS SAR interferometry, *J. Glaciol.*, 48 (163) (2002) 559–565.

[48] K. S. Tomar, S. Kumari, A. J. Luis, Seasonal ice flow velocity variations of Polar Record Glacier, East Antarctica during 2016–2019 using Sentinel-1 data, *Geocarto Int.*, (2021) 1–12.

[49] C. Zhou, Y. Zhou, F. Deng, S. Ai, Z. Wang, E. Dongchen, Seasonal and interannual ice velocity changes of Polar Record Glacier, East Antarctica, *Ann. Glaciol.*, 55 (66) (2014) 45–51.

[50] E. Rignot, R. H. Thomas, Mass balance of polar ice sheets, *Science*, 297 (5586) (2002) 1502–1506.

[51] B. Scheuchl, J. Mouginot, E. Rignot, Ice velocity changes in the Ross and Ronne sectors observed using satellite radar data from 1997 and 2009, *Cryosphere*, 6 (5) (2012) 1019–1030.

[52] D. Floricioiu, K. Jezek, M. Baessler, W. Abdel Jaber, Geophysical parameters estimation with TerraSAR-X of outlet glaciers in the Transantarctic Mountains, *Int. Geosci. Remote Sens. Symp.*, (2012) 1565–1568.

[53] J. Wuite, K. C. Jezek, X. Wu, K. Farness, R. Carande, The velocity field and flow regime of David Glacier and Drygalski Ice Tongue, Antarctica, *Polar Geogr.*, 32 (3–4) (2009) 111–127.

[54] G. Wendler, K. Ahlnäs, C. S. Lingle, On Mertz and Ninnis glaciers, East Antarctica, *J. Glaciol.*, 42 (142) (1996) 447–453.

[55] R. A. Massom, A. B. Giles, R. C. Warner, H. A. Fricker, B. Legrésy, G. Hyland, L. Lescarmontier, N. Young, External influences on the Mertz Glacier Tongue (East Antarctica) in the decade leading up to its calving in 2010, *J. Geophys. Res. Earth Surf.*, 120 (3) (2015) 490–506.

[56] X. Li, E. Rignot, M. Morlighem, J. Mouginot, B. Scheuchl, Grounding line retreat of Totten Glacier, East Antarctica, 1996 to 2013, *Geophys. Res. Lett.*, 42 (19) (2015) 8049–8056.

[57] K. Lindbäck, G. Moholdt, K. W. Nicholls, T. Hattermann, B. Pratap, M. Thamban, K. Matsuoka, Spatial and temporal variations in basal melting at Nivlisen ice shelf, East Antarctica, derived from phase-sensitive radars, *Cryosphere*, 13 (10) (2019) 2579–2595.

[58] T. Liu, M. Niu, Y. Yang, Ice velocity variations of the Polar Record Glacier (East Antarctica) using a rotation-invariant feature-tracking approach, *Remote Sens.*, 10 (1) (2018).

[59] P. H. Pandit, S. D. Jawak, A. J. Luis, Estimation of velocity of the Polar Record Glacier, Antarctica using synthetic aperture radar (SAR), in *Multidiscip. Digit. Publ. Inst. Proc.*, 2 (7) (2018) 332.

[60] D. Massonnet, K. L. Feigl, Radar interferometry and its application to changes in the earth's surface, *Rev. Geophys.*, 36 (4) (1998) 441–500.

[61] C. W. Chen, H. A. Zebker, Phase unwrapping for large SAR interferograms: Statistical segmentation and generalized network models, *IEEE Trans. Geosci. Remote Sens.*, 40 (8) (2002) 1709–1719.

[62] T. A. Scambos, M. J. Dutkiewicz, J. C. Wilson, R. A. Bindschadler, Application of image cross-correlation to the measurement of glacier velocity using satellite image data, *Remote Sens. Environ.*, 42 (3) (1992) 177–186.

[63] T. Heid, A. Kääb, Evaluation of existing image matching methods for deriving glacier surface displacements globally from optical satellite imagery, *Remote Sens. Environ.*, 118 (2012) 339–355.

[64] S. D. Jawak, M. Joshi, A. J. Luis, P. H. Pandit, S. Kumar, S. F. Wankhede, A. T. Somadas, Mapping velocity of the Potsdam Glacier, East Antarctica using Landsat-8 data, *Int. Arch. Photogramm. Remote Sens. Spat. Inf. Sci.*, XLII–2/W13 (2019) 1753–1757.

[65] H. Anschütz, O. Eisen, H. Oerter, D. Steinhage, M. Scheinert, Investigating small-scale variations of the recent accumulation rate in coastal Dronning Maud Land, East Antarctica, *Ann. Glaciol.*, 46 (2007) 14–21.

[66] R. Dietrich, R. Metzig, W. Korth, J. Perlt, Combined use of field observations and SAR interferometry to study ice dynamics and mass balance in Dronning Maud Land, Antarctica, *Polar Res.*, 18 (2) (1999) 291–298.

13 Multi-Temporal SAR Interferometry
Theory, Processing, and Applications

Devara Meghanadh and Ramji Dwivedi

CONTENTS

13.1 INTRODUCTION

Since the beginning of geodesy, the humans have been curious to know the earth, its size, its shape, and causes of various phenomena taking place over and under the earth. Remote sensing technology, capable of collecting information from distance, has changed the ways of visualizing and observing the earth. Satellite remote sensing, a technique to observe the earth from space, has revolutionized the space sector and research in the field of geodesy. Large numbers of satellites equipped with high-capacity sensors are playing a crucial role in our development, affecting our daily lives and programs. Satellite remote sensing is mainly benefitted by its wider coverage and availability of various powerful sensors providing low- to high-resolution data acquisitions, which make it suitable to effectively address real world problems.

Data acquisition by satellites is performed in two modes: passive and active remote sensing. Passive remote sensing methods record electromagnetic radiation reflecting from the earth that is originally produced by the sun; active remote sensing methods have their own source of illumination. Passive remote sensing techniques include multispectral and hyperspectral imaging, thermographic imaging, radiometers, etc., while active remote sensing includes radar, LiDAR, synthetic aperture radar, laser altimeter, scatterometer, etc. The following sections present underlying concepts of SAR, geometric distortions in SAR, and an extensive discussion on SAR processing methods.

13.2 SYNTHETIC APERTURE RADAR (SAR)

The first civil and scientific application of radar started in 1946 in the field of radio astronomy; its first application to earth was shown by Graham in 1974 through topographic mapping. Synthetic aperture radar (SAR) satellites, since the launch of SEASAT (1978), have become the source of information for earth observations. Several satellites from different countries have been launched for providing information regarding sea waves, sea ice, wind, rainfall, and changes in land surfaces, etc. SAR is an efficient sensor for the detection of the aforementioned events since it is sensitive to minor changes in surface roughness on the order of the radar wavelength. Spaceborne SAR, an active microwave remote sensing technology, is capable of imaging earth in all weather conditions, irrespective of day and night, due to the microwaves' ability to pierce clouds. Additionally, SAR also has the advantage of providing significant control by manipulating several important parameters, such as incidence angle, phase, frequency, power, swath width, and spatial resolution, while extracting quantitative information. After the launch of the first civilian SAR satellite SEASAT in June 1978, Canada, Europe, and Japan have placed SAR satellites Radarsat-1, ERS-1/2 (European remote sensing), ENVISAT, and JERS, respectively, for observing land and sea surfaces. With the ongoing satellite missions of Radarsat-2, Sentinel-1A, and Sentinel-1B, SAR data will be available for the next 10–15 years.

SAR is a pulsed radar system that performs two-dimensional coherent imaging by preserving the phase information of backscattered reflectivity. Complex SAR processing algorithms result in the form of a SLC (single look complex) image, a 2D array of complex numbers, representing the phase and brightness of the scatterers on the earth or moon surface. When the magnitude of the processed pulse, representing the backscattered signal strength, is displayed in both range (perpendicular to flight direction) and azimuth (parallel to the flight direction), then we see a radar image. SAR instruments collect information about both phase and amplitude of the return signal. In a SLC image, 'single look' informs that the data has no averaging to provide the highest possible spatial resolution, and 'complex' tells us that the value stored in each pixel contains both amplitude and phase (in phase and quadrature phase) value [1]. The phase information for a single, independent scene is meaningless if the ratio between resolution cell size (metres) and SAR signal wavelength (centimetres) is too high, making the phase values random, moving from one pixel to another [2]. On a computer, a pixel of an SLC image is a complex value represented by $a + ib$ (32-bit real numbers). The amplitude of a pixel is calculated as $\sqrt{a^2 + b^2}$, and the phase is calculated as $\tan^{-1}\left(\dfrac{b}{a}\right)$. At first, a SAR image may look like an optical image. However, a closer look reveals several differences subject to understanding of how radar interacts with targets. A sample SAR image is shown in Figure 13.1. One could clearly differentiate a SAR image from an optical image in terms of geometric distortion produced due to the look angle and the slope or height of the target. The terrain area captured in an SAR resolution cell is influenced by the topography of the terrain. It depends on the terrain slope of the plane perpendicular to the orbit and the azimuth direction.

13.3 GEOMETRIC DISTORTIONS IN SAR

SAR imaging system produces mapping of three-dimensional coordinates to two-dimensional SAR images with azimuth and range, which is completely different from nadir looking optical imaging systems. This type of geometry produces geometric distortion in SAR images. These distortions are termed foreshortening, layover, and shadow and are dependent on SAR parameters such as PRF, antenna design, and incidence angle. Foreshortening describes the fact that slopes facing the look direction of the satellite appear squeezed in the SAR image. The ground resolution cell dimension

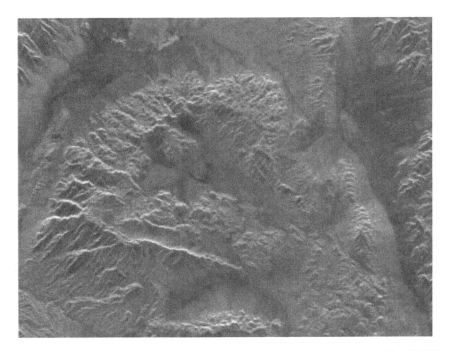

FIGURE 13.1   Intensity image of mountain range in Mojave Desert, CA, USA, captured by ERS [3].

varies as the terrain slope increases in accordance to the horizontal surface. This distortion is explained in Figure 13.2(a), which shows points A and B will appear closer than they are actually in SAR images as both will return pulses at similar time because of the same slant range. However, one cannot differentiate points C and D in the SAR scene because their return would be at same time to the sensor. When the slope of the terrain surpasses the radar off-nadir angle, then the scatterers are imaged in opposite order and overlaid on the impact from other locations. This is known as a layover effect. This distortion is explained in Figure 13.2(b), which shows return from B will arrive prior to A, and hence, point B will be laid over A irrespective of their actual position on the ground. Shadow generally occurs in steep mountainous regions where the radar beam is unable to illuminate the areas behind the steep slopes. The same can be explained from Figure 13.2(c), where region B is too steep to be illuminated by radar waves. Notably, foreshortening has a significant influence on the amplitude information in acquired SAR images. Due to a steeper incidence angle and larger resolution cell, foreshortened areas appear brighter. All of these distortions are shown in Figure 13.3 for a better understanding.

13.4   SAR INTERFEROMETRY (INSAR)

The SAR interferometry (InSAR) technique is one of the principal applications of SAR technology [5–7]. It is based on the difference of phase measurement between two SAR images obtained from distinct orbital locations or at different epochs. In principle, unique interferometric configurations are defined by the distribution of the receiving/transmitting antennas. In particular, conventional InSAR configurations (mono-static) utilize two antennas observing the investigated scene at:

- the same time and different locations, spaced in the across-track direction (across-track interferometry);
- different times and the same locations (along-track interferometry);
- different times and different locations (repeat-pass across-track interferometry).

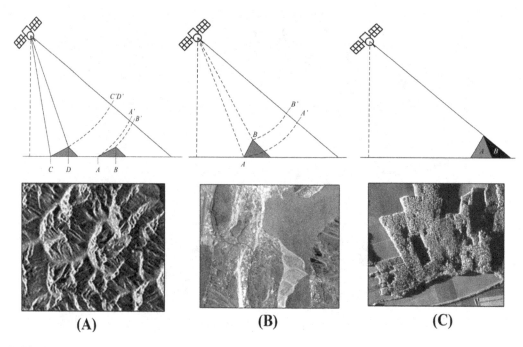

FIGURE 13.2 (a), (b), and (c) represent geometric distortions in SAR images that are foreshortening, layover, and shadow effects [4].

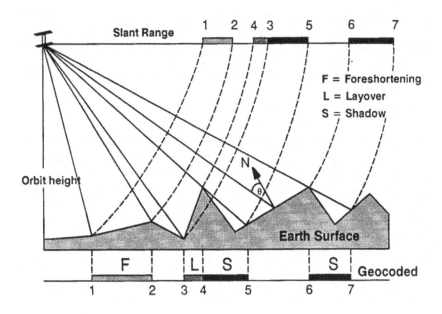

FIGURE 13.3 Effect of terrain changes on SAR image [3].

SAR interferometry configurations where receiving and transmitting antennas are on board different moving platforms, i.e., bi-static and multi-static, are also investigated [8–10].

Basic InSAR geometry is presented in Figure 13.4, which shows two sensor acquisitions from S1 and S2 that are separated by a perpendicular baseline $B_\perp$ and interferometric baseline B. In an ideal

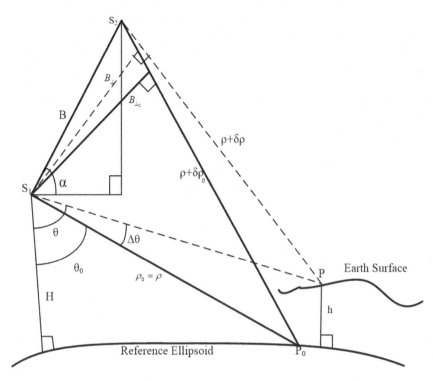

FIGURE 13.4 Basic InSAR geometry. The extra path length (δρ) between S2 and P represents the interferometric phase. The dashed triangle and bold triangle represent InSAR geometry with respect to the earth's surface and the ellipsoid respectively. Subscript '0' refers to ellipsoidal geometry. H and h are ellipsoid height of the sensor and point P respectively. θ and θ_0 are the look angles for point P and P_0 respectively. The angle between horizontal at point S1 and baseline is denoted by α.

environment free from error sources, the phase measured at both S1 and S2 is directly proportional to the range measured ρ and ρ + δρ, respectively.

The advantage of single-pass interferometry over repeat-pass interferometry is that the images are acquired under almost the same weather conditions, resulting in a high degree of coherence in the SLC images prepared from them. On the other hand, in repeat-pass interferometry, the images are acquired on different dates and different atmospheric conditions, resulting in a temporal decorrelation in the SLCs formed. Single-pass interferometry is limited due to its length of antenna.

InSAR uses the differential phase between the phase information acquired by two or more SAR scenes over the same area either simultaneously or at different times with slightly different imaging angles for deriving high-resolution spatial information. The basic principle of interferometry relies on the fact that the fact of the SAR images is a modulo 2π measure of the sensor–target distance. The phase value is uncertain relative to an individual pixel in a single SAR image that cannot be directly exploited. The phase difference between two SAR images may be used to calculate distance variations. This is estimated by multiplying the reference image (master) by the complex conjugated of another image (slave). The slave SLC image should be precisely co-registered and resampled with respect to master SLC [11]. After multiplication, the resultant images are called interferograms [2]. The interferometric phase results in interference fringes because of coherent sources imaging from different positions. The geometric position between sensors is related to the number of fringes that will appear in an image.

Two SAR images acquired from same orbital track imply that the temporal baseline between the two acquisitions will remain stable, i.e., 35 days for ERS-1/2 and ENVISAT. If a target remains coherent for a period of time and does not decorrelate significantly, the repeat-pass interferometry is possible for such a temporal baseline. In general, targets decorrelate temporally, i.e., condition of water and snow changes between seasons; vegetation is affected by weather and human intervention. Further, the geometrical decorrelation is directly proportional to the perpendicular baseline ($B_\perp$). The fringe rates and occurrence of interferogram fringes also increase with an increase in the perpendicular baseline ($B_\perp$). A critical baseline is also defined in InSAR that is related to a fringe rate greater than modulo 2π for a resolution cell that is not useful in InSAR [4]. The following are the contributing parameters to the InSAR phase:

(i)   The baseline between satellite positions ($\Delta\phi_{Base}$)
(ii) Topographic structures such as hills and valleys ($\Delta\phi_{Topographic}$)
(iii) The deformation between two acquisitions ($\Delta\phi_{Deformation}$)
(iv) The atmospheric delay on electromagnetic waves ($\Delta\phi_{Atmp}$)
(v)   Noise ($\Delta\phi_{Noise}$)

The InSAR phase mathematical model can be written as follows:

$$\Delta\phi = \Delta\phi_{Base} + \Delta\phi_{Topographic} + \Delta\phi_{Deformation} + \Delta\phi_{Atmp} + \Delta\phi_{Noise}. \tag{13.1}$$

$\Delta\phi$ represents the interferometric phase, which is the phase difference of two SAR SLC scenes. Ignoring any atmospheric and decorrelation effects, the estimated phase difference ($\Delta\phi$) is directly related to the change in path range ($\delta\rho$) in the satellite line of sight (LOS):

$$\Delta\phi = \frac{-4\pi}{\lambda}\Delta\rho, \tag{13.2}$$

where λ is SAR wavelength and the negative sign depicts the phase delay, which decreases as $\delta\rho$ increases. For topographical mapping, all terms except the phase contribution – because of baseline ($\Delta\phi_{Base}$) and topography ($\Delta\phi_{Topographic}$) – are treated as noise. Equation (13.3) computes the duo [11]:

$$\Delta\phi_{Topographic} + \Delta\phi_{Base} = \frac{-4\pi}{\lambda}B\sin(\theta - \alpha), \tag{13.3}$$

where θ is look angle and α is angle of baseline with horizontal plane (Figure 13.4). InSAR was primarily developed for mapping earth topography; in fact, the shuttle radar topographic mission (SRTM) has been developed on the concept of InSAR technology [12]. The only limitation is that the interferometric phase is modulo 2π, and in order to obtain a continuous topographic map, the differential phase needs to be integrated between all neighbourhood pixels over the interferogram. The integration process to obtain a continuous interferogram phase map is referred to as phase unwrapping. The phase due to topography can also be computed from the external digital elevation model (DEM). If it is subtracted from the interferometric phase while ignoring the decorrelation and atmospheric effects, the resulting phase will be due to deformation between the two acquisitions and can be written as follows:

$$\Delta\phi = \frac{-4\pi}{\lambda}D_{LOS}, \tag{13.4}$$

where D_{LOS} is the deformation of the earth crust along the satellite LOS.

Interferometry using SAR has been extensively investigated for mapping slow-moving landslides. It becomes more deadly when one or more of the triggering elements become activated [13 –16]. MT-InSAR processing techniques involve multi-temporal SAR acquisitions resulting into a time-series information of 1D-LOS displacements by reducing spatial uncorrelated phase components from the interferometric phase. The produced time-series displacement maps could be a critical input for early warning systems [17–19]. The first proposed multi-temporal InSAR technique, PSInSAR™, is based on the selection of permanent scatterers by using amplitude dispersion [20].The technique became most successful in estimating urban region deformation trends, but it failed in non-urban areas [20-21]. Researchers have also investigated other variations, such as amplitude dispersion and different coherence criteria [22–24]. A novel method based on phase criterion was proposed by [25] – the Stanford method for persistent scatterer interferometry (StaMPS) – for selecting persistent scatterer (PS). The MT-InSAR based on StaMPS has been extensively utilized in deformation investigations [25–28]. This method gives displacement information for PS pixels that have a steady phase history throughout the observation period.

13.5 MT-INSAR (ADVANCED INSAR TECHNIQUE) PROCESSING CHAIN

Initially, InSAR was used in a variety of natural hazard applications due to its excellent spatial resolution and vast area coverage [20, 29, 30]. However, due to various errors in interferometric phase, such as spatial and temporal decorrelation and satellite orbit errors, the technique's credibility is always a concern [31]. [5] introduced differential InSAR (DInSAR), which made it possible to employ SAR to measure ground displacement. Earthquake modelling, volcanology, landslide investigation, glaciology, and ground deformation mapping are the core disciplines in which the technique has been used [2, 32–34]. Although the technique outperforms traditional InSAR, it is limited by factors such as spatial and temporal decorrelation and atmospheric effects, which decrease the effectiveness of the method in areas covered by water bodies, vegetation, and forests, where the geometrical characteristics change frequently from time to time. The multi-temporal InSAR technique, which uses time-series acquisitions to analyse the temporal evolution of detected displacements, generates deformation time-series. In recent years, time-series InSAR approaches for retrieving the deformation component from pixels with various scattering properties have been developed. SBAS (small baseline) and PS methods are two types of multi-temporal InSAR algorithms currently available. However, naming convention for the two categories is inconsistent, in that PS-InSAR extracts a particular pixel over the study region, while a SBAS method refers to the formation of interferograms. Many variations of these proposed methods are also available in the literature, which can be directly observed by means of the diversity attempted in pixel selection criteria, baseline configuration, or assumptions in deformation behaviour. For pixel selection, various thresholds and indices are proposed, for example, amplitude dispersion index, coherence, phase criterion, statistical homogeneity test, or concept of quasi or cousin PS [21, 24, 35–36]. In baseline configurations, researchers have attempted single master or multi-master, or thresholds on baselines such as small baseline. Similarly, many methods have considered assumptions of linear deformation in time, while some of them have considered spatial smoothness. An extensive discussion on MT-InSAR approaches can be found in [17], and different MT-InSAR techniques are provided in Table 13.1.

13.5.1 StaMPS: Stanford Method for Persistent Scatterers

Hooper [48] developed the StaMPS approach, which is an advanced method of the earlier developed PS-InSAR methods by [21] and [25]. It comprises four steps, i.e., generation of interferograms, estimation of phase stability, selection of PS, and displacement estimation.

13.5.1.1 Generation of Interferogram

StaMPS selects a master scene on the basis of criteria of maximizing sum correlation of all the master–slave pairs and further uses the DORIS program to generate single master interferograms. Equation (13.5) represents the expression of the correlation as a product of four variables, where

TABLE 13.1
A Summary of Various MT-InSAR Approaches [17]

MT-InSAR Approaches	Selection Criterion	Baseline Configuration	Deformation Type
[20-21]	Amplitude dispersion	Single master	Linear deformation in time
[22]	Coherence	Small baselines	Spatial smoothness
[37]	Coherence	Small baselines	Spatial and temporal smoothness
[23]	Coherence	Small baselines	Linear deformation in time
[24]	Amplitude dispersion & spectral phase diversity	Single master	Linear deformation in time
[38-39]	Amplitude dispersion, coherence, spectral coherence	Small baselines	Linear deformation in time
[25]	Amplitude and phase criterion	Single master	Spatial smoothness
[40]	Coherence	Small baselines	Stepwise linear function in time
[41]	Amplitude dispersion & signal to clutter ratio	Single master	Different types of deformation models
[42]	Coherence	Small baselines	Spatial smoothness
[43]	Statistical homogeneity test	Single master after triangulation	Deformation model in time
[35]	Quasi-PS approach	Target-dependent interferogram subset	Linear deformation in time
[44]	Coherence	Small baselines	Different types of deformation models
[45]	Amplitude dispersion	Single master	Different types of deformation
[46]	Statistical homogeneity test	Small baselines	Linear deformation in time
[47]	Statistical homogeneity test	Single master	Linear deformation in time
[36]	Amplitude dispersion & Cousin PS	Small baselines	Spatial smoothness

$\rho_{temporal}$ refers to temporal correlation, $\rho_{spatial}$ to spatial correlation, $\rho_{doppler}$ to doppler frequency correlation, and $\rho_{thermal}$ to noise correlation. Oversampling is used to avoid aliasing and to determine the dominant scatterer's subpixel position in a resolution cell. In StaMPS, oversampling the data is an option that is done by default by a factor of two, and more pixels are spotted for higher rate of oversampling.

$$\rho_{total} = \rho_{temporal} * \rho_{spatial} * \rho_{doppler} * \rho_{thermal}. \tag{13.5}$$

The PS-InSAR strategy, which is based on StaMPS, uses the DInSAR technology to create interferograms with an existing DEM to remove the phase owing to topography contribution. The height of the SRTM DEM is transformed to the equivalent topographic phase after it is radar coded (range, azimuth). Following the DInSAR principles, the phase due to topography is eliminated from each interferogram. Using accurate orbit information, the contribution to interferometric phase due to orbital inaccurate information is computed. Finally, residual phase remains as the consequence of removing the phase due to orbit errors and topographic phase. A geocoded interferogram stack is the result of the initial interferometric processing.

13.5.1.2   PS Selection
The next step is to choose a candidate PS after the generation of the interferograms. The amplitude dispersion index D_A, which is the ratio of σ_A (standard deviation) and μ_A (mean) of the amplitude values for every pixel in the stack of SLC images, is used to make a preliminary PS candidate selection (Equation 13.6). A high D_A pixel value implies that the pixel has maintained amplitude stability

during the interferometric processing period. This assists in the filtering of pixels that are not PS candidates. Highly decorrelating pixels, such as those of water bodies and vegetation areas, are excluded by setting a threshold on this number index [49].

$$D_A = \frac{\mu_A}{\sigma_A}. \tag{13.6}$$

After performing several simulations and understanding the relationship between D_A and phase standard deviation, [48] revealed that a threshold on $D_A \leq 0.4$ includes almost all PS candidates.

13.5.1.3 Phase Stability Estimation

After selection of PS candidates, phase analysis is performed by calculating phase stability for each PS candidate. For an xth pixel in an ith interferogram, wrapped phase $\varphi_{x,i}$ could be represented as:

$$\varphi_{x,i} = w\left\{\phi_{D,x,i} + \phi_{A,x,i+} + \phi_{S,x,i} + \phi_{\theta,x,i} + \phi_{N,x,i}\right\}, \tag{13.7}$$

where $\Delta\phi_{D,x,i}$ refers to the contribution of pixel motion in phase change due to the direction of radar line of sight, $\Delta\phi_{A,x,i}$ is the phase caused by atmospheric delay, $\Delta\phi_{S,x,i}$ represents the residual phase caused by inaccuracies in orbit of the satellite, $\Delta\phi_{\theta,x,i}$ is the look angle error contribution in phase, $\Delta\phi_{N,x,i}$ is the noise term, and w is the wrapping operator denoting wrapped phase value to modulo 2π [48]. Residual errors $\Delta\phi_{S,x,i}$ and $\Delta\phi_{\theta,x,i}$ are errors in the precise information of orbit and external DEM. Finally, the pixels with least value of estimated noise are selected as PS pixels. Further, the phase stability (γ_x) is computed as:

$$\gamma_x = \frac{1}{N}\left|\sum_{i=1}^{N} \exp\left\{j\left(\varphi_{x,i} - \tilde{\varphi}_{x,i} - \Delta\phi_{D,x,i}\right)\right\}\right|, \tag{13.8}$$

where $\tilde{\varphi}_{x,i}$ is a wrapped estimate of the spatially correlated parts of the interferogram phase $\varphi_{x,i}$, namely the atmospheric error, the satellite inaccuracy error, and the look angle error. The term $\Delta\phi_{\theta,x,i}^{u}$ is the unwrapped estimate of the residual topographic phase error, and N is the number of interferograms. The spatially uncorrelated look angle (SULA) error, commonly known as the DEM error, persists in the chosen PS pixels. This is accomplished by removing the estimated residual topographic phase error from the phase of the chosen PS pixels and then performing phase unwrapping. After phase unwrapping, the spatially correlated look angle (SCLA) error in the PS pixels of the interferograms is computed. The SCLA error is calculated by using a high-pass filter over the unwrapped phase values in time and a low-pass filter in space. Finally, we remove the SCLA error from the remaining phase value to get an estimate of the phase owing to deformation. The interferograms include phase values wrapped to modulo 2 (because of the fact that microwave pulses are sinusoidal and repeat their pattern after a period of two). Thus, the phase values in the interferograms represent the values left in the microwave signal's last cycle.

13.5.1.4 Phase Unwrapping and Displacement Estimation

The wrapped phase values must be adjusted by adding the necessary number of 2π cycles, a process called phase unwrapping, in order to recover the original phase difference in the interferograms' pixels. Surface deformation magnitudes higher than five centimetres induced by any event, for example earthquake, can be successfully determined regardless of the time period of occurrence if the area maintains coherence across time and reliable 2D or 3D phase unwrapping could be

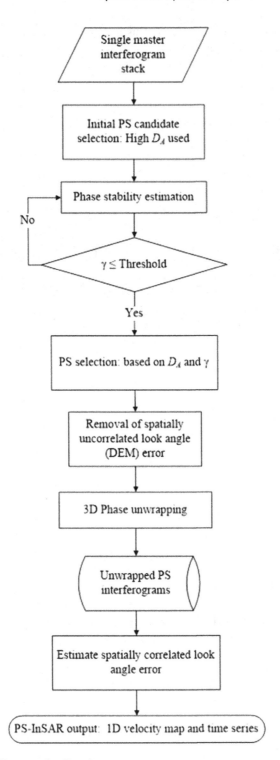

FIGURE 13.5 PS-InSAR processing flowchart.

employed to unwrap the interferograms [20, 50]. The StaMPS approach preserves coherence by employing only PS pixels with good coherence, and it employs 3D phase unwrapping algorithms to estimate larger deformations. Figure 13.5 shows the complete methodology.

13.5.1.5 SBAS

Initially, the SBAS technique, proposed by [22], showed its capabilities in investigating deformation in several cases, mostly by exploring ERS SAR data [51–53]. In particular, the standard SBAS technique works with interferograms that are first multi-looked and then individually phase unwrapped. It was originally developed to extract large spatial scale displacement with lower resolution. The key to any SBAS method is the selection of interferogram pairs for which temporal and spatial separation between the acquisitions are minimum and, hence, minimizing the temporal and spatial decorrelation. However, it has been realized in previous research work that, although SBAS takes advantage of multiple master interferograms with less spatial and temporal baselines, extraction of measurement pixels was dependent on the features of the terrain [52]. For non-urban terrain, SBAS methods failed to extract too many measurement pixels.

To begin, let us review the fundamental theoretical premise of the conventional SBAS approach and consider that for a stack of N + 1, SAR images of the same area are imaged at different times $(t_0, \ldots \ldots t_N)$. M differential interferograms are generated while reducing the decorrelation phenomena. To generate M interferograms, SAR image pairs with minimal spatial and temporal baselines, and low doppler centroids frequencies are used. To retrieve the time-series displacement, independent interferogram formation leads to several small baseline subsets that must be properly linked. Since the phase information is modulo 2π, the interferometric phase is processed to obtain the true phase. This phenomenon is called phase unwrapping.

Now, let us identify a generic or reference pixel in the SAR image in the azimuth and range direction represented as (x, r) and assume the phase signal of each interferogram (unwrapped) is a reference to a high coherence pixel with a known deformation pattern (or a pixel in the non-deforming area). Improper selection of this reference pixel will impact the overall results. An expression for the ith interferogram formed between SAR image acquisitions at time t_B and t_A with perpendicular baseline $B_\perp$, look angle θ, and slant range can be written as:

$$
\begin{aligned}
\Delta\phi_i(x,r) &= \phi(t_B,x,r) - \phi(t_B,x,r) \\
&= \frac{4\pi}{\lambda}\left(d(t_B,x,r) - d(t_A,x,r)\right) \\
&\quad + \frac{4\pi}{\lambda}\frac{B_{\perp j}\Delta z}{r\sin\theta} + \frac{4\pi}{\lambda}\left(\phi_{atmp}(t_B,x,r) - \phi_{atmp}(t_A,x,r)\right) + \Delta n_j
\end{aligned}
\tag{13.9}
$$

where $\Delta\phi_i$ is the phase difference for the ith interferogram for generic pixel (x, r), $d(t_B,x,r), d(t_A,x,r)$ are the radar line-of-sight projection of deformation at time t_B and t_A respectively, $\phi_{amp}(t_B,x,r)$ is the atmospheric error, and Δn_j is the noise for decorrelation effect. Equation (13.9) leads us to define a system of M equations in the N unknowns $\phi(t_1,x,r)$, which can be rearranged using matrix concept as follows:

$$
I\phi = \delta\phi,
\tag{13.10}
$$

where I is an incidence-like matrix with values of 1,−1 for a particular interferogram pair and 0 otherwise. The system of equations may be manipulated in such a manner that the current unknowns are replaced by mean phase velocity (adjacent acquisitions). The new unknowns could be shown as following:

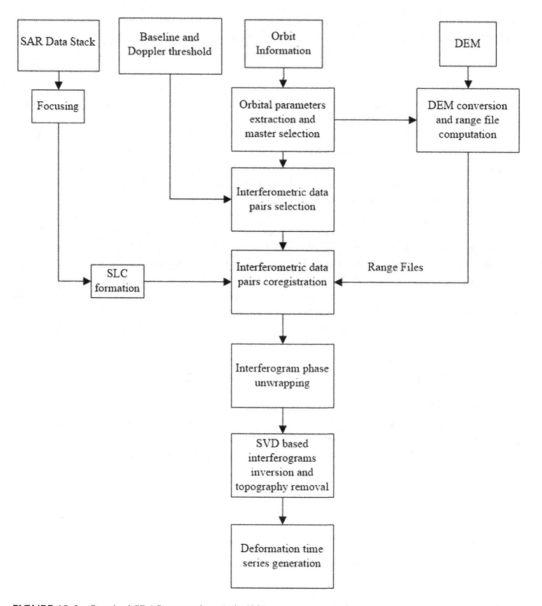

FIGURE 13.6 Standard SBAS processing chain [22].

$$v = \left[v_i = \frac{\phi(t_1, x, r)}{t_1 - t_0} \right], \ldots\ldots, v_N = \frac{\phi(t_N, x, r) - \phi(t_{N-1}, x, r)}{t_N - t_{N-1}}. \qquad (13.11)$$

Equation (13.10) becomes:

$$Bv = \delta\phi, \qquad (13.12)$$

where B represents an M × N matrix. Further, in case of rank deficiency of matrix B, use of singular value decomposition (SVD) allows us to estimate the inverse of B, providing the L2-norm solution of Equation (13.12). The abovementioned standard SBAS method is summarized in Figure 13.6.

13.6 MONITORING OF LANDSLIDES IN NAINITAL (UTTARAKHAND, INDIA) USING STAMPS

Due to the capability of imaging the earth in all weather conditions irrespective of day and night, with high resolution and benefits over conventional monitoring technologies such as GPS, levelling etc., SAR interferometry (InSAR) has been broadly employed for deformation monitoring [31]. The processing of 13 ENVISAT ASAR SLCs of Nainital (Figure 13.7) using StaMPS resulted in 12 interferograms that are geocoded, illustrated in Figure 13.8. At first, candidates of greater than 100,000 PS were chosen based on the basis of DA threshold value, resulting in 5606 PS pixels. The processing resulted in the generation of a mean velocity map in LOS direction of satellite, as depicted in Figure 13.9 in cold and warm colours, corresponding to motions toward and away from the satellite. The obtained mean velocity of PS pixels varies between (-17.8 mm year^{-1} to 26 mm year^{-1}). In Figure 13.9, pixels in the north-eastern and eastern parts of Nainital lake (Sher-ka-danda) are displayed in warm colours, suggesting migration away from the satellite. These locations were historically impacted by subsidence and landslide activity as a result of the slope's instability.

FIGURE 13.7 Study area: Nainital, Uttarakhand, India: (a) Google earth imagery of Nainital township around lake, (b) view of golf course landslide (top left), Google earth footage (top right) and ground fissures over (bottom left) golf course landslide; Aloo khet and Hari Nagar area in Nainital township (bottom right) [54].

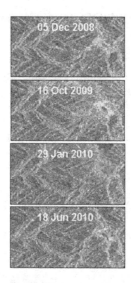
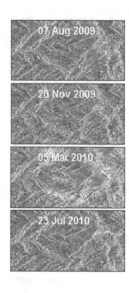

FIGURE 13.8   Interferograms for the Nainital region [55].

Although this region has been steady for a few years, a sufficient number of PS pixels with warm colours are retrieved in this area. In Figure 13.9, an unstable area, a golf course landslide, is identified and circled (shown in pink) in the southwestern part of Nainital lake. According to a previous geotechnical study conducted in 2007–2008 for the southwestern portion of the Raj Bhawan complex's golf course in Nainital, the subsidence-affected zone of the golf course edge was located at the vertical cliff. At the golf course's edge, toppling of rock blocks and rock slide were noticed as a result of intersecting joints. Additionally, it was determined that subsidence is manifested by earth fractures and seepage caused by a buried drain. Despite the extensive vegetation, StaMPS processing was successful in extracting PS pixels from that region and identifying subsidence activity. After conducting a geotechnical evaluation and validating the results with StaMPS, this location has been designated as a critical zone. Additionally, subsidence in the neighbourhood of Nainital lake is depicted in warm colours in Figure 13.9. Mallital, the area surrounding Nainital lake, is the township's primary shopping area. Additionally, on the south-eastern side of Nainital lake, and along the Balia Nala, Hari Nagar, and Aloo khet rivers, there are two hilly places that have formed a valley as a result of intense shearing. These two sites are also designated as zones prone to landslides. Although PS densities are slightly lower in these two places, at least 10–12 pixels are identified with warm colours. The DMMC study [54] also includes a map of landslide danger zonation (Figure 13.10) that was created by combining multiple thematic maps created using satellite imagery and other data sources. The areas surrounding Balia Nala and the golf course are classified as high-hazard zones, which further verify the PS results.

13.7   MONITORING OF LANDSLIDES IN NAINITAL (UTTARAKHAND, INDIA) USING STAMPS

Various ways for preparing LSMs have been proposed by researchers. They have considered various characteristics including distance to faults, distance to rivers, distance to roads, stream power index, texture, soil type, precipitation, geomorphology, LULC, lithology, curvature, slop, aspect, and

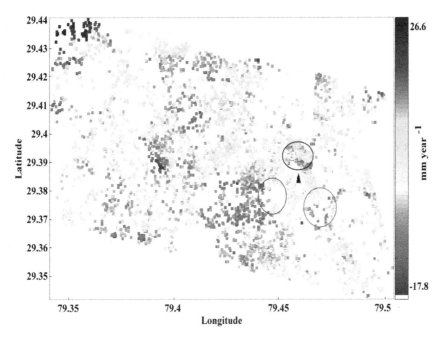

FIGURE 13.9 1D-LOS mean velocity plot of Nainital region [55]. Nainital lake is shown with a black triangle. A black circle shows the Tallital area of Nainital town; a blue circle shows the Aloo khet and Hari Nagar area. A pink circle shows the Raj Bhawan complex.

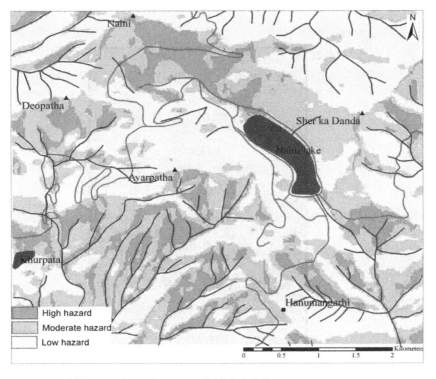

FIGURE 13.10 Landslide hazard zonation map of Nainital [54].

elevation for landslide susceptibility mapping [56–57]. However, it has been found that when input parameters are given weights, approaches become biased. As a result, the analytical hierarchy process (AHP) was developed to address this problem [58–60]. AHP fuzzy logic has also been used by several researchers to give weight priorities [61–62]. It has also been discovered that 1D-LOS surface displacement rates are not taken into consideration while generating LSMs. Researchers have employed MT-InSAR to prepare landslide inventories on their own. However, no effort has been made to investigate the role of the MT-InSAR estimates along with other parameters in the LSM generation. [63] used hotspot analysis to find unstable zones using a 1D-LOS velocity map obtained by MT-InSAR processing. The authors advocated for the inclusion of other criteria, including in-situ measurements and optical imaging, in order to classify moving regions as landslide prone zones (LSZs). [64] used the random forest (RF) method of machine learning to apply an SBAS-InSAR approach to the findings of LSM optimization. [65] developed a method for mapping landslide inventories using MT-InSAR results from multi-constellation SAR datasets, SAR intensity images, and DEM-derived products. [66] suggested a method for detecting active deformation areas (ADAs) based on Cruden and Varnes' landslide nomenclature [67]. Given that MT-InSAR is a potent tool for investigating slow-moving landslides, its estimation can be a crucial input for identifying susceptible zones when combined with elements influencing and initiating landslides such as aspect, slope, geomorphology, rainfall, LULC, and lithology.

The two SLC stacks (Stack-1: 20 ENVISAT and ERS1/2 scenes; Stack-2: 60 Sentinel-1A TOPS scenes) were processed of the Srinagar–Rudraprayag region using the MT-InSAR technique to obtain LSZs (Figure 13.11). Both stacks' masters were chosen by determining the sum correlation of all feasible single master interferometric pairings. As a result, 19 interferograms are formed from Stack-1 and 59 interferograms from Stack-2. Further, the topographic signal is eliminated via the SRTM DEM (90 m). From interferometric processing, ~11500 and ~3600 PS pixels from the two stacks are detected, respectively. Figures 13.12(a–d) depict a 1D-LOS mean displacement rate map from the ERS1/2 and ENVISAT datasets with a deformation rate ranging from −4.35

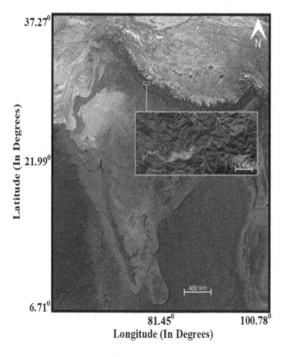

FIGURE 13.11   Srinagar–Rudraprayag region [68].

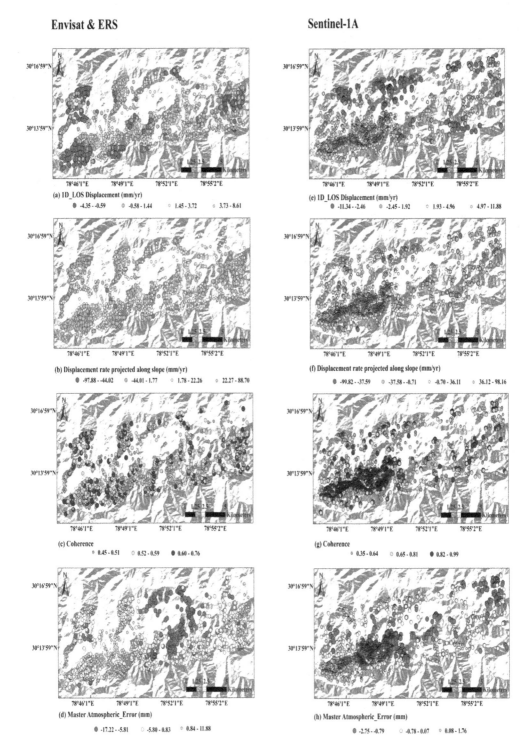

FIGURE 13.12 (a–d) Results obtained from MT-InSAR processing of ERS1/2 & ENVISAT: 1D-LOS displacement estimates, displacement rate projected along slope, coherence, and master atmospheric error. (e–h) Results obtained from MT-InSAR processing of Sentinel-1A: 1D-LOS displacement estimates, displacement rate projected along slope, coherence, and master atmospheric error [68].

to 8.71 mm year⁻¹ along with displacement rate projected to slope direction, coherence map and master atmospheric error. PS pixels that are stable deform at a rate of -1.5 mm year⁻¹ to 1.5 mm year⁻¹. A preliminary examination of the MT-InSAR data in conjunction with pre-existing LSM generated by NLSM (GSI) shows the presence of unstable zones next to LSZs. The 1D-LOS mean displacement map derived from Sentinel-1A data processing by using MT-InSAR method is shown in Figures 13.12(e–f), along with displacement rate projected to slope direction, coherence map, and master atmospheric error. The rate of deformation ranges between -11.34 and -1.5 mm year⁻¹. High negative deformation rates range from -11.34 mm to -1.5 mm year⁻¹ with a mean of -4.42 mm year⁻¹ emphasizing the presence of unstable zones. The analysis of the results from both 1D-LOS mean velocities suggests the presence of subsidence and uplift in the investigated area.

Additionally, PS pixels detected in the vicinity of Srinagar city indicate movement toward the satellite's line of sight. PS pixels in the study area's south-east region demonstrate movement away from the satellite's line of sight. These identified movements imply that the region is not stable. A preliminary examination of the MT-InSAR data in conjunction with pre-existing LSM generated by NLSM (GSI) shows the presence of unstable zones next to LSZs. However, the identified moving zones cannot be classified as LSZs only on the basis of this research. Other critical aspects, such as DEM derivatives, geomorphology, optical imagery datasets, lithology, LULC maps, rainfall, the presence of faults, and distance from highways, must be taken into account. Elevation, slope, aspect, LULC, geomorphology, and lithology are all regarded as possible considerations and are therefore included in multi-criteria decision analysis. Each subfactor of each factor is weighted to account for its effect on the decision-making process during reclassification. For example, steep slopes and areas at a high elevation are generally more prone to landslides than other places within both layers. SE

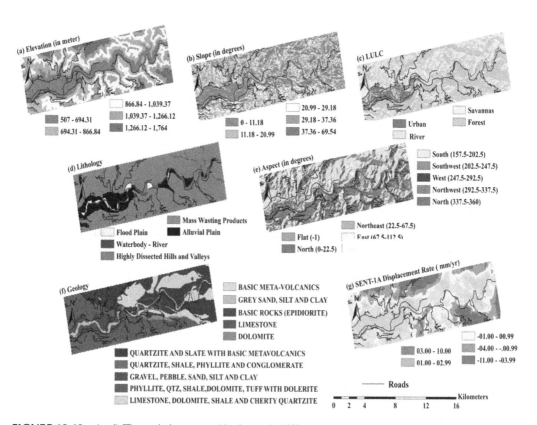

FIGURE 13.13 (a–d) Thematic layers used in the study [68].

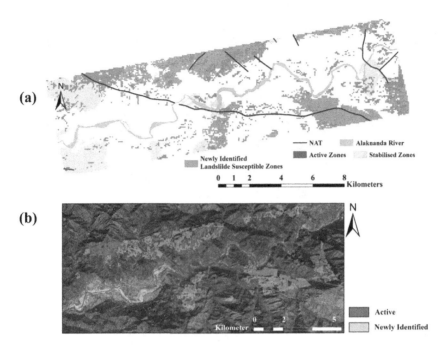

FIGURE 13.14   Status of detected landslide susceptible zones (LSZs) [68].

and NW directions are preferred in aspect, as [69] discovered a NW–SE deformation tendency in the study area. Quartzite, limestone, phyllites, and dolomite are widespread in the study area, which consists of high incidence of landslides. As a result, the aforementioned subfactors are prioritized during reclassification. Similarly, in the geomorphology layer, the piedmont alluvial plain and severely dissected structural hills and valleys are given high priority, and LULC prioritizes forest, mixed forest, and savannas. All thematic layers used are shown in Figure 13.13. Initially, AHP has been used for weight assignments to each layer, and therefore the pairwise comparison matrix has been prepared according to the significance of the thematic layers. After weight assignment, LSM is generated using multi-criteria decision analysis for both the Stack-1 and Stack-2. By comparing the new LSM (produced using Sentinel-1A data) to the LSM generated earlier using ENVISAT and ERS1/2 data, 502 medium and 131 high LSZs were found. The current status of LSZs is depicted in Figure 13.14.

13.8   SURFACE DEFORMATION MEASUREMENT OF THE L'AQUILA REGION

In this section, 14 ENVISAT ASAR SLC images of the L'Aquila region, Italy, are processed using PS-InSAR and SBAS methods, and obtained results are discussed with their interpretations. Using PS-InSAR method (StaMPS), 13 single master geocoded interferograms are generated, which resulted in generation of 21103 PS pixels (see Figure 13.15). The obtained 1D-LOS mean velocity plot shows displacement in the warm and cold colours from −47.79 to 42.53 mm year^{-1} (Figure 13.16). The 1D-LOS mean velocity plot highlights a pattern of deformation in south–east and north–west moving opposite to the earthquake epicentre and in proportion to the normal fault.

Using the SBAS approach, 54 interferograms are generated with no isolated cluster. All spatial baselines are below 400 m and temporal baselines less than one year. At the end, 4886 measurement pixels are selected as SDFP (slowly decorrelating filtered phase) pixels by this method. Hence, it is observed that fewer pixels are detected by the SBAS method in comparison to the PS-InSAR method. However, it should also be considered that both are optimized for two unlike scattering

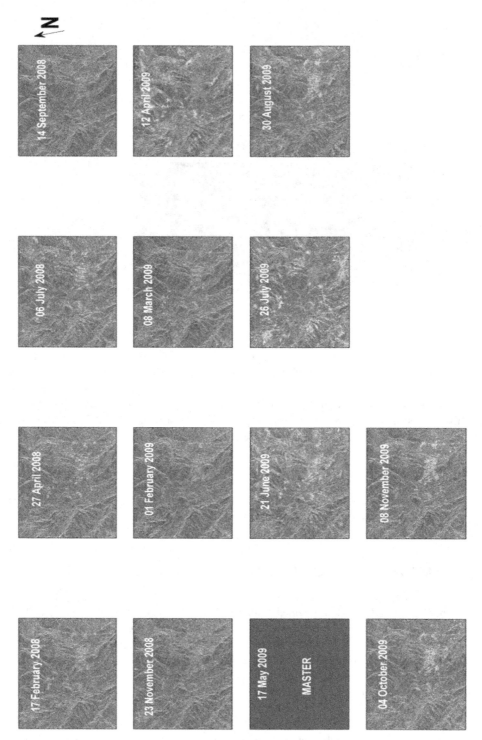

FIGURE 13.15   Unwrapped interferograms of the L'Aquila earthquake. Master image date: 17 May 2009 [70].

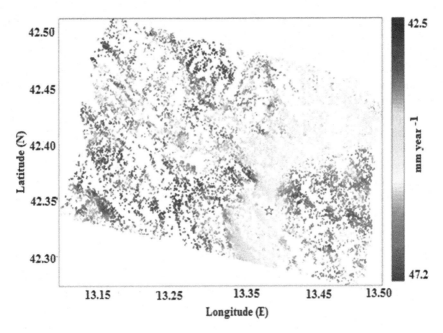

FIGURE 13.16   1D-LOS mean velocity plot for L'Aquila region after PS-InSAR processing. The star mark denotes the epicentre [70].

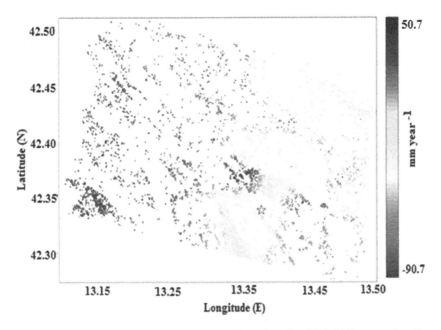

FIGURE 13.17   1D-LOS mean velocity plot for L'Aquila region after PS-InSAR processing. The star mark denotes the epicentre [70].

models. The 1D-LOS velocity map (Figure 13.17) obtained from the StaMPS-based SBAS method shows a displacement rate in the range from −90.7 to 50.7 mm year⁻¹ in cold and warm colours.

A total of 833 common pixels are selected in 4886 SDFP pixels due to low decorrelation for scatterers even though range and azimuth filtering was performed. Although both methods differ by means of processing and in tackling various errors, the obtained result has 21 pixels, only showing a 1D-LOS mean velocity greater than 50 mm year^{-1}, moving away from the satellite. The mean velocity difference in roughly 62% (517 pixels) of the typical 833 pixels is less than 3 mm year^{-1}, and 66% of the pixels have a difference in mean velocity of less than 5 mm year^{-1}. This might be because the phase of the chosen pixels produced by both approaches differs, and 3D phase unwrapping is currently under investigation to offer an accurate approximation. The extraction of the number of pixels in the research region covered by snow and vegetation, in which PS-InSAR appears to be the superior of the two approaches, is one notable feature of this work. Furthermore, the spatial density of measurement pixels is critical for isolating the atmospheric phase term and removing it from the interferometric phase utilizing the atmospheric phase's spatial correlation and temporal decorrelation properties [50]. In areas with a high density of dominating scatterers, the SBAS method's inability to identify a significant number of measurement pixels renders it less successful than PS-InSAR.

13.9 CONCLUSIONS

Multi-temporal SAR interferometry is a well-established technique for surface monitoring, particularly for a slow-moving deformation body. The chapter presented an extensive discussion of basics of SAR and InSAR for critical monitoring and detection of natural hazards along with important limitations. The chapter highlighted the major MT-InSAR processing algorithms, namely PS-InSAR and SBAS, which identify measurement pixels to extract the deformation signal and estimate magnitude of deformation at millimetre level. The chapter, in general, addresses three applications: monitoring of landslides in Nainital, landslide susceptibility mapping for the Srinagar–Rudraprayag region and estimation of co-seismic deformation pattern in the L'Aquila region, which suffered a massive earthquake. The short revisit time of SAR satellite missions, for example 12 (6) days for Sentinel-1A or 1B (A & B), has strengthened the application area of natural hazards monitoring, leading InSAR towards being a potential technique for landslide forecasting.

REFERENCES

[1] P. Tarikhi, Synthetic aperture radar persistent scatterer interferometry (PS-InSAR), in *ISNET/CRTEAN Training Course on Synthetic Aperture Radar (SAR) Imagery: Processing, Interpretation and Applications*, 13 May 2010, 1–67.

[2] P.M. Mather, *Computer Processing of Remotely-Sensed Images: An Introduction*, 3rd edition. Great Britain: John Wiley & Sons, Ltd, 2004.

[3] R. Bamler, Principles of synthetic aperture radar, *Surveys in Geophysics*, 21(2) (2000) 147–157.

[4] M.L. Jonathan, GPS and PSI integration for monitoring urban land motion, PhD thesis report, University of Nottingham, UK (2010).

[5] A.K. Gabriel, R.M. Goldstein, H.A. Zebker, Mapping small elevation changes over large areas: Differential radar interferometry, *Journal of Geophysical Research: Solid Earth*, 94(B7) (1989) 9183–9191.

[6] D. Massonnet, K.L. Feigl, Radar interferometry and its application to changes in the Earth's surface, *Reviews of Geophysics*, 36(4) (1998) 441–500.

[7] R. Bürgmann, P.A. Rosen, E.J. Fielding, Synthetic aperture radar interferometry to measure Earth's surface topography and its deformation, *Annual Review of Earth and Planetary Sciences*, 28(1) (2000) 169–209.

[8] G. Krieger, A. Moreira, Spaceborne bi-and multistatic SAR: potential and challenges, *IEE Proceedings-Radar, Sonar and Navigation*, 153(3) (2006) 184–198.

[9] S. Duque, P. López-Dekker, J.J. Mallorqui, Single-pass bistatic SAR interferometry using fixed-receiver configurations: Theory and experimental validation, *IEEE Transactions on Geoscience and Remote Sensing*, 48(6) (2010) 2740–2749.

[10] G. Krieger, H. Fiedler, J. Mittermayer, K. Papathanassiou, A. Moreira, Analysis of multistatic configurations for spaceborne SAR interferometry, *IEEE Proceedings-Radar, Sonar and Navigation*, 150(3) (2003) 87–96.

[11] H.A. Zebker, R.M. Goldstein, Topographic mapping from interferometric synthetic aperture radar observations, *Journal of Geophysical Research: Solid Earth*, 91(B5) (1986) 4993–4999.

[12] T.G. Farr, P.A. Rosen, E. Caro, R. Crippen, R. Duren, S. Hensley, M. Kobrick, M. Paller, E. Rodriguez, L. Roth, D. Seal, S. Shaer, J. Shimada, J. Umland, M. Werner, M. Oskin, D. Burbank, D. Alsdorf, *The Shuttle Radar Topography Mission. Reviews of Geophysics*, 45(3) (2007).

[13] M. Polcari, M. Palano, J. Fernández, S.V. Samsonov, S. Stramondo, S. Zerbini, 3D displacement field retrieved by integrating Sentinel-1 InSAR and GPS data: the 2014 South Napa earthquake, *European Journal of Remote Sensing*, 49(1) (2016) 1–13.

[14] A. Tiwari, A.B. Narayan, R. Dwivedi, A. Swadeshi, S. Pasari, O. Dikshit, Geodetic investigation of landslides and land subsidence: Case study of the Bhurkunda coal mines and the Sirobagarh land-slide, *Survey Review* (2018).

[15] P.J. González, M. Bagnardi, A.J Hooper, Y. Larsen, P. Marinkovic, S.V. Samsonov, T.J. Wright, The 2014–2015 eruption of Fogo volcano: Geodetic modeling of Sentinel-1 TOPS interferometry, *Geophysical Research Letters*, 42(21) (2015) 9239–9246.

[16] Y. Zhang, X. Meng, C. Jordan, A. Novellino, T. Dijkstra, G. Chen, Investigating slow-moving landslides in the Zhouqu region of China using InSAR time series, *Landslides*, 15(7) (2018), 1299–1315.

[17] M. Crosetto, O. Monserrat, M. Cuevas-González, N. Devanthéry, B. Crippa, Persistent scat-terer interferometry: A review, *ISPRS Journal of Photogrammetry and Remote Sensing*, 115 (2016) 78–89.

[18] A. Hooper, D. Bekaert, K. Spaans, M. Arıkan, Recent advances in SAR interferometry time series analysis for measuring crustal deformation, *Tectonophysics*, (2012), 514, 1–13.

[19] E. Intrieri, F. Raspini, A. Fumagalli, P. Lu, S. Del Conte, P. Farina, N. Casagli, The Maoxian landslide as seen from space: detecting precursors of failure with Sentinel-1 data, *Landslides*, 15(1) (2018) 123–133.

[20] A. Ferretti, C. Prati, F. Rocca, Analysis of permanent scatterers in SAR interferometry. In *IGARSS 2000, IEEE 2000 International Geoscience and Remote Sensing Symposium. Taking the Pulse of the Planet, The Role of Remote Sensing in Managing the Environment, Proceedings (Cat. No. 00CH37120) IEEE*, 2 (2000, July) 761–763.

[21] A. Ferretti, C. Prati, F. Rocca, Permanent scatterers in SAR interferometry, *IEEE Transactions on Geoscience and Remote Sensing*, 39(1) (2001) 8–20.

[22] P. Berardino, G. Fornaro, R. Lanari, E. Sansosti, A new algorithm for surface deformation monitoring based on small baseline differential SAR interferograms, *IEEE Transactions on Geoscience and Remote Sensing*, 40(11) (2002) 2375–2383.

[23] O. Mora, J.J. Mallorqui, A. Broquetas, Linear and nonlinear terrain deformation maps from a reduced set of interferometric SAR images, *IEEE Transactions on Geoscience and Remote Sensing*, 41(10) (2003) 2243–2253.

[24] C. Werner, U. Wegmuller, T. Strozzi, A. Wiesmann, Interferometric point target analysis for deformation mapping. In *IGARSS 2003, 2003 IEEE International Geoscience and Remote Sensing Symposium, Proceedings (IEEE Cat.No. 03CH37477)*, 7 (2003, July) 4362–4364.

[25] A. Hooper, H. Zebker, P. Segall, B. Kampes, A new method for measuring deformation on volcanoes and other natural terrains using InSAR persistent scatterers, *Geophysical Research Letters*, 31(23) (2004).

[26] W. C. Hung, C. Hwang, Y.A. Chen, C.P. Chang, J. Y. Yen, A. Hooper, C.Y. Yang, Surface deformation from persistent scatterers SAR interferometry and fusion with leveling data: A case study over the Choushui River Alluvial Fan, Taiwan, *Remote Sensing of Environment*, 115(4) (2011) 957–967.

[27] M. Motagh, J. Beavan, E.J. Fielding, M. Haghshenas, Postseismic ground deformation following the September 2010 Darfield, New Zealand, earthquake from TerraSAR-X, COSMO-SkyMed, and ALOS InSAR. *IEEE Geoscience and Remote Sensing Letters*, 11(1) (2013) 186–190.

[28] M.C. Cuenca, A.J. Hooper, R.F. Hanssen, Surface deformation induced by water influx in the abandoned coal mines in Limburg, the Netherlands observed by satellite radar interferometry, *Journal of Applied Geophysics*, 88 (2013) 1–11.

[29] J.F. Dehls, M. Basilico, C. Colesanti, Ground deformation monitoring in the Ranafjord area of Norway by means of the permanent scatterers technique. In *IEEE International Geoscience and Remote Sensing Symposium, IEEE*, 1 (2002, June) 203–207.

[30] H.A. Zebker, J. Villasenor, Decorrelation in interferometric radar echoes, *IEEE Transactions on Geoscience and Remote Sensing*, 30(5) (1992) 950–959.

[31] M. Nengwu, C. Weiyan, L. Shuangping, Z. Min, H. Ping, J. Zonghuang, … & L. Tao, Landslide monitoring by PS-InSAR along Qing river. In *2012 Second International Workshop on Earth Observation and Remote Sensing Applications IEEE*, (2012, June) 235–239.

[32] C. Colesanti, A. Ferretti, C. Prati, F. Rocca, Seismic faults analysis in California by means of the permanent scatterers technique, *Retrieval of Bio-and Geo-Physical Parameters from SAR Data for Land Applications*, 475 (2002, January) 125–131.

[33] C. Meisina, F. Zucca, D. Notti, A. Colombo, A. Cucchi, G. Savio, M. Bianchi, Geological interpretation of PSInSAR data at regional scale, *Sensors*, 8(11) (2008) 7469–7492.

[34] V. Greif, J. Vlcko, Application of the PS-InSAR technique for the post-failure landslide deformation monitoring at Lubietova site in central Slovakia. In *Landslide Science and Practice*. Berlin: Springer (2013) 15–23.

[35] D. Perissin, T. Wang, Repeat-pass SAR interferometry with partially coherent targets, *IEEE Transactions on Geoscience and Remote Sensing*, 50(1) (2011) 271–280.

[36] N. Devanthéry, M. Crosetto, O. Monserrat, M. Cuevas-González, B. Crippa, An approach to persistent scatterer interferometry, *Remote Sensing*, 6(7) (2014) 6662–6679.

[37] D.A. Schmidt, R. Bürgmann, Time-dependent land uplift and subsidence in the Santa Clara valley, California, from a large interferometric synthetic aperture radar data set, *Journal of Geophysical Research: Solid Earth*, 108(B9) (2003).

[38] J. Duro, J. Inglada, J. Closa, N. Adam, A. Arnaud, High resolution differential interferometry using time series of ERS and ENVISAT SAR data, *FRINGE 2003 Workshop*, 550 (2004, June) 72.

[39] M. Crosetto, E. Biescas, J. Duro, J. Closa, A. Arnaud, Generation of advanced ERS and Envisat interferometric SAR products using the stable point network technique, *Photogrammetric Engineering & Remote Sensing*, 74(4) (2008) 443–450.

[40] M. Crosetto, B. Crippa, E. Biescas, Early detection and in-depth analysis of deformation phenomena by radar interferometry, *Engineering Geology*, 79(1–2) (2005) 81–91.

[41] B.M. Kampes, *Radar Interferometry* (Vol. 12). The Netherlands: Springer (2006) 12.

[42] P. López-Quiroz, M.P. Doin, F. Tupin, P. Briole, J.M. Nicolas, Time series analysis of Mexico City subsidence constrained by radar interferometry, *Journal of Applied Geophysics*, 69(1) (2009) 1–15.

[43] A. Ferretti, A. Fumagalli, F. Novali, C. Prati, F. Rocca, A. Rucci, A new algorithm for processing interferometric data-stacks: SqueeSAR, *IEEE Transactions on Geoscience and Remote Sensing*, 49(9) (2011) 3460–3470.

[44] E.A. Hetland, P. Musé, M. Simons, Y.N. Lin, P.S. Agram, C.J. DiCaprio, Multiscale InSAR time series (MInTS) analysis of surface deformation. *Journal of Geophysical Research: Solid Earth*, 117(B2) (2012).

[45] F.J. Van Leijen, Persistent scatterer interferometry based on geodetic estimation theory (2014).

[46] K. Goel, N. Adam, A distributed scatterer interferometry approach for precision monitoring of known surface deformation phenomena, *IEEE Transactions on Geoscience and Remote Sensing*, 52(9) (2013) 5454–5468.

[47] X. Lv, B. Yazıcı, M. Zeghal, V. Bennett, T. Abdoun, Joint-scatterer processing for time-series InSAR, *IEEE Transactions on Geoscience and Remote Sensing*, 52(11) (2014) 7205–7221.

[48] A. Hooper, Persistent scatterer InSAR for crustal deformation analysis, with application to VolcanAlcedo, Galapagos, *J. Geophys. Res., B*, 112(7) (2007) 1–19.

[49] S.P. Agram, F. Casu, H.A. Zebker, R. Lanari, Comparison of persistent scatterers and small baseline time-series InSAR results: A case study of the San Francisco bay area, *IEEE Geoscience and Remote Sensing Letters*, 8(4) (2011) 592–596.

[50] C. Colesanti, G. B. Crosta, A. Ferretti, C. Ambrosi, Monitoring and assessing the state of activity of slope instabilities by the permanent scatterers technique. In *Landslides from Massive Rock Slope Failure*. Dordrecht: Springer (2006) 175–194.

[51] R. Lanari, G. De Natale, P. Berardino, E. Sansosti, G.P. Ricciardi, S. Borgstrom, C. Troise, Evidence for a peculiar style of ground deformation inferred at Vesuvius volcano, *Geophysical Research Letters*, 29(9) (2002) 6–1.

[52] R. Lanari, F. Casu, M. Manzo, G. Zeni, P. Berardino, M. Manunta, A. Pepe, An overview of the small baseline subset algorithm: A DInSAR technique for surface deformation analysis, *Deformation and Gravity Change: Indicators of Isostasy, Tectonics, Volcanism, and Climate Change*, (2007) 637–661.

[53] L. Cascini, S. Ferlisi, G. Fornaro, R. Lanari, D. Peduto, G. Zeni, Subsidence monitoring in Sarno urban area via multi-temporal DInSAR technique, *International Journal of Remote Sensing*, 27(8) (2006) 1709–1716.

[54] DMMC, Slope instability and geo-environmental issues of the area around Nainital. A DMMC publication. [Online]. Available: http://dmmc.uk.gov.in/files/pdf/Nainital_Enviornmental_Degradation.pdf,(2011).

[55] R. Dwivedi, P. Varshney, A. Tiwari, A.B. Narayan, A.K. Singh, O. Dikshit, K. Pallav, Monitoring of landslides in Nainital, Uttarakhand, India: Validation of PS-InSAR results, In *2015 Joint Urban Remote Sensing Event (JURSE), IEEE*, (2015, March) 1–4.

[56] Y. Hong, Y. Hong, R. Adler, G. Huffman, Use of satellite remote sensing data in the mapping of global landslide susceptibility, *Natural Hazards*, 43(2) (2007) 245–256.

[57] T. Xiao, S. Segoni, L. Chen, K. Yin, N. Casagli, A step beyond landslide susceptibility maps: A simple method to investigate and explain the different outcomes obtained by different approaches, *Landslides*, 17(3) (2020) 627–640.

[58] T. Kavzoglu, E.K. Sahin, I. Colkesen, Landslide susceptibility mapping using GIS-based multi-criteria decision analysis, support vector machines, and logistic regression, *Landslides*, 11(3) (2014) 425–439.

[59] I. Semlali, L. Ouadif, L. Bahi, Landslide susceptibility mapping using the analytical hierarchy process and GIS, *Current Science*, 116(5) (2019) 773.

[60] A. El Jazouli, A. Barakat, R. Khellouk, GIS-multicriteria evaluation using AHP for landslide susceptibility mapping in OumErRbia high basin (Morocco), *Geoenvironmental Disasters*, 6(1) 3(2019).

[61] Y. Noorollahi, S. Sadeghi, H. Yousefi, A. Nohegar, Landslide modelling and susceptibility mapping using AHP and fuzzy approaches, *Int. J. Hydro.*, 2(2) (2018) 137–148.

[62] E. Tazik, Z. Jahantab, M. Bakhtiari, A. Rezaei, S.K. Alavipanah, Landslide susceptibility mapping by combining the three methods fuzzy logic, frequency ratio and analytical hierarchy process in Dozain basin, *International Archives of Photogrammetry, Remote Sensing and Spatial Information Sciences*, 40(2) (2014) 267.

[63] L. Solari, M. Del Soldato, R. Montalti, S. Bianchini, F. Raspini, P. Thuegaz, N. Casagli, A Sentinel-1 based hot-spot analysis: Landslide mapping in north-western Italy, *International Journal of Remote Sensing*, 40(20) (2019) 7898–7921.

[64] F. Zhao, X. Meng, Y. Zhang, G. Chen, X. Su, D. Yue, Landslide susceptibility mapping of Karakorum highway combined with the application of SBAS-InSAR technology, *Sensors*, 19(12) (2019) 2685.

[65] X. Liu, C. Zhao, Q. Zhang, J. Peng, W. Zhu, Z. Lu, Multi-temporal loess landslide inventory mapping with C-, X-and L-band SAR datasets – a case study of Heifangtai Loess Landslides, China, *Remote Sensing*, 10(11) (2018) 1756.

[66] L. Solari, S, Bianchini, R. Franceschini, A. Barra, O. Monserrat, P. Thuegaz, F. Catani, Satellite interferometric data for landslide intensity evaluation in mountainous regions, *International Journal of Applied Earth Observation and Geoinformation*, 87 (2020) 102028.

[67] D.M. Cruden, D.J. Varnes, Landslides: investigation and mitigation, Chapter 3-Landslide types and processes, *Transportation Research Board Special Report*, (247) (1996).

[68] M. Devara, A. Tiwari, R. Dwivedi, Landslide susceptibility mapping using MT-InSAR and AHP enabled GIS-based multi-criteria decision analysis. *Geomatics, Natural Hazards and Risk*, 12(1) (2021) 675–693.

[69] S. Khanduri, K.S. Sajwan, A. Rawat, C. Dhyani, S. Kapoor, Disaster in Rudraprayag District of Uttarakhand Himalaya: A special emphasis on geomorphic changes and slope instability, *Journal of Geography and Natural Disasters*, 8(1) (2018) 1–9.

[70] A. Tiwari, R. Dwivedi, O. Dikshit, A.K. Singh, A study on measuring surface deformation of the L'Aquila region using the StaMPS technique, *International Journal of Remote Sensing*, 37(4) (2016) 819–830.

14 SAR for Cultural Heritage Monitoring

Vignesh Kandasamy and Shashi Kumar

CONTENTS

14.1 REMOTE SENSING FOR CULTURAL HERITAGE SITES

The use of remote sensing for archaeological and cultural heritage started in 1981 when SIR-A (shuttle image radar) found subsurface valley and pale channels in the eastern Sahara [1]. The radar image, taken as part of AIRSAR Pacific Rim deployment in 1996, reveals the hidden temple of Angkor and its water system. AIRSAR has the benefit of long-wavelength P-band data, which can penetrate the soil surface to detect subsurface features, and was flown with the TOPSAR instrument in a DC-8 Aircraft; the TOPSAR uses radar interferometry to generate very high-resolution topographic maps [2]. As Angkor is densely covered with vegetation, the P-band SAR data was able to show significant details of the temple site. LiDAR technology is revolutionizing the field of archaeology with its unparalleled ability to penetrate the canopy of dense forests. LiDAR-based studies help in tropical environments where dense forest is often seen. The study reveals a low-density settlement complex, such as those found in ancient Mesoamerican urbanization in Caracol, Cayo, Belize, and Angamuco, Michoacán, Mexico [3]. The LiDAR-based study on Angkor reveals the greater undocumented details of the ancient cities. The small structure, densely covered in vegetation, and the magnitude of anthropogenic changes were revealed [4]. The cultural heritage site of Rome is widely known for its structural beauty. A two-scale, multi-sensor SBAS-DInSAR-based approach to find deformation from 1992 to 2000 was carried out with the help of ERS-1&2 and ENVISAT ASAR data [5]. Tapete and Cigna [6] proposed a multi-spatial/temporal hazard assessment for cultural heritage sites using rapid mapping and deformation analysis of PSI. The proposed methodology

DOI: 10.1201/9781003204466-14

313

was applied over Pitigliano and Bivigliano, located in northern and southern Tuscany, Italy [6]. The study carried out by Kumar et al. [7] gives a detailed analysis of deformation mapping of Angkor Wat for 12 years; the study used the Japan Aerospace Exploration Agency's (JAXA) data ALOS PALSAR-1 and ALOS PALSAR-2. The study uses all-weather monitoring satellites, such as microwave, to compute Angkor Wat's deformation using advanced persistent scatter interferometric synthetic aperture radar (PSInSAR) technique [8]–[11]. The PSInSAR uses permanent scatters [8], [10], [12] to find deformation, as the scatter will not change depending on the time. The study found that the Angkor Wat temple was stable from 2007 to 2009 and from 2014 to 2018. The study also found a negligible upliftment in Angkor Wat that might be due to the imbalance recharge of water around the moats and barays of Angkor Wat [7].

14.2 STUDY AREA

The ancient city of Angkor is located in Cambodia to the north of Lake Tonle Sap. Angkor is famous for its remnants of an ancient temple complex, which was constructed in laterite blocks, sandstones, and bricks [13]. The city of Angkor was 400 sq. km, and it was the political and spiritual heart of the Khmer Empire from the 9th to 15th centuries [14]. Angkor was home to hundreds of temples (see Figure 14.1); at the peak of the empire, the Khmer civilization expanded its power to most of Southeast Asia [15]. Angkor and its medieval temple complex have been a focus of intensive scholarly research and conservation for more than a century [14], [16]–[18]. Angkor had low-density urbanization [19] that could have held more than 5,00,000 people [4]. Understanding the urban morphology of Angkor will help researchers to understand the sustainability of urban landscapes. The advancement of remote sensing paved the way to discover the archaeological topography of the settlement complex, irrespective of the vegetation cover [20]. Using LiDAR, the study of the Greater Angkor project revealed that the city of Angkor extends over at least 35 km², further than the extent of the walls of Angkor Thom (9 km²) [4]. The LiDAR survey revealed a well-constructed gridded pattern of cities with canals and moats [14], [21]. The decline of Angkor might have resulted from the increasing trade opportunities in the 14th–15th century, which might have pulled elites to the southern coastal regions [22].

14.2.1 ANGKOR WAT

Angkor Wat was built by Khmer King Suryavaraman II in the early 12th century. Angkor Wat faces west rather than east as it was originally dedicated to Lord Vishnu, and then was transformed into

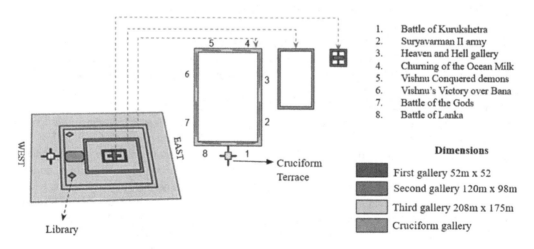

FIGURE 14.1 The structure Angkor Wat shown in a 2D image [7].

a Buddhist temple in the 12th century. The description of the temple given by Zhou Dagun in the 1290s provides the significance and importance of the temple and urban landscape during the period [14]. The integration of Angkor Wat into the central area of the low-density urban complex of Greater Angkor [23], [24] refused the convention modeled by Angkor of a series of small walled cities [14]. Angkor Wat is located to the south of Angkor Thom between East Baray and West Baray [24] at the coordinate 13.4125 N, 103.8670 E. In 1992, UNESCO declared Angkor Wat a World Heritage site due to its significance of structural beauty and its cultural heritage [25], [26]. Angkor Wat measures about 162.2 hectares (402 acres) with classical Khmer architecture as a temple mountain named Mount Meru, which is said to be the home of gods in Hindu and Buddhist mythology. The quincunx of the tower symbolizes the five peaks of the mountain, and the moat and the wall symbolize the mountain ranges and ocean [27]. Angkor Wat is a standing example of 12th-century Khmer architects skilled in the use of sandstone. The main building is made of sandstone, and the laterite is used for outer walls and hidden structures [28].

14.2.2 STRUCTURE

The Angkor Wat outer wall, which is made up of laterite with dimensions of 1,024 m × 802 m and stands 4.5 m high, is surrounded by a moat of 190 m wide and over 5 kilometers in perimeter, with an apron of open ground [21], [28]. The open space is covered with trees; the LiDAR survey from the Greater Angkor project found the orthogonal series of the mound that surrounded the temple and beyond the eastern moat [4], [21]. The moat is 5 km long and extends 1.5 kilometers from east to west and 1.3 kilometers from north to south [28], [29]. The outer wall encloses about 230 acres, including the temple and a low-density populated city, while in the north of Angkor Thom there is a royal palace. As the city was built using perishable materials rather than stones, only the outline of this structure remains under the forest [20]. A terrace raises the temple higher than the city. Angkor Wat is made up of three rectangle galleries, shown in Figure 14.1; each gallery is higher than the last. Each rectangle gallery has a gopura at the corners, and the inner galleries have towers forming a quincunx shape [14], [28], [30]. The lotus structure invokes the mythical Mount Meru [14], [31]. Towers connected by galleries are the basic elements of Khmer architecture [18]. The outer wall, which is made of laterite, also modified between the 13th and 17th centuries, perhaps for defensive purposes [29].

14.2.3 HYDRAULIC NETWORK

Bernard-Philippe Groslier of the École Française d'Extrême-Orient (EFEO) was the first researcher to focus on Angkor's remnants of a hydraulic network, which had been partially mapped in the first half of the 20th century [23]. The barays, or reservoirs, had inlets and outlets that were connected to a network of channels and embankments. Angkor Wat was connected with four inlets and one outlet canal. [16] recognized the southwest outlet as the Angkor canal that flows to the lake [21].

The extensive hydrological networks were well built for the extensive agriculture activity. The agricultural land might be interconnected with the local temple and the ponds surrounding the farmland. The pond in the city of Angkor might have been renovated and reused by the Khmer population until its decline. The Siem Reap river is engraved into the Angkorian flood plain to 5–8 m, which was a major canal up to the 14th century. The canal is filled with cross-bedded sands that indicates the rapid movement of sediments [24]. Many sites in South and Southeast Asia need to be examined using remote sensing to understand the heritage and trade aspects, particularly in tropical fields such as Anuradhapura and Polonnaruwa in Sri Lanka, Borobudur in Indonesia, Sambor Prei Kuk and Koh Ker in Cambodia, and Sukhothai in Thailand [23].

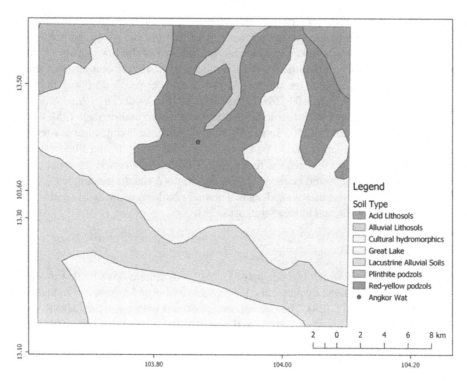

FIGURE 14.2   The soil type map of Angkor Wat.

14.2.4 GEOMORPHOLOGICAL

The geomorphological analysis from the 2015 trenches found that the Angkor Wat enclosure was part of the alluvial plain [32]. The alluvial plain is the highest productivity soil compared to other soil as it is highly porous [33]. The alluvium plain is usually covered with tall grasses, vegetation, and forest [34]. The geological aspect shown in Figure 14.2 and the tropical climate are favorable for the trees to grow. The gradual decline of the Angkorian Empire has led to the city of Angkor remaining untouched for centuries, thus possibly explaining the thick forest cover.

Angkor Wat was raised from the ground surface and flattened as a mound depression grid system [22]. The near-surface geology of Angkor was determined in 1994 by conducting a drill core, which revealed that the ancient and impermeable sandstone is overlaid by highly permeable quaternary sediments up to 80 m deep [13], [35].

Figure 14.3 shows Angkor Wat in multiple spaceborne SAR satellites. Figure 14.3(a) shows the Sentinel-1 image, which is a C-band satellite with a central wavelength of 5.54 cm. The C-band penetration capability is limited; in vegetation, the radar signals scatter from the canopy. The Angkor central building is shown as bright as high backscatters are seen. The L-band ALOS PALSAR shown in Figure 14.3(b) shows the advantage of L-band sensors, which have high penetration capability in dense vegetation. The long-wavelength SAR data will have high penetration, which gives higher coherence than other spaceborne SAR data [7]. The ALOS PALSAR-1 satellites have a central wavelength of 23.62 cm. All three galleries of Angkor Wat are visible from ALOS PALSAR images. The X-band Terra SAR-X, which is a high-resolution satellite from the German Space Agency (DLR), is shown in Figure 14.3(c). TerraSAR-X has a central X-band wavelength of 31 mm. The Angkor Wat gallery and its structure is seen in Figure 14.3(c). Compared to Sentinel-1 and ALOS PALSAR, the resolution and wavelength of TerraSAR and Tandem-X give an advantage for monitoring the heritage site.

Synoptic view of Angkor Wat from multiple Space borne SAR satellite:

FIGURE 14.3 Multifrequency SAR images: (a) C-band, (b) L-band, (c) X-band.

FIGURE 14.4 Intensity image of (a) Terra SAR-X, (b) Tandem-X.

TABLE 14.1
Different SAR Satellites and Their Details

Satellite	Band	Resolution (range by azimuth resolution)	Wavelength
Sentinel-1	C	5 × 20 m	5.54 cm
ALOS PALSAR-1	L	4.68 × 3.13 m	23.62 cm
ALOS PALSAR-2	L	4.29 × 3.97 m	22.9 cm
TerraSAR – X	X	1.36 × 1.86 m	31 mm

The Terra and Tandem images were acquired on 23 April 2011 from an ascending orbit, which is shown in Figure 14.4. The image was acquired in a strip map. The co-registered single look slant-range complex (COSSC) product was acquired by a right-facing antenna with a near incidence angle of 43.16 degrees and a far incidence angle of 45.50 degrees. The resolution of the TerraSAR-X is shown in Table 14.1

Figure 14.5 shows the coherence estimation of Angkor Wat from 2011 to 2013. The coherence image demonstrates structural changes with time. The higher the coherence, the less the change in

coh_HH_23Apr2011_23Apr2011 [coherence]

0.1   0.53   0.96

FIGURE 14.5   InSAR coherence map of Angkor Wat.

the structure, i.e., higher coherence of the phase of return signals will be preserved. In Figure 14.5, it is visible that the temple structure, which is a man-made feature, has very high coherence. The vegetation, which changes with respect to weather, has less coherence. The moat, which contains water, shows much less coherence. The Angkor Wat galleries, pathway, and western entrance can be detected from the coherence image.

Figure 14.6(a) shows the phase of the interferogram of Angkor Wat in the X-band TerraSAR-X data. TerraSAR-X and TanDEM-X are twin satellites that can acquire the interferometric acquisition without temporal decorrelation by operating these two satellites with an appropriate InSAR baseline. COSSC data are those products that were acquired by the satellites TerraSAR-X and TanDEM-X without any temporal gap in different polarimetric combinations. In June 2010, TanDEM-X joined the TerraSAR-X satellite to perform interferometric acquisitions as per the requirements [36]. The zero temporal decorrelation ensures the accuracy in the interferometric phase can be used for interferometric applications, mainly related to height estimation. However, the phase of the interferogram will have some noise due to atmospheric disturbances such as water vapor. These disturbances can be estimated and removed. Once the atmospheric disturbance is removed, the image will be free from errors and can be used to find the deformation. Figure 14.6(b) shows the phase of interferogram after atmospheric removal; the fringes are seen clearly, and such phase information is used to find the time series for the deformation monitoring of the cultural heritage site.

14.3   DATASET

The PSInSAR monitoring of Angkor Wat over a period of 15 years has been done in three time periods: (a) 2006 to 2009, (b) 2014 to 2018, and (c) 2017 to 2021.

(a) 2006 to 2009: Seven interferometric single look complex (SLC) data of JAXA ALOSPALSAR-1 from 2006 to 2009 were acquired in fine bean single polarization mode.

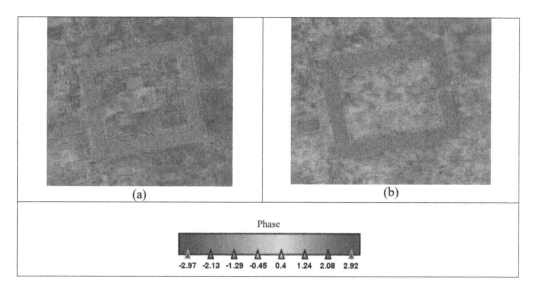

FIGURE 14.6 Interferogram of Angkor Wat.

The master image was taken on 31 December 2007. The highest spatial baseline of 1500 m can be seen from the data that was acquired on 28 December 2006, and the highest temporal baseline of 414 days can be seen from the data of 17 February 2009.

(b) 2014 to 2018: Ten interferometric SLC data of ALOS PALSAR-2 from 2014 to 2018 were acquired in fine bean double polarization mode. The master image was taken on 17 February 2016, and the highest spatial baseline of 300 m can be seen from the data of 15 February 2017.

(c) 2017 to 2021: Forty-nine SLC data of Sentinel-1 data were collected in interferometric wide (IW) swath mode from 2017 to 2021. The 49 data were acquired in ascending orbit, as all of the data need to be in the same orbit. The master image was selected on 14 May 2019. The largest spatial baseline of 77.56 meters can be seen on 14 December 2017, and the maximum temporal variation of 792 days can be seen on 13 March 2017. The temple structure seen in Figure 14.3 shows the mean amplitude of the study area from various satellites.

The temple structure, galleries, dense vegetation, and moat (a waterlogged area) are distinguishable in the image as the radar signal scatters these features differently [37]. The master image is selected based on comparatively minimal temporal and geometrical decorrelation [38].

14.4 PSINSAR PROCESSING OF SENTINEL DATA

PSInSAR processing to find the displacement over Angkor Wat is done using the SNAP-StaMPS workflow [39]. The entire process of estimating the surface deformation is shown in Figure 14.9 and these steps are explained.

The SNAP-StaMPS workflow is a semi-automated script that is written in Python 2 for PSInSAR processing. Once the master image is selected, basic pre-processing such as applying orbit file and TOPSAR split are done for all the images using slave_split.py. The co-registration of master and slave images is done and the co-registered image is used for interferometric processing. This interferogram, which has useful phase information, helps in further processing to find the long temporal pattern. An important step of this processing is to export the interferogram results to StaMPS [40] readable format; the export is done with the help of the stamps_export.py script. The advantage of PSInSAR is that the displacement is calculated using permanent features that have high coherence. The permanent candidates are selected based on the permanent scattering nature of the features [10],

Date	Bperp (m)	Btemp (days)	Date	Bperp (m)	Btemp (days)	Date	Bperp (m)	Btemp (days)	Date	Bperp (m)	Btemp (days)
28-Dec-16	1500	368	13-Mar-17	-8.77	792	05-Aug-18	25.95	282	15-Jan-20	28.48	-246
12-Feb-07	200	322	30-Apr-17	4.91	744	16-Sep-18	-27.88	240	14-Feb-20	13.96	-276
31-Dec-07	0	0	24-May-17	60.57	720	10-Oct-18	29.55	216	15-Mar-20	-19.49	-306
15-Feb-08	-900	46	29-Jun-17	4.07	684	03-Nov-18	15.29	192	14-Apr-20	-17.4	-336
01-Apr-08	-700	92	11-Jul-17	43.66	672	03-Dec-18	15.63	162	20-May-20	32.78	-372
02-Jan-09	750	368	04-Aug-17	-16.67	648	08-Jan-19	-13.22	126	13-Jun-20	0.9	-396
17-Feb-09	470	414	21-Sep-17	13.69	600	01-Feb-19	-0.8	102	19-Jul-20	13.04	-432
01-Oct-14	75	504	15-Oct-17	-14.37	576	15-Mar-19	18.36	60	18-Aug-20	51.21	-462
10-Dec-14	165	434	20-Nov-17	7.01	540	08-Apr-19	10.47	36	05-Sep-20	11.11	-480
18-Feb-15	-80	364	14-Dec-17	75.56	516	14-May-19	0	0	05-Oct-20	4.14	-510
30-Sep-15	-80	140	19-Jan-18	3.99	480	13-Jun-19	28.08	-30	04-Nov-20	6.32	-540
17-Feb-16	0	0	12-Feb-18	11.89	456	13-Jul-19	12.1	-60	04-Dec-20	-17.8	-570
28-Sep-16	-150	224	20-Mar-18	66.4	420	18-Aug-19	-34.98	-96	03-Jan-21	8.16	-600
15-Feb-17	300	364	25-Apr-18	17.17	384	17-Sep-19	13.04	-126	02-Feb-21	-15.82	-630
19-Jul-17	10	518	07-May-18	15	372	23-Oct-19	-21.77	-162	10-Mar-21	27.29	-666
29-Sep-17	30	590	12-Jun-18	-11.15	336	10-Nov-19	5.39	-180	ALOS PALSAR-1	ALOS PALSAR-2	Sentinel -1
31-Jan-18	175	714	18-Jul-18	-5.11	300	16-Dec-19	17.7	-216	Master Image		

FIGURE 14.7 Dataset used for the study of Angkor Wat monitoring.

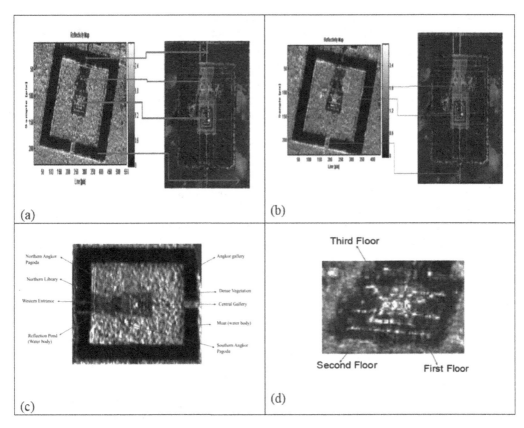

FIGURE 14.8   Appearance of Angkor Wat in SAR imageries: (a) ALOS PALSAR-1, (b)ALOS PALSAR-2, (c) Sentinel-1, and (d) central temple from ALOS PALSAR-1.

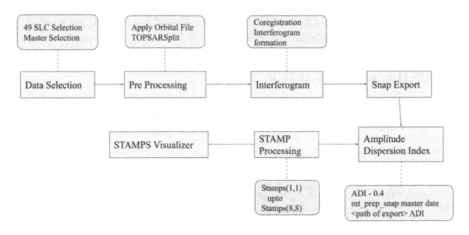

FIGURE 14.9   Workflow diagram of PSInSAR study using SNAP-StaMPS.

[41], [42]. The amplitude dispersion index (ADI) is defined as the temporal standard deviation to the temporal mean of the amplitude [38]. An amplitude dispersion value of 0.4 is chosen as this gives a good number of pixels with minimum decorrelation noise. The selection of an ADI of 0.4 gave way to select the high amplitude stability index. As the size of the study area is smaller, the numbers of

permanent scatters are minimal for ADI of 0.25. This can be due to the resolution of the image and noise due to the dense vegetation. So, an ADI of 0.4 is chosen.

The exported results are imported in Matlab for further processing. StaMPS helps to select the permanent scatters and also removes the weed pixels that are hindered by the atmosphere. The total stable pixels are 182 after the removal of weed pixels. After the removal, the remaining pixels are stable and have the phase that gives unambiguous phase information. The deformation can be measured by elimination of the other phase information except for the phase due to the ground movement [43].

14.5   RESULTS

The methodology described in the previous section is used to find the deformation of the temple from 2006 to 2009, 2014 to 2018, and 2017 to 2021. From Figure 14.13, it is found that the temple is stable. The mean amplitude image in Figure 14.8 shows the temple structure, library, western entrance, and moat.

14.5.1   PS IDENTIFICATION

There were 353 persistent scatterer (PS) points identified for ALSO PALSAR-1 from 2006 to 2009, and 805 points are identified from 2014 to 2018 using ALOS PALSAR-2. The amplitude stability index (ASI) of 0.8 is used for 2006 to 2009 and an ASI value of 0.7 to find the persistent scatters. After the APS removal, the number of scatters is reduced to 168 for 2006 to 2009 and 204 for 2014 to 2018.

More than 5400 pixels are selected using an ASI of 0.6 for Sentinel-1 data from 2017 to 2021. There are a total of 492 PS candidates that are selected in this step of StaMPS processing. Among the 492 PS candidates, only 267 PS are selected after the re-estimation of coherence. The temporal coherence is high for the temple structure, as seen in Figure 14.5, as the man-made features are not affected by any temporal variation [44], [45].

The advantage of SAR is its all-weather property, which helps to monitor the cultural heritage site in seasonal conditions, but the water vapor in the atmosphere causes some noise. The noise due to the atmosphere is estimated and removed. After the removal of weed pixels, the number of stable pixels is 182 in all the interferograms.

14.5.2   LOS DISPLACEMENT OF 2006 TO 2009

The line-of-sight (LOS) displacement of Angkor Wat is analyzed from 2006 to 2009 with seven SLC data from the ALOS PALSAR-1 satellite. The deformation analysis is done with the help of

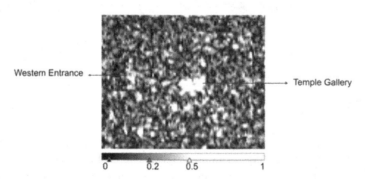

FIGURE 14.10   Coherence image of Angkor Wat.

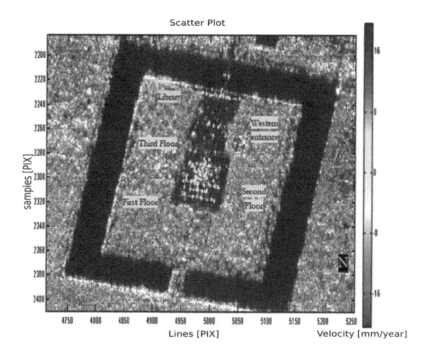

FIGURE 14.11   LOS displacement of Angkor Wat from 2006 to 2009.

the PSInSAR technique to the displacement in mm scale. The deformation ranges from −20 mm/ year to +20 mm/year. The positive values indicate the movement towards the sensor, and the negative value indicates the movement away from the sensor. From Figure 14.11, the first galleries and second galleries with the green dot say that the galleries are stable. The third gallery seems to be stable with minor upliftment near the northern entrance. The Angkor Wat structure is stable between 2006 to 2009.

14.5.3   LOS DISPLACEMENT OF 2014 TO 2018

The LOS displacement of Angkor Wat is analyzed from 2014 to 2018 with ten SLC data from the ALOS PALSAR-2 satellite. The deformation analysis is done with the help of the PSInSAR technique to the displacement in mm scale. The deformation ranges from −20 mm/year to +20 mm/year. The positive values indicate the movement towards the sensor and the negative value indicates the movement away from the sensor. From Figure 14.12, there seems to be an upliftment of 8 mm near the northern side of the second gallery. The western entrance also shows some upliftment of 16 mm, which could be due to the water recharge work carried out by the APSARA foundation.

14.5.4   LOS DISPLACEMENT 2017 TO 2021

The LOS displacement over Angkor Wat is analyzed from 2017 to 2021 with 49 SLC data from the Sentinel-1 satellite. The displacement analysis is done with the help of the PSInSAR technique to find displacement at the mm scale. The displacement ranges from −4 mm/ year to 5 mm/year. The positive values indicated movement towards the sensor and the negative values indicate movement away from the sensor. The −4 mm is represented as dark red, which indicates subsidence, and + 4 mm is represented as dark blue, which indicates upliftment. Figure 14.13 shows the displacement over Angkor Wat and its surroundings.

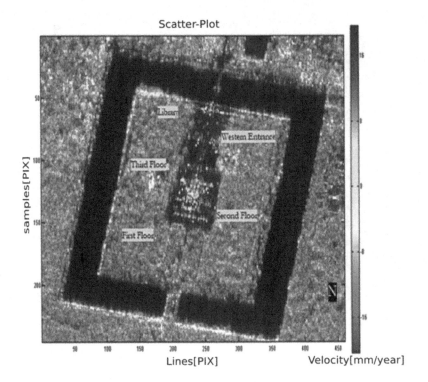

FIGURE 14.12 LOS displacement of Angkor Wat from 2014 to 2018.

FIGURE 14.13 LOS displacement of Angkor Wat from 2017 to 2021.

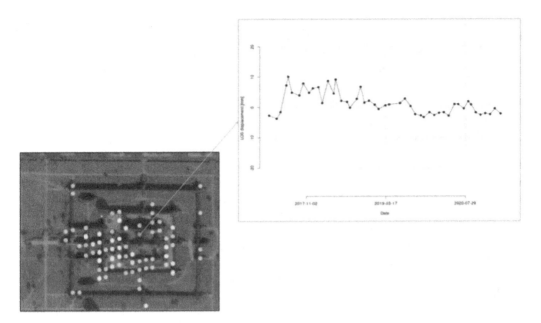

FIGURE 14.14 LOS displacement of Angkor Wat galleries and time-series information of central tower from 2017 to 2021.

The second and third gallery look stable as they are represented by green dots. The first gallery is also stable as it is represented by the green dot. The western entrance, which is 230 m long [28], is represented as a pale blue dot that indicates upliftment of less than 2 mm.

Figure 14.14 shows the time-series information from 2017 to 2021 over the central tower in the first gallery. The linear trend seems to points toward subsidence. But the subsidence is very low at less than −2 mm/year. The southern Angkor pagoda shown in Figure 14.14 seems to have a subsidence of higher than −4 mm.

14.6   DISCUSSION

The monitoring of Angkor Wat using advanced remote sensing techniques helps to protect the heritage site. The monitoring of Angkor Wat from 2011 to 2013 with high-resolution data such as TerraSAR/TanDEM shows an annual deformation of −3 mm to +3 mm [13]. The monitoring of Angkor Wat using L-band ALOS PALSAR-1 from 2006 to 2009 and ALOS PALSAR-2 from 2014 to 2018 shows deformation ranges from + 4 mm to +16 mm and −4 mm to −10 mm. The 12 years of monitoring in [7] uses a maximum of only seven images from 2014 to 2018 due to the availability of ALOS PALSAR-1 over the study area and the high cost of ALOS PALSAR-2 data acquisition. The PSInSAR analysis required a minimum of 20 images for accurate estimation of deformation [39]. The ESA sentinel open data policy gave a way to use 49 Sentinel-1 SLC images for 2017 to 2021. This gives a reliable estimate of deformation over Angkor Wat from 2017 to 2021. The deformation analysis of Angkor Wat shown in Figure 14.14 says the temple is stable from 2017 to 2021. The deformation ranges from −4 mm/year to +5 mm/year, which nearly matches with the Tomo-InSAR work done by [13] using TerraSAR-X and TanDEM -X.

The temple center tower in the first gallery has minimum subsidence that is seen only in this study. The western entrance, which shows some upliftment, is seen in the previous study from 2014 to 2018. This upliftment is also correlated with restoration work such as "Enhancing and restoring water systems in Angkor World Heritage Site and Siem Reap City" [7], [46]. Several research works have addressed the issues related to water extraction near Angkor due to the booming tourism, but the global tourism sector is very weak due to Covid-19, so such extraction of water may be neglected for at least a year from March 2020. The subsistence of −4 mm seen in the building near the Angkor temple can be set aside as the deformation is minimum. The software used for PSInSAR analysis is developed to remove most possible errors, but we cannot neglect the error associated with different sources of the InSAR measurement and estimation of PSI [47], [48].

14.7 CONCLUSION

In this study, advanced InSAR monitoring such as PSInSAR is used to monitor the deformation of Angkor Wat from March 2017 to March 2021. A stack of 49 interferograms is used in this study to monitor the deformation. From 2017 to 2021, the temple is found to be stable with a negligible deformation range of −4 mm/year to +5 mm/year. The increase in the number of images helps to give an accurate view of the deformation over Angkor Wat. The booming of tourism is always speculated [20] as a cause for the deformation monitoring of Angkor Wat and its surrounding areas. The recent global lockdown due to Covid-19, which has led to a weak tourism sector in Cambodia, is also a factor in neglecting the water extraction factor for deformation. But these correlations can be made only with reliable water extraction data over the Siem Reap and its surroundings. The importance of an open data policy is stated in this research work. The ancillary data of the cultural heritage sites and their surroundings need to be collected and stored regularly. These open data will lead to high-quality research with multiple correlation factors in and around the cultural heritage sites. After a pandemic like Covid-19, the importance of data and open data policies need to be seriously taken into consideration even for cultural heritage sites. The monitoring of cultural heritage sites is necessary to preserve the ancient remains in the modern world, and such work needs to be encouraged among younger generations for continued monitoring of Angkor and its surroundings.

REFERENCES

[1] J. F. McCauley et al., "Subsurface valleys and geoarcheology of the Eastern Sahara revealed by shuttle radar," *Science (80-).*, vol. 218, no. 4576, pp. 1004–1020, Dec. 1982.

[2] A. Freeman and S. Hensley, "Analysis of radar images of Angkor," *IEEE*, pp. 2572–2574, 1999.

[3] A. F. Chase, D. Z. Chase, C. T. Fisher, S. J. Leisz, and J. F. Weishampel, "Geospatial revolution and remote sensing LiDAR in Mesoamerican archaeology," *Proc. Natl. Acad. Sci. U. S. A.*, vol. 109, no. 32, pp. 12916–12921, 2012.

[4] D. H. Evans et al., "Uncovering archaeological landscapes at Angkor using lidar," *Proc. Natl. Acad. Sci. U. S. A.*, vol. 110, no. 31, pp. 12595–12600, 2013.

[5] G. Zeni et al., "Long-term deformation analysis of historical buildings through the advanced SBAS-DInSAR technique: The case study of the city of Rome, Italy," *J. Geophys. Eng.*, vol. 8, no. 3, 2011.

[6] D. Tapete and F. Cigna, "Rapid mapping and deformation analysis over cultural heritage and rural sites based on persistent scatterer interferometry," *Int. J. Geophys.*, vol. 2012, no. September, 2012.

[7] S. Kumar, S. K. Vignesh, A. Babu, P. K. Thakur, and S. Agrawal, "PSInSAR-based surface deformation mapping of Angkor Wat cultural heritage site," *J. Indian Soc. Remote Sens.*, vol. 7, no. Kabirdoss 2017, 2020.

[8] P. Gonnuru and S. Kumar, "PsInSAR based land subsidence estimation of Burgan oil field using TerraSAR-X data," *Remote Sens. Appl. Soc. Environ.*, vol. 9, no. November, 2017, pp. 17–25, 2017.

[9] L. Solari, A. Ciampalini, F. Raspini, S. Bianchini, and S. Moretti, "PSInSAR analysis in the Pisa urban area (Italy): A case study of subsidence related to stratigraphical factors and urbanization," *Remote Sens.*, vol. 8, no. 2, 2016.

[10] A. Ferretti, A. Fumagalli, F. Novali, C. Prati, F. Rocca, and A. Rucci, "A new algorithm for processing interferometric data-stacks: SqueeSAR," *IEEE Trans. Geosci. Remote Sens.*, vol. 49, no. 9, pp. 3460–3470, 2011.

[11] A. Hassan et al., "Land subsidence monitoring using persistent scatterer InSAR (PSInSAR) in Kelantan catchment."

[12] J. W. Bell, F. Amelung, A. Ferretti, M. Bianchi, and F. Novali, "Monitoring aquifer-system response to groundwater pumping and artificial recharge," *First Break*, vol. 26, no. 8, pp. 85–91, 2008.

[13] F. Chen et al., "Radar interferometry offers new insights into threats to the Angkor site," *Sci. Adv.*, vol. 3, no. 3, p. 9, 2017.

[14] R. Fletcher, D. Evans, C. Pottier, and C. Rachna, "Angkor Wat: An introduction," *Antiquity*, vol. 89, no. 348, pp. 1388–1401, 2015.

[15] F. R. Evans Damian and Hanus Kasper, "The story beneath the canopy: An airborne Lidar survey over Angkor, Phnom Kulen and Koh Ker, Northwestern Cambodia," in *Across Space and Time Papers from the 41st Conference on Computer Applications and Quantitative Methods in Archaeology*, 2013, no. March, pp. 25–28.

[16] C. Pottier, "Some evidence of an inter-relationship between hydraulic Features and Rice field patterns at Angkor during ancient times (the hydraulic city in Asia: The huge monuments in terms of the relationship between agriculture and water)," *Journal of Asian Studies*, no. 18 2000.

[17] S. Kak, "The solar number in Angkor Wat," *Indian J. Hist. Scinece*, vol. 34, no. 2, p. 127, 1999.

[18] G. Croci, "Structural damage and remedial measures for the temples of Angkor, Cambodia," *Struct. Eng. Int.*, vol. 11, no. 4, pp. 234–236, 2001.

[19] A. Carter, P. Heng, M. Stark, R. Chhay, and D. Evans, "Urbanism and residential patterning in Angkor," 2018.

[20] F. Chen, "Radar remote sensing for the Angkor World Heritage site," 2015. [Online]. Available: http://earth.esa.int/heritage/2015-events/15m38/Presentations/29_Chen.pdf. [Accessed: 20-Jul-2018].

[21] D. Evans and R. Fletcher, "The landscape of Angkor Wat redefined," *Antiquity*, vol. 89, no. 348, pp. 1402–1419, 2015.

[22] A. K. Carter et al., "Temple occupation and the tempo of collapse at Angkor Wat, Cambodia," *Proc. Natl. Acad. Sci. U. S. A.*, vol. 116, no. 25, pp. 12226–12231, 2019.

[23] D. Evans et al., "A comprehensive archaeological map of the world's largest preindustrial settlement complex at Angkor, Cambodia," *Proc. Natl. Acad. Sci. U. S. A.*, vol. 104, no. 36, pp. 14277–14282, 2007.

[24] R. J. Fletcher et al., "Redefining Angkor: Structure and environment in the largest, low density urban complex of the pre-industrial world," *Udaya J. Khmer Stud.*, vol. 4, no. October 2018, pp. 107–121, 2003.

[25] J. Wager, "Environmental planning for a world heritage site: Case study of Angkor, Cambodia," *J. Environ. Plan. Manag.*, vol. 38, no. 3, pp. 419–434, 1995.

[26] W. H. Committee, "Convention concerning the protection of the world cultural and natural heritage. Santa Fe.," Santa Fe, USA, 1992.

[27] M. S. Falser, *Cultural Heritage as Civilizing Mission: From Decay to Recovery*. Springer International, 2011.

[28] M. Petrotchenko, *Focusing on the Angkor Temples: The Guidebook*, 4th ed. Cambodia, 2017.

[29] D. Brotherson, "The fortification of Angkor Wat," *Antiquity*, vol. 89, no. 348, pp. 1456–1472, 2015.

[30] Glaize Maurice, *A Guide Book to the Angkor Monuments*, 4th ed. Siem Reap, 2009.

[31] C. Higham, *Encyclopedia of Ancient Asian Civilizations*. New York, Facts On File, 2004.

[32] W. C. Rasmussen and G. M. Bradford, *Ground-Water Resources of Cambodia*. US, 1977.

[33] K. C. Anup and S. Kalu, "Chapter 11 – soil pollution status and its remediation in Nepal," K. R. Hakeem, M. Sabir, M. Öztürk, and A. R. B. T.-S. R. and P. Mermut, Eds. San Diego: Academic Press, 2015, pp. 313–329.

[34] A. Dwevedi, P. Kumar, P. Kumar, Y. Kumar, Y. K. Sharma, and A. M. Kayastha, "15 – soil sensors: Detailed insight into research updates, significance, and future prospects," A. M. B. T.-N. P. and S. S. Grumezescu, Eds. Academic Press, 2017, pp. 561–594.

[35] T. F. Sonnemann, D. O'Reilly, C. Rachna, R. Fletcher, and C. Pottier, "The buried 'towers' of Angkor Wat," *Antiquity*, vol. 89, no. 348, pp. 1420–1438, 2015.

[36] T. Fritz, H. Breit, C. Rossi, U. Balss, M. Lachaise, and S. Duque, "Interferometric processing and products of the TanDEM-X mission," in *2012 IEEE International Geoscience and Remote Sensing Symposium*, 2012, pp. 1904–1907.

[37]   M. Ouarzeddine, B. Souissi, and A. Belhadj-Aissa, "Classification of polarimetric SAR images based on scattering mechanisms," *5th Int. Symp. Spat. Data Qual. SDQ 2007, Model. Qual. Sp. time*, vol. XXXVI, no. 2-C43, pp. 1–6, 2007.

[38]   A. Ferretti, C. Prati, and F. Rocca, "Permanent scatters in SAR interferometry," *IEEE Trans. Geosci. Remote Sens.*, vol. 39, no. 1, pp. 8–20, 2001.

[39]   M. Foumelis et al., "ESA SNAP – stamps integrated processing for Sentinel-1 persistent scatterer interferometry," *Int. Geosci. Remote Sens. Symp.*, vol. 2018, no. July, pp. 1364–1367, 2018.

[40]   A. Hooper, "StaMPS/MTI Manual Version 3.1," Delft Institute of Earth Observation and Space Systems, Delft University of Technology, 2009.

[41]   M. Crosetto, O. Monserrat, A. Jungner, and B. Crippa, "Persistent scatterer interferometry: potential and limits," 2010.

[42]   N. Devanthéry, M. Crosetto, O. Monserrat, M. Cuevas-González, and B. Crippa, "An approach to persistent scatterer interferometry," *Remote Sens.*, vol. 6, no. 7, pp. 6662–6679, 2014.

[43]   R. F. Hanssen, "Satellite radar interferometry for deformation monitoring: A priori assessment of feasibility and accuracy," *Int. J. Appl. Earth Obs. Geoinf.*, vol. 6, pp. 253–260, 2004.

[44]   A. Babu and S. Kumar, "SBAS interferometric analysis for volcanic eruption of Hawaii island," *J. Volcanol. Geotherm. Res.*, vol. 370, pp. 31–50, 2019.

[45]   P. Gonnuru and S. Kumar, "PsInSAR based land subsidence estimation of Burgan oil field using TerraSAR-X data," *Remote Sens. Appl. Soc. Environ.*, vol. 9, pp. 17–25, Nov. 2017.

[46]   C. Sok, "Enhancing and restoring water systems in Angkor world heritage site and Siem Reap city," 2017.

[47]   P. J. González and J. Fernndez, "Error estimation in multitemporal InSAR deformation time series, with application to Lanzarote, Canary Islands," *J. Geophys. Res. Solid Earth*, vol. 116, no. 10, pp. 1–17, 2011.

[48]   J. Tu, D. Gu, Y. Wu, and D. Yi, "Error modeling and analysis for InSAR spatial baseline determination of satellite formation flying," *Math. Probl. Eng.*, vol. 2012, p. 140301, 2012.

15 Extraction and Evaluation of Lineaments From DEMs Generated from Different Bands of Microwave Data and Optical Data
A Case Study for Jahazpur Area, Bhilwara, India

Pralay Bhaumik, Himanshu Govil, Shashi Kumar, and Sankaran Rajendran

CONTENTS

DOI: 10.1201/9781003204466-15

15.1 INTRODUCTION

Lineaments are linear or near-linear features of different types on the earth's surface (Han et al., 2018). In remote sensing, lineaments are linear features that include cultural features and man-made structures such as canals, dams, roads, etc. (Farahbakhsh et al., 2018). Lineaments represent different geological features, such as shear zones/faults, fold axial traces, lines of sedimentary facies change, alignment of water channels, streams, and valleys, and zones of mineralization (Karaca and Bozcu, 2019). Usually, lineaments are substantially long, which makes them difficult to measure by field surveys, and can only be adequately exploited with the help of remote sensing data (Nyaberi et al., 2019). Many times, the lineaments are covered by deep vegetation and soil and are located in an area that is difficult to access and investigate (Han et al., 2018). These can be mapped and studied with the help of remote sensing data that covers a large area.

Mapping of lineaments can be carried out using both optical and synthetic aperture radar (SAR) data (Abdelkareem et al., 2020). However, the manifestation of a lineament is dependent on the scale of observation and dimensions involved (Javhar et al., 2019; Mohammadi et al., 2020). Recent studies have shown that digital elevation models (DEMs) generated from SAR data are suitable to extract lineaments (Fentahun et al., 2021). Also, DEMs outperform in the extraction of lineaments from raw satellite data in terms of accuracy and consistency of length of the lineaments extracted (Das et al., 2018; Soliman and Han, 2019).

Visualization of DEM in terms of shaded relief helps to bring out many important features of the geology of an area, those that otherwise may remain unnoticed. Shaded relief maps can be generated from different sun azimuth angles and then combined to identify the lineaments accurately. In this process, the combined image brings out a higher edge gradient value (in terms of DN values of boundary pixels), which can subsequently be used in edge detection and lineament extraction. Lineaments can be extracted from shaded relief maps by visual or digital interpretation of DEMs (Rajasekhar et al., 2018). Visual extraction and interpretation of lineaments are time consuming and subject to personal biases and experiences, while digital interpretation and mapping methods are fast, consistent, and more objective (Farahbakhsh et al., 2018). Automatic lineament extraction by digital mapping methods is popularized by the introduction of computing facilities and robust algorithms (Barkah and Daud, 2021).

In this method, the use of SAR imaging has advantages when compared with optical data since images can be acquired both day or night and under all weather conditions, and can further be used to identify small topographic reliefs with relatively high resolution (Tsuchida et al., 1990; Moreira et al., 2013; Inggs and Lord, 2015; Priya and Pandey, 2021).

High resolution and highly accurate DEMs can be generated from interferometric SAR data, where "two SAR images acquired in the same area with a nearly identical incidence angle (one usually regarded as master and the other slave) are combined to produce a phase interference image called an interferogram" (Ba et al., 2012; Grohmann, 2018). The separation of the antennas, called the baseline measurement, is the most important criterion for DEM generation (Wegmüller, 1997; Venkataraman et al., 2006). The baseline measurement should be large enough to have the required height accuracy; at the same time, it should be small enough to get rid of large decorrelation. A trade off between accuracy and decorrelation is required to achieve an optimum value (Zhang et al., 2019).

However, there will always be some differences between lineaments extracted automatically from DEMs generated from different data sources, for example, DEMs generated from microwave data and those generated from optical data (Razoki et al., 2019; Army and Saepuloh, 2020). The major share of these differences is attributable to quality of the DEMs used, in terms of both resolution (spacing) and vertical accuracy (Soliman and Han, 2019; Ferreira and Cabral, 2021).

This study aims to extract the lineaments of the Jahazpur area, Bhilwara, India, which is a hydrothermal alteration zone for mineralization. The study extracts and maps the general pattern of linear features from DEMs generated using C-band SAR data, L-band SAR data, and optical data and evaluates using lineament density maps and rose diagrams.

15.2 STUDY AREA

The study area is located at Jahazpur, within the Bhilwara district of Rajasthan state, India (as shown in Figure 15.1 below). The Jahazpur area is associated with several major to minor hillocks in random order. The average height of the study area from mean sea level (MSL) is approximately 324 m. The altitude variation of the study area is from 247 m to 505 m above sea level, which represents moderate relief. The extent of the study area in terms of latitude and longitude is 25°17′ N–25°54′ N and 74°51′ E–75° 23′ E. The total area of the study site is about 3,500 km². The main river flowing through the study area is Banas River.

15.2.1 GEOLOGICAL SETTINGS OF THE STUDY AREA

The area of study is divided into three parts based on geological settings, namely Jahazpur group, Mangalwar complex, and Hindoli group of rocks (Tripathi, 2019b). The Jahazpur group is further divided into two parts: the Eastern Jahazpur belt and the Western Jahazpur belt (Tripathi, 2019a). The Jahazpur group of rocks is covered by the Hindoli group of rocks on the eastern side, while the western side is surrounded by Mangalwar complex, which belongs to the Archaean age (Tripathi and Govil, 2019). Two parallel dolomitic quartzite ridges are striking from NW to SE. The Banas River is filled with deposition of quaternary sediments, which intercept the ridges at various places

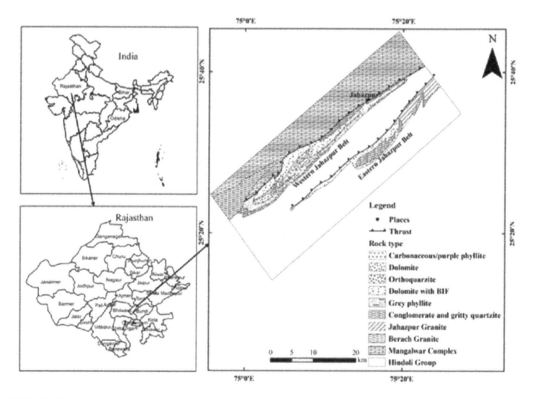

FIGURE 15.1   Map of study area.

in NE–SW and west–east directions (Tripathi, 2019c). There are three major rock types, namely the dolomite, quartzite, and phyllite. The dolomite is associated with banded iron formations (BIFs) in some places. The major minerals of the area are talc, clay, marble, mica, quartz, feldspar, and copper (Govil et al., 2018).

15.3 DATA USED

15.3.1 MICROWAVE DATA

In this study, the C-band data (frequency 5.405 GHz) of Sentinel-1A and L-band data (frequency 1270 MHz) of PALSAR of ALOS-1 have been used. Data acquired during the monsoon period and post-monsoon period were deliberately shelved to have minimum decorrelation within the interferometric pairs caused by atmospheric disturbances or vegetation outgrowth. While choosing the interferometric pairs, we noted the separation of antennas, called the baseline measurement. This is one of the important features to identify correlation between the members of an interferometric pair. Two interferometric pairs with the most suitable baseline measurements were identified and studied, both of which, incidentally, were acquired during the winter months.

15.3.1.1 Sentinel-1A

Sentinel-1 is a space mission of the Copernicus Programme of the European Space Agency (ESA) consisting of the constellation of two satellites. The payload of Sentinel-1 is a SAR in C-band that provides continuous imagery with a repeat cycle of 12 days. Single look complex (SLC) product captured in interferometric wide (IW) swath mode has been used in the current study. SLC product was used as it includes single look in each dimension using the full transmit signal bandwidth and consists of complex samples preserving the phase information. IW mode captures three sub-swaths using terrain observation with progressive scans SAR (TOPSAR). In the TOPSAR technique, in addition to steering the beam in range, the beam is also electronically steered from backward to forward in the azimuth direction for each burst, resulting in homogeneous image quality throughout the swath. Description of Sentinel-1A data used in the present study is furnished in Table 15.1.

15.3.1.2 ALOS-I PALSAR

The advanced land observation satellite (ALOS) is a satellite observation program by Japan Aerospace Exploration Agency (JAXA). ALOS-I phased array type L-band synthetic aperture radar

TABLE 15.1
Description of Sentinel-1A Data

Date	Mode	Type	Pass	Orbit	Base
05.12.2018	IW	SLC	Desc	24883	144 m
17.12.2018	IW	SLC	Desc	25058	

TABLE 15.2
Description of ALOS-I PALSAR Data

Date	Mode	Type	Pass	Orbit	Base
02.01.2007	FBS	SLC	Asc	5013	1,784 m
17.02.2007	FBS	SLC	Asc	5684	

TABLE 15.3
Data Used in This Chapter

Serial No.	Data	Date	Type of Data	Referred to Here as
1.	Sentinel-1A	05.12.2018 and 17.12.2018	Raw satellite imagery	Sentinel-1A (generated)
2.	ALOS-1 PALSAR	02.01.2007 and 17.02.2007	Raw satellite imagery	ALOS data (generated)
3.	ALOS-1 PALSAR	02.01.2007 and 17.02.2007	DEM	ALOS DEM (downloaded)
4.	ALOS PRISM		DEM	AW3D30 (downloaded)
5.	Google Earth	29.12.2020 and 13.12.2018	Raster data and Terrain altitude	Google Earth

(PALSAR) is a satellite-based SAR sensor that operates in the L-band and has a temporal resolution of 46 days. This sensor utilizes the L-band frequency (1.27 GHz, 24 cm) with an incident angle of 34.3°. The selected scene of fine beam single (FBS) mode acquisition has a product level of 1.5 and contains 10 m of spatial resolution. The data used here are able to enhance the near-surface structures. Description of ALOS-I PALSAR data used in the present study is furnished in Table 15.2.

ALOS-I PALSAR satellite images can be used for producing a DEM (Bannari et al., 2016). In addition to the raw data of ALOS-I PALSAR, high resolution (12.5 m) DEMs generated from ALOS-I PALSAR data are also available in open source. This downloaded DEM provides an additional benchmark for the extraction of lineaments and further comparison with the other results of this study.

15.3.2 OPTICAL DATA

15.3.2.1 ALOS World 3D-30m (AW3D30)

ALOS World 3D-30m (AW3D30) is a global DEM dataset generated from the panchromatic remote sensing instrument for stereo mapping (PRISM) onboard the ALOS satellite, which was operational from 2006 to 2011. The AW3D project generated a DEM or digital surface model (DSM) with a spatial resolution of approximately 5 m, which is the densest global-scale elevation raster available commercially (Sedeek, 2019). AW3D30 is a free global DSM dataset with a spatial resolution of approximately 30 m (1 arcsec in latitude and longitude). It is a resampled version of the 5-meter mesh of the AW3D DSM dataset (Japan Aerospace Exploration Agency, 1997). Recent studies have shown the suitability of AW3D DEM with other open source DEMs (Sedeek, 2019; Takaku et al., 2014). In some other research, the AW3D30 has been used as reference data because of the unavailability of ground control points (Soliman and Han, 2019). In the present study, AW3D30 has been utilized as a benchmark elevation raster. Google Earth web portal has also been used for interpretation and validation of results.

The datasets used in this study are provided in Table 15.3

15.4 METHODOLOGY

The methodology of this study is as follows, which has been graphically represented in Figure 15,2.

15.4.1 GENERATION OF DEM

In this study, DEMs were generated from interferometric SAR data of C-band (Sentinel-1A) and L-band (ALOS PALSAR). One advantage of using the L-band image is its ability to see through vegetation canopies owing to the penetration capability of microwave pulses having a long wavelength (23.62 cm) (Maghsoudi et al., 2018).

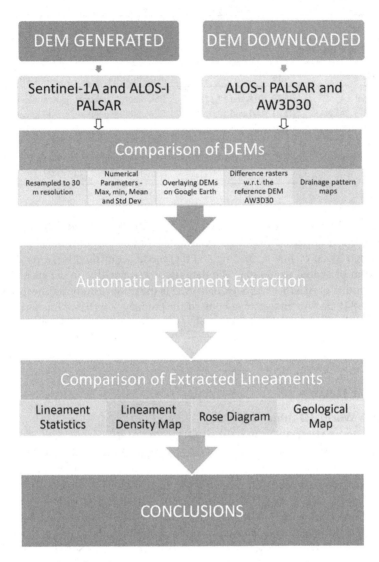

FIGURE 15.2 Methodology flow chart.

15.4.1.1 Sentinel-1A

As per the extent of the study area, Sentinel-1A data sub-swath IW3 and bursts 5 to 8 were found to be adequate; hence, this portion of the data was split from both the raw scenes. The following steps were applied in ESA SNAP software to generate DEM from Sentinel-1A interferometric pair:

1. S1 TOPS co-registration
2. Creating interferogram
3. Debursting
4. Goldstein phase filtering
5. Exporting to Snaphu, unwrapping, and importing back
6. Phase to elevation
7. Range-doppler terrain correction

Sentinel-1A precise orbit files and SRTM 3 sec DEM were auto-downloaded during processing.

15.4.1.2 ALOS-I PALSAR

The ALOS-I PALSAR data of the study area is covered in two parts, namely Frame 490 and Frame 500, and thus DEMs were also generated in two parts in this study. The following steps were applied in ESA SNAP software to generate DEM from ALOS-I PALSAR interferometric pair:

(1) DEM-assisted co-registration
(2) Interferogram formation
(3) Phase filtering
(4) Exporting to Snaphu, unwrapping, and importing back
(5) Phase to elevation
(6) Range-doppler terrain correction

SRTM 3 sec DEMs were auto-downloaded during processing of ALOS-I PALSAR interferometric data. Two partial DEMs were blended to form the whole DEM of the study area.

15.4.2 COMPARISON OF DEMs

The four DEMs included in this study are: (i) the DEM generated from Sentinel-1A data, (ii) the DEM generated from ALOS-I PALSAR data, (iii) the downloaded ALOS-I PALSAR DEM (pertaining to the same date of acquisition), and (iv) the downloaded AW3D30. All DEMs were resampled to 30 m resolution and subset to study area before comparison. All the images were registered in the WGS84 UTM Zone 43N coordinate system. The DEMs were examined in terms of their basic numerical parameters, namely, maximum elevation, minimum elevation, mean, and standard deviation of elevation values, by overlaying them on Google Earth web portal, and through computation of difference rasters with respect to the reference DEM (AW3D30). In addition, the drainage pattern maps were extracted from each DEM and superimposed on the same map. Thus, the consistency of the DEMs was assured. The DEM comparison tasks were carried out using ArcGIS and Global Mapper software.

The differences between the DEM generated from ALOS-I PALSAR data and the corresponding downloaded DEM (available in the open source) were found to be negligible. This very fact indirectly supported correctness of the ALOS-I PALSAR DEM generated as part of this chapter.

15.4.3 AUTOMATIC LINEAMENT EXTRACTION

To enhance accurate detection of lineaments, shaded relief maps were generated using sun azimuths at $0°$, $45°$, $90°$, and $135°$. The final shaded relief maps were prepared by combining the rasters from the four different azimuth angles into a single raster. The combined shaded relief map for each DEM is processed through the LINE algorithm available in PCI Geomatica software. The software automatically extracts the lineaments using six parameters, namely the radius of filter in pixels (RADI), threshold for edge gradient (GTHR), threshold for curve length (LTHR), threshold for line fitting error (FTHR), threshold for angular difference (ATHR), and threshold for linking distance (DTHR). Several combinations of parameter settings were tried, and a suitable combination of parameters was chosen to be used in this study. It was found that by changing the value of GTHR to 30 (from default value 100) and keeping the other values as default, a substantially good correspondence was achieved between the automatically extracted lineaments and those detected by visual inspection. In brief, the GTHR represents edge gradient threshold, which is the minimum value of gradient (jump or drop in DN value) to be considered as an edge during edge detection. Thus, by reducing the value of GTHR parameter to 30, the algorithm became capable of detecting some additional lineaments, which are otherwise dull and obscured because of vegetation growth or view angle. In each case, the minimum length of extracted lineament was 900 m as all datasets were resampled to 30 m resolution, and the LTHR parameter in PCI Geomatica (which signifies the minimum length of curve, in pixels) was fixed at 30 pixels.

15.4.4 COMPARISON OF EXTRACTED LINEAMENTS

The extracted lineaments are first examined in terms of fundamental statistics calculated from them, namely the number of lineaments, total length, maximum length, and then in terms of the lineament density maps. In the final stage, the results are studied with the geological map of the study area.

15.5 RESULTS

Figure 15.3 shows the DEM generated from Sentinel-1A data and overlaid on the Google Earth image. Here all the water channels and high ground are depicted at their correct locations. We examined all the DEMs and verified in the same manner. Figure 15.4 shows the ALOS-I PALSAR DEM, resampled to 30 m resolution and clipped to the common area.

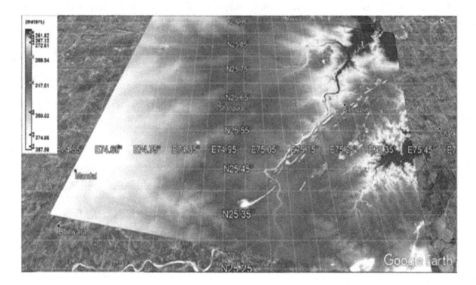

FIGURE 15.3   DEM generated from Sentinel-1A data overlaid on Google Earth.

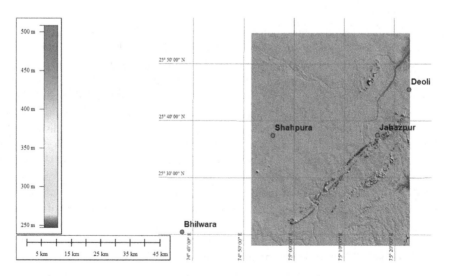

FIGURE 15.4   DEM generated from ALOS-I PALSAR, resampled to 30 m resolution, and clipped to the common area of overlap.

The statistics calculated from the elevation figures, namely the maximum, minimum, mean, and standard deviation of all four DEMS, are summarized in Table 15.4. It shows that all the DEMs generated from microwave data exhibit absolute consistency. However, there is a discrete gap of around 50 m in the case of the elevation values projected by the DEM generated from optical data (AW3D30). The average height of AW3D30 is approx. 50 m higher than the other three DEMs, while the standard deviation values are extremely close to each other. The maximum and minimum values can be ignored due to the fact that one odd point can be missed out or misrepresented in any of the steps involved.

In some parts of the study area, especially in the top right corner along the water channel, there are sporadic bright and dark outlier points in the AW3D30 DEM, as shown in Figure 15.5 below. However, all DEMs generated from microwave data do not show any such deformity.

Further, in the direction of consistency among the DEMs, calculations resulted in extremely close values of standard deviation, which is a measure of dispersion. It signifies that the datasets might have different absolute values. However, the relative differences among values within any particular dataset are more or less the same. In other words, the deviation in elevation values is a classical "shift of origin" problem without any impact on the scale. To prove this point beyond any doubt, difference rasters were generated where each of the microwave DEM rasters was subtracted from AW3D30 elevation values. The difference rasters along with the associated histograms are shown in Figures 15.6(a)–(f).

TABLE 15.4
Comparison of Statistics

DEM	Max	Min	Mean	Std Dev
Sentinel-1A (generated)	501	248	301.94	19.99
ALOS data (generated)	508	247	301.93	20.04
ALOS DEM (downloaded)	518	245	301.93	20.13
AW3D30 (downloaded)	587	218	354.15	19.94

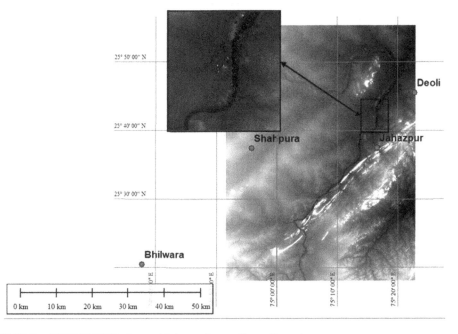

FIGURE 15.5 AW3D30 DEM along with inset of sporadic outlier points.

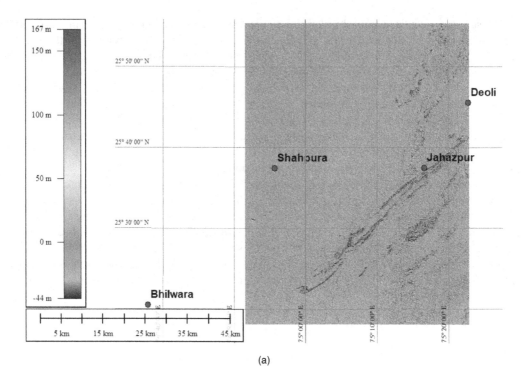

(a)

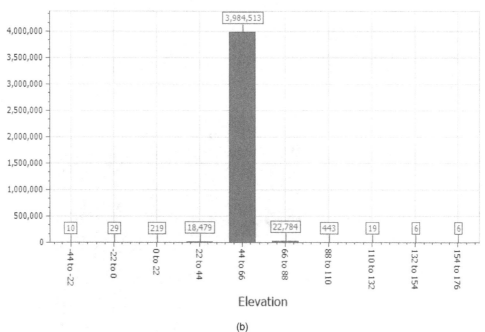

(b)

FIGURE 15.6(a)   Difference raster AW3D30 – Sentinel-1A.
FIGURE 15.6 (b)   Histogram generated from the difference of elevation values AW3D30 – Sentinel-1A.

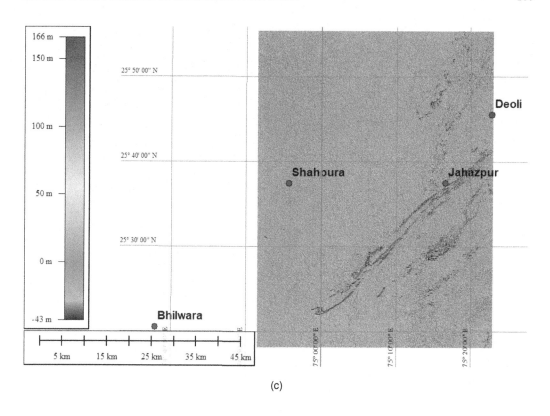

(c)

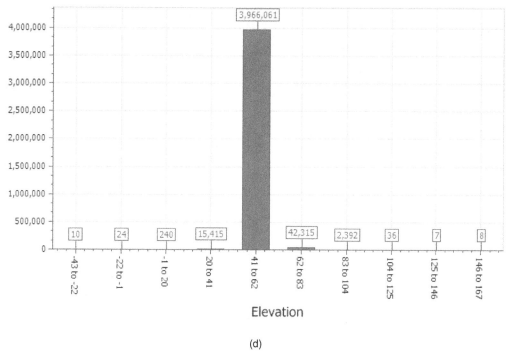

(d)

FIGURE 15.6(c)   Difference raster AW3D30 – ALOS DEM (generated).
FIGURE 15.6(d)   Histogram generated from the difference of elevation values AW3D30 – ALOS DEM (generated).

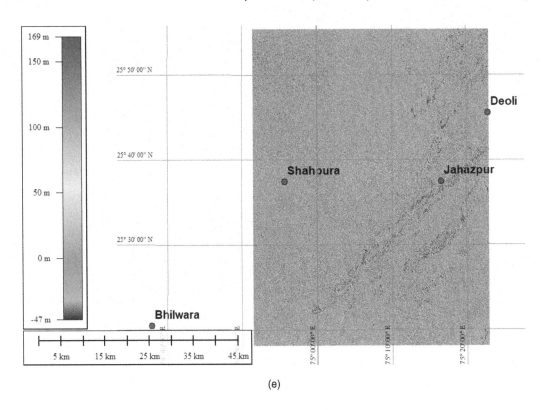

(e)

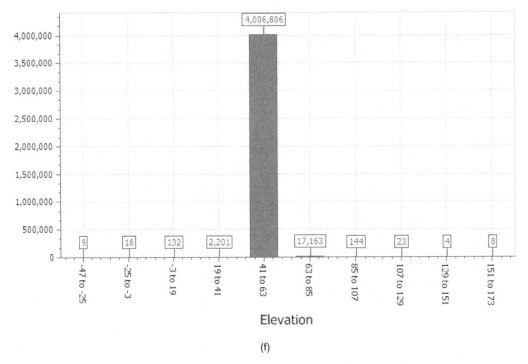

(f)

FIGURE 15.6(e)   Difference Raster AW3D30 – ALOS DEM (Downloaded).
FIGURE 15.6 (f)   Histogram Generated from the Difference of Elevation Values AW3D30 – ALOS DEM (Downloaded).

In all of Figure 15.6(a)–(f), it is evident that there is a discrete gap of around 50 m in elevation values. To further evaluate the relative accuracy of the DEMs, analysis of drainage patterns was taken up for the individual DEMs through ArcGIS software. In every single case, streams up to the order of 5 were extracted by the software, and the general pattern of the streams agreed with each other. As a sample, the drainage pattern extracted from the downloaded ALOS DEM and the combined drainage patterns are shown in Figures 15.7(a) and 15.7(b) respectively.

Lineaments extracted automatically from these DEMs also show the same general pattern only with varying densities of lineaments, as shown in Figures 15.8(a)–(d).

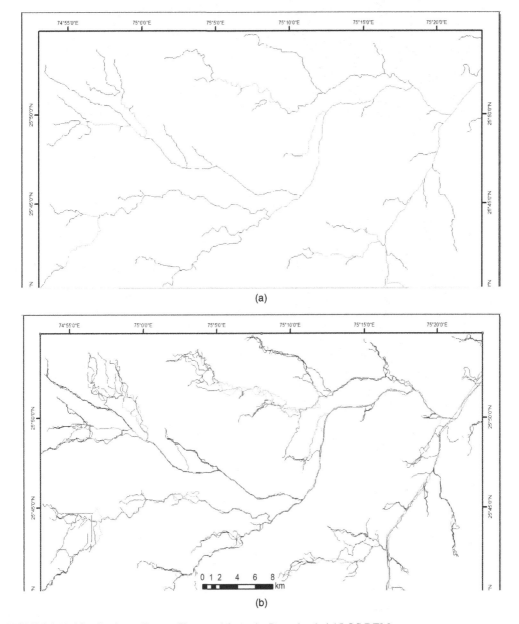

(a)

(b)

FIGURE 15.7(a)   Drainage Pattern Extracted from the Downloaded ALOS DEM.

FIGURE 15.7(b)   Superimposed Drainage Patterns Extracted from Sentinel-1A DEM (generated), ALOS DEM (generated), ALOS DEM (downloaded), and AW3D30 (downloaded).

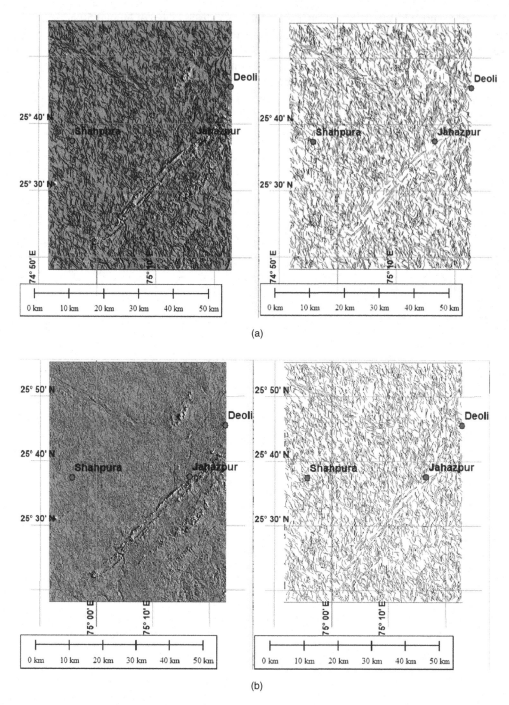

FIGURE 15.8(a) Automatically Extracted lineaments from Sentinel-1A DEM (generated) overlaid on the same DEM (left) and the same lineaments against a white background (right).

FIGURE 15.8(b) Automatically extracted lineaments from ALOS DEM (generated) overlaid on the same DEM (left) and the same lineaments against a white background (right).

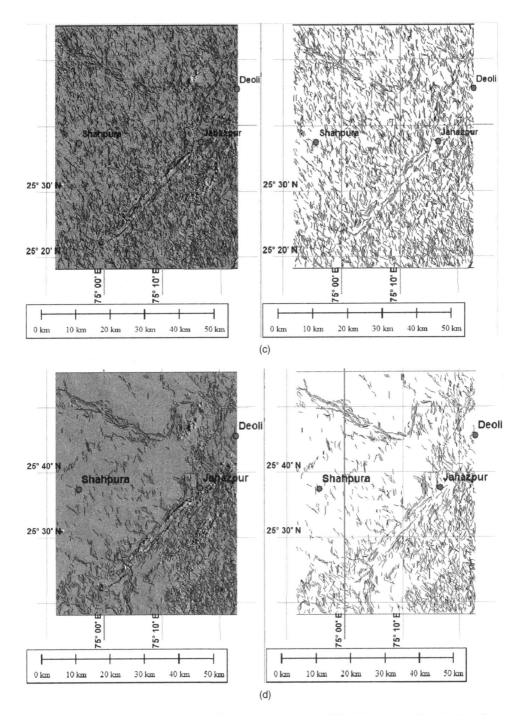

FIGURE 15.8(c) Automatically extracted lineaments from ALOS DEM (downloaded) overlaid on the same DEM (left) and the same lineaments against a white background (right).

FIGURE 15.8(d) Automatically extracted lineaments from AW3D30 (downloaded) overlaid on the same DEM (left) and the same lineaments against a white background (right).

TABLE 15.5
Comparison of Lineament Statistics

DEM	No. of Lineaments	Total Length (m)	Max. Length (m)
Sentinel-1A (generated)	3624	6304523	12138
ALOS data (generated)	3531	6125923	13464
ALOS DEM (downloaded)	2771	4666574	11670
AW3D30 (downloaded)	1729	2995694	13508

The statistics calculated from extracted lineaments are summarized in Table 15.5. It is noticed that the lineaments extracted from AW3D30 DEM (generated from optical data) are less in number than the lineaments extracted from the other DEMs (all generated from SAR data). The lineament map generated from AW3D30 looks cleaner on the mid-left side. This difference might have been caused due to fundamental differences in methods to generate DEMs from optical and microwave data. It is interesting to note that a water channel slightly left of the mid-bottom of the study area has been picked up in all four cases. This channel was deliberately included in parts, at the edge of the study area, to check the efficiency of the extraction method.

The lineaments extracted from ALOS DEM (downloaded) are less in number than the lineaments extracted from the other two DEMs, both generated from raw SAR data. This difference might have been caused by smoothening filters applied while generating the ALOS DEM (downloaded). It is interesting to note that DEMs generated from C-band and L-band, once resampled to the same spacing, are equally capable of extracting lineaments. The lineament maps generated from these two DEMs are very similar both visually and numerically (difference in total length approx. 2.8%). Lineament density maps were generated from all four DEMs, and the results are shown in Figures 15.9(a)–(d). Furthermore, rose diagrams were generated for trend analysis from all four DEMs, and the results are shown in Figures 15.10(a)–(h). Rose diagrams in Figures 15.10(a), (c), (e), and (g) are based on frequency (as percentage of the total population), while those in Figures 15.10(b), (d), (f), and (h) are based on length (as percentage of total lineation length).

The relevant details from rose diagrams are furnished in Table 15.6.

TABLE 15.6
Details of Lineaments from Rose Diagrams

Raster layer	Population	Total Length of All Lineations	Max Bin Length
Sentinel-1A (generated)	11,588	12,609,166.15	790,865.21
ALOS DEM (generated)	11,421	12,251,965.53	764,353.37
ALOS DEM (downloaded)	8,764	9,333,267.17	607,719.12
AW3D30 (downloaded)	5,001	5,991,509.4	350,868.29

The lineament density maps indicate the geological formations that are depicted in the published geological map of the study area (Figure 15.1). In each DEM, the density of lineaments near the bottom right corner of the study area is found to be more than the average density, which can be explained by the presence of faults and folds in the Mangalwar complex, as depicted in the geological map.

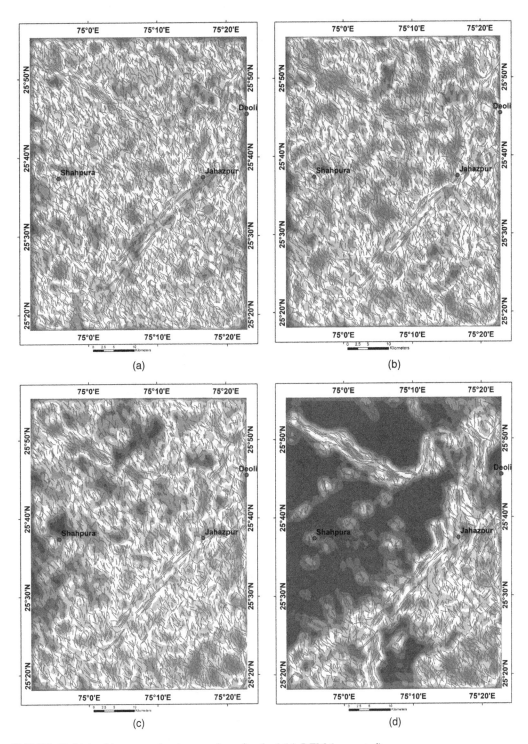

FIGURE 15.9(a) Lineament density map from Sentinel-1A DEM (generated).

FIGURE 15.9(b) Lineament density map from ALOS DEM (generated).

FIGURE 15.9(c) Lineament density map from ALOS DEM (downloaded).

FIGURE 15.9(d) Lineament density map from AW3D30 DEM (downloaded).

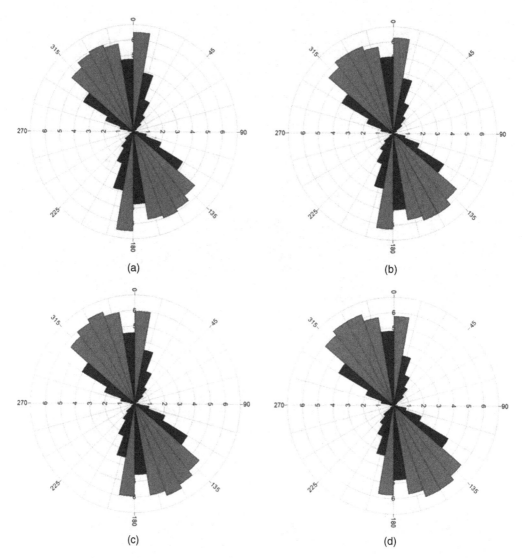

(a)   (b)

(c)   (d)

FIGURE 15.10(a)   Rose diagram from Sentinel-1A DEM (generated) based on frequency (as percentage of total population).

FIGURE 15.10(b)   Rose diagram from Sentinel-1A DEM (generated) based on length (as percentage of total lineation length).

FIGURE 15.10(c)   Rose diagram from ALOS DEM (generated) based on frequency (as percentage of total population).

FIGURE 15.10(d)   Rose diagram from ALOS DEM (generated) based on length (as percentage of total lineation length).

Both types of rose diagram (based on frequency and based on length) show excellent consistency for every DEM considered in this study. This consistency in turn supports the correctness of the lineaments identified in the previous steps of our chapter. The general trend of the rose diagrams is the same in all the cases. Taking into account the total length of lineations, it is observed that the DEMs generated from SAR data (Sentinel-1A and ALOS PALSAR) give us the longest lineaments. This may be explained by the fact that these DEMs were generated in the course of this particular chapter, and no smoothening filters were used on them. These generated DEMs are in raw format. Next in the order of total length of lineations comes the ALOS PALSAR DEM (downloaded), while

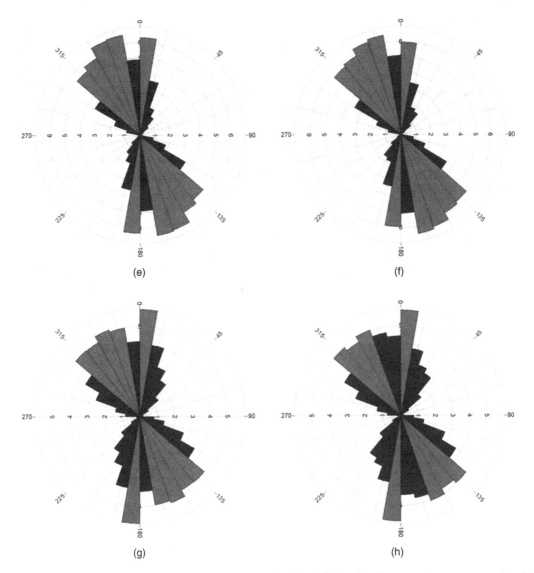

FIGURE 15.10(e) Rose diagram from ALOS DEM (downloaded) based on frequency (as percentage of total population).
FIGURE 15.10(f) Rose diagram from ALOS DEM (downloaded) based on length (as percentage of total lineation length).
FIGURE 15.10(g) Rose diagram from AW3D30 DEM (downloaded) based on frequency (as percentage of total population).
FIGURE 15.10(h) Rose diagram from AW3D30 DEM (downloaded) based on length (as percentage of total lineation length).

the smallest total length of lineations corresponds to the AW3D30 DEM (downloaded). ALOS PALSAR DEM is generated through the process of interferometry, which can capture even the finest of differences in altitude, and hence helps to identify more lineaments than the AW3D30 DEM, which relies on photogrammetric methods applied to a stereo pair of optical data. It may be worth mentioning here that the downloaded files of AW3D30 DEM appear smoother in comparison to the downloaded files of ALOS PALSAR DEM. All the results mentioned earlier are perfectly matching and supporting each other, hence providing the accurate geology of the study area.

15.6   CONCLUSIONS

This study extracted and evaluated the lineaments from DEMs generated from microwave data and optical data of the Jahazpur area, Bhilwara. The results show that both C-band and L-band microwave data are capable of generating good-quality DEMs and provided appropriate baseline measurement during the selection of interferometric pairs. The accuracies of these DEMs are commensurate with each other despite their intrinsic difference in spacing. The study of baseline measurements of 144 m and 1,784 m shows that these are sufficient to generate accurate DEM from Sentinel-1A C-band data and ALOS PALSAR L-band data, respectively, in cases of moderate relief. In this particular study, there was a discreet shift of around 50 m in elevation between the standard DEM generated from optical data and the other three DEMs (all generated from SAR data). It is quite extraordinary that except for this shift, all four DEMs conform to each other very precisely. The lineaments automatically extracted from different DEMs are significantly influenced by the wavelength. Due to their longer wavelength, C-band and L-band microwave data can bring out lineaments that are not visible in optical data. The fundamental difference of methodology, namely interferometry vis-à-vis photogrammetry, has a greater contribution to the overall difference of the extracted lineaments. The study shows that the smoothening filters applied on DEM influences the number of extracted lineaments since it diminishes the sharpness of contrast between a lineament and its neighboring pixels. Despite the differences in the number of extracted lineaments, the general trend of the lineament density maps, generated from all the DEMs, matches precisely with the geological map of the study area.

ACKNOWLEDGMENTS

This work is supported by Space Application Center, Indian Space Research Organization Grant No. EPSA/3.1.1/2017. The SAR data were downloaded from Alaska Satellite Facility (ASF).

REFERENCES

Abdelkareem, M., Bamousa, A.O., Hamimi, Z., Kamal El-Din, G.M., 2020. Multispectral and RADAR images integration for geologic, geomorphic, and structural investigation in southwestern Arabian Shield, Al Qunfudhah area, Saudi Arabia. *Journal of Taibah University for Science* 14, 383–401. doi:10.1080/16583655.2020.1741957

Army, E.K., Saepuloh, A., 2020. Field verifications of geological structures related to SAR detected lineaments. *IOP Conference Series: Earth and Environmental Science* 417. doi:10.1088/1755-1315/417/1/012012

Ba, D.N., Tran, G., Huong, T., 2012. Comparison of elevation derived from InSAR data with DEM from topography map in Son Dong, Bac Giang, Viet Nam. *Science and Technology* 30, 25–29.

Bannari, A., El-battay, A., Saquaque, A., Miri, A., 2016. PALSAR-FBS L-HH mode and Landsat-TM data fusion for geological mapping 246–268. doi:10.4236/ars.2016.54020

Barkah, A., Daud, Y., 2021. Identification of structural geology at the Tangkuban Parahu geothermal area, West Java based on remote sensing and gravity data. *AIP Conference Proceedings* 2320. doi:10.1063/5.0038809

Das, S., Pardeshi, S.D., Kulkarni, P.P., Doke, A., 2018. Extraction of lineaments from different azimuth angles using geospatial techniques: a case study of Pravara basin, Maharashtra, India. *Arabian Journal of Geosciences* 11. doi:10.1007/s12517-018-3522-6

Farahbakhsh, E., Chandra, R., Olierook, H.K.H., Scalzo, R., Clark, C., Reddy, S.M., Dietmar, R.M., 2018. Computer vision-based framework for extracting geological lineaments from optical remote sensing data 1–17.

Fentahun, T.M., Bagyaraj, M., Melesse, M.A., Korme, T., 2021. Seismic hazard sensitivity assessment in the Ethiopian Rift, using an integrated approach of AHP and DInSAR methods. *Egyptian Journal of Remote Sensing and Space Science*. doi:10.1016/j.ejrs.2021.05.001

Ferreira, Z., Cabral, P., 2021. Vertical accuracy assessment of ALOS PALSAR, GMTED2010, SRTM and Topodata digital elevation models 116–124. doi:10.5220/0010404001160124

Govil, H., Tripathi, M.K., Diwan, P., Guha, S., Monika, 2018. Identification of iron oxides minerals in Western Jahajpur Region, India using aviris-ng hyperspectral remote sensing. *International Archives of the Photogrammetry, Remote Sensing and Spatial Information Sciences – ISPRS Archives* 42, 233–237. doi:10.5194/isprs-archives-XLII-5-233-2018

Grohmann, C.H., 2018. Evaluation of TanDEM-X DEMs on selected Brazilian sites: Comparison with SRTM, ASTER GDEM and ALOS AW3D30. *Remote Sensing of Environment* 212, 121–133. doi:10.1016/j.rse.2018.04.043

Han, L., Liu, Z., Ning, Y., Zhao, Z., 2018. Extraction and analysis of geological lineaments combining a DEM and remote sensing images from the northern Baoji loess area. *Advances in Space Research* 62, 2480–2493. doi:10.1016/j.asr.2018.07.030

Hobbs, W.H., 1912. *Earth Features and Their Meaning*. New York: McMillan.

Inggs, M.R., Lord, R.T., 2015. Applications of satellite imaging radar. *Applications of Satellite Imaging Radar* 1–22.

Japan Aerospace Exploration Agency, E.O.R.C., 1997. ALOS Global Digital Surface Model "ALOS World 3D – 30m (AW3D30)" – Product Description. Japan Aerospace Exploration Agency.

Javhar, A., Chen, X., Bao, A., Jamshed, A., Yunus, M., Jovid, A., Latipa, T., 2019. Comparison of multi-resolution optical Landsat-8, Sentinel-2 and radar Sentinel-1 data for automatic lineament extraction: A case study of Alichur area, SE Pamir. *Remote Sensing* 11, 1–29. doi:10.3390/rs11070778

Karaca, Ö., Bozcu, M., 2019. Çizgisellikler Yardımı ile Tektonik ve Volkanik Yapıların Belirlenmesi: Çan-Etili (Çanakkale) Linyit Havzası Örneği. *Türkiye Jeoloji Bülteni / Geological Bulletin of Turkey* 62, 247–262. doi:10.25288/tjb.570362

Maghsoudi, Y., Meer, F. Van Der, Hecker, C., Perissin, D., Saepuloh, A., 2018. Using PS-InSAR to detect surface deformation in geothermal areas of West Java in Indonesia. *Int J Appl Earth Obs Geoinformation* 64, 386–396. doi:10.1016/j.jag.2017.04.001

Mohammadi, F.A., Amin, Z.M., Ahmad, A. Bin, 2020. Lineament assessment of Aynak Copper mine using remote sensing approach. *IOP Conference Series: Earth and Environmental Science* 540. doi:10.1088/1755-1315/540/1/012034

Moreira, A., Prats-iraola, P., Younis, M., Krieger, G., Hajnsek, I., Papathanassiou, K.P., 2013. A tutorial on synthetic aperture radar. *IEEE Geoscience and Remote Sensing Magazine*.

Nyaberi, D., Barongo, J., Kariuki, P., Ogendi, G., Basweti, E., 2019. Groundwater resource mapping through the integration of geology, remote sensing, geographical information systems and borehole data in arid–subarid lands at Turkana South sub-county, Kenya. *Journal of Geoscience and Environment Protection* 7, 53–72. doi:10.4236/gep.2019.712004

Priya, T., Pandey, A.C., 2021. Geoinformatics-based assessment of land deformation and damage zonation for Gorkha earthquake, 2015, using SAR interferometry and ANN approach. *SN Applied Sciences* 3, 1–16. doi:10.1007/s42452-021-04574-9

Rajasekhar, M., Raju, G.S., Raju, R.S., Ramachandra, M., Kumar, B.P., 2018. Data on comparative studies of lineaments extraction from ASTER DEM, SRTM, and Cartosat for Jilledubanderu river basin, Anantapur district, A. P, India by using remote sensing and GIS. *Data in Brief* 20, 1676–1682. doi:10.1016/j.dib.2018.09.023

Razoki, B., Yazidi, M., Kaid Rassou, K., Chakiri, S., Khaddari, A., Bejjaji, Z., Hmidi, F. El, Hadi, H. El, Allouza, M., 2019. Extraction of lineaments using optical and radar images: the case of Tan-Tan Province, Morocco. *International Journal of Civil Engineering and Technology (IJCIET)* 10, 1147–1155.

Sedeek, A., 2019. Accuracy assessment of DEMs using modern geoinformatic methods. *Geoinformatica – An International Journal (GIIJ)* 6, 13–22.

Soliman, A., Han, L., 2019. Effects of vertical accuracy of digital elevation model (DEM) data on automatic lineaments extraction from shaded DEM. *Advances in Space Research* 64, 603–622. doi:10.1016/j.asr.2019.05.009

Takaku, J., Tadono, T., Tsutsui, K., 2014. Generation of high resolution global DSM from ALOS PRISM. *International Archives of the Photogrammetry, Remote Sensing and Spatial Information Sciences – ISPRS Archives* 40, 243–248. doi:10.5194/isprsarchives-XL-4-243-2014

Tripathi, M.K., 2019a. Comparative evaluation threshold parameters of spectral angle mapper (SAM) for mapping of Chhabadiya Talc minerals, Jahajpur, Bhilwara, Rajasthan using Hyperion hyperspectral remote sensing data, *2019 2nd International Conference on Intelligent Communication and Computational Techniques (ICCT)* 72–74.

Tripathi, M.K., 2019b. Lithological mapping using digital image processing techniques on Landsat 8 OLI remote sensing data in Jahajpur, Bhilwara, Rajasthan, *2019 2nd International Conference on Intelligent Communication and Computational Techniques (ICCT)* 43–48.

Tripathi, M.K., 2019c. Petrography, XRD Analysis and Identification of Talc Minerals near Chhabadiya Village of Jahajpur Region, Bhilwara, India through Hyperion hyperspectral remote sensing data, *2019 2nd International Conference on Intelligent Communication and Computational Techniques (ICCT)* 75–78.

Tripathi, M.K., Govil, H., 2019. Evaluation of AVIRIS-NG hyperspectral images for mineral identification and mapping. *Heliyon* 5, e02931. doi:10.1016/j.heliyon.2019.e02931

Tsuchida, S., Yamaguchi, Y., Hase, H., 1990. Investigation of lineaments from remote sensing data. *ISPRS* 619–628.

Venkataraman, G., Rao, Y.S., Rao, K.S., 2006. Application of SAR interferometry for Himalayan glaciers. European Space Agency, (Special Publication) ESA SP. doi:10.1111/j.1365-246X.1986.tb04513.x

Wegmüller, U., 1997. Land applications of SAR interferometry. In: *Microwave Physics and Techniques SE – 17*, pp. 235–250. doi:10.1007/978-94-011-5540-3_17

Zhang, B., Li, J., Ren, H., 2019. Using phase unwrapping methods to apply D-InSAR in mining areas. *Canadian Journal of Remote Sensing* 45, 225–233. doi:10.1080/07038992.2019.1583097

16 Scatterer-Based Deformation Monitoring Induced Due to Coal Mining by DInSAR Techniques

Vinay Kumar, Nyamaa Tserendulam, and Rajat Subhra Chatterjee

CONTENTS

16.1 INTRODUCTION

The Jharia coal field is one of the major coal mine belts in India where coal is extracted by two mining approaches: open cast and underground [1]. In underground mining techniques, either bord-and-pillar or longwall, large rectangular blocks of coal are extracted. Strips of coal are excavated by protecting the coal gallery with hydraulic supports. Once the coal block is fully extracted, the void becomes too large to support itself, which causes its roof to sag; finally, the roof and overlying rock collapse into the void. This typically results in horizontal and vertical movement at the land surface, which can extend beyond the mine footprint. These risks associated with mining voids is causing subsidence at the land surface, which affects surface infrastructure. The magnitude and extent of subsidence is dictated by the extent of coal extraction, the depth of the coal seam, and the thickness of the excavated material (the height of the void) [2].

Underground mining can result in a shallow, flat-bottomed rectangular trough at the surface, sometimes accompanied by cracking, heaving, buckling, humping, and stepping. These effects can impact built environments such as roads and buildings as well as cause disturbances to river courses and other surface water features. Generally, uniform vertical movement does not cause surface damage, but differential vertical movement does. This damage is caused by tilting and horizontal displacement of the overburden, which accompanies the lowering of the land surface [3].

In the Jharia coalfield area, subsurface coal fires occur mostly at shallow depths (<40 m) [4]. In the Jharia coalfield, land subsidence occurs primarily due to underground mining and subsurface coal fires. The causes, that is, different types of underground mining, such as bord-and-pillar, long-wall mining, depillaring, and caving; water logging of the abandoned underground mine workings; and subsurface coal fire, are diverse in nature and spatio-temporally haphazard, and give rise to irregular and complex deformation patterns [5].

The Jharia coalfield is facing subsidence problems due to the presence of old workings, which are generally waterlogged; around a dozen of these have subsided in recent times, causing severe damage to in the form of wide cracks, large depressions, sinkholes (potholes), blockage of road and rail, and general damage to buildings and other surface properties. Coal fire–related subsidence is an important aspect of the Jharia coal field. The main characteristics of these subsidence include indications on the surface area that seen only a few hours in advance; they do not follow any pattern, cause marked depressions with wide cracks and steppings, and are associated with a rumbling sound [6].

To detect and derive subsidence-related parameters in the earth's surface because of coal mining activities, both ground-based and space-based techniques can be used. These techniques should be applied for more frequent and repeated observations in order to know how the subsidence pattern evolves over time in the mine footprint [7].

The techniques used for observing and measuring subsidence depend on the spatial extent of the anticipated deformation and the magnitude of the expected subsidence. Among available spaceborne techniques, DInSAR appears to be very efficient in terms of spatial and temporal resolution of measurements vs feasibility [8]. PSInSAR (permanent scatterers interferometric synthetic aperture radar) is an advanced form of DInSAR that uses multiple interferograms created from a stack pf multiple SAR images [9]. In PSInSAR, pixels that display stable radar reflectivity characteristics throughout every image of the dataset are referred to as permanent scatterers (PS) [10]. This algorithm was developed to overcome the errors produced by atmospheric artifacts on signal phase. Once these errors are removed, a history of motion can be created for each target, allowing the detection of both linear and non-linear motion. PSInSAR measures ground movement with millimeter accuracy. Persistent scatterer interferometry (PSI) is more suitable than the DInSAR time series for identifying most stable scattering pixels where pixel properties do not vary with time and look angle, in a stack of SAR images rather than a DInSAR time series process [11]. PSI allows individual point targets' temporal analysis of the interferometric phase. The PSI technique provides better accuracy for measurement of surface target displacement than does the DInSAR process [9], [12]. PSI also reduces the consequences of phase path delay, which occurs during SAR image acquisition as a result of atmospheric heterogeneity [13]. The phase unwrapping process in the PSInSAR technique is very important to accurately determine ground movement. Also, PSI has limited capability for the detection of high movement rates of displacement [14]. However, PSInSAR combines with the DInSAR time series process to allow the detection of high rates of linear and non-linear deformations [15].

The minimum displacement detection in the PSI technique depends on the spatial density of the scatterers: the temporal resolution and the wavelength of SAR signal. To accomplish millimeter-level precision of land displacement measurement in the PSInSAR technique, greater than SAR pairs are required to generate a sufficient number of interferograms. Moreover, real-time monitoring is not possible in the PSI technique [14].

The objective of this study is time series analysis by DInSAR for monitoring of linear and non-linear motions for characterization of subsidence due to underground mining and/or coal fire.

16.2 STUDY AREA AND DATA USED

16.2.1 STUDY AREA

The study area chosen for analyzing surface deformation occurring in the Jharia coal field is situated in Dhanbad, in the state of Jharkhand. The Jharia coal field is located in the Damodar River Valley and covers an area of 447 km². The coal field is situated between 23°40′00″ and 23°50′00″ N latitude and 86°10′00″ to 86°30′00″ E longitude. These coal mines, which are the largest coal producer of bituminous coal in India, consist of 23 underground and nine open cast mines. Dhanbad, which is known as the Coal Capital of India, is the major city situated in the study area. Surrounding townships of Dhanbad are Maheshpur and Katrasgarh in the north, and Jharia, Dobari, and Bokaro steel city in the east. It is also surrounded by the Damodar river to the south [16].

16.2.2 DATASETS USED

In this project, ALOS PALSAR-2, fine mode dual (FBD) polarization, and level 1.1 single-look complex (SLC) time series SAR data (Tables 16.1 and 16.2) are used for advanced DInSAR processing for deformation monitoring [17].

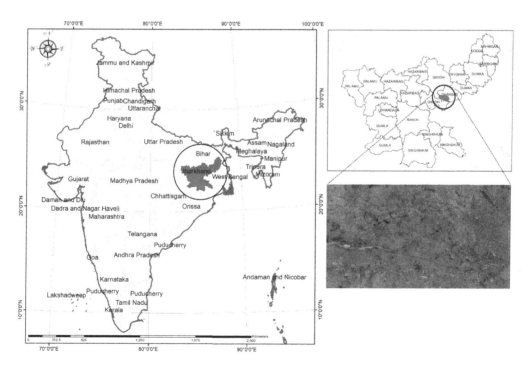

FIGURE 16.1 Location map of study area, Jharia coal field, Dhanbad, Jharkhand.

TABLE 16.1
Description of Used Dataset Used

Specification	ALOS PALSAR-2
Sensor mode	FBD
Wavelength	L-band, 23.5 cm
Scene width (km)	70
Polarization	HH
Interferometric wide-swath mode	70 km swath
Date	2016–2019
Range and azimuth resolution	9.1 × 5.3 m
pass	Ascending

TABLE 16.2
List of ALOS PALSAR-2 Data Used for the PSInSAR Analysis of the Study Area, the Master Scene (Highlighted)

No	Mission	Product	Date	Perpendicular Baseline	Temporal Baseline
1			2014.10.04	−389.12	728.00
2			2015.02.21	336.75	588.00
3			2015.10.03	−111.60	364.00
4			2016.02.20	216.73	364.00
5			2016.10.01	221.05	140.00
6			2017.02.18	0.00	0.00
7	ALOS PALSAR-2	SLC	2017.09.30	229.17	−224.00
8			2018.02.03	25.41	−350.00
9			2018.03.03	55.83	−378.00
10			20190119	118.70	−700.00
11			20190302	22.63	−742.00

16.3 METHODOLOGY

This study involves time series SAR data processing using L-band SAR datasets for monitoring land deformation; this uses an advanced differential interferometric synthetic aperture radar (DInSAR) algorithm referred as the persistent scatterer (PS) InSAR technique (Figure 16.2). The advantage of using PSInSAR is that it deals with both decorrelation and atmospheric delay errors of conventional InSAR and provides deformation history with sub-centimeter accuracy [8], [15].

16.3.1 BASELINE ESTIMATION

The baseline is the distance, in three-dimensional space, between the satellite positions at different acquisitions – that is, the distance between two SAR platforms. The distance between the satellite location at the second acquisition and a point along the range direction of the satellite at the first acquisition is the perpendicular baseline. Baseline estimation is required to understand the exact location of the satellite along its orbital path each time it acquires radar data over the targeted swath. Baseline estimation is also important because if the perpendicular baseline between a master

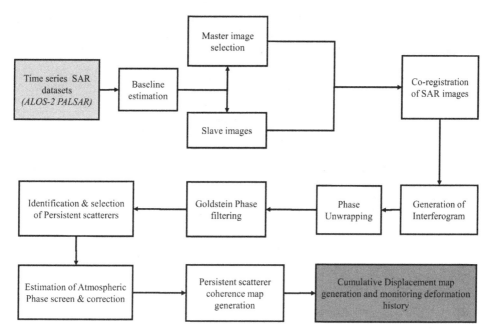

FIGURE 16.2   Flowchart for PSInSAR processing using time series SAR data.

image and any slave image is larger than the critical baseline, then there will be a loss of coherence between the pair and, therefore, a loss of InSAR capabilities [15].

16.3.2   Co-registration

Co-registration is one of the essential steps for the spatial alignment of multiple SAR images geographically. Image pixels with similar coordinates are referenced to one another. For InSAR processing, two or more SAR images must be co-registered with each other to sub-pixel accuracy. One image is selected as the master image, and the other SAR images are treated as the slave images [18]. PSInSAR processing begins with the co-registration of all slave images with the master image in the interferometric stack. In order to superimpose the pixels of each image in slant-range geometry, co-registration takes care of any translational, rotational, or scaling differences between the stack of SAR images. To co-register the stack of SAR images, a digital elevation model (DEM) is also required [19].

16.3.3   Generation of Interferogram

The interferogram is generated by cross-multiplication of the master image with the complex conjugate of the slave image. The amplitude of both SAR scenes is multiplied, and the phase represents the difference in phase between the two SAR images. After co-registration, the interferograms were generated by computing the Hermitian product of master and slave images.

Interferometric fringes normally represent a 2π cycle, whereas fringes appear as cycles of arbitrary colors, and every cycle represents half the sensor's wavelength. Relative surface movement between two points can be computed by counting the fringes and by multiplication with half of the wavelength. The closer the fringes, the larger the strain on the surface [18], [21].

The interferometric phase of each SAR scene pixel depends on the difference in the travel paths from the two SAR images. The variation in interferometric phase $\Delta\phi$ is directly proportional to the range difference ΔR and divided by the wavelength λ.

$$\phi_1 = \frac{4\pi R}{\lambda}, \ \phi_2 = \frac{4\pi(R+\Delta R)}{\lambda}.$$
$$\Delta\phi = \phi_2 - \phi_1 = \frac{4\pi\Delta R}{\lambda}$$

The generated interferograms indicated the phase difference between co-registered master and slave SAR scenes. The difference in the phase is due to the topography and is seen in the form of interferogram fringes.

Five different sources contribute in the phase difference:

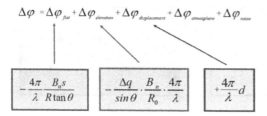

- $\Delta\phi_{flat} \rightarrow$ Phase contribution due to the earth curvature, also referred to as the flat earth phase.
- $\Delta\phi_{elevation} \rightarrow$ Phase contribution due to topography.
- $\Delta\phi_{displacement} \rightarrow$ Phase contribution due to surface deformation.
- $\Delta\phi_{atmosphere} \rightarrow$ Phase contribution due to atmospheric noise. This was introduced due to the atmospheric pressure, temperature, and humidity change between the two acquisitions.
- $\Delta\phi_{noise} \rightarrow$ Phase contribution due to noise by scatterers, temporal change, different look angle, and volume scattering.

InSAR processing tries to eliminate other sources of error in order to be left with only the contributor of interest, which is typically the elevation or displacement. During the formation of the interferogram, the first step is to remove the flat earth phase, which is due to the curvature of the earth's surface. This phase is estimated using orbital information and subtracted from the interferogram [20].

16.3.4 COHERENCE ESTIMATION

The coherence (γ) between two co-registered master and slave SAR images is defined as the absolute value of the normalized complex cross-correlation between the two SAR signals:

$$\Upsilon = \frac{\sum_N P_1.P_2^*}{\sqrt{\sum_N |P_1|^2 \sum_N |P_2|^2}},$$

where,
N = no. of pixels in the N-sample moving window,
P_1 = complex master SAR image,
P_2 = complex slave SAR image,
P_2^* = complex conjugate of slave SAR image.

The coherence value ranges between 0 (incoherence or noise) and 1 (completely coherent signal). It is a function of systematic spatial decorrelation, natural image decorrelation, and additive noise. Therefore, pixels that are highly coherent will have nominal decorrelation and nominal noise. The two major purposes of coherence data are:

- To determine the quality of the interferometric phase measurement. InSAR pairs with low coherence cannot be used for deriving reliable phase measurements.
- To extract thematic information related to surface features and their temporal changes.

The purpose of adaptive filtering is to eliminate the pixels that display low coherence or high noise from the generated interferogram. The coherence threshold is directly used in adaptive filtering and is a user-defined variable. [22]

The coherence image shows how similar each pixel is between the master and slave images in a scale ranging from 0 to 1. Highly coherent areas will appear bright and areas with poor coherence values will appear dark. In the coherence image, vegetation is normally shown as with poor coherence values and buildings with very high coherence.

16.3.5 TOPOGRAPHIC PHASE REMOVAL

The interferogram needs to be flattened for removing the topographic phase. This can be done by simulating an interferogram based on a reference DEM and needs to be subtracted from processed interferogram. Generation of a flattened interferogram via DEM excludes the topography. The number of fringes in the final interferogram is reduced and now excludes local topographic information.

The flattened interferograms with fringes are only related to changes in elevation along with surface displacement atmosphere and noise. In this step, the phase due topography is removed from the residual phase [23].

The phase corrected for the earth's curvature effect is given by:

$$\Phi_{flat} = \frac{4\pi}{\lambda} \Big[B\sin(\theta - \alpha) - B\sin(\theta_0 - \alpha) \Big]$$

$$\Phi_{flat} = \frac{4\pi}{\lambda} \Big[B'\sin(\theta - \alpha) - B'\sin(\theta_0 - \alpha) \Big].$$

16.3.6 PHASE UNWRAPPING

The phase unwrapping process resolves 2π ambiguity of the SLC phase data, and wrapped phase values are translated to absolute phase values. The SAR receiver records the phase as a function of location along the wavelength and phase ranges from 0 to 2π. Once the phase reaches a value of 2π, it automatically resets to 0. Phase unwrapping is required to create an absolute, continuous phase signature by reconstructing the wrapped phase into a continuous phase ramp. The absolute phase is used to calculate the change in distance between satellite and pixels of the imaged area.

The interferometric phase in the interferogram is ambiguous and within 2π. The phase must be unwrapped to relate the interferometric phase to topographic height. Altitude of ambiguity h_a is defined as the difference in altitude that generates an interferometric phase change of 2π after flattening of the interferogram [23].

$$h_a = \frac{\lambda R sin\theta}{2B_n}.$$

Phase unwrapping unravels the ambiguity by integrating difference in phase between neighboring pixels. The variation in phase between two points on the flattened interferogram provides accurate measurement of the actual variation in altitude, after deleting the integer no. of altitudes of ambiguity.

The quality and reliability of the unwrapped phase are dependent on the input coherence. The results are reliable only in areas with high coherence [18].

16.3.7 Phase Filtering

Phase filtering is required as interferometric phases are affected by noise due to temporal decorrelation, geometric decorrelation, volume scattering, and processing error. Many scatterers present per resolution cell and their temporal changes introduce phase noise. The interference pattern is lost when there is loss of coherence. The signal-to-noise ratio needs to be better by filtering the phase for proper phase unwrapping. The ultimate objective of interferogram filtering is phase noise reduction, which makes the phase unwrapping simple, robust, and efficient [18], [23].

16.3.8 Identification and Selection of Persistent Scatterers

PSInSAR is an interferometric stacking technique that measures small ground deformations for a long period of time [24]. The PSInSAR procedure involves almost all of the InSAR processing steps, but the results differ due to the fundamental purpose of PSInSAR:

- This technique searches consistently coherent features in the study area throughout the image stack. Surface features that are relatively stable (no spatial or temporal decorrelation) are consistently coherent.
- This can be combined with a backscattering mechanism that has high-amplitude radar returns (e.g. single- or double-bounce).

Earth surface features that fulfill these criteria are normally manmade features, like buildings, bridges, roads, dams etc., and some natural features that lack vegetation like rock outcrops or cliff faces. These features that yield high radar returns consistently are called persistent scatterers (PS) and are the only points with surface displacement information in the result – all other non-PS pixels, which do not qualify, are discarded and provide no output information [10].

16.3.9 Atmospheric Phase Screen Estimation and Its Correction

The earth's atmosphere is a mixture of many gases, with its own physical properties, and contains fine suspended particles. The atmosphere has different layers, namely troposphere, stratosphere, mesosphere, thermosphere, and exosphere; of these, troposphere and ionosphere are the main cause of delay in SAR signal. The SAR wave passes twice to these atmospheric layers, which have varying refractive indices and cause propagation delays, which results in excess path length [25]. After PS's selection in PSInSAR processing, it estimates and corrects the troposphere- and ionosphere-induced range errors. The delay in the tropospheric phase that causes APS was removed for each image that was obtained during the SAR acquisition time. The atmospheric changes that caused phase delay were analyzed, and their estimation was based on the variation in the residual phase between the connected PS candidates.

After calculation and subtraction of the APS for every acquisition, the success rate of unwrapping increases. The APS has been estimated with the PS technique using ALOS-2 PALSAR time series SAR data in the Jharia coal field. The master atmosphere and orbit error phase are computed at the same time [24].

16.3.10 Persistent Scatterer Coherence Map Generation

The phase noise can be computed from the InSAR pair with the help of the local coherence γ. The γ is the cross-correlation coefficient of the InSAR pair computed on a moving window of few pixels in range and azimuth, after all the deterministic phase components due to the terrain elevation are corrected. As a first approximation, the deterministic phase components in a small window are linear, in both slant-range and azimuth direction. This can be estimated from the interferogram using the frequency detection of complex sinusoids in noise. The coherence image of the data is then generated by calculating the absolute value of γ on a moving window that covers the complete SAR image.

The amount of correlation between the PSCs in different interferograms was estimated in the process of identification of PS candidates and removal of the APS error. The PS coherence map was produced by analyzing the images over different time periods. The coherence value 0 indicates that interferometric phase is just noise, whereas 1 indicates absence of phase noise. The relationship between the coherence and interferometric phase dispersion can be found using complicated mathematical computations [9].

16.3.11 Generation of Cumulative Displacement Map and Monitoring Deformation History

Deformation velocity estimation for the cumulative displacement map is the final step for generating deformation map. This process consists of computation of deformation velocity from the time series data. The final result is a deformation map, deformation velocity, and the deformation accumulated at each acquisition time. The deformations estimated are in the direction of satellite LOS.

The aim of monitoring deformation induced due to mining:

- Measurement to derive subsidence parameters, which can further be related to causing damage for buildings, roads, bridges, railways, and other manmade features and landforms.
- To provide information for planning and designing future mine layout for subsidence mitigation [19].

16.4 RESULTS AND DISCUSSION

The results obtained from time series ALOS-2 L-band SAR data are shown and discussed in this section. Differential interferograms generated and vertical displacement land subsidence maps were prepared from pairs of ALOS-2 PALSAR data (Figure 16.3). DInSAR-based LOS displacement rates were determined for the mining localities; the deformation fringes were observed at various locations. The deformation fringes are very clear and prominent in L-band DInSAR (Figure 16.3).

From differential interferograms generated for each year's vertical displacement map, it was observed that every year the rate of vertical displacement is increasing around the mining area in the Jharia coal field (Figure 16.4).

In this study, the biggest subsidence fringes were observed in and around Joyrampur, East Basuriya, Kujama, Rajapur, and North and West Tisra minings, the surrounding settlements. In the study area, land subsidence rates in different mining sites were obtained from the cumulative displacement map. As per the results, the rate of subsidence observed in different mining sites varies from a few centimeters to tens of centimeters per year.

The results from spaceborne DInSAR and PSInSAR were validated using ground-based precision leveling and GPS observations in the Joyrampur and East Basuriya test sites, seen in Table 16.3. The observed results from the ALOS-2 time series SAR analysis were found to be similar to the

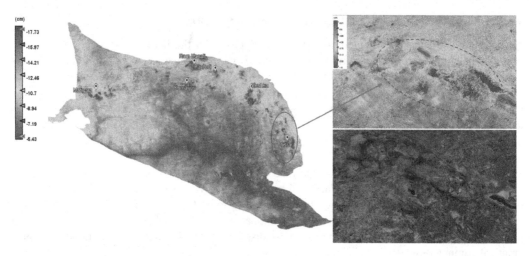

FIGURE 16.3   Vertical displacement map using ALOS-2 PALSAR differential interferograms.

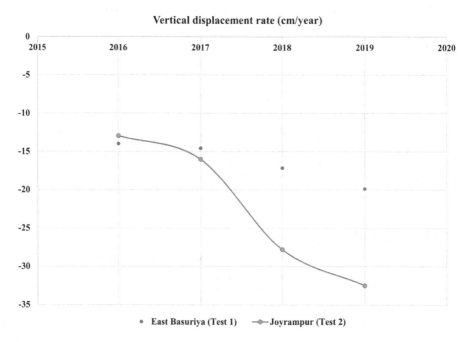

FIGURE 16.4   Vertical displacement rate using ALOS-2 PALSAR time series datasets.

ground observations. The rate of land subsidence observed in and around the mines was almost ± 30 cm/year in the Jharia coal field.

16.5   CONCLUSION

The study was carried out to obtain a cumulative displacement map of the Jharia coal field from multi-temporal time series L-band SAR data of 2016–2018 using the advanced DInSAR technique PSInSAR. The highest rates of subsidence were observed in and around mining areas and their surrounding settlements. The rate of land deformation observed was almost ± 30 cm/year in the

TABLE 16.3
Validation with Ground Observation

TEST SITES	Spaceborne observation ALOS-2 PALSAR L-band DInSAR, vertical displacement (cm/year)	Ground- based observation Vertical displacement rate by precision leveling (cm/year)	Spaceborne observation ALOS-2 PALSAR L-band PSInSAR, horizontal displacement (cm/year)	Ground- based observation Horizontal displacement rate by GPS (cm/year)
East Basuriya	19.86177	16.6	8.5	8.9
Joyrampur	32.47769	33.1	10.5	9.2

Jharia coal field mining area. The deformation fringes are much clearer and more prominent and the subsidences were well detected in the cumulative displacement map obtained from the L-band time series SAR data. The results were validated using ground observations and two mining sites were considered for comparison. It can be concluded from the results that the ALOS-2 L-band time series SAR data for accurately monitoring the deformation history of the mine-induced subsidence. Since the PSInSAR approach uses time series SAR data, it can provide a cumulative displacement map, and the rate of deformation is more accurate, up to mm level. So, the adopted methodology can be used for detection, mapping, and monitoring of deformation history in the affected coal mining areas where the causes of subsidence are due to mining. This approach will also help in suitability planning and designing of surface characterization and other structural development activities in the mining areas and delineate future scenes of mining. Information related to the subsiding areas' spatial extent and subsidence rate can help in identification of the deformed areas for recommending possible mitigation measures for any further hazards.

REFERENCES

[1] G. B. Stracher, A. Prakash, and E. V. Sokol, Eds., "Chapter 9 – impact of mining activities on land use land cover in the Jharia coalfield, India," in *Coal and Peat Fires: A Global Perspective*, Boston: Elsevier, 2015, pp. 263–279.

[2] T. M. Barczak, "Research developments that contributed to the landscape of longwall roof support design over the past 25 years," in *Advances in Coal Mine Ground Control*, Elsevier, 2017, pp. 1–34.

[3] Commonwealth of Australia, "Background review – subsidence from coal mining activities," p. 82.

[4] T. K. Mukherjee, "Detection and delineation of depth of subsurface coalmine fires based on an airborne multispectral scanner survey in a part of the Jharia coalfield, India*," National Academies and TRB, p. 5.

[5] V. K. R. Karanam, M. Motagh, and K. Jain, "Land subsidence in Jharia coalfields, Jharkhand, India – detection, estimation and analysis using persistent scatterer interferometry," EGU General Assembly 2020, 4–8 May 2020, EGU2020-21118, doi: 10.5194/egusphere-egu2020-21118.

[6] A. I. Johnson, International Association of Hydrological Sciences, and International Symposium on Land Subsidence, Eds., *Land Subsidence: Proceedings of the Fourth International Symposium on Land Subsidence, held at Houston, Texas, 12–17 May 1991*. Wallingford: IAHS Press, 1991.

[7] X. Cui, Y. Zhao, G. Wang, B. Zhang, and C. Li, "Calculation of residual surface subsidence above abandoned longwall coal mining," *Sustainability*, vol. 12, no. 1528, p. 12, 2020.

[8] S. Dong, H. Yin, S. Yao, and F. Zhang, "Detecting surface subsidence in coal mining area based on DInSAR technique," *J. Earth Sci.*, vol. 24, no. 3, pp. 449–456, Jun. 2013, doi: 10.1007/s12583-013-0342-1.

[9] V. Tofani, F. Raspini, F. Catani, and N. Casagli, "Persistent scatterer interferometry (PSI) technique for landslide characterization and monitoring," *Remote Sens.*, vol. 5, no. 3, pp. 1045–1065, Mar. 2013, doi: 10.3390/rs5031045.

[10] C. Văduva, C. Dănişor, and M. Datcu, "Joint SAR image time series and PSInSAR data analytics: An LDA based approach," *Remote Sens.*, vol. 10, no. 9, p. 1436, Sep. 2018, doi: 10.3390/rs10091436.

[11] J. C. Mura et al., "Monitoring of non-linear ground movement in an open pit Iron Mine Based on an Integration of advanced DInSAR techniques using TerraSAR-X Data," *Remote Sens.*, vol. 8, no. 5, p. 409, 2016.

[12] H. Jia and L. Liu, "A technical review on persistent scatterer interferometry," *J. Mod. Transp.*, vol. 24, no. 2, pp. 153–158, Jun. 2016, doi: 10.1007/s40534-016-0108-4.

[13] M. Crosetto, O. Monserrat, M. Cuevas-González, N. Devanthéry, and B. Crippa, "Persistent scatterer interferometry: A review," *ISPRS J. Photogramm. Remote Sens.*, vol. 115, pp. 78–89, May 2016, doi: 10.1016/j.isprsjprs.2015.10.011.

[14] P. J. V. D'Aranno, A. Di Benedetto, M. Fiani, M. Marsella, I. Moriero, and J. A. Palenzuela Baena, "An application of persistent scatterer interferometry (PSI) technique for infrastructure monitoring," *Remote Sens.*, vol. 13, no. 6, p. 1052, Mar. 2021, doi: 10.3390/rs13061052.

[15] Y. Wang et al., "Ground deformation analysis using InSAR and backpropagation prediction with influencing factors in Erhai Region, China," *Sustainability*, vol. 11, no. 10, p. 2853, May 2019, doi: 10.3390/su11102853.

[16] R. S. Chatterjee, J. Roy, and A. K. Bhattacharya, "Mapping geological features of the Jharia coal-field from Landsat-5 TM data," *Int. J. Remote Sens.*, vol. 17, no. 16, pp. 3257–3270, Nov. 1996, doi: 10.1080/01431169608949142.

[17] "Archive | ALOS-2/PALSAR-2 | PASCO CORPORATION." http://en.alos-pasco.com/offer/alos-2_palsar-2_archive.html (accessed Apr. 15, 2021).

[18] Z. Li and J. Bethel, "Image coregistration in SAR interferometry," *ISPRS Archives*, vol. XXXVII, no. B1, p. 6, 2008.

[19] W. Duan, H. Zhang, C. Wang, and Y. Tang, "Multi-temporal InSAR parallel processing for Sentinel-1 large-scale surface deformation mapping," *Remote Sens.*, vol. 12, no. 22, p. 3749, Nov. 2020, doi: 10.3390/rs12223749.

[20] L. Veci, "Interferometry Tutorial," no. March 2015, pp. 1–20, 2016.

[21] M. Furuya, "SAR interferometry," in *Encyclopedia of Solid Earth Geophysics*, H. K. Gupta, Ed. Dordrecht: Springer Netherlands, 2011, pp. 1041–1049.

[22] R. Touzi, A. Lopes, J. Bruniquel, and P. W. Vachon, "Coherence estimation for SAR imagery," *IEEE Trans. Geosci. Remote Sens.*, vol. 37, no. 1, pp. 135–149, Jan. 1999, doi: 10.1109/36.739146.

[23] Hoonyol Lee and Jian Guo Liu, "Topographic phase corrected coherence estimation using multi-pass differential SAR interferometry: differential coherence," in *IGARSS 2000. IEEE 2000 International Geoscience and Remote Sensing Symposium. Taking the Pulse of the Planet: The Role of Remote Sensing in Managing the Environment. Proceedings (Cat. No.00CH37120)*, Honolulu, HI, USA, 2000, vol. 2, pp. 776–778, doi: 10.1109/IGARSS.2000.861700.

[24] M. Costantini, S. Falco, F. Malvarosa, and F. Minati, "A new method for identification and ana-lysis of persistent scatterers in series of SAR Images," in *IGARSS 2008 – 2008 IEEE International Geoscience and Remote Sensing Symposium*, Boston, MA, USA, Jul. 2008, pp. II-449–II–452, doi: 10.1109/IGARSS.2008.4779025.

[25] Z. Qiu, Y. Ma, and X. Guo, "Atmospheric phase screen correction in ground-based SAR with PS technique," *SpringerPlus*, vol. 5, no. 1, p. 1594, Dec. 2016, doi: 10.1186/s40064-016-3262-6.

17 An Insight to the Lunar Surface

Characterization From the L- and S-Band Polarimetric Data

Awinash Singh, Shashi Kumar, and Ling Chang

CONTENTS

DOI: 10.1201/9781003204466-17

17.1 INTRODUCTION

The moon is the brightest celestial body seen from the earth and the most fascinating to see in the night sky. The exploration of the moon asks us to investigate our existence right start from the birth of the universe. The earth's moon is our planet's only natural satellite, and hereafter it will be referred to simply as the moon.

In our solar system, there are approximately 200 moons belonging to our planets and dwarf planets that have been discovered to date [1]. Jupiter alone has 53 confirmed moons and 26 provisional moons; its total of 79 moons makes it the largest in our solar system [1]. The birth of the moon always sparks questions. Was it separated from the earth by a massive asteroid, or did something else happen? Some have conclusive evidence about its birth, but the question remains unanswered as questions about the birth of the solar system are still being explored. As this is quite a debatable topic, we shall stick to our moon. The moon is 384,400 km from the earth, and it is the nearest celestial body. So, it is easy for us to explore and investigate unanswered questions about its existence and its relation to the earth. We have been gathering information for centuries, starting from Galileo and extending to the recent lunar missions; we have come a long way in understanding the unexplored lunar surface and its components.

17.2 THE MOON: A CATAPULT FOR FUTURE SPACE MISSIONS

The moon (or *luna*, in Latin) is a fascinating celestial body and is also nearest to the earth, meaning it is the brightest and largest we can see in the clear night sky. It is the earth's only natural satellite and sits at a distance of approximately 384,400 kilometers from earth; it is the only place outside of our planet that human beings have reached and explored the surface [2]. Exploration of the lunar surface is quite interesting and profound to us in a lot of ways, but a question always arises: why is the moon important to us? The answer to this is thoroughly instructive. The moon is believed to have formed around 4.5 billion years ago when a Mars-sized object, Theia, hit the earth's surface; this event caused the birth of our moon in this vast solar system. The moon's importance plays major role as earth's satellite, as its gravity controls the earth's spin axis; at time of the moon's formation, the earth's spin was much faster, around five hours, in comparison to the present day [3]. It is also believed that the moon and earth once shared the same magnetic field but must have lost it completely by 1.5 billion years ago [4].

The existence of the moon and its evolution played a vital role in the existence of our planet, as a large celestial body revolving around our planet made the orbit of the earth stable. Another role is that of tidal effects, which reduced the spin of the earth from around five hours to around 24 hours, as earlier our planet was spinning too fast. Most important are the lunar tides, whence the marine life in our seas came into existence; in this case, this also resulted in the origination of life of land, too [3].

The moon is also a source of most of mineralogical resources, which can be used for future space missions, specifically as good products for fuel substitutes to be used for future deep space explorations and the colonization of mankind on the lunar surface [5]. Recent findings of water ice content at the moon's poles – which is believed to be buried or mixed with the regolith – and water ice content outside the poles also offer hope for achieving our goals in the near future as we inch towards our desire for deep space exploration [6]–[9]. While to date dependence on extraction of minerals, and economic activity related to it, has been limited to earth, lunar resources can be used for exploration of the lunar surface as well as for the scientific and economic activity of both the moon and the earth – to say nothing of exploration of the other celestial bodies in the solar system. Recent studies have discussed the potential resources on the lunar surface – mainly solar wind implanted volatiles, Helium-3, water, oxygen, metals (platinum group metals), iron and siderophile elements, titanium, aluminum, silicon, rare earth elements, thorium, and uranium [5]. The continued exploration of the lunar surface will produce positive results for the goals that we hope can soon be achieved.

17.2.1 IMPORTANCE OF THE MOON IN THE INDIAN SPACE PROGRAM

The father of the Indian space program, Dr. Vikram Sarabhai, once said, "There are some who question the relevance of space activities in a developing nation; to us, there is no ambiguity of purpose." This is also relevant to the current scenario; India as a developing nation, has come a long way in its space program – from the initial days of the first rocket launch in 1963 to the launch Chandrayaan-2 in 2019. In 2014, it made it as far as the red planet, Mars, achieving its goal on the first attempt, a feat that had not been accomplished by any other nation [10]. Chandrayaan-1, the first deep space exploration mission of the Indian space program, was initiated in 2008, making India one of the first developing nations to send its orbiter to the moon to study topography, mineral, and chemical mapping of the lunar surface and also to search for water. The detection of abundant water in the form of OH/H20, involving solar wind interaction, was a major achievement in this mission. The success of this mission has led to the exploration of other planetary bodies like Mars.

17.2.2 HUMAN FOOTPRINTS ON THE MOON: THE MANNED MISSIONS ON THE LUNAR SURFACE

The thirst for exploring the lunar surface increased with the missions carried out in earlier stages of exploration by different nations. Visiting the lunar surface, exploring, and returning to the earth with samples increased the information about the lunar surface and made a vast difference in understanding the structure and geology of the lunar surface. The closeness of the moon has made it possible to access its surface easily and continuously, unlike any other deep space destination. The first manned mission carried out in 1968 was Apollo 8 (Table 17.1), which was a crewed orbiter mission; the last, Apollo 17, was of the same era and was a crewed lander mission in 1972. There has subsequently been an almost five-decade halt in manned missions, but with the upcoming Artemis missions, returning to the moon will occur in the coming years.

17.2.3 THE CHRONICLE OF LUNAR EXPLORATION: LANDER, ORBITER, AND IMPACTOR

Interest in exploring Luna dates to the first telescopic observation in August 1609, by an Englishman named Thomas Harriott; Galileo followed in 1610. Earlier, there were many speculations regarding the moon – that it has life and oceans, for instance. It was also believed that the composition of the lunar surface was rhyolite; this belief persisted into the early 20th century, until exploration of the lunar surface enabled making observations, collecting samples during the Apollo era, and doing analyses on these samples once they were returned to earth. This led to a detailed understanding of our nearest celestial body.

TABLE 17.1
Apollo Series Description (Credits-NASA) [11]

Mission Name	Launch Date and Landing Site	Objectives
Apollo 8	December 21, 1968	Illustrate command and service module performance in cislunar and lunar orbit. Demonstrate communications, tracking lunar distances, and photographs of the proposed landing site.
Apollo 9	March 3, 1969	Test lunar module, spacecraft launch, and vehicle adapter, demonstrate extravehicular activity (EVA), and perform system functions.
Apollo 10	May 18, 1969	Verification of lunar module system in the lunar environment, refinement of the lunar gravitational potential.
Apollo 11	July 16, 1969, & Mare Tranquillitatis	Observe properties of lunar regolith, EVA to collect samples, and science experiments to investigate soil mechanics, solar winds, passive seismic, lunar dust detector, lunar surface magnetometer.
Apollo 12	November 14, 1969, & Ocean of Storms	Deploy the Apollo Lunar Surface Experiments Package (ALSEP), selenological inspection, surveys, and samplings in landing areas, development of techniques for precision-landing capabilities, further evaluations of the human capability to work in the lunar environment for a prolonged period.
Apollo 14	January 31, 1971 & Fra Mauro	Lunar field geology investigations, collection of surface material samples for return to Earth, communications tests using S-band and VHF signals to determine reflective properties of the lunar surface, tests to determine variations in S-band signals.
Apollo 15	July 26, 1971, & Hadley-Appennius	Perform selenological inspections, surveys, and sampling of materials and surface features of the landing site.
Apollo 16	April 16, 1972 & Descartes formation	Perform geological inspection, survey, and sampling of materials and surface features in the landing site, to emplace and activate surface experiments, and to conduct inflight experiments and photographic tasks.
Apollo 17	December 7, 1972	Obtain samples of highland material that were older than the Imbrium impact, heat flow experiment; lunar seismic profiling, or LSP; lunar surface gravimeter, or LSG; lunar atmospheric composition experiment, or LACE; and lunar ejecta and meteorites, or LEAM.

The first mission carried out was Luna-1, launched by the Soviet Union on January 3, 1959; this was a flyby mission, from which it was discovered that the lunar surface does not have any global magnetic field. Luna-9 in 1969 became the first mission in which a spacecraft landed on any celestial body; before this, the missions were only flyby or impactors. A recent mission to the moon was Chang'e-5, launched by China in November 2020, in which samples were collected after around 44 years – the last samples collected had been in 1976, by Luna-24. The urge to explore the lunar surface (Table 17.2) is never-ending; upcoming missions by different nations are a prime example of this. There is no need to engage in any space race if we can go hand in hand to achieve good results for mankind.

17.2.4 FUTURE LUNAR MISSIONS

Lunar exploration in the future will aid the leap to deep space exploration. The space agencies of various countries, including USA, Russia, China, India, Japan, and South Korea, are actively

TABLE 17.2
Lunar Exploration Timeline

Mission Name	Launch Time	Operation Mode
Luna 1	Jan 2, 1959	Flyby
Pioneer 4	Mar 3, 1959	Flyby
Luna 2	Sep 12, 1959	Impact
Luna 3	Oct 4, 1959	Probe
Ranger 1	Aug 23, 1961	Attempted test flight
Ranger 2	Nov 18, 1961	Attempted test flight
Ranger 3	Jan 26, 1962	Attempted impact
Ranger 4	Apr 23, 1962	Impact
Ranger 5	Oct 18, 1962	Attempted impact
Luna 4	Apr 2, 1963	Flyby
Ranger 6	Jan 30, 1964	Impact
Ranger 7	Jul 28, 1964	Impact
Ranger 8	Feb 17, 1965	Impact
Ranger 9	Mar 21, 1965	Impact
Luna 5	May 9, 1965	Impact
Luna 6	Jun 8, 1965	Attempted lander
Zond 3	Jul 18, 1965	Flyby
Luna 7	Oct 4, 1965	Impact
Luna 8	Dec 3, 1965	Impact
Luna 9	Jan 31, 1966	Lander
Luna 10	Mar 31, 1966	Orbiter
Surveyor 1	May 30, 1966	Lander
Lunar Orbiter 1	Aug 10, 1966	Orbiter
Luna 11	Aug 24, 1966	Orbiter
Surveyor 2	Sep 20, 1966	Attempted lander
Luna 12	Oct 22, 1966	Orbiter
Lunar Orbiter 2	Nov 6, 1966	Orbiter
Luna 13	Dec 21, 1966	Lander
Lunar Orbiter 3	Feb 4, 1967	Orbiter
Surveyor 3	Apr 17, 1967	Lander
Lunar Orbiter 4	May 8, 1967	Orbiter
Surveyor 4	Jul 14, 1967	Attempted lander
Lunar Orbiter 5	Aug 1, 1967	Orbiter
Surveyor 5	Sep 8, 1967	Lander
Surveyor 6	Nov 7, 1967	Lander
Surveyor 7	Jan 7, 1968	Lander
Luna 14	Apr 7, 1968	Orbiter
Zond 5	Sep 15, 1968	Return probe
Apollo 7	Oct 11, 1968	
Zond 6	Nov 10, 1968	Return probe
Apollo 8	Dec 21, 1968	Crewed orbiter
Apollo 9	March 3, 1969	Crewed orbiter
Apollo 10	May 18, 1969	Orbiter
Luna 15	Jul 13, 1969	Orbiter
Apollo 11	Jul 16, 1969	Crewed lander
Zond 7	Aug 7, 1969	Return probe
Apollo 12	Nov 14, 1969	Crewed lander
Apollo 13	Apr 11, 1970	Crewed lander (aborted)

(continued)

TABLE 17.2 (Continued)
Lunar Exploration Timeline

Mission Name	Launch Time	Operation Mode
Luna 16	Sep 12, 1970	Sample return
Zond 8	Oct 20, 1970	Return probe
Luna 17/Lunokhod 1	Nov 10, 1970	Rover
Apollo 14	Jan 31, 1971	Crewed lander
Apollo 15	Jul 26, 1971	Crewed lander
Luna 18	Sep 2, 1971	Impact
Luna 19	Sep 28, 1971	Orbiter
Luna 20	Feb 14, 1972	Sample return
Apollo 16	Apr 16, 1972	Crewed landing
Apollo 17	Dec 7, 1972	Crewed landing
Luna 21/Lunokhod 2	Jan 8, 1973	Rover
Luna 22	Jun 2, 1974	Orbiter
Luna 23	Oct 28, 1974	Lander
Luna 24	Aug 14, 1976	Sample return
Hiten	Jan 24, 1990	Flyby, orbiter, and impact
Clementine	Jan 25, 1994	Orbiter
AsiaSat 3/HGS-1	Dec 24, 1997	Lunar flyby
Lunar Prospector	Jan 7, 1998	Orbiter and impact
SMART 1	Sep 27, 2003	Orbiter
Kaguya (SELENE)	Sep 14, 2007	Orbiter
Chang'e 1	Oct 24, 2007	Orbiter
Chandrayaan-1	Oct 22, 2008	Orbiter
Lunar-A	Canceled	Orbiter and penetrators
LRO	Jun 18, 2009	Orbiter
LCROSS	Jun 18, 2009	Impact
Chang'e 2	October 1, 2010	Orbiter
ARTEMIS	2010	Orbiter
GRAIL	September 8, 2011	Orbiter
Chang'e 3	December 1, 2013	Lander and rover
LADEE	May 2, 2013	Orbiter
Delta IV-Orion (EFT-1)	September, 2014	Orbiter
SLS-Orion (EM-1)	2017	Orbiter
Constellation Altair Lander (canceled)	2018	Lander
SELENE-2 (canceled)	2018	Orbiter and lander with rover
Chang'e 4	May 20, 2018	Lander and rover
Chandrayaan-2	2019	Orbiter and lander
Chang'e 5	2019	Sample return

Credit: Lunar and Planetary Institute (LPI)

participating in exploration of the lunar surface, for instance by planning to send probes that contain an orbiter, lander, rover, or sample return mission. The first crewed mission in almost five decades is being planned by NASA; their Artemis-3 mission is planned for 2024. Detailed descriptions of future lunar missions are explained in Table 17.3, while an interpretation of future lunar missions is shown in Figure 17.1.

TABLE 17.3
Future Lunar Missions

Name	Country and Agency	Expected Launch Date	Nature of Mission
Artemis 1	USA & NASA	16 December, 2021	Orbiter
CAPSTONE	USA & NASA	2021	Orbiter
Peregrime Mission-1	USA & NASA	2021	Lander
Luna-25	Russia & Roscosmos	2021	Lander
IM-1	USA & NASA	2021	Lander
LunaH-MAP	USA & NASA	2021	Orbiter
Lunar Flashlight	USA & NASA	2021	Orbiter
Lunar Ice Cube	USA & NASA	2021	Orbiter
LunIR	USA & NASA	2021	Orbiter
Cislunar Explorers	USA & NASA	2021	Orbiter
OMOTENASHI	Japan & JAXA	2021	Lander
EQUULEUS	Japan & JAXA	2021	Orbiter
SLIM	Japan & JAXA	2022	Lander
Korea Pathfinder Lunar Orbiter	South Korea & KARI	2022	Orbiter
Prime-1	USA & NASA	2022	Lander
Chandrayaan-3	India & ISRO	3rd Quarter, 2022	Lander
XL-1 Lander	USA & NASA	2023	Lander
VIPER	USA & NASA	2023	Rover
Artemis-2	USA & NASA	September 2023	Orbiter
Chang'e-6	China & CNSA	2023–24	Lander, orbiter, sample return
Lunar Trailblazer	USA & NASA	2024	Orbiter
Artemis-3	USA & NASA	2024	Crewed lander mission
Luna-26	Russia & Roscosmos	Expected 2024	Orbiter
Chang'e-7	China & CNSA	Expected 2024	Lander, orbiter, rover, sample return
Luna-27	Russia & Roscosmos, European Space Agency	2025	Lander
Luna-28	Russia & Roscosmos	2026	Lander
Chang'e-8	China & CNSA	TBD	Unknown
Luna-29	Russia & Roscosmos	2028	Lander

Credit: NASA-NSSDC & LPI

FIGURE 17.1   Future lunar missions (Credit: LPI) [12].

17.3 THE NEW ERA OF SAR-BASED MISSIONS FOR THE LUNAR SURFACE

17.3.1 CHANDRAYAAN-1

Chandrayaan-1's mission of the Indian Space Research Organisation took place in 2008 and consisted of several payloads, which included Mini-SAR as well. The major scientific objective of this instrument was to detect water ice in the permanently shadowed region (PSR) on the lunar poles, up to a depth of a few meters [5]. The Mini-SAR used the S-band and has a wavelength of 12.6 cm and an incidence angle of 35°. The spatial resolution of the image strips is 75 meters per pixel [13]. Preliminary results concluded from the Mini-SAR data were that the circular polarization ratio (CPR) values in the north polar regions were in the range of 0.1–0.3. A group of craters was identified that showed a high CPR value between 0.6–1.7 in the interior of the crater, but this was less in the exterior of the rim of the crater, which was around 0.2–0.4. In the South Pole–Aitken basin, the massifs that make up the rim of the basin showed high CPR. The small craters of the south pole, namely Shoemaker and Faustini, also showed high CPR values. Apart from the non-polar regions that showed a high CPR value was Sulpicius Gallus, which has fine-grained pyroclastic deposits near it. Craters such as Aratus and Aristarchus, which are fresh craters, have high CPR values. The average combined CPR of mare and highland terrain is ~0.32 ± 0.11 [9], [14].

17.3.2 LUNAR RECONNAISSANCE ORBITER

The lunar reconnaissance orbiter (LRO) was launched in 2009 with a developed version of the Chandrayaan-1 mission's SAR instrument on board, i.e., Mini-RF. The Mini-RF instrument has a hybrid polarimetry architecture operating at two bands, i.e., S- and X-band, whose wavelengths are 12.6 cm and 4.2 cm, respectively. It focuses on the lunar poles that went previously unexplored for possible locations of ice deposits, volatiles, impacts, and volcanic processes on the moon. It has also mapped the PSR of the lunar poles for polar volatiles [15], as well as the roughness of the lunar surface, and it can see the ejecta that is not visible in optical images. The major science objective of Mini-RF is to investigate the vertical distribution of water; the form and abundance of water ice; how impacts expose and break down rocks to produce regolith on the moon and other airless bodies; the present rate of regolith gardening; and how lunar volcanism has evolved [16].

17.3.3 CHANDRAYAAN-2

The DFSAR instrument aboard Chandrayaan-2 is a dual-frequency monostatic system operating at L-band (24 cm) and S-band (12 cm) at an altitude of 100 km. One of the main features of this radar sensor is that it is the first L-band polarimetric SAR utilized for lunar studies, which will be used for deeper penetration into the regolith, and it is also the first fully polarimetric SAR to orbit the moon. The instrument can also acquire imaging in single, dual, and hybrid-circular polarimetry and resolution capacities from 2 m to 75 m in the slant range, with incidence angles ranging from 9.6° to 36.9° [17], [18]. The fully polarimetric mode in this aims for unambiguous detection and the characterization and quantitative estimation of the water ice in the PSR region of the lunar poles.

The DFSAR will also address the ambiguities detected in depicting high values of the CPR for water ice that was found in the earlier missions that were caused by surface roughness. The advantage of full-polarimetric data over any arbitrary polarization state like circular, linear, and hybrid modes is that it contains more scattering information. Chandrayaan-2 DFSAR data with different incident angles 10° and 35°, steep and moderate respectively, can be used to calculate the surface roughness of the regolith. The configuration of DFSAR is shown in Figure 17.2.

The major scientific objectives of the DFSAR instrument are (a) Detection and estimation of water–ice deposits in the permanently shadowed regions of the moon, using dual-frequency and full-polarimetric imaging at multiple viewing angles. (b) Regolith dielectric

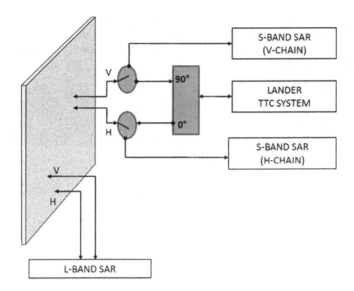

FIGURE 17.2   SAR configuration with lander communication [20].

constant and surface roughness estimation over the lunar surface using multi-frequency data. (c) Investigation of geo-morphological features especially in the polar regions and preparation of geomorphological maps and high-resolution crater floor maps. (d) Quantitative estimation of regolith thickness and distribution over selected regions using data from dual-frequency radiometer mode. [19]

17.4   CRATER FORMATION

Impact craters usually occur to all celestial bodies in the solar system that have solid surfaces in nature. Earth has a thick atmosphere, however, so meteoroids that enter the atmosphere are blasted off due to friction generated by the earth's gravity upon entry [20]. An impact crater is formed when energy is instantly transferred from the impactor to the target. As two bodies in a solar system approach each other at high velocity, kinetic energy is provided from the relative orbital motion of the colliding bodies and gravitational energy from the gravitational field. Impact craters can be much larger because of collisions that can be very energetic. On the moon, the only geological activity that takes place is impact cratering.

17.4.1   TYPES OF CRATERS

The craters can be divided into four classes based on their morphology: namely, micro craters or pits, small or simple craters, large craters, and multi-ring basins. Micro or pit craters are formed when micrometeoroids or high velocity cosmic dust grains cause these craters at the sub-centimeter scale on rocky surfaces. The center of these craters is covered with glass, and they are found on astronomical bodies that do not have an atmosphere. Small or simple-shaped craters are those whose depth is approximately one-fifth of their diameter, and these craters are in bowl-shaped structures. Large craters are also called complex craters because of their structures. The base area of these craters is smooth, but there is a peak in its center, and the rim looks like a terrace. The diameter of these craters can range from a few tens to a few hundred kilometers. In multi-ring basins, these craters cover a much larger area than the large craters as they are made up of several concentric circles, and the inner ring has a hill [21].

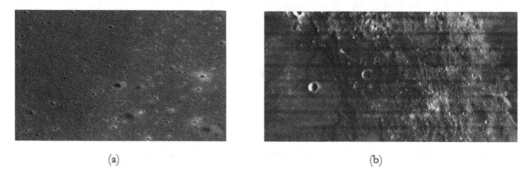

(a)   (b)

FIGURE 17.3   Lunar pyroclastic deposit: (a) Aristarchus Plateau (b) Rima Bode (Credit: NASA/ Goddard/ Arizona State University/ USGS Astrogeology Science Center).

17.5   LUNAR PYROCLASTIC DEPOSITS

Pyroclastic deposits are the evident source of early volcanism in lunar history and contain metal oxides and volatiles that can be used in the future. In total, there are more than 100 mapped regions of pyroclastic deposits on the lunar surface, and some of them range to an extent of 49,000 sq. km [22], [23]. They are generally related to the mare boundaries, volcanism centers, and the fractures that lie in the impact craters [22]. Lunar pyroclastic deposits can be classified into two types: namely, localized dark mantling deposits and regional dark mantling deposits (RDMDs). Localized dark mantling deposits are related to endogenic dark haloed craters. These pyroclastic deposits are divided into three classes. Class 1 consists of highlands materials with minor olivine and volcanic glass. Class 2 is made up of fragmented mare basalts, and Class 3 is of mafic materials in which olivine and pyroxene are in abundance [24]. RDMDs are comprised of picritic glasses of volcanic origin [24], [25]. Based on spectral data, RDMDS are also categorized into two types. Glasses that show Fe2+ are one type; an example is Aristarchus plateau (Figure 17.3(a)). The ilmenite-rich black beads or spheres of the pyroclastic region are the second type; an example is the Apollo 17 site, which is the Taurus-Littrow valley [26]. The other examples include Rima Bode (Figure 17.3(b)) and the southern Mare Vaporum regions. The age of the Apollo 17 landing site in the Taurus-Littrow valley dates back to 3.48–3.66 Ga ago [22]. Ferrous iron (Fe2+), which are volcanic glass beads and/or black crystallized beads, was found at Taurus-Littrow, Aristarchus, and Sulpicius Gallus. The Apollo landing site also has orange glasses and crystallized beads. The pyroclastic deposits have various resource possibilities; they are fine-grained and boulder-free, so they can be used for future lunar outposts. So, it will be time and cost effective for machinery. It has also been stated in various studies that these deposits can be used for producing oxygen. Other resources include volatiles implanted from the solar wind, such as H, He, He-3, C, and other noble gases, that could be used for life support materials and other agricultural activities [24], [27].

17.6   LUNAR RILLES

The lunar surface comprises several geological structures apart from the craters, which include lunar rilles. Rilles are referred to as *rima* in Latin, plural *rimae*. These rilles look like dried riverbeds and are categorized into three types: sinuous, straight, and arcuate [28]. Sinuous rilles are considered to be formed by collapsed lava tubes and appear as a meandering river. A magma source region on the mantle would likely have created these depressions when magma reached the surface. At one time, it was considered that these channel-like features were created by surface or subsurface erosion from flowing water or erosion due to ash flows, collapsed lava tubes, or the intersection of fracture patterns. But now, the better assumption is that their formation is because of lava flow and erosion

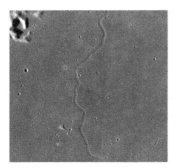 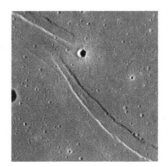 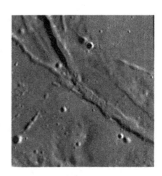

FIGURE 17.4 Lunar Rilles: (a) sinuous rille – Rima Sharp, (b) straight rille – Rima Cauchy, (c) arcuate rille – Rimae Sulpicius Gallus (Credit: NASA, GSFC, Arizona State University).

from the collapsed lava tubes [29]. The sinuous rille is the most common rille-type feature found on the lunar surface. Figure 17.4(a) shows an example of a sinuous rille, which is Rima Sharp; its rille length is around 276 km. The second type is the straight rille, which is formed by tectonic forces. When a block of crust descends to the valley floor, the surface of the crust separates under extensional forces, which are called graben. The largest straight rille is found in the Oceanus Procellarum, also known as Ocean of Storms, situated on the near side of what is known as Rima Sirsalis, and stretches to 400 km [28]. Figure 17.4(b) shows an example of a straight rille, which is Rima Cauchy. The arcuate rille is the third type, which is formed along the margins of maria within some basins as curved formations, similar to parentheses or bows (without the arrows). Arcuate rilles are likely the result of mare basalts sagging toward the center, causing the edges to pull apart. This is why the rille shape closely follows the basin's circular shape [28]. Figure 17.4(c) shows an example of arcuate rille, which is Rimae Sulpicius Gallus, and its total rille length is around 80 km.

17.7 SOUTH POLE

The geology of the moon is quite fascinating and makes us curious as human beings, as most of it is still unexplored and unanswerable. The existence and findings of water ice deposits at both of poles and especially in the south polar region makes the south pole an interesting exploratory area because most of this part is in the PSR. The south pole lies in one of the largest and oldest basins of our solar system recognized to date, that is, the South Pole–Aitken (SPA) basin [30]–[32]. SPA is situated on the far side of the moon, and the basin is around 2500 km in diameter and averages around 12 km in depth, which belongs to the pre-Nectarian period [33]. The moon's mineralogy consists of a mixture of feldspar, pyroxene, olivine, and ilmenite. It was found that pyroxene and plagioclase are major carriers of iron and aluminum, respectively, while clinopyroxene is present in most of the mare deposits that are also in the SPA basin. Orthopyroxene is majorly present near the rim of the SPA basin, especially between the Lyman and Antoniadi craters. The Apollo basin in the SPA, which is rich in anorthite but low in FeO, also has a major presence of orthopyroxene. Olivine is significantly low in the SPA basin compared to the other lunar surfaces [30]. Lucey et al. [31] also concluded that the SPA basin's floor is a mixture of lower crust, which consists of low-K Fra Mauro (LKFM) mafic rock, and the upper mantle, which contains 10–20 wt% of FeO and approximately 0.1 wt% TiO_2 [31]. It was revealed that the crust of the SPA basin is comparatively thinner (20 km) than the average thickness (68 km) of the far side. The center region of the SPA basin is rich in Ca, Fe pyroxene, and Mg rich pyroxenes are predominant in the rest of the central SPA. The outer region of the SPA, which is SPA exterior, is highly feldspathic [34].

The south pole region, which is just inside the main rim of the SPA basin, is located in the heavily cratered region of the southern highlands [35]. The geological interpretation of this region is very

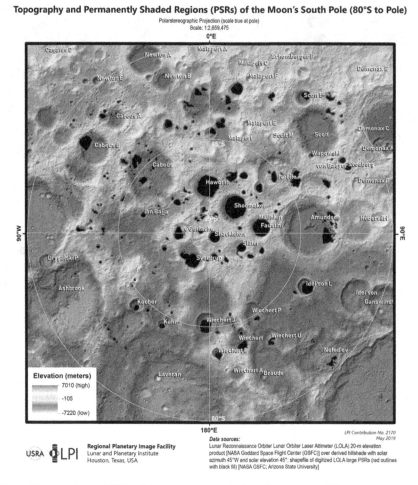

Topography and Permanently Shaded Regions (PSRs) of the Moon's South Pole (80°S to Pole)

Polarstereographic Projection (scale true at pole)
Scale: 1:2,659,475

FIGURE 17.5　Topography and PSR of the lunar south pole (Credit: Lunar and Planetary Institute).

difficult because of the lunar spin axis as the sunlight is always at low angles in the polar region, especially in the south pole, making most of it in the PSR (Figure 17.5). Leibniz β is the large massif platform-like structure and is the most prominent feature in the inner ring of the basin [35]. As earlier mentioned, this area belongs to the pre-Nectarian period, and the terrain in this region is highly informal because of the SPA basin itself. The area is covered in various irregular craters, and there is a collection of craters, too. The average annual temperature of the lunar south pole is around 38K, which is very low, and the PSR is very cold, it is cold enough to have water ice deposits. The hydrogen concentrations in the PSR have been measured by the lunar energetic neutron detector (LEND), which is around 0.3–0.5 wt% water equivalent hydrogen (WEH) [36]. The south pole consists of the Schrodinger impact basin, which consists of the Schrodinger crater; this basin is of much interest because of its structure, as it is one of the last two impact basins to be formed on the lunar surface. The basin has several features; there is a deposit of dark material around a volcanic vent that is one of the largest individual volcanic features on the moon. This dark, spectrally similar material can be seen on the Apollo 17 landing site in the Taurus-Littrow valley, which is near the southeastern edge of Mare Serenitatis; it resembles glass-like structures called pyroclastic material [37]. Overall, it can be said that the SPA basin has a high possibility for the existence of more water ice deposits and other mineral-rich components because of its structure, as it is one of the largest and oldest impact basins in the solar system [38].

17.8 CIRCULAR POLARIZATION RATIO

CPR is one of the most important parameters for measuring water ice content on the surface of the moon. According to the formula, SC is the ratio between the received power in the same sense (SC) and the transmitted power in the opposite sense (OC) [39], [40]. Due to the incident radar wave bouncing multiple times, rough surfaces have a high CPR value since they generate more same-sense signals. Usually, in surface scattering, the CPR value is less than unity. The main issue of using CPR alone is if a high CPR value is obtained from the rough surface such that rocks, lava flows. So, in this scenario, a radar signal is transmitted (left circular polarization (LCP)) and, after hitting a boulder, changes into right circular polarization (RCP), before again rebounding to another boulder and changing polarization from RCP to LCP and then to the receiver (see Figure 17.6). This results in double-bounce scattering, which can be a misleading result for interpretation of water ice content [39]. The relation of CPR with the stokes parameter is given in Equation (17.1).

$$CPR = \left(s_1 - s_4\right) / \left(s_1 + s_4\right). \tag{17.1}$$

High CPR caused by surface roughness scattering

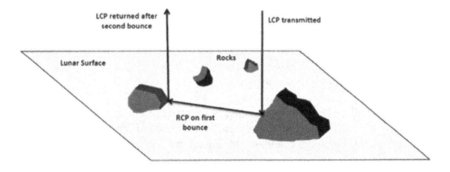

High CPR caused by ice/volume scattering

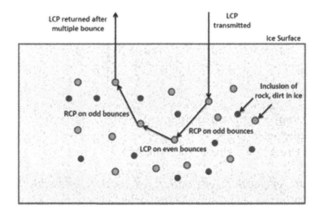

FIGURE 17.6 Higher CPR caused by planetary ice (volume) or roughness due to surface scattering [39].

17.9 DECOMPOSITION TECHNIQUES

The major decomposition techniques used in the study of the lunar surface are m-chi (m-χ), m-delta (m-δ), and m-alpha (m-α) for hybrid polarimetry data, and fully polarized data H-alpha decomposition.

So, from stokes, child parameters m, δ, and χ are calculated and the degree of polarization (m) is calculated from Equation (17.2).

$$m = \frac{\sqrt{S_2^2 + S_3^2 + S_4^2}}{S_1}. \tag{17.2}$$

The degree of polarization for a completely polarized wave is 1 and for a completely unpolarized wave is 0.

The relative phase (δ) denotes double-bounce scattering and is calculated per Equation (17.3).

$$\delta = \tan^{-1}\left(\frac{S_4}{S_3}\right). \tag{17.3}$$

The ellipticity parameter (χ) is sensitive to double-bounce scattering compared to surface scattering and is calculated per Equation (17.4).

$$\mathrm{Sin}\, 2\chi = \frac{-S_4}{mS_1}. \tag{17.4}$$

17.9.1 M-δ DECOMPOSITION

These decompositions allow land and oceanographic researchers to distinguish surface scattering and double-bounce scattering. The parameters in this decomposition are m, relative phase, and orientation angle (δ) [41]. These are calculated by Equations (17.5), (17.6), and (17.7).

$$s = \left[mS_1 \frac{(1+\sin\delta)}{2}\right]^{\frac{1}{2}}, \tag{17.5}$$

$$v = \left[S_1(1-m)\right]^{\frac{1}{2}}, \tag{17.6}$$

$$d = \left[mS_1 \frac{(1-\sin\delta)}{2}\right]^{\frac{1}{2}}, \tag{17.7}$$

where,
s = odd-bounce scattering or surface scattering,
v = volumetric scattering, and
d = even-bounce scattering or double-bounce scattering.

The parameters are dependent mainly on two components: δ and degree of polarization (m). δ differentiates between surface and double-bounce, which makes it an important parameter. So, the positive value of δ shows signs of the dominance of surface scattering and the negative value for double-bounce scattering dominance.

17.9.2 M-χ Decomposition

From the lunar surface, this decomposition is widely applied when separating even-bounce scattering from odd-bounce scattering; the parameters that are used are m, χ, and δ [40]. This decomposition technique was first used by Raney in hybrid polarimetric data [41]. Calculations of the parameters in this decomposition are shown in Equations (17.8), (17.9), and (17.10).

$$s = \left[mS_1 \frac{(1 - sin2\chi)}{2} \right]^{\frac{1}{2}}, \tag{17.8}$$

$$v = \left[S_1 (1 - m) \right]^{\frac{1}{2}}, \tag{17.9}$$

$$d = \left[mS_1 \frac{(1 + sin2\chi)}{2} \right]^{\frac{1}{2}}, \tag{17.10}$$

where,
s = odd-bounce scattering or surface scattering,
v = volumetric scattering, and
d = even-bounce scattering or double-bounce scattering.

17.9.3 M-α Decomposition

The parameter m and polarization angle (α) are determined by the H-α method of decomposition, which consists of eigenvalues.
  α is calculated from Equation (17.11) [42].

$$A = 2|\chi|. \tag{17.11}$$

m-α decomposition is calculated by Equations (17.12), (17.13), and (17.14).

$$s = \left[mS_1 \frac{(1 + cos2\alpha)}{2} \right]^{\frac{1}{2}}, \tag{17.12}$$

$$v = \left[S_1 (1 - m) \right]^{\frac{1}{2}}, \tag{17.13}$$

$$d = \left[mS_1 \frac{(1 - cos2\alpha)}{2} \right]^{\frac{1}{2}}, \tag{17.14}$$

where,
s = odd-bounce scattering or surface scattering,
v = volumetric scattering, and
d = even-bounce scattering or double-bounce scattering.

  The value of alpha (α) is in the range of 0 and π/2. If the value of α is equal to 0, then it shows surface scattering; if it is in the range of π/4, then it shows volume scattering; and if it is equal to π/2, then it is double-bounce scattering.

17.10   STUDY AREA AND DATASETS

17.10.1   SHACKLETON CRATER

Shackleton crater is situated on the interior basin massif of the South Pole–Aitken (SPA) basin. The south pole is situated inside the topographic rim of the SPA basin and is one of the oldest and largest impact craters on the moon [43]. The size of the Shackleton crater is 20 km in diameter and 4.2 km deep, and it is the largest impact crater situated within 1° of the south pole of the moon. Initially, the age of this crater was found to be of Eratosthenian age (1–3.2 Gyr before present), but after the studies, it was concluded that it is of Imbrian age (3.2–3.8 Gyr before present). The age of the Shackleton crater is 3.6 Gyr, which is older than the mare surface of the Apollo 15 (3.3 Gyr) landing site, but relatively younger than the Apollo 14 landing site (3.85 Gyr) [35], [44]. The location of the Shackleton crater is 89° 54′ 0″ S, 0° 0′ 0″ E, and it is nearly coincident with the lunar south pole, whose interior is almost completely in permanent sun shadow. The crater walls are smoother, as the surface roughness is at a scale of 20–50 m, and the crater floor can be divided into two regions, a flat portion and an elevated terrain [45]. Subsequently, as it is in permanent shadow, it may have dealt as a cold trap to congregate volatiles as both the poles of the moon show inflated amounts of hydrogen content, and if it is present in the form of water ice and these can be present in the permanently shadowed areas, this makes Shackleton crater a plausible candidate of such water ice deposits [35].

17.10.2   ERLANGER CRATER

The diameter of the Erlanger crater is around 10 km, and its coordinates are 86.94 N and 28.62 E. It is situated between two large craters, Peary and Byrd. This crater is also in the PSR, as most of the craters do not get sunlight [46].

17.10.3   SLATER CRATER

Slater crater is another crater situated at the lunar south pole, with most of its area in the PSR. Its coordinates are 88.08°S 111.29°E. A summit between the Shackleton crater and Slater crater has

FIGURE 17.7   Shackleton crater (Credit: NASA/GSFC/Arizona State University).

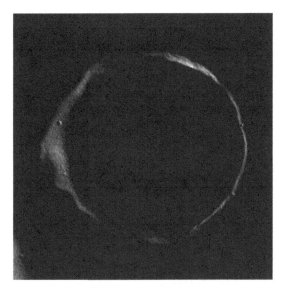

FIGURE 17.8 Erlanger crater (Credit: NASA/GSFC/Arizona State University).

FIGURE 17.9 Slater crater (Credit: LPI, Lunar Orbiter Photo Gallery, Lunar Orbiter 4).

been identified as a possible landing site for NASA's upcoming Artemis mission. The site is identified as site 007 (see Figure 17.9).

17.10.4 RIMAE SULPICIUS GALLUS

The Rimae Sulpicius Gallus is situated in the Mare Serenitatis region and is well known to be of a lunar mare, which means it has large dark basaltic plains. The pyroclastic deposits near the Sulpicius Gallus are estimated to be 50 m thick and contain both mare and highlands terrain.

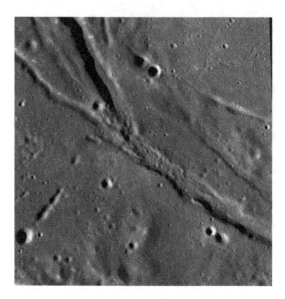

FIGURE 17.10   Rimae Sulpicius Gallus (Credit: NASA/GSFC/Arizona State University).

17.11   RESULTS

This work involves the characterization of three craters that are situated at the south pole and the north pole of the lunar surface: Shackleton and Slater at the south pole and the Erlanger crater at the north pole. These craters all lie in the PSR of the lunar surface. It also includes the characterization of a rille, i.e., Rimae Sulpicius Gallus.

17.11.1   Shackleton Crater

Shackleton crater is situated in the south pole region, and it is in the PSR. The characterization of this crater is on three decomposition techniques and CPR for LRO hybrid pol data that is of S-band (Table 17.4).

17.11.1.1   m-δ (Delta) Decomposition

Figure 17.11 (d) shows the RGB composite of the m-δ decomposition of Shackleton crater along with the components of scattering mechanisms, namely double-bounce, volume, and surface scattering. As seen in Figure 17.11 (b), volume scattering is dominant in this decomposition technique. Surface scattering is visible on the right side of the crater wall. However, the presence of the rough surface makes the crater dominant in volume scattering, which is a diffuse scattering pattern due to absorption in the crater walls. Double-bounce scattering is also visible on the crater but is relatively lower than volume and surface scattering. Surface scattering is dominant outside of the crater, which can be seen. The mean values of the surface scattering are 0.16, 0.136 for volume scattering and 0.124 for double-bounce scattering.

17.11.1.2   m-χ (chi) Decomposition

The m-χ decomposition separates the odd and even-bounce scattering and enhances it. It also differentiates the ejecta and their relative thickness. As shown in Figure 17.12(d), the RGB composite of the m-χ decomposition, the surface scattering, and double-bounce scattering are dominant on the right side of the crater wall and part of the crater base. The outer rim of the crater also shows

TABLE 17.4
Dataset Details of Hybrid Polarimetry Data Used in This Work

Sr No.	Sensor Name	Product ID	Study Area	Band	Resolution in (m/pixel)
1	LRO Mini-RF	LSZ_02261_1CD_OKU_89S140_V1	Shackleton	S	7.5
2	Chandrayaan-1 Mini-SAR	FSB_01299_1CD_OIU_86N326_V1	Erlanger	S	75
3	LRO Mini-RF	LSZ_02615_1CD_XKU_22N010_V1	Rimae Sulpicius Gallus	S	7.5

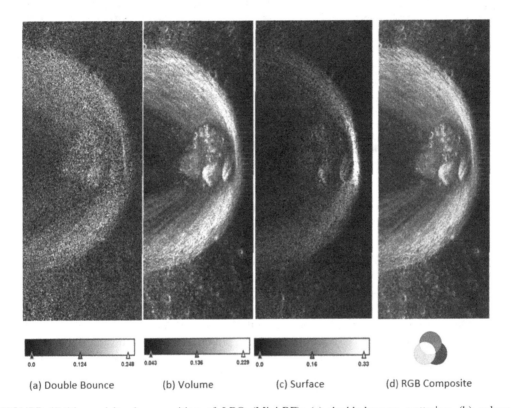

(a) Double Bounce (b) Volume (c) Surface (d) RGB Composite

FIGURE 17.11 m-delta decomposition of LRO (Mini-RF): (a) double-bounce scattering, (b) volume scattering, (c) surface scattering, and (d) RGB color composite.

double-bounce scattering. Volume scattering is seen in the crater walls and parts of the crater base, which may be because of the presence of rough material in the crater walls, while double-bounce scattering may be because of natural dihedrals in the surroundings. The mean values of surface scattering are 0.143, which is highest in comparison to double-bounce scattering, which is 0.14, and 0.136 for the least volume scattering.

17.11.1.3 m-α (Alpha) Decomposition

This decomposition technique is based on eigenvector analysis of hybrid pol data, and it is close to H/α decomposition of fully polarimetric data. In this angle, α is derived from the stokes parameter.

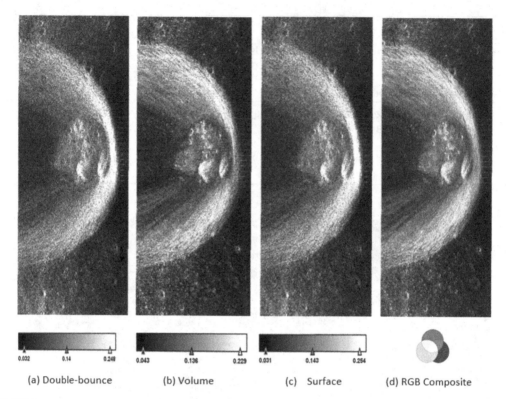

0.032 0.14 0.248	0.043 0.136 0.229	0.031 0.143 0.254	
(a) Double-bounce	(b) Volume	(c) Surface	(d) RGB Composite

FIGURE 17.12   m-chi decomposition of LRO (Mini-RF): (a) double-bounce scattering, (b) volume scattering, (c) surface scattering, and (d) RGB color composite.

The polarization angle of 0° is sensitive to double-bounce scattering; surface scattering is sensitive to 90°, and volume scattering is sensitive to predominant depolarized backscatter.

Figure 17.13 (d) shows the RGB composite of the m-α decomposition. Surface scattering is quite dominant in this decomposition technique and is visible in the crater walls, base, and outside the rim. Double-bounce scattering is quite low in this decomposition, and the presence of volume scattering is greater than surface scattering due to the presence of the rough surface. High volume scattering is quite visible in the crater walls. The mean values of the double-bounce scattering are very low, i.e., 0.0055, which is visible only in the small area at the right side of the crater. The mean value of volume scattering is 0.136, and for surface scattering, it is 0.2.

17.11.2 ANALYSIS OF CPR

Figure 17.14 shows the values of CPR in the crater. The high values of CPR, which is more than 1 in the Shackleton crater, depict that the crater has some areas that are a probable location of water ice deposits. Values below 1 relate to the lunar regolith and other materials. The high values of CPR can be also due to scattering by rough surfaces, which may be because of double-bounce scattering or volume scattering. The locations on the right side of the crater walls show low CPR, and it was observed that it showed surface scattering in these regions. The CPR value, which is close to 1.99 in some areas, is present in the crater walls and some areas outside the crater rim.

17.11.3 SLATER CRATER

In this study, the scene that covers the Slater crater is of L-band DFSAR of Chandrayaan-2 (Table 17.5), and as earlier stated in this chapter, this region lies in the PSR of the lunar south pole.

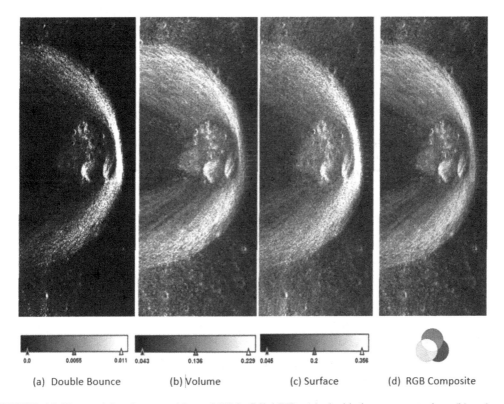

(a) Double Bounce   (b) Volume   (c) Surface   (d) RGB Composite

FIGURE 17.13   m-alpha decomposition of LRO (Mini-RF): (a) double-bounce scattering, (b) volume scattering, (c) surface scattering, and (d) RGB color composite.

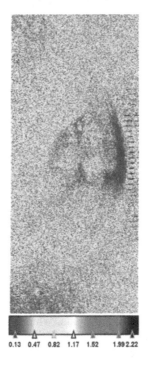

FIGURE 17.14   Value of CPR for Shackleton crater for LRO (Mini-RF).

TABLE 17.5
Dataset Details of Fully Polarimetric Data Used in This Work

Sr No.	Sensor Name	Product ID	Date of Acquisition	Study Area	Band	Azimuth & Range Resolutions (meters)
1	Chandrayaan-2 DFSAR	ch2_sar_ncxl_ 20191103t150253267_d_fp_d18	03-11-2019	Slater	L	0.59 & 9.59
2	Chandrayaan-2 DFSAR	ch2_sar_ncxl_ 20191112t100519040_d_fp_gds	12-11-2019	Erlanger	L	0.55 & 9.59

FIGURE 17.15   Barnes decomposition for Chandrayaan-2 (DFSAR): (a) full scene of the data covering Slater crater and (b) zoomed view of the PSR region.

Here, Barnes decomposition technique is used to characterize different types of scattering, namely volume.

17.11.3.1 BARNES DECOMPOSITION

Figure 17.15 shows the RGB composite image of Barnes decomposition of Slater carter in the south pole of the DFSAR of Chandrayaan-2 data, which is single look complex (SLC) data. Figure 17.15(a) shows the scene that covers two PSR regions, including the PSR region of the Slater crater. Figure 17.15(b) shows the zoomed in version of the scene of the PSR encircled in yellow, which is shown to clearly distinguish the crater and its scattering mechanism; its PSR_ID is SP_

88100_1147820. Figure 17.15 (c) shows the zoomed in image of the Slater crater whose PSR_ID is SP_874430_1188390. The wall of the crater shows volume scattering depicting the crater walls to be of a rough surface, and some areas of the walls depict surface scattering. The floor of the crater shows volume scattering, which is seen in green, which also depicts that the floor is rough. The PSR_ID SP_88100_1147820 shows volume scattering in the crater floor and also in the crater walls, which depicts that these regions are rough.

17.11.4 ERLANGER CRATER

Erlanger crater is one of the small craters situated at the north pole on the lunar surface. It also lies in the PSR region. The characterization of this crater is likewise based on three decomposition techniques and CPR for hybrid pol data of Chandrayaan-1, which is of S-band. For fully polarimetric data of L-band DFSAR of Chandrayaan-2, the Barnes decomposition technique has been used to analyze the different polarimetric scattering.

17.11.4.1 m-δ (Delta) Decomposition

Figure 17.16 (d) shows the RGB composite of the m-δ decomposition of the Erlanger crater, which shows the dominance of volume scattering in the crater walls, whereas the crater base and the surrounding area around the rim show the dominance of surface scattering and double-bounce scattering. The crater base and the surrounding areas are smooth, so surface scattering is more prominent in these regions. Double-bounce scattering is visible in the crater base and outside the crater rim, which could be because of the natural dihedral structure in the surroundings. The mean values of volume scattering are 0.114; for surface and double-bounce it is the same at 0.1.

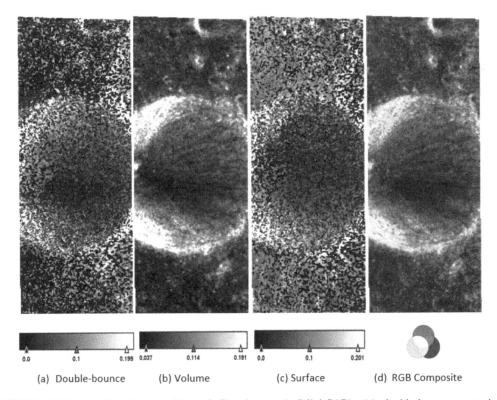

(a) Double-bounce   (b) Volume   (c) Surface   (d) RGB Composite

FIGURE 17.16 m-delta decomposition of Chandrayaan-1 (Mini-SAR): (a) double-bounce scattering, (b) volume scattering, (c) surface scattering, and (d) RGB color composite.

17.11.4.2 m-χ (chi) Decomposition

Figure 17.17 (d) shows the RGB composite of the m-χ decomposition of the Erlanger crater, which shows that dominance of volume scattering is found in the crater walls, suggesting that the walls of the crater are of a rough surface, as was seen in m-δ decomposition. The crater base has double-bounce and surface scattering in dominance. The magenta color in the crater base and the surrounding around the rim shows the combination of double-bounce and surface scattering. The mean values of the volume scattering are 0.114, and for double-bounce and surface scattering is the same, at 0.099, which was also seen in the m-δ decomposition.

17.11.4.3 m-α (Alpha) Decomposition

Figure 17.18 (d) shows the RGB composite of m-α decomposition of Erlanger crater. High volume scattering is seen in the crater walls, as in the other two decompositions, i.e., m-δ and m-χ. But in this, the crater base shows a dominance of surface scattering, and it is also seen on the outside of the crater rim. A very small scattering of double-bounce is seen in the rim connected to the crater, which could be because of the presence of natural dihedrals in the region. The small craters in the region outside the crater also show volume scattering; the surface scattering outside the crater shows the area to be smooth, which was not in the case of the other two decompositions. The mean value of volume scattering is 0.114, which is similar in all the decompositions; surface scattering is 0.14, whereas the mean value of double-bounce scattering is very low at 0.00103.

17.11.4.4 Analysis of CPR

Figure 17.19 shows the values of CPR in the crater. The high values of CPR, which is more than 1 in the Erlanger crater, depict that the crater has some areas that may be a probable location of water

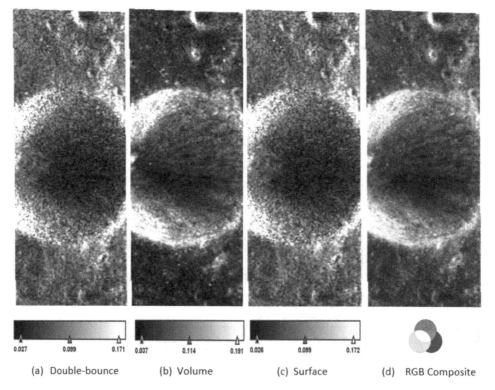

(a) Double-bounce   (b) Volume   (c) Surface   (d) RGB Composite

FIGURE 17.17 m-chi decomposition of Chandrayaan-1 (Mini-SAR): (a) double-bounce scattering, (b) volume scattering, (c) surface scattering, and (d) RGB color composite.

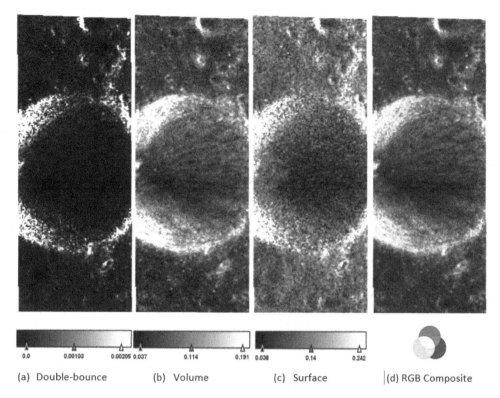

(a) Double-bounce (b) Volume (c) Surface |(d) RGB Composite

FIGURE 17.18 m-alpha decomposition of Chandrayaan-1 (Mini-SAR): (a) double-bounce scattering, (b) volume scattering, (c) surface scattering, and (d) RGB color composite.

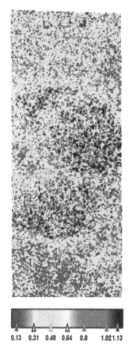

FIGURE 17.19 Value of CPR for Erlanger crater for LRO (Mini-RF).

ice deposits. Values that are below 1 relate to the lunar regolith and other materials. The high values of CPR may be also due to scattering by the rough surface, which can be because of double-bounce scattering or volume scattering. The locations of the crater walls show high CPR, of 1.02 to 1.13, particularly in the crater walls but not on the floor of the crater. The areas outside of the crater show low CPR values, which can be caused by surface scattering.

17.11.4.5 Barnes Decomposition

Figure 17.20 shows the RGB composite image of Barnes decomposition of Erlanger crater of DFSAR of Chandrayaan-2 data, which is SLC data. Figure 17.20(a) shows the scene that covers three PSR regions, including the PSR region of the Erlanger crater. Figure 17.20(b) shows the zoomed version of the scene of two PSR, in which one, whose PSR_ID is NP_877350_0169810, has the crater is encircled in black; while the other, whose PSR_ID is NP_875450_0179490, has the crater encircled in blue, which is shown to clearly distinguish the crater and its scattering mechanism. Figure 17.20 (c) shows the zoomed in image of the Erlanger crater whose PSR_ID is NP_869610_0287570. The wall of the crater shows volume scattering in dominance, depicting the crater walls to be of a rough surface. The floor of the crater shows surface scattering, which is seen in blue, and also depicts that the floor is smooth; this was seen as well from the other decomposition techniques used on the S-band of Mini-SAR and Mini-RF. The walls also show some regions to be in blue, which gives an interpretation that some regions in the crater walls are smooth. The area outside the crater rim shows

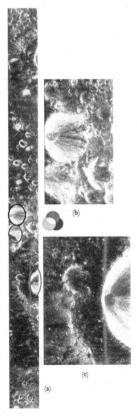

FIGURE 17.20 Barnes decomposition for Chandrayaan-2 (DFSAR): (a) full scene of the data covering Erlanger crater, (b) zoomed view of the two PSR region, and (c) zoomed view of Erlanger crater.

the ejecta of the crater, which is seen in green and depicts volume scattering in these regions. The scene also shows different craters that can be easily identified as in green, while some regions show in blue that are smooth in nature.

17.11.5 *RIMAE SULPICIUS GALLUS*

The Rimae Sulpicius Gallus is the lunar rille that contains pyroclastic deposits in its surrounding areas. The characterization of this area is done by the m-χ decomposition technique for the hybrid pol data of LRO Mini-RF and values of CPR.

Figure 17.21 shows the RGB composite of the m-χ decomposition in which the area where the rille, i.e., the Rimae Sulpicius Gallus, is seen shows the dominance of double-bounce scattering in the surrounding region, including a part that shows volume scattering. In this, it can be seen that the mean values of all the scattering mechanisms are quite similar, which are 0.12 for double-bounce scattering, 0.12 for surface scattering, and 0.11 for volume scattering.

For any surface, if the CPR value is greater than 1, this indicates that due to the presence of diffuse scatterers or volume scattering, it shows the same sense polarization. The area that showed volume scattering in the decomposition has a higher value of CPR, which is around 1.17 in these regions. The pyroclastic deposits in the region show the presence of high volume scattering along with double-bounce scattering.

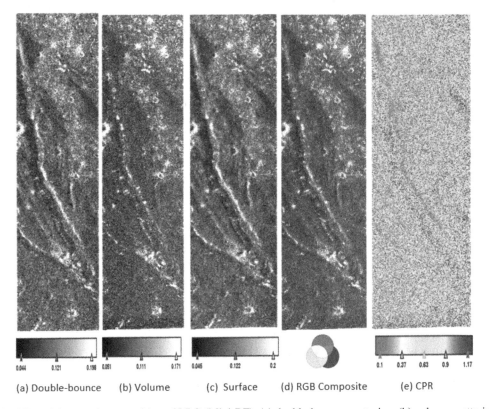

(a) Double-bounce   (b) Volume   (c) Surface   (d) RGB Composite   (e) CPR

FIGURE 17.21 m-χ decomposition of LRO (Mini-RF): (a) double-bounce scattering, (b) volume scattering, (c) Surface scattering, (d) RGB color composite, and (e) CPR values.

17.12   CONCLUSIONS

This study shows an attempt to identify and characterize the region of the lunar poles and the PSR region of the lunar surface, which also includes the lunar rille present in the Mare Serenitatis region. This study gives an idea about the craters in the lunar poles and gives an interpretation of the scattering in these regions by different decomposition techniques used on hybrid polarimetric data and fully polarimetric data. The m-chi decomposition used in characterizing different scattering mechanisms gives a better interpretation to identify these regions in hybrid polarimetric data. The use of CPR value indicates the regions in the crater where the surface is rough or smooth, as well as an initial interpretation of the region regarding the possible locations of water ice deposits. The fully polarimetric data of L-band DFSAR characterizes the crater in a more-detailed manner in comparison to the S-band. The DFSAR also characterizes the scattering of the Slater crater, which is also in the PSR region of the lunar surface. For future studies, this study recommends that the craters be identified for surface characterization and identification of lunar volatiles and surface and subsurface features present in the lunar regolith, which can offer an advancement for the future exploration of these areas.

REFERENCES

[1] NASA, "In depth | Moons – NASA solar system exploration." https://solarsystem.nasa.gov/moons/in-depth/ (accessed Sep. 14, 2021).

[2] NASA, "In-depth | Earth's Moon – NASA solar system exploration." https://solarsystem.nasa.gov/moons/earths-moon/in-depth/ (accessed Apr. 05, 2021).

[3] I. A. Crawford, "Lunar resources: A review," *Prog. Phys. Geogr.*, vol. 39, no. 2, pp. 137–167, 2015, doi: 10.1177/0309133314567585.

[4] NASA, "Earth and moon once shared a magnetic shield." https://www.nasa.gov/feature/earth-and-moon-once-shared-a-magnetic-shield-protecting-their-atmospheres (accessed Apr. 01, 2021).

[5] N. Bhandari and N. Srivastava, "Active moon: Evidences from Chandrayaan-1 and the proposed Indian missions," *Geoscience Letters*, vol. 1, no. 11, Dec. 01, 2014, doi: 10.1186/s40562-014-0011-y.

[6] W. C. Feldman et al., "Evidence for water ice near the lunar poles," *J. Geophys. Res. E Planets*, vol. 106, no. E10, pp. 23231–23251, 2001, doi: 10.1029/2000JE001444.

[7] P. O. Hayne, O. Aharonson, and N. Schörghofer, "Micro cold traps on the moon," *Nat. Astron.*, vol. 5, pp. 169–175, 2021, doi: 10.1038/s41550-020-1198-9.

[8] S. Li et al., "Direct evidence of surface exposed water ice in the lunar polar regions," *Proc. Natl. Acad. Sci. U. S. A.*, vol. 115, no. 36, pp. 8907–8912, 2018, doi: 10.1073/pnas.1802345115.

[9] P. D. Spudis et al., "Evidence for water ice on the moon: Results for anomalous polar craters from the LRO Mini-RF imaging radar," *J. Geophys. Res. Planets*, vol. 118, no. 10, pp. 2016–2029, Oct. 2013, doi: 10.1002/jgre.20156.

[10] B. Harvey, H. H. F. Smid, and T. Pirard, *Emerging Space Powers*. 2010.

[11] NASA, "The Apollo Missions." https://www.nasa.gov/mission_pages/apollo/missions/index.html (accessed Sep. 17, 2021).

[12] LPI, "Lunar Mission Timeline." https://www.lpi.usra.edu/lunar/missions/ (accessed Sep. 17, 2021).

[13] L. Carter et al., "The MiniSAR imaging radar on then Chandrayaan-1 on the Moon," *Lunar Planet. Sci. Conf.*, vol. 40, no. 1098, pp. 7–8, 2009.

[14] D. Spudis et al., "Results of the Mini-SAR imaging radar, Chandrayaan-1 mission to the moon p," 2010. [Online]. http://lunarscience2009.arc.nasa.gov/node/73 (accessed Oct. 30, 2020).

[15] R. Vondrak, J. Keller, G. Chin, and J. Garvin, "Lunar reconnaissance orbiter (LRO): Observations for lunar exploration and science," *Space Sci. Rev.*, vol. 150, no. 1–4, pp. 7–22, 2010, doi: 10.1007/s11214-010-9631-5.

[16] S. S. Bhiravarasu, T. Chakraborty, E. Heggy, and R. Kumar, "Characterizing the scattering properties of the moon with the LRO Mini-RF and Chandrayaan-2 DFSAR radars," in *51st Lunar and Planetary Science Conference*, the Woodlands, Texas, Mar. 2020, pp. 1–3.

[17] D. Putrevu, S. Trivedi, A. Das, and D. Pandey, "L- and S-band polarimetric synthetic aperture radar on Chandrayaan-2 mission," *Curr. Sci.*, vol. 118, no. 2, pp. 226–233, 2020.

[18] G. W. Patterson et al., "Characterizing the scattering properties of the moon with the LRO Mini-RF and Chandrayaan-2 DFSAR radars," 2020. [Online]. https://ui.adsabs.harvard.edu/abs/2020 LPI....51.2507P/abstract (accessed Nov. 20, 2020).

[19] D. Putrevu, A. Das, J. G. Vachhani, S. Trivedi, and T. Misra, "Chandrayaan-2 dual-frequency SAR: Further investigation into lunar water and regolith," *Advances in Space Research*, vol. 57, no. 2, pp. 627–646, 2015, doi: 10.1016/j.asr.2015.10.029.

[20] C. Koeberl, "Remote sensing studies of impact craters: how to be sure?," vol. 336, pp. 959–961, 2004, doi: 10.1016/j.crte.2004.05.001.

[21] L. M. Jozwiak, J. W. Head, M. T. Zuber, D. E. Smith, and G. A. Neumann, "Lunar floor-fractured craters: Classification, distribution, origin and implications for magmatism and shallow crustal structure," *J. Geophys. Res. Planets*, vol. 117, no. E11, 2012, doi: 10.1029/2012JE004134.

[22] L. M. Carter, B. A. Campbell, B. R. Hawke, D. B. Campbell, and M. C. Nolan, "Radar remote sensing of pyroclastic deposits in the southern Mare Serenitatis and Mare Vaporum regions of the Moon," *J. Geophys. Res*, vol. 114, p. 11004, 2009, doi: 10.1029/2009JE003406.

[23] L. R. Gaddis, M. I. Staid, J. A. Tyburczy, B. R. Hawke, and N. E. Petro, "Compositional analyses of lunar pyroclastic deposits," *Icarus*, vol. 161, no. 2, pp. 262–280, 2003, doi: 10.1016/S0019-1035(02)00036-2.

[24] S. Lawrence and B. Hawke, "Lunar pyroclastic deposits: An accessible and quantifiable lunar resource," *Proc. Lunar Planet. Sci. Conf. 39th*, 2008, p. 1804.

[25] C. K. Shearer and J. J. Papike, "Basaltic magmatism on the Moon: A perspective from volcanic picritic glass beads," *Geochim. Cosmochim. Acta*, vol. 57, no. 19, pp. 4785–4812, 1993, doi: 10.1016/0016-7037(93)90200-G.

[26] L. R. Gaddis, C. M. Pieters, and B. Ray Hawke, "Remote sensing of lunar pyroclastic mantling deposits," *Icarus*, vol. 61, no. 3, pp. 461–489, 1985, doi: 10.1016/0019-1035(85)90136-8.

[27] G. Chin et al., "Lunar reconnaissance orbiter overview: The instrument suite and mission," *Space Sci. Rev.*, vol. 129, no. 4, pp. 391–419, 2007, doi: 10.1007/s11214-007-9153-y.

[28] "Rilles and rilles: Sinuous, straight, and arcuate | Lunar reconnaissance orbiter camera." http://lroc.sese.asu.edu/posts/1147 (accessed Sep. 22, 2021).

[29] D. M. Hurwitz, J. W. Head, and H. Hiesinger, "Lunar sinuous rilles: Distribution, characteristics, and implications for their origin," *Planet. Space Sci.*, vol. 79–80, no. 1, pp. 1–38, 2013, doi: 10.1016/j.pss.2012.10.019.

[30] P. G. Lucey, "Mineral maps of the moon," *Geophys. Res. Lett.*, vol. 31, no. 8, Apr. 2004, doi: 10.1029/2003GL019406.

[31] P. G. Lucey, G. J. Taylor, B. R. Hawke, and P. D. Spudis, "FeO and TiO_2 concentrations in the South Pole-Aitken basin: Implications for mantle composition and basin formation," *J. Geophys. Res. Planets*, vol. 103, no. E2, pp. 3701–3708, Feb. 1998, doi: 10.1029/97JE03146.

[32] NASA, "South Pole – Aitken Basin." https://www.nasa.gov/mission_pages/LRO/multimedia/lroimages/lola-20100409-aitken.html (accessed Mar. 09, 2021).

[33] K. J. Kim et al., "The South Pole–Aitken basin region, Moon: GIS-based geologic investigation using Kaguya elemental information," *Adv. Sp. Res.*, vol. 50, no. 12, pp. 1629–1637, Dec. 2012, doi: 10.1016/j.asr.2012.06.019.

[34] D. P. Moriarty and C. M. Pieters, "The character of South Pole–Aitken Basin: Patterns of surface and subsurface composition," *J. Geophys. Res. Planets*, vol. 123, no. 3, pp. 729–747, Mar. 2018, doi: 10.1002/2017JE005364.

[35] P. D. Spudis, B. Bussey, J. Plescia, J. L. Joset, and S. Beauvivre, "Geology of Shackleton Crater and the south pole of the Moon," *Geophys. Res. Lett.*, vol. 35, no. 14, 2008, doi: 10.1029/2008GL034468.

[36] J. Flahaut et al., "Regions of interest (ROI) for future exploration missions to the lunar South Pole," *Planet. Space Sci.*, vol. 180, p. 104750, Jan. 2020, doi: 10.1016/j.pss.2019.104750.

[37] S. E.M., R. M.S., and E. E.M., "The South Pole region of the moon as seen by Clementine," *Am. Assoc. Adv. Sci.*, vol. 266, no. 5192, pp. 1851–1854, 1994, doi: DOI: 10.1126/science.266.5192.1851.

[38] R. A. Yingst and J. W. Head, "Geology of mare deposits in South Pole–Aitken basin as seen by Clementine UV/VIS data," *J. Geophys. Res. Planets*, vol. 104, no. E8, pp. 18957–18979, Aug. 1999, doi: 10.1029/1999JE900016.

[39] S. Mohan, A. Das, and M. Chakraborty, "Studies of polarimetric properties of lunar surface using Mini-SAR data," *Curr. Sci.*, vol. 101, no. 2, pp. 159–164, 2011.

[40] P. N. Calla, S. Mathur, and M. Jangid, "Study of equatorial regions of Moon with the help of backscattering coefficient obtained from LRO data," *J. Earth Syst. Sci.*, vol. 123, no. 2, pp. 433–443, 2014, doi: 10.1007/s12040-014-0407-2.

[41] R. Raney Keith, J. T. S. Cahill, G. Patterson Wesley, and D. B. J. Bussey, "The m-chi decomposition of hybrid dual-polarimetric radar data with application to lunar craters," *J. Geophys. Res. E Planets*, vol. 117, no. 5, 2012, doi: 10.1029/2011JE003986.

[42] K. S. Tomar, "Hybrid polarimetric decomposition for aboveground biomass estimation using semi-empirical modelling," Univ. of Twente, Enschede, The Netherlands, p. 70, 2015.

[43] N. E. Petro and C. M. Pieters, "Surviving the heavy bombardment: Ancient material at the surface of South Pole–Aitken basin," *J. Geophys. Res. E Planets*, vol. 109, no. 6, pp. 1–13, 2004, doi: 10.1029/2003JE002182.

[44] B. J. Thomson, D. B. J. Bussey, J. T. S Cahill, C. Neish, G. W. Patterson, and P. D. Spudis, "The interior of Shackleton crater as revealed by Mini-Rf orbital radar," *Science (80-.).*, pp. 10–11, 2011.

[45] M. T. Zuber et al., "Constraints on the volatile distribution within Shackleton crater at the lunar south pole," *Nature*, vol. 486, no. 7403, pp. 378–381, 2012, doi: 10.1038/nature11216.

[46] K. B. Bhavya, "Polarimetric modeling of lunar surface for scattering information retrieval using Mini-SAR data of Chandrayaan-1," Univ. of Twente, Enschede, The Netherlands, 2013.

18 Synthetic Aperture Radar (SAR) Data Calibration and Validation

*P. V. Jayasri, K. Niharika, H. S. V. Usha Sundari Ryali,
and E. V. S. Sita Kumari*

CONTENTS

18.1 INTRODUCTION

Recent advances in microwave remote sensing have seen the development of synthetic aperture radar (SAR) satellites because of their capability to obtain information independent of weather conditions and external illumination source; these characteristics have made them potentially important, particularly in the tropics, where persistent cloud cover limits the use of data from optical and near infrared satellite sensors. As there are many potential applications of spaceborne SAR systems, including crop monitoring, forest monitoring, soil moisture measurement, sea ice classification, etc., this requires that the system be well calibrated, particularly in terms of radiometric and geometric

DOI: 10.1201/9781003204466-18

calibration. However, because of coherent SAR imaging, the presence of speckles in radar images makes it relatively difficult to identify point targets, with known geographic locations, that needed for geometric and radiometric corrections. Moreover, polarimetric SAR systems have necessitated an increasing interest in the remote sensing community, since they are able to provide much more information than the conventional single polarization systems. There are several spaceborne PolSAR missions already in space, such as RADARSAT-2, TERRASAR-X, ALOS PALSAR, and EOS-04, and hence reliable polarimetric calibration procedures and techniques are highly relevant. Therefore, corner reflectors to suit SAR and PolSAR are considered for proper radiometric, geometric, and polarimetric calibration of SAR missions.

18.2 SIGNIFICANCE OF SAR CALIBRATION

To investigate the long-term stability of the spaceborne SAR system, there is a general need for accurate SAR calibration in order to support application-oriented research programmers. SAR calibration and validation begin as the stage on which the integrity of all data subsequently derived will be based. Without such calibration and validation, the data may be at best being qualitative. Validation is usually a measure of how well the derived product from a given SAR describes a given geophysical entity as measured by independent means. Validation involves significantly more than the original concept of ground truth or surface truth. It takes into account a broad range of variables not considered in the early developmental phases of satellite-derived data and information. Slight changes that may occur in either the calibration of a sensor or its validated product may generate erroneous data records unless the data are of very high quality. The elements of both calibration and validation are required in order to have knowledge on whether the changes in the product are due to changes in the instrument or a change in the environment.

The purposes of calibration are twofold:

(a) Conversion of the radar output units into predetermined reference units.
(b) The measurement of dynamic system characteristics, which fluctuate throughout the life of the system to enable correction of the final product for such features.

In particular, it is important to know whether SAR calibration is constant over the mission life. Absolute calibration of SAR data allows the user to interpret imagery in a quantitative manner. For example, a pixel value within a calibrated SAR image may be attributed to a backscattering coefficient for the corresponding area on the ground. Geophysical parameters, such as soil moisture, can then be extracted through the use of suitable backscatter models. Also, absolute calibration is essential if comparison of data from different sensors is to provide useful information. Absolute calibration allows taking into account all the contributions in the radiometric values that are not due to the target characteristics. This permits the differences in the image radiometry to be minimized and makes any SAR images obtained from different incidence angles, ascending/descending geometries, and/or opposite look directions easily comparable and even compatible to acquisitions made by other radar sensors. Precise calibration needs to be performed in order to properly correct the errors introduced by the transmitter and the receiver into the scattering data.

For calibration and validation, the following payload characteristics measurements are considered:

- SAR high power amplifier (HPA) stability
- Pulse replica characteristics/stability
- Dynamic range
- Noise equivalent sigma naught (NES0)
- Spatial resolution
- Integrated side lobe ratio (ISLR)

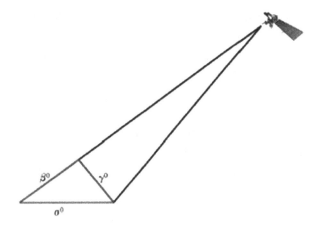

FIGURE 18.1 Depiction of γ_0, β_0, σ_0.

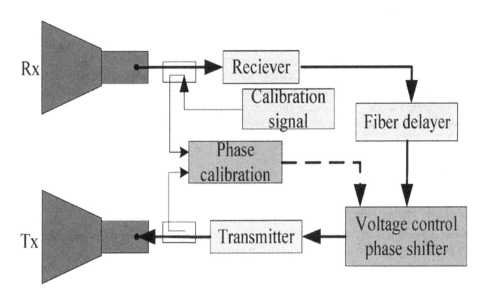

FIGURE 18.2 Hardware architecture of active radar calibrator.

- Peak side lobe ratio (PSLR)
- Georeferencing (absolute, scale, skew etc)
- Radiometric calibration (absolute and relative)

Note: Frequently used terminology is further defined in Appendix .

A SAR processor is calibrated when the coefficients required for accurate radiometry have been determined, but an image is calibrated when those coefficients have been applied. Calibrating a SAR image is the process of converting a linear amplitude image into a radiometrically calibrated power image. The input image is in units of digital numbers (DNs), whereas the output image is in units of β_0, γ_0 or σ_0, which is the ratio of the power that comes back from a unit area of ground to the power sent to a unit area of ground. The application will determine which of these calibration units to choose. Scientists are generally interested in quantitative measures that are referring to the ground, i.e., they work with σ_0 values. For calibration purposes, γ_0 values are preferred because they are equally spaced. Finally, system design engineers would choose β_0 values, as these values are independent from the terrain covered.

$$\gamma_0 = \sigma_0/\cos(\text{incidence angle}) \tag{18.1}$$

$$\beta_0 = \sigma_0/\sin(\text{incidence angle}) \tag{18.2}$$

Radiometric stability is the standard deviation of the (time series) measurements of the radar cross-section of a calibration target (using the same calibration constant) and the radiometric accuracy as the (time series) average of the absolute difference between the nominal radar cross-section and the measured radar cross-section (using the same calibration constant) of a calibration target.

18.3   TYPES OF SAR CALIBRATIONS

The measured radar backscatter is uniquely related to a geophysical property of the targets. Any change in the geophysical property can therefore be determined by the measurement of its backscatter. However, this measurement assumes that the system is calibrated in such a way that any changes in backscatter due to variations in system gain have been removed. To assess the stability of the SAR system, period calibration is envisaged based on the mission requirements. After the launch, during commissioning and the initial phase, all the imaging modes envisaged by SAR mission will be exercised and calibration of all modes in various polarizations will be performed. To have long-term stability of the SAR system, SAR calibration exercises will be done quarterly or half-yearly or, if the system prompts for any change onboard or SAR processing software, then calibration is carried in campaign mode. To ensure highly accurate data products, there are mainly two types of calibration techniques to calibrate the in-orbit performance, namely:

(a)   Internal calibration.
(b)   External calibration.

18.3.1   INTERNAL CALIBRATION

Spaceborne systems include methods for internal calibration, which usually involve the transmission of a precisely generated signal through the transmitter–receiver system.

To achieve high quality of data product, regular health monitoring and characterization of SAR raw data is required. The data contains calibration data in terms of replica, noise, transmit high power SSPA (HPA), which comes in the beginning of the imaging session, followed by cal operations of low noise amplifier (LNA), noise, and replica, which come at the end of each imaging session. The replica is an ideal chirp, which depicts the transmitted power by the transmitted antenna, and noise cal depicts the noise floor of the receiver. HPA gives the gain imbalance and transmit path gain and phase information. The LNA cal pulses gives the gain information in the receiver paths. These parameters are required to be consistent with reference to the onboard cal data observed. If the behaviour of these parameters is beyond threshold levels, then relevant alarms will be provided to concern payload teams to take corrective action.

A linearly frequency modulated signal (chirp signal) is generated onboard, which will be passed through the transmitting chain containing power amplifiers (like SSPA, high power amplifiers), while the receiving chain contains LNA. However, such methods fail to include the gain of the antenna and ignore propagation losses. Also, internal calibration systems on occasion can introduce errors or even fail completely.

A method of overcoming this is to use external calibration targets, i.e., targets of accurately known radar cross-section, to use these as a check on the internal calibration system, and to provide overall system calibration. In addition, external targets provide a means of referring measurements made by one system to another, thus maintaining continuity. External targets are particularly important in verifying the antenna gain pattern. This pattern is based on ground-based measurements made prior to launch, and its accuracy depends on the stiffness of the antenna support structure and deployment mechanism. For a steered beam phased array antenna, the pattern will generally vary from one beam to another, and this requires each individual beam to be calibrated.

18.3.2 External Calibration

The effectiveness of external calibration depends entirely on the accuracy with which the deployed target cross-section is known. Not only must the cross-section be measured or derived to a given accuracy or tolerance, it is also important that the stability of the target cross-section be known especially because SAR missions are expected to have a long life of five years or more.

The success of an external calibration procedure is directly influenced by five characteristics of the radar calibration target, which include:

(a) Large radar cross-section (RCS).
(b) Wide RCS pattern.
(c) Small physical size.
(d) Stable RCS.
(e) Insensitive RCS to the surrounding environment.

Calibration targets need to have a cross-section that is sufficiently large to enable them to be accurately measured against the background. The RCS should be stable with an accuracy that can be stated within specified limits. Sometimes ground targets acts as primary calibration sources. Agricultural analysis requires images that are not only internally consistent (dependent on accurate processing) but should be comparable with others. This entails calibration of SAR images to a fixed reference. For carrying out SAR calibration, a feature with known RCS is identified in an image and then the "brightness" of the image in correspondence to the "brightness" of the identified known feature is adjusted. In general, there are three possible types of ground targets that are preferred for external calibration to yield better operational performance of SAR systems. Those are point targets (namely active targets and passive targets) and distributed targets. The following sections describe the characteristics and usability of each type of target to aid in complete SAR system calibration.

18.3.2.1 Active Targets

Active transponders placed on ground can be used for external calibration of SAR systems whereby the incident radiation is amplified and returned. This has the advantage of being able to provide a signal that is much higher than the background, making it much easier to locate and allowing more accurate calibration of the image. Active transponders provide better ratio of signal clutter, which provides better calibration accuracy. Transponders with high RCS provide accurately defined point targets within the SAR image. Transponders offer a greater range of RCS levels.

The main building blocks of a transponder are a receive antenna, a high-precision amplifier, and a transmit antenna (Figure 18.2). The main advantages of a transponder over a corner reflector are its small size and therefore portability and the possibility of easily changing receive and transmit polarizations. The main disadvantage lies in the fact that a precise electronic amplification for a relatively large temperature range is difficult to implement. The transponders are equipped with an internal temperature compensation to allow an operation in winter (say $-15°$ C) and summer ($35°$ C) scenarios.

18.3.2.2 Passive Targets

Passive calibration point targets offer several advantages over active transponders. They can be built with high radiometric accuracies, do not delay the reflected signal, which is the desired property for

FIGURE 18.3 Structure of 75 cm trihedral and 100 cm dihedral corner reflectors, including mounting pedestal.

geometric calibration, and are relatively robust for field use during the calibration campaigns. They are inherently stable and relatively inexpensive to construct. On the other hand, they are bulky and cannot easily be moved to a new location, and they obviously do not allow for data recording.

The simplest kind of known feature would be a metallic reflective sheet positioned such that the normal to the plane of the sheet is accurately pointing at the satellite, which would be a difficult proposition. A metallic sphere can provide the same RCS from any incidence angle, but the disadvantage with this is that a sphere naturally scatters most incident radiation away from the incident direction, making it very "dim" and difficult to discern from the background scatter.

Corner cube retro reflectors (Figure 18.3) are passive targets that offer one of the best solutions for calibration. The corner reflector consists of three sheets of metal or gauze arranged to form a right-angled corner whereby incident radiation entering the corner reflector reflects off each of the three surfaces in turn before being redirected towards the source of the radiation. Corner reflectors still need to be pointed towards the satellite, but the accuracy of the pointing is much less critical than for a flat metallic sheet reflector.

18.3.2.3 Distributed Targets

Calibration with distributed targets requires use of a distributed target (such as a field of grass or well-ploughed field) for which the RCS is well known. The RCS can be predicted if one carefully controls the distributed target characteristics to duplicate a well-known and measured target. This is very difficult to do at best, as there are many variables to control. Fields with different roughness levels can be prepared to study the behaviour with respect to surface roughness. Distributed target calibration refers to external calibration using natural targets of large areas with homogeneous backscattering properties. A fundamental assumption is that the scattering properties of these areas are stable or that the variation is well characterized. This permits the image characteristics associated with the target scattering to be decoupled from the sensor performance. The Amazon rainforest is an established distributed target for SAR data calibration, as announced by the SAR subgroup of the Working

Group on Calibration and Validation (WGCV) of the Committee on Earth Observation Satellite (CEOS). The Amazon rainforest was used for ERS-1/2, J-ERS-1, RADARSAT-1/2, ENVISAT, RISAT-1, Sentinel-1A/1B, EOS-04, RADARSAT Constellation Mission (RCM), etc., providing a large isotropic backscattering reference over a wide range of incidence angle.

18.4   CORNER REFLECTORS

A corner reflector is the most commonly used object for generating an impulse response in a test SAR image. A good impulse response has a relatively large value for the pixel that maps the point scatterer location, and very small values for all surrounding pixels. The impulse response is a basic building block in describing given radar's imaging performance, since an image is built up from the linear combination of impulse responses from all individual scatterers illuminated by the radar. Corner reflectors have the property to reflect incident radiation directly back to the source, independent of the angle of the incidence of the radiation on the reflector. Corner reflectors are found to be very attractive radar targets as they exhibit a large bistatic and monostatic RCS over a wide angular range. Relevant input factors for designing and deploying corner reflectors, including the background from surrounding areas, pointing angles from SAR, contribution from multipath, the dimensions, material, shapes, polarization dependency, etc., are considered. Though triangular trihedral reflectors are found to be most suitable [9], the optimum sizes for corner reflectors are arrived at with minimum fabrication errors as the physical sizes of the planes depend on the radar operating frequency, average power required to identify the target in the image, reflector mounting mechanism, etc. Calibration targets need to have a cross-section that is sufficiently large to enable them to be accurately measured against the background for different frequency bands (X, C, S, L). For proper identification of CR in SAR image, it is highly required to maintain good signal to clutter ratio (SCR), which is determined by deploying corner reflectors in an area with low background radiation. Based on the frequency of operations, corner reflector dimensions are chosen that have an RCS that will satisfy the SCR criteria, i.e., better than 30 dB, so as to guarantee good phase stability.

18.4.1   TYPES OF CORNER REFLECTORS

There are basically two main types of corner reflectors, i.e., dihedral and trihedral corner reflectors, which are generally used for external calibration. Dihedral corner reflectors have two surface planes orthogonal to each other, whereas trihedral has three surface planes exactly perpendicular to each other with all three surfaces either shaped triangular or square as shown in Table 18.1.

18.4.1.1   Trihedral Corner Reflectors

Generally, trihedral corner reflectors are used for calibration. They are chosen because of the wide aspect angle over which their cross-section is reasonably constant and because of the cross-section can be accurately determined from a precise measurement of their dimensions. Trihedral corner reflectors are relatively insensitive to misalignment, which is a main reason for their use.

The advantage of trihedral targets is their simplicity, relatively lower cost, and the fact that they can be used as an absolute calibration reference without cross-calibration against standard targets. The beam width of a trihedral CR is rather broad (having a 3 dB beam width of 40° in both elevation and azimuth), so trihedral CRs are fairly tolerant to installation errors. However, the peak RCS is reduced if the trihedral CR is not optimally deployed.

The triangular trihedral consists of three sides of triangular aluminium panels. Each panel has a small hole on it to drain rainwater and minimize the effect of strong wind. The longest side of each triangular panel is reinforced with angular bars to minimize surface curvature. The panels are then attached perpendicular (90°) to each other by bolts and nuts [6].

TABLE 18.1

Radar Cross-Sections and Surface Areas of Different Types of Corner Reflectors

Type of Corner Reflector	Figure	Radar Cross-Section (σ)	Surface Area	Remarks
Dihedral		$8\pi a^4/\lambda^2$	$2a^2$	Medium RCS
Triangular trihedral		$4\pi a^4/3\lambda^2$	$1.5a^2$	Low RCS
Square trihedral		$12\pi a^4/\lambda^2$	$3a^2$	High RCS

The uncertainty of the RCS is mainly governed by the following factors.

- Misalignment from cardinal direction
- Interplate orthogonality error
- Plate curvature deviation
- Surface irregularities

18.4.1.2 Corner Reflectors for Polarimetric Calibration

One measured scattering matrix is usually not sufficient to solve the polarimetric calibration problem where four complex unknowns must be retrieved. A simple way to obtain different scattering matrices with only one reflector is to rotate the reflector around the line of sight provided that its scattering matrix differs from the identity matrix. Experimentally, it is much easier to calibrate with one reflector where the scattering matrices are measured at the same range. Only an accurate alignment must be performed. Therefore polarimetrically advantageous, the rotation of the dihedral around the line of site allows one to receive a maximum voltage, for co-polar measurement at angle α_1 and for cross-polar measurement at angle α_2. With all these considerations, the rotatable dihedral corner reflector is a suitable solution for a polarimetric calibration, but the use of dihedral corner demands an alignment more precise than is needed for a trihedral corner reflector. Backscatter response from corner reflectors across various frequency does not have significant radiometric variability because deployment of suitable RCS corner reflector during calibration. However, CR response will vary according to its scattering matrix coefficient in co-cross polarizations. In case of trihedral, cross-polarization response is negligible, whereas in dihedral, at 45° azimuth offset, cross-polarization response is maximum. So, based on required polarization response, CRs are chosen and oriented accordingly.

18.4.1.3 Dihedral Corner Reflectors

Even though trihedral corner reflectors have the property to provide a high backscattering RCS response for a wide range of incidence angles, which is necessary due to the broadness of the synthetic aperture, nevertheless this calibrator lacks a cross-polar response, making it limited for a complete polarimetric calibration. Hence, dihedral corner reflectors as shown in Figures 18.4 and 18.5 are used for full calibration, although they have orientation angle dependence. Generally, polarization selective dihedrals are used for the polarimetric calibration. While natural extended targets such as forest have been largely used for polarimetric calibration of synthetic aperture radars, it requires some assumptions in the target's polarimetric scattering properties, and there might be some uncertainty in them. On the other hand, if an appropriate combination of point targets of different polarization selectiveness is available and they have accurate polarimetric scattering properties and fairly large RCS, it is more straightforward to use them for polarimetric calibration.

There are four different types of dihedral corner reflectors, namely

(a) 45° rotated dihedral.
(b) 22.5° rotated dihedral.
(c) H-polarization selective dihedral (Figure 18.4).
(d) V-polarization selective dihedral (Figure 18.5).

Dihedral can be rotated with a 45° angle around the line of sight to maximize the return in cross-polarization. This will reflect the cross-polarized component of the wave that is incident on it. So, a 45° rotated dihedral is seen only in HV or VH image. Dihedral can be rotated with a 22.5° angle around the line of sight to get the return in both co-polarization and cross-polarization. So, 22.5° rotated dihedral is seen in all HH, VV, VH, and HV images.

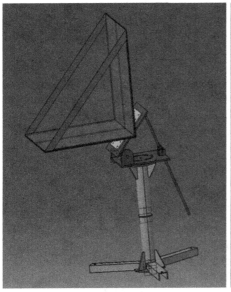

FIGURE 18.4 Dihedral corner reflector.

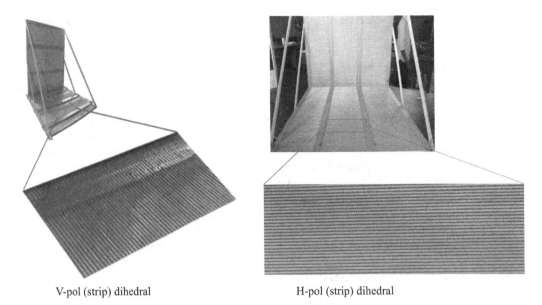

V-pol (strip) dihedral   H-pol (strip) dihedral

FIGURE 18.5 V-pol (strip) dihedral and close-up view of strips and H-pol (strip) dihedral and close-up view.

18.4.1.4 Polarization Selective Dihedrals

The main issue of the polarimetric SAR systems is that when using trihedrals for calibration, the received scattering data shows the same behaviour for both flat terrain and for the trihedral, due to the equivalent number of "reflection jumps" (1 and 3 respectively) that the reflected scattering data has carried out. This can be avoided if double "reflection jump" (typically 2) calibrators could be fabricated, like the dihedral corner reflector, but without the incidence angle dependence. Therefore, different polarization selective dihedrals are made with thin wires/strips placed in the direction of polarization to be reflected, horizontal (H) or vertical (V), as shown in Figure 18.5(b). So, a dihedral made with horizontally placed strips will reflect H only components and a dihedral made with vertically placed strips will reflect V only components. So, an H-pol selective dihedral is seen only in HH images and a V-pol selective dihedral is seen only in VV images.

The wire aligned dihedrals proposed for Pi-SAR (having X-band SAR) have a thin dielectric frame to hold the wires, requiring no base material [1], [4], [5]. Here one can expect better polarization selectiveness because of less dielectric area, which may cause unnecessary reflection to degrade the calibration accuracy as here it does not require any dielectric base to hold the wires. The corner reflectors are also useful to determine phase calibration coefficients, i.e., phase imbalances between polarimetric channels in the radar hardware. Calibration techniques that require known depolarizing targets such as dihedral corner reflectors often lead to complexity in target orientation and knowledge of theoretical values of the scattering matrix. Misalignment of these targets may lead to greater error in the calibration.

18.4.1.5 Interferometric SAR Calibration

Various methods are available for interferometric SAR data calibration. Trihedral corner reflectors networks can be deployed in deformation areas for millimeter deformation validation. This demands a large infrastructure with many corner reflectors at differential heights for better accuracy. Networks of geodetic GPS (which gives point measurement) are also used for validation to determine X, Y, Z displacement to compute accurate deformation. This network is usually deployed in deformation-prone areas. In places where GPS network is not available, geological information from authorized agencies will be considered for validation.

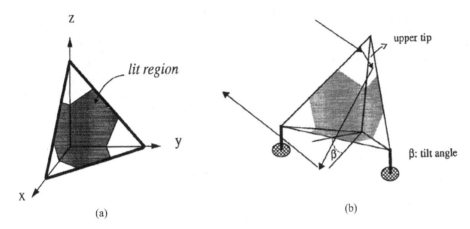

(a) (b)

FIGURE 18.6 (a) The geometry of lit region on a triangular corner reflector and (b) the interaction of a triangular corner reflector with the ground plane.

18.4.1.6 Self-Illuminating Corner Reflectors

For a triangular corner reflector at bore sight incidence, only a portion of each panel is illuminated, as shown in Figure 18.6.

In characterization of lit regions of a triangular corner reflector, it is noticed that at bore sight incidence phi = 45° and theta = 54.7° where the RCS is maximized. Only two-thirds of the area in each panel is lit and gives rise to the maximum RCS. The geometry of each panel is a pentagon, as shown in Figure 18.6; one obvious advantage of a corner reflector with pentagonal panels, which will be referred to as a pentagonal corner reflector, is reduction in the surface area (weight) by one-third without reducing the maximum RCS.

An important feature of a corner reflector when considered as a calibration target for imaging radars is its interaction with the ground plane. Since the reflected rays from the tips of the trihedral corner reflectors are not captured by the other panels, they may interact with the scatterers on the ground plane and give rise to some unknown backscatter contribution. For high angles of incidence, where the lower panel is almost parallel with the ground plane, the specular reflection from the ground plane illuminates the upper tip of the corner reflector, which again will increase its RCS. For the pentagonal corner reflector, on the other hand, all the rays that enter the reflectors' cavity experience the triple reflection and return to the radar. Therefore, its interaction with the ground plane is expected to be minimal.

Self-illuminating corner reflectors offer two major improvements over the widely used triangular corner reflectors.

(a) The uncertainty in the RCS of self-illuminating corner reflectors, caused by the interaction of the ground plane with the corner reflector, is significantly smaller than that of the triangular corner reflectors.

(b) For a specified RCS, the panel area is two-thirds of that of the triangular one.

18.4.2 Construction and Fabrication of Corner Reflectors

Corner reflectors are used for many reasons because of very high RCS for its small size. The high RCS is maintained over a wide incidence angle, and an exact solution is known for their RCS. If the corner reflectors are precisely surveyed with differential GPS, they will be well suited for geometric calibration. Corner reflectors are used as control points for geocoding of SAR data. Corner reflectors are easy to make from metal sheet, but with due care to ensure that the surfaces join exactly at 90°, and robust enough to maintain good flatness, because the error analysis manifested a drop in excess of 5 dB in the level of maximum RCS when one of the three angles of the corner reflector is aligned ±89° instead of 90°. The corner reflector will produce maximum RCS when it is aligned at a 45° incidence angle. This maximum RCS will be maintained over a wide range of incidence angles with approximately 10° displacement on either side. Photogrammetry is used to measure surface irregularities, orthogonality errors, and surface curvature for the reflector faces, as mechanical imperfections will lead to a reduction of the theoretical value of RCS. An accurate measurement of the reflector size is also can be made.

Definite conditions to be followed for better RCS of corner reflectors:

(a)   They must be robust enough to maintain good flatness.
(b)   Care must be taken to be sure that the surfaces join at exactly at 90°.
(c)   Orthogonality of the corner reflectors must be better than 0.2°.
(d)   Plate surface curvature – less than 0.4 mm.
(e)   Plate surface irregularity – less than 0.2 mm.

Different types of manufacturing materials, like aluminium and glass fibre reinforced plastic (GFRP) and base material made of Styrofoam or plywood are recommended for easy deployment and robust characteristics of corner reflectors.

18.4.3   Selection of Calibration Site and Deployment of Corner Reflectors

Due to errors in orientation of the reflectors and the presence of multipath, sometimes the corner reflectors could not be identified in the SAR image. Errors in the orientation of the reflector considerably reduce the backscatter of the reflector resolution cell, resulting in the absence of a bright target in the image. The presence of multipath, such as nearby housing structures and power lines, confuses which bright target in the image is the reflector. Additional considerations are also included, such as deploying CRs away from buildings, the satellite-facing slope of hills, mountains, and obscuring dense vegetation, since all of them can produce a bright response. The calibration fields have to be situated well away from bright objects in order to minimize uncertainties due to erroneous background contributions. Areas that are at least 100 metres away from objects with potential "double-bounce" effect and those where backscatter contribution from its land cover is presumably small can be selected as deployment sites.

If the calibration targets are deployed over a surface with nonzero backscatter, it is required that the RCS of the target is much larger than the direct backscatter of the terrain and also that the coherent interaction of the target and the terrain is as small as possible. The wide RCS pattern or insensitivity of the target alignment to the radar coordinate and the small physical size requirements are needed to assure the ease of target deployment under the field conditions. As these reflectors will be used in field conditions, they should withstand all type of thermal, wind, and rain load. When compared to bare soil, grass provides the more suitable calibration site. As the background of the soil fields is brighter and more variable than that of the grass field, the grass field is less sensitive to soil moisture. In order to accurately position and align the targets with the main beam of the SAR instrument, differential GPS receivers, precise compasses, and inclinometers are used (Figure 18.7).

When corner reflectors are deployed in hilly terrain, the CR backscatter response suffers from geometric distortions like foreshortening, layover, and shadow effects and also depends on incidence angle. Hence, when deployed in hilly regions, the acquisition plan should be considering incidence angle, terrain slope, and descending/ascending imaging. This will help in conducting calibration exercises in hilly terrains. In case of airborne SAR calibration, special attention should be taken while orienting the reflectors because an airborne SAR system will operate at high incidence

FIGURE 18.7   Inclinometer and deployment strategy during orientation of corner reflector.

FIGURE 18.8   Deployment of corner reflectors in Cal_Val site having low backscatter response.

angles leading to very low elevation angles (sometimes, it may go up to $-20°$). So, the CR must have the arrangement in design itself to adjust for low elevation angles as well (Figure 18.8). Based on the terrain height, the incidence angle varies, and hence the elevation angle of CR varies accordingly.

18.5   TYPES OF SAR CALIBRATION AND VALIDATION

The objective of the calibration process is to characterize the system with sufficient accuracy that the properties of the imaged target area (as measured through its electromagnetic interaction with the radiated signal) can be derived from the image data values using some systematic analysis procedure. Calibration of the SAR end-to-end data system presents a formidable challenge to both the radar and ground processor designs. The uncertainty in the characterization of each element in the data system must be established, and an overall error model developed to determine if the expected system performance meets the specification. The process of radiometrically calibrating the SAR image data can be reduced to the estimation of the bias and scale factors that relate the backscatter coefficient to the image data number (DN). The calibration can be done in terms of absolute or relative measures.

The literature survey on SAR calibration and validation shows that the previous SAR missions proposed various methodologies for radiometric and geometric calibration. The variation in the methodology is basically due to SAR payload architecture, imaging modes capability, the elements involved in SAR processing system, data product format, and levels of data products. Ideally, all the data products generated by the SAR correlator are absolutely calibrated such that an image pixel intensity is directly expressed in terms of the mean surface backscatter coefficient. This requires the signal processor to adaptively compensate for all spatial and time dependent variations in the radar system transfer characteristics referred to as radiometric correction or compensation.

The SAR system provides high resolution images of radar backscattered signal from the targets. The SAR calibration process involves measuring the system transfer function and correcting the data products such that they directly represent the target backscatter coefficient. However, an accurate estimate of the target reflectivity requires precise knowledge of the relative geometry between sensor and target. So, calibration of the SAR system involves primarily radiometric and geometric calibration.

The ground calibration sites should consist of a combination of point targets (e.g., corner reflectors, transponders) and distributed targets of known homogenous backscatter characteristics (e.g., Amazon rainforest and Congo rainforest). For distributed target analysis, the Amazon rainforest is considered as the most suitable site for SAR radiometry-related observations and calibration. Gamma backscatter for the Amazon rainforest (CEOS calibration site) is determined to be around −6.5 dB for C-band measurement, providing stable radiometry of the order of ±1 dB. The statistical analysis in the literature shows that the seasonal variation of backscatter at the Amazon is better than 0.25 dB.

18.5.1   Radiometric Calibration

For the estimation of radar backscatter coefficient, radiometric calibration of image is essential. The radiometric calibration procedure provides a reference mechanism between SAR DN values and known RCS of a deployed standard target or distributed target. Absolute radiometric accuracy can be defined as 1 sigma uncertainty resulting from the measurement of targets with known backscatter coefficient when the instrument is working in its specified operational conditions. Radiometric stability, also referred to as relative radiometric accuracy, can be defined as the standard deviation of repeated backscatter coefficient measurements of one or a series of targets' location on the earth and acquired within specified operational conditions that were sufficiently sampled over a given time space "T". Then it can be stated as radiometrically stable over "T".

Radiometric calibration involves

(a)   Point target analysis.
(b)   Distributed target analysis.

Point target analysis is performed on point targets, which are specular scatters of known RCS such as corner reflectors and active radar calibrators (ARC). Point targets span a geometric area much smaller than a resolution cell, but exhibit an RCS that is bright with respect to the total backscattered power from the surrounding target area within the resolution cell. Point target analysis (Figure 18.9) includes the estimation of calibration constant and image quality parameters viz. PSLR, ISLR, spatial resolution, and background to peak ratio using point targets.

Distributed target calibration refers to external calibration using natural targets of large areas with homogeneous backscattering properties. A fundamental assumption is that the scattering properties of these areas are stable or that the variation is well characterized. This permits the image

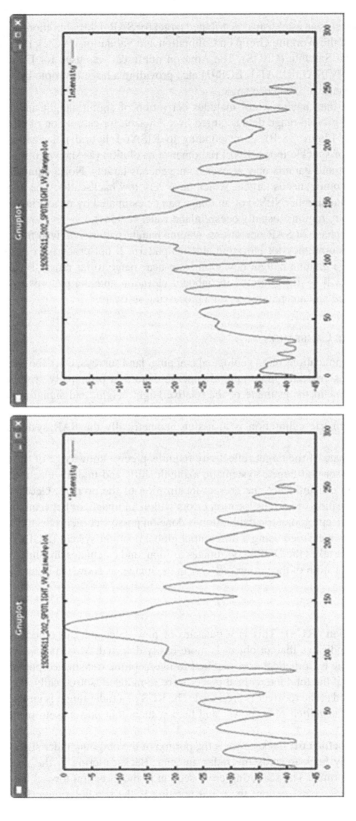

FIGURE 18.9   Along-track and across-track impulse response function of a point target.

characteristics associated with the target scattering to be decoupled from the sensor performance. The Amazon rainforest is an established distributed target for SAR data calibration, as announced by the SAR subgroup of the Working Group on Calibration and Validation (WGCV) of the Committee on Earth Observation Satellite (CEOS). The Amazon rainforest was used for ERS-1/2, J-ERS-1, RADARSAT-1/2, ENVISAT, RISAT-1, EOS-04 etc., providing a large isotropic backscattering reference over a wide range of incidence angle.

Distributed target data analysis tool includes derivation of sigma naught and gamma naught patterns on SLC and ground range data acquired over Amazon for estimation of elevation antenna pattern as shown in Figure 18.10, corresponding to RISAT-1 hybrid polarization data. It also includes estimation of speckle index, ENL, radiometric resolution (as shown in Figure 18.11 and 18.12), sigma naught and gamma naught over homogeneous targets. Noise equivalent sigma zero is derived from the homogeneous targets, which have very low backscatter. The upper limit to the noise equivalent sigma naught (NES0) of an image can be estimated by measuring the radar cross-section of low intensity regions (usually ocean/inland water regions).

During the initial phase of SAR operations, gamma naught patterns derived from images of the Amazon signify the correctness of elevation antenna pattern. If not properly compensated, it will be reflected as a large gamma naught deviation from near range to far range. Based on the feedback, improvement will be incorporated in onboard elevation antenna patterns by uplink biased coefficients or updated antenna patterns in data processing software.

18.5.2 Geometric Calibration

For many scientific applications (e.g., geological mapping, land surveys, etc.), the geometric fidelity of the data product is critically important. Geometric distortion principally arises from platform ephemeris errors, error in the estimate of the relative target height, and signal processing errors. Geometric calibration consists of the estimation of absolute geometric accuracy of the point targets. The purpose of geometric calibration is to assign geometrically the SAR system to the earth's surface.

An accurate estimate of the target reflectivity requires precise knowledge of the relative geometry between the sensor and target. Systematic azimuth shifts and internal electronic delay of the reference instrument can influence the correct localization of the product. Geometric calibration refers to the determination of various location errors within an image, or between multiple images. To surmount these effects, geometric calibration is done on passive corner reflectors with their geographical coordinates measured using a differential global position system (DGPS) with a few cm accuracy. The module takes the DGPS coordinates as input and calculates absolute geometric location accuracy w.r.t. location of the corner reflector in the image, as shown in Figure 18.13.

APPENDIX

Radar cross-section (RCS): This is a measure of how detectable an object is with a radar. A larger RCS indicates that an object is more easily detected. More precisely, the RCS of a radar target is the hypothetical area required to intercept the transmitted power density at the target such that if the total intercepted power were re-radiated isotropically, the power density actually observed at the receiver is produced. The RCS of a radar target is an effective area that intercepts the transmitted radar power and then scatters that power isotropically back to the radar receiver.

Backscattering coefficient: Backscatter is the portion of the outgoing radar signal that the target redirects directly back towards the radar antenna. Backscattering is the process by which backscatter is formed. The scattering cross-section in the direction toward the radar is called the backscattering cross-section; the usual notation is the symbol sigma. It is a measure of

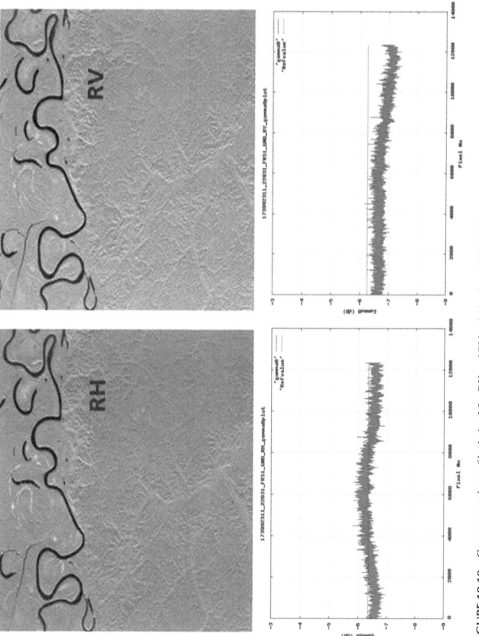

FIGURE 18.10 Gamma naught profile derived for RH and RV polarization of RISAT-1.

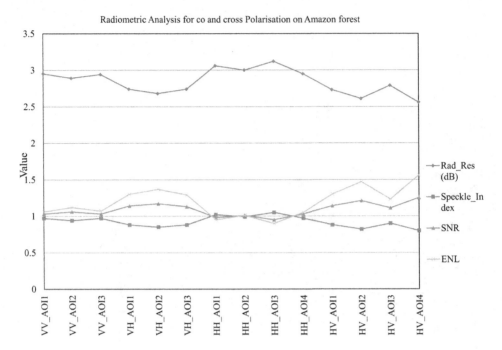

FIGURE 18.11 Radiometric analysis for co -and cross-polarization of the Amazon rainforest.

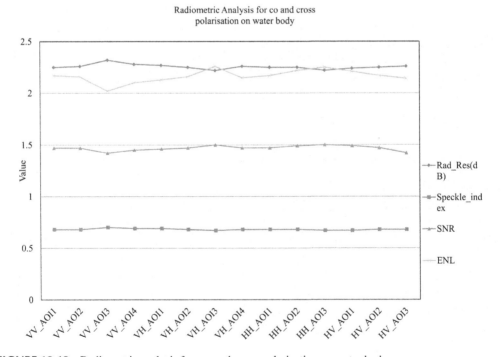

FIGURE 18.12 Radiometric analysis for co- and cross-polarization on water body.

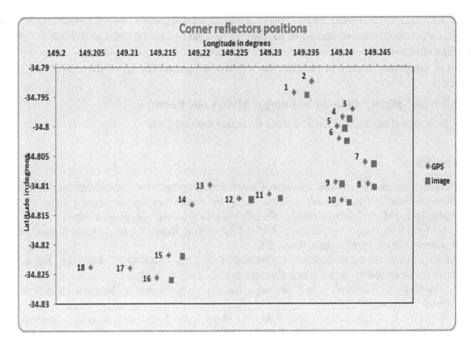

FIGURE 18.13 Corner reflector positions in image and GPS for the image for RISAT-1.

the reflective strength of a radar target. The normalized measure of the radar return from a distributed target is called the backscatter coefficient, or sigma naught, and is defined as per unit area on the ground. If the signal formed by backscatter is undesired, it is called clutter. Other portions of the incident radar energy may be reflected and scattered away from the radar or absorbed.

Dynamic range: A description of the variety of signal amplitudes available in a system. Dynamic range is specified either (i) to be within minimum and maximum values or (ii) with respect to the ratio of maximum to minimum values.

Spatial Resolution: The spatial resolution reflects the capability of the system to resolve adjacent objects. The impulse response function (IRF) (or the point target response) of a SAR system is the 2-D image of a point target in either slant range or ground range representation, neglecting effects of background clutter and thermal noise. Spatial resolution (IRF) is derived from the width of the main lobe at a power level, 3 dB down the peak of the impulse response function in pixels or in metres in both azimuth and range directions.

Peak side lobe ratio (PSLR): It describes the power resolution between the main lobe and side lobe. If a SAR system has a poor PSLR, the side lobe of a strong target will be misclassified as false targets. It is derived by estimating the ratio of the highest side lobe power to the peak power in the main lobe. It is given by:

$$PSLR = 20 * \log10 * (P_{sidelobe}/P_{mainlobe}).$$

In this module, both left and right PSLR are also calculated for studying detailed IRF characteristics on both sides of the main lobe. These are given by:

$$LPSLR = 20 * \log10 * (P_{leftsidelobe}/P_{mainlobe}).$$
$$RPSLR = 20 * \log10 * (P_{rightsidelobe}/P_{mainlobe}).$$

As per RISAT-1 specifications, PSLR should be better than −17 dB.

Integrated side lobe ratio (ISLR): ISLR describes the extent to which energy spread around main lobe. If a SAR system has a poor ISLR, the response from a sufficiently strong target will submerge several weak targets and result in misclassification (loss of detection). Also, in a multi-target environment, spread of the energy beyond resolution units will result in enhanced background noise level, which will impair the contrast of the image. ISLR is computed by the ratio of integrated energy of the side lobes to the integrated energy of the main lobe. ISLR is given by

ISLR = 20 * log10 * (Side Lobe Energy/ Main Lobe Energy).

A typical one-dimensional ISLR should be better than −13 dB.

REFERENCES

[1] Development of Polarization Selective Corner Reflectors and Its Experiment for Calibration of Airborne Polarimetric Synthetic Aperture Radar by Makoto Satake, Toshihiko Umehara, Akitsugu Nadai, Hideo Maeno, Seiho Uratsuka, Takeshi Matsuoka, and Hiroaki Honma, Japan.

[2] Long Term Radiometric Calibration of ERS-1 SAR by G.E. Keyte, P.J. Bird, D.R.D Kenward Defence Research Agency, Farnborough, Hants, UK

[3] An Experiment for the Radiometric Calibration of the ERS-1 SAR by P.J. Bird, G.E. Keyte, D.R.D. Kenward Defence Research Agency, Farnborough.

[4] ALOS PALSAR Calibration and Validation Results from Sweden by Swedish Defense Research Agency, Sweden.

[5] Polarimetric Calibration Experiment of ALOS PALSAR with Polarization Selective Dihedrals.

[6] Assessment of Small Passive Corner Reflectors for Geometric Correction of RADARSAT Fine Mode SAR Data by Donald M. Ugsang, Kiyoshi Honda and Genya Saito.

[7] Expendable Trihedral Corner Reflectors for Target Enhancement and Position Control in RADARSAT-1 Fine Beam Mode SAR Imagery: *Results from an Exercise Narwhal Pre-Trial Deployment* Jason Norris, Paris W. Vachon, David Schlingmeier, Ryan English, and Lloyd Gallop

[8] Optimum Corner Reflectors for the Calibration of Imaging Radars by Kamal Sarabandi, Senior Member, IEEE and Tsen-Chieh Chiu.

[9] SAR Data Processing (Curlander and McDonough 1991), IGPP 2000, ASF 2000

Index

Note: Figures are indicated by *italics*.

Printed in the United States
by Baker & Taylor Publisher Services